The Economics of Networks

The International Library of Critical Writings in Economics

Series Editor: Mark Blaug

Professor Emeritus, University of London, UK
Professor Emeritus, University of Buckingham, UK
Visiting Professor, University of Amsterdam, The Netherlands

This series is an essential reference source for students, researchers and lecturers in economics. It presents by theme a selection of the most important articles across the entire spectrum of economics. Each volume has been prepared by a leading specialist who has written an authoritative introduction to the literature included.

A full list of published and future titles in this series is printed at the end of this volume.

Wherever possible, the articles in these volumes have been reproduced as originally published using facsimile reproduction, inclusive of footnotes and pagination to facilitate ease of reference.

For a list of all Edward Elgar published titles visit our site on the World Wide Web at
www.e-elgar.com

The Economics of Networks

Edited by

Mark Casson

Professor of Economics
University of Reading, UK

and

Marina Della Giusta

Senior Lecturer in Economics
University of Reading, UK

THE INTERNATIONAL LIBRARY OF CRITICAL WRITINGS IN ECONOMICS

An Elgar Reference Collection
Cheltenham, UK • Northampton, MA, USA

Published by
Edward Elgar Publishing Limited
Glensanda House
Montpellier Parade
Cheltenham
Glos GL50 1UA
UK

Edward Elgar Publishing, Inc.
William Pratt House
9 Dewey Court
Northampton
Massachusetts 01060
USA

A catalogue record for this book is available from the British Library

Library of Congress Control Number: 2007942979

ISBN 978 1 84720 365 6

Printed and bound in Great Britain by MPG Books Ltd, Bodmin, Cornwall

Contents

Acknowledgements vii

Introduction Mark Casson and Marina Della Giusta ix

1. Harald Baldersheim, Jan Bucek and Pawel Swianiewicz (2002), 'Mayors Learning across Borders: The International Networks of Municipalities in East-Central Europe', *Regional and Federal Studies*, **12** (1), Spring, 126–37 1
2. Ashok Deo Bardhan and Subhrajit Guhathakurta (2004), 'Global Linkages of Subnational Regions: Coastal Exports and International Networks', *Contemporary Economic Policy*, **22** (2), April, 225–36 13
3. René Belderbos and Leo Sleuwaegen (1996), 'Japanese Firms and the Decision to Invest Abroad: Business Groups and Regional Core Networks', *Review of Economics and Statistics*, **78** (2), May, 214–20 25
4. Mark Brayshay, Mark Cleary and John Selwood (2005), 'Interlocking Directorships and Trans-national Linkages within the British Empire, 1900–1930', *Area*, **37** (2), 209–22 32
5. Ronald S. Burt (1999), 'Private Games are too Dangerous', *Computational and Mathematical Organization Theory*, **5** (4), December, 311–41 46
6. Mark Casson and Howard Cox (1997), 'An Economic Model of Inter-Firm Networks', in Mark Ebers (ed.), *The Formation of Inter-Organizational Networks*, Chapter 7, Oxford: Oxford University Press, 174–96 77
7. Howard Cox, Simon Mowatt and Martha Prevezer (2003), 'New Product Development and Product Supply within a Network Setting: The Chilled Ready-Meal Industry in the UK', *Industry and Innovation*, **10** (2), June, 197–217 100
8. Niek de Jong and Rob Vos (1995), 'Regional Blocs or Global Markets? A World Accounting Approach to Analyze Trade and Financial Linkages', *Weltwirtschaftliches Archiv*, **131**, 748–73 121
9. Sarah Drakopoulou Dodd and Eleni Patra (2002), 'National Differences in Entrepreneurial Networking', *Entrepreneurship and Regional Development*, **14** (2), January, 117–34 147
10. Peter Sheridan Dodds, Duncan J. Watts and Charles F. Sabel (2003), 'Information Exchange and the Robustness of Organizational Networks', *Proceedings of the National Academy of Sciences of the United States of America*, **100** (21), October, 12516–21 165
11. Mika Kallioinen (2004), 'Information, Communication Technology, and Business in the Nineteenth Century: The Case of a Finnish Merchant House', *Scandinavian Economic History Review*, **LII** (1), 19–33 171
12. Douglas S. Massey (1987), 'Understanding Mexican Migration to the United States', *American Journal of Sociology*, **92** (6), May, 1372–403 186

13. Larry Neal and Stephen Quinn (2001), 'Networks of Information, Markets, and Institutions in the Rise of London as a Financial Centre, 1660–1720', *Financial History Review*, **8** (1), April, 7–26 218
14. M.E.J. Newman and Juyong Park (2003), 'Why Social Networks are Different from other Types of Networks', *Physical Review E*, **68** (3), 036122, 1–8 238
15. Lucy Newton (2003), 'Capital Networks in the Sheffield Region, 1850–1885', in John F. Wilson and Andrew Popp (eds), *Industrial Clusters and Regional Business Networks in England, 1750–1970*, Chapter 7, Aldershot, UK: Ashgate Publishers, 130–54 246
16. Rebeca Raijman, Silvina Schammah-Gesser and Adriana Kemp (2003), 'International Migration, Domestic Work, and Care Work: Undocumented Latina Migrants in Israel', *Gender and Society*, **17** (5), October, 727–49 271
17. Kenneth D. Roberts and Michael D.S. Morris (2003), 'Fortune, Risk, and Remittances: An Application of Option Theory to Participation in Village-Based Migration Networks', *International Migration Review*, **37** (4), Winter, 1252–81 294
18. Janet W. Salaff and Arent Greve (2004), 'Can Women's Social Networks Migrate?', *Women's Studies International Forum*, **27**, 149–62 324
19. Ma Ángeles Serrano and Marián Boguñá (2003), 'Topology of the World Trade Web', *Physical Review E*, **68** (1), 015101, 1–4 338
20. David A. Smith and Michael F. Timberlake (2001), 'World City Networks and Hierarchies, 1977–1997: An Empirical Analysis of Global Air Travel Links', *American Behavioral Scientist*, **44** (10), June, 1656–78 342
21. Barney Warf (1995), 'Telecommunications and the Changing Geographies of Knowledge Transmission in the Late 20th Century', *Urban Studies*, **32** (2), 361–78 365
22. Tamar Diana Wilson (1998), 'Weak Ties, Strong Ties: Network Principles in Mexican Migration', *Human Organization*, **57** (4), 394–403 383

Name Index 393

Acknowledgements

The editors and publishers wish to thank the authors and the following publishers who have kindly given permission for the use of copyright material.

Ashgate Publishing for excerpt: Lucy Newton (2003), 'Capital Networks in the Sheffield Region, 1850–1885', in John F. Wilson and Andrew Popp (eds), *Industrial Clusters and Regional Business Networks in England, 1750–1970*, Chapter 7, 130–54.

American Physical Society for articles: Ma Ángeles Serrano and Marián Boguñá (2003), 'Topology of the World Trade Web', *Physical Review E*, **68** (1), 015101, 1–4; M.E.J. Newman and Juyong Park (2003), 'Why Social Networks are Different from other Types of Networks', *Physical Review E*, **68** (3), 036122, 1–8.

Blackwell Publishing Ltd for articles: Kenneth D. Roberts and Michael D.S. Morris (2003), 'Fortune, Risk, and Remittances: An Application of Option Theory to Participation in Village-Based Migration Networks', *International Migration Review*, **37** (4), Winter, 1252–81; Ashok Deo Bardhan and Subhrajit Guhathakurta (2004), 'Global Linkages of Subnational Regions: Coastal Exports and International Networks', *Contemporary Economic Policy*, **22** (2), April, 225–36; Mark Brayshay, Mark Cleary and John Selwood (2005), 'Interlocking Directorships and Trans-national Linkages within the British Empire, 1900–1930', *Area*, **37** (2), 209–22.

Elsevier Ltd for article: Janet W. Salaff and Arent Greve (2004), 'Can Women's Social Networks Migrate?', *Women's Studies International Forum*, **27**, 149–62.

MIT Press Journals for article: René Belderbos and Leo Sleuwaegen (1996), 'Japanese Firms and the Decision to Invest Abroad: Business Groups and Regional Core Networks', *Review of Economics and Statistics*, **78** (2), May, 214–20.

Larry Neal and Stephen Quinn for their own article: (2001), 'Networks of Information, Markets, and Institutions in the Rise of London as a Financial Centre, 1660–1720', *Financial History Review*, **8** (1), April, 7–26.

National Academy of Sciences of the United States of America for article: Peter Sheridan Dodds, Duncan J. Watts and Charles F. Sabel (2003), 'Information Exchange and the Robustness of Organizational Networks', *Proceedings of the National Academy of Sciences of the United States of America*, **100** (21), October, 12516–21.

Oxford University Press for excerpt: Mark Casson and Howard Cox (1997), 'An Economic Model of Inter-Firm Networks', in Mark Ebers (ed.), *The Formation of Inter-Organizational Networks*, Chapter 7, 174–96.

Sage Publications, Inc. via the Copyright Clearance Center for articles: David A. Smith and Michael F. Timberlake (2001), 'World City Networks and Hierarchies, 1977–1997: An Empirical Analysis of Global Air Travel Links', *American Behavioral Scientist*, **44** (10), June, 1656–78; Rebeca Raijman, Silvina Schammah-Gesser and Adriana Kemp (2003), 'International Migration, Domestic Work, and Care Work: Undocumented Latina Migrants in Israel', *Gender and Society*, **17** (5), October, 727–49.

Society for Applied Anthropology for article: Tamar Diana Wilson (1998), 'Weak Ties, Strong Ties: Network Principles in Mexican Migration', *Human Organization*, **57** (4), 394–403.

Springer Science and Business Media for article: Ronald S. Burt (1999), 'Private Games are too Dangerous', *Computational and Mathematical Organization Theory*, **5** (4), December, 311–41.

Springer-Verlag GmbH for article: Niek de Jong and Rob Vos (1995), 'Regional Blocs or Global Markets? A World Accounting Approach to Analyze Trade and Financial Linkages', *Weltwirtschaftliches Archiv*, **131**, 748–73.

Taylor and Francis Ltd (http://www.informaworld.com; http://www.tandf.no/economichistory) for articles: Barney Warf (1995), 'Telecommunications and the Changing Geographies of Knowledge Transmission in the Late 20th Century', *Urban Studies*, **32** (2), 361–78; Sarah Drakopoulou Dodd and Eleni Patra (2002), 'National Differences in Entrepreneurial Networking', *Entrepreneurship and Regional Development*, **14** (2), January, 117–34; Harald Baldersheim, Jan Bucek and Pawel Swianiewicz (2002), 'Mayors Learning across Borders: The International Networks of Municipalities in East-Central Europe', *Regional and Federal Studies*, **12** (1), Spring, 126–37; Howard Cox, Simon Mowatt and Martha Prevezer (2003), 'New Product Development and Product Supply within a Network Setting: The Chilled Ready-Meal Industry in the UK', *Industry and Innovation*, **10** (2), June, 197–217; Mika Kallioinen (2004), 'Information, Communication Technology, and Business in the Nineteenth Century: The Case of a Finnish Merchant House', *Scandinavian Economic History Review*, **LII** (1), 19–33.

University of Chicago Press for article: Douglas S. Massey (1987), 'Understanding Mexican Migration to the United States', *American Journal of Sociology*, **92** (6), May, 1372–403.

Every effort has been made to trace all the copyright holders but if any have been inadvertently overlooked the publishers will be pleased to make the necessary arrangement at the first opportunity.

In addition the publishers wish to thank the Library of Indiana University at Bloomington, USA and the Library of the University of Warwick, UK, for their assistance in obtaining these articles.

The editors and publishers gratefully acknowledge the assistance of Professor Michael Katz and Professor Carl Shapiro during the early stages of this project.

Introduction

Mark Cusson and Maria Della Giusta

A network age?

This collection examines networks as a relevant concept for the analysis of both local and global economic activities. It complements two other reference sources on networks: Grabher and Powell (2004), which focuses on social networks, and Cave, Majumdar and Vogelsang (2002–5), which focuses on telecommunications networks. Our collection aims to illustrate the fact that networks possess a significant economic dimension, in that they facilitate economic transactions. It is therefore possible to analyse them, from the point of view of economic agents, in terms of costs and benefits of belonging to them. Curiously, mainstream economics has only recently discussed networks in terms of their possible configurations and their related costs and benefits (Economides and Encaoua, 1996); previously the subject had remained in the realm of geographers and historians. This is surprising since the shift from markets to networks and from ownership to access has been at the core of the political analysis of current processes of globalisation (Rifkin, 2000), in which having the right connections increasingly matters more than owning physical resources.

The first part of our collection contains papers that illustrate the network concept and its applicability to a variety of settings, from chemical reactions and neural networks to networks of scientific collaborations and businesses. We also include a collection of papers that make use of the concept in a more or less formal manner in the context of economics, showing the wide range of applications to processes of diffusion of information, trust building, learning and entrepreneurship.

The second part of the collection includes papers that use the concept of networks to describe connectivity and flows of information, including trade and migration. This has been predominantly the field of enquiry of economic geographers, although a literature on sustainability and interdependence is beginning to emerge which makes use of the same concepts (see the New Economic Foundation, 2006).

Networks are studied by almost every social science, and by the physical sciences too. In *physics*, there are electrical circuits; in *civil engineering*, structures like bridge trusses; in *information technology* there are telephones and the Internet; while in *geography* there are transport systems, such as motorways and railway systems. Agriculture and industry depend upon distribution systems (pipelines, electricity grids) and disposal systems (drainage ditches, sewage systems). In *biology*, the brain is analysed as a network of neurons, and in *anthropology*, family networks are created and sustained through reproduction. *Economists* refer to networks of trade, investment and technology transfer when discussing international and inter-regional resource flows. *Sociologists* analyse social groups in terms of inter-personal networks, and use network effects to explain 'chain migration' flows, while *business strategists* analyse networks of strategic alliances between firms. Networks also appear in drama and fiction – in terms of the connections between the different characters in the play or story.

The ubiquity of networks suggests that a major economy of thought can be effected by standardising terminology to facilitate intellectual arbitrage between different disciplines. Economic and social history can be enriched using ideas originating in biology or information technology, for example, while insights gained from history can be exported to other disciplines.

A common feature of all network concepts is connectivity. In abstract terms a network is most conveniently defined as a set of elements which are connected to each other. The basic principles of network representation are set out in the mathematical theory of graphs (Biggs, Lloyd and Wilson, 1986; Diestel, 1997). Direct connections link pairs of elements; these connections can be joined up in various ways to create a range of paths. There may be several different paths between any given pair of elements in the network.

Although graph theory claims to be general, it involves a number of simplifying assumptions which restrict its application in the social sciences. There are a number of simple refinements which will facilitate the wider application of network theory.

From an economic and social perspective, there are four key aspects of networks:

- the *types of element* that belong to the network;
- the *diversity* of the elements, in terms of the number of different types of specialised elements that belong to the network;
- the *types of relationship* that connect the elements; and
- the *configuration* of the network, which describes the pattern in which the different elements are connected up.

Network theory and economics

The first part of our collection covers the theory of networks as they are discussed in the scientific literature, and unveils important properties that networks possess. We begin with a selection of more technical papers on networks in general and then move to papers describing the network concept as it is used in economics.

Particular attention has been given to the study of the statistical properties of different natural networks, such as chemical reaction networks, neural networks, food webs, social networks, scientific collaboration networks and computer networks (Amaral et al., 2000), which can all be modelled as so-called 'small-world' networks, i.e. networks that are neither fully random nor regular. Newman and Park (2003, Chapter 14, this volume) identify two distinctive characteristics of social networks: a positive degree of correlation between adjacent vertices, i.e. assortative mixing according to group membership; and clustering, i.e. a propensity for vertex pairs to be connected if they share a mutual neighbour. These properties distinguish them from other types of networks and are accounted for by the division of social networks into groups or communities, as exemplified by scientific collaborations and business networks.

As information exchange lies at the heart of the interest for networks in economics, we also include a technical paper focusing specifically on network properties that are pertinent for the optimisation of information exchange. Dodds, Watts and Sabel (2003, Chapter 10, this volume) focus specifically on information exchange, and illustrate how different network configurations perform differently under varying conditions of information exchange. Working with a basic hierarchical structure, they highlight multi-scale networks – that is, networks in which connectivity between nodes or elements occurs both at the local and the global level, although the density of links is not uniform and rather decreases with depth. Such networks have the highest robustness to information exchange, in that both the likelihood of congestion-related failure for individual nodes and the likelihood of system failure when a node fails are simultaneously minimised. These results resonate well with findings from simulations in the economic sociology literature, which concern the social context for the development of trust in interactions between people.

Burt (1999, Chapter 5, this volume) illustrates how cooperation requires maximum density networks, and how trust and distrust cannot be understood independently of the context in which they are produced, so that thinking of private games between two people independently of context cannot produce useful results compatible with observed reality. In the context of private games (dyadic relationships) sociologists tend to explain trust as emerging from past exchanges, whereas economists look to the incentives of future exchanges. Public games are instead interaction sequences in which two people display their behaviour to one another, but are mindful of their reputation with friends and acquaintances observing the game. The paper makes a number of specific arguments in this context: a balance argument (people have a preference for consistency between relationships adjacent in a network); a reputation argument (strong indirect connections through third parties as a medium for enforcement of social norms of cooperation); and a gossip argument (etiquette-biased information amplifying predispositions towards trust and distrust).

Within the economic literature networks have mostly been studied by institutional theorists in the context of the theory of the firm and of entrepreneurship. Casson and Cox (1997, Chapter 6, this volume) demonstrate that networks can be an efficient institutional solution to a coordination problem arising in the organisation of economic transactions, and concentrate particularly on the modelling of contractual aspects of resource flows between different production plants. The price mechanism as a vehicle of communication works only if the distribution of ownership is appropriate for motivating the honest sharing of information and if property rights are secure. The classic organisational solution to this problem is internalisation (replacement of the market by a firm), but it is also possible to have moral incentives generating reliable information through a network linkage, which relies on trust between the parties sustained by moral incentives. Networks can therefore be described as a high-trust coordination mechanism. The point is illustrated by Britain's nineteenth-century, international business networks, based on the social institutions in which late-Victorian Britain invested heavily (the missionary movement, the 'old school tie' alumni networks, the regimental and other military affiliations of explorers and business adventurers, etc.). The free-standing company (that is, companies floated in the UK but operating abroad) and the merchant house system constituted an organisational form based on a mixture of contractual arrangements between groups of connected individuals.

These networks are at the centre of the study of London-based bankers in the seventeenth century by Neal and Quinn (2001, Chapter 13, this volume), who illustrate the ways in which bankers acquired the ability to take advantage of exchange-rate differentials using networks of merchants, with different efficacy depending on the different nations' legal systems. They argue that this credit nexus sustained the long-run development of trade relationships in northern Europe, and illustrate the difference between Amsterdam, which had an exchange bank, and London, which relied instead on networks of bankers who offered mutual acceptance and systemic monitoring as a group and arranged international monitoring through their networks of foreign agents. To prevent misbehaviour Blackwell, for example, had only one agent per city, thereby generating considerable business with a trusted agent who had little incentive to misbehave as the opportunity cost would have been too great. Bankers therefore generated an information flow concerning reputations to make sure that news of malfeasance would spread fast, with merchants as the conduits of such information through their correspondence, which they kept as proof of their good name; they also kept bills of exchange to make sure default could be traced back to its roots.

The role of particular intermediating figures in a network is discussed by Newton (2003, Chapter 15, this volume) in her analysis of the role of business networks in managing the changing economic and institutional conditions facing the financial sector in the Sheffield region in the nineteenth century. She describes the highly embedded networks resulting from the running of totally integrated mills, which led to an industrial network of complex linkages reinforced by intermarriage and social networking, extending to banking and finance, and focusing on the role of company promoters using their contacts to raise subscriptions. These actors were particularly interesting in that they had often a bad reputation for being unscrupulous, and yet played an important role in promoting joint stock companies. The need for intermediation had arisen because of the growing number of investors, and their lack of knowledge of the law. The paper includes an analysis of the networks used by three promoters involved in setting up 90 different companies, which illustrates how investors were drawn from geographical and occupational groups that were bound by trust-based relationships.

Networks interaction in the diffusion of new technologies is the subject of a historical study by Kallioinen (2004, Chapter 11, this volume), who analyses the impact of the telegraph on international trade in the nineteenth century, illustrating path dependence in the adoption of the telegraph. The progress of information technology was accompanied by the extension of merchants' personal business networks, and these together reduced information costs by improving speed and reliability of information diffusion. Relevant and recent information is necessary for interaction, and the paper asks what kind of information was transmitted by the telegraph and whether it displaced correspondence between business partners. The case study contained in the paper is that of a merchant house in Turku, Finland, which is interesting because it was peripheral and because the telegraph was adopted relatively late. The research findings indicate that personal correspondence remained very important for transmitting delicate information on liquidity or the reputation of business partners, whereas the telegraph was used for sharing information on prices, freight charges and the security of transport routes.

Cultural factors exert an influence on networking too, and the paper by Dodd and Patra (2002, Chapter 9, this volume) conducts an analysis of entrepreneurial networking in Greece and compares it with findings from other nations to assess the significance of culture in explaining observed patterns of entrepreneurial networking. Entrepreneurship theory sees networking as a mechanism for exploring the creation and development of new ventures. The study finds that Greek entrepreneurs include many more family and friends and fewer business ties in their strong-tie networks, which give them access to larger secondary networks than Japanese, American, Irish, Italian and Swedish entrepreneurs. Correspondingly, they spend a lot more time in network maintenance, confirming that network affiliation entails costs as well as benefits and that an affiliation strategy has high opportunity cost.

Cox, Mowatt and Prevezer (2003, Chapter 7, this volume) study the effects on innovation and learning from belonging to networks, starting from the observation that the 1990s have witnessed a sharp rise in the incidence of the network form of business organization, with implications for industrial structure and the nature of competition. Their analysis of vertical networks within the chilled ready-meal sector of the food processing industry helps to identify a control network (based on the ownership of inventory management software by supermarkets which extends considerable control over food producers and manufacturers) and a network of innovation (based on the collection of data on customers which are shared with food processors and packaging firms on a cooperative basis for the purposes of innovation). At the centre of each network is access to data on purchasing patterns, which is under the control of supermarkets. However, the structure of the innovation network is based on alliances and cooperation, whereas the control network has evolved from vertical integration to subcontracting.

The effects of network affiliation on learning are studied in a variety of contexts, and to illustrate this we have included a paper by Baldersheim, Bucek and Swianiewicz (2002, Chapter 1, this volume) which describes the characteristics of networking by mayors from eastern European cities, and explicitly conceptualises networking as a learning process. The authors investigate stages of learning corresponding to mayors' study visits, twinning initiatives and visits by foreign experts and advisors. They identify the forces driving learning networks as push factors (local problems and pressures), pull factors (opportunities and incentives) and facilitating factors (personal resources, political styles and cultures). They find that study visits and twinning follow similar geographical patterns, whereas consultancies do not, because they are part of specific programmes. It is interesting to note that only half of the mayors say that the consultancies are useful; the other half find consultancies either only partially useful or not useful at all. Regression analysis finds pull factors to be the most important ones, with the mayor's view of the local economy mattering most.

Global networks: trade, information and people

Over the last ten years a number of studies have been conducted on the effects of the ICT revolution on knowledge transmission. The geography literature has made explicit use of the network concept to explain the growth of world cities, the expansion of offshore banking centres and the globalisation of back offices (Warf, 1995, Chapter 21, this volume). The effect of the Internet on the geography of worldwide services is at the centre of the paper, which suggests on the one hand that some features of the development of the World Wide Web are akin to those of other transport networks, and on the other hand that the expectation that space would be eliminated as a relevant dimension have not been borne out. On the contrary, the author suggests that much can be learned from analysing the specific ways in which new nodes and old trading centres have combined to generate the current map of world centres of trade, particularly in finance.

The paper by Smith and Timberlake (2001, Chapter 20, this volume) provides an attempt to map empirically the hierarchy of major world cities. They start from a series of assumptions: that global processes are grounded in what geographically situated people do; that what they do involves relations across space involving the transport of material goods, the transmission of information and the movement of people themselves; and finally, that relations are structured by historical development of geographic localities. These localities are sites for social interaction, production, reproduction, consumption and exchange. They refer to Sassen's work on global cities as nodes that both attract and repel (Sassen, 2002), and Castells's prediction that global cities will become dominant by developing the infrastructure needed to capture information flows, leading to spatially defined urban hierarchies (Castells, 2004). The paper uses network analysis to map the world city system with data on flows of air passengers, and provides measures of equivalence for grouping cities together according to similar patterns of exchange and of centrality in order to understand the role of particular nodes. Cohesion analysis is used to chart changes and stability of membership in cliques over time, and equivalence analysis to identify central actors. The authors find stability over the 1980s and 1990s, with a fall in the importance of Mumbai and Buenos Aires and a rise in importance of several East Asian cities, together with evidence of polarization rather than convergence.

Serrano and Boguñá (2003, Chapter 19, this volume) apply network theory to the world trade web and show how it can be characterised as a complex network with the corresponding properties of scale-free degree distribution (degrees being the number of edges emanating from a vertex), small world (the average path length between any pair of vertices growing logarithmically with size of system) and high clustering coefficient (neighbours of a vertex having high probability of being interconnected). They use their results to prove that, through the progressive removal of constraints during globalisation, the trade system has become a self-organised complex system.

Network analysis is used in a slightly different way by de Jong and Vos (1995, Chapter 8, this volume), who develop a world accounting matrix to highlight trade and finance linkages between countries and to assess the degree of regionalisation of international trade and finance. They provide an analysis of the degree of regionalisation of commodity and finance flows, revealing that strongly regionalised patterns of trade and investment exist and that there has been a weakening of regional concentration of commodity trade in the 1980s. They also find that finance flows are regionally concentrated, but not in quite the same way as trade flows.

Brayshay, Cleary and Selwood (2005, Chapter 4, this volume) use networks to reconstruct the social connections behind historical patterns of economic globalisation, and provide a study of the networks of the elite owners and managers of twelve transnational corporations at the start of the twentieth century. They concentrate specifically on the social spheres in which directors lived in order to understand the context in which information was created, valued and exchanged. Multiple directorships increased in percentage terms between 1899 and 1900 and between 1929 and 1930, from less than 30 per cent to more than 40 per cent. However, board sizes did not change, suggesting the occurrence of a growing concentration of power in a small elite, as demonstrated by the growing number of intercorporate linkages between a small number of key directors which developed over the same period. The directors shared a similar education: predominantly at Eton or Harrow and then Oxford or Cambridge (more than 80 per cent), and common club affiliations (Carlton Club, Athenaeum, Brook's, Marlborough Club and White's) – often belonging to several clubs, even at opposite ends of the political spectrum. The authors conclude that, although few companies were truly transnational, there were already many global connections in the UK corporate elite that spanned the world and helped to create the social web onto which transnational corporations subsequently transplanted.

Similar results confirming the importance of inter-firm links to the process of internationalisation are found across time and cultures, and as a contemporary example we have included a paper by Belderbos and Sleuwaegen (1996, Chapter 3, this volume) which studies the process of internationalisation undergone over recent decades by Japanese firms. The authors conduct an inquiry into the reasons for Japanese decisions to invest abroad, highlighting particularly factors related to their networks of inter-firm linkages in the major regions of outward investment (US and Western Europe and Asia). They find that, whereas firms' specific intangible assets are important in determining investment in western industrialised countries, it is actually inter-firm linkages that help lower barriers to investment in Southeast Asia, within both horizontal and vertical business groups.

The remainder of the papers in this section explore the human dimensions to networks, starting with a study of the global linkages of US coastal regions by Bardhan and Guhathakurta (2004, Chapter 2, this volume). This study focuses on variations in trading patterns of different states in the US, and analyses the differences between determinants of exports from the West and the East coast economic regions. California and New York are the largest immigrant states of the US, as a significant number of immigrants arrive and settle there, and there is a high concentration of transnational business linkages based along the coast (involving both foreign direct investments and more informal business-to-business contacts). The Atlantic coast has a longer history of industrial development and older immigrant concentrations (from Europe, Africa and Latin America), whereas the Pacific coast has newer industries and more recent immigrants (from Mexico and Asian countries). By using a gravity model including transnational networks (contacts that bind foreign-born immigrants to their country of birth) and international business networks (intra-firm commercial transactions connecting affiliates, subsidiaries, offices and headquarters across national borders), the study finds evidence that immigrants can help reduce risk and transaction costs associated with international trade (which are higher than those associated with local trade) by capitalising on the ethnic capital embodied in their communities. The study also finds evidence that business-to-business ties reduce transaction costs. Both regions show a high propensity to trade with the Asia-Pacific region. The social networks coefficient is positive and significant for the West coast (and makes distance insignificant), where immigrants are also better educated, and insignificant for the East coast.

There is a vast literature on migrants' social networks, analysing the effect of culture and social networks in determining the socioeconomic advancement of migrants (e.g. Pang and Lau, 1998; Polloni et al., 2001; Borjas and Bronars, 1991). The literature illustrates how networks are anchored in the home community and require the support of kin in the community to maintain network vitality, which assists migrants by expanding their opportunities. Roberts and Morris (2003, Chapter 17, this volume), for example, describe remittances to the home community as a cost of accessing social networks and as a payment for the option of participating in employment networks based in the village.

Massey (1987, Chapter 12, this volume) is one of the first studies to identify migrant networks as a source of social capital which help migrants to accumulate and acquire other forms of capital. A number of writers agree that people are part of social networks through non-random selection processes in which social and economic variables determine both the membership of a network and the propensity to migrate.

More detailed work on types of social networks is reported in Wilson (1998, Chapter 22, this volume), which analyses the dispersion and clustering of immigrants originally from the same community in terms of five network principles: multiple locality of networks (networks that encompass a variety of geographical destinations); work sites and work types as anchoring points of networks; strength of weak ties in network expansion (information about employment opportunities passed from acquaintances); diffuse networks as social capital; and dense networks as social capital (information and aid exchanged through these connections).

Salaff and Greve (2004, Chapter 18, this volume) ask whether the impact of social capital on women migrants is different from that on men, and focus on the immigration to Canada of middle-class, highly educated people from China. They analyse how migration alters the family support system, how migrant couples adapt to reduced social capital for childcare and how this impedes the career opportunities of skilled women migrants in particular. It is generally believed that kinship ties are especially important for working-class immigrants. Salaff and Greve (2004), however, find that, while highly educated people are more likely to seek collegial and organisational ties for equivalent positions in the host country, kinship ties continue to be important to highly educated women migrants, as transnational motherhood also occurs amongst them. They also find that links of social networks between spheres (work, family, community) differ by gender. Men's social networks span work and community more effectively, while women's span work and family, enabling them to work but falling short of getting them good jobs.

A further and recently expanding theme within this literature relates to so-called transnational care networks, and the many dilemmas resulting from it (Raijman, Schammah-Gesser and Kemp, 2003, Chapter 16, this volume). The impact of such situations for the well-being of the women who have left children behind in their home countries to care for children and adults in developed countries has been considered in a number of studies (Ehrenreich and Hochschild, 2002; Mattingly, 2001). Many studies find that women who leave their families behind are less able to settle and integrate into the host communities than when they bring their children with them, although the logistics of their own childcare requirements may then become overwhelming. In this context, the availability of social networks for caring becomes relevant in defining their opportunities for work in the country of immigration (Salaff and Greve, 2004).

A further issue highlighted in this literature concerns the relationship between immigrant women and local women, as the increased participation of local women in the workforce in the recipient countries, their continued responsibility for a majority of the domestic chores (Hersch and Stratton, 2002), and the lack of affordable childcare facilities has resulted in increasing dependence on immigrant workers to help out within the household (Ehrenreich and Hochschild, 2002). This domestic 'outsourcing' strategy has enabled local women to go out to work, while delegating their 'reproductive' activities to others. The availability to migrant workers of social networks for care (use of a network of family or friends to look after their children while they are out at work) means that they are able to charge less for the job that they do than if they had to pay for childcare. Thus, Salaff and Greve (2004, p. 29) argue that, 'work-family role conflicts are public issues needing institutional solutions, but few countries define them this way. Societies rarely acknowledge the work that people do to mesh institutional structures: people draw on personal relations to resolve inconsistent demands'.

This introduction has shown that networks of all kinds are crucial to the performance of the economy. Physical networks transport goods and people, distribute energy, and assist with the disposal of waste. Social networks coordinate the division of labour, allowing the individual specialists throughout the economy to harmonise their individual decisions (Granovetter, 1985; Castells, 2004). Whatever institutional arrangement of coordination is used – firm, market, government, club, etc. – a network of some kind is involved. Different types of network relationship, and different types of network configuration, are suited to different tasks. Better understanding of networks will make it easier to understand why different institutions are used for different purposes (Doreian and Stokman, 1997). Where physical networks are concerned, a better understanding of networks will make it easier to understand why certain types of activity agglomerate, why these agglomerations are located in the places that they are, and why centres of agglomeration tend to remain so stable while other factors change.

References

Amaral, L.A.N., A. Scala, M. Barthelemy and H.E. Stanley (2000), 'Classes of Small-world Networks', *Proceedings of the National Academy of Sciences of the United States of America*, **97** (21), 11149–11152.

Biggs, Norman L., E. Keith Lloyd and Robert Wilson (1986), *Graph Theory, 1736–1936*, Oxford: Oxford University Press.

Borjas, G.J. and S.G. Bronars (1991), 'Immigration and the Family', *Journal of Labor Economics*, **9** (2), 123–148.

Castells, Manuel (2004), *The Network Society*, Cheltenham: Edward Elgar.

Cave, Martin, S. Majumdar and I. Vogelsang (eds) (2002–5), *Handbook of Telecommunications Economics*, Amsterdam: Elsevier.

Diestel, Reinhard (1997), *Graph Theory*, New York: Springer.

Doreian, Patrick and Frans N. Stokman (1997), *Evolution of Social Networks*, Amsterdam: Gordon and Breach.

Economides, N. and D. Encaoua (eds) (1996), 'Special Issue on Networks Economics: Business Conduct and Market Structure', *International Journal of Industrial Organization*, **14**, 669–671.

Ehrenreich, B. and A. Russell Hochschild (eds) (2002), *Global Woman: Nannies, Maids, and Sex Workers in the New Economy*, New York: Henry Holt and Company, Metropolitan Books.

Grabher, Gernot and Walter W. Powell (eds) (2004), *Networks*, Cheltenham: Edward Elgar.

Granovetter, Mark (1985), 'Economic Action and Social Structure: The Problem of Embeddedness', *American Journal of Sociology*, **91** (3), 481–510.

Hersch, Joni and Leslie S. Stratton (2002), 'Housework and Wages', *Journal of Human Resources*, **37** (1), 217–229.

Mattingly, D.J. (2001), 'The Home and the World: Domestic Service and International Networks of Caring Labour', *Annals of the Association of American Geographers*, **91** (2), 370–86.

New Economic Foundation (2006), *UK Interdependence Report 2006*, http://www.neweconomics.org/gen/z_sys_PublicationDetail.aspx?pid=220.

Pang, M. and A. Lau (1998), 'The Chinese in Britain: Working towards Success?', *International Journal of Human Resource Management*, **9** (5), 862–874.

Polloni, A., D.S. Massey, M. Ceballos, K. Espinosa and M. Spittel (2001), 'Social Capital and International Migration: A Test Using Information on Family Networks', *American Journal of Sociology*, **106** (5),1262–1298.

Rifkin, Jeremy (2000), *The Age of Access: How the Shift from Ownership to Access is Transforming Modern Life*, London: Penguin.

Sassen, S. (ed.) (2002), *Global Networks: Linked Cities*, London: Routledge.

[1]

Mayors Learning across Borders: The International Networks of Municipalities in East-Central Europe

HARALD BALDERSHEIM, JAN BUCEK and PAWEL SWIANIEWICZ

The age of internationalization has also reached local government. Leaders of local authorities are increasingly in touch with their opposite numbers in other countries. The cross-border networks between cities, towns and regions seem to grow denser day by day (Goldsmith and Klausen, 1997, Baldersheim and Ståhlberg, 1999a). East and Central European mayors are very much a part of this trend. However, not all municipalities and mayors are equally involved in this pattern of cross-border networking. To the extent that important information, economic resources, or strategic advantages flow from membership of such networks, those who cannot or will not take part may be disadvantaged.

In this article, we shall address three issues related to these networks: (1) What precisely are the activities mayors engage in when taking part in international networks? (2) How far-flung are the networks of the East-Central European mayors? What are the geographical patterns? (3) And what are the forces driving international networking? What are the characteristics of the cosmopolitan mayor and municipality? The material we use comes from a survey of mayors in the Czech Republic, Poland and Slovakia carried out in 1997. Between 300 and 500 mayors were surveyed in each country (see Table 8 for details of the respective samples). The survey was in some respects a repeat of a 1991 study reported in Baldersheim, Illner, Offerdal, and Swianiewicz, 1996.

To us, it seems appropriate to conceptualize international networking as a learning process. This choice of perspective seems especially appropriate with regard to the East-Central European mayors under study here. They were only the second cohort of democratically elected mayors since the fall of communism in 1989. They were responsible for running new institutions established in 1990, a task for which most of them had had little chance of preparation. Their lot was very much one of learning by trial and error once in office. Many of them rose to the occasion and have managed admirably

---

Harald Baldersheim, University of Oslo; Jan Bucek, Comenius University, Bratislava; Pawel Swianiewicz, University of Warsaw.

Regional and Federal Studies, Vol.12, No.1, Spring 2002, pp.126–137
PUBLISHED BY FRANK CASS, LONDON

(Surazska, 1997, Baldersheim *et al.*, 1996). Others have felt that the routines of day-to-day management were not quite what they had imagined in the heyday of the velvet revolutions and have therefore left local politics.

In theories of organizational learning a series of sophisticated concepts has been developed to characterize various types of learning (such as problem-driven and solution-driven search, single loop and double loop learning, deutro learning, and superstitious learning: see Cyert and March, 1963, Argyris and Schön, 1978, Levitt and March, 1988). These concepts mostly define learning by reference to the outcomes or contents of the processes of learning. For our purposes the focus is limited to the process as such. We divide the process into three steps of deepening learning or commitment to learning. The first step is feeling a need to acquire new or more information about ways of solving problems in the municipality, or starting a search process. The second step is focusing the search on a particular part of the environment where relevant information may be found and entering into a committed search. The third step is actually to commit resources to achieve change in one's own organization. In this study the operationalization of these three steps are (1) the mayor's study visits abroad, (2) twinning initiatives and other co-operative relations between municipalities, and (3) visits from foreign experts and advisors to the mayor's municipality as consultants in the actual change process.

However, as mentioned above, not all mayors are equally active in international networking. The motives for establishing international contacts and taking part in learning networks may vary, of course. The motives may have to do with variations in problems, opportunities, locations, politics or institutional factors. Some mayors may be driven by the force of the problems they face in their municipality; others may be chiefly interested in financial or other forms of support that may be gained from international contacts or international funds, such as EU or Phare funds; others again may hope that contacts with internationally prestigious institutions may rub off on them and add to their own personal status. There may also be variations in terms of opportunities to establish international contacts. Mayors in large cities or municipalities close to borders may have easier access to such contacts and also more exposure to information about opportunities. Variations may also arise because of factors related to the mayor as a person or political figure – an academic education or language skills may help a mayor in international contacts. Political style and political culture may also matter: the extrovert style associated with the New Political Culture (Clark, 1983; Clark and Hoffmann-Martinot, 1998), for example, may predispose a mayor to establish more international contacts, whereas a traditional political boss may seek solutions to problems in other contacts than those of international partners. Mayors from municipalities characterized by a civic culture that generates social capital or trust in the manner suggested by Robert Putnam (1993) might also be expected to enter into cross-border networks more readily than those functioning in a low-trust culture. Finally, institutional differences may affect learning behaviour. The position of mayor is not the same in the three countries (Baldersheim, Blaas, Horvath, Illner and Swianiewicz, 1996). Slovakia has a directly elected mayor. In the Czech Republic, the mayor is elected by the council among the council members. Polish councils may find their mayors also outside their own ranks, among professional managers. The directly elected Slovak mayor may have the greatest scope for acting on their own and taking initiatives regarding international contacts.

To sum up, following Marks *et al.*, 1994, the forces driving learning networks may be divided into push factors such as local problems and pressures, or pull factors such as opportunities and incentives. To these two sets we will add a third one, facilitating factors such as personal resources, political style and culture, and institutional features (Baldersheim and Ståhlberg, 1999b). Facilitating factors are intervening variables that serve to enhance the impacts of push and pull factors

FEATURES OF CROSS-BORDER LEARNING NETWORKS

Study tours and twinning relations

The first step in the learning process is that of starting a search for information. The search may start in many different ways, and going on a study trip abroad may be a rather special and sophisticated way of initiating a process of improvement. Consequently, it is not something that it is reasonable to expect every mayor to do. But precisely how many or how few engage in this sort of activity? This is brought out in Table 1, which is based on responses to the question 'Have you been abroad on study tours during your term of office?'

More than half of all mayors have been abroad on study trips. Foreign tours are more usual in Poland and Slovakia than in the Czech Republic. Nearly half of all Polish and Slovak mayors have been on such trips more than once whereas only a third of the Czech mayors have done so.

TABLE 1
MAYORS' STUDY TOURS TO FOREIGN DESTINATIONS (%)

	Czech Republic	Poland	Slovakia
None	53	31	27
Once	17	22	28
Several times	30	48	46
N	516	513	311

Establishing twinning links with foreign partners, the second step in the operationalization of the learning sequence, is also quite common. Between a third and a half of the municipalities have established such relations. The proportion with such links is, however, somewhat smaller in Poland than in the other two countries. So the relative reticence of Czech mayors with regard to study tours may be said to be compensated for by their municipalities' greater propensity to take twinning initiatives.

TABLE 2
TWINNING OR OTHER FORMAL CO-OPERATIVE RELATIONS WITH FOREIGN MUNICIPALITIES (%)

	Czech Republic	Poland	Slovakia
None	53	64	57
Yes	47	36	43
N	516	513	311

Destinations

Where do the mayors go when they go on study tours? What are their destinations? Is the geographical pattern the same for study tours and twinning relations? If it is, then it may be concluded that the mayors, when they start a process of search for information, also often find something that is useful and that is followed up in the form of more long-term relationships. Or do the geographical patterns seem haphazard so that the mayors' contacts appear as whims of the moment, tourist adventures rather than strategic, long-term initiatives?

TABLE 3
COUNTRIES OF DESTINATION FOR MAYORS' STUDY TOURS (PERCENTAGE OF MAYORS WHO TRAVELLED TO:)

	Czech Republic	Poland	Slovakia
Russia	0.4	2.3	1.9
Other Central-East	5.2	20.2	24.6
Western Europe:			
Austria	16.2	6.7	45.4
Germany	20.6	44.9	18.8
France	8.9	24.6	12.5
United Kingdom	5.4	3.5	8.0
Benelux	11.0	10.9	19.5
Nordic countries	10.6	20.9	8.0
Other West European	13.9	10.9	20.4
USA	4.2	1.9	5.4
Canada	0.2	0.2	0.3
Other non-European	0.4	1.0	1.9

Table 3 suggests that travels to the closest Western neighbours dominate. For the Czech Republic the most frequent destinations of travels are: Germany (over 20% of interviewed mayors) and Austria (16%); Belgium and the Netherlands and the remaining West European countries are much less frequent destinations. For Poles, travels to Germany are the most frequent (almost half of mayors). France and the Nordic countries are next in rank and are much more important for the Poles than for Czechs and Slovaks. The long tradition of Polish–French ties probably plays an important role in the former and relative geographical proximity in the latter case. For Slovak mayors Austria is definitely the most frequent destination of study tours (almost half of all mayors travelled there).

It is characteristic that travels to East-Central European neighbours are much rarer than to West European countries. This is particularly striking in the case of the Czech Republic, while in Poland and Slovakia such contacts are more frequent.

A map of formal twinning links shows much the same features as one for study tours (table not presented). In Poland over 20% of municipalities have German partners, around 7% have French ones, around 7% have partners in Nordic countries, and 10% in other East-Central European states.

The Polish case suggests a definite regional pattern to the intensity of international contacts with individual countries. Some of the regional differences are simple to explain – they depend on geographical distance from the partner. Sometimes the explanation can be found in deeper historical traditions, while in some cases it may be difficult to find any logical explanation. Polish local governments' contacts with other East-Central European countries are the most frequent in regions located close to Polish borders. Local governments from Southern Poland have the most contacts with the Czech Republic, Slovakia and Hungary, while those in Eastern Poland often have links with Lithuania, Belorussia and Ukraine. Municipalities located in close vicinity of the Kaliningrad region have the largest number of contacts with Russia.

Links with Austria are most frequent in south-eastern Poland, which in the nineteenth century belonged to the Habsburg empire. Not surprisingly, contacts with Germany are the most common in western and northern Poland. Travels to Nordic countries are the most frequent from municipalities located near the Baltic seashore. Links with France, Netherlands and Belgium are more evenly distributed, although an above-average frequency is found in the Poznan region (in mid-western Poland).

Foreign experts and assistance

The use of foreign experts mapped here refers to experts coming from a foreign municipality or the visit of a consultant from an international aid programme or consultancy organization. Such contacts are relatively rare. Overall, less than a fifth report such visits. Use of foreign experts seems to be the most common in Slovakia, where almost a third of the mayors indicated their presence (see Table 4). The proportion of Czech or Polish municipalities which benefited from foreign assistance is considerably smaller.

TABLE 4
MUNICIPALITIES USING FOREIGN EXPERTS/ASSISTANCE (%)

	Czech Republic	Poland	Slovakia
None	86	85	72
Aid from foreign municipality	7	4	17
Aid programme	7	11	11

We do not have information about the tasks performed by the foreign experts or the results of their services, for example the change achieved. However, we did ask the mayors about their experience with the experts, i.e. how useful they thought the expert aid was. To a certain extent, this may be regarded as an 'outcome' measure. The work of foreign consultants is usually perceived as useful, although there are some exceptions to this rule. Over half of the respondents admit the assistance was useful and 30–40% thought it was partially useful. It seems that Polish local governments were the least satisfied – 15% of mayors claimed the foreign experts' advice was not useful, while the percentage of disappointed mayors in the Czech and Slovak Republics was well below 10%.

TABLE 5
MAYORS' OPINIONS ON FOREIGN ASSISTANCE (%)

	Czech Republic	Poland	Slovakia
Useful	62	51	51
So, so (not very useful)	34	34	41
Not useful	5	15	8

Note: Only mayors with experience of foreign assistance/aid programme are counted in this table.

Where did the foreign consultants come from? First of all, their origins are quite different from that of the other forms of international contacts. The origins of consultants are obviously related to the presence of long-term international programmes for local governments, which are financed either by the European Union (mostly through the PHARE programme) or by individual governments (such as USAID, British Know-How Fund) or by semi-public foundations from Western Europe (for example, the Adenauer or Ebert foundations from Germany). In the Czech Republic slightly over 50% of the experts came from Western Europe and the rest were usually from the USA. Western Europe provided about two-thirds of consultants working in Poland and over three-quarters of those working for Slovak local governments. Unfortunately, more precise information cannot be given here since many mayors did not distinguish clearly between donor agencies (such as PHARE, Know-How Fund, and German foundations).

Intensity of cross-border learning

In this section, we summarize the intensity of international contacts. The index of cross-border learning is based on the summary of answers to the three issues that were analysed separately above: International study tours (no = 0, once = 1, more = 2); twinning arrangements (no = 0, yes = 2); and international experts (no = 0, yes = 2).

The index may vary from 0 (no international contacts detected) to 6 (intensive contacts). The proportion of '0' varies from 18% of municipalities in Slovakia to 26% in Poland and 34% in the Czech Republic. The proportion of '6' (the most intensive contacts) ranges from 7% in Czech Republic to 8% in Poland and 18% in Slovakia. The average scores of the index are 2 in the Czech Republic, 2.19 in Poland and 2.62 in Slovakia.

The index is significantly correlated with the size of municipalities in all three countries (see Table 6). The table confirms that local governments in Slovakia have the most international contacts. However, a comparison of Poland and Slovakia is not so straightforward. Although the average index is higher for Poland, it seems to be very much dependent on the larger size of Polish local governments. When we compare Czech and Polish local governments of similar size, we may observe the reverse relationship – Czech local governments are more internationally active.

TABLE 6

'INDEX OF INTERNATIONALISM' ACCORDING TO SIZE OF MUNICIPALITIES

	Czech Republic	Poland	Slovakia
< 2,000	0.80	2.00	1.65
2,000 – 10,000	1.79	1.60	2.85
10,000 – 20,000	3.42	2.41	4.17
20,000 – 50,000	3.77	3.76	4.67
> 50,000	5.07	4.64	5.00

WHAT DRIVES CROSS-BORDER LEARNING?

Above, it was suggested that participation in international learning networks might be driven by a variety of forces, divided into pull, push and facilitating factors. The push factors included the performance of the local economy, which is mapped through items such as the rate of unemployment and the establishment of new firms. The expectation is that the worse the performance of the local economy the greater is the pressure on the mayor to act since the municipal finances are influenced by people's ability to pay taxes and by taxes paid by local firms.

Pull factors create opportunities or expose the municipalities to information about opportunities in international networks. Here, such items include membership in regional municipal associations (that often spread information about international network opportunities), the size of the municipalities (mayors of large urban municipalities are more exposed to opportunities), centrality (distance to the information networks of central cities), proximity to international borders, and the affluence of the municipalities (those which can afford to pay for the mayor's trips abroad).

Facilitating factors enhance the impacts of push and pull factors. Here, they include the mayor's education, age, gender and political style. Education is expected to work as a general asset in establishing international contacts (language skills, knowledge of other countries). With regard to gender, the expectation is that female mayors will be more active in international networks than their male counterparts. Female mayors are generally newer to the political game and can be expected to be less firmly integrated into established old-boy networks and traditional role models for mayors; they may therefore be more inclined to look abroad for new ideas about how to run the municipality and therefore more easily drawn into such international networks. Furthermore, younger mayors may be more inclined to try out or establish new relationships across borders. The pursuit of international contacts is also expected to be associated with a modern political style, such as an aptitude for working with the media (newspapers, radio) or a propensity to engage in dialogue with individual citizens rather than organized groups (a populist rather than a corporatist inclination, as suggested by the theory of the New Political Culture, Clarke and Hoffmann-Martinot, 1998).

Regression analyses have been carried out with the individual aspects of international networking as dependent variables rather than the overall index. This is because the facilitating factors are regarded as more appropriate in explaining the mayor's personal behaviour (study tours abroad) and less relevant for aspects of aggregate municipal behaviour such as formal twinning arrangements and visits from foreign experts.

TABLE 7A
FACTORS EXPLAINING INTERNATIONAL CONTACTS – REGRESSION ANALYSIS

	Mayor's travels abroad		
	PL	CR	SK
R	.470	.420	.386
R^2	.221	.176	.149
sign. F	.0000	.0000	.0000
Push factors			
Unemployment[a]	*		
New firms[b]	***	***	**
Pull factors			
Member of associations[c]	**	***	*
Centrality[d]	***		
Size[e]		**	
High budget[f]	***		
Proximity to borders[g]	*		
Personal/facilitating factors			
Sex			
Age			
Education	*	*	*
Contacts with journalists important for mayor[h]		*	
Citizen influence should be through political parties[i]	*		

* – significant on .05 level, ** – on .01 level, *** – on .001 level

Notes:
[a] Information supplied by surveyed mayors
[b] Information supplied by surveyed mayors
[c] Membership of municipal associations; information by surveyed mayors
[d] In Poland: distance from a city of 300,000 inhabitants or more; in Czech Republic: distance from Prague, Brno or Ostrava; in Slovakia: distance from Bratislava or Kosice
[e] Number of inhabitants
[f] Budget per capita
[g] In kilometers
[h] Mayors agreeing to the statement that 'Contacts with journalists are important for doing my job'
[i] Mayors agreeing to the statement that 'Citizens who want to influence local decision-making should be members of political parties'

The results of regression analyses are reported in tables 7A and 7B. In sum, the variables introduced into the equations yielded significant r^2s for all dependent variables in all three countries. International networking is influenced both by push and pull as well as facilitating factors. Overall, pull factors seem the most important ones. Memberships of municipal associations and size seem to be of general importance. Centrality is most important in Poland and least so in Slovakia. Proximity to borders is also

TABLE 7B
FACTORS EXPLAINING INTERNATIONAL CONTACTS – REGRESSION ANALYSIS

	Formal twinning			Visits of foreign experts		
	PL	CR	SK	PL	CR	SK
R	.451	.441	.433	.364	.388	.372
R^2	.204	.192	.166	.133	.151	.115
sign. F	.0000	.0000	.0000	.0000	.0000	.0000
Push factors						
Unemployment						
New firms	***	**	***	**	**	***
Pull factors						
Member of associations	***	***		*	**	**
Centrality	*	**		**		
Size	***	***	*	***	***	*
High budget	***	***				
Proximity to borders	**		*			

* – significant on .05 level, ** – on .01 level, *** – on .001 level

a driving force in Poland but it also has some significance in Slovakia with regard to twinning. Budgets matter most in Poland and the Czech Republic.

Education is the most important of the facilitating factors; better educated mayors go more often on study tours abroad. This is true in all three countries. However, political style also has some significance. Czech mayors who emphasize contacts with journalists (a New Political Culture indicator) as important for their jobs also go abroad more often. Polish mayors who think political parties are the most appropriate channel for citizen influence (a Traditional Culture indicator) rather than more direct contacts also travel more. The latter is rather against what we expected. The age and gender of the mayor are of little consequence.

Of the push factors as introduced into the analyses it is the mayor's view of the local economy that matters most. There are more international contacts in localities with an ability to attract new firms, whereas the opposite was expected. Thus, the local economy seems to work more as a pull factor than a push factor. A growing local economy may create learning opportunities for the mayor and the municipality. The municipality is pulled along on a wave of external contacts. It could, of course, also be that the mayor's contacts abroad help establish new firms in the locality. Undoubtedly, this is what mayors would like to think. Our data do not allow us to say that they are not right.

CONCLUSIONS

We have found that mayors and municipalities in East-Central Europe are extensively involved in cross-border networks with their counterparts in other European countries. The political upheavals of ten years ago have reached down to the local levels and produced fundamental re-orientations in patterns of co-operation. The patterns point strongly towards an emphasis on co-operation with West European counterparts. East-Central European municipalities are thus very much a part of the ongoing process of European integration that also drives much of the cross-border co-operation between municipalities in other parts of Europe. In this process, aspects of geographical location and historical ties matter for the relations that are established. However, the nature of the mayor as a person and a political operator also makes a difference. The extent of involvement in learning networks also depends on personality and political style. Consequently, who the citizens elect as their mayor may make a great deal of difference for their city's involvement in European integration. Mayors matter.

REFERENCES

Argyris, C. and D. Schön (1976), *Organizational Learning*. Reading, Mass.: Addison-Wesley.

Baldersheim, H. and K. Ståhlberg, eds. (1999a), *Nordic Region-Building in a European Perspective*. Aldershot: Ashgate.

Baldersheim, H. and K. Ståhlberg (1999b), 'The Internationalisation of Finnish and Norwegian Local Government', in H. Baldersheim and K. Ståhlberg (eds), *Nordic Region-Building in A European Perspective*. Aldershot: Ashgate.

Baldersheim, H.M. Illner, A. Offerdal, L. Rose and P. Swianiewicz (eds) (1996), *Local Democracy and the Processes of Transformation in East-Central Europe*. Boulder, Col.: Westview Press.

Baldersheim, H.G. Blaas, T.M. Horvath, M. Illner and P. Swianiewicz (1996), 'New institutions of Local Government. A Comparison', in H. Baldersheim, M. Illner, A. Offerdal, L. Rose and P. Swianiewicz (eds), *Local Democracy and the Processes of Transformation in East-Central Europe*. Boulder, Col.: Westview Press.

Clark, T.N. and V. Hoffmann-Martinot (eds) (1998), *The New Political Culture*. Boulder: Westvew Press.

Clark, T.N. and L. Ferguson (1983), *City Money*. New York: Columbia University Press.

Cyert, R.M. and J.G. March (1963), *A Behavioral Theory of the Firm*. Englewood Cliffs, NJ: Prentice-Hall.

Goldsmith, M.J.F. and K.K. Klausen (eds) (1997), *European Integration and Local Government*. Cheltenham: Edward Elgar.

Levitt, B. and J.G. March (1988), 'Organizational Learning', *Annual Review of Sociology*, Vol.14, pp.319–40

Marks, G., F. Nielsen, L. Ray and J. Salk (1994), 'Competencies, Cracks, and Conflicts: Regional Mobilization in the European Union'. Ch.3 in G. Marks, F.W. Scharpf, P.C. Schmitter and W.S. Streck (eds), *Governance in the European Union*. London: Sage.

Putnam, R. (1993), *Making Democracy Work: Civic Traditions in Modern Italy*. Princeton: Princeton University Press.

Surazska, W. (1997), *Balu burmistra*. Warsaw: Rzeczpospolita.

APPENDIX
DISTRIBUTION OF SAMPLES ACCORDING TO POPULATION SIZE OF MUNICIPALITIES (%)

	<2,000	2,000 to 10,000	10,000 to 20,000	20,000 to 50,000	>50,000	Total sample – responses (N)
Czech Republic						
Sample distribution	14.5	67.8	10.6	4.2	2.97	711–519
Nation-wide distribution	84	13	2	1	0.6	
Poland						
Sample distribution	0.6	64.1	15.8	15.2	4.3	1500–513
Nation-wide distribution	0.2	66	21	9	4	
Slovakia						
Sample distribution	37.1	49.2	5.8	5.8	2.2	550–313
Nation-wide distribution	86	11	1	1	0.4	

Source: Responses are based on questionnaires mailed to mayors in 1997. The surveys were carried out by national teams based in Bratislava, Prague and Warsaw, financed by a grant from the Norwegian Research Council plus national sources in the respective countries.

[2]

GLOBAL LINKAGES OF SUBNATIONAL REGIONS: COASTAL EXPORTS AND INTERNATIONAL NETWORKS

ASHOK DEO BARDHAN and SUBHRAJIT GUHATHAKURTA*

This article explores the determinants of exports of the two coastal regions of the continental United States and the differences between them. The authors evaluate the contribution of international sociocultural and business networks to exports of the two major coastal regions of the United States, the West Coast and the East Coast, and examine their geographic trading affinities. The article finds that although transnational business ties play a significant positive role in boosting overall exports of both coasts, social networks of foreign-born immigrants play a similar role only for the West Coast. The study also suggests that the significance of distance as a proxy for transportation costs is somewhat diminished once these networks are taken into account. Both regions seem to share a propensity for exports to the Asia-Pacific region. (*JEL* R0, F10, F 20)

I. INTRODUCTION

Trade issues have traditionally been analyzed at the level of the nation-state. Indeed, in international trade literature a country functions largely as a monolithic black box. For a large country, such as the United States, this aggregate level of analysis may obscure some underlying regional economic features and attributes. The latter have acquired increasing significance because growing global economic integration has given an added impetus to forces of agglomeration and specialization within nations. The study of international trade of subnational regions offers the possibility of gaining insight into the building blocks of macro-trading affinities. For example, export data, available for constituent states of the United States, allows one to study variations in trading patterns among different states and regions of the union. The trading affinities of regional economies would also be helpful in assessing their vulnerability to foreign shocks and in determining changes in competitiveness relative to the national and other subnational economies. The objective here is to study the differences between and the determinants of exports from the two coastal economic regions of the United States: the West Coast economic region, comprising the contiguous coastal states of California, Oregon, and Washington, and the East Coast economic region, consisting of the states of Florida, Georgia, South Carolina, North Carolina, Virginia, Maryland, Delaware, New Jersey, New York, and the New England states minus land-locked Vermont.

This article is motivated by several factors. The first arises out of the increasing emphasis placed by regional and state authorities on stimulating exports. The number of international trade and investment offices as well as export promotion offices of various states has been increasing annually until recently. States regularly schedule trade missions led by senior officials. Indeed, there has been a trickle-down effect of this policy initiative on the part of state officials, with city mayors now promoting their metropolitan exports. The

*The authors gratefully acknowledge the advice, suggestions, and help from Raj Datta, Jeffrey Frankel, David Howe, Dwight Jaffee, Cynthia Kroll, Raka Ray, seminar participants at UC Berkeley, Stanford, and Indian Institute of Management, Ahmedabad. The suggestions of three anonymous referees are also much appreciated. The study was partially funded by the the Fisher Center for Real Estate and Urban Economics, UC Berkeley, and the Herberger Center for Design Excellence, Arizona State University.

Bardhan: Haas School of Business, F-602 University of California, Berkeley, CA 94720. Phone 1-510-643-7355, Fax 1-510-6113-7357, E-mail bardhan@haas.berkeley.edu

Guhathakurta: School of Planning and Landscape Architecture, Arizona State University, Tempe, A2 85287. Phone 1-602-965-6343, E-mail: subhro.guha@ asu.edu

ABBREVIATIONS

GDP: Gross Domestic Product

NAFTA: North American Free Trade Association

Contemporary Economic Policy
(ISSN 1074-3529)
Vol. 22, No. 2, April 2004, 225–236

DOI: 10.1093/cep/byh016

primary factor behind this emergent enthusiasm for trade has been the realization, particularly in the coastal states, that exports are increasingly a very sizable part of the gross regional product. The second is the size of the two regional economies—the West Coast and the East Coast economies of the United States, which are larger than all but a few of the world's economies—and the sizable geographic distance separating the two. If these regions are indeed significantly different in their trading patterns and have different influences impacting these patterns, then this study could also contribute to the debate about the role of the nation-state vis-à-vis its constituent regions in the age of increasing globalization.

This article looks at exports as well as other global linkages of these coastal economies, such as transnational immigrant and business networks. The coastal states are entrepôts not just to trade and investment flows but also to the impact of international social (immigrant) and business networks. Indeed, the two major coastal states, California and New York, are also the largest immigrant states of the union. A significant proportion of the flow of immigrants arrives in these coastal regions; but more importantly, a sizable number of them choose to settle down there. The ease of international travel and the entrepôt nature of the coastal ports also leads to a high concentration of transnational business linkages based along the coasts, in the form of foreign direct investment as well as various other forms of business-to-business contacts.

Contiguous coastal states belonging to one region share common attributes that distinguish them from the inland states. In contrast to inland states, coastal states are generally the transshipment points for the majority of goods imported and exported, as well as for international flows of people. The two coastal regions are also different; a priori one would expect the Atlantic coast to have trading affinities with Europe and South America, and the Pacific coast to be the entrepôt for most of the trade with Asia. The distinctions between the two coasts have been sustained by different historical contexts and separate industrial trajectories. The Atlantic coast has a longer history of industrial development and older immigrant concentrations, whereas the Pacific coastal states have attracted newer industries and mostly recent immigrants. Regardless, the existing immigrant concentrations in the Atlantic coastal states have continued to draw immigrants from Europe, Africa, and Latin America through established social networks. Similar networks are also operational on the Pacific coast but for immigrants who arrive mostly from Mexico and Asian countries. The composition, structure, and age of these immigrant communities in the two regions lead to differences in the nature of contacts they have with their countries of origin. Similarly, the international business ties of these regions have traversed different paths. One would expect the trading patterns of these regions to be impacted by the significant differences in the makeup of the resident population and the dominant industrial structure.

The methodological tool in this article is a stripped-down version of the gravity model. Some formulation of the gravity model has been a familiar and widely used method of studying international and interregional trade relationships. In recent years its usage has been extended to assess the impact of trade and openness on national or regional growth and income (Frankel et al., 1996b) and to discover natural trading blocs (Frankel et al., 1996a). Here, instead of applying a traditional gravity model to the United States as a whole, the authors employ a modified version of the model to exports of the two coastal regions of the United States. The traditional gravity model is also modified to check for the influence of other quasi-economic trading stimuli, such as transnational business and social ties and networks in determining the direction and volume of exports. By transnational social ties and networks, the authors mean the contacts that bind foreign-born immigrants to their countries of birth. International business networks are understood as intrafirm commercial transactions connecting affiliates, subsidiaries, offices, and headquarters across national borders. The exact formulations are explained later.

In the context of a gravity model, the choice of subnational regions instead of the nation as an object of study helps one arrive at a more accurate measure of distance with the regions' trading partners. It also allows one to test for differential trading affinities of the two coastal seaboards, far removed from each other, and geographically closer to different parts of the world—Asia-Pacific region in the case of the West Coast, and Europe/South America in the case of the East Coast.

The questions that are addressed are: what are the similarities and differences in the relationships between exports and their determinants, such as social/business networks, for the two coastal regions and the nation as a whole, and what are the global regional exporting affinities of these coastal economies? This approach—that is, the study of trading patterns of subnational regions—though accounting for the ties and networks that bind local and regional economies to the larger global economy, helps one look at the regional economy as an integral part of the global economy.

The article is organized in the following fashion. Section II summarizes the relevant literature, and section III highlights the theoretical considerations that go into the empirical methodology. These are followed by section IV, the data section; section V, which discusses the estimation results, and section VI, which contains the concluding remarks.

II. LITERATURE REVIEW

Rapid advances in information and communications technologies and intensifying global economic integration are rendering the nation-state somewhat less meaningful as an economic unit. Paul Krugman (1991), among other economists, has been advocating an integrated look at regional economics, macroeconomics, and international economics under the aegis of economic geography. The economic strands connecting regional economies to the global economy have usually been examined through the prism of regional competitiveness, development of local industry, and impact on local labor markets. Shift-share techniques have been usefully employed to assess trade-related job changes at the regional level, as well as for evaluating regional advantage (Noponen et al., 1993; Sihag and McDonough, 1989).

Various studies have explored the impact of foreign-born immigrants on issues relating to wages, employment, welfare, and business formation (Simon, 1992). Social scientists have also thrown considerable light on the creation, maintenance, and role played by transnational social networks formed due to ties with the country of origin of foreign-born immigrants in the United States, on the determinants of immigrant concentration and on the microstructure of migration networks (Castles and Miller, 1993; Massey and España, 1987; Belanger and Rogers, 1992; Bartel, 1989). Studies have also looked at the relationship between movement of people and movement of capital and goods (Sassen, 1988, 1998) and the role played by immigrant networks in sustaining business and economic ties with the country of origin (Borjas, 1994; Matthei, 1996; Ho, 1993; Saxenian, 1999).

The relationship between immigrant populations and trade is an emerging area of research in economic and sociological literature. A number of studies have shown that the size of the foreign-born populations contributes significantly to trade between the country of origin and the adopted country (Gould, 1994; Head and Ries, 1998). Rauch (2001) reviews this body of literature and suggests that there is evidence pointing to the role of transnational business and social networks in promoting international trade due to mitigation of contract enforcement problems and enhancement of information flows. Gould's (1994) study of U.S. trade with 47 partner countries showed that immigrants facilitated the expansion of trade to their countries of origin, with exports being more strongly influenced than imports. A similar study of Canadian trade with partner countries reaffirmed the positive influence of immigrants on trade (Head and Reis, 1998). An innovation of the Canadian study was the disaggregation of migrants by type, showing that immigrants who were independents (mostly professionals) had a more pronounced impact on trade than entrepreneurs and refugees.

Dunlevy and Hutchinson's (1999) study of the historical impact of immigrants on American imports for the period between 1870 and 1910, which examines the contribution of migrant stock to imports from their countries of origin and is disaggregated both by exporting regions and by commodity type, corroborates the trade-enhancing effects of immigrants in the more recent cases reported earlier. The results show considerable variation in the influence of migrants by their region of origin on U.S. imports and note the impact of migrants only for finished and differentiated goods, such as manufactures and foodstuffs.

The evidence provided in this body of literature suggests that there is a positive relationship between migrant flows and trade flows. However, more disaggregated analyses have shown that this relationship is conditioned by a number of contextual factors. Given that studies have been only available for two countries

(United States and Canada) and that most of these studies were conducted at the national level, generalization of these results is limited. In addition, questions remain regarding the robustness of these results. It is possible, for example, that some key geographical region of the United States accounted for the results, or that the variation could have been explained by the type of immigrants and by the type of commodities traded. For example, Rauch (1999) presents evidence that common language/colonial ties and networks due to proximity are more important for differentiated products.

Another branch of international trade literature provides one more set of networks that can potentially impact trade flows. Foreign direct investment and direct investment abroad have generated a debate whether these kinds of investment activities substitute or complement trade between the country where investment originates and the host country (Konan, 2000; Roy and Viaene, 1998). Wilamoski and Tinkler (1999) show that there is a rise in intrafirm exports and imports between the United States and Mexico as a result of U.S. foreign direct investment in Mexico. Similarly, theoretical studies have found that vertical investment across borders complements rather than substitutes for trade, because of intrafirm trade in intermediates (Konan, 2000). Clausing (2000) finds evidence that supports the conclusion that multinational activity and trade are complementary activities, particularly multinational activity and intrafirm trade.

However, most of the empirical literature on this topic looks at the issue of complementarity or substitutability between *local* sales in a foreign country of, say, foreign affiliates of U.S. multinationals and *exports* from the United States to that foreign country. The idea in those studies is to examine whether those local sales of multinational affiliates displace the exports that were previously being shipped from the home country. The literature does not examine a related issue—whether exports by multinationals from the home country augment the overall exports from the home country, that is, whether there is a positive spillover effect of intrafirm trade on arm's-length trade.

III. THEORETICAL CONSIDERATIONS

Economists have derived the gravity equation from basic principles of international economics. The equation postulates that bilateral trade between two countries would be proportional to the product of their respective outputs and declining in distance between them. Deardorff (1995), in a seminal article, shows how the basic Heckscher-Ohlin model of international trade can lead to a gravity specification for bilateral trade. When countries produce distinct goods with complete specialization or for a whole range of other assumptions and preferences, trade takes place according to the standard gravity model and declines with distance, with the latter being a rough measure of transportation costs. Harrigan (2001) reviews the theoretical and empirical literature on gravity models and similarly stresses the role played by relative as well as absolute transportation and other trade and transaction costs. In the empirical literature, the extensions to the standard version of the model have generally come in the form of variables that would impact trade, transportation, and transaction costs. Regional dummy variables have been used to both capture the relative transportation costs of trading with a particular region of the world and highlight trading affinities. The rationale for using foreign-born immigrants in the gravity model in this study is precisely because their presence alleviates the costs of doing business between their country of origin and the host country.

Immigrants impact trade because of their kinship ties and their implicit knowledge about the customs, language, and social norms of their country of origin. Immigrants can substantially reduce the hidden costs of foreign trade by identifying potential customers and business partners and by deftly navigating the plethora of local customs, laws, and business practices in their home country. In fact, the social and economic conditions, which give rise to issues of trust at the national level, are more pronounced in the sphere of international trade. If agents cannot indulge in complete contracting (even in the domestic market) with far better information and legal machinery and reputational threats at their disposal, one can conjecture that international markets are fraught with greater risk in terms of incomplete contracts and high transaction costs. In other words, "economizing on transactions costs," a concept that lies at the core of the theories of Williamson (1998), seems to be one appropriate theoretical framework for understanding the relationship between immigrants and trade. Also related to these issues is the proposition that immigrant populations capitalize on the ethnic capital embodied in their communities (Borjas, 1995), and one of the manifestations of this capitalization is expressed in ties and trade flows with the country of origin. Insofar as trade is information-dependent, in the sense of knowledge about foreign markets, regulations, and contacts, then the pool of immigrants in the United States constitutes a large information bank that can be drawn on to tap foreign markets

In the present case, the authors bring two different strands of literature together by including a variable that captures transnational business ties as well as the transnational social ties of newly arrived immigrants. Insofar as business-to-business ties enhance business information flows across countries and reduce transaction costs, one would expect them to impact the prices faced by the importers and consequently the amount of trade between any bilateral set of countries. Unlike the literature cited earlier, the approach here is somewhat different. In this article, a variable that proxies for transnational business-to-business ties is used to test if these ties have a positive and significant impact on overall exports from the coastal regions. The variable used is the proportion of exports to different countries that is carried out by multinationals or the ratio of intrafirm exports to total exports. Therefore, unlike the extant literature, which studies complementarity between multinational activity *within the domain* of a foreign country and exports from the United States, here the authors test for complementarity between intrafirm exports and total exports.

Studies of intrafirm activities have focused mostly on transfer pricing issues and on the connection between foreign direct investment and trade. The magnitude of intrafirm trade by country has become increasingly evident with the publication of survey articles and data by the U.S. Department of Commerce in 1997. The large proportion of intrafirm trade signifies a strengthening and deepening of cross-country business ties. Inclusion of a variable as a proxy for these networks in a gravity model can help one ferret out the spillover effects that within-firm trade can have on arm's-length transactions.

The authors bring together these independent strands of literature on impact of immigrants and business networks on trade flows in the context of exports of subnational regions of the United States. Because of the variation in the type and composition of foreign-born immigrants settled on the two seaboards, as well as the differences in the industrial paths taken by the geographically and historically distinct regional economies, it is possible to simultaneously account for both of these effects and assess the differential impact these kinds of global linkages have on the international trade flows of these regional, coastal economies.

The equation estimated is:

$$\begin{aligned} Log([\Sigma_i StateExports]_n) &= constant + \alpha \mathrm{Log}(GDP_n) \\ &\quad + \beta Log(GDP\ per\ Capita_n) \\ &\quad + \gamma Log(Distance[West\ or\ East]_n) \\ &\quad + \lambda\, Log(\Sigma_i Foreign\ Born)_n \\ &\quad + \theta(Intrafirm\ Export\ Ratio)_n \\ &\quad + Region\ Dummy_n. \end{aligned}$$

This version of the gravity model is built on exports alone, because import data for subnational regions of the United States is not available. The model estimated is therefore a stripped-down version of the standard model because the authors are not looking at bilateral trade of all countries that a gravity model is usually associated with. The state exports were summed (over i states) separately for both coasts by importing country (n), and their logs were taken. Similarly, the foreign-born immigrants, resident in states of the two coastal regions, were summed up by their country of origin. For both the West and East Coasts, pooled ordinary least squares regressions with fixed effects were carried out for the cross-sectional panel of importing countries. Pooled, time-dummy fixed-effects specification was chosen to neutralize year-specific effects for the three years of data, 1994–96. The dependent variable is the log of goods exports of the two regions.

A few further clarifications are in order. All the independent variables are in log form, which helps in interpreting the estimated coefficients as elasticities. Because the intrafirm export variable is already expressed in percentage terms, the authors follow general convention in many log-linear models and retain it in its untransformed state. To isolate the effect of these networks, the authors need some more control variables apart from the ones already included, such as gross domestic product (GDP) and distance. Frankel et al. (1995) note that as countries "become more developed they tend to specialize more and to trade more." The authors control for this level of development by including a GDP per capita variable, which is widely used as a control variable in gravity trade equations. Also, as with many trade-related papers using the gravity model with a view to highlighting trade affinities, the authors include regional dummies (see Rose, 2000; Frankel et al., 1995). The latter are in binary form and take the value 1, in the case of the Asia-Pacific region dummy, whenever the country in question belongs to one of the following: Japan, China, Hong Kong, Korea, Taiwan, Singapore, Malaysia, Indonesia, the Philippines, Thailand, Vietnam, Australia, or New Zealand, and zero otherwise. Although the Asia-Pacific trade block does not formally exist as yet, papers by Frankel and co-workers (1995) and others have pointed out that by nature of its intraregional trade and ties, it does so in a de facto sense. Similarly, the European Union can be thought to have formalized the already-existing intraregional ties. These dummies are of course different from the time dummies for 1994, 1995, and 1996 used in a fixed-effects context, where only the constant in the regression, or the intercept, is affected.

IV. THE DATA

A. *State/Regional Export Data*

Export data for the coastal regions have been calculated from state-level export data available from the U.S. Department of Commerce, which has an arrangement with the Massachusetts Institute for Social and Economic Research. This institute has been generating the state export database since 1987 under an agreement with the U.S. Census Bureau's Foreign Trade Division. Known as the Origin of Movement series, it is estimated from shippers' export declaration documents at customs points and ports of exit. An imputational algorithm is utilized to allocate missing data to states. Unlike Canadian data on interprovincial trade, there is no comparable U.S. data on exports and imports between states.

The authors use data for country-wise goods exports of the coastal states listed earlier, for the years 1994–96. These three years were the most recent common years for the entire sample of countries for which there were complete and reliable data on all the relevant variables. Moreover, the Asian crisis erupted in 1997, causing major fluctuations in exchange rates and disrupting global trade flows. There are 51 countries in our sample, roughly accounting for more than 95% of total exports worldwide by these coastal regions. This number was ultimately dictated by the availability of intrafirm trade data for different countries. The total number of panel obeservations for the three years is therefore 153.

Although the two coasts of the continental United States are mismatched in the number of states along the coastline, the total amount of exports from these two coastal regions are comparable. The three states along the West Coast exported $122 billion worth of merchandise to 62 major markets around the globe in 1996. That year, the 14 East Coast states exported merchandise worth $148.5 billion to the same markets. Exports from the two coastal regions accounted for a little over 40% of total U.S. exports in 1996. Table 1 lists the top export markets for the two coastal regions.

B. *Social Networks*

Because the contacts and information networks of immigrants in their home country would presumably wither away after a few generations, the authors incorporate only zero-generation or foreign-born immigrants with a "fresh memory." Data come from Table 144 of the Social and Economic Characteristics series of the 1990 U.S. Census, which publishes the number of foreign-born residents, that is, the stock of foreign-born immigrants in the United States by each state and by country of birth. In the case of a number of newly independent countries, such as the successor states to the former Yugoslavia and Soviet Union, the authors have allocated the numbers from the parent state to the successor states in proportion to the population.

An examination of the number of foreign-born inhabitants by state and region shows that the overwhelming majority of them have chosen to locate in California. Although this is expected given the size of the state, it is intriguing that California has more foreign-born residents than the entire East Coast region. The second most important destination for immigrants is the state of New York, which has less than half of the foreign-born population of California. Except the states of California, New York, and Florida, no other state had a

TABLE 1
Major Export Markets for the U.S. Coastal Regions

	East Coast Markets			West Coast Markets		
		1996	1994–96 Change (%)		1996	1994–96 Change (%)
Rank	East Coast Total	$148,486,457	20	West Coast Total	$122,130,065	20
1	Canada	30,057,370	17	Japan	27,508,250	23
2	Japan	14,247,600	17	Canada	13,904,692	27
3	United Kingdom	9,372,337	20	South Korea	10,328,151	58
4	Germany	7,217,902	34	Mexico	8,095,028	25
5	Mexico	6,632,665	1	Taiwan	7,337,162	11
6	South Korea	6,506,785	23	United Kingdom	6,629,061	3
7	Brazil	5,323,318	61	Germany	5,028,104	11
8	Belgium	5,209,059	9	Hong Kong	4,761,672	31
9	Netherlands	4,503,667	17	Malaysia	3,720,411	11
10	Switzerland	4,102,525	95	China	3,493,194	2
11	France	3,932,039	22	Netherlands	3,088,411	−3
12	Hong Kong	3,756,049	11	Thailand	2,910,523	55
13	Taiwan	3,314,439	−1	France	2,888,642	−1
14	Israel	2,838,635	26	Australia	2,773,599	5
15	China	2,826,473	25	Philippines	2,409,870	55

TABLE 2
Foreign-Born Population in Coastal States of U.S.

	East Coast Immigrants		West Coast Immigrants	
Rank	Country of Origin	Population	Country of Origin	Population
1	Italy	313,862	Mexico	2,549,937
2	Dominican Republic	298,347	Philippines	512,803
3	Canada	282,229	Vietnam	294,701
4	Jamaica	270,087	El Salvador	282,628
5	Germany	247,431	South Korea	227,000
6	United Kingdom	238,738	China	225,886
7	China	185,462	Canada	211,611
8	Colombia	177,858	United Kingdom	159,488
9	Poland	161,350	Guatemala	136,843
10	South Korea	156,859	Germany	131,199
11	India	147,991	Japan	114,650
12	Mexico	133,078	Taiwan	110,798
13	Philippines	131,684	India	89,110
14	Portugal	130,106	Hong Kong	69,501
15	Ireland	96,346	Nicaragua	58,979

Source: 1990 Census of Population and Housing: Social and Economic Characteristics, table 144.

foreign-born population of more than 500,000 in 1990. The country-wise distribution of foreign-born immigrants on the two coasts is significantly different, with consequences that shall be commented on in the next section. Whereas immigrants settled on the West Coast seem to be mostly from the Asia-Pacific region, the East Coast presents a more nuanced picture, with an apparent tilt toward Europe and the Americas (see Table 2).

C. *Transnational Business Networks and Ties*

As a proxy for the intensity of business ties connecting the coastal regions with our sample of countries, the authors use intrafirm export ratios calculated by the Bureau of Economic Analysis of the Department of Commerce in the February 1997 edition of the *Survey of Current Business*. The intrafirm export ratios by country is the proportion of U.S. exports to that country transacted by U.S. parent firms to their affiliates in that country or by foreign affiliates to their parent firms outside the United States. The ratios range widely by country, from highs of 74% for Switzerland and 70% for Japan to less than 3% for Greece, Turkey, and Poland.

D. Distance

The authors use the traditional great circle distance (in kilometers) between San Francisco for the West Coast and New York for the East Coast and usually the largest city of the other country, with some exceptions. In countries that cover large geographic areas, such as Russia, India, Australia, and China, the article takes into account the geographic spread of economic activity. The basic motivation was to measure distances from the West Coast's geographic center of economic activity, around San Francisco, to the corresponding center in the other country, which was done on a case-by-case basis. Microsoft's Encarta software was used for calculating the distances.

E. GDP and GDP per Capita

Data on the GDP and GDP per capita were obtained from the selective Data Query segment of the World Development Indicators database of the World Bank online at http://devdata.worldbank.org/data-query. The GDP figures were available directly, whereas the GDP per capita figure has been calculated from the former and the population data accessed from the same source. These data as well as the export figures for the coastal regions of the United States are in current U.S. dollars.

V. RESULTS

Table 3 shows the estimation results of the model. The year-specific intercepts for the three years, which are the result of the fixed-effects, time-dummy specification, are not shown. The first columns show the results for the most basic form of the gravity model that includes the GDP, the per capita income, and the distance variables, and they seem to fit the regional export data quite well. For the West Coast region, the signs of all the variables—GDP, GDP per capita, and distance—are as expected

TABLE 3
Regressions for West and East Coasts

	West			East		
Explanatory Variables	**I**	**II**	**III**	**I**	**II**	**III**
GDP	0.918*	0.593*	0.52*	0.563*	0.521*	0.44*
	(0.054)	(0.054)	(0.062)	(0.037)	(0.057)	(0.054)
GDP per capita	0.047	0.258*	0.22*	−0.04	−0.009	−0.04
	(0.067)	(0.054)	(0.068)	(0.058)	(0.06)	(0.075)
Distance	−0.557*	−0.077	0.119	−0.682*	−0.92*	−0.757*
	(0.24)	(0.231)	(0.272)	(0.09)	(0.175)	(0.165)
Foreign-born (social networks)		0.239*	0.262*		0.059	0.086
		(0.058)	(0.057)		(0.068)	(0.067)
Asia		1.51*	1.44*		0.929*	0.81*
		(0.151)	(0.158)		(0.158)	(0.16)
NAFTA		1.48*	1.54*		0.332	0.458+
		(0.28)	(0.29)		(0.26)	(0.241)
Intrafirm export ratio (business networks)			1.13*			1.24*
			(0.56)			(0.495)
Adj R^2	0.64	0.85	0.86	0.50	0.59	0.61
N	153	153	153	153	153	153

Notes: Dependent variable: log of exports. All variables (except dummies and intrafirm export ratio) in logs. Coefficients on time dummies/year controls not shown. White heteroscedasticity-consistent standard errors in parentheses. Pooled least squares regression, 1994–96.

*Significant at 5%. +Significant at 10%.

in the most truncated equation (1). The per capita variable is not significant, although that changes in subsequent equations. The results are somewhat similar in the case of the East Coast, and again the coefficient on the per capita variable is not significant. Gravity models that incorporate bilateral, paired, export and import data usually find the sign to be positive and significant. In this article, only one-way data, that is, exports, are used. Moreover, the income elasticity of goods exported from the coastal economies to other countries might be quite low.

The augmented model includes the international social network variable and regional dummies for the North American Free Trade Association (NAFTA) and the Asia-Pacific region. The countries listed in the latter region have been mentioned before, and in addition to the reasons given there for the inclusion of this dummy variable, the rationale for choosing a region that is not formally a trade bloc also stems from its location vis-à-vis the West Coast, as well as the increasing role played by this region in international trade.

The coefficient on the social network variable is positive and significant for West and positive and insignificant for East. Apparently, at least for West, the transnational ties and contacts of the foreign-born immigrants resident there have a positive impact on the exports of the region. A 1% increase in immigrants settled on the West Coast tends to increase the region's exports by over 0.2%. This seems to buttress the initial hypothesis about the competitive value of the knowledge bank embodied in the foreign-born population. The difference between the coasts in terms of the impact of this variable lies in both the different industrial structure of the regions and the composition of the immigrants, their countries of origin, and their occupations. Interestingly enough, the Asian dummy is significant for both coasts, whereas the NAFTA dummy is positive but significant only for the West. The Europe dummy was tried but found to be insignificant for both regions. Previous gravity models have found little evidence for a NAFTA effect for the United States as a whole, despite the existence of a Canada–U.S. Free Trade Pact of 1989 and NAFTA itself, which became operational in 1994 (Krueger, 2000). The strong impact of the Asian dummy formalizes anecdotal evidence about the role of the region in trade with the United States. The fastest growing region of the world until the 1997 Asian crisis, its rapidly developing economies have been participating ever more actively in global trade. Also, the U.S. recession of the early 1990s boosted outsourcing to countries in Asia, resulting in an increase in trade in inputs, both of the intrafirm as well as arm's-length variety. This leads logically to the next version of the estimated model that includes the intrafirm variable.

An additional singularity in the results for equation (2) for the West Coast is that the coefficient on the distance variable loses its significance once the foreign-born variable is introduced, suggesting that distance (and consequently transportation costs) do not have their traditional negative drag on exports once the social networks are taken into account. This is somewhat tentative evidence that relative transportation costs between the West Coast and different countries don't vary enough to make much of a difference. The behavior of the coefficient on the distance variable cannot be accounted for in the absence of any significant degree of correlation between number of foreign-born immigrants and distance, which would have explained why the latter drops out after inclusion of the former. Noninclusion of Mexico, the major contributor to West Coast immigration numbers, does not significantly change the results. Trade economists using gravity models have acknowledged that the principal natural barriers to trade may be cultural or perhaps logistical in origin, and it was thought that variables for distance or proximity could adequately reflect such intangibles (Frankel et al., 1995). One could also conjecture that contacts and ties to the home country are themselves independent of distance and that frequent travel home serves more than one purpose, thus spreading out the fixed costs. This prompts another explanation for the different behavior of the coasts when it comes to the effect of immigrants on trade. There is suggestive evidence that foreign-born immigrants settled on the West Coast tend to travel more frequently and in greater numbers to their countries of origin. Again, this is possibly due to the different mix of dominant countries of origin of immigrants of both coasts. Borjas (1991) also refers to the shifts in the national origin mix of the immigrant flow. It should be noted that the two different regions covered in this article are home to a different mix, both in terms of the

TABLE 4
Educational Attainment of Foreign-Born Persons 25 Years of Age and Over

Country	Percent with Bachelors Degree
Philippines	34.6
Hong Kong	28.0
India	26.6
Taiwan	26.1
Japan	24.8
South Korea	22.2
Thailand	19.5
China	15.4
France	14.0
Oceania	13.2

Source: 1990 Census.

national origin of immigrants, as well as their educational levels. Table 4, read together with Table 2, suggests that the shift in the national origin mix has other implications as well; the West Coast is home to a better-educated foreign-born population, when taking into account the Asian bias of the immigrant population there, which would be another reason for the different behavior of the coasts in international trade. Because the data on educational attainment does not cover a significant number of countries in the data set and is not available at a finer geographical detail at the level of individual states and regions, one cannot include it in the regressions.

The third equation includes the measure of business ties across borders—the intrafirm export ratio. It is positive and significant for both East and West, suggesting that there are strong complementarities and spillover effects from intrafirm trade for exports overall. The greater the proportion of total trade that is conducted within multinational firms, the greater the overall exports to the country where the affiliate/headquarters are located, that is, arm's-length exports seem to be positively impacted by intrafirm exports from the coasts.

The theory of intraindustry trade suggests that like trades with like, or that most of the trade of a developed economy is with other developed economies because of the similarity in their industrial structures, leading to intense trade in differentiated goods and intermediate inputs for complex production processes. Most intrafirm trade is often also intraindustry trade, except in the case of firms-conglomerates or international trading companies that deal in a whole range of goods. Although the authors have controlled for the standard of living with the per capita variable, the coefficient on the intrafirm export ratio variable is robustly positive and significant.

An explanation can perhaps be found by looking deeper into the kind of goods being traded. International trade of intermediate inputs explains a large proportion of within-firm trade. Global economic integration has led to a proliferation of plants manufacturing intermediate inputs in an increasingly diverse set of countries. The traditional cross-border intrafirm trade involving only the rich countries—the United Kingdom, Netherlands, United States, and Japan—is now being supplemented by more dispersed intrafirm trade. In fact, global economic integration has allowed multinationals to create sequential production processes by locating their intermediate production activities in various parts of the world. Together with such fragmented production comes an intensive trade in intermediate inputs for the purpose of production of the final manufactured good and a network of spillover ties both in the host country, as well as the home country (see Arndt and Kierzkowski, 2001). The story involving trade in intermediate inputs could explain why the Asian effect remains significant in the third regressions (albeit with diminished magnitude), suggesting that it cannot be just intrafirm trade with this region that accounts for this trading affinity but possibly some kind of complementarity of industrial structures, expressed in cross-Pacific supply chains and production networks.

The authors carry out another check by running the last equation with a different dependent variable—the log of computer and electronics product exports from the two regions (see Table 5). Though the results for the East Coast region are largely similar to the earlier ones, the West Coast trends are further confirmed, whether it is the phenomenon of "disappearing distance," the role of "ethnic capital," the weight of the Asia-Pacific region in the coast's foreign markets, or even the spillover effect of intrafirm exports. The persistence of the Asia-Pacific effect underscores the possibility, already mentioned, of cross-Pacific production ties and trade in

TABLE 5
Dependent Variable: Log of West and East Coast Exports of Computer and Electronic Products

Explanatory Variables	West	East
GDP	0.742*	0.504*
	(0.06)	(0.041)
GDP per capita	0.24⁺	0.09⁺
	(0.12)	(0.048)
Distance	0.015	−0.77*
	(0.11)	(0.16)
Foreign-born	0.341*	0.016
	(0.042)	(0.015)
Asia	1.78*	0.92*
	(0.144)	(0.20)
NAFTA	1.52*	0.58*
	(0.31)	(0.24)
Intrafirm export ratio	1.35*	1.25*
	(0.39)	(0.47)
Adj. R^2	0.89	0.74
N	153	153

Notes: All variables (except dummies and intrafirm export ratio) in logs. Coefficients on time dummies/year controls not shown. White heteroscedasticity-consistent standard errors in parentheses. Pooled least squares regression, 1994–96.

*Significant at 5%.

⁺Significant at 10%.

high-tech intermediate inputs being the driving force behind this phenomenon. Feenstra (1998) points to the simultaneous integration of world markets through increased trade but a disintegration of the production process, with manufacturing activity being scattered globally. Traditional, domestic, vertical integration, and Fordist models are giving way to arm's-length outsourcing or transnational integration, which involves intrafirm trade in intermediate inputs, a phenomenon that is getting increasingly widespread, particularly in the high-tech sectors.

VI. CONCLUDING REMARKS

The two large coastal regional economies of the United States appear to have different trading affinities, although both share a propensity for trade with the Asia-Pacific region. Variables used as proxies for social and business contacts appear to be just as important as the minimalist geographical attribute of distance, certainly for the West Coast, and transportation costs seem to matter less, when other gravitational forces are taken into account. In all likelihood, this is due to a combination of factors, such as trade in intermediate inputs particularly of an intrafirm nature, linking the West Coast and the Asia-Pacific economies, the complex chains of international production, highly integrated trade ties, and transnational social connections that characterize the West Coast economy, as well as some specific attributes of the West Coast economy. By "specific attributes" we mean the increasingly "weightless" nature of high-tech products, that is, their high price-to-weight ratio.

Foreign-born immigrants settled on the West Coast of the country seem to constitute a formidable bank of competitive power, an observation shared by other social scientists. Also, business networks set up by multinational firms, cross-border family enterprises, their subsidiaries, and affiliates have a powerful and positive impact on overall exports from the coasts, suggesting that there are spillover effects of foreign direct investment. The economic space created by the interaction of affiliates, subsidiaries, and the parent firm tends to have an energizing effect on arm's-length transactions as well.

This study of the international trade of a subnational region, together with the social and business networks that bind it to other national economies, is in effect a look at a regional economy as an integral part of the global. Literature on international trade has either ignored subnational regions or treated them as fractal or self-similar to the national economy. At a time when national economies and global markets are getting more closely integrated, a look inside the black box reveals the singular attributes of ties that bind different subnational regions to the global economy.

REFERENCES

Arndt, S. W., and H. Kierzkowski (eds.). *Fragmentation: New Production Patterns in the World Economy*, Oxford: Oxford University Press, 2001.

Bartel, A. P. "Where Do the New U.S. Immigrants Live?" *Journal of Labor Economics*, 7(4), 1989, 371–91.

Belanger, A., and A. Rogers. "The Internal Migration and Spatial Redistribution of the Foreign-Born in the United States: 1965–1970 and 1975–1980." *International Migration Review*, 4, 1992, 1342–69.

Borjas, G. J. "Immigrants in the U.S. Labor Market: 1940–80." *American Economic Review*, 81(2), 1991, 287–91.

Borjas, G. J. "The Economics of Immigration." *Journal of Economic Literature*, 32(4), 1994, 1667–717.

———. "Ethnicity, Neighborhoods, and Human-Capital Externalities." *American Economic Review*, 85(3), 1995, 365–90.

Castles, S., and M. J. Miller. *The Age of Migration: International Population Movements in the Modern World*. London: Macmillan, 1993.

Clausing, K. A. "Does Multinational Activity Displace Trade?" *Economic Inquiry*, 38(2), 2000, 190–205.

Deardorff, A. "Determinants of Bilateral Trade: Does Gravity Work in a Neoclassical World?" NBER Working Paper 5377, Cambridge, MA. December 1995.

Dunlevy, J. A., and W.K. Hutchinson. "The Impact of Immigration on American Import Trade in the Late Nineteenth and Early Twentieth Centuries." *Journal of Economic History*, 59, 1999, 1043–62.

Feenstra, R. C. "Integration of Trade and Disintegration of Production in the Global Economy." *Journal of Economic Perspectives*, 12(4), 1998, 31–50.

Frankel, J. A., E. Stein, and S. Wei. "Trading Blocs and the Americas: The Natural, the Unnatural, and the Super-Natural." *Journal of Development Economics*, 47(1), 1995, 61–95.

———. "Regional Trading Arrangements: Natural or Supernatural?" *American Economic Review*, 86(2), 1996a, 52–56.

Frankel, J. A., D. Romer, and T. Cyrus. "Trade and Growth in East Asian Countries: Cause and Effect?" NBER Working Paper Series 5732, Cambridge, MA. 1996.

Gould, D. "Immigrant Links to the Home Country: Empirical Implications for U.S. Bilateral Trade Flows." *Review of Economics & Statistics*, 76(2), 1994, 302–16.

Harrigan, J. "Specialization and the Volume of Trade: Do the Data Obey the Laws?" *Staff Report No. 140, New York Federal Reserve*, November 2001.

Head, K., and J. Ries. "Immigration and Trade Creation: Econometric Evidence from Canada." *Canadian Journal of Economics*, 31, 1998, 47–62.

Ho, C. G. T. "The Internationalization of Kinship and the Feminization of Caribbean Migration: The Case of Afro-Trinidadian Immigrants in Los Angeles." *Human Organization*, 52, 1993, 32–40.

Konan, D. E. "The Vertical Multinational Enterprise and International Trade." *Review of International Economics*, 8(1), 2000, 113–25.

Krueger, A. "NAFTA's Effects: A Preliminary Assessment." *World Economy*, 23(6), 2000, 761–75.

Krugman, P. *Geography and Trade*. Boston: MIT Press, 1991.

Massey, D. S., and F. G. España. "The Social Process of International Migration." *Science*, 237, 1987, 733–38.

Matthei, L. M. "Gender and International Labor Migration: A Networks Approach." *Social Justice*, 23(3), 1996, 38–53.

Noponen H., J. Graham, and A. Markusen (eds.). *Trading Industries, Trading Regions: International Trade, American Industry, and Regional Economic Development*. New York: Guilford Press, 1993.

Rauch, J. E. "Networks versus Markets in International Trade." *Journal of International Economics*, 48(1), 1999, 7–35.

———. "Business and Social Networks in International Trade." *Journal of Economic Literature*, 39(4), 2001, 1177–203.

Rose, A. "One Money, One Market: The Effect of Common Currencies on Trade." *Economic Policy*, 15(30), 2000, 7–46.

Roy, S., and J-M. Viaene. "On Strategic Vertical Foreign Investment." *Journal of International Economics*, 46(2), 1998, 253–79.

Sassen, S. *The Mobility of Labor and Capital: A Study in International Investment and Labor Flow*. London: Cambridge University Press, 1988.

———. *Globalization and its Discontents: Essays on the New Mobility of People and Money*. New York: New Press, 1998.

Saxenian, A. *Silicon Valley's New Immigrant Entrepreneurs* San Francisco: Public Policy Institute of California, 1999.

Sihag, B. S., and C. C. McDonough. "Shift-Share Analysis: The International Dimension." *Growth & Change*, 20(3), 1989, 80–88.

Simon, J. L. "Immigrants and Alien Workers." *Journal of Labor Research*, 13(1), 1992, 73–78.

Survey of Current Business. Bureau of Economic Analysis, U.S. Department of Commerce, February 1997.

Wilamoski, P., and S. Tinkler. "The Trade Balance Effects of U.S. Foreign Direct Investment in Mexico." *Atlantic Economic Journal*, 27(1), 1999, 24–37.

Williamson, O. E. "Transaction Cost Economics: How It Works; Where It Is Headed." *Economist-Leide*, 146(1), 1998, 23–58.

[3]

JAPANESE FIRMS AND THE DECISION TO INVEST ABROAD: BUSINESS GROUPS AND REGIONAL CORE NETWORKS

René Belderbos and Leo Sleuwaegen*

Abstract—The determinants of the decision by Japanese firms to set up manufacturing plants in Southeast Asia, Europe and North America are analyzed using micro-data on the behavior of firms in the electronics industry. While firm-specific intangible assets based on R&D and marketing efforts are positively related to the decision to invest in Europe and North America, investment in Southeast Asia is mainly related to human resources and driven by inter-firm ties within horizontal and vertical business groups. The empirical results suggest that membership of horizontal *keiretsu* relaxes liquidity constraints, while the manufacturing networks of horizontal and vertical *keiretsu* in Southeast Asia facilitate the establishment of manufacturing plants by member firms.

I. Introduction

THE sharp increase of Japanese Direct Foreign Investment (DFI) in manufacturing industries of North America and Europe over the last decade has provoked a substantial amount of research into the determinants of Japanese DFI. There is now an extensive body of literature suggesting that Japanese investments in industrial countries are explained by similar factors, mainly firm-specific advantages, as those that explain foreign investments by U.S. or European firms.[1] Across industries, Japanese DFI is positively related to industry traits such as R&D and advertising intensity (as proxies for firm-specific intangible assets owned by firms in the industry), while import barriers also have induced investments. Recent analysis of investment decisions by individual Japanese firms in the United States by Chang and Kogut (1993) and Hennart and Park (1994) found that previous experience in operating manufacturing plants abroad induces subsequent investments, results which are again similar to those found for U.S. firms (Yu (1990)).

While the importance of firm-specific advantages in explaining Japanese DFI is thus well established, there are at least two issues which have largely been left untouched in the literature (see Caves (1993)). Firstly, there are indications that there is a role to play for interfirm linkages within Japanese business groups, or *keiretsu*. For instance, Kashyap and Scharfstein (1992) found that firms that are members of one of the six bank-centered (horizontal) *keiretsu* are significantly less liquidity constrained in their investment decisions than non-member firms. This could imply that membership of horizontal business groups also helps to facilitate financing of risky foreign ventures. In another recent study, Head, Ries and Swenson (1994) showed that the choice of the location of Japanese firms' U.S. manufacturing plants can be partly explained by the presence of existing plants established by member firms of the same manufacturer-centered (vertical) *keiretsu* in the area. This raises the question whether the presence of group activities also gives a separate inducement to DFI by other group firms.[2]

A second shortcoming of the existing empirical literature is the almost complete limitation of analysis to DFI in the United States. At the same time as the surge in Japanese DFI in Western industrialized countries, Japanese firms established themselves as dominant investors in Southeast Asia (Gold et al. (1991)). The larger Japanese multinational enterprises (MNEs) are the main forces behind this trend by establishing "regional core networks" of complementary manufacturing plants in different countries in Southeast Asia, making use of comparative locational advantages in labour costs and skills (Nakakita and Urata (1991)). However, a distinctive characteristic of Japanese DFI in this region is the equally important role of small and medium-sized Japanese companies, which in many cases lack strong firm-specific advantages (MITI (1990, p. 45)).[3] Gold et al. argue that historical, political, and, in particular, cumulative economic ties between Southeast Asian countries have now given rise to the formation of a trade and investment bloc, in which the economic distance between participating countries and therewith the barriers firms face in establishing production subsidiaries abroad are greatly reduced. The implication is that firm-specific advantages are much less important in explaining Japanese DFI in this region.

This paper addresses the above two issues. Using micro data on Japanese firms in the broadly defined electronics and precision machinery sector, it examines whether the determinants of Japanese DFI in Asia are different from the determinants of DFI in North America and Europe, and tests for the influence of inter-firm relationships in both bank-centered horizontal business groups and manufacturer-centered vertical business groups. The next section develops the arguments concerning the determinants of Japanese DFI, including the effects of inter-firm relationships within Japanese business groups. Section III describes the empirical model and the data used. Results are presented in section IV, and section V concludes.

Received for publication November 5, 1993. Revision accepted for publication June 3, 1995.

* Hitotsubashi University and University of Sussex; and Catholic University Leuven and Erasmus University, respectively.

We would like to thank Tomiko Nojima and Shigeru Nishiyama for assistance in gathering and processing the data. We received helpful comments from Giovanni Capanelli, Martin Carree, Kyoji Fukao, Yui Kimura, Morio Kuninori, Jeroen Potjes, Shujiro Urata, Hideki Yamawaki, Ippei Yamazawa, and two anonymous referees. René Belderbos received support from the Japanese Ministry of Education, the Japan-German Berlin Center, the Tinbergen Institute at Erasmus University Rotterdam, and the Bank of Japan; Leo Sleuwaegen's research was funded by FKFO Grant Number 2.0052.92.

[1] An incomplete listing is Chang and Kogut (1993), Fukao et al. (1994), Hennart and Park (1994), Kimura, Kragas and Pugel (1993), Drake and Caves (1992), Sleuwaegen and Yamawaki (1992), Kogut and Chang (1991), and Kimura (1989).

[2] Hennart and Park (1994) found a positive effect of parent firms' investments in the United States in 1984 on investment by second tier *keiretsu* members in 1986. The effect was not significant, though, which they attribute to the relative paucity of Japanese investments at the time.

[3] This pattern has been observed since the 1960s and gave rise to a literature describing Japanese DFI as induced by changes in comparative advantage instead of induced by firm-specific advantages (Kojima (1978)).

II. Determinants of Japanese DFI in Southeast Asia, Europe and North America

Hypotheses concerning the determinants of the decision to invest abroad are developed in relation to mainstream internalization theory, theories of corporate finance, and particular traits of inter-firm linkages within Japanese business groups.

Internalization Theory

Mainstream theory of the MNE considers a firm's possession of intangible assets such as special technological, management or marketing skills as the central determinant of DFI.[4] Firms need to possess some kind of competitive advantage over foreign rivals to overcome the inherent disadvantages of operating abroad in an unfamiliar environment. There are strong incentives to exploit intangible assets themselves (internalisation), since these are by their nature hard to capitalize in arm's length markets. The decision to set up a foreign plant and not to export from the home country is explained by locational factors such as high transportation costs, relative production cost and, increasingly important, various tariff and other barriers impeding exports to foreign markets.

Empirical studies have shown that Japanese DFI in the United States follows this logic. In addition, it is conceivable that Japanese firms also possess a more specific type of intangible asset that is based on an efficient organisation of manufacturing processes. Efficient use of human resources, just-in-time delivery of components, and strict quality control are all elements of such organisational skills. Experience has shown that these skills can be transferred abroad to foreign manufacturing ventures (Caves (1993)).

While Japanese DFI in Western industrialized countries will follow this logic, it can be argued that firm-specific advantages play a much lesser role in the decision to invest in Southeast Asia. Traditionally, active government support and the assistance of Japanese trading houses (*Sougou Sousha*) reduced costs, risks, and informational requirements of investing in Southeast Asia.[5] With the increasing economic integration between Japan and Southeast Asia in which the "regional core networks" of established MNEs play a major role, and with the active policy of Southeast Asian countries to attract Japanese DFI, the barriers to foreign investment are further reduced. This, coupled with the relative absence of strong local competing firms in Southeast Asian markets, suggests that Japanese firms may be stimulated to invest in this region even if they lack the firm-specific advantages accruing from substantial investments in R&D and marketing that are often necessary to compete in Western industrial markets.

Corporate Finance

In early theories of DFI based on capital market imperfections, the MNE is primarily seen as engaging in capital cost arbitrage in a world with imperfect capital markets (e.g., Aliber (1970)). The hypothesis that firms invest abroad because they have capital cost advantages over foreign firms, has appeal in explaining Japanese DFI, since Japanese firms are often seen as having access to low cost capital (Hodder (1991)). In the late 1980s, these capital cost advantages stemmed mainly from high levels of liquidity in Japanese firms.[6] Since in a world of imperfect capital markets, internally generated funds are available at lower costs to the firm than external funds, liquidity is often found to influence investment decisions (Hoshi, Kashyap and Scharfstein (1992), Belderbos (1992)). This will apply in particular to decisions to invest abroad for which the costs and benefits are more uncertain (Caves (1993)). The hypothesis follows that firms that possess a large enough pool of internally generated funds have a capital cost advantage which can be transferred abroad.

Horizontal Business Groups

Horizontal business groups are large bank-centered diversified groups of basically independent firms. The advantages of group relationships are seen as derived from stable supply and demand through long-term business relationships, a relaxation of capital constraints for risky investments through the monitoring function of the main bank, and information exchange on new markets and technologies (Flath (1993), Nakatani (1984), Goto (1982)). As argued by Hoshi, Kashyap and Scharfstein (1992) and Flath (1993), the monitoring function of the main bank can solve part of the agency problems of debt by allowing for a better assessment of investment projects than the market could have made. Member firms can rely on the main bank of the group to finance investment projects which would otherwise have been hard to finance through arm's length markets. It follows that members of horizontal groups are less likely to be hindered by lack of funds to finance risky foreign ventures than non-member firms. The relationship between liquidity and DFI is expected to be weak or absent.

It is conceivable that members of a horizontal business-group may also benefit from the experience of other member firms and the group trading firms in doing business and operating manufacturing plants abroad. Informational requirements (with respect to market trends, location, recruiting employees, etc.) and lack of experience are important bar-

[4] DFI may also occur through internalisation of the market for intermediate inputs other than intangibles, if it involves vertical integration to reduce transaction costs (Hennart (1982)).

[5] It is argued that the Japanese government saw the relocation in Southeast Asia of manufacturing activities for which Japan had lost its comparative advantage as an indispensable part of industrial (restructuring) policy in the 1960s and 1970s (see Kojima (1978) and Ozawa (1979)). DFI was promoted via tax breaks and through such institutions as the Export-Import Bank of Japan, which provided assistance and low interest loans.

[6] This coincided with a wave of Japanese acquisitions of U.S. firms (Kester (1991)).

riers to foreign investment but can be overcome by information sharing within a horizontal business group. Moreover, firms might find it easy to sell their foreign produce to member firms in the region with which they have a long-term business relationship, or let marketing be handled by one of the trading firms belonging to the group. A study by Yamamura and Wassman (1989) found that investment in the United States by members of horizontal business groups tends to be clustered in specific areas, suggesting that overseas networks of the group are important in choosing the location of DFI. In the present study it will be examined whether the presence of group manufacturing activities overseas has an impact on the decision to invest abroad by members firms.

Vertical Business Groups

Vertical business groups are groups of subcontractors, satellite firms and trading firms around major large-scale assembly-type manufacturers such as Toyota and Hitachi. Here the "leading" or "core" firm usually exerts control over the management of the other firms in the group, enforced by shareholding, financial ties and the dispatch of managers. DFI by firms in vertical business groups is likely to be even more strongly affected by information exchange and supplier linkages than DFI by members of horizontal groups. In North America and Europe, formal and informal pressure on Japanese firms to increase the local content of their manufacturing activities has given Japanese subcontractor firms an important incentive to establish production plants abroad to supply their core firms with locally produced components. Investment by subcontractor firms is facilitated by the core company which may provide assistance and an exclusive market for the firm's components. In Asia the regional core networks of major automobile and electronics firms may play a similar facilitating role for subcontractor firms' investments. The hypothesis follows that the presence of overseas networks of vertical business groups exerts a positive influence on subcontractor firms' decisions to invest abroad.

III. The Empirical Model

The hypothesis that the determinants of the decision to invest in Southeast Asia differ from those to invest in Western industrial countries is tested at the firm level, against statistical data on Japanese firms, listed at Japanese stock exchanges in 1989, and active in the broad electronics and precision machinery sector. In this sector the number of firms is relatively large, DFI in both Western countries and Southeast Asia is prominent, and there is a large variety in firm size.

In order to analyze the determinants of the decision to invest abroad in different regions, all foreign investments up to June 1989 are taken into account and firms are classified as belonging to one of three firm types:

1. domestic firms without any foreign production;
2. firms with at least one manufacturing subsidiary in Southeast Asia but without manufacturing investments in other regions, for reasons of convenience hereafter referred to as "Asia-bound MNEs";
3. firms with at least one manufacturing subsidiary in Europe or North America referred to as "West-bound MNEs"; they may or may not operate manufacturing subsidiaries in Southeast Asia as well.[7]

Of the total of 204 listed firms 65 are classified as domestic firms, 60 as Asia-bound MNEs and 66 as West-bound MNEs. Of the 66 West-bound MNEs, 53 also operate manufacturing plants in Southeast Asia.

A multinomial logit model is used to relate the probabilities that a firm belongs to one of these three types (or states) to a set of features of the firm:

$$P_i^s = \frac{\exp[\alpha^s + \beta^s X_i + \gamma^s X_i^s]}{\sum_{q=1}^{3} \exp[\alpha^q + \beta^q X_i + \gamma^q X_i^q]} \tag{1}$$

where P_i^s is the probability that firm i belongs to state s, α^s are constants, X_i are firm-specific variables with coefficients β^s, and X_i^s are variables that are firm- and state-specific with coefficients γ^s. To identify the model, the coefficients α, β, and γ have to be normalized to zero for one state.

Explanatory Variables

The explanatory factors include the following firm characteristics related to the possession of *firm-specific intangible assets:* R&D intensity (*RDINT*, measured as the ratio of R&D expenditures over value added), sales cost intensity (*MARKINT*, direct and indirect sales costs as a percentage of sales), and human resource intensity (*HUMRES*, labour cost of non-factory employees over total labour cost).[8] The inclusion of sales force expenditures in addition to advertising outlays in *MARKINT* arguably makes the variable a better proxy for reputation and marketing expertise in the industrial electronics sector, where direct sales costs tend to be high. *HUMRES* is a proxy for the availability and quality of managerial and staff workers who could be expatriated to transfer organisational skills to foreign plants.

In addition, a high capital intensity of production indicated by a high capital to labour ratio (*CAPLAB*, the value of fixed, depreciable capital over total labour cost) may indicate possession of intangible assets as well. The rise of Japanese electronics firms as global competitors is often claimed to be related to the adoption of highly efficient, productivity raising mass production techniques (Franko (1983)). Also,

[7] North America includes the United States and Canada. Europe includes EFTA, EC, and Eastern European countries. Southeast Asia includes South Korea, Taiwan, Hong Kong, the ASEAN countries (the Philippines, Indonesia, Malaysia, Thailand, Brunei, and Singapore), and China.

[8] All these variables are calculated on the basis of average data over fiscal years 1986–1988. A description of data and data sources can be obtained from the authors on request.

the most capital intensive firms are in a better position to benefit from comparative advantages of Western industrial countries where capital is a relatively abundant factor. *RDINT*, *MARKINT*, *HUMRES*, and *CAPLAB* are all expected to have a strong impact on the decision to become a West-bound MNE but a weaker impact on the decision to become an Asia-bound MNE.

In addition to the above-mentioned structural characteristics of the firm, it is useful to control for *firm size* (*EMPL*, measured by the logarithm of employment[9]). The main effect firm size is expected to pick up is that a certain firm size is usually required for carrying the overhead cost associated with setting up a foreign organization and international communication network.

From the perspective of *corporate finance*, firms which possess capital cost advantages in the form of a large pool of internally generated funds are expected to show a higher probability to invest abroad. As the best proxy for the availability of internally generated funds for investment abroad, the variable *INTFUNDS* divides pre-tax profits (including non-operating revenues) by domestic fixed capital outlays over the last three years.

In order to establish the effects of inter-firm linkages in *horizontal business groups*, the firms in the sample were classified as belonging to one of the 6 large horizontal *keiretsu*.[10] A dummy variable, *HORGROUP*, is included which takes on the value 1 if a firm is considered a member of one of these horizontal business groups. Since there may be general benefits of belonging to horizontal business groups through information exchange and risk reduction, *HORGROUP* is expected to have a positive effect on the propensity to invest abroad. In addition, since member-firms may be less liquidity constrained, liquidity is expected to have a weaker effect on DFI decisions. To capture this effect, an interactive term combining *INTFUNDS* with *HORGROUP* is included in the model. The coefficient is expected to be negative.

Member-firms of horizontal business groups may also find it more easy to invest abroad if other member firms have already established networks there. To account for this factor, the number of manufacturing subsidiaries established by all other member-firms of the group in the electronics industry in Southeast Asia (*HORASIA*) and North America/Europe (*HORWEST*), respectively, are included as explanatory variables. Since *HORASIA* and *HORWEST* are state-specific variables,[11] which are only expected to influence the decision to invest in, respectively, Southeast Asia and Europe/North America, the coefficients of these variables for other states are restricted to zero in the estimating model.

Firms are considered to be affiliated subcontractors (*SUBCON* dummy = 1) if they belong to a *vertical business group;* i.e., if they are partially or wholly controlled via equity ownership or dispatch of personnel by the core firm with which they have a subcontracting or original equipment manufacturing (*OEM*) relationship. Since subcontracting firms' manufacturing operations are integrated in the core firms' domestic network, and their dependence on the core firm may make them unable to define an overseas investment strategy independently, *SUBCON* is expected to have a negative sign. However, in case the core firm has established a manufacturing network abroad, the same link with the core firm will lower barriers to foreign investment. To capture this effect, two variables are included, *VERASIA* and *VERWEST*, which count the number of manufacturing subsidiaries of the core firm in Southeast Asia and North America/Europe, respectively.

Besides the firm-specific and group-specific variables mentioned above, a set of *industry dummies* is used to capture the effect of differences in industry environment and industry-wide locational factors, including various kinds of barriers to trade. Seven industries corresponding to broad product groups are distinguished: consumer electronics (*CONSUM*), office equipment and computers (*OFFCOMP*), telecommunications equipment (*TELCOM*), part and components (*COMPO*), automation and control equipment (*AUTOM*), medical and scientific equipment (*MEDICAL*) and heavy electrical equipment (*HEAVY*).

IV. Empirical Results

Table 1 presents the estimation results. The first two columns present the estimated coefficients and t-ratios for the probability that a firm is a West-bound or Asia-bound MNE, respectively, with domestic firm taken as reference state. The third column contains the differences between the coefficients for West-bound and Asia-bound MNEs and corresponding t-ratios.

The results for the probability that a firm is a West-bound MNE broadly confirm the hypotheses based on internalization theory: the coefficients of *RDINT*, *MARKINT*, *HUMRES*, and *CAPLAB* all have a positive sign and are significantly different from zero. Japanese DFI in Western industrialized countries thus has similar driving forces as DFI by Western firms, a finding which is in accordance with previous empirical work on Japanese DFI in the United States. In addition, firm size is important for the decision to become a West-bound MNE, which is likely to be related to the high fixed setup costs of establishing overseas manufacturing subsidiaries and communication networks. The significantly positive effect of *INTFUNDS* supports the view that the availability of internally generated funds is often necessary to finance risky foreign investment projects.

[9] Rather than sales, employment is used as a measure of firm size. Since Japanese electronics firms differ in the extent to which they rely on upstream vertical integration, subcontracting, or independent parts suppliers, sales is not a straightforward measure. For similar reasons value added was used as the factor to scale R&D expenditures.

[10] The Dodwell (Industrial Groups in Japan) classification was preferred over other available sources because it applies the strictest standards to group ties and therefore provides the best test whether systematic differences between members and non-members in foreign investment decisions exist. Seventy-two firms were classified as members of horizontal business groups.

[11] The estimated coefficients for *HORASIA* and *HORWEST* are of the form γ^{i} in equation (1).

TABLE 1.—MULTINATIONAL LOGIT OF THE PROBABILITY THAT JAPANESE ELECTRONICS FIRMS ARE DOMESTIC FIRMS, WEST-BOUND MNEs OR ASIA-BOUND MNEs

Reference State	West-bound MNE Domestic Firm	Asia-bound MNE Domestic Firm	West-bound MNE Asia-bound MNE
log *EMPL*	2.24[c]	0.96[b]	1.28[c]
	(5.07)	(2.58)	(3.80)
RDINT	8.09[c]	0.92	7.16[c]
	(2.66)	(0.36)	(2.66)
MARKINT	0.27[a]	0.08	0.25[b]
	(1.84)	(0.03)	(2.43)
CAPLAB	1.09[b]	0.06	1.06[b]
	(2.11)	(0.07)	(2.28)
HUMRES	4.17[a]	5.63[c]	−1.47
	(1.84)	(2.99)	(−0.78)
INTFUNDS	0.56[b]	0.28	0.29
	(2.55)	(1.60)	(1.62)
*HORGROUP***INTFUNDS*	0.57	−1.35[b]	1.92[c]
	(0.88)	(−2.56)	(3.00)
HORGROUP	−0.43	0.10	−0.53
	(−0.36)	(0.10)	(−0.48)
*HORGROUP***HORASIA*		0.07[b]	
		(2.23)	
*HORGROUP***HORWEST*	0.02		
	(0.27)		
SUBCON	−4.62[c]	−4.72[c]	0.09
	(−2.58)	(−3.29)	(0.08)
*SUBCON***VERASIA*		0.43[c]	
		(2.64)	
*SUBCON***VERWEST*	0.54[a]		
	(1.88)		
Constant and Industry Dummies:			
CONSTANT	−23.14[c]	−10.25[c]	−12.89[c]
	(−5.95)	(−3.39)	(−4.21)
CONSUM	4.66[c]	3.40[b]	1.26
	(2.90)	(2.46)	(1.14)
OFFCOMP	1.81	0.68	1.13
	(1.44)	(0.66)	(0.97)
TELCOM	−1.57	−1.24	−0.30
	(−1.11)	(−1.19)	(−0.23)
COMPO	3.72[c]	2.69[c]	1.02
	(3.64)	(3.38)	(1.14)
AUTOM	2.03	1.78	0.26
	(1.50)	(1.49)	(0.22)
MEDICAL	1.44	1.14	0.30
	(1.44)	(1.49)	(0.32)
Observations	204		
McFadden's R^2	0.43		
Log-likelihood	190.7 [c]		

Notes: Asymptotic *t*-ratios are in parentheses. Coefficients in the third column are differences between the coefficients in the first and second column. The omitted industry dummy is *HEAVY*.
[a] Significant at the 0.10 level.
[b] Significant at the 0.05 level.
[c] Significant at the 0.01 level.

The variables related to horizontal business groups do not contribute to the explanation of investment decisions in Western industrialized countries. The coefficient for *HORGROUP* has a negative sign but is insignificant. The coefficient of the interactive term *HORGROUP*INTFUNDS* and the coefficient of *HORWEST* fail to reach significance either. While horizontal *keiretsu* networks may influence the *location* of manufacturing plants in Western industrialized countries, the results do not indicate that they play a major role in the *decision* to invest in these countries.

On the other hand, membership of a vertical business group does have a significant effect on the probability that firms become West-bound MNEs. The coefficient for *SUBCON* is negative and significant: subcontractors in a vertical business group are, all things equal, less likely to take the decision to become a West-bound MNE. However, the results also indicate that this general effect may be offset if the core firm has invested extensively in manufacturing operations in Europe and North America: the coefficient of *VERWEST* has a positive sign and is significant at the 10% level. This lends support to the hypothesis that subcontractors are invited by their core firms to set up manufacturing plants in Europe and North America, often as a response to formal and informal local content requirements.

Among the industry dummies, the coefficients of *CONSUM* and *COMPO* are significantly positive, relative to the base case (*HEAVY*). Firms in the consumer electronics and electronics components industries are more likely to have invested in Europe and North America than can be explained by firm characteristics only. This can be related to trade restricting measures taken in the United States and the EC against Japanese imports (e.g., colour televisions and semiconductors). It is also likely to reflect the relatively strong competitive advantages of Japanese firms vis-à-vis North American and European firms that allow Japanese firms to compete with Western firms on their home ground.

The second column of table 1 shows the effects of firm characteristics on the probability of firms to be an Asia-bound MNE. In sharp contrast to the results for the decision to become a West-bound MNE, none of the firm characteristics except *HUMRES* and *EMPL* exert a significant influence on the probability to become an Asia-bound MNE. The possession of intangible assets, apart from human resources, evidently is not a prerequisite to setting up manufacturing plants in Southeast Asia. This is in accordance with the view that both the relative absence of strong competing firms and cumulative economic ties between Japan and Southeast Asia have reduced barriers to DFI in the region. The positive effect of *HUMRES* indicates that DFI in Southeast Asia is facilitated if the firm can draw on human resources and transfer organisational skills to foreign plants. The positive effect of *EMPL* indicates that a certain threshold size of the firm is necessary to become an Asia-bound MNE, although the coefficient is significantly lower than the coefficient of *EMPL* found for the decision to become a West-bound MNE. The coefficient of *INTFUNDS* has the expected positive sign but is insignificant. Liquidity plays a lesser role in the decision to invest in Asia, which may be related to smaller risk factors attached to investments in Asia.

The results for the variables related to horizontal and vertical business groups strongly confirm the importance of interfirm linkages in explaining the decision to invest in Southeast Asia. While membership of a horizontal business group, as such, does not exert an influence on the decision to become an Asia-bound MNE (the coefficient for *HORGROUP* is insignificant), the significantly negative coefficient for the interactive term between *INTFUNDS* and *HORGROUP* suggests that members of horizontal business groups are not liquidity constrained in their decision to invest in Asia. This conforms with the view that member firms can borrow at relatively low cost from their main bank and group-related financial institutions to expand in Asia. The significantly positive effect of *HORASIA* confirms that the presence of group firms in Southeast Asia may reduce informational constraints for potential investors, lead to transfer of experience in manufacturing abroad, and facilitate marketing of the products through long-term supplier linkages with other member firms and the trading firm active in the region.

The negative coefficient for *SUBCON* again suggests that subcontractor firms which are dependent on their core firm are generally less likely to invest abroad. On the other hand, the size of the regional network of the core firm in Southeast Asia, *VERASIA*, has the expected positive effect with the coefficient significant at the 1% level. This result demonstrates the importance of regional core networks established by the major electronics firms in Southeast Asia in reducing the barriers for related subcontractor firms to set up manufacturing plants there.[12]

Among the industry dummies, again the coefficients of *COMPO* and *CONSUM* are significantly positive, though smaller than for the decision to become a West-bound MNE. Higher than average DFI in Southeast Asia in these industries is likely to reflect that in the consumer electronics industry and related components industries, as well as in the semiconductor industry, the production process can be separated into stages which make substantially different uses of capital, skilled labour, and unskilled labour (Nakakita and Urata (1991)). This has driven the development of regional core networks in Southeast Asia which in turn act as catalysts for investment by other firms.

The coefficients in the third column of table 1 are the differences in the coefficients of the first and second column with corresponding t-ratios. They show the effects of firm characteristics on the probability that a firm is a West-bound MNE and not an Asia-bound MNE. The coefficients of *EMPL*, *RDINT*, and *CAPLAB* are positive and significantly different from zero at the 5% or 1% (*EMPL*) level, while the coefficients of *MARKINT* and *INTFUNDS* are significant at the 10% level. Clearly, the decision to invest in Europe or North America is governed by different factors than the decision to become an Asia-bound MNE. *HUMRES*, a measure of human resources within the firm, is the only variable that does not differentiate West-bound MNEs from Asia-bound MNEs.

Finally, it was investigated to what extent the results are sensitive to the timing of investment by splitting up the sample for firms which invested abroad before 1986 and those which invested more recently. The statistical results did not indicate a significant change in the regime of the model for early versus late investors.[13]

V. Concluding Remarks

While the possession of *firm-specific* intangible assets remains a prerequisite for Japanese investment in Western industrialized countries, the basic finding that *inter-firm* linkages help to lower barriers to invest abroad, in particular for firms investing in Southeast Asia, has an interesting parallel with previous empirical results with respect to the role of firm-specific experience in the process of DFI (Hennart and

[12] Of the possible interactive effects of business group membership with explanatory variables, only a positive interaction effect of *RDINT* with *SUBCON* tended to reach levels of statistical significance. This result is suggestive of a complementary relationship between core firms' and subcontractors' R&D also found by Suzuki (1993).

[13] The results are available from the authors. The minor differences that can be discerned appear related to the modern development of Japanese industry, i.e., a diminished importance of internal funds for DFI decisions of late investors is likely to be related to deregulation and development of the Japanese financial sector.

Park (1994), Chang and Kogut (1993) and Yu (1990)). The results here suggest that at least part of the experience in doing business abroad is not necessarily tied to the firm but transferable to other firms through inter-firm linkages within horizontal and vertical business groups.

It is difficult to assess to what extent the findings are specific to Japanese MNEs. While the organization of firms in horizontal and vertical *keiretsu* may be particular to Japanese industry, the importance of inter-firm ties such as long-term supplier linkages is not. Regional differences are also likely to exist in the determinants of DFI by American and European firms within their respective trade blocs (NAFTA and EU) versus DFI outside these blocs. These issues offer ample scope for further research.

REFERENCES

Aliber, Robert Z., "The Theory of Direct Foreign Investment," in Charles P. Kindleberger (ed.), *The International Corporation* (Cambridge and London: MIT Press, 1970).

Belderbos, René A., "Large Multinational Enterprises Based in a Small Economy: Effects on Domestic Investment," *Weltwirtschaftliches Archiv* 128 (1992), 543–557.

———, "Strategic Trade Policy and Multinational Enterprises: Essays on Trade and Investment by Japanese Electronics Firms," Ph.D. Thesis, Erasmus University, Rotterdam (1994).

Caves, Richard E., *Multinational Enterprise and Economic Analysis* (Cambridge: Cambridge University Press, 1982).

———, "Japanese Investment in the United States: Lessons for the Economic Analysis of Foreign Investment," *The World Economy* 16 (1993), 279–300.

Chang, Sea Jin, and Bruce Kogut, "Platform Investments and Volatile Exchange Rates: Japanese Direct Investment in US Electronic Industries," mimeograph, New York University (1993).

Drake, Tracey A., and Richard E. Caves, "Changing Determinants of Japan's Foreign Investment in the United States," *Journal of the Japanese and International Economies* 6 (1992), 228–246.

Flath, David, "Shareholdings in the Keiretsu, Japan's Financial Groups," this REVIEW 75 (1993), 249–257.

Foundation for Economic Research of the University of Amsterdam, *Manual Logit-JD* (Amsterdam: University of Amsterdam, 1988).

Franko, Lawrence G., *The Threat of Japanese Multinationals: How the West Can Respond* (Chichester: Wiley, 1983).

Fukao, Kyoji, et al., "R&D Investment and Overseas Production: An Empirical Analysis of Japan's Electric Machinery Industry Based on Corporate Data," *Bank of Japan Monetary and Economic Studies* 12 (1994), 1–60.

Gold, David, Persa Eonomou and Telly Tolentino, *Trade Blocs and Investment Blocs: The Triad in Foreign Direct Investment and International Trade* paper presented at the annual meeting of the Academy of International Business, Miami (Oct. 19, 1991).

Goto, Akira, "Business Groups In a Market Economy," *European Economic Review* 19 (1982), 53–70.

Head, Keith, John Ries, and Deborah Swenson, "Agglomeration Benefits and Location Choice: Evidence from Japanese Manufacturing Investments in the United States," NBER Working Paper Series No 4767, Cambridge, MA (1994).

Hennart, Jean-François, *A Theory of Multinational Enterprise* (Ann Arbor: University of Michigan Press, 1982).

Hennart, Jean-François, and Y. R. Park, "Location, Governance, and Strategic Determinants of Japanese Manufacturing Investments in the United States," *Strategic Management Journal* 15 (1994), 419–436.

Hodder, James E., "Is the Cost of Capital Lower in Japan?," *Journal of the Japanese and International Economies* 5 (1991), 86–100.

Hoshi, Takeo, Anil Kashyap, and David Scharfstein, "Corporate Structure, Liquidity, and Investment: Evidence from Japanese Industrial Groups," *The Quarterly Journal of Economics* 107 (1992), 33–60.

Kester, W. Carl, *Japanese Takeovers: The Global Contest for Corporate Control* (Boston: Harvard Business School Press, 1991).

Kimura, Yui, "Firm-Specific Strategic Advantages and Foreign Direct Investment Behaviour of Firms: The Case of Japanese Semiconductor Firms," *Journal of International Business Studies* 20 (1989), 296–314.

Kimura, Yui, Erik S. Kragas and Thomas A. Pugel, "Further Evidence on Japanese Direct Investment in US Manufacturing," IMRI Working Paper 002/1993, International Management Research Institute, International University of Japan (1993).

Kogut, Bruce, and Sea-Jin Chang, "Technological Capabilities and Japanese Foreign Direct Investment in the United States," this REVIEW 73 (1991), 400–413.

Kojima, Kiyoshi, *Direct Foreign Investments: A Japanese Model of Multinational Business Operations* (London: Croom Helm, 1978).

Ministry of International Trade and Industry (MITI), *White Paper on Small Business 1990* (Tokyo: MITI, 1990).

Nakakita, Toru, and Shujiro Urata, "Industrial Adjustment in Japan and its Impact on Developing Countries," paper presented at the Conference on Industrial Adjustment of Developed Countries and its Impact on Developing Countries, Institute of Developing Economies, Tokyo (Feb. 1–2, 1991).

Nakatani, Iwao, "The Economic Role of Financial Corporate Grouping," in Masahiro Aoki (ed.), *The Economic Analysis of the Japanese Firm* (Amsterdam: North Holland, 1984), 227–258.

Ozawa, Terutomo, *Multinationalism, Japanese Style: The Political Economy of Outward Dependency* (Princeton: Princeton University Press, 1979).

Sleuwaegen, Leo, and Hideki Yamawaki, "Foreign Direct Investment and Intra-Firm Trade: Evidence from Japan," in A. Koekkoek and L. Mennes (eds.), *International Trade and Global Development* (London: Routledge, 1992).

Suzuki, Kazuyuki, "R&D Spillovers and Technology Transfer among and within Vertical Keiretsu Groups: Evidence from the Japanese Electrical Machinery Industry," *International Journal of Industrial Organization* 11 (1993), 573–591.

Yamamura, Kozo, and Ulrike Wassmann, "Do Japanese Firms Behave Differently?: The Effects of Keiretsu in the United States," in Kozo Yamamura, *Japanese Investment in the United States: Should We Be Concerned?* (Washington, D.C.: Society for Japanese Studies, 1989).

Yu, Chwo-Ming Joseph, "The Experience Effect and Foreign Direct Investment," *Weltwirtschaftliches Archiv* 126 (1990), 561–580.

[4]

Area (2005) 37.2, 209–222

Interlocking directorships and trans-national linkages within the British Empire, 1900–1930

Mark Brayshay*, Mark Cleary and John Selwood†**

*School of Geography, University of Plymouth, Plymouth PL4 8AA

Email: mbrayshay@plymouth.ac.uk

**Office of the Vice-chancellor, University of Plymouth, Plymouth PL4 8AA

†Department of Geography, University of Winnipeg, Winnipeg, Manitoba R3B 2E9, Canada

Revised manuscript received 12 December 2004

Recent research has highlighted the value of employing the idea of networks to describe the interrelatedness of today's globalizing economy. Networks facilitate flows of knowledge, ideas, managerial techniques and capital between firms both within and across political borders. This paper argues that the reconstruction of social connections through which information is created, given value and exchanged is fundamental to an understanding of not only contemporary but also historical patterns of economic globalization. We focus on the networks of the capitalist elite running 12 major multinational enterprises, active across British imperial territories, between c.*1900 and* c.*1930. An examination is made of the economic and spatial interlocks between firms created by board members who were multiple directors. Social underpinnings of multiple directorates are examined by exploring the common, overlapping social spheres within which individuals engaged. A clearer grasp of the ways in which corporate activity operated in the early 1900s can provide a better understanding of the social context of global economic operations.*

Key words: *British Empire, trans-national, multiple and interlocking directorships, social networks, capitalist biographies*

Introduction

The recent growth of theoretical and empirical studies of globalization is indicative of the importance attached to understanding the origins, nature and context of global economic activity and the emergence of global capitalist networks. At the heart of much of this literature is, perhaps inevitably, a real uncertainty about the nature and value of the models of globalization that have been developed (Giddens 2000; Guillén 2001; Sklair 2001). That uncertainty, reflected in elusive terms such as *internationalization*, the *global economy* or *global information flows*, is equally present in historical analyses of the interconnected growth patterns in the world economy.

The analysis of global flows of commodities, capital and ideas, and the extent to which such flows have become more spatially interconnected, is central to any understanding of how globalization has developed and how 'an economy with the capacity to work as a unit in real time on a planetary scale' emerged (Castells 1996, 92). In historical terms, analyses have focused predominantly on the economic underpinnings of particular networks of exchange, whether in exotic goods, precious metals or, more recently, plantation products (Wolf 1982; Walvin 1997; Ogborn 2000). However, alongside these mainly economic studies, and recognizing that the historical geography of globalization is also concerned with flows of information, ideas and

ISSN 0004-0894

influence, increased attention has also been given to social networks. This acknowledges that, to trace the evolution of greater integration in the global economy, research is needed on the social relationships between the actors involved in developing global capitalism. The reconstruction of networks through which information was created, given value and exchanged is fundamental not only to an understanding of historical patterns of economic exchange but, equally, can highlight parallels with contemporary globalization processes (Gertler 2001; O'Hagan and Green 2002a 2002b).

The half-century preceding the 1914–18 war was an especially dynamic time for the development of the global economy when a range of revolutions in physical transport networks (railways and steamships), information flows (the telegraph) and the institutions supporting the trading economy (from banking to the stock exchange) made it possible for multinational enterprises to operate and expand (Kieve 1973; Barty-King 1979; Standage 1998; Wilkins 1998; Hirst and Thompson 1999). The argument is not that this period marked the onset of globalization: as Guillén notes, 'there is no agreement as to whether it was with Magellan and Mercator, James Watt and Captain Cook, Nixon and Kissinger or Thatcher and Reagan that globalisation started' (2001, 237–8), but rather that the revolution in interchange of knowledge allowed far-flung elements of a business enterprise to share virtually real-time information, thereby enabling the growth and geographical expansion of multinationals. Building on these developments, albeit interrupted by war and economic depression, the internationalization and globalization of the economy was a marked feature of the early twentieth century (Robertson 2003). In addition to revolutionary changes in the efficiency of commodity flows, the political context of internationalization was also especially significant during this period. Supported by the hegemonic European empires, trade followed the flag and investment and trading patterns were shaped by the dual forces of the search for profit and the protective shelter of imperial power (Lewis 1981; Corley 1994; Wilkins 1998).

To investigate the importance of a *social* as well as an *economic* dimension to globalization, this paper provides a preliminary discussion of a larger on-going study of the networks of directors who ran major companies between *c.*1900 and *c.*1930. Our contention is that to understand how the economy both internationalized and globalized in that period, there is a need to identify and analyse the networks through which information, ideas and managerial techniques were exchanged, trust was negotiated, goods were traded, and capital was transferred between firms, and within and across political borders.

The firm in its social context

Our prime focus is on the composition and interactions of directors of a small sample of multinational companies, active in British imperial territories between 1899–1900 and 1929–1930. Rather than seeking to examine all facets of a company's visible activities, the paper explores connections between, and engendered by, company directors. If we can grasp more fully the ways in which corporate activity was structured and articulated in the past, a better general understanding of the social context of global economic operations is possible.

Concepts developed in studies of today's capitalist elite by authors such as Kay (1993) and Scott (2003) of the 'architecture' of the firm suggest that the corporate community operates within complex sets of networks and contacts. While there is an important 'internal architecture' of relationships amongst the managers and employees within a particular company (Kay 1993), our focus is on elements of the 'external architecture' of linkages connecting an enterprise to its customers, suppliers and other firms. Scott (2003) suggests that three significant types of linkage exist within this 'external architecture'. First, *personal* links support a web of connections binding the elite together; these might include educational experience, family ties or social club membership. Second, *commercial* links, shaped by company alliances, foster information sharing and connections through mutual experience at board level. Third, there are *capital* links, which are social networks facilitating and channelling investment from the banking community towards particular enterprises (Scott and Griff 1985a; Scott 1991). This corporate architecture underpins the activities of the capitalist elite whereby alliances are built within a range of structures thereby facilitating flows of information, ideas and capital between different companies. The need to extend work on the capitalist elite onto the global stage was acknowledged by Scott himself, who noted that a weakness of existing research is that it has been 'resolutely national in its orientation and perhaps the time for a global perspective has come' (2003, 171).

While the role and contribution of directors may well have varied markedly from company to company and individual to individual, they provide an initial basis for analysing how social networks might have influenced company activity in this, and later, periods. Contemporary sociological work on the capitalist elite emphasizes the role of directors as the starting point for delineating the social sinews underlying company activity (Glasberg and Schwartz 1983; Scott 1991; Tomka 2001). An understanding of links between company boards is therefore a first step in unpacking the social milieu within which were embedded the economic actors who drove the internationalization of the economy in the early twentieth century. In this context, the notion of 'embeddedness' signifies the process of building 'personal relationships of trust' amongst key individuals who shaped the trans-national economy (Hess 2004, 176).

The interactions of company directors can be 'mapped' in a number of ways. One approach is to 'read back' from the *networks* to the *individuals* in order to construct personal biographies germane to their corporate activities. Education, family background, class background and social interactions can thus help in building profiles of key players. Combining this information with evidence drawn from personal biographies, company histories, letters and diaries offers invaluable insights into their connectedness. Equally, however, it is appropriate to 'map forward' from the names of directors to those other companies on whose boards a director may have served. Directors very often held *multiple* directorships (membership of the boards of several different companies) and, through those directorships, established what are usually termed *interlocking* directorships, or *interlocks*, which were potentially exploitable links between different companies. The term interlock has been used to describe dyadic links between directors drawn from two different firms who are associated by mutual membership of the board of a third company. Equally, however, the term interlock is used to describe the linking of two firms through the person of a single director who serves on both boards. In this paper, we focus primarily on the second definition. Our research explores connections between firms and argues that their development was a product of both the common, overlapping social spheres within which directors moved (from public school to Oxbridge, for example) and a deliberate corporate strategy to create interlocks perceived to be mutually beneficial. Directors holding seats on more than one company board provided channels for what is increasingly described as 'tacit knowledge transfer', that is, the sharing of personal, informal insights and information which might secure competitive advantages or business opportunities (O'Hagan and Green 2002b).

Sampling early twentieth-century multinational enterprises

A first stage in the research is the identification of a sample of enterprises within which to examine multiple directorships. The total population of companies in existence was estimated using the annual *Stock Exchange Yearbook* listings of businesses quoted on the London Stock Exchange (Skinner 1900a 1930a). These lists record all companies whose shares could be publicly traded. To establish an overall idea of the number of companies with international interests in 1899–1900 and 1929–1930, a sample of approximately 25 per cent of the *Yearbook* entries was extracted. On this basis, it is estimated that 34 per cent of the 7004 companies had at least some international interests in 1899–1900. Although by 1929–1930 the number of companies had risen to 7465, the proportion with international interests (33 per cent) remained stable. These percentages seem remarkably high, but it should be noted that the majority of companies had interests in only one other country. Indeed, a mere 90 companies (less than 4 per cent) operated in more than one other country or colony in 1929–1930. Of these, just a handful – for example, Dunlop, Lever Brothers, Shell, ICI, Ford Motors and Cable and Wireless – were truly worldwide enterprises. Because our central objective is to examine a sample of companies with growing overseas, especially colonial, interests, the total from which a selection could be made was relatively small. Our choice was further guided by the need to identify companies continuously in business from 1899–1900 until 1929–1930, with headquarters in London, and with extant company archives. To encompass different aspects of directorship linkages, a sample yielding an even mix of banking, shipping, trading and primary producer enterprises, with a range of sizes of boards of directors, was required. The notion that the growing multinationals of the early twentieth century were heirs of the great chartered companies of a previous imperial era prompted the inclusion of one of the latter, namely the Hudson's Bay Company (Newman 1987; Selwood 2000). Another 11 companies were then added: Dalgety &

Co. Ltd, Barclays Bank, the Bank of Australasia, the Chartered Bank of India, Australia & China, the Foreign & Colonial Investment Trust, P & O, the Australian United Steam Navigation Co. Ltd, Elder Dempster & Co., the Consolidated Goldfields Corporation, the British North Borneo Company and Millars' Timber & Trading Company.

Identifying multiple directorships

Previous contributions by geographers to historical studies of corporate networks are rare (for the contemporary period see Taylor 2001; Beaverstock *et al.* 2002). Most literature is by sociologists and economists. For example, the 1976 work of the Research Group on Intercorporate Structure on multiple directorships amongst leading companies in ten countries (including Britain) provides a snapshot of trans-company interlocks which then existed (Stokman *et al.* 1985). Analysis for Britain was extended to 1904, 1938 and 1992 (Scott and Griff 1985a; Scott 1985 2003), and Fennema and Schijf (1985) explored trans-national interlocks within the 1976 data. In general, however, there is a dearth of work on the interconnectedness of early twentieth-century *multinational* enterprises.

In order to set the context for an exploration of interlocks with other firms generated by the 12 multinationals selected for this study, the total number of multiple directorships in 1899–1900 and 1929–1930 was estimated. Based on a 5 per cent sample of entries in the 1899–1900 *Directory of Directors* (929 names), fewer than 30 per cent (270) of company directors appear to have held more than one directorship (Skinner 1900b 1930b). These 270 multiple directors generated 893 company linkages. In 1929–1930, again drawing on a 5 per cent sample (1516 names), the proportion of directors who were multiples had significantly increased to more than 40 per cent, or 634 names, together generating 2801 company interlocks (an increase from 3.3 to 4.4 links per multiple director). This appears to confirm trends noted by previous authors suggesting that the proportion of directors holding other directorships in early twentieth-century companies was a relatively large and growing phenomenon (Scott 1985 2003).

Examining the membership of the boards of the sample companies reveals that together they comprised 123 directors in 1899–1900, rising to 139 by 1929–1930: a modest overall increase of 13 per cent, almost entirely accounted for by the substantial expansion in the Barclays' directorate (Figure 1). By 1929–1930, as well as its Dominions & Colonial Bank, Barclays had subsidiaries in France, Italy and Canada. Key directors of these subsidiaries occupied seats on the expanded board of the parent business. By contrast, confirming trends revealed by Scott's (1985) work on Britain's top 250 companies (for the period 1904–1938), the boards of five of the 12 companies had become smaller by 1929–1930 than they had been 30 years before; the rest had remained static. Thus, notwithstanding the special case of Barclays, there was a growing concentration of economic power in the hands of a small elite group.

In 1899–1900, directors of the sample companies were associated as board members with a total of 255 other firms; by 1929–1930, the number had risen to 497. This increase suggests that a growing mesh of intercorporate linkages between a small number of key directors was developing. To facilitate an exploration of the nature of the linkages, we recorded the name of each of the other companies interlocked with the 12 'core' enterprises, their business sector (in one of 14 general categories), their principal product or service and the main country or colony where their interests were focused. Comparing 1899–1900 and 1929–1930, the total number of company interlocks generated by the multiple directors of the 12 firms grew by 114 per cent from 333 to 713, or an increase in the ratios of 2.7 to 5.1 per multiple director (Figure 1).

Economic and spatial character of company interlocks

The economic and spatial spread of the links created by multiple directorships provides an indication of not only the corporate character, but also the geographical reach of early twentieth-century multinationals. Table 1 shows the 1929–1930 distribution of each company's interlocks across the range of 14 key business sectors noted above. Underlining the importance of the *capital architecture* of firms, links with financial businesses stand out: more than a third of all interlocks were with companies in that sector (Lisle-Williams 1984a 1984b; Scott and Griff 1985b; Chapman 1986; Cassis 1988; Scott 2003). In the case of the shipping, trading and primary production multinationals, as well as interlocks with banks and financial service providers, other directorships predictably clustered in similar or closely related businesses. For example, 66 of the

	Authorized Capital £m		Key Executive Directors	
	1900	1930	1899–1900	1929–1930
1. Australian United Steam Navigation Co.	0.6	0.745	Sir Edwin Dawes (Ch)	Lord Inchcape (Ch)
2. Bank of Australasia	1.6	6.0	Sir Richard Jeans (MD)	Lord Aldenham (MD)
3. Barclays Bank * Includes new European and Colonial subsidiaries of the Bank.	6.0	20.0 (32.0)*	Francis Bevan (CH) Samuel Buxton (ViceCH)	Frederick Goodenough (Ch) William Tuke (ViceCh) Sir Henry Hambling (DepCh) Edwin Fisher (Mgr) Henry Mitchell (Mgr) Walter Stevenson (Mgr)
4. British North Borneo Company	2.0	3.6	Sir Richard Martin (Ch) Sir Charles Jessel (ViceCh) William Cowie (MD)	Major General Sir Neill Malcolm (Pres) Dougal Malcolm (VicePres) Hon. Mountstuart Elphinstone (MD)
5. Chartered Bank of India, Australia and China	0.8	3.0	John Gwyther (Ch) C Lewis (Mgr) W Main (Mgr)	Sir Montague Turner (Ch) J S Bruce (Mgr) G Miller (Mgr)
6. Consolidated Goldfields Corporation	3.25	5.0	Lord Harris (Ch)	Lord Brabourne (Ch)
7. Dalgety	4.0	7.0	Edmund Doxat (Ch & MD) Charles Churchill (DepCh)	Hon. Edmund Parker (Ch) Edward Reid (MD)
8. Elder, Dempster & Co.	1.0	10.5	Alfred Jones (Ch)	Lord Kylsant (Ch)
9. Foreign & Colonial Investment Trust	1.25	4.0	Lord Cecil (Ch)	Sir Evelyn Cecil (Ch) Arthur Crichton (Mgr)
10. Hudson's Bay Co.	2.0	4.5	Lord Strathcona (Governor) Earl of Lichfield (Dep Governor) D Kemp (Mgr)	Charles Sale (Governor)
11. Millars' Timber & Trading Company	0.5	2.0	Sir George Paget (Ch) Charles Temperley (MD)	James White (CH)
12. P & O	3.5	7.65	Sir Thomas Sutherland (Ch & MD)	Lord Inchcape (Ch & MD) Viscount Glenapp (Joint DepCh & MD) Hon. Alexander Shaw (Joint DepCh & MD) Frank Ritchie (MD)

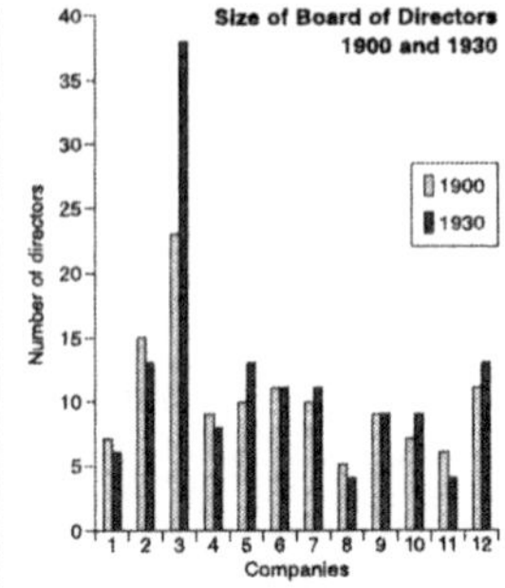

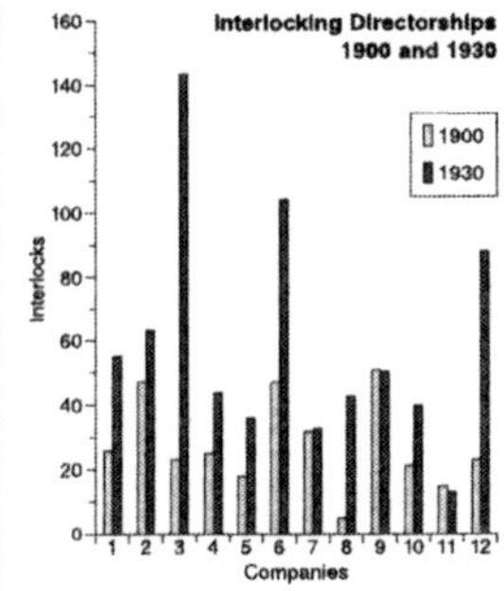

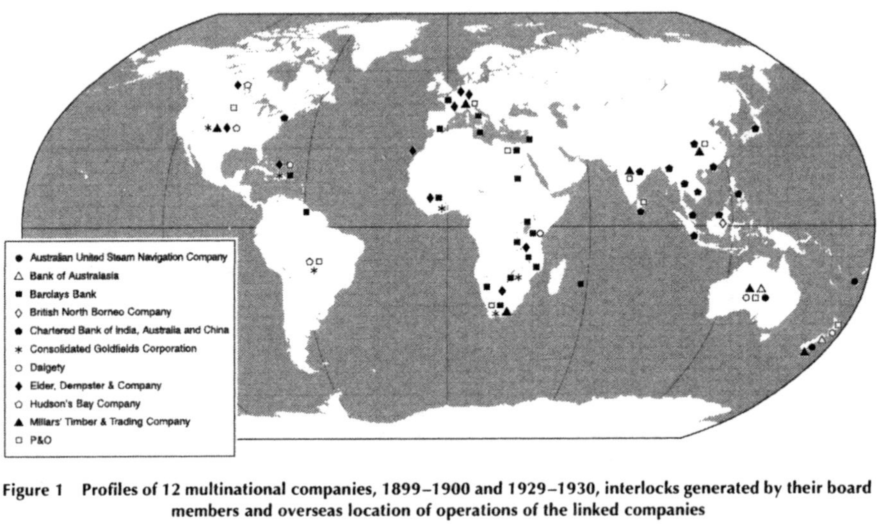

Figure 1 Profiles of 12 multinational companies, 1899–1900 and 1929–1930, interlocks generated by their board members and overseas location of operations of the linked companies

Table 1 Company interlocks by business sector, 1929–1930

	Australian United Steam Navigation Company	Bank of Australasia	Barclays Bank	British North Borneo Company	Chartered Bank of India, Australia and China	Consolidated Goldfields Corporation	Dalgety	Elder, Dempster and Company	Foreign and Colonial Investment Trust	Hudson's Bay Company	Millars' Timber and Trading Company	P & O	Totals
Transport	25	0	43	6	5	0	10	32	7	1	2	39	170
Financial services	14	25	49	14	15	20	14	8	42	17	1	24	243
Plantations	3	1	4	7	7	0	1	0	1	0	2	5	31
Agriculture	1	4	1	2	0	0	2	0	0	0	0	1	11
Mining and construction	2	18	10	6	0	66	1	1	0	0	6	2	112
Land and property	1	1	7	0	0	4	0	0	0	0	0	2	15
Manufacturing	1	6	10	3	2	4	4	0	0	4	0	2	36
Trade	2	1	3	0	2	1	0	1	0	1	1	2	14
Industry	3	3	8	1	1	2	1	1	0	1	0	3	24
Services	1	0	3	1	0	1	0	0	0	12	0	1	19
Oil and gas	0	3	1	0	3	4	0	0	0	1	0	0	12
Utilities	0	0	4	3	1	2	0	0	0	0	0	2	12
Development	0	0	1	1	0	0	0	0	0	3	1	0	6
Communications	2	1	0	0	0	0	0	0	0	0	0	5	8
Total	55	63	144	44	36	104	33	43	50	40	13	88	713

104 interlocks generated by the 11-strong 1929–1930 board of the Consolidated Goldfields Corporation were with mining and construction businesses. Nevertheless, the Corporation's directors held seats on company boards spread across another seven of the 14 business sectors.

Linkages generated by Barclays' directors stand out both numerically and sectorally. The penetration of the Bank is striking, particularly when it is noted that more than 20 other multiple directorships on the boards of the four Barclays overseas subsidiaries are omitted from the figures. The links of the two largest shipping enterprises in the sample, namely the Australian United Steam Navigation Company and P & O, though numerically smaller, were not only widespread, but also remarkably similar to each other in their sector distribution. While they were dominated by ties to financial and other transport businesses, a spread of linkages with plantation, agriculture, land and property, trade, industrial, and communications businesses suggests alliances strategically placed to support the 'commercial links' component of the external architecture of the firm.

Given this paper's emphasis on the social and geographical dynamics that shaped the operation of early multinationals, it is appropriate to examine the spatial character of the company interlocks generated by the sample multiple directors. While 38 per cent of the 1929–1930 interlocks were with UK-focused companies, the remainder comprised links with businesses engaged in localities spread throughout the world (Table 2). Directors of the Consolidated Goldfields Corporation illustrate the point. Although a majority of the Corporation's connections were with companies (mostly mining) engaged in Africa, the board's members also generated links with businesses operating in several European countries, as well as in Australia, Canada, the USA, and South and Central America. The global reach of company interlocks generated by directors of Barclays, the Bank of Australasia, and the Chartered Bank of India, Australia and China is notable, but so too is the distinct pattern of connections with enterprises operating, respectively, in South America, Australasia and Asia. Elder Dempster, known for its widespread West African maritime fiefdom (Davies 1973; Sherwood 1997), also had links with transportation companies engaged in business in Southeast Asia, Australia and the Americas.

The complex spatial web of connections generated by the board of P & O is even more remarkable. In addition to linkages with businesses spread across Europe, in 1929–1930, P & O directors interlocked the company with other firms operating in the Middle East (Egypt and Iraq), India and Ceylon (Sri Lanka), and Australia – a geography that closely mirrored P & O's intercontinental shipping routes and its network of agencies. Directorships were also held in global communications companies (including Cable and Wireless Ltd), marine assurance companies, and equipment manufacturing businesses in the UK. There was an interlock with the Suez Canal Lighterage Company, and two apiece with the Euphrates and Tigris Steam Navigation Company and the Eastern & Australian Steamship Company. In South Asia, an interlock existed with the Ceylon Steamship Company and two with the Ceylon Wharfage Company. P & O directors were on the boards of a number of Indian railway and river steam navigation companies, and held five interlocks with enterprises operating tea plantations in India. Through its board, particularly its executive directors, P & O therefore exercised potentially far-reaching corporate influence not only over the means of insuring, communicating with and servicing its ships in distant locations, and transporting potential cargoes and passengers to the quayside, but also the production of some of the key commodities that it contracted to carry. In the case of emergent multinationals, it is clear that, in addition to the three components of company 'architecture' noted above, interlocks were also established for geographical reasons and this represents a fourth *spatial* component of a firm's external architecture.

The corporate elite of early twentieth-century multinational enterprise

There is a seductive and perhaps dangerous appeal in the exploration of networks of multiple directorships that is engendered in part by the accessibility of the necessary information. Even the application of sophisticated network analysis to define power blocs or to distinguish between the linkages of executive and non-executive directors can easily lead to conclusions about a 'concentration of corporate influence' where *positions* are taken to imply *power* (Scott 1985, 1). Nevertheless, exploring multiple directorships is an important step in any investigation of the structuration of the capitalist class. As noted earlier, company interlocks represent the channels available for sharing business information amongst enterprises and people (Useem 1984; Scott 1991).

Table 2 Company interlocks by main geographical area of interest of other companies, 1929–1930

	Australian United Steam Navigation Company	Bank of Australasia	Barclays Bank	British North Borneo Company	Chartered Bank of India, Australia and China	Consolidated Goldfields Corporation	Dalgety	Elder, Dempster and Company	Foreign and Colonial Investment Trust	Hudson's Bay Company	Millars' Timber and Trading Company	P & O	Totals
UK	27	25	87	9	11	18	17	20	39	17	0	3	273
Europe	1	5	8	2	2	5	3	1	0	3	0	41	71
Africa	0	5	2	15	0	53	1	11	0	1	9	0	97
Middle East	4	0	1	0	0	0	1	0	0	0	0	3	9
South Asia	16	1	2	1	7	0	0	0	0	0	0	29	56
Southeast Asia	0	1	5	8	11	0	0	1	1	0	3	0	30
Asia (general)	2	0	0	0	1	0	1	0	0	2	0	5	11
Australasia	3	13	2	1	0	2	6	2	0	2	1	2	34
Central America	0	5	0	2	1	6	0	0	3	0	0	0	17
South America	0	4	20	6	0	10	1	6	0	2	0	0	49
USA	0	3	6	0	1	9	2	1	5	1	0	0	28
Canada	0	0	8	0	0	1	1	0	2	12	0	1	25
Global	2	1	3	0	2	0	0	1	0	0	0	4	13
Total	55	63	144	44	36	104	33	43	50	40	13	88	713

However, because the mere existence of a connection reveals little about either the quality or the quantity of information that was transmitted, or the strength of a social relationship, it will be necessary for us to explore in future papers the character of the networks that such analyses imply and to understand the active agency of the people and the collectivities involved.

It has been argued that Britain's late nineteenth- and early twentieth-century corporate elite was drawn predominantly from the land-owning, business and professional classes and that there was little mobility into the group from outside (Meisel 1958; Useem 1984; Jeremy 1984; Kay 1993). The occupants of 'top command situations' tended to be 'integrated through interaction and association' (Scott 2003, 157). Their cohesiveness was reinforced through common experiences of schooling, higher education, intermarriage and social activities (Rosenberg 1987). Shared values of profit seeking and corporate expansion further strengthened the ties that bound together an inner circle of mutually connected people who dominated the largest enterprises (Useem 1984; Sklair 2001). To explore these ideas in the context of the 12 multinationals, data were sought on the educational background, club and society membership, as well as the status, honours and official positions of the companies' directors. Although the existence of social connections does not prove that they influenced personal or commercial activity within the business world, research of this kind underlines the notion that economic geographies can be understood only by examining the social and cultural geographies within which they are embedded (Dicken *et al.* 2001).

Tracking the schools and universities attended by the directors in our samples was not an easy task. The six-volume *Dictionary of Business Biography* (Jeremy 1984), obituaries in *The Times*, entries in the *Dictionary of National Biography* and specific biographies, provide only a partial picture. However, the schools attended by 116 sample directors (44 per cent) have been established. While some 31 different institutions occur in the data, in both 1899–1900 and 1929–1930, an education at either Eton or Harrow predominated. Together these elite institutions accounted for 52.4 and 48.7 per cent of the schools known in 1899–1900 and 1929–1930, respectively. The universities or other post-school educational establishments attended are known in 30 per cent of cases. Some 21 different further and higher education institutions are named, including the Royal Military Academies at Sandhurst and Woolwich, and the Britannia Naval College at Dartmouth. The old East India Company training establishment, Haileybury College, features in the 1899–1900 sample, and overseas institutions, such as the universities of Zurich and Toronto and the Otago School of Mines in New Zealand, occur in the 1929–1930 list. However, the dominance of Oxbridge stands out. In both 1899–1900 and 1929–1930, of all directors for whom evidence has been recovered, past attendance at either Oxford or Cambridge universities accounted for more than 80 per cent of the cases. Moreover, Trinity College Cambridge alone accounted for 36.7 per cent of the sample in 1899–1900 and 31.3 per cent in 1929–1930.

Further research is required to reveal more fully the links between public schools and the Oxbridge colleges that trained the business elite and the recruitment of directors to company boards. Key questions include, for example, how frequently an Eton and Trinity College background enhanced opportunities for securing a directorship, and whether a shared educational experience influenced decisions made by those who offered appointments. Ultimately, answers will be found only by reconstructing particular individual behaviour patterns. Exploring memberships of clubs and societies, however, can provide further circumstantial evidence of group cohesion and social interaction (Meisel 1958; Jeremy 1984; Kay 1993).

Club and society memberships held by the sample directors in 1899–1900 and 1929–1930 of any of 65 different organizations were investigated (Nevill 1969; Cowell 1976; Lejeune and Lewis 1979). The most prominent affiliations were to the Carlton Club, the Athenaeum, Brooks's, the Marlborough Club and White's. Memberships held by 43 of the 1899–1900 sample directors (37 per cent) and 76 of the 1929–1930 sample (56 per cent) are known. It was common for top directors to belong to several clubs, sometimes at opposite ends of the political spectrum. Although a full analysis of all the social connections suggested by club memberships cannot be presented here, it is clear that numerous 'within-board' and 'between-board' networks existed. For example, in 1929–1930, 20 directors (i.e. more than a quarter of the total sample of memberships) belonged to the influential Carlton Club (Phelps 1983) (Table 3). Four of these were directors of Barclays; four were on the board of the Chartered

Table 3 The Carlton Club and social networks of corporate power, 1929–1930

Director's name Member of Carlton Club	School (if known)	University (if known)	Core company directorship	Other directorships (ordinary)	Other directorships (executive)	Total interlocks
Lord Aldenham	Eton	Cambridge	Bank of Australasia	20	6	26
Mr Arthur Allen			Foreign & Colonial Investment Trust	1	0	1
Lord Brabourne	Eton	Cambridge	Consolidated Goldfields Corporation	16	0	16
Mr Colin Campbell JP	Eton		Chartered Bank of India, Australia & China	1	3	4
Sir Evelyn Cecil MP, PC	Eton	Oxford	Foreign & Colonial Investment Trust	4	4	8
Hon. Arthur Crichton	Eton	Oxford	Foreign & Colonial Investment Trust	10	2	12
Lord Ebury	Harrow		Hudson's Bay Company	3	0	3
Mr Stephen Fairbairn	Geelong	Cambridge	Dalgety	0	0	0
Sir James Fortescue-Flannery MP, JP	Liverpool School of Science		Barclays Bank	3	8	11
Sir William Goschen JP	Eton		Chartered Bank of India, Australia & China	1	3	4
Sir Henry Hambling JP			Barclays Bank	4	3	7
Mr Oliver Hoare	Harrow	Oxford	Consolidated Goldfields Corporation	20	0	20
Lord Inchcape	Elgin		P & O	15	12	27
Lord Kylsant			Elder, Dempster & Company	5	32	37
Mr Edward Mackay	Edinburgh		Chartered Bank of India, Australia & China	1	0	1
Earl of Midleton PC	Eton	Oxford	Bank of Australasia	4	2	6
Sir William Mitchell MP, JP	Privately		Chartered Bank of India, Australia & China	4	1	5
Hon. Henry Mond MP, PC	Winchester		Barclays Bank	6	3	9
Mr John Pender MP	Eton		P & O	5	2	7
Lord Rochdale	Shrewsbury	Cambridge	Barclays Bank	1	5	6
				124	86	210

Note: MP – Member of Parliament; PC – Privy Councillor; JP – Magistrate

Bank of India, Australia and China; two represented P & O and the Australian United Steam Navigation Company, three were from the Foreign & Colonial Investment Trust; two each were from the Bank of Australasia and the Consolidated Goldfields Corporation; and there was one each from the Hudson's Bay Company, Elder Dempster and Dalgety's. The Carlton was clearly an important nexus of contact for ten of the 12 sample enterprises upon which this paper focuses.

All but one of the Carlton members were major multiple directors: between them, they engendered 210 company interlocks, or an average of around 11 each. Moreover, 86 interlocks were as chairman, deputy-chairman or managing director of the other companies. Table 3 tentatively indicates further complex layers of social connection amongst the 20 Carlton Club members. For instance, as a group comprising seven members of the House of Lords and five MPs, there was evident potential for social interaction through political activity. Service as a magistrate by five of the Carlton members indicates yet another set of interconnections. Membership of the Athenaeum, Brooks's, White's and the Marlborough clubs reveals other intricate sets of interconnections and suggests important avenues for future papers.

Biographies of capitalism

It was earlier noted that one approach to 'mapping' the socio-spatial role of company directors in shaping the international economy is to focus specifically on the relationships of *individual* members of the corporate elite. The demands of this approach are clear: sampling just 12 companies (albeit large multinational enterprises) yielded a dataset comprising more than 100 directors for both 1899–1900 and 1929–1930. The need to select a smaller sub-sample of individuals is therefore clear. Our ultimate objective is to explore the operational use made of their own networks by those directors engendering the largest number of company interlocks, defined as those with more than eight other directorships. In 1929–1930, this criterion confines the sample to 27 individuals headed by Lord Kylsant (Chairman, Elder, Dempster & Co.) and Lord Inchcape (Chairman and Managing Director, P & O). To demonstrate the scope and potential value of our evidence, Figure 2 offers a summary of the business and spatial networks of Kylsant and Inchcape. In just a few cases, where appropriate information has survived, the use of personal archival material is beginning to indicate further, more precise ways in which the engagement of top directors with businessmen and allied companies were exploited. Such connections were actively employed to secure specific commercial aims engendering economic and spatial impacts. Again, future research will pursue these issues in greater depth.

Conclusion

Literature exploring contemporary globalization points to novel changes occurring in the structure and dynamics of the business elite (Sklair 2001). It argues that a new 'trans-national capitalist class' is emerging whose members have specific relations with other businessmen, agencies and institutions not only within their own country, but also in other countries. This paper reinforces the contention that, in the early twentieth century, although genuinely trans-national enterprises were rare, there already existed an interconnected corporate elite running large companies whose interests were spread across the world (Jones 2002; Robertson 2003). Our results suggest that many multiple directors were by then enmeshed within complex sets of relations with other businessmen and agencies not only in London and the UK, but also spread across the British Empire and other countries. This brief preliminary study indicates the importance of acknowledging the existence at least a century ago of a nascent trans-national capitalist class. It also underlines the value of employing the idea of networks to understand the economic globalization processes of the early twentieth century and the interwar era. We point to the need to examine further the social and cultural geographies within which key players in the world's internationalizing economy were embedded. Indeed, we argue that historical studies of human agency and human interrelations (often impossible to reveal in full until the passage of time has drawn back the veils of individual privacy) are central to an understanding of how the economy both internationalized and globalized.

Acknowledgements

This research is part of a project funded by the Economic and Social Research Council (Grant No. RES-000-22-0208). Thanks are due to Simon Francis for assembling primary data, to Pauline Framingham for data processing assistance, to Jamie Quinn for the artwork and to Richard Perkins for comments on an early draft of the paper.

Owen Cosby Philipps, Lord Kylsant, 1863–1937 (Elder Dempster) 1929–1930: 37 interlocks

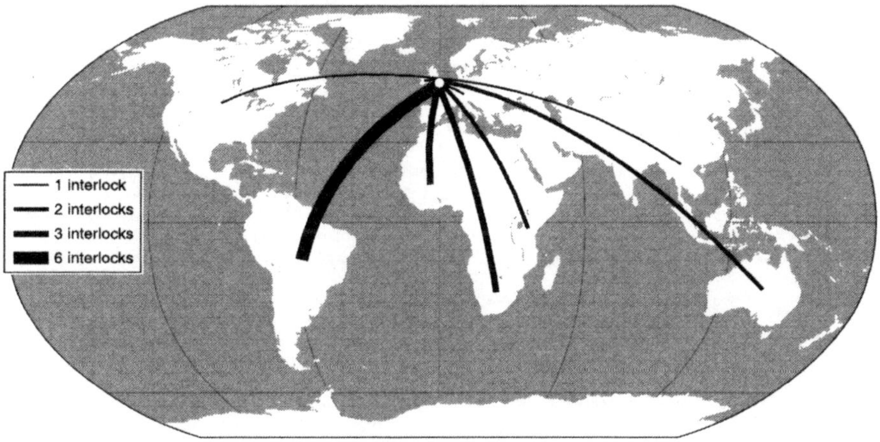

James Lyle Mackay, Earl of Inchcape, 1852–1932 (P&O) 1929–1930: 27 interlocks

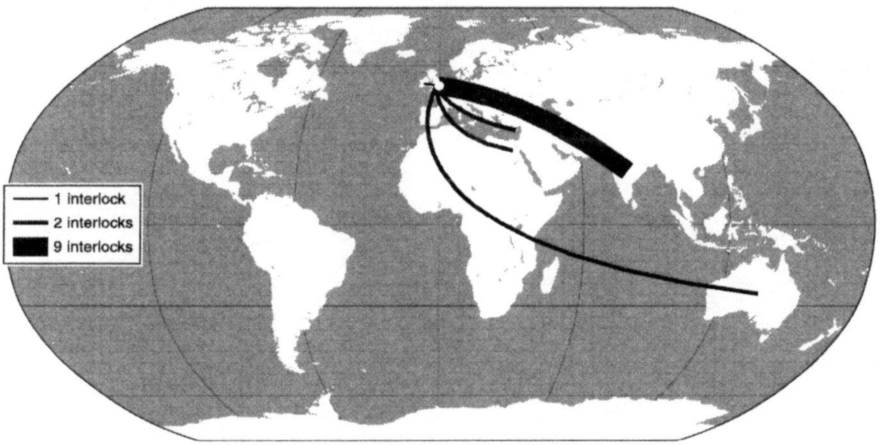

Figure 2 Constructing biographies of capitalism: overseas areas of operation of companies with which Lord Kylsant and the Earl of Inchcape were 'interlocked' (1929–1930). Note: interlocks with companies operating in the UK and Europe are not shown

References

Barty-King H 1979 *Girdle round the earth: the story of Cable and Wireless and its predecessors* Heinemann, London

Beaverstock J V, Doel M A, Hubbard P J and Taylor P J 2002 Attending to the world: cooperation and connectivity in the World City network *Global Networks* 2 111–32

Cassis Y 1988 Merchant bankers and City aristocracy *British Journal of Sociology* 39 114–20

Castells M 1996 *The rise of the network society* Blackwell, Oxford

Chapman S D 1986 Aristocracy and meritocracy in merchant banking *British Journal of Sociology* 37 180–93

Corley T A B 1994 Britain's overseas investments in 1914 revisited *Business History* 36 71–88

Cowell F R 1976 *The Athenaeum: the club and social life in London 1824–1974* Heinemann, London

Davies P N 1973 *The trade makers: Elder Dempster in West Africa, 1862–1972* George Allen & Unwin, London

Dicken P, Kelly P F, Olds K and Wai-Chung Yeung H 2001 Chains and networks, territories and scales: towards a relational framework for analysing the global economy *Global Networks* 1 89–112

Fennema M and Schijf H 1985 The transnational network in **Stokman F N, Ziegler R and Scott J** eds *Networks of corporate power: a comparative analysis of ten countries* Polity Press, Cambridge 250–67

Gertler M S 2001 Tacit knowledge and the economic geography of context or the undefinable tacitness of being (there) Paper presented at the Nelson and Winter DRUID summer conference, Aalborg Denmark 12–15 June (http://www.utoronto.ca/progris/recentpub.htm) Accessed 4 July 2002

Giddens A 2000 *Runaway world: how globalization is reshaping our lives* Routledge, New York

Glasberg D S and Schwartz M 1983 Ownership and control of corporations *Annual Review of Sociology* 9 311–32

Guillén M F 2001 Is globalization civilizing, destructive or feeble? A critique of five key debates in the social science literature *Annual Review of Sociology* 27 235–60

Hess M 2004 'Spatial' relationships? Towards a reconceptualization of embeddedness *Progress in Human Geography* 28 165–86

Hirst P and Thompson G 1999 *Globalization in question* Polity Press, London

Jeremy D J 1984 Anatomy of the British business elite 1860–1980 *Business History* 26 3–24

Jones G 2002 Business enterprises and global worlds *Enterprise and Society* 3 Dec 581–605

Kay J 1993 *Foundations of corporate success: how business strategies add value* Oxford University Press, Oxford

Kieve J 1973 *The electric telegraph: a social and economic history* David and Charles, Newton Abbot

Lejeune A and Lewis M 1979 *The Gentlemen's Clubs of London* Marboro, London

Lewis A 1981 The rate of growth of world trade, 1830–1973 in **Grassman S and Lundberg E** eds *The world economic order: past and prospects* Macmillan, Basingstoke 11–74

Lisle-Williams M 1984a Beyond the market: the survival of family capitalism in the English merchant banks *British Journal of Sociology* 35 241–71

Lisle-Williams M 1984b Merchant banking dynasties in the English class structure: ownership, solidarity and kinship in the City of London, 1850–1960 *British Journal of Sociology* 35 333–62

Meisel J H 1958 *The myth of the ruling class* University of Michigan Press, Ann Arbor

Nevill R H 1969 *London Clubs: their history and treasures* Chatto and Windus, London

Newman P C 1987 *Company of adventurers. Vol 3: Merchant princes* Viking Press, Toronto

O'Hagan S B and Green M B 2002a Interlocking directorates: an example of tacit knowledge transfer *Urban Geography* 23 154–79

O'Hagan S B and Green M B 2002b Tacit knowledge transfer via interlocking directorates: a comparison of Canada and the United States *Geografiska Annaler* 84 49–63

Ogborn M 2000 Historical geographies of globalisation c1500–1800 in **Graham B and Nash C** eds *Modern historical geographies* Prentice Hall Longman, Harlow 34–69

Phelps B 1983 *Power and the party: a history of the Carlton Club, 1832–1982* Macmillan, London

Robertson R 2003 *Three waves of globalization: a history of a developing global consciousness* Zed Books, London

Rosenberg H 1987 The kitchen and the multinational corporation: an analysis of the links between household and global corporations *Journal of Business Ethics* 6 179–94

Scott J 1985 Theoretical framework and research design in **Stokman F N, Ziegler R and Scott J** eds *Networks of corporate power: a comparative analysis of ten countries* Polity Press, Cambridge 1–19

Scott J 1991 Networks of corporate power: a comparative assessment *Annual Review of Sociology* 17 181–203

Scott J 2003 Transformations in the British economic elite *Comparative Sociology* 2 155–73

Scott J and Griff A 1985a *Directors of industry* Polity Press, Cambridge

Scott J and Griff A 1985b Bank spheres of influence in the British corporate network in **Stokman F N, Ziegler R and Scott J** eds *Networks of corporate power: a comparative analysis of ten countries* Polity Press, Cambridge 215–34

Selwood J 2000 An early example of globalisation: The Hudson's Bay Company's interlocking directorships *Prairie Perspectives* 3 1–16

Sherwood M 1997 Elder Dempster and West Africa 1891–c1940: the genesis of underdevelopment *The International Journal of African Historical Studies* 30 253–76

Skinner T 1900a *The Stock Exchange yearbook* Cassell Petter and Galpin, London

Skinner T 1900b *Directory of directors* Thomas Skinner and Company, London

Skinner T 1930a *The Stock Exchange yearbook* Cassell Petter and Galpin, London

Skinner T 1930b *Directory of directors* Thomas Skinner and Company, London

Sklair L 2001 *The transnational capitalist class* Blackwell, Oxford
Standage T 1998 *The Victorian Internet: the remarkable story of the telegraph and the nineteenth-century on-line pioneers* Wiedenfeld and Nicolson, London
Stokman F N, Ziegler R and Scott J 1985 eds *Networks of corporate power: a comparative analysis of ten countries* Polity Press, Cambridge
Taylor P J 2001 Specification of the World City network *Geographical Analysis* 33 181–94
Tomka B 2001 Interlocking directorships between banks and industrial companies in Hungary at the beginning of the twentieth century *Business History* 43 25–43
Useem M 1984 *The inner circle* Oxford University Press, New York
Walvin J 1997 *Fruits of empire: exotic produce and British trade, 1660–1800* Macmillan, Basingstoke
Wilkins M 1998 Multinational enterprises and economic change *Australian Economic History Review* 38 103–34
Wolf E R 1982 *Europe and the people without history* University of California Press, Berkeley CA

[5]

Computational & Mathematical Organization Theory 5:4 (1999): 311–341

Private Games are too Dangerous

RONALD S. BURT
Graduate School of Business, University of Chicago, Chicago, IL 60637, USA; INSEAD, Boulevard de Constance, 77305 Fountainbleu Cedex, France
email: ron.burt@gsb.uchicago.edu

Abstract

Given the difficulty of observing interpersonal relations as they develop within an organization, I use iterated prisoner's dilemma games to simulate their development. The goal is to understand how trust could develop as a function of private games, that is, as a function of interaction sequences between two people independent of their relationships with other people. My baseline is Axelrod's results with TIT for TAT showing that cooperation can emerge as the dominant form of interaction even in a society of selfish individuals without central authority. I replicate Axelrod's results, then show that the results only occur in a rare social context—maximum density networks. Where people form less dense networks by withdrawing from unproductive relationships, as is typical in organizations, the competitive advantage shifts from TIT for TAT to abusive strategies. A devious PUSHY strategy wins in moderate to high density networks. A blatantly HOSTILE strategy wins in less dense networks. Abusive players do well in sparse networks because their abuse is lucrative in the initial exchanges of a relationship—before the other person knows to withdraw. Wise players avoiding the abusive players leaves the abusive players free to concentrate on naive players (con men thrive in big cities). The implication is that what keeps abusive players at bay are friends and acquaintances warning managers away from people known to exploit their colleagues. I reinforce the point with illustrative survey data to conclude that private games are not only too dangerous, but also too rare and too slow to be the foundation for trust within organizations. The results are an evidential call for the sociological intuition that trust and distrust cannot be understood independent of the network context in which they are produced.

Keywords: trust, organization, social network, density, prisoner's dilemma

1. Introduction

There are two ways to think about the probability of trust within a relationship. The simpler is to think in terms of private games—that is, in terms of interaction sequences between two people independent of their relationships with other people. Trust emerges between the two people as a function of their history and future with one another. Two prominent examples of this thinking in sociology are Homans' (1961) analysis of social behavior, and Blau's (1964) analysis of social exchange (see Blau, 1994: 152–172, for Blau's contemporary view, esp. pp. 156–158, explaining his continued focus on dyadic exchange). Blau (1964: 112–113) argues that trust develops because social exchange involves unspecified obligations for which no binding contract can be written. When you exchange sensitive information with someone, for example, trust is implicit in the risk you now face that the other person might leak the information. Putting aside Blau's moral obligation aspect of exchange to focus on parameters of cost-benefit calculation (cf. Ekeh, 1974: 175), Coleman (1990: Chap. 5) captured trust more concretely for his systems of two-party exchange: Trust is committing to an exchange before you know how the other person will behave. You anticipate cooperation from the other person, but you commit to the exchange before you know how the other person will behave. This is trust, pure and simple. Anticipated cooperation is a narrow segment in the spectrum of concepts spanned by richer images such as Barber's (1983) distinctions between trust as moral order, competence, and obligation. However, anticipated cooperation is much of the trust essential to people in organizations. The issue isn't moral. It is flexible cooperation (e.g., Macauley, 1963; Uzzi, 1996).

Viewed as anticipated cooperation, trust is twice created by repeated interaction; from the past and from the future. From the past, repeated experience with a person is improved knowledge of the person. Cooperation in today's game is a signal of future cooperation. Across repeated games with cooperative outcomes, you build confidence in the other person's tendency to cooperate. At minimum, the cumulative process can be cast as a statistical decision problem in which you become more certain of the other person across repeated samples of his or her behavior. The repetition of cooperative exchange promotes trust. More generally, the cumulative process involves escalation. From tentative initial exchanges, you move to familiarity, and from there to more significant exchanges. The gradual expansion of exchanges promotes the trust necessary for them. Whatever the cumulative process, past cooperation is a basis for future cooperation (cf. Zucker, 1986, on process-based trust; Larson, 1992; on the importance of the long term for trust between firms; Lawler and Yoon, 1996, for laboratory evidence; Stinchcombe, 1990: 164–165, on the information advantages of current suppliers for building trust; Gulati, 1995; Gulati and Garguilo, Forthcoming, for empirical evidence). Further, the history of cooperation is an investment that would be lost if either party behaved so as to erode the relationship—another factor making it easier for each party to trust the other to cooperate. Blau (1968: 454) summarized the process as follows: "...social exchange relations evolve in a slow process, starting with minor transactions in which little trust is required because little risk is involved and in which both partners can prove their trustworthiness, enabling them to expand their relation and engage in major transactions. Thus, the process of social exchange leads to the trust required for it in a self-governing fashion." Where sociologists explain trust emerging from past exchanges (e.g., Coleman, 1990; Granovetter, 1992), economists look to the incentives of future exchanges (e.g., Kreps, 1990; Gibbons, 1992: 88ff). The expectation that violations of trust will be punished in the future leads players to cooperate even if defection would be more profitable in a single play of the game. The information contained in past experience and the potential for future interactions are inextricably linked. A player's willingness to forego short-term gains is based on the expectation that his or her current behavior will be used to predict his or her behavior in the future.

The alternative is to think more broadly in terms of public games—interaction sequences in which two people display their behavior to one another, but are mindful of their reputation with friends and acquaintances observing the game. Relationships play out in a social context of friends, acquaintances, and enemies who are third parties to the relationship and transform what was private into public. Three network arguments describe how third parties to a relationship can be expected to affect trust within the relationship. There is a balance argument in which people are presumed to have a preference for consistency between relationships adjacent in a network (e.g., Heider, 1958; Davis, 1970), a reputation argument in which strong indirect connections through third parties are a medium through which social norms of cooperation can be enforced (e.g., Granovetter, 1985, 1992; Coleman, 1988, 1990; Kreps, 1990, Greif, 1993; Putnam, 1993), and a gossip argument in which etiquette-biased information amplifies predispositions toward trust or distrust (e.g., Burt and Knez, 1995; Burt, 1999a, 1999b; Sobel, 1999). The gossip argument reproduces the first two in predicting that third parties increase the probability of trust within strong relationships, and contradicts them in predicting that third parties also increase the probability of distrust within weak relationships. Evidence consistent with the gossip argument is beginning to appear as scholars test for network effects on negative relationships (e.g., Burt and Knez, 1995, on distrust associated with third parties within organizations; Labianca et al., 1998, on perceptions of conflict associated with third parties; Gulati and Westphal, Forthcoming, on third-party interlocks amplifying positive and negative predispositions to alliance between organizations; Burt, 1999c, on three generic research findings supporting the gossip argument).

Whatever the cross-sectional and historical evidence of association between trust and third parties, the evidence needed to establish third-party effects in an authoritative way is a study of interpersonal networks over time to see how variation in the structure of third parties around a relationship affects its development. The problem is that such observation typically involves (a) substantial cost within an organization of even moderate size, and (b) the distortions associated with intrusive observers. The problem must be more serious toward the top of the organization where much of trust is an implicit understanding and so not easily calibrated over time. Systematic evidence from the field has been limited to cross-sectional data showing that trust and distrust are more likely in relations embedded in third-party ties (Gulati and Westphal, 1999, Gulati and Garguilo, 1999, are rare exceptions that use panels of archival data on relations between organizations). How relations develop as a function of third parties remains unknown, so causal inferences are accordingly suspect (Burt and Knez, 1995: 284–285).

Where observation over time is difficult, simulations can be a productive complement to cross-sectional data. I use iterated prisoner's dilemma games between eight game strategies to simulate the development of relationships among kinds of managers within an organization. My baseline is Axelrod's (1980a, 1980b, 1984) widely-known use of such simulations to argue that cooperation can emerge as the dominant form of interaction even in a society of selfish individuals without central authority.

Two points are established with the simulations. I first replicate Axelrod's tournament results on cooperation. TIT for TAT is the most successful kind of player. The TIT for TAT strategy is to begin with cooperation, then reciprocate whatever move your partner made in the prior game.

Second, I show that TIT for TAT's success is limited to dense networks. The simulated network of Axelrod's tournament was dense in two ways rare in organizations: repeated games with every other person, and no exit from a bad relationship. This is a network characteristic of families more than organizations. I make the simulation more relevant to organizations by shifting to a sparse network in which relations rarely have a chance to develop beyond initial exchanges and players can withdraw from a bad relationship. The result is a change in the quality of relationships and the relative success of player strategies. Relations in the sparse network are on average more rewarding and more pleasant because players can withdraw from bad relationships. The irony is that the higher quality relations serve most to benefit nasty players, players who exploit cooperative partners. In anything less than maximum-density conditions, the advantage shifts from TIT for TAT players to the cautiously exploitative PUSHY players. Just before the network disintegrates to a condition more sparse than dense, the advantage quickly shifts to the more aggressively exploitative HOSTILE players, who dominate all populations more sparse than dense. Nasty players do well in sparse networks because they do well in the initial games of a relationship, and few relations in a sparse network develop beyond the initial games.

I use the term density as it is usually used in network analysis, but let me be clear about it at the outset because density is a key variable in what follows. A dense network is one in which each person has a strong (positive or negative) relationship with every other person. At the other extreme, a sparse network is one in which relations are often weak or absent. When I allow in the simulation for people to play only few games with specific others, and withdraw from unproductive relationships, I transform what were dense networks into sparse networks. There are other ways in which a sparse network could occur, but in this paper I only study the consequences of infrequent interaction and withdrawal. It is useful to keep separate the condition of a network (e.g., dense versus sparse) from the many processes by which the network could have come to its current condition.

2. Private Games in Dense Networks

To ensure that the substantive content of the simulations is clear, let me take a moment to describe the prisoner's dilemma game. Hardin (1990: 364) provides a delightful glimpse into the game's origin: "This game was discovered or invented—it is not clear which is the more apt term here—by Merrill Flood and Melvin Dresher, two early game theorists who were trying to test bargaining theories with experimental games. Oddly, two of the games with which Flood experimented before the prisoner's dilemma involved simple exchanges—of old cars for money. He seems not to have seen that his prisoner's dilemma game was a simplification and generalization of such exchanges. Unfortunately, this association got lost in the later naming of the game by A.W. Tucker, who saw in the game a perverse analog of American criminal justice, in which prosecutors extract confessions on the promise of reduced sentences." The analog is illustrated in figure 1 with an anecdote often used, in this or similar form, to introduce the game.[1]

You are a prisoner deciding whether to confess. The best outcome for you (ego) and your partner (alter) occurs if you cooperate with one another and don't confess, but cooperation is not the optimum strategy for you personally. If your partner confesses, you are better off confessing (five years in prison versus ten if you don't confess). If your partner doesn't confess, you are still better off confessing (no years in prison versus five if you don't confess). Regardless of your partner's behavior, you personally are better off confessing. Trust is the essential tension of the game. You have to decide to cooperate before you know how your partner will reciprocate. Can you trust your partner to keep his mouth shut? In the absence of trust, the optimum choice is to defect.[2]

		Alter's Move	
		Cooperate	**Defect**
Ego's Move	**Cooperate**	E gets 3, A gets 3 Reward for mutual cooperation	E gets 0, A gets 5 Sucker's payoff and temptation to defect
	Defect	E gets 5, A gets 0 Temptation to defect and sucker's payoff	E gets 1, A gets 1 Punishment for mutual defection

The prosecutor has two suspects in jail. The suspects are questioned separately and cannot communicate with one another. There is insufficient evidence to convict the suspects of their crime, but the prosecutor has sufficient evidence to convict them both of a lesser offense. If neither suspect confesses, then neither will be convicted of their serious crime but both will be convicted of the lesser offense. If both confess, then both will be convicted of the serious crime. Playing the two suspects against one another, the prosecutor tells each that he will go free if he is the first to testify against the other. The informer will go free. The other person will get the book thrown at him.

Figure 1. The Prisoner's dilemma.

The optimum strategy is less obvious across repeated games. Today's game has implications for tomorrow's game. With respect to the prisoner anecdote, there will be future games in prison or on the street with the partner betrayed today (not to mention the future disdain of peers—no one likes a snitch).

Axelrod took a behavioral approach to determining the optimum strategy. Whatever the initial value of the approach, it is productive for the ease with which it extends to more complex network settings. Experts were invited to submit strategies for a computer tournament to determine the optimum strategy (Axelrod, 1980a: 7): "In a computer tournament, each entrant writes a program which embodies a decision rule to select the cooperative or noncooperative choice on each move. The program has available to it the history of the game so far, and may use this history in making a choice. Because the participants are recruited primarily from those who have written on game theory and especially the prisoner's dilemma, the entrants are assured that their decision rule will be facing rules of other experts. Such recruitment also guarantees that the state of the art is represented in the tournament." There are obvious questions about who would enter such a tournament, and there were few submissions to the initial tournament.[3] However, the results of the first tournament were sufficiently intriguing (Axelrod, 1980a) to draw 63 contestants for a second tournament (Axelrod, 1980b).

2.1. Network Model

The 63 contestants were not completely different. Qualities of some strategies appear in other strategies. I wrote a computer program to simulate the behavior of eight strategies, or kinds of players, that span significant distinctions in Axelrod's tournament. Game outcomes are proportional to the rewards in Axelrod's tournament and figure 1 (10 points for mutual defection, 30 points for mutual cooperation, 50 points to the player who defects against a cooperating partner, and 0 points to the player who cooperates with a partner who defects).

Table 1 is a summary of the simulations. Cell (A, B) is the average outcome for player A in games with player B (cf. Axelrod, 1980a: 11, 1980b: 387, 1984: 194, 197–199). There are eighty, not eight, players in the table. Table 1 is a summary of relations in an eighty-person network where each relation is based on games transacted at random within the network. The table begins with each relation z_{ij} from row i to column j equal to zero. Pick one of the rows i at random to play a game. Pick column j at random to be the other player. The two players make moves according to their respective strategies. The results are added to the appropriate two cells of the table: If i and j both cooperate, add 30 points to relations z_{ij} and z_{ji}. If i and j both defect, add 10 points to relations z_{ij} and z_{ji}. If i cooperates but j defects, then add 50 points to relation z_{ji}, nothing to z_{ij}. Draw a second random pair of players for game two. Make each player's move. Add the results to the appropriate two relations in the table. Draw a third random pair of players, and so on. Continue for 800,000 games. Each relation is the cumulative result of an average of 250 repeated games. To get the average outcome for player i in a game with player j, divide the summed pay-offs in relation z_{ij} by the number of games summed in the relation. Cell (A, B) in Table 1 is the average of the 100 relations between the ten players of row kind A with the ten players of column kind B. The standard deviation of average outcomes across the 100 relations in each cell is reported in parentheses. The number in brackets is the average number of games played to define each of the relations (slightly more than 250 because the 10 self-relations z_{ii} in each diagonal cell are excluded). In network analysis terms, Table 1 is a density table of the simulated relations between the eighty players.

Note that these results do not describe an N-way game; they describe two-person games in a system of N players. In an N-way game, each player is engaged in a game with the $N - 1$ other players. As N increases, monitoring the other players is more difficult, and cooperation is less likely because so many players have to cooperate at the same time. This is the central point of Hechter's (1987) argument for the importance of control mechanisms to enforce cooperation. In fact, Knez and Camerer (1994) describe experiments in which adding one person to a two-person coordination game significantly erodes cooperation. The network summarized in Table 1 is limited to two-person games. It is the network implicit in Axelrod's simulations. Players do not monitor all $N - 1$ other players, and there is no indirect monitoring through third parties. The only games known to a player are the games in which he or she is a participant.[4]

2.2. Nonresponsive Players

The first three kinds of players in Table 1 are nonresponsive in the sense that they give no attention to the behavior of their partner. HAPPY cooperates. HOSTILE defects. ERRATIC

Table 1. Average rewards from private games.

	1	2	3	4	5	6	7	8	Row averages
1. HAPPY (Always cooperate)	30.0 (0.0) [256]	0.0 (0.0) [253]	14.8 (0.8) [254]	30.0 (0.0) [255]	30.0 (0.0) [252]	30.0 (0.0) [252]	27.1 (0.6) [257]	15.0 (0.0) [255]	22.1
2. HOSTILE (Never cooperate)	50.0 (0.0) [253]	10.0 (0.0) [253]	29.6 (1.3) [254]	10.2 (0.0) [254]	10.3 (0.0) [253]	10.2 (0.0) [253]	10.2 (0.0) [255]	10.2 (0.0) [252]	17.6
3. ERRATIC (Random)	40.2 (0.6) [254]	5.1 (0.3) [254]	22.3 (1.3) [254]	22.3 (0.6) [250]	31.2 (0.9) [252]	5.4 (0.3) [254]	20.7 (0.7) [253]	22.3 (0.7) [254]	21.2
4. TIT for TAT (Reciprocate)	30.0 (0.0) [255]	10.0 (0.0) [254]	22.2 (0.6) [250]	30.0 (0.0) [251]	30.0 (0.0) [253]	30.0 (0.0) [252]	11.7 (1.3) [248]	30.0 (0.0) [255]	24.3
5. OTHER CHEEK (Tit for two tats)	30.0 (0.0) [252]	9.9 (0.0) [253]	18.5 (0.6) [252]	30.0 (0.0) [253]	30.0 (0.0) [255]	30.0 (0.0) [253]	25.1 (4.2) [252]	15.0 (0.0) [249]	23.6
6. RIGHTEOUS (Never forgive)	30.0 (0.0) [252]	10.0 (0.0) [253]	29.5 (1.1) [254]	30.0 (0.0) [252]	30.0 (0.0) [253]	30.0 (0.0) [253]	10.9 (0.8) [254]	10.3 (0.0) [254]	22.6
7. SNEAKY (Up to 10% deceit)	32.0 (0.4) [257]	10.0 (0.0) [255]	23.0 (0.8) [253]	11.9 (1.3) [248]	29.4 (5.3) [252]	10.9 (0.8) [254]	11.0 (0.5) [257]	12.2 (1.6) [253]	17.6
8. PUSHY (Up to 50% deceit)	40.0 (0.0) [255]	10.0 (0.0) [252]	22.3 (0.8) [254]	30.0 (0.0) [255]	40.0 (0.0) [249]	10.1 (0.0) [254]	12.0 (1.6) [253]	29.8 (0.0) [251]	24.3

NOTE—Each cell represents 100 relations between ten players of the row kind and ten players of the column kind (except diagonal cells which exclude the ten self-relations of players with themselves). The relation from player i to player j is the average pay-off for player i in repeated games with player j. Average outcomes at the top of the table are the average of 790 relations from each kind of player. The three numbers in cell (A, B) of the table are: the average of the 100 row A relations with column B players, the standard deviation of the relations (in parentheses), and the average number of games played to define each relation [in brackets].

is equally likely to cooperate or defect. Always cooperating, HAPPY players always earn 30 points in games with one another. Always defecting, HOSTILE players always earn 10 points from one another. HOSTILE does well against HAPPY because HAPPY continues to cooperate despite HOSTILE's defections. The outcome of these games are 50 points to HOSTILE, 0 to HAPPY. HOSTILE also does well against random play. When ERRATIC cooperates with HOSTILE he earns nothing and when he defects he earns 10 points. Half his moves are cooperation, so his average profit from a game with HOSTILE is only 5 points. On the other side, HOSTILE earns 50 points when ERRATIC cooperates and 10 points when he defects, for an average profit of 30 points.

HOSTILE is the most successful of the three nonresponsive players. Axelrod presents two kinds of evidence for such conclusions; expected outcomes and ecological survival. In terms of expected outcomes, HOSTILE is most successful. These games equally distributed across the three nonresponsive players yield an average profit to HOSTILE of 29.9 (divide by three the row sum from Table 1 of 50.0, plus 10.0, plus 29.6). The other two nonresponsive players earn less—14.9 for HAPPY, and 22.5 for ERRATIC.

2.3. *Nice Players*

The next three players in Table 1 are what Axelrod (1980b: 389) termed "nice" players. Nice players respond to their partner, but are never the first to defect. TIT for TAT begins with cooperation, then reciprocates the other person's last move—cooperates in response to cooperation, defects in response to defection. This was Anatol Rapoport's submission, and won the tournament (Axelrod, 1980b: 389–390). OTHER CHEEK begins with cooperation, then reciprocates, but turns the other cheek in response to a defection, allowing the other person two defections before retaliating. This tit-for-two-tats strategy was John Maynard Smith's submission to the Axelrod tournament. RIGHTEOUS cooperates until the other person is discovered to be dishonest, then never again cooperates with that person. This strategy consistent with the legal philosophy of the Puritan Massachusetts Bay Colony was James W. Friedman's submission to the Axelrod tournament (cf. Gibbons, 1992: 91ff, on the "trigger" strategy).

RIGHTEOUS players are the most successful among these six kinds of players, but no one kind of player is dominant. The players in descending order of expected profit are RIGHTEOUS (26.6 mean outcome), TIT for TAT (25.4), OTHER CHEEK (24.7), HAPPY (22.5), ERRATIC (21.1), and HOSTILE (20.1). HOSTILE is now the least successful player because his constant defection denies him the cooperation benefits shared by the nice players. Further, nice players reciprocate HOSTILE's defection so he can't exploit them like he exploits HAPPY. The primary difference among the nice players is their relative success against random play. RIGHTEOUS does best against ERRATIC. As soon as RIGHTEOUS discovers that ERRATIC defects against a cooperative partner, it never cooperates again. Thereafter, RIGHTEOUS earns at least 10 points per game with ERRATIC.

2.4. *Nasty Players*

Nasty players defect against a cooperating partner. HOSTILE players are the pure form; they defect in all games with all players. ERRATIC players are a weak form in the sense that they do sometimes defect against a cooperating partner. The last two players in Table 1 are strategic forms. They respond to their partner's behavior, but they look for opportunities to get away with defecting against a cooperating partner.

SNEAKY looks for a little extra from a tit-for-tat strategy. The strategy is to play the TIT for TAT strategy, but occasionally defect against a cooperating partner. If the other player defects, SNEAKY defects. If the other cooperates, SNEAKY cooperates at random 90% of the time. In other words, SNEAKY's deceit can go as high as defecting in 10% of his moves against a cooperating partner. This was Johann Joss's submission to the Axelrod tournament (JOSS in Axelrod, 1980a: 14, 23; 1984).

PUSHY tries to exploit, but backs away if threatened. PUSHY defects on the first move to test the other player. If the other player cooperates, then PUSHY cooperates on the second move and defects on alternate subsequent moves (4, 6, 8, etc.). If the other defects, PUSHY apologizes by cooperating on the next move and playing TIT for TAT for the rest of the game. In other words, PUSHY's deceit can go as high as 50% against a cooperating partner. This was David Gladstein's submission to the Axelrod tournament (TESTER in Axelrod, 1980b: 391; 1984).

The nasty players reveal important differences between nice players. SNEAKY reveals the importance of forgiveness (Axelrod, 1980a: 14–18). RIGHTEOUS never forgives, TIT for TAT forgives after retaliating with a punishment, and OTHER CHEEK is the most forgiving in the sense that he turns the other cheek and waits for a second defection before retaliating. The result is that SNEAKY drags RIGHTEOUS and TIT for TAT into an unproductive equilibrium state of mutual retaliation while OTHER CHEEK does well. The average outcome of games between SNEAKY and TIT for TAT are 11.7 points to TIT for TAT, 11.9 points to SNEAKY. The expected outcome varies as much as it does because it depends on the timing of SNEAKY's initial defection. When SNEAKY does defect, TIT for TAT retaliates, then SNEAKY retaliates in return, and the two players are thereafter in an equilibrium state of mutual retaliation. In contrast, when SNEAKY defects against OTHER CHEEK, there is no immediate retaliation and SNEAKY is unlikely to defect twice in a row, so OTHER CHEEK usually forgives the one defection with SNEAKY's subsequent cooperation. Two results: (a) SNEAKY players get more from their games with OTHER CHEEK because defections earn them 50 points and give OTHER CHEEK nothing (29.4 mean outcome for SNEAKY versus 25.1 mean outcome for OTHER CHEEK). (b) OTHER CHEEK makes money while the other nice players get runner-up awards (25.1 mean outcome for OTHER CHEEK versus 11.7 and 10.9 mean outcomes for TIT for TAT and RIGHTEOUS). It pays to forgive.

It also pays to punish. PUSHY reveals the importance of provocability (Axelrod, 1980b: 391–393). RIGHTEOUS and TIT for TAT retaliate immediately against a defection, OTHER CHEEK waits. The result is that PUSHY drags RIGHTEOUS into an unproductive equilibrium of mutual retaliation, exploits OTHER CHEEK, and does well with TIT for TAT. On the first point, RIGHTEOUS never trusts a PUSHY player after PUSHY's opening defection, so they both end up with minimum profit (10.3 points to RIGHTEOUS in Table 1, 10.1 to PUSHY, slightly higher for RIGHTEOUS because PUSHY apologizes with two cooperative moves before going into permanent defection). Second, the largest gains are against OTHER CHEEK. PUSHY never defects twice in a row, so OTHER CHEEK never punishes his defections. Games alternate between mutual cooperation (30 points to both players) and exploitation (50 points to PUSHY, zero to OTHER CHEEK), giving PUSHY the advantage on average (40.0 points to PUSHY and 15.0 to OTHER CHEEK in Table 1). Third, TIT for TAT does well against PUSHY because he punishes PUSHY immediately for his opening defection, after which PUSHY cooperates with TIT for TAT. The average outcome of their games is 30.0 points to both PUSHY and TIT for TAT. This is also why PUSHY does so well against players of his own kind. After earning only 10 points with their initial defections against one another, PUSHY players cooperate and earn 30 points per game (29.8 mean across two 10-point and 249 30-point games).

Having SNEAKY and PUSHY players in the population affects the relative success of the nice players. TIT for TAT is the most successful player, and ultimately dominant, but not by much. Average outcomes are reported at the top of Table 1. These are the average relation for each row kind of player with all players (an average of 790 relations from each row kind of player). The four most successful players are TIT for TAT (24.3 mean outcome), PUSHY (24.3), OTHER CHEEK (23.6), and now the least successful of the nice players, RIGHTEOUS (22.6 mean outcome).

2.5. *Ecological Results*

The simulation also replicates Axelrod's ecological results. Allow two reasonable baseline assumptions: players breed in proportion to the expected outcome of their games with one another (i.e., successful players are more numerous in the next generation), and players die in proportion to their numbers (death affects all players equally).

Then, the results in Table 1 can be used to project the mix of players in the population across successive generations. Where P_1 and P_2 are the proportions of HAPPY and HOSTILE players in a population, then $P_1 P_2$ is the proportion of random games between HOSTILE and HAPPY, and 50.0 is the expected outcome for the HOSTILE player. Therefore, since players breed in proportion to their expected outcomes, expected player i births, B_i, are:

$$B_i \text{ in next generation} = \Sigma_j P_i P_j Z_{ij} \quad (1)$$

where z_{ij} is the average outcome in Table 1 for player i in a game with player j (e.g., z_{21} is 50.0, the average outcome for a HOSTILE player against HAPPY). Let players die in proportion to their numbers, say a 25% death rate to speed the ecological process to equilibrium. Player i proportion in the next generation is the current number minus deaths, $(1 - .25)N_i$, plus births, B_i, quantity divided by the new population total:

$$P_i \text{ in next generation} = (.75N_i + B_i)/\Sigma_j(.75N_j + B_j). \quad (2)$$

For example, consider a population of 10 HAPPY, 10 HOSTILE, and 10 ERRATIC players. The first generation will produce five new HAPPY players, $(30.0 + 14.8)/9$, ten new HOSTILE players, and seven and a half new ERRATIC players. A death rate of 25% will claim two and half players of each kind in the first generation. Therefore, from proportions

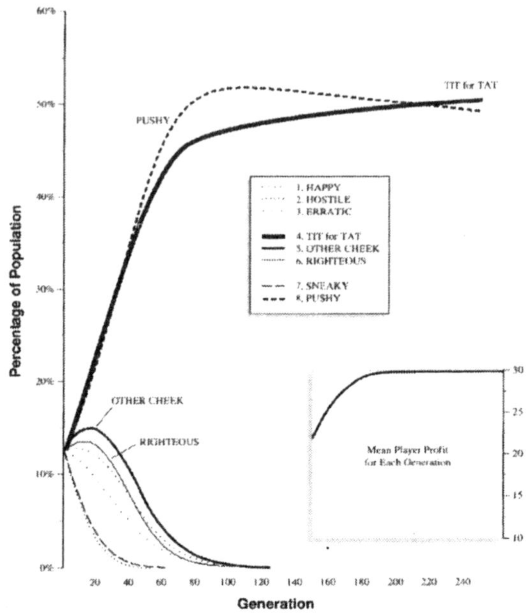

Figure 2. Survival in Private Games.

of .33, .33 and .33 in the first generation, the population shifts to proportions of .28, .39, and .33 in the second generation. The second generation contains more HOSTILE players and fewer HAPPY players because games between these two kinds of players favor HOSTILE.

Figure 2 shows what happens when all eight kinds of players in Table 1 interact across generations. The two most successful strategies, TIT for TAT and PUSHY, quickly replace the other players. There are slightly more PUSHY players at that point because they do better at exploiting OTHER CHEEK and HAPPY players. Once PUSHY's victims are dead, however, all games are among PUSHY and TIT for TAT players. PUSHY players are at a slight disadvantage that ultimately destroys them. TIT for TAT players do slightly better with one another because they always cooperate. The opening move in which PUSHY tests the other player lowers their gains from one another (29.8 between PUSHY players versus 30.0 between TIT for TAT). That slight disadvantage multiplies through time to eliminate the PUSHY players. The population is about equally composed of PUSHY and TIT for TAT players in the 200th generation, then 44% PUSHY by the 500th generation, 36% by the one thousandth generation, and so on until the last PUSHY player dies in generation 74,296. The dominance of TIT for TAT isn't affected by the initial numbers of players, but the number of generations required to reach dominance is affected. The smaller the (non-zero) proportion of TIT for TAT players in the initial population, the more generations that pass before TIT for TAT players replace all others.[5]

3. From Voice to Exit

The simulated exchange network summarized in Table 1, and the kindred density tables in analyses such as Axelrod's tournament, are maximum-density networks. Every person plays *many* repeated games with *every* other person in the network.

Networks are rarely this dense in organizations. Managers do have contacts with whom they meet frequently, or trust because of previous frequent meetings. But more often than not, life in a complex organization involves work with new contacts and people met only rarely—senior managers, peers in other functions, colleagues in other firms. Play in a sparse network involves relations defined by fewer games, and choice between alternative partners. Instead of many repeated games with every person, players complete introductory games with many people, and limit their numerous repeated games to a few preferred people.

The cooperation implications of a sparse network are not clear. The effect of few games is well known. Defection is the optimum prisoner's dilemma move against a partner you won't meet again. The implications of choice between alternative partners is less obvious. Tullock (1985: 1076) noted on the surprising lack of attention to a withdrawal option in prisoner's dilemma games; "All of the previous articles that I have seen are situations in which the individual does not have a choice of partners. Either he is stuck with his colleague, like the two prisoners in the initial story, or the state of nature is such that he cannot change partners." Tullock (1985: 1080–1081) concluded that introducing the threat of withdrawal will generate cooperation:

> "...the main theme of this discussion has been that the prisoner's dilemma, strictly speaking, occurs only in a rather narrow area. Where there are a number of potential players available, the dilemma is proportionately weakened. Indeed, here we have what amounts to a mapping of the usual economic distinction between monopoly on the one side and competition on the other. If there is only one person with whom I can play the game, both he and I very likely will decide not to cooperate. As the number of people playing increases, the prospect that either he or I can get another partner, if we find our current partner objectionable, exerts steadily increasing pressure to always play cooperatively.... Where the market is broad and there are many alternatives, you had better cooperate. If you choose the noncooperative solution, you may find you have no one to noncooperate with."

Another view is to think in terms of Hirschman's (1970) contrast between voice and exit. In dense networks, players respond to uncooperative partners with voice. The responsive players in Table 1 are petulant in the sense that they punish uncooperative partners by being uncooperative in return. This is their only communication option since they are obliged to continue the relationship whether it is productive or not. In contrast, players in sparse networks can respond to uncooperative partners with exit. They are not obliged to waste time on uncooperative partners. They can punish by avoiding uncooperative partners. The exit option, however, has the potential to be a private solution to a collective problem. Ego rejecting an uncooperative partner is likely to do better with a different partner, but what does that leave the uncooperative partner free to do to other players? What it does is free nasty players to focus on the most cooperative players, and so earn maximum gains from each round of completed games.

4. Private Games in Sparse Networks

Table 2 summarizes game play in a sparse network. As in Table 1, each cell in Table 2 is the average outcome for row players in games with the column players. The average game outcome for a kind of player is reported at the top of the table.

Table 2 differs from Table 1 in two ways. First, fewer games define relations (16,000 games were played to construct Table 2, versus 800,000 to construct Table 1). The average relation in Table 2 is defined by five games, but almost a fifth of the relations are defined by only one or two games, and 14 pairs of players never meet one another—versus the 253 game average, and 201 game minimum in Table 1. In contrast to the relations in Table 1 defined by a long history of repeated games, Table 2 describes relations based primarily on the initial games in a relationship.[6]

Second, and this is the more consequential difference from Table 1, players in a sparse network can choose between alternative partners, so they can punish uncooperative partners by rejecting them in future games.[7] Retaliatory defection in Table 1 is replaced by rejection in Table 2. For example, TIT for TAT in Table 1 retaliates by defecting when the other person defects. In Table 2, TIT for TAT rejects the defecting person as a partner the next time he is assigned to a game with the person. TIT for TAT picks someone else to be their partner.[8] TIT for TAT in Table 1 forgives after one retaliatory defection. TIT for TAT in Table 2 forgives after one retaliatory rejection. The other responsive players in Table 2 similarly correspond to players in Table 1. OTHER CHEEK rejects a partner after the other defects in two successive games, then forgives. RIGHTEOUS rejects a partner after the other defects once, and continues to reject them thereafter. SNEAKY and PUSHY use TIT for TAT's retaliation rule.[9]

4.1. Result 1: Better Relationships

I draw three conclusions from the simulation. First, the sparse-network relations are of higher quality. This is so in two ways, both due to players being able to choose between alternative partners.

Relations in the sparse network are more rewarding. Not everyone gains more, but the average game in Table 2 yields a higher outcome than the average game in Table 1. Players earn 27.0 points on average in the 6,320 games defining the sparse network summarized in Table 2. In the dense network summarized in Table 1, the average outcome is significantly lower (21.6 points; 23.7 t-test, $P < .001$).

Relations in the sparse network are also more pleasant, in the sense that there are fewer games with uncooperative players. Players have numerous repeated games with every other player in a dense network. The only way to punish is to be uncooperative, so many relations degenerate into a permanent cycle of retaliation. This happens in organizations, but not often. Vindictive behavior is a self-indulgence I associate with managers past the productive segment of their careers. If efforts to build a cooperative relationship with someone are met

Table 2. Game rewards in a sparse network.

	1	2	3	4	5	6	7	8	Row averages
1. HAPPY (Always cooperate)	30.0 (0.0) [5, -]	0.0 (0.0) [7, -]	13.8 (6.6) [6, -]	30.0 (0.0) [5, -]	30.0 (0.0) [5, -]	30.0 (0.0) [6, -]	28.2 (3.2) [6, -]	16.3 (2.9) [6, -]	21.6
2. HOSTILE (Never cooperate)	50.0 (0.0) [7, -]	10.0 (0.0) [8, -]	30.8 (9.3) [7, -]	50.0 (0.0) [4, -]	50.0 (0.0) [5, -]	50.0 (0.0) [1, -]	47.7 (4.8) [4, -]	39.0 (3.8) [4, -]	37.0
3. ERRATIC (Random)	40.9 (4.4) [6, -]	4.8 (2.3) [7, -]	22.3 (7.3) [7, -]	41.5 (4.7) [4, -]	41.4 (5.1) [5, -]	43.7 (6.3) [2, -]	37.8 (6.7) [5, -]	31.5 (4.9) [5, -]	30.2
4. TIT for TAT (Reciprocate)	30.0 (0.0) [5, -]	0.0 (0.0) [4, 3]	12.7 (7.1) [4, 2]	30.0 (0.0) [6, -]	30.0 (0.0) [6, -]	30.0 (0.0) [7, -]	26.1 (3.7) [5, 1]	21.9 (4.7) [5, 1]	24.3
5. OTHER CHEEK (Tit for two tats)	30.0 (0.0) [5, -]	0.0 (0.0) [5, 2]	12.9 (7.6) [5, 1]	30.0 (0.0) [6, -]	30.0 (0.0) [5, -]	30.0 (0.0) [6, -]	27.6 (3.5) [6, 0]	16.4 (2.4) [6, -]	22.6
6. RIGHTEOUS (Never forgive)	30.0 (0.0) [6, -]	0.0 (0.0) [1, 6]	9.4 (9.5) [2, 6]	30.0 (0.0) [7, -]	30.0 (0.0) [6, -]	30.0 (0.0) [8, -]	25.9 (5.2) [6, 1]	0.0 (0.0) [1, 5]	26.7
7. SNEAKY (Up to 10% deceit)	31.2 (2.2) [6, -]	0.6 (1.2) [4, 3]	15.7 (8.1) [5, 2]	32.6 (2.5) [5, 0]	31.6 (2.3) [6, -]	32.7 (3.5) [6, 0]	28.7 (3.6) [4, 1]	23.2 (6.2) [5, 1]	25.6
8. PUSHY (Up to 50% deceit)	39.2 (1.9) [6, -]	2.7 (0.9) [4, 3]	18.8 (7.9) [5, 1]	35.4 (3.2) [5, -]	39.0 (1.6) [6, -]	50.0 (0.0) [1, 1]	33.0 (6.0) [5, 0]	26.8 (1.5) [7, -]	29.4

NOTE—Each cell represents 100 relations between ten players of the row kind and ten players of the column kind (except diagonal cells which exclude the ten self-relations of players with themselves). The relation from player i to player j is the average pay-off for player i in repeated games with player j. Average outcomes at the top of the table are the average of 790 relations from each kind of player. The results describe the 6,306 relations in which one or more games were played (six cells contain one pair of disconnected players, four cells contain two pairs). The numbers in cell (A, B) of the table are: the average of row A relations with column B players, the standard deviation of the relations (in parentheses), the average number of games played to define each relation [first number in brackets], and the average number of times that each row player rejected each column player as a partner [second number in brackets, "-" means never].

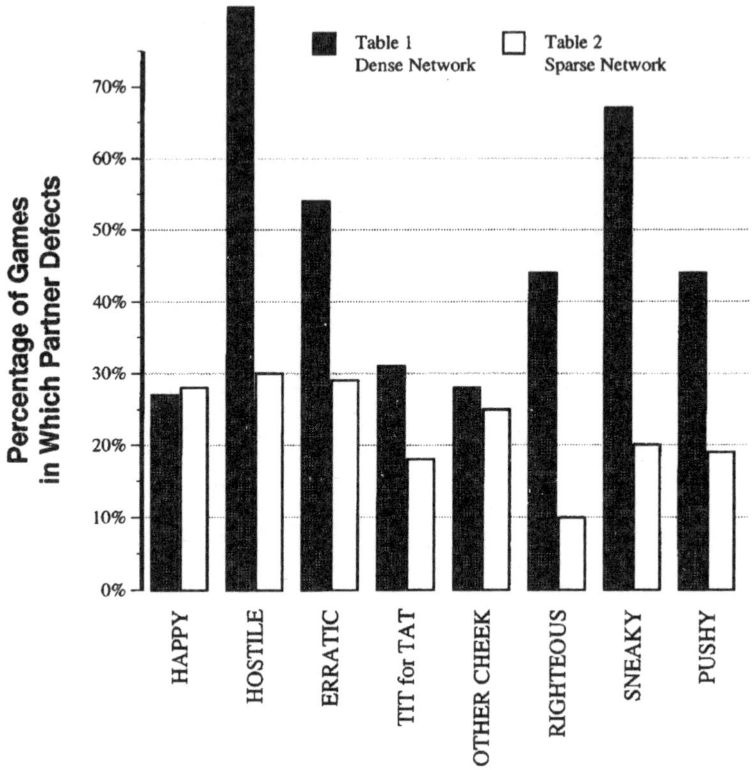

Figure 3. Games with uncooperative partners in dense and sparse networks.

with abuse, managers don't spend time punishing the person. They avoid her. They shift to more productive relationships.

The more pleasant aspect of relations within the sparse network is illustrated in figure 3. Bars show the proportion of games in which the other person defects. Dark bars describe games in dense networks (Table 1). Defections are high because of the obligatory repeated games with uncooperative partners in dense networks. Almost half of the games in Table 1 are with an uncooperative partner (47%). Defection is most often against HOSTILE and SNEAKY players. HOSTILE players elicit defections from all responsive players, so they have the highest proportion of games with uncooperative partners (81%). SNEAKY players often get caught making their occasional defection, so they have the next highest proportion (67%). White bars describe games in the sparse network (Table 2). Less than a quarter of the games are with an uncooperative partner (23%). Almost every kind of player benefits. Of the nice players, RIGHTEOUS players benefit most. Their Puritanical standard of never forgiving embroils them in mutual retaliation relations in the Table 1 dense network. In the sparse network, they can stay away from the partners they despise. Their 44% of games with uncooperative partners in the dense network drops to 10% in the sparse network. Even HOSTILE players have more positive games in a sparse network. They face uncooperative partners in only 30% of their games, down from 81% in the dense network. Their behavior is no less aggressive, but other players now avoid them. The result is that HOSTILE players in a sparse network are more often in games with naive partners.

4.2. *Result 2: Nasty Player Advantage*

The irony is that the more rewarding and pleasant relations in a sparse network most benefit the nasty players. Nasty players do well in sparse networks because they do well in the initial games of a relationship, and few relations in a sparse network develop beyond the initial games. Given relations based on preliminary games, players can go either of two ways: (a) treat the initial games as a honeymoon in which you are cooperative to encourage trust within the relationship, or (b) treat the initial games as a window of opportunity to exploit your partner. In private games, the player who takes the latter course dominates.[10]

The nasty player advantage is illustrated in figure 4. The vertical axes are cumulative average outcomes in repeated games between two kinds of players. The top graph shows what happens between HOSTILE and TIT for TAT. HOSTILE earns 50 points in the opening game by defecting against TIT for TAT's cooperation. TIT for TAT earns nothing. On the second move, TIT for TAT is uncooperative in retaliation and the HOSTILE remains uncooperative. They each earn 10 points. The average outcome after the second game is 30 points to HOSTILE (average of 50 and 10), and five points to TIT for TAT (average of zero and 10). Additional games move their average outcomes to the 10 points expected in a continuing relation of mutual retaliation (cells 2,4 and 4,2 in Table 1). Games between PUSHY and RIGHTEOUS in figure 4 illustrates the same point with slightly more complex players. PUSHY earns 50 points in the first game by defecting against a cooperative RIGHTEOUS, who earns nothing. RIGHTEOUS never trusts PUSHY again, defecting in every subsequent game. PUSHY cooperates on games two and three, then retaliates with defection. Additional games move their average outcomes to the 10 points expected in mutual retaliation (cells 6,8 and 8,6 in Table 1).

What is different in a sparse network is that the figure 4 relations between nice and nasty players never develop beyond the first game. The nice player exits after the first exploitative move. When a HOSTILE player defects in the first game, for example, TIT for TAT refuses the next assigned game with that player. Note the game frequencies in Table 2. The first number in brackets is the average number of games played between row and column players. The second number in brackets is the average frequency of a row player rejecting a game with a column player. The [4, 3] in the second column of row four means that each TIT for TAT player, on average, completes four games with each HOSTILE player, and refuses the player three times as a partner.

But after rejecting HOSTILE, TIT for TAT forgives. TIT for TAT is open for a new first game with HOSTILE—who again exploits TIT for TAT. The games are infrequent, but the outcomes are consistently no points for TIT for TAT, 50 points for HOSTILE (cells 4,2 and 2,4 respectively in Table 2).

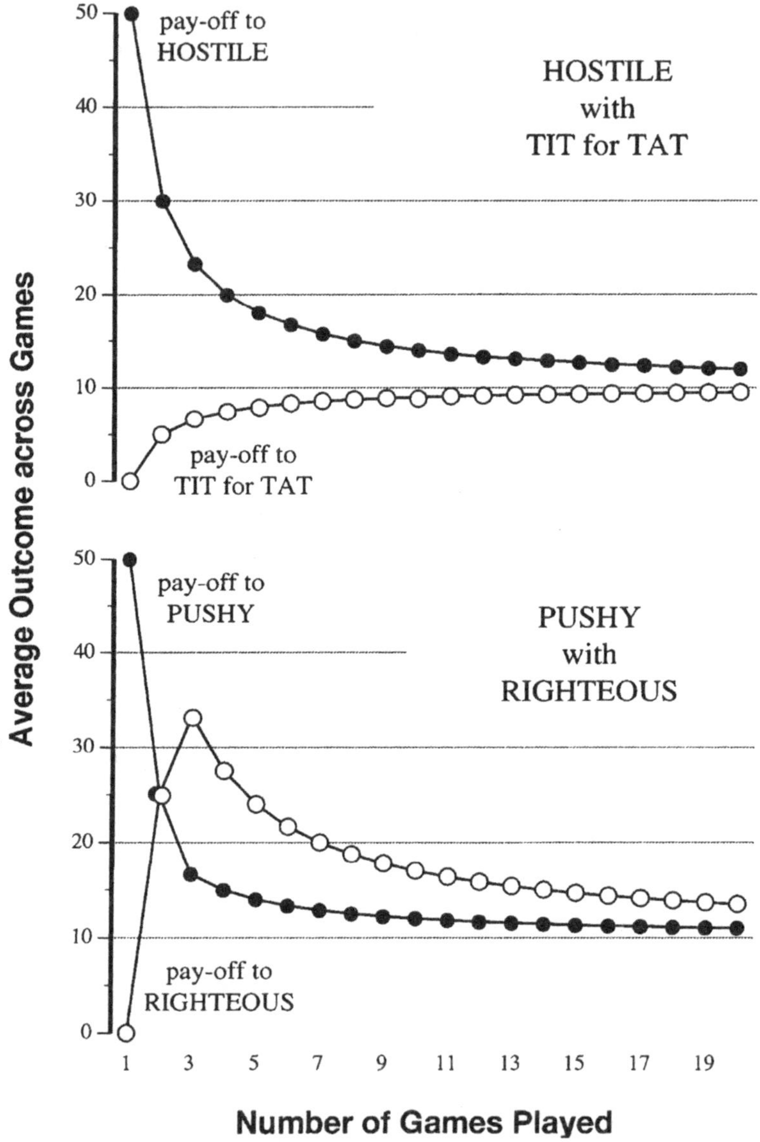

Figure 4. Nasty players do well in the initial games of a relationship.

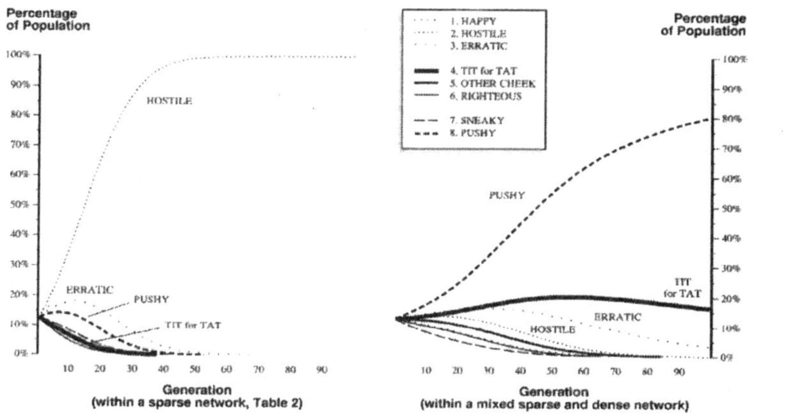

Figure 5. Survival in a sparse network.

RIGHTEOUS is the optimum nice strategy in a sparse network because it is never exploited twice by the same partner (26.7 row average at the top of Table 2, versus 24.3 and 22.6 for TIT for TAT and OTHER CHEEK). HOSTILE's initial defection is never forgiven. The [1, 6] frequency in the second column of row six of Table 2 means that HOSTILE plays only one game with RIGHTEOUS, after which RIGHTEOUS refuses all future games (an average of six times). Similarly, each RIGHTEOUS player completes only one game with each PUSHY player ([1, 5] in row six, column eight). Responding to PUSHY's initial defection, RIGHTEOUS rejects all subsequent games.

But RIGHTEOUS is the best of a bad lot. Paired against nasty players in a sparse network, nice players lose. The most successful are HOSTILE (37.0 row average at the top of Table 2), ERRATIC (30.2), and PUSHY (29.4).

The survival graphs in figure 5 provide more dramatic illustration. The left-hand graph describes what happens in a population that remains sparse across generations; something like the city-street society of strangers. Nice players die quickly (bold solid lines). The two runner-up nasty players then disappear (bold dashed lines), leaving a population of HOSTILE players. If there is even one HOSTILE player in the initial population, his advantage is sufficient to eventually replace the other seven kinds of players. And the other players disappear quickly. In dense-network figure 2, more than 100 generations pass before TIT for TAT and PUSHY jointly dominate the dense network, and thousands more pass before the population is entirely TIT for TAT players. In sparse-network figure 5, almost everyone is a HOSTILE player (99%) within 50 generations.[11]

The graph to the right of figure 5 describes what happens in a mixture of sparse and dense networks.[12] Nice players have the advantage in established relations (Table 1). Nasty players have the advantage with new acquaintances (Table 2). Like a confidence man in the big city, nasty players can thrive if sufficient new players enter the population. The established relations sustaining nice players means that it takes longer for the nice players to disappear, but they do. The last TIT for TAT player dies in generation 224. HOSTILE doesn't do as well because exploiting partners in dense networks results in low-yield relations of mutual retaliation (figure 4). PUSHY is more careful about defecting against cooperating partners, and so dominates the mixed sparse and dense population (80% by 100th generation in figure 5, 99% by the 400th generation).

4.3. Result 3: Mixtures of Dense and Sparse

The mixture graph to the right in figure 5 is one specific mixture of dense and sparse. New generations are 25% new players because I use a 25% death rate. I use the outcomes in Table 2 to describe sparse-network games with new players, so the mix in figure 5 is 75% dense to 25% sparse. In a mixture of 75% dense, the graph to the right in figure 5 shows that PUSHY players are dominant.

In different mixtures of dense and sparse, other players are dominant. The results in figure 6 tie together the results at specific alternative mixtures of dense and sparse.[13] The horizontal axis is a continuum from 0% dense networks to 100% dense. The graphs shows how dominance shifts from HOSTILE, to PUSHY, to TIT for TAT players as density increases. Maximum density is to the right. Survival in this population is described by the graph in figure 2 and the outcomes in Table 1. TIT for TAT is ultimately dominant, but at 47% is still less than PUSHY in the 100th generation (indicated by the gap above the end of the bold line at the right in figure 6). Minimum density is to the left in the graph. HOSTILE players are dominant. Survival is described by the graph to the left in figure 5 and the outcomes in Table 2. The .75 density population in figure 6 lies between the extremes. This is the population described by the graph to the right in figure 5. PUSHY players are ultimately dominant, but are only 80% of the population in figure 5 by the 100th generation, which is the generation reported in figure 6.

TIT for TAT Requires Maximum Density. Three points are illustrated in figure 6. First, TIT for TAT is dominant only in the maximum density conditions—the conditions in Axelrod's tournament, and kindred analyses such as the simulations summarized in Table 1. Give players a choice between alternative partners for their relationships, which is the usual situation for managers in an organization, and TIT for TAT loses to PUSHY. The lower the density, the faster TIT for TAT loses to PUSHY. This is indicated in figure 6 by the rapid decline in percent TIT for TAT at lower levels of density levels below 1.0 (bold line); 46% TIT for TAT at .99 density, drops to 40% at .95 density, and 34% at .90 density.

Not indicated in figure 6 is the fact that TIT for TAT players do not survive in populations that are anything less than maximum density. Their disappearance requires more generations at higher levels of density. The specific number of generations is trivial because that changes if the death rate is changed, but the increasing relative numbers of generations is stable.[14] At .8 density, TIT for TAT declines to one percent of the population after 567 generations. At .9 density, they decline to one percent after 1,495 generations. At .95 density, they last for 6,750 generations. At .96 density, they last for 32,073 generations. The advantage then shifts. TIT for TAT players begin to hold a minority equilibrium position against a PUSHY majority. At .97 density, they decline to 22.5% of the population after seventy thousand

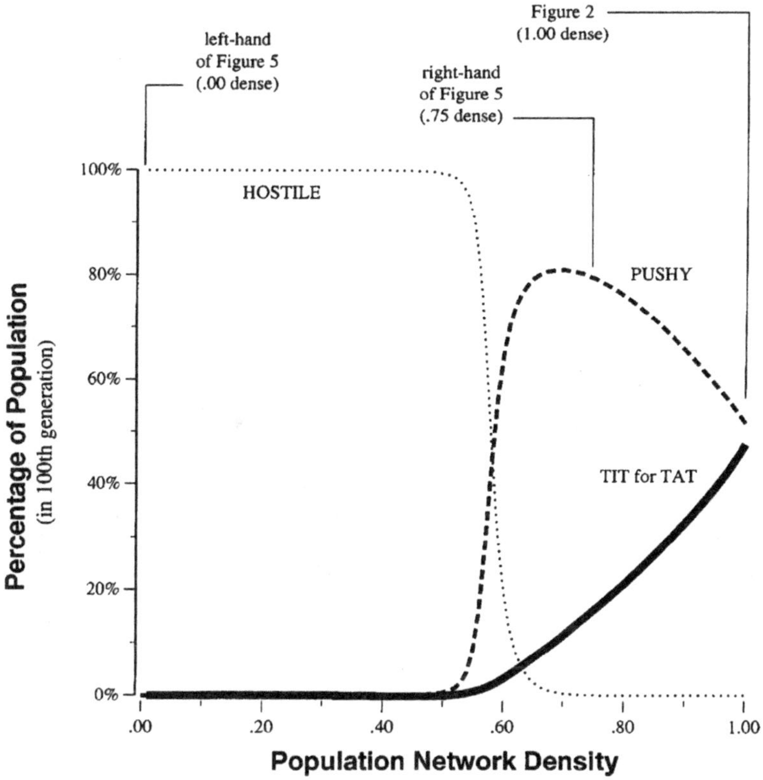

Figure 6. Flash-point shift in a sparse network between PUSHY and HOSTILE.

generations, then remain at that proportion in subsequent generations. At .98 density, they reach an equilibrium of 47.6% after sixty thousand generations. At .99 density, they reach an equilibrium of 73.4% after twenty-five thousand generations. Only at 1.0 density, as in Table 1 and figure 2, do TIT for TAT players expand to eventually replace all others.

PUSHY Dominates Populations More Dense than Sparse. Second, the cautious exploitation by PUSHY players is the dominant strategy in mixed populations more dense than sparse. PUSHY players speed to dominance faster as the dense network disintegrates to sparse—reaching their peak at .7 density (bold dashed line in figure 6). At .7 density, PUSHY is 81% of the population by the 100th generation (reported in figure 6), and 99% after 300 generations. Then, quickly, the advantage shifts to more aggressively exploitative players.

HOSTILE Is Dominant in Most Mixtures of Dense and Sparse. Third, HOSTILE is the dominant strategy in predominantly sparse populations (dotted line in figure 6). The advantage shifts from PUSHY to HOSTILE within a narrow range of density (where the dotted and dashed lines cross in figure 6). The critical range is .6 to .5 density. Here are the numbers plotted in figure 6 (population network density, proportion HOSTILE, and proportion PUSHY in 100th generation):

.60	.20	.65
.59	.31	.57
.58	.46	.44
.57	.65	.29
.56	.81	.16
.55	.90	.08

At .60 density, PUSHY players are dominant. They are 65% of the population in the 100th generation, 99% after 250 generations. A few decimal points later, at .55 density, the advantage has shifted to HOSTILE. They are 90% of the population in the 100th generation, 99% after 130 generations. The dotted line in figure 6 shows that the advantage stays with HOSTILE players at all lower levels of network density.

5. Conclusion and Discussion

To determine the value of understanding trust as a function of public rather than private games, relationships can be studied over time to see how variation in the structure of third parties around a relationship affects its development. The problem is that such observation is expensive and intrusive. Therefore, systematic empirical evidence from the field has been limited to cross-sectional data showing that trust and distrust are more likely in relations embedded in strong third-party ties. How trust and distrust developed as a function of the third parties remains unknown, and causal inferences are accordingly suspect.

Where observation over time is difficult, simulations can be a productive complement to cross-sectional data. I have used iterated prisoner's dilemma games between eight game strategies to simulate the development of relationships among kinds of managers within an organization. My baseline has been Axelrod's widely-known use of such simulations to argue that cooperation can emerge as the dominant form of interaction even in a society of selfish individuals without central authority.

Two points have been established. First, the simulations replicate Axelrod's results on cooperation. TIT for TAT is the most successful kind of player (Table 1, figure 2). The TIT for TAT strategy is to begin with cooperation, then reciprocate whatever move your partner made in the prior game. TIT for TAT players are successful because they are: *nice* (they never defect before the other person), *forgiving* (punished partners are presumed rehabilitated), and *easily provoked* (immediate retaliation). As Axelrod summarized the virtues of a TIT for TAT strategy (1980b: 403): "Its niceness prevents it from getting into unnecessary trouble. Its provocability discourages the other side from persisting whenever defection is tried. And its forgiveness helps restore mutual cooperation."

Second, TIT for TAT's success is limited to dense networks. The simulated network of Axelrod's tournament was dense in two ways rare in organizations: repeated games with every other person, and no exit from a bad relationship. This is a network characteristic of families more than organizations. I made the simulation more relevant to organizations by shifting to a sparse network in which relations rarely have a chance to develop beyond initial exchanges and players can withdraw from a bad relationship. The result is a change in the quality of relationships and the relative success of player strategies (Table 2, figures 3, and 6). Relations in the sparse network are on average more rewarding and more pleasant because players can withdraw from bad relationships. The irony is that the higher quality relations serve most to benefit nasty players, players who exploit cooperative partners. In anything less than maximum-density conditions, the advantage shifts from TIT for TAT players to the cautiously exploitative PUSHY players. Just before the network disintegrates to a condition more sparse than dense, the advantage quickly shifts to the more aggressively exploitative HOSTILE players, who dominate all populations more sparse than dense. Nasty players do well in sparse networks because they do well in the initial games of a relationship, and few relations in a sparse network develop beyond the initial games.

The results in sparse networks are less surprising that they are an important reminder. The effect of fewer games is well known. Defection is the optimum prisoner's dilemma move against a partner you won't meet again. Sparse networks are a merely social context in which exploiting cooperative partners can be the optimum strategy.

My conclusion is that trust is unlikely within an organizations based on private games. The rewards of cooperation depend on being able to avoid unproductive relations before they begin. The key to cooperation in a sparse network is not the threat that partners will withdraw from bad relationships. Exploitative players in a large network of private games can always find new partners. The key is the threat that potential partners will avoid unproductive relationships. What keeps nasty players at bay are the friends and colleagues who warn managers away from people known to exploit their partners.[15]

Two findings from illustrative survey data reinforce the point. First, private games are rare in the sense that manager relationships are typically embedded in relations with third parties. The amount of embedding varies between relationships, but all tend to involve some third-party presence. For example, a probability sample of 284 senior managers in a large American electronic components and computer manufacturer surveyed in 1989 cited 3,015 colleagues they deemed to be key contacts for information, personal advice, and political support within the organization (Burt, 1992, 1999c). Two thirds of the 3,015 relationships were embedded in relations with one or more mutual friends close to the manager and the colleague (65%), and every cited colleague had some third-party connection with the manager citing them. Similar network questions were given in 1996 to a representative sample of 317 staff officers in two large American financial services firms (Burt et al., 1998; Burt, 1999c). The 317 staff officers cited 3,324 key colleague contacts, of whom almost two-thirds were embedded in relations with mutual friends (64%), and again, every cited colleague had some third-party connection with the manager citing them. The same network questions were given in 1997 to a representative sample of 60 senior managers in a large French chemicals firm (Burt et al., 1998). The 60 managers cited 656 key colleague contacts, of whom slightly more than two-thirds were embedded in relations with mutual friends (68%), and only nine (2%) were with colleagues who had no third-party connection

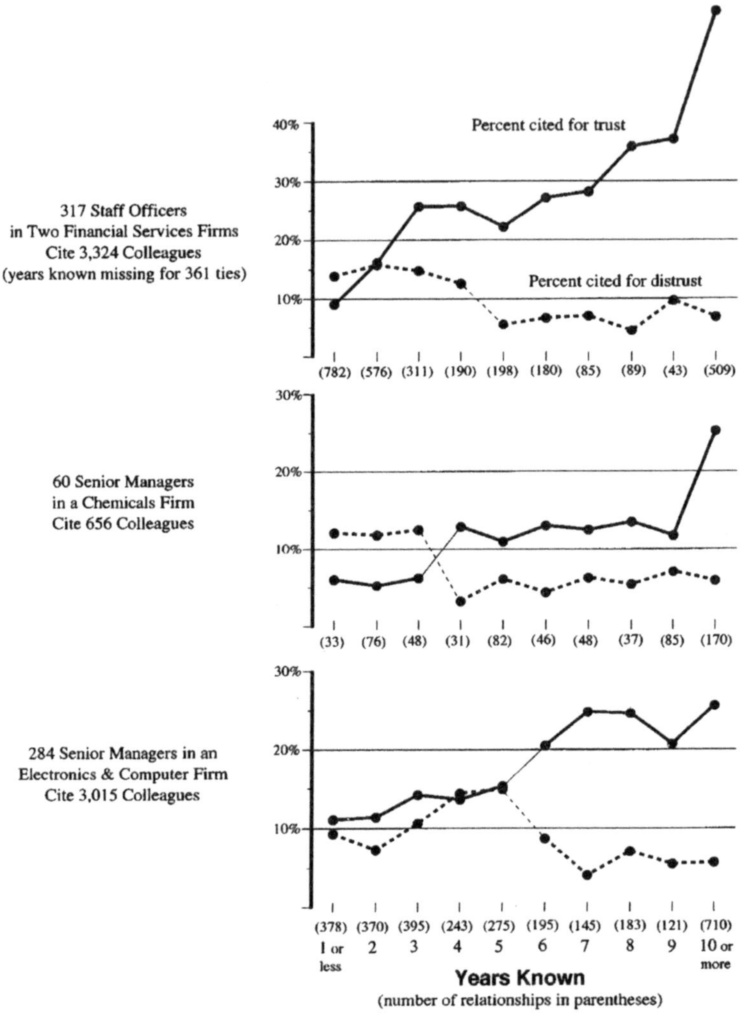

Figure 7. Probability of trust increases with time.

with the manager citing them. These are only illustrative data, but they agree on the tendency for manager relationships to be embedded in relations with third parties. Nothing is private at the top of organizations. What begins in private, is unlikely to stay private.

Second, the probability of trust increases with the age of a relationship as expected in private games, but the change involves several years. Figure 7 shows the probability of a colleague being cited for trust or distrust as a function of relationship age in each of the three study populations in the preceding paragraph. The substantive content of the trust and distrust indicators is beyond the scope of this paper (see Burt and Knez, 1995). Most of the cited relationships in the three study populations (4,831 of 6,995) were cited for neither trust nor distrust. Trust is indicated by a manager citing a colleague as someone with whom s/he would discuss potentially damaging personal information, and the increasing bold lines in figure 7 show that older relationships are more likely to be cited for trust. Distrust is indicated by a manager citing someone as his or her most difficult colleague and the decreasing dashed lines show that recent relationships are more likely to be cited for distrust. The sign of the association between trust and time is not the point here. The point is that several years pass before the association occurs. In the electronics and computer firm at the bottom of figure 7, trust and distrust were equally likely for the first five years of a relationship. Relations more than five years old are significantly more likely to be cited for trust, but there is no correlation with age for the first five years and no correlation with age after five years. Colleagues seem to be sorted into two groups after five years (a period about equal to two job assignments in this firm); those you trust and with whom you maintain relations, versus others you allow to drift away. The same pattern appears in the chemicals firm except that the watershed number of years is three, after which trust is more likely (and colleagues are especially likely to be cited for trust in relations that have lasted for a decade). The same pattern appears in tendency for staff officers to cite colleagues for distrust except that the watershed number of years is four, after which distrust is much less likely. Only the staff officers show continuous increase in the probability of trust as a relationship ages. Regardless of trust being significantly more likely in relationships that have lasted for three (chemicals firm), four (financial services firms), or five years (electronics and computer firm), the point here is that years is too long a gestation period. Managers typically have to decide over the course of a few days whether to trust a colleague. There is no time to accumulate a history with the colleague. The expedient course is to ask mutual friends and acquaintances about their history with the colleague, whereupon the game is public.

Thus, private games are not only too dangerous, they are too rare and too slow to be the foundation for trust within organizations. Managers are protected from exploitation by the information third parties provide, they more often than not have mutual friends to whom they can turn as third parties, and they can get that information quickly. It seems safe to conclude that trust and distrust cannot be understood independent of the network context in which they are produced.

Acknowledgment

This material was the subject of a 1994 session of James Coleman's Mathematical Sociology Seminar at the University of Chicago. I am grateful to Kazuo Yamaguchi and James Coleman for comments that guided my revision of the initial manuscript.

Notes

1. Hardin's note here is a citation to Flood (1958), and a citation to an earlier Rand Corporation research memorandum RM-789-1 (20 June 1952), which is, to his knowledge the first instance of the appearance of

the prisoner's dilemma. Hardin also reports, from private communication with Merrill Flood, that Flood gives Tucker credit for giving the game its current name (which must have been an informal communication because I have yet to see a Tucker publication credited as the source).

2. There is a voluminous literature on behavior in prisoner's dilemma games as a function of players (e.g., sex, occupation, nationality, personality), the magnitude of the temptation to defect, and the relation between the player (e.g., previous experience, opportunities to communicate). Rapoport et al. (1976) provide a useful review of results, Rapoport (1987) is a succinct overview of issues, Roth (1995: 26–30) provides behavioral economics review, Oskamp (1971) focuses on results with experiment subjects playing against programmed players, and Lomborg (1996: 278–283) provides a contemporary review of the sociology of iterated prisoner's dilemma games.
3. There are also questions about the validity of simulated play. In his behavioral economics review, Roth (1995: 29) calls attention to inconsistency between the success of cooperation in Axelrod's simulations and the negative results in some experiments with human subjects, and "suspects" that the inconsistencies reflect the learning that occurs with human subjects (see Macy, 1991: 818–820, for negative results in simulations that allow for ego learning across repeated play; cf., Roth and Erev, 1995). I am not concerned with the validity of simulated play for two reasons: First, sociologists are well beyond the issue of simulation versus experiments with human subjects because published research goes straight to the trust phenomenon in vivo with field data on senior managers (as cited in the text). Second, I study the simulations as a social fact, not as reality. Axelrod's results are widely cited as evidence of trust emerging from private games. They need to be put into perspective. I replicate his results, then show their implausibility in the sparse networks that characterize organizations.
4. Marwell and Oliver (1993: Chap. 5) illustrate the logical next step in their simulations of exchange network solutions to the collective goods problem. Their strategy is to have every player be an entrepreneur monitoring the feasibility of becoming an "organizer." Each player only knows the other players with whom he or she has direct contact. Contact is established at random between players (constrained to a lognormal distribution of network sizes within the system). Players calculate whether they could write a contract providing a collective good paid with contributions from contacts such that the cost of each contact's contribution is less than the benefit each would receive from the collective good. Marwell and Oliver compare systems restricting games to different social structures of pairing players to see how the structures affect the probability of the collective good. In addition to significant results on covariate effects of interest and resource heterogeneity, their central result is that centralized systems are more likely to provide themselves with the collective good because there is more likely to be a player with a large network who can bring together the most rewarding set of contributors. The players in Table 1 are less sophisticated than Marwell and Oliver's in the sense that they do not transfer experience across relationships. A next step for the simulations in this paper would be to allow players to learn how to behave in a relationship from their experience in other relations and from successful players elsewhere in the network (see footnote 9).
5. Initial numbers matter for other mixtures of players (a less circulated result from Axelrod's tournament, 1980b: 401–403; 1984: 40, 48). If the population begins with equal numbers of only the first six kinds of players in Table 1, it evolves to an equilibrium of multiple players. After ninety generations, the HOSTILE and ERRATIC players are all dead, and the population is stable at 16% HAPPY, 27% TIT for TAT, 23% OTHER CHEEK, and 34% RIGHTEOUS. There is no ecological pressure on the four finalists after the ERRATIC players disappear. All four finalists cooperate with one another and so breed in proportion to their existing numbers. The RIGHTEOUS players become most numerous because they profit most from games with ERRATIC players. The two key variables are: (a) the relative advantage of nice players in games with ERRATIC players—strong to weak in Table 1 are RIGHTEOUS, then TIT for TAT, then OTHER CHEEK, and (b) the relative numbers of nice players in the initial population. On the first point, more ERRATIC players in the initial population means a higher proportion of RIGHTEOUS players at equilibrium. On the second point, a kind of nice player that begins with a numerical disadvantage might not expand fast enough to overtake the other nice players before all of the available ERRATIC players are consumed. For example, a population composed of twenty OTHER CHEEK players to ten each of the other five kinds evolves to an equilibrium in which OTHER CHEEK is most numerous (21% TIT for TAT, 28% RIGHTEOUS, 37% OTHER CHEEK). A population initially composed of twenty TIT for TAT players to ten each of the others moves to an equilibrium in which TIT for TAT is most numerous (42% TIT for TAT, 26% RIGHTEOUS, 19%

OTHER CHEEK). Population composition notwithstanding, I am interested in a composition as in Table 1 that spans the space of Axelrod's contestants and replicates his results, because my goal is to show why the results do not generalize to the sparse networks typical within organizations.

6. Drawing pairs of players at random is now a stronger assumption than in Table 1. Drawing players at random for Table 1 imposes independence on the timing and number of games. However, differences between relations in their number of games is trivial because all relations are defined by a large number of games. Table 2 is more complex. Pairs of players vary in the extent to which they develop a relationship. It is now a strong assumption to say that the number of games is independent between relations. Available work on network dynamics is of little use here because the work remains largely abstract and methodological, guided by little or no substantive research on network dynamics (e.g., Burt, 1979; Marsden, 1983; Zeggelink, 1994; Stokman and Zeggelink, 1996 for illustrative models and literature review). Turning to common sense, there is reason to believe at minimum that the initial games of adjacent relations are not independent. The factors that result in me first interacting with you, lead me to meet the people with whom you interact. When someone meets you in the hall, for example, they also meet the people you meet in the hall. This implies that the probability of games between persons i and j should increase with the extent to which i and j play games with the same people (instead of being independent of games with other people). Looking for information on a functional form for the contingency, I studied network data on manager relationships in three study populations (figure 7). A manager cites two people j and k especially close with each other. How does the manager's frequency of meeting person j change as meetings with person k become more frequent? If either person is within the manager's work group, frequency is contingent (11.6 chi-square, 4 d.f., $P = .02$). Managers meet more often the people that their immediate co-workers meet often. Beyond the immediate workgroup, however, frequency is independent in adjacent relationships, and more cited colleagues are beyond the immediate work group, so frequency in the aggregate is independent in adjacent relationships (5.1 chi-square, 4 d.f., $P = .27$). Managers are involved in such a diversity of events that the frequency with which they meet one key colleague is independent of the frequency with which they meet other key colleagues close to the first. Therefore, it is not unreasonable to draw players at random for Table 2. A next step would be to draw players in sparse networks as a function of their ties to other players (see footnote 9 on learning, footnote 11 on allowing players to select productive relationships).

7. By more consequential, I mean that larger differences are created. Here are correlations between the corresponding 64 cells in four density tables:

1.00	.70	.35	.37	dense, no withdrawal (Table 1)
	1.00	.66	.69	sparse, no withdrawal
		1.00	.87	dense, allowing withdrawal
			1.00	sparse, allowing withdrawal (Table 2)

If players were not allowed to reject partners in Table 2, then average outcomes in the table would be correlated .70 with the averages in Table 1. The outcomes would be almost as correlated, .69, with the outcomes in Table 2. If the dense relations in Table 1 were defined by games in which players could reject partners, average outcomes would be correlated .87 with the outcomes reported in Table 2. Limiting the number of games defining relations has an effect (Table 2 no rejection is more correlated than Table 1 with the last two tables), but allowing rejections creates the largest differences from Table 1 (.35 and .37 are the lowest correlations).

8. In a population of fixed size, exit doesn't guarantee an acceptable partner. How many partners can a player reject before having to play with the next partner drawn? I constructed Table 2 allowing different numbers of rejections: none, one, two, three, and so on, allowing up to nine rejections before a player had to play with the tenth partner drawn. There is a .676 correlation between corresponding cells in the tables allowing none versus one rejection, a .985 correlation between cells in the tables allowing one versus two rejections. The correlation increases to .993 for two versus three rejections, .998 for three versus four rejections, .999 and higher between tables allowing more rejections. I also constructed dense networks allowing different numbers of rejections. The correlation between corresponding cells in the aggregate table are .508 for none versus one rejection (Table 1 describes the network allowing no rejections), .994 for one versus two, .992 for two versus three, .997 for three versus four, .999 and higher between tables allowing more rejections. Limiting rejections to a specific number has different implications for different kinds of players in different

networks, but in eighty-person dense and sparse networks, I get similar aggregate structures with limits of five percent or more of the network (four person limit is five percent of the eighty-person network). I use a ten percent limit for Table 2. Players can reject up to eight random partners before they have to play with the ninth.

9. Limiting players to exit in place of defection excludes most of the learning I expect in a sparse network. Given a choice between alternative partners, players should learn to avoid hostile partners and seek out cooperative partners. I do not model this because I want to hold the strategies in Table 1 constant to see what happens to their relative success in a sparse network. The next step is to see if the same outcomes result when players can learn their neighbor's strategy where it helps distinguish hostile from cooperative partners. Macy (1991: 834ff) offers a promising lead for such work with his simulations of a sparse network in which players select future partners on the basis of prior games (also Boone and Macy, 1998, with undergraduates). Lomborg (1996) offers results on players learning to replace their strategy with more productive strategies (also Macy and Skvoretz, 1998, on strategies diffusing through game play). Lomborg's two central modifications to the Axelrod simulations are that ego learns (a random sample of players compare themselves to a randomly selected other player and switches to the other player's strategy if the other player is earning higher payoff) and a veil of noise obscures ego's vision of alter's moves (random error in perceiving alter's move; alter is paid according to his actual move, but ego responds to the misperceived move). He shows that learning makes it possible for cooperation to emerge and be sustained even with substantial amounts of misunderstanding due to noise. A particularly nice point is that learning generates higher levels of cooperation than would occur with TIT FOR TAT playing against itself because a TIT FOR TAT player misperceiving the other player's move triggers a continuing exchange of defections (Lomborg, 1996: 289–290; also see the next footnote on noisy networks).
10. The TIT for TAT strategy has been criticized in recent simulations for being too quick to punish when moves cannot be interpreted clearly. Add a random function to the simulation so that ego occasionally misperceives alter's move. If alter cooperates, but ego believes that the move was a defection, then ego playing a TIT for TAT strategy punishes with a defection on the next move, which triggers a subsequent defection by alter playing a TIT for TAT strategy, and so locks the two players into a perpetual exchange of reprisals. Strategies more forgiving than TIT for TAT can avoid the exchange of reprisals, and so dominate TIT for TAT where noise is an issue (see Bendor et al., 1991, 1996; Kollak, 1993, 1996). An alternative is to have players learn to switch to more productive game strategies as in Lomborg's (1996) simulations discussed in the preceding footnote. A sparse network probably involves a greater amount of noise than a dense network, because there is less experience with alter to rely upon, but the generosity that is a solution to noise is not a solution to the problems of low density. In a sparse network, strategies more forgiving than TIT for TAT will be eaten alive. The nice strategy that fares best is RIGHTEOUS, which never forgives a defection. As for learning, the strategies most likely to be learned under a criterion of who is earning the largest payoffs are abusive strategies, HOSTILE and PUSHY.
11. The results would be different if players could "lock-in" productive relationships. Stanley et al. (1994) show in theory that allowing exit in what I here describe as a sparse network can lead to cooperative players dominating the network if they can lock-in productive relationships in the sense that once they find a cooperative partner they can stay in that relationship for subsequent games. Boone and Macy (1998) present empirical results with undergraduates in a computer laboratory card game that suggest behavioral qualifications to the theoretical conclusion, but the theoretical point remains that each cooperative player should eventually all pair with another cooperative player, leaving nasty players to games with one another, which means that nasty players disappear in an evolutionary graph such as figure 6. Locking-in productive relationships makes sense in a marriage market, but what managers stay working with the same contacts across their career? Successful managers are continually meeting new people and forming new work relationships, with new relations seeming to emerge almost independently beyond the immediate work group (footnote 6). Networks within organizations are obviously not random, but neither are they a marriage market in which successful managers can withdraw into relationships with a few friends. The "lock-in" solution is not a realistic solution, for managers, to the competitive advantage of nasty players in sparse networks (reputation is; see Rapoport et al. (1995), demonstration with students playing against all other students in a laboratory network that mutual cooperation and mutual defection relations tend to "lock-in" when students know their partner's history of behavior with other students in the group).

12. Generations are projected for the left-hand graph in figure 5 as described in the text by Eqs. (1) and (2). Player i proportion in the next generation for figure 5 is the current number, minus deaths, plus births, quantity divided by the new population total (cf. Eq. (2)): $(.75N_i + B_i)/\text{NTOT}$, where NTOT is the new total of players in the population, $\Sigma_j(.75N_j + B_j)$, and births are a function of player i success in games with each other kind of player j (cf. Eq. (1)):

$$B_i \text{ in next generation} = \Sigma_j P_i P_j Z_{ij} = \Sigma_j P_i[(.75N_j + B_j)Z_{ij}]/\text{NTOT}, \tag{3}$$

where Z_{ij} is cell (i, j) in Table 2. This is what happens when little knowledge is carried from one game to the next. In relations with more history, these results are less reasonable because players have to be too forgiving. For example, a TIT for TAT player in Table 2 plays four games with each HOSTILE player, rejecting the player once between each game. The cycle with HOSTILE is play game, get exploited, punish by refusing to take the person as a partner in the next game, then forgive. Four times with each HOSTILE player. TIT for TAT has the forgiveness of a saint. Generations are projected for the right-hand graph in figure 5 allowing a mix of dense and sparse networks. Births are computed with the following equation:

$$B_i \text{ in next generation} = \Sigma_j P_i[.75N_j Z_{ij(1)} + B_j Z_{ij(2)}]/\text{NTOT}. \tag{4}$$

Players breed in proportion to their success in dense games with experienced players and their success in sparse games with new players (where $Z_{ij(1)}$ and $Z_{ij(2)}$ are cells (i,j) in Tables 1 and 2 respectively).

13. Generations are projected for each population with weighted averages of Tables 1 and 2 and the populations all begin with equal numbers of the eight kinds of players. I tried linking the tables to new and old players as in the preceding footnote, then manipulating the death rate as a way to mix dense and sparse. This turned out to be a poor strategy because more changes than the mix between dense and sparse. A 0% death rate in the preceding footnote, for example, doesn't generate the graph in figure 2 for survival in dense networks. It generates a population extremely slow to change because older players never leave. Generations are projected for figure 6 by simply averaging the outcome matrices in Tables 1 and 2:

$$B_i \text{ in next generation} = \Sigma_j P_i P_j[(\text{Density})Z_{ij(1)} + (1 - \text{Density})Z_{ij(2)}]. \tag{5}$$

where density is the population network density on the horizontal axis of figure 6 and P_i is defined as in the preceding footnote. Generations are projected for each of 101 populations distinguished by density increments of .01 from zero to one inclusive. The proportional numbers of HOSTILE, PUSHY, and TIT for TAT players are reported in figure 6.

14. The specific numbers of generations in this paragraph are trivial because they change with the death rate, but their relative numbers are significant. The three results in the paragraph are: (1) TIT for TAT eventually disappears in a population below .97 density, (2) TIT for TAT goes to an equilibrium proportion at densities .97 to .99, and (3) at 1.0 density, TIT for TAT eventually replaces all other players. If I replace the 25% death rate in the text with the maximum, a 100% death rate, I get the same results but in fewer generations. At .9 density, for example, TIT for TAT players decline to one percent of the population after 375 generations (versus 1,495 in the text). But in populations with a 100% death rate, it is still true that: (1) TIT for TAT disappears in all populations less than .97 density, (2) TIT for TAT goes to an equilibrium of 22.5% at .97 density, 47.6% at .98 density, and 73.4% at .99 density, and (3) at 1.0 density, TIT for TAT eventually replaces all other players.

15. My purpose in this paper has been to simulate a baseline model of trust in a sparse network of private games to support the conclusion that trust is unlikely without making the games in some way public so that new partners can signal their trustworthiness to one another. My preference at this point is to return to field data on managers to learn how trust is associated with third parties in public games (e.g., Burt and Knez, 1995; Burt, 1999c). Alternatively, one could continue with the network simulation by adding assumptions about how trust might be facilitated by embedding games in a broader social structure (Willer and Skvoretz, 1997, outline directions for such work). For example, Macy and Skvoretz (1998) induce cooperation in a sparse network of simulated prisoner's dilemma games by adding assumptions to define a neighborhood around each player, define certain players as "like-minded," assume that trust is more likely between "like-minded neighbors," and define probabilities with which players interact with neighbors rather than strangers outside the neighborhood. Trust emerges within neighborhoods, then expands between neighborhoods.

References

Axelrod, R. (1980a), "Effective Choice in the Prisoner's Dilemma," *Journal of Conflict Resolution*, 24, 3–25.

Axelrod, R. (1980b), "More Effective Choice in the Prisoner's Dilemma," *Journal of Conflict Resolution*, 24, 379–403.

Axelrod, R. (1984), *The Evolution of Cooperation*. Basic Books, New York.

Barber, B. (1983), *The Logic and Limits of Trust*. Rutgers University Press, New Brunswick, NJ.

Bendor, J., R. Kramer and S. Stout (1991), "Cooperation in a Noisy Prisoner's Dilemma," *Journal of Conflict Resolution*, 35, 691–719.

Bendor, J., R. Kramer and P. Swistak (1996), "Cooperation Under Uncertainty: What is New, What is True, and What is Important," *American Sociological Review*, 61, 333–338.

Blau, P.M. (1964), *Exchange and Power in Social Life*. John Wiley, New York.

Blau, P.M. (1968), "Interaction: Social Exchange," in *The International Encylopedia of the Social Sciences*, Vol. 7, Free Press and Macmillan, New York, pp. 452–458.

Blau, P.M. (1994), *Structural Contexts of Opportunities*. University of Chicago Press, Chicago, IL.

Boone, R.T. and M.W. Macy (1998), "Dependence, Selectivity, and Cooperation," Paper presented at the annual meetings of the American Sociological Association.

Burt, R.S. (1979), "Relational Equilibrium in a Social Topology," *Journal of Mathematical Sociology*, 6, 211–252.

Burt, R.S. (1992), *Structural Holes*. Harvard University Press, Cambridge, MA.

Burt, R.S. (1999a), "Entrepreneurs, Distrust, and Third Parties," in L. Thompson, D. Messick and J. Levine (Eds.), *Shared Cognition in Organizations*, Mahwah, NJ: Lawrence Erlbaum Associates.

Burt, R.S. (1999b), "Trust and Gossip on the Path to Equilibrium," in A. Casella and J.E. Rauch (Eds.), *Network and Market Models of the Economy*, New York: Russell Sage Foundation.

Burt, R.S. (1999c), "Evidence of Density, Distrust, and Character Assassination," Graduate School of Business, University of Chicago.

Burt, R.S., J.E. Jannotta and J.T. Mahoney (1998), "Personality Correlates of Structural Holes," *Social Networks*, 20, 63–87.

Burt, R.S., R.M. Hogarth and C. Michaud (1998), "The Social Capital of French and American Managers," Graduate School of Business, University of Chicago.

Burt, R.S. and M. Knez (1995), "Kinds of Third-Party Effects on Trust," *Rationality and Society*, 7, 255–292.

Coleman, J.S. (1988), "Social Capital in the Creation of Human Capital," *American Journal of Sociology*, 94, S95–S120.

Coleman, J.S. (1990), *Foundations of Social Theory*. Harvard University Press, Cambridge, MA.

Davis, J.A. (1970), "Clustering and Hierarchy in Interpersonal Relations: Testing Two Graph Theoretical Models on 742 Sociograms," *American Sociological Review*, 35, 843–852.

Ekeh, P.P. (1974), *Social Exchange Theory*. Harvard University Press, Cambridge, MA.

Flood, M. (1958), "Some Experimental Games," *Management Science*, 5, 5–26.

Gibbons, R. (1992), *Game Theory for Applied Economists*. Princeton University Press, Princeton, NJ.

Granovetter, M.S. (1985), "Economic Action, Social Structure, and Embeddedness," *American Journal of Sociology*, 91, 481–510.

Granovetter, M.S. (1992), "Problems of Explanation in Economic Sociology," in N. Nohria and R.G. Eccles (Eds.), *Networks and Organization*, Boston, MA: Harvard Business School Press.

Greif, A. (1993), "Contract Enforceability and Economic Institutions in Early Trade: The Maghribi Traders Coalition," *American Economic Review*, 83, 525–548.

Gulati, R. (1995), "Familiarity Breeds Trust? The Implications of Repeated Ties for Contractual Choice in Alliances," *Academy of Management Journal*, 38, 85–112.

Gulati, R. and M. Gargiulo (1999), "Where do Interorganizational Networks Come From?" *American Journal of Sociology*, 104, 1439–1493.

Gulati, R. and J.D. Westphal (1999), "Cooperative or Controlling? The Effects of CEO-Board Relations and the Content of Interlocks on the Formation of Joint Ventures," *Administrative Science Quarterly*, 44, 473–506.

Hardin, R. (1990), "The Social Evolution of Cooperation," in K.S. Cook and M. Levi (Eds.), *The Limits of Rationality*, Chicago, IL: University of Chicago Press.

Hechter, M. (1987), *Principles of Group Solidarity*. University of California Press, Berkeley, CA.
Heider, F. (1958), *The Psychology of Interpersonal Relations*. John Wiley, New York.
Hirschman, A.O. (1970), *Exit, Voice, and Loyalty*. Harvard University Press, Cambridge, MA.
Homans, G.C. (1961), *Social Behavior*. Harcourt, Brace & World, New York.
Knez, M. and C. Camerer (1994), "Creating Expectational Assets in the Laboratory: Coordination in Weakest-Link Games," *Strategic Management Journal*, 15, 101–119.
Kollock, P. (1993), "An Eye for an Eye Leaves Everyone Blind: Cooperation and Accounting Systems," *American Sociological Review*, 58, 768–786.
Kollock, P. (1996), "The Logic and Practice of Generosity," *American Sociological Review*, 61, 341–346.
Kreps, D.M. (1990), "Corporate Culture and Economic Theory," in J.E. Alt and K.A. Shepsle (Eds.), *Perspectives on Positive Political Economy*, New York: Cambridge University Press.
Labianca, G., D.J. Brass and B. Gray (1998), "Social Networks and Perceptions of Intergroup Conflict: The Role of Negative Relationships and Third Parties," *Academy of Management Journal*, 41, 55–67.
Lawler, E.J. and J. Yoon (1996), "Commitment in Exchange Relations: Test of a Theory of Relational Cohesion," *American Sociological Review*, 61, 89–108.
Larson, A. (1992), "Network Dyads in Entrepreneurial Settings: A Study of the Governance of Exchange Relationships," *Administrative Science Quarterly*, 37, 76–104.
Lomborg, B. (1996), "The Evolution of Social Structure in the Iterated Prisoner's Dilemma," *American Sociological Review*, 61, 278–307.
Macaulay, S. (1963), "Non-Contractual Relations in Business: A Preliminary Study," *American Sociological Review*, 28, 55–67.
Macy, M.W. (1991), "Learning to Cooperate: Stochastic and Tacit Collusion in Social Exchange," *American Journal of Sociology*, 97, 808–843.
Macy, M.W. and J. Skvoretz (1998), "Trust and Cooperation Between Strangers," *American Sociological Review*, 63 (in press).
Marwell, G. and P. Oliver (1993), *The Critical Mass in Collective Action*. Cambridge University Press, New York.
Marsden, P.V. (1983), "Restricted Access in Networks and Models of Power," *American Journal of Sociology*, 88, 686–717.
Oskamp, S. (1971), "Effects of Programmed Strategies on Cooperation in the Prisoner's Dilemma and Other Mixed-Motive Games," *Journal of Conflict Resolution*, 15, 225–229.
Putnam, R.D. (1993), *Making Democracy Work*. Princeton University Press, Princeton, NJ.
Rapoport, A. (1987), "Prisoner's Dilemma," in J. Eatwell, M. Milgate and P. Newman (Eds.), *Game Theory*, Macmillan Press, New York.
Rapoport, A., M. Guyer and D. Gordon (1976), *The 2 × 2 Game*. University of Michigan Press, Ann Arbor, MI.
Rapoport, A., A. Diekmann and A. Franzen (1995), "Experiments with Social Traps IV: Reputation Effects in the Evolution of Cooperation," *Rationality and Society*, 7, 431–441.
Roth, A.E. (1995), "Introduction to Experimental Economics," in J.H. Kagel and A.E. Roth (Eds.), *The Handbook of Experimental Economics*, Princeton, NJ: Princeton University Press.
Roth, A.E. and I. Erev (1995), "Learning in Extensive-Form Games: Experimental Data and Simple Dynamic Models in the Intermediate Term," *Games and Economic Behavior*, 8, 164–212.
Sobel, J. (1999), "Another View of Trust and Gossip," in A. Casella and J.E. Rauch (Eds.), *Network and Market Models of the Economy*, New York: Russell Sage Foundation.
Stanley, E., D. Ashlock and L. Tesfatsion (1994), "Iterated Prisoner's Dilemma with Choice and Refusal of Partners," in C.G. Langton (Ed.), *Artificial Life III*, Vol. 7, New York: Addison-Wesley.
Stinchcombe, A.L. (1990), *Information and Organizations*. University of California Press, Berkeley, CA.
Stokman, F.N. and E.P.H. Zeggelink (1996), "Self-Organizing Friendship Networks," in W.B.G. Liebrand and D.M. Messick (Eds.), *Frontiers in Social Dilemmas Research*, Berlin: Springer-Verlag.
Tullock, G. (1985), "Adam Smith and the Prisoner's Dilemma," *Quarterly Journal of Economics*, 99, 1073–1081.
Uzzi, B. (1996), "The Sources and Consequences of Embeddedness for the Economic Performance of Organizations: The Network Effect," *American Sociological Review*, 61, 674–698.
Willer, D. and J. Skvoretz (1997), "Games and Structures," *Rationality and Society*, 9, 5–35.
Zeggelink, E.P.H. (1994), "Dynamics of Structure: An Individual Oriented Approach," *Social Networks*, 16, 295–333.

Zucker, L.G. (1986), "Production of Trust: Institutional Sources of Economic Structure, 1840–1920," *Research in Organizational Behavior*, 8, 53–111.

Ronald S. Burt is the Hobart W. Williams professor of sociology and strategy at the University of Chicago and the Shell Professor of Human Resources and Organisational Development at INSEAD. His work is on the social structure of competitive advantage in careers, organizations, and markets.

[6]

An Economic Model of Inter-Firm Networks

MARK CASSON AND HOWARD COX

INTRODUCTION

Advocates of networking often commend networks as being more fair and more democratic than alternative organizational forms. This chapter uses the principles of economic theory to show that they are often more efficient too. It examines the conditions under which a network can be expected to emerge as an efficient institutional solution to a co-ordination problem. This means embedding the analysis of inter-firm networks within a more general economic theory of institutional choice. Implementing such an approach makes it necessary to identify the main alternatives to the network and to explain why, under certain conditions, these alternatives are inferior to the network itself. Identifying these conditions allows us to provide an explanation for why international business networks, which linked together an array of independent firms, developed out of Britain in the nineteenth century.

The chapter proceeds as follows. To begin with, the economic logic of a network linkage is explored, the importance of information flows is recognized, and the role of trust is identified as a key element in allowing for the transmission of reliable information. It is shown that trust can be based either on the rule of law or on moral imperatives. The importance of the distinction between warranted and unwarranted trust is emphasized. The concept of intermediation is then introduced. Intermediation is shown to be of considerable importance in facilitating economic co-ordination across a variety of institutional settings.

An analytical model is then presented to demonstrate the way in which various institutional frameworks deal with the problems of organizing economic transactions. The model identifies the role of an intermediator as a channel of communication and explains the circumstances under which inter-firm networks will emerge as an efficient response to the issue of co-ordination. Finally, the chapter turns to consider the actual operation of a particular form of inter-firm networking arrangements, centred on nineteenth-century Britain, which allowed for the co-ordination of a wide variety of international economic transactions. It identifies the social underpinnings of these networks, illustrating the important role played by intermediators based mainly in the City of London.

CO-ORDINATION AND COMMUNICATION

Networks mean different things to different people. A simple definition of a network is a set of linkages which either directly or indirectly connect every member of a group to every other member of the group. But what is the basic unit from which such groups are formed? And what exactly qualifies as a linkage?

When examining inter-firm networks it may seem obvious to take the firm as the basic unit of analysis, and to study how networks are constructed by linking firms together. But it is actually more useful to focus on individual plants instead. Following conventional economic usage, the concept of a plant includes not only factory buildings and machinery, but also warehouses, shops, and any location-specific operation that adds value to the flow of a product. The reason for focusing on the plant level is that the multiplant firm is an alternative to a network operated by independent single-plant firms. The rationale of a network hinges on why a set of separate firms linked together is superior to a single integrated firm, and this can only be understood by going right down to the plant level (Casson 1992).

However, because of their complexity, inter-plant networks are difficult to describe in literal terms. Complications must be avoided by bold simplifications which abstract from inessential characteristics. The difficulty is to know what is essential and what is not. This chapter tackles the issue by using a schematic diagram to summarize the physical flows of resources (goods, services, and so on) between the plants.

The physical configuration of resource flows is dictated mainly by technology. Technology determines what inputs are required in what proportions to generate a given output, and whether or not this transformation affords economies of scale. Geography is important too. The location of raw materials and energy inputs relative to final demand governs transport requirements. Geography also determines the main modal options that are available for freight traffic and, together with transport technology, determines how far consignments need to be consolidated and fed into trunk systems before reaching their destination (Casson 1990: Chapter 2).

The study of networks as an organizational mechanism, however, is concerned mainly with the contractual aspects, rather than with the physical aspects of these flows. Contractual arrangements are dictated by co-ordination requirements rather than by technology. Decisions taken about the different flows need to be co-ordinated in order to optimize the performance of the network. In the context of this paper, the relevant performance criterion is the value added by network operations as a whole. Co-ordination involves intensive information flows which must occur prior to the flow of resources. At any instant of time the current flow of resources is the result of past co-ordination, whilst the current flow of information relates to future flows of resources. The only information flows that are concerned with current resource flows are those which involve checking that plans are being fulfilled, and rectifying errors when they are not.

In analysing networks it is thus the flow of information needed to co-ordinate the flow of resources, and not the flow of resources itself, that is crucial. Successful co-ordination depends on intelligible and reliable information flow. Intelligibility requires a common language, compatible communications equipment, and so on, while reliability requires the information exchanged to be accurate and reasonably robust. Because the environment is in a constant state of flux, knowledge must be continually updated if current decisions are to take full account of changes that have just occurred.

Sources of relevant information are widely distributed. Certain people have access to some information before others do, according to where they are based. One reason for this is that information is often generated as a by-product of another activity—thus the production engineer who rectifies faults has privileged information about the kind of design improvements in capital equipment that might be made; the sales assistant may detect a pattern in 'lost sales' which suggests an addition to the product line, and so on.

Such individual items of information are usually of little value unless they are synthesized. It may be impossible to produce the new line which customers want unless design improvements are made in production equipment, for example. Thus information on demand and supply must be combined in order to realize value from them. In economic analysis this is the conventional role of the price mechanism, and such information will be communicated in the form of changing relative prices.

For the price mechanism to work, however, the distribution of ownership must be appropriate to the co-ordination problem concerned. An inappropriate structure will not motivate the honest sharing of information. For example, rival owners may have an incentive to distort information in order to exploit market power. Thus where the owner of an upstream plant and the owner of a downstream plant are locked into a bilateral monopoly, the synthesis of information that is required for the efficient co-ordination of the resource flow may be impaired by mutual misrepresentation in the negotiation of the price. This would not occur if the plants concerned were both under the ownership of a single firm. Thus where price distortion is a serious problem, internalization of the linkage within a firm, that is, common ownership, may be the best solution to the co-ordination problem.

In addition to the issue of the distribution of ownership, the question of security of property rights must also be considered. This means not only that property rights must be well defined, but also that the exchange of rights involved in a contract must be safe. Ownership becomes particularly vulnerable when it changes hands. One approach is simply to restructure the ownership of the plants, as above, so that the product does not change ownership in the course of its flow. This eliminates the incentive to default and is essentially the internalization strategy, in which co-ordination by an integrated firm replaces co-ordination by the market.

The alternative to internalization is to leave ownership unchanged but to design powerful incentives to prevent deception and default. This can be done in two ways. One approach is simply to strengthen the law, to make conventional markets work better. The other is to invoke moral incentives which generate reliable information flows without recourse either to the law or to internalization. Morality can create a climate of interpersonal trust, and it is this climate of trust, it is suggested here, which is the hallmark of the network solution.

Thus in answer to the question raised at the outset, concerning the nature of a network linkage, it may be said that a network linkage is one which relies on a trust between the parties sustained by moral incentives. Thus short-term contracting qualifies as a network phenomenon if the two parties expect to remain loyal to each other, and neither attempts to exploit the other's loyalty by driving too hard a bargain with them. Informal contracts of all kinds, based on a handshake rather than a written agreement, also qualify as network arrangements.

The network may therefore be characterized as a high-trust co-ordination mechanism linking independent owners. In Table 7.1, the two main alternatives to the network, the market and the firm, are characterized as a low-trust mechanism involving independent owners and a mechanism based on integrated ownership, respectively.[1]

[1] An interesting point here is that the firm itself can apparently occur in both high-trust and low-trust variants. This is highlighted in Table 7.1, where the contrast in the top line between the market and the network is mirrored in the bottom line by the distinction between the high-trust and low-trust firm. This distinction can be related to a number of distinctions which have been made by other writers. In early twentieth-century Britain, for example, it was common to distinguish between paternalistic (high-trust) and bureaucratic (low-trust) organizations—not just amongst firms, but in public services and government too. McGregor's differentiation of theory X and Y in managerial leadership highlights a similar phenomenon, as does the familiar distinction between US-type and Japanese-type firms (Ouchi 1981; Aoki 1988). This illustrates the important point, which will not be pursued further here, that networks can be found within firms as well as between them. It raises the interesting possibility that firms with high-trust corporate cultures, which network internally, may also be better at networking externally, because the strategies governing internal and external relations are then alike. Conversely, firms that have low-trust corporate cultures may have difficulty participating in inter-firm networks as the principles of networking are not well understood (see the discussion of US-Japanese joint ventures in Casson 1992).

Table 7.1. A simple typology of co-ordinating mechanisms

Ownership	Interpersonal trust	
	Low	High
Distributed	Market	Network
Consolidated	Low-trust firm	High-trust firm

THE CONCEPT OF TRUST

Several different concepts of trust can be found in the sociological literature. There is, for example, the well-known distinction between calculative trust and non-calculative trust. There is also the distinction between resilient trust and fragile trust employed by Ring (see Chapter 5). The concept of trust employed in this chapter is related to both non-calculative trust and to resilient trust, but is not completely coincident with either of them.

Following Casson (1991), this chapter takes an economic approach to trust, which means that it analyses trust in terms of rational action. Everything is therefore calculative in this context. Unlike most other economic models, however, this model explicitly recognizes affective as well as material rewards. Affective rewards are morally framed; people reward themselves affectively for doing what they believe to be right and punish themselves affectively for doing what they believe to be wrong. Morality therefore provides an incentive structure quite distinct from the material dimension. In this context calculative trust, as described by sociologists, may be categorized as trust underpinned by material incentives (e.g. pecuniary sanctions and rewards), while non-calculative trust is trust underpinned by moral incentives. It is therefore preferable to distinguish between material trust and moral trust rather than to invoke a distinction based upon calculation.

Moral trust is resilient in the sense that it is able to survive occasional unanticipated outcomes and other setbacks. The strength of moral trust lies in its social endogeneity. Material trust, on the other hand, is fragile because it depends for its support on an enforcement system which is exogenous to the parties engaged in trade. Here, unanticipated outcomes which cannot be speedily resolved by an effective legal system will quickly undermine material trust. However, if the law is equipped with effective policing and a sufficiently punitive set of sanctions, then under these conditions it may engender stronger trust than moral incentives can. Which is the stronger, moral or material trust, depends upon which mechanism society has made the greater investment in.

Reduced to its basics, trust involves a belief that the other person will be honest. Trust is warranted when this belief is true. Trust, whether warranted or not, is vital to any transaction. There is no point in attempting to negotiate a deal with someone who is never likely to fulfil their side of it. Since it takes two to make a deal, mutual trust is required. A deal, once negotiated, will only go through as planned, however, when each party validates the other party's trust in them. Successful transactions therefore depend on warranted trust, and warranted trust must be mutual. For this condition to be met, each party must not only believe the other to be trustworthy, but must also be trustworthy themselves. A social equilibrium then prevails because each party's beliefs about the other are validated, and so there is no reason for them to change their beliefs in the future. If this condition is not satisfied, a trading equilibrium cannot be sustained. This highlights a distinction between warranted and unwarranted trust, which has received insufficient attention in the literature.

The thrust of this chapter can now be stated in the following way: the basic relation upon which networks are built is a relation of mutual warranted moral trust. The situation is illustrated in Table 7.2.

The two main alternative mechanisms, based on material and moral incentives, are indicated by the two columns, whilst the distinction between warranted and unwarranted trust is indicated by the two rows. Each type of mechanism is associated with a distinctive kind of investment: an investment in monitoring and the enforcement of sanctions in the case of the material mechanism, and investment in an 'invisible infrastructure' of social bonds in the case of the moral mechanism. The first is exemplified by the legal system, and by the internal discipline of the hierarchical firm, whilst the second is exemplified by bonding between members of a business élite, or between members of a cohesive management team within a firm.

Table 7.2. A classification of trust

			MECHANISM	
	INVESTMENT		*Material*	*Moral*
		Type of:	Monitoring and sanctions	Moral rhetoric and social bonding
		Level of:		
STATUS	*Unwarranted*	Too little	Defective property rights	Untrustworthy relations
	Warranted	Adequate	Law-based trust	Interpersonal trust

No investment of any kind will generate no trust at all. Too little investment will generate unwarranted trust—those inclined towards an optimistic view of other people will find themselves the victims of cheating. Once their trust in other people is betrayed, rational calculation will suggest that it is better for them not to attempt to trade at all. Too little investment in a legal system generates a problem of defective property rights, as shown in the top left-hand quadrant of Table 7.2, whilst too little investment in a social system leads to untrustworthy social relations, as indicated in the top right quadrant of Table 7.2. It is only adequate investment in monitoring and sanctions that creates a viable system of law, as indicated in the bottom left quadrant, whilst only adequate investment in social infrastructure generates the high-trust relation shown in the bottom right quadrant of Table 7.2. It is this latter high-trust relation which is the model for the network relation described in this chapter.

THE ROLE OF INTERMEDIATION

One of the obstacles to using moral incentives in support of business transactions is that these mechanisms tend to work best in small, stable, compact groups. Table 7.3 summarizes the main kinds of group in which such socialization can occur.

Table 7.3. Social groups that support business networks

Institution	Specific economic functions		Affiliation strategy
	Technical training	Moral education	
Family	Passes on tacit business skills useful for self-employment	Provides basic moral teaching	Marry in
	Inheritance system develops useful concentration of business capital	Inculcates respect for age and experience (ambivalent effect)	Become an adopted protégé
Church	Reading of scriptures improves literacy	Ligitimates morality	Conversion
		Encourages concept of personal accountability to ancestors, God, etc. as well as to peers Perpetuates tradition (ambivalent effect)	

(continued overleaf)

Table 7.3. *continued*

Institution	Specific economic functions		Affiliation strategy
	Technical training	Moral education	
School, university, qualification	Develops analytical decision-making skills	Inculcates loyalty (in both pupils and alumni) Emphasizes achievement through hard work Values ability and competence	Study to gain entry (where appropriate)
Military service	Teaches tactical and engineering skills	Teaches discipline, respect for authority, and how to cope with risky situations	Conscription or volunteering
Trade unions, professional associations, etc.		Promote craftsmanship and professional standards Values solidarity (ambivalent effect)	Gain appropriate work experience
Clubs (sporting, charitable, hobbies, etc.)	Self-improvement through friendly competition	Value of teamwork (in team sports)	Attain sufficient proficiency, respectability, etc. (where appropriate)
	Develops management skills by participating in collective decision-making, etc.	Value of caring (in charitable activities—ambivalent effect)	
Political party	Make contacts linking public and private sectors	Cynical morality—'the end justifies the means', etc. (negative effect)	Very easy to join
	Acquire 'charismatic leadership' skills by standing as candidate		

It also compares the kind of training in technical skills and moral values that the different groups provide. With some types of group multiple affiliation is possible, but not with others. Thus while a person may switch by conversion from one religion to another, they cannot credibly adhere to two different religions at the same time; by changing affiliation they distance themselves from the group to which they originally belonged. On the other hand, a person can quite credibly belong to two different local clubs or societies, and may indeed perform a valuable service in brokering between what might otherwise be two non-overlapping social groups.

Multiple affiliation is important in the development of business networks by entrepreneurs. The wider the range of an individual's affiliations, the greater will be his or her personal network of trusted contacts. This applies particularly to people with varied work experience and leisure interests ('playing hard' may be just as strategically important as working hard where the 'networked' entrepreneur is concerned). There is, of course, a trade-off between breadth and depth of attachments: people who change jobs frequently, or spread their leisure time thinly across several societies, are unlikely to become as strongly bonded to their colleagues as those who maintain steady allegiance to a small number of social groups. So far as business networking is concerned, however, a wide range of relatively superficial attachments can always be strengthened by subsequent social contact in the course of business negotiations.

In order for a social network to support a business network it is necessary for the members of the social network to be in place where the business operations require them. The economic logic of the business network will normally dictate where members of the social network need to be placed, rather than the other way round. If a social network is to fulfil a business role, its members therefore need to display a degree of mobility. The mobility required to operate an international network is, of course, much greater than that required for, say, a purely local one. It may be questioned whether a social network can really be effective over long distances, because opportunities for face-to-face contact will be very limited. The answer is that many of the social networks used for business purposes came into existence when people who were once together disperse. The school and the local community, for example, effect emotional bonding before a person's business career begins. The emotional intensity of togetherness amongst young people may be sufficient to bind them together for a considerable time after they have left school. Once they have revitalized their association for business purposes, the limited contact experienced in the normal course of business dealings may then be sufficient to keep the bond intact indefinitely.

One way of interpreting the role of the social groups illustrated in Table 7.3 is to say that they provide a mechanism through which their members may establish high-trust interpersonal relations. There may be cases, however, where members of different groups may stand to benefit from forming high-trust business links based on moral trust. In these cases an intermediator, in the form of a reputable individual who holds multiple affiliation, may be a way of extending the role of trust beyond the immediate group members.

Intermediation of this kind can take a variety of forms. In order to sustain trade, for example, the intermediator may buy a good from a seller and resell it to a buyer. This can build a chain of trust between the buyer and the seller where no direct trust exists between them. The buyer does not trust the seller to supply high quality goods. The buyer trusts the intermediator, however, because of the intermediator's reputation, whilst the intermediator has sanctions over the seller that the buyer does not. Trade can therefore proceed because quality assurance is provided by the intervention of the intermediator in the trade.

Intermediation is important in other ways as well. It was noted at the outset that successful co-ordination normally depends upon a synthesis of information. This process of synthesis often benefits from intermediation. The intermediator specializes in the task of combining information from diverse sources. This reduces the overall cost of co-ordination. Having effected a synthesis, the intermediator can then feed back to the appropriate parts of the system the particular information needed to ensure harmonization. Intermediation is a very general method of improving co-ordination. Unlike internalization, discussed earlier, which is concerned specifically with the replacement of a market by a firm, intermediation is relevant to all three modes of co-ordination—the firm, the market, and the network.

SCHEMATIC REPRESENTATION OF NETWORKS

This section extends the simple scheme for the representation of business systems used in Casson (1992) to examine strategic issues connected with networks. It begins by considering the problems which may arise in using the price mechanism to co-ordinate business transactions. It then considers the way in which the alternative mechanisms of the firm (formal internalization) and the network are able to perform the co-ordinating role. Using this framework, the chapter then illustrates why the network approach was especially appropriate for the co-ordination of Britain's international business networks in the nineteenth century.

The starting-point for the analysis of co-ordination mechanisms, as suggested above, is at the plant level where the basic linkage is that of product flow. The left-hand side of Fig. 7.1 illustrates a system comprising four plants.

A plant is indicated by a square, and is identified by a number. The flow

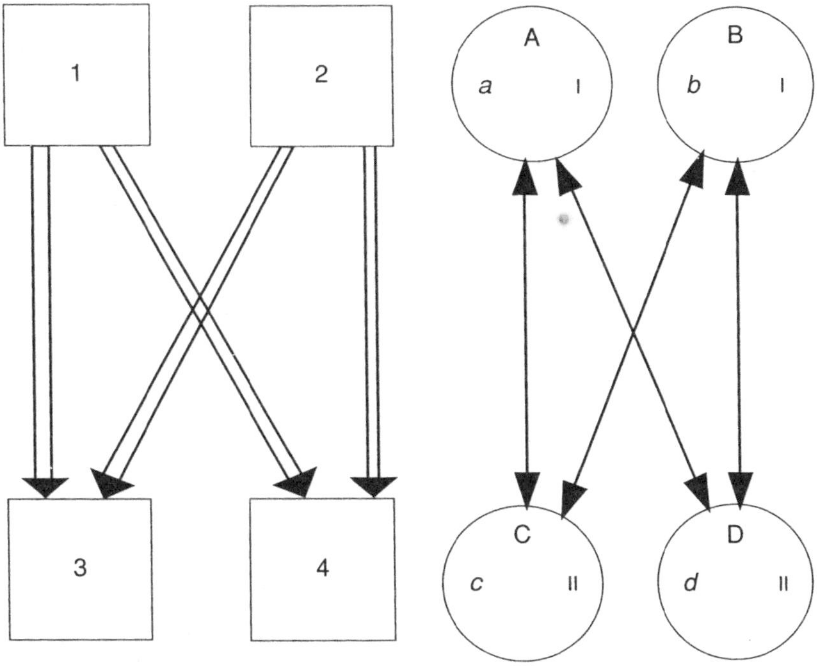

Fig. 7.1. Resource flows and information flows

of a product between the plants is shown by a double line, with the direction of flow indicated by an arrow. The figure shows two upstream plants, 1 and 2, located in Britain, which supply intermediate products to two downstream plants, 3 and 4, located abroad. The upstream plants may in turn receive raw materials from other plants at an earlier stage of the sequence. Likewise, the downstream plants will either supply a further stage of production, or sell to final consumers instead. These other flows are not illustrated because they are not part of the system being analysed. Since almost any system can be thought of as being part of a larger system, the use of artificial boundaries to limit the field of analysis in this way is usually unavoidable.[2]

Thus, in Fig. 7.1 the downstream plants 3 and 4 receive complementary inputs from the upstream plants 1 and 2. Each downstream plant may be a mining concern, for example, procuring two inputs from specialized pro-

[2] It is assumed that there is normally a flow of money payments in the opposite direction whenever the plants involved are owned by different firms (or, in the case of joint ventures, by a different consortium of firms). Equally, it is assumed that notional payments are only involved if the plants are owned by the same firms (or the same consortium of firms).

ducer good manufacturers. The first input is produced in plant 1; its supplies to plants 3 and 4 are substitutes for each other. The second input is produced in plant 2; its supplies to 3 and 4 are also substitutes for each other. When the plants are independently owned, this pattern of complementarity and substitution creates two markets, one for each input. The role of the network is to operate these markets more efficiently than ordinary impersonal mechanisms would do.

Each downstream firm has the job of seeing that the inputs are combined in suitable proportions, and of bidding for these inputs to their upstream suppliers. In turn, the upstream firms must decide how much of their product to supply to each of their downstream customers. If all the plants had a single common owner, then the co-ordination of product flow would be an internal affair. Whether internal or external, however, the co-ordination process involves a two-way information flow which must be completed before the products can be delivered.

Information flows connected with co-ordination are indicated by a single line. An arrow at either end of the line indicates that the flow is two-way. Information, however, flows between people; for this reason, people are distinguished from plants by the use of a circle rather than a square. A crucial feature of the scheme set out in this paper is that information flows used for co-ordination are represented on a separate diagram. They are not superimposed on the representation of the product flows. Thus, in Fig. 7.1 the information flows are represented on the right-hand side of the diagram. The figure illustrates four individuals each linked to two of the others by a two-way information flow.

Not only does separation make the diagrams more intelligible to the eye; it also facilitates a full recognition of the fact that information flows between people rather than the plants themselves. The information flows mainly to and from people who make decisions. These people are, in turn, often motivated to make good decisions by having ownership of a particular plant. But the relationship between individuals and plants is certainly not one to one in general. For example, the person who makes day-to-day decisions about a plant may be a manager employed for this purpose by the owner of the firm. Thus it is positively misleading in many instances to draw information flows as if they go from plant to plant, rather than from one person to another.

Individuals are identified by lower case letters and the firm for whom they work by upper case letters. If the same letter is used to identify both an individual and a firm, then it means that the individual is the sole owner of the firm. In order to match up the resource flow scheme with the information flow scheme, it is necessary to identify which particular individual controls which plant. In Fig. 7.1 this is done visually. Individuals and plants that occupy the same position in the figure are assumed to be related, in the sense that the plant is controlled by the individual concerned. For example, if the right-hand diagram were superimposed on the left-hand diagram, then individual *a* (the owner of firm A) would overlay plant 1, and this is taken to indicate that he or she controls it. Individuals who do not control any plant are positioned in the information flow diagram so that they would not overlay any plant in the resource flow diagram.

The scheme also identifies the social relations which exist between the individuals who are involved in the process of information exchange. The lower case letters (denoting the individual located at the plant) are followed by a roman numeral, indicating the social group to which the individual belongs, or a string of numerals in the case of multiple membership of groups. An ordinary roman numeral indicates a fully integrated group in which every member trusts every other member not to default. A roman numeral followed by a plus or minus indicates a subgroup; a minus indicates a low-status subgroup and a plus indicates a high-status élite. The members of the high-status group have a reputation with the members of the low-status group (and with each other), which means that they are trusted by everyone in the group, whereas the members of the low-status group are not trusted by the élite of the group. Members of a high-status élite are not trusted by anyone outside the group to which they belong.

The central issue to be explored in the information flow diagram is the accuracy of the information exchanged. Accurate and undistorted flows of information will be characteristic of intra-firm flows created through the internalization of markets. It will also be a feature of information exchange between parties who trust each other because they belong to a well-defined social group. A situation of undistorted information flows is indicated by attaching a second arrowhead to a line of information flow. This means that the sender will supply information which is as accurate as possible, either because the two parties are part of the same firm or because they trust one another. If information flows are neither intra-firm nor intra-group, then information may be unreliable and co-ordination will suffer as a result.

INTEGRATION AND INTERMEDIATION

The main value of these conventions is that they facilitate a detailed comparison of alternative sets of contractual arrangements which may underpin a given set of physical resource transactions. Not all possible arrangements can be compared, however, because there are just too many of them. This section follows an informal step-wise approach which investigates a sequence of arrangements, each of which has the potential to improve upon its predecessor.

The starting-point is a critique of the contractual arrangements portrayed on the right-hand side of Fig. 7.1. The diagram assumes that co-ordination depends upon information flows between people from different social groups (I and II) who do not display moral trust in one another. If the costs of using the price mechanism are substantial due to market imperfections, then internalization theory suggests that the natural response will be vertical integration.

Integration can be effected either forwards or backwards. The downstream producers are more vulnerable than the upstream producers in the sense that they combine two complementary inputs, so that a shortage of either one could seriously disrupt production. The upstream producers, on the other hand, each face two sources of demand for their product, so that if one declines there may well be scope to expand supplies to the other. It therefore seems reasonable to assume that, on balance, backward integration is more likely than forward integration in this case.

There is a difficulty, however, in that both the downstream firms cannot acquire outright ownership of both upstream firms. If one of them did succeed in acquiring both, then this firm would be able to hold the other firm to ransom by threatening to cut off its supplies. If, on the other hand, they each acquired one of the firms, then each would be able to hold the other to ransom. Thus the left-hand diagram in Fig. 7.2 illustrates a scenario in which the owners of firms C and D, who belong to social group II, form a partnership to jointly take control of firms A and B. The information flows between the four individuals now take place under common ownership and are thus reliable.

If *c* and *d* do not belong to the same social group, however, then such a partnership will not be viable. In this case nothing short of full integration will do. In principle, any one of the four firms could take the initiative to do this. Nevertheless, it is more useful to introduce a fifth player, *e*, whose firm E would take over the other four. Individual *e* then intermediates between *a*, *b*, *c*, and *d*, who become employee managers of their plants, reporting to a headquarters run by *e*. What is important here is to illustrate that gains from internalization can be reaped by an agent who is not directly involved in the actual process of physical product flow. This is illustrated in the right-hand diagram of Fig. 7.2.

This internalization-based solution to the problem of market imperfections may be contrasted with the network arrangement which would be possible if all the independent owners were members of the same social group. Such a situation is illustrated in the left-hand diagram of Fig. 7.3. All the lines now carry double arrows. Everyone trusts everyone else and coordination proceeds smoothly: everyone compromises over price and no one ever defaults.

Although the case of the overseas Chinese in South East Asia provides examples of such network arrangements (Redding 1990), such harmony between buyers and sellers is somewhat unusual because buyers and sellers typically belong to different social groups. In the absence of such social homogeneity, what is required to sustain the network of trust is a

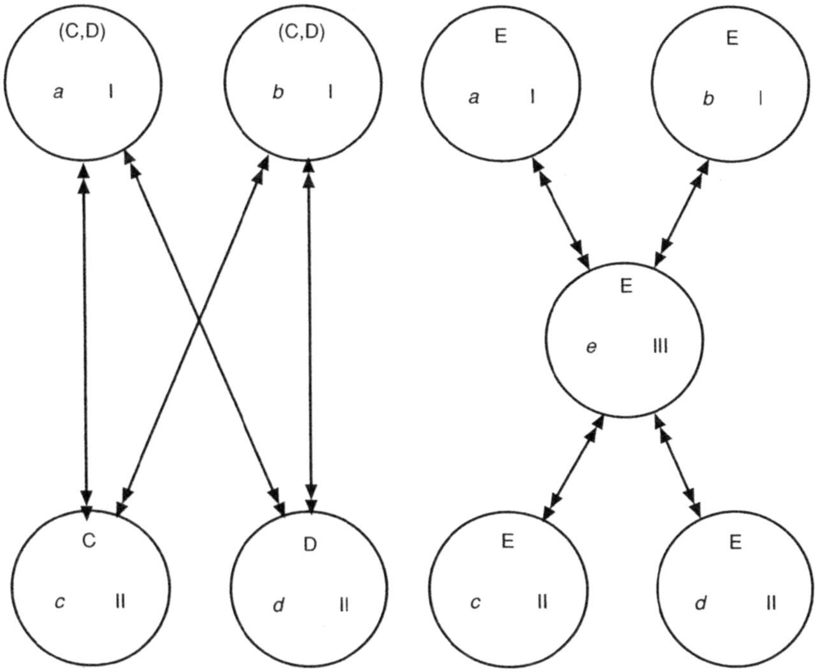

Fig. 7.2. Two internalization-based solutions to market imperfections

middleman who belongs to two or more social groups. Such dual membership creates a chain of trust linking pairs of producers who could not otherwise trust each other. This is the role played by the middleman, *e*, in the middle diagram of Fig. 7.3.

Middlemen typically engage in trade continuously, whilst the customers and suppliers with whom they trade often do so only intermittently Thus middlemen tend to acquire a reputation which others lack. They become a social élite, in the sense that they are trusted by others, and by each other, but do not necessarily trust those with whom they trade. Such a situation is illustrated in the right-hand diagram of Fig. 7.3, where the social groups I and II have each been split into two subgroups, one comprising a reputable élite and the other comprising the rest of the group. The middleman, *e*, belongs to the élites of both I and II, and is therefore trusted by buyers and sellers alike.

Comparing the left-hand and right-hand diagrams in Fig. 7.3 highlights the significance of intermediation so far as networks are concerned. It shows

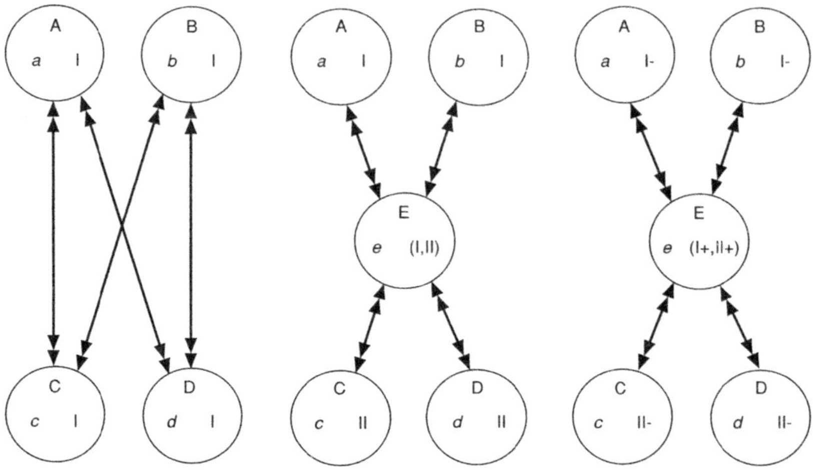

Fig. 7.3. Intermediation based on dual group membership and élite status

that a reputable intermediator can successfully overcome the problems of social segmentation without himself needing to trust any of the people with whom he deals. All that is required is his membership of an élite and that this be recognized by both the groups concerned.

The other point to re-emphasize is that the channelling of information through the intermediator does not necessarily require the channelling of the product through the intermediator's hands as well. In some cases the intermediator does indeed handle the product (as with most retail outlets), but in other cases, such as the merchant houses described in the example below, they do not.

BRITAIN'S NINETEENTH-CENTURY INTERNATIONAL BUSINESS NETWORKS

It was suggested earlier that investment in social institutions would reduce the cost of networking relative to other forms of co-ordination. Late Victorian Britain invested heavily in social institutions of the kind listed in Table 7.3, and these institutions provided the basis for international business networks which linked together the activities of independent firms. Thus, although they were not specifically tailored to the promotion of imperial development, these institutions indirectly served the cause of international business by creating a climate in which long-distance clusters of inter-firm networks could flourish.

At the heart of these networks was the family, the bastion of middle-class respectability. It provided a social foundation for the paternalistic family capitalism which was characteristic of late Victorian enterprise. An important ritual element in respectable family life was Sunday churchgoing. The Church of England underwent a spiritual revival in mid-century, under the twin influences of the Evangelical movement and the Oxford movement, leading to an upsurge in emotional commitment and missionary zeal. Indeed, missionary activity played a major role in legitimizing imperial expansion. Where trade developed, the missionaries followed, and this in turn fostered colonization (Stanley 1990).

Schooling was also high on the Victorian agenda. Compulsory attendance was introduced, and new schools built to accommodate a growing population. The Sunday School movement, reinforced by city church-building and revivalism, had a major (if short-lived) impact on the working classes. Of greatest significance for imperial development, however, was the role of the public schools in inculcating the virtues of leadership through self-discipline. Intense social bonding at school created the phenomenon of the 'old school tie'—an allegiance formed in youth which could be exploited for business purposes throughout a person's career (Jones 1993: 44–5). The school, the church, and the family all provided links between those in the colonies and those at home, allowing business transactions to proceed in a high-trust atmosphere even though the parties concerned were thousands of miles apart.

The role of the armed forces should not be overlooked either. Many explorers and business adventurers had a military background and could use these connections to raise capital when suitable opportunities arose, so that the military represented a significant group among the shareholders in imperial enterprises (Davis and Huttenback 1988: 162–82). The armed forces themselves were glamorised by their part in the rituals of imperialism. Whig historians placed the military successes of the early nineteenth century into a broader context of national progress. Parallels were drawn between the economic and social progress under Queen Victoria and the national revival under Queen Elizabeth three centuries earlier.

This sense of continuity with the past was not, however, purely subjective. Cain and Hopkins (1993) have formally charted the significant continuity of the British élite during this time. In late Victorian Britain this élite intermediated across a powerful international network which channelled capital raised in London into a vast number of business opportunities overseas.

Through the course of the nineteenth century, it was the service sector of the British economy in general, and the financial service sector in particular, which exerted an increasing influence on the shape of Britain's economic development (Rubinstein 1993). Despite the wealth generated in the north of England by the rapid growth of industrial production during the first half of the nineteenth century, important elements of the landed aristocracy succeeded in reconsolidating their dominant economic status through the development of financial and mercantile activities grouped around the south-east of the country. In transferring the basis of its power from the ownership of land to the control of finance, this aristocratic élite succeeded in creating, in Cain and Hopkins's terminology, a regime of 'Gentlemanly Capitalism' which dominated the subsequent pattern of Britain's international economic relations. As these writers explain, the members of this group exhibited a strong degree of cultural homogeneity, providing an ideal terrain in which to germinate interpersonal business linkages.

> High finance, like high farming, called for leadership from 'opinion-makers' and trust from associates and dependants. A gentleman possessed the qualities needed to inspire confidence; and because his word was his bond, transactions were both informal and efficient. Shared values, nurtured by a common education and religion, provided a blueprint for social and business behaviour. The country house led to the counting house; the public school fed the service sector; the London club supported the City. Gentlemanly enterprise was strongly personal, and was sustained by a social network which, in turn, was held together by the leisure needed to cultivate it (Cain and Hopkins 1993: 36).

Augmenting these indigenous social networks were a variety of continental elements attracted to London as the commercial centre of the world. By the latter half of the nineteenth century, the networks fostered within the City had become sufficiently dispersed internationally to be considered as representing a cosmopolitan bourgeoisie (Jones 1987).

Together with their role of financing and facilitating international commodity trade, these mercantile groups also began to engage in international investment, notably through the promotion of so-called free-standing companies. According to Wilkins (1988: 261), during the period under consideration the free-standing company was probably the most typical mode of British direct investment abroad and was the form in which much investment previously considered as portfolio in nature was actually transferred.

Free-standing companies were joint-stock companies, registered in Britain (usually in London, but occasionally in Scotland) and with capital denominated in sterling, but which were designed to finance investment in a productive venture overseas (Casson 1994). They were free-standing in the sense that they were not developed in relation to any parallel operation within Britain itself, unlike the overseas subsidiaries of a conventional multinational corporation. Both the range of countries and the economic activities in which they were involved varied widely; with respect to the latter, Wilkins points out that free-standing companies were to be found in agriculture, timber, cattle raising, mining, oil production, manufacturing, transportation, public utilities, banking, land mortgages, and land development.

The central actor in the formation of a free-standing company was the promoter. Promoters were individuals with connections abroad, or the staff of City institutions such as merchant banks, or what Chapman (1985) has termed 'investment groups'. One merchant bank which helped to promote a cluster of free-standing companies in the mining industry was Rothschilds, which was instrumental in the formation of a mining engineering consultancy company called the Exploration Company. During the 1890s, the officers of the Exploration Company promoted many new mining concerns that were formed to exploit the growing number of mineral discoveries which became viable following the development of deep-mine technology (Turrell and van Helten 1986). Thus, during the late nineteenth century many of the operations which made up the international mining industry took the form of intermediated networks rather than integrated multinational corporations.

The clustering of individual free-standing companies around a particular merchant house created a set of inter-firm linkages that afforded scope economies in marketing and in the use of information regarding the level of reserves. In fact, clustering was a phenomenon which represented a hallmark of free-standing companies. The recurrence of the same providers of legal and accounting services in the promotion of the companies, for example, is a feature that provides important empirical evidence of the networking tendency displayed by this form of international economic co-ordination. Wilkins has noted, for example, that certain firms of solicitors (such as Ashurst's, Linklater's, and Freshfield's) were used frequently for the purposes of establishing free-standing companies. The services of a select group of accountants were utilized both for verifying accounts and auditing overseas operations in a quasi-management role. Mining engineering companies, such as Bewick, Moreing & Co., and John Taylor and Sons, provided many of the extractive-based free-standing companies with engineering and management services (Wilkins 1988: 266).

The board of directors of free-standing companies often included the representatives of indigenous firms from the industry in question. This gave investors confidence in the enterprise being promoted, and allowed domestic entrepreneurs the opportunity to 'go abroad' without relocating their own enterprises. Thus another clustering of firms tended to revolve around individuals with links to particular industries.

Thus an important function of the free-standing company is that it provided an alternative for British-based firms to international vertical integration. As such, it provided a means of international integration through a mixture of contractual arrangements, but one which featured recurring groups of connected individuals, rather than the impersonal links of the market process or the administrative hierarchies of the corporate firm.

Using the conventions set out in the previous two sections, Fig. 7.4 shows the role of the promoter, *e*, based in a London financial institution, *E*, as an

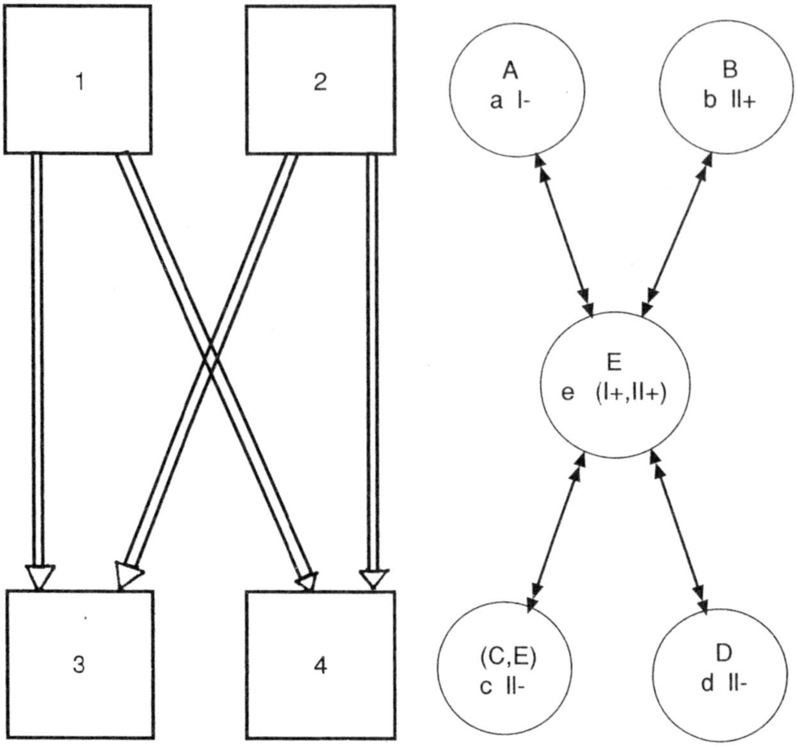

Fig. 7.4. Stylized representation of late nineteenth-century international business network

Notes

1. Capital equipment factory in Midlands or North of England owned by Co. A.
2. Professional practice of consulting engineers, solicitors, accountants, etc., owned by Co. B.
3. South African mine owned jointly by Co. C and Co. E.
4. Latin American plantation owned by Co. D.

a British industrialist.
b Senior partner in professional practice.
c Colonial expatriate.
d British-educated member of local social élite.
e Promoter, e.g. partner in London-based financial institution.

A British manufacturing firm producing capital equipment.
B Professional partnership of accountants, etc.
C Free-standing firm operating a mine in South Africa, part owned by London-based financial institution, E.
D Free-standing firm operating a plantation in Latin America.
E London-based financial institution engaged in company promotions.

I– New middle class formed by entrepreneurial craftsmen and their descendants.
II– Poorer gentlemen who socialized with élite gentlemen at English public school.
I+, II+ Wealthy élite drawn from both middle and upper classes including aristocratic financiers, assimilated immigrants, and 'self-made' men.

intermediating mechanism linking firms in Britain (A, B) that supplied goods and services to operating companies located in the overseas market (C, D).

Hence the promoter provides the means of intermediating information flows, while product and service flows move directly between the plants (1, 2) in Britain (owned by firms A, B) and the activities (3, 4) abroad (activity 3 is jointly owned by C and E and activity 4 is owned by D).

The figure illustrates how individuals *c* and *d*, who lack reputation with *a* and *b*, gain access to them via *e*, who has a reputation with everyone owing to his membership of the London élite. Since *e* trusts *c* and *d* less than they trust him, however, *e* may require equity control, which (in the case of Fig. 7.4) *c* is willing to accede to by sharing ownership. Individuals *a* and *b* then trust *c* and *d* indirectly because of the latter's relationship with *e*.

In practice there seems to have been a fairly high degree of trust in the parties involved in firms C and D in any case, which meant that *e* allowed them considerable discretion in the day-to-day management of affairs. This facilitated efficient and responsive local management at a time when communication with head office was still relatively slow. Decentralization within the free-standing firm also allowed head office overheads to be kept to a minimum.

CONCLUSION

This chapter has attempted to explore how the existence of interpersonal networks which straddled national boundaries provided the basis for international business networks during the nineteenth century. The development of these networks involved the creation of a large number of independent free-standing companies which were floated in the UK but which actually operated in countries abroad. The setting-up, financing, and provisioning of these free-standing companies relied upon the ability of key actors in Britain to play the role of intermediator, and thus to co-ordinate independent firms abroad with the appropriate economic agents in the metropolitan country. These intermediators were able to perform this function because they held influential positions in a range of the social networks which were a hallmark of Britain's, and especially London's, nineteenth-century economic structure.

During the twentieth century, these networks increasingly gave way to the internalized managerial structures of the industry-specific multinational corporations. To date, the general failure of such networks to hold sway after 1914 has been attributed by US business historians to the functional shortcomings of this specific institutional form—especially its inability to transfer adequate managerial know-how (Wilkins 1988; Chandler 1990). On the contrary, the analysis of this chapter leads us to suggest that the explanation for their general demise needs to be sought in the changing international social relations which arose in the wake of World War I, rather than as a result of any purely functional shortcomings stemming from this particular organizational form.

In concluding, it is clear that the example of Britain's international inter-firm networks represents only one of many instances of the business network phenomenon, and that this institutional form has experienced a resurgence over recent years. In contrast to many of the more contemporary examples of inter-firm business networks which are discussed in this book, those described above tended to be founded upon social institutions and networks which already existed, such as the family and Britain's school system. Of the more recent examples, it has tended to be the existence of ongoing inter-firm relations which themselves have facilitated interpersonal relationships. Upon these interpersonal relationships many new instances of inter-firm networks have been founded. As in the past, however, they rely for their efficacy upon the existence of bonds of moral trust between the participants.

Clearly, the specific social circumstances of networks will vary over space and time, and their sociological implications can usefully be studied on a case-by-case basis. What this chapter has attempted to do is to illustrate that there are general economic principles which allow networks to be understood purely as an efficient institutional response to the problem of coordination. Whilst one implication of this analysis is that economists are no longer able to proceed on the assumption that economic transactions can be studied as if social relations between the participants do not matter, the basic analytical framework of economic theory remains well equipped to provide a rigorous explanation of the network phenomenon.

REFERENCES

Aoki, M. 1988. *Information, Incentives, and Bargaining in the Japanese Economy*. Cambridge: Cambridge University Press.

Cain, P. J., and Hopkins, A. G. 1993. *British Imperialism: Innovation and Expansion 1688–1914*. London: Longman.

Casson, M. C. 1990. *Enterprise and Competitiveness: A Systems View of International Business*. Oxford: Clarendon Press.

—— 1991. *Economics of Business Culture: Game Theory, Transaction Costs and Economic Performance*. Oxford: Clarendon Press.

—— 1992. 'Internalization Theory and Beyond'. In Buckley, P. J. (ed.). *New Directions in International Business Research: Priorities for the 1990s*. 4–27. Aldershot: Edward Elgar.

——1994. 'Institutional Diversity in Overseas Enterprise: Explaining the Free-Standing Company'. *Business History*. 36 (4): 95–108.

Chandler, A. D. 1990. *Scale and Scope: The Dynamics of Industrial Capitalism*. Cambridge, Mass.

Chapman, S. D. 1985. 'British-Based Investment Groups before 1914'. *Economic History Review*. 2nd series. 38: 230–51.

Davis, L. E., and Huttenback, R. A. 1988. *Mammon and the Pursuit of Empire: The Economics of British Imperialism*. Cambridge: Cambridge University Press.

Jones, C. A. 1987. *International Business in the Nineteenth Century: The Rise and Fall of a Cosmopolitan Bourgeoisie*. Brighton: Wheatsheaf Books.

Jones, G. 1993. 'British Multinational Banking Strategies over Time'. In Cox, H., Clegg, J., and Ietto-Gillies, G. (eds.). *The Growth of Global Business*. 38–61. London: Routledge.

Ouchi, W. 1981. *Theory Z: How American Business Can Meet the Japanese Challenge*. Reading, Mass.: Addison-Wesley.

Redding, S. G. 1990. *The Spirit of Chinese Capitalism*. Berlin: De Gruyter.

Rubinstein, W. D. 1993. *Capitalism, Culture and Decline in Britain, 1750–1990*. London: Routledge.

Stanley, B. 1990. *Bible and the Flag: Protestant Missions and British Imperialism in the Nineteenth and Twentieth Centuries*. Leicester: Apollos.

Turrell, R. V., and van Helten, J.-J. 1986. 'The Rothschilds, the Exploration Company and Mining Finance'. *Business History*. 28: 181–205.

Wilkins, M. 1988. 'The Free-standing Company, 1870–1914: An Important Type of British Foreign Direct Investment'. *Economic History Review*. 2nd series. 41: 259–82.

[7]

Industry and Innovation, Volume 10, Number 2, 197–217, June 2003

Carfax Publishing
Taylor & Francis Group

New Product Development and Product Supply within a Network Setting: The Chilled Ready-meal Industry in the UK

Howard Cox, Simon Mowatt and Martha Prevezer

It is now widely acknowledged that the 1990s witnessed a sharp rise in the incidence of network forms of business organization. From an economic perspective, the ability of firms to exploit inter-organizational networks has clearly led to new forms of business-to-business transacting, but it has also had significant implications both for industrial structure and the nature of competition and innovation more generally. The purpose of the present paper, therefore, is to review new evidence regarding the function played by inter-firm networks, and in particular to present a detailed analysis of the operation of vertical network arrangements within the chilled ready-meals sector of the food processing industry. The paper identifies and analyses the operation of two distinct inter-organizational network types that operate in this sector: a control network and a network for innovation.

Interest in the study of business networks has evolved along various fronts, and across different disciplines. Within economic study, the regional level analysis stemming from Marshall's concept of externalities has been the basis for the study of industrial districts and cluster analysis. At the firm level the transactions cost paradigm (Coase 1937; later developed by Williamson 1975, 1985) has been important as a basis for the analysis of "hybrid" forms of organization between markets and hierarchies (Powell 1990). The influence of sociological studies of business networks, focusing on the process of intermediation and relationships between specific actors, has allowed for a more sophisticated understanding of network processes within and between firms (for a review see Grabher 1993; Grandori and Soda 1995; Ebers 1997). Towards the end of the last decade, elements of all these approaches have been present in studies of network organizations (see Ebers 1997 for a review also of this literature). In these approaches the boundaries of a firm are blurred by cooperative agreements (Sachwald 1998), and the flow of tacit information between firms (Casson and Wadeson 1998). The emphasis has moved away from considering the boundaries of the firm to examining information flows within networks (Casson 1997). This literature focuses on the mechanisms that ensure the quality of information in networks, with an emphasis on the development and economic function of trust (Casson and Cox 1997; also see Lane and Bachmann 1998 for a review of trust in network organizations).

Recent studies have attempted to move beyond the identification and taxonomy of

1366-2716 print/1469-8390 online/03/020197-21 © 2003 Taylor & Francis Ltd
DOI: 10.1080/1366271032000096644

network forms towards an understanding of their role in the innovation process, principally in high-technology industries. This approach is especially prevalent in the study of research and development (R&D) and cluster studies (Swann *et al.* 1998). These industries, characterized by telecommunications, pharmaceuticals and biotechnology, are not often representative of many other sectors, especially those characterized as low-tech. Focus has turned therefore to networks and innovation within traditional industries. There has been an acknowledgement that relationships between suppliers and manufacturers within the automotive sector have been transformed by network relationships (such as the dynamic network of Dicken 1998), particularly those driven by new information communications technologies (ICTs) such as electronic data interchange (EDI). Jarillo (1993) and (particularly) Abernathy *et al.* (1999) have extended the understanding of these processes into other sectors such as the textiles industry. Competition and innovation are increasingly being undertaken simultaneously between firms involved in vertical and horizontal network relationships. The role of vertical chains is most evidently expounded in studies of international systems of disintegrated manufacture, commodity chains (Gereffi 1994; and the allied concept of the differentiated network, Nohria and Ghoshal 1997), and in studies of cooperative innovation between firms in the supply chain (Tether 2000). Several studies have examined the innovation process within these types of vertically non-integrated production systems. In these analyses, the role of customers driving innovation often implicitly assumes the customer to be another firm within the vertical chain, typically a downstream manufacturer (as in Clark *et al.* 1987; Harabi 1998) rather than the final consumer.

Our paper extends the analysis of network forms and the innovation processes between firms in vertical relationships. The paper seeks to understand how organizational structures and innovation might be altered within a traditional sector that has introduced new ICT-based technologies. We have sought to do this by means of detailed research into the UK food processing and retailing industry, where during the past decade the competitive dynamics have been transformed as a result of the introduction of networks and EDI systems by the large-scale multiple retailers (supermarkets). Studies in the 1980s by Senker (1986, 1988) identified that the impetus for innovation in processed food was beginning to move from branded manufacturers to retailers. This shift has continued, and the introduction of generic ICTs has further strengthened the position of the multiple retailers relative to manufacturers (Cox *et al.* 2002). The present paper finds that there are two complementary networks engendered by the use of new ICTs, one based on innovation and the other on control. An interesting aspect of the network systems depicted in this paper is that they encompass and are partly driven by the final consumer, as well as by producers themselves.

APPROACH AND METHODOLOGY

During the mid-1980s Senker (1986, 1988) examined the newly identified role of UK food retailers in new product development (NPD) in order to test whether contemporary economic theories could account for this pattern of innovative activity, and found that they lacked explanatory power. Recent developments in the study of business networks, outlined in the introduction, have widened theoretical approaches so as to examine both networks and innovation. This paper draws on network theory's contribution to economic analysis to enable an examination of retailer-centred vertical chains in the chilled ready-meals sector. The principal theoretical framework used in this paper follows the economic network-theory approach developed by Mark Casson (Casson 1997; Casson and Cox 1997), which emphasizes the centrality of information within an economic framework. In moving beyond the conventional axioms of transaction cost theory (Williamson 1975, 1985), network theory allows for more complex relations between ownership boundaries and the effective locus of control, and addresses how such relations are facilitated through its systems of information management. As such, the focus on networks anticipates greater flexibility in the ownership boundaries of firms within industries, with the optimal configuration emerging as the dynamic outcome of the interplay between technological change and the exigencies of the competitive process. Furthermore, this information-based approach incorporates an understanding of the role of social mechanisms in creating, guaranteeing and perpetuating trust from an economic perspective. This is particularly useful in examining networks that involve informal organizations such as those identified in this paper, and can help develop an analysis of detailed case study examples. From an historical perspective, Chandler's approach (1977, 1990, 2000) to examining business structure also provides our study with a useful framework to understand organizational and industrial change.

The theoretical approach used to identify the changes within the food processing industry and the relationships between firms has been supplemented by more detailed study of specific sets of vertical relationships. In order to test the validity of our characterization of the contemporary network relationships and innovation process in the sector we also undertook a series of semi-structured interviews designed to substantiate and augment our findings and to build up a detailed knowledge of the functioning of networks. To examine the processes of control and innovation, we selected one of the vertical chains in the industry that we deemed to be representative. This vertical chain related to a retailer,[1] Retailer A, which accounted for a significant share of the final market for chilled ready-meals. For the examination of the control network in this vertical chain we interviewed general managers from logistics contractors that we termed M (General Manager Development Consumer Europe) and N (Development Director, Europe) the Project Manager for Chilled and Perishable Goods in Retailer A. For the innovation network we followed a similar methodology to the interview-based approach used by Senker (1988). Senker made detailed case studies of the main UK grocery retailers in order to examine how they were able to develop products during the mid-1980s when these retailers were beginning to establish novel own-brand products. Through interviews with retailers in the sector she found that some retailers were innovating products and processes, whilst others were merely contracting suppliers to create own-label versions of branded products. The true innovators directly promoted the manufacture of novel products by adopting closer

1 Because of the sensitive nature of competition and inter-firm relationships in the industry, we are not able to reveal the names of the companies and individuals who helped with this study.

relations with their suppliers, and setting up (or extending) their own internal product development departments.[2]

This paper builds a similarly detailed picture of the innovation network in the sector through interviews with Retailer A's[3] NPD section (principally the Senior Trading Manager for Fresh Foods) and representatives of supplier firms and contractors. Interlocking testimony was used to verify information given by interview subjects, which was particularly successful in this case because of the nature of the career path within the industry (there was some overlap at times between actors simultaneously involved in both networks). The interviews had a built-in variety as it was common for actors to have experience at different stages of the value chain, and for retailers, contractors and suppliers to have worked for other companies in the sector.[4] In this way, and by a brief examination of the retailer innovation network of another food retailer, designated as Company E, the representative nature of the selected vertical chain was corroborated. In addition to this programme, supporting interviews were held with those holding a global and long-term view of the industry, namely industry trade journal editors (e.g. *Frozen and Chilled Foods*, *Food Manufacture*) and trade association officials.[5]

THE INNOVATION NETWORK

The characteristics and structure of the chilled ready-meals market

The emergence of network structures in the food processing and retailing sector can be best understood in the context of two primary factors: first, the food retailers'

2 Senker divided retailers into two main categories: acceptors (who commissioned suppliers to replicate products, accepting supplier standards) and intervenors (who were intimately involved in the product development process with suppliers). The mechanism by which firms dealt with suppliers or managed product development in food was through the establishment of their hygiene departments and food technicians. M&S and J. Sainsbury's food hygiene departments underwent a radical change in the 1970s, increasing the number of staff, shifting their emphasis to quality control, product development, packaging technology and machinery. From the table below it can clearly be seen that in the early 1980s Tesco moved from being an acceptor to following M&S and J. Sainsbury's strategy of intervention. In this process a hygiene department is vital to gain technical capacity and to learn about rival products and supplier operations. By 2000 all the major UK grocery multiples have become intervenors.

Retailers and their NPD strategies in the mid-1980s

Retailer	Hygiene dept. established	Internal food technicians 1970	Internal food technicians 1985	Strategy
M&S	1948	30	69	Intervenor
J. Sainsbury	1920	100	130	Intervenor
Tesco	1973	—	112	Intervenor
Safeway	1964	8	27	Acceptor
Asda	1970	8	27	Acceptor

Source: Senker (1988: 111, Table 4.4).

3 Which included staff with direct knowledge of working with supplier development research, as well as at national and foreign subsidiaries.

4 For example, one of two managers interviewed at Contractor A had worked in a similar role for both Retailer C and Supplier B, and Retailer A's logistics manager had worked previously for Retailer C.

5 The trade association officials involved wished to stay anonymous due to the nature of relationships within the industry.

TABLE 1: UK RETAIL SALES OF CHILLED READY-MEALS, 1993–99

Year	£m	Index
1993	340	100
1994	380	112
1995	435	130
1996	475	140
1997	497	146
1998	551	162
1999	596	175

Source: Key Note Report (2001).

adoption of new ICTs, and second, the example of the system of relational contracting established by the clothing and foodstuffs retailer Marks and Spencer (M&S), which described itself as "a manufacturer without factories". M&S's practice of relational contracting was transferred from its clothing and textiles activities to its food business, and then to the supermarket grocery sector in general, as retailers sought to emulate M&S's differentiation strategy and suppliers adopted their quality standards and systems in order to supply the supermarket sector.

The chilled ready-meals market sector was pioneered by M&S, and the major UK[6] multiples developed their own lines in the 1990s in response to this. Chilled ready-meals are high value-added premium convenience products, which have displayed rapid growth during the 1990s (see Table 1). They are ready-prepared complete meals or meal centres that need only heating by oven or microwave[7] and are chilled, not frozen, for freshness. As the meals are highly perishable, and have a very limited shelf life, they require a sophisticated chill chain which can deliver meals from manufacturer to point of retail in a few days.

The appeal of the sector is not only convenience, but also its ability to provide quality substitutes to restaurant meals. Variety is therefore a key aspect of the sector, and retailers need to be able to respond not only to the market demand in terms of allocation, but with a corresponding array of new products. The sector is largely controlled by six retailers that account for some 95 per cent of the market by sales (see Table 2).

Retailers use chilled ready-meals as part of their own-brand differentiation strategy, a strategy that has been a key to competitive success within the sector.[8] Retailers therefore attempt to follow customer eating trends closely and the range of products offered by firms within the sector is very large—despite the low volume sales in

6 The UK accounted for 49 per cent by value of the European chilled ready-meals market in 1998. Germany and France accounted for 21 and 20 per cent, respectively. The bulk of the products for France and Germany is accounted for by chilled Pizzas, which are qualitatively quite different from ready-meals in general. *Source*: Vickers (1999).

7 This "dual-ovenable" product characteristic is one that demands leading-edge materials technology in terms of hygiene and packaging. This also requires that the manufacturers, packagers, and retailers develop the product packaging closely together, as the packaging also forms part of the retailer's generic own-branding strategies.

8 Own-label products are where retailers source the supply of lower-price alternative products to compete with branded manufacturers' products, usually at the bottom end of the market (Burt and Sparks 1997). Own-brand goods are those products developed *by the retailer* to strengthen their brand as retailers, and were developed chiefly in the UK market (Fernie and Pierrel 1996) where their influence is strongest.

TABLE 2: UK RETAIL SHARE OF CHILLED READY-MEALS, 1995–2000

	1995	1996	1997	1998	1999	2000
Own label, of which	*95*	*95*	*95*	*95*	*95*	*95*
M&S	45	42	40	37	35	32
J. Sainsbury's	20	23	25	22	23	23
Tesco	14	16	17	22	23	23
Asda	4	5	5	6	8	8
Safeway	5	4	4	4	4	4
Waitrose	5	4	3	3	3	3
Other own label	2	1	2	1	1	1
Branded	*5*	*5*	*5*	*5*	*5*	*5*

Note: Figures in columns may not sum to 100 due to rounding.
Source: Key Note Report (2001).

TABLE 3: MAINSTREAM "ETHIC" MEAL RECIPES, QUARTER 4, 1999

	M&S	J. Sainsbury	Tesco	Asda	Waitrose
Indian	18	12	15	12	26
Oriental	13	11	18	9	14
Tex-Mex	12	4	12	5	3

Source: Mintel (2000), Key Note Report (2001) and industry sources.

many individual product lines. Retailer A offered a total of 141 different chilled ready-meals in 2000, having introduced some 44 new products in 1999 alone. Some indication of this variety can be taken from the number of products the top five retailers offer in the "ethnic" market (the majority of the market being comprised of British and Italian recipes) shown in Table 3.

In contrast to the dominant position of the leading retailers, the manufacture of chilled ready-meals is widely diffused, with branded manufacturers accounting for less than 5 per cent of total production. In the UK the sector is supplied by over 180 firms ranging from specialist micro-kitchens employing less than five people to a few large companies such as Northern Foods and Hazlewood (*Grocer* 1997). The largest firms supplying the sector may produce other chilled products in addition to ready-meals, but these are the exception.[9] As product development in the sector is retailer-led, suppliers exhibit some distinctive features in terms of nature and composition. Retailers tend to source from a great number of suppliers in order to respond quickly to new restaurant trends with new recipes, exploiting the flexibility of small suppliers. Many of these recipes, especially in the "ethnic" area, are initially developed by very small specialist companies some of whom, such as Noon Foods, have become major firms through their association with the retail sector. Table 4 indicates the largest suppliers to the sector and gives some indication of their main customers.[10] The range

9 Geest and Hazlewood, for example, are manufacturers of other chilled products, such as pasties and chilled pizzas. Northern Foods supplied M&S exclusively with chilled ready-meals until 1999, but supplied other retailers with chilled products.

10 Data in this sector is extremely difficult to obtain due to the intense competition within the retail sector, and the sensitive nature of customer-supplier relationships. We are not able to give confidential information released to us by firms used to inform this investigation, but have attempted to give publicly available information wherever possible. The data in this table therefore shows publicly known links and the largest supplier firms and is not comprehensive.

of dishes is also dependent on access to many specialist suppliers, as the production of ready-meals spans different product bases (poultry, fish, meats, vegetables), market segments (healthy eating, luxury, etc.) and ethnic recipes (traditional British, oriental, French, Italian, Thai, Tex-Mex). As Table 4 indicates, the specialist suppliers are mostly smaller companies. The largest volume of production, however, is sourced from a small group of manufacturers; Northern Foods for example supplies about 30 per cent of M&S convenience foods and Hazlewood Foods produces 20 per cent of all chilled ready-meals. Because the major volume manufacturers have developed in

TABLE 4: MAJOR OUTSIDE OWN-BRAND SUPPLIERS IN 2000. *SOURCE*: VARIOUS[a]

Supplier	£m[b]	Specialization	Major customer (firm-specific specialization indicated)
Northern Foods	1,285.9	General	M&S,[c] Sainsbury's, Asda, Tesco
—Recipe Dish Company		General	M&S
—Cavaghan & Grey		Vegetarian/fish/poultry	M&S
Hazlewood Foods	788.9	General	Safeway, Tesco, Waitrose, Somerfield
Van de Bergh	763.8	Oriental	Tesco
Geest	522.1	General	Tesco (Indian), Sainbury's (Italian), Waitrose (British, Italian)
Sun Valley	268.0	Poultry	M&S
Bluecrest Freebooter[d]	169.3	Fish	Tesco
Headland	164.0	General	Major supermarkets
S&A	60.13	Indian/Oriental	Asda, Waitrose, Safeway, Morrison
Katsouris	60.0	Indian/Vegetarian	Tesco, Waitrose, Somerfield
Marlow Foods	56.6	Quorn	Sainsbury's, Tesco
Noon Foods	52.1	Indian/Oriental	Waitrose, Sainsbury's
Pinney's	51.0	Fish	M&S, Sainsbury's
Oscar Mayer	42.6	General	Sainsbury's
Ferndale	25.0	Tex-Mex	Asda
Ethic Cuisine	19.3	Vegetarian	Sainsbury's
Grampian Country Foods	15.4[e]	Poultry	M&S
Perkins	12.8[f]	Vegetarian	Not known
RF Brookes	9.0	Italian/Vegetarian	M&S
Daloon	8.3	Indian/Oriental	Major supermarkets
Cherry Valley	6.0	Poultry	Waitrose, Morrison

[a]Data derived from company annual reports, Mintel (2000), Key Note Report (2001), FAME and AMADEUS databases and industry sources.

[b]Turnover has been provided wherever possible at the level of the firm, subsidiary or division producing chilled ready-meals.

[c]Until 2000 Northern Foods exclusively supplied M&S with chilled ready-meals. After M&S's change in policy on long-term relational contracts, Northern Foods began to supply other supermarkets, although the Recipe Dish Company and Cavagham & Grey remain exclusive subsidiaries for supplying M&S.

[d]Bluecrest Freebooter, which until 1998 was a subsidiary of Booker Foods, along with Grampian Country Foods (GCF) appear to be the only supermarket contract suppliers which also offer a range of chilled ready-meals under their own brand name. Their total branded market share is less than 1 per cent.

[e]GCF Group turnover is £851.2 million in 2001, however, most of this is derived from the group's primary activity of meat processing. This estimate relating to turnover of chilled ready-meals is taken from the *GCF Group Director's Report and Consolidated Financial Statements for the Year Ended 31 May 2001*, the chicken convenience food division having a total turnover of £147.9 million and supplying prepared meats and sandwiches.

[f]Turnover indicated is that of Simply Fresh Foods Ltd. This company is a subsidiary of Perkins Chilled Foods, whose overall turnover for the period was £303 million. *Source*: Industry sources and FAME for turnover data.

conjunction with retailers, they often have an exclusive relationship with them. In some cases larger producers supply several retailers, but in different product areas with little overlap.[11] Where overlap exists, manufacturers may have dedicated plants for each retailer, producing meals to their specification.[12] No manufacturer supplies the *same* product to multiple customers.

Profits in the chilled ready-meals market are not derived primarily from the economies of standardization. Rather, variety, novelty, and quality are the key elements. The chilled ready-meal NPD process therefore needs to be rapid and responsive to changing customer tastes. The organizational solution to this problem in the sector is an inter-organizational trust-based network rather than a strategy of internalization. The large retailers are in a position to gain marketing information directly via their intimate relationship with the customer through point of sale (POS) monitoring, customer loyalty schemes (exploited by sophisticated data mining centres maintained by the retailers) and their own market research. The aim is to identify new market niches, and fill them with new differentiated products as quickly as possible, and thereby respond effectively to new eating trends. Thus the critical information required to develop new products is obtained by retailers, who then use this knowledge to leverage control over the innovative process as a whole. Retailers in the UK are able to coordinate the development of new products as they have internal hygiene and product development departments, even though they do not have any production capacity of their own (Senker 1986, 1988; Hughes and Merton 1996; Fernie 1997).

Coordinated new product development through strategic alliances: Retailer A's innovation network

Retailer A is an example of a firm that has been able to exploit its proximity to the consumer to develop new products more effectively than firms higher up the value chain. Retailer A derives knowledge about consumer trends through the innovation network, especially from expert sources of information and small specialist companies, in addition to its own consumer-based information. Retailer A accepts that "many new product ideas come from our suppliers and we work very closely with some of the top chefs ... so we follow those consumer trends which are very fashionable". The relationships engaged in this sector are best understood as inter-organizational networks whereby manufacturers and packaging firms develop new products in conjunction with retailers. Figure 1 depicts the NPD network.

Retailer A claims to have a "very long term relationships with [its] suppliers". Trust within long-term relationships is critical (Lane and Bachmann 1998). Retailer A has no capital stake in suppliers, and there are few formal contracts between retailers and food suppliers in the chilled ready-meal sector but instead many strategic alliances based on mutual advantage. Relations essentially take the form of a "gentleman's agreement" and this is made possible by the structure of the industry created by the

11 Geest, for example, supplies Tesco with Indian, Sainsbury's with Italian, and Waitrose with British recipes.

12 Northern Foods has two production plants dedicated to M&S at Sheffield and Grantham; Geest has separate plants for Tesco (Button Bridge and Spalding), Sainsbury's (Sun Valley) and Waitrose (Tilbrook), and Noon has dedicated centres for its customers.

FIGURE 1: THE INNOVATION NETWORK.

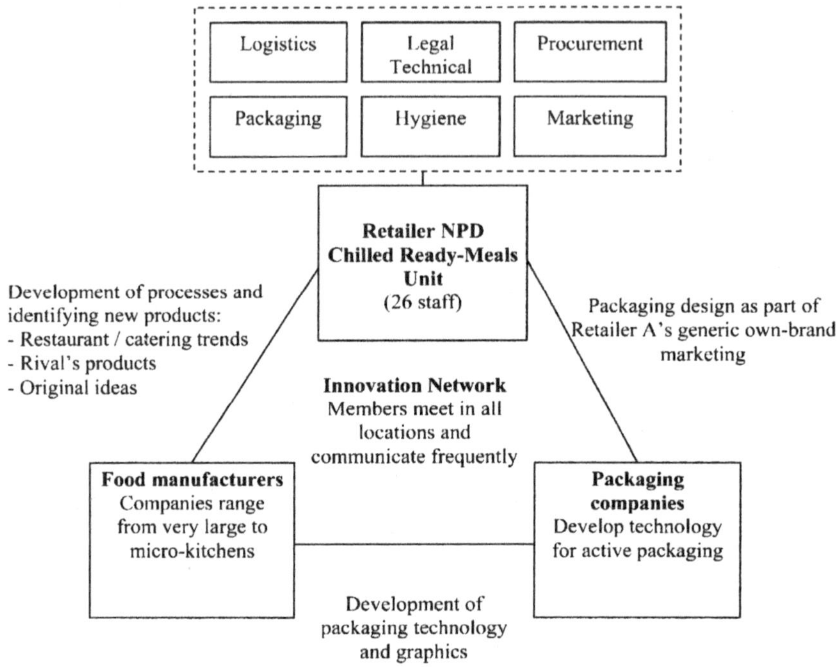

innovation network itself. Retailer A uses many small suppliers to ensure it has access to a large variety of recipes, but relies on Supplier Z for 50 per cent of its ready-meals by sales volume. As is typical with the larger suppliers in the sector, Supplier Z has a dedicated factory for Retailer A, guaranteeing confidentiality and exclusivity. Details of products, specifications and recipes developed for specific retailers and retailer's sensitive information remain confidential, as suppliers rely on retailers' loyalty and support in an oligopolistic final market comprised of few firms. This trust has enabled Retailer A to move from business plans of typically 3 years to longer terms of 5 years, and implement joint investment plans. These plans range from non-contractually based agreements in which Retailer A agrees to "deliver a volume of business to a manufacturer for five years and the manufacturer invests in a dedicated factory", to arrangements to supply small firms with technical assistance in return for access to new recipes. For this process to be effective the retailer must ensure that its quality standards and processes are adopted and integrated with its packaging and, crucially, own-brand marketing strategy. Information needs to be passed between the partners in this network. The "relationships in this sector are different than when you are working with the big branded suppliers as we work very closely with ready-meal suppliers and the confidences that we tell them we wouldn't do on the branded side". This is especially significant for small-scale suppliers (whose continued existence is crucial to the retailer in developing new products quickly) where the retailer is their sole client.[13] In certain examples, retailers can help lower the asset specificity risks and information costs of suppliers by lending specialist staff, information, equipment, and money in return for dedicated investments. This series of very close relations binds the network firms into mutual dependencies whereby it becomes more profitable for firms to act without opportunism, having redefined the pay-off structures to reward cooperative approaches. In the case of large manufacturers the relationship centres on negotiation over exclusivity agreements, the use and development of dedicated manufacturing centres, and the coordination of new hygiene technologies and processes, such as the development of specific packaging systems. Relations with smaller firms, many of which could be termed "micro-kitchens" employing less than 10 staff, were characterized more by an exchange of hygiene technician staff to coordinate basic standards and to transfer technological information, especially information about production systems from manufacturers, from the retailer to small producers.

Managing production in the innovation network

Relations within and between firms in the innovation network are "fluid and dynamic". Retailer A's chilled ready-meal NPD unit is part of the fresh foods division and incorporates buyers responsible for recipe development. The chilled ready-meals unit is headed by the Senior Trading Manager for Fresh Foods[14] and has a permanent team of 26 people that includes a product development team, working on recipe development with suppliers, and 6 buyers who are responsible for the day-to-day administrative, commercial side of the business. The unit works with the fresh foods division staff that liaise with the food technicians in the hygiene department (who have a total staff of 198), logistics, marketing, procurement, legal/technical department and packaging technologists. This organization is mirrored in suppliers. The chilled ready-meals NPD unit and their supplier counterparts spend around 50 per cent of their time in each other's firms or in central meeting grounds. "Some of the factories now are like large hotel kitchens, because it has become more and more specialised and the runs have become smaller" and in these cases the ongoing exchange of staff and knowledge for development and monitoring is especially important. This is of special importance in this segment, as the technical requirements of the packaging are so demanding. The NPD unit therefore coordinates internal departments, external manufacturers and third-party packaging firms.[15] In the case of a micro-kitchen, Retailer A supplies access to its packaging and food hygiene and production experts through the chilled ready-meals unit and "really do work very closely together".

---

13 The difference in relationships between the largest and smallest suppliers is something that the literature has not focused on, and which this study did not directly address. However, this, and the issue of firm growth through relational contracting in dependent network relations, is an area worthy of future attention. This study found little differences in the transaction cost issues for smaller suppliers.

14 The senior trading manager was our main interview respondent for the innovation network within Retailer A.

15 In the case of larger manufacturers packaging is managed specifically for each customer, and often through third-party specialist firms as well. Where large manufacturers do produce packaging this is in close development with the retailer's hygiene, marketing, procurement and packaging departments through the chilled ready-meal NPD unit.

THE CONTROL NETWORK

Retailers' control networks differ from the open-ended relational networks that they have established for innovation, and are characterized more by formal contractual arrangements. The radical changes that have occurred in the UK grocery supply chain have been well documented, especially from the fields of logistics and supply-chain management (Fernie and Pierrel 1996; Burt and Sparks 1997). By focusing on the economic relationships and drawing on our detailed interview-based research with Retailer A's internal logistics department and external contractors, we offer new insights to the processes at work. Retailers' control of the supply chain represents a sophisticated form of network organization that is essentially one of subcontracted coordination. Although at first glance this system appears similar to conventional subcontracting, a closer examination of the linkages reveals a system that more closely resembles a form of upstream franchising, with novel solutions to organization problems. Under traditional subcontracting arrangements, the retailer devolves process and operations to a logistics subcontractor. The true costs and risks are obscured by the problems of information impactedness and asset specificity, as when the contractor buys or builds dedicated facilities such as warehouses. Much of the economics-based literature on the management of the supply chain focuses on these issues and the mix between internalization and externalization (Buck 1990; Ross 1997; Bourlakis 1998). However, this approach underplays the changing nature of the modes of externalization employed, and the ways in which transaction cost problems centring on uncertainty and opportunism have been addressed in novel and sophisticated ways. In the control network, the retailer seeks to resolve these problems by retaining ownership of the key assets and by controlling the coordination of information and supplier processes directly throughout the network via their command of the computer information system. In the following sections we will first examine the development of the supply chain in the UK food retail industry, and following this we concentrate on examining Retailer A's control network.

From a warehouse-based to a replenishment-based supply chain

Grocery retailers in the UK have achieved control over IT-based systems of supply-chain coordination. This has changed the nature of the supply chain from a warehouse-based system to one where retailers manage their inventory on a replenishment-based just-in-time system with little stock holding. This not only enables retailers to economize on warehousing costs, but also allows them to correlate demand and supply with unprecedented accuracy. Managing the logistics of product distribution emerged in the early 1980s as a major objective of the food retailers in the UK (Quarmby 1988), in particular, the goal of centralizing their logistics and distribution operations to use "logistical competency to gain competitive advantage" (Bowersox 1998). The retailer J. Sainsbury pioneered the development of dedicated regional distribution centres (RDCs) in the 1970s as an intermediate stage in the distribution process. These RDCs operated on Sainsbury's behalf but were owned by one of the growing number of specialist distributors through a process of subcontracting whereby contractors were guaranteed fixed-term management fees. Transportation of products from the RDCs to the stores was then largely undertaken directly by Sainsbury's own fleet of vehicles (McKinnon 1989).

By the 1990s, the RDC pattern had become established with British food retailers, although they increasingly owned the RDCs, which they had either built themselves, or bought from contractors at the end of contract periods. In addition, retailers began to encourage the development of primary consolidation centres (PCCs) to which manufacturers were able to deliver increasingly small batch-driven loads, prior to their transfer to the RDCs. These allowed very small crate (rather than pallet) based deliveries to be made. Crates can accommodate partial boxes, ideal for the delivery of very short shelf-life low-volume, high value-added products such as ready-meals. The efficiency therefore does not come from standardized delivery and economies of scale. Indeed, as the logistics manager of Retailer A notes, the drawback of the system is that "you are moving more air" but the compensating advantage is derived from the degree to which it is possible to accurately match supply and demand. Larger manufacturers can coordinate the collection of stock from small suppliers for delivery into the PCC. Therefore, as long as the retailers use their transparent EDI system to coordinate and control this process they can manage the supply chain from beginning to end. Under this system of organization, the RDCs no longer carry out a warehousing function, but consolidate goods for demand-driven direct delivery to retail outlets. The distribution and logistic structure, using both RDCs and PCCs, allows small manufacturers to join the supply chain efficiently, and for large manufacturers to supply products on demand, rather than by bulk delivery.

The mechanism by which coordination has been achieved is via ICT-based communication and information exchange systems. The gradual adoption of electronic point of sale (EPOS) replenishment systems in the early 1980s, and scanning technology in the mid-1980s allowed the supply chain to be managed in a more efficient way.[16] Grocery retailers, constrained by the perishable nature of certain products, were at the forefront of the move from inventory-based systems to customer-driven systems (MacDonald 1994). The ability to use EDI between organizations in real time is a key feature of being able to manage inter-firm systems of coordination (Hughes and Merton 1996; Mason-Jones and Towill 1998). This ability to manage the supply chain allowed retailers to switch to customer demand-driven[17] systems of replenishment (Ody and Newman 1991; Smart 1995; Fernie and Pierrel 1996; Winters 1996), and encouraged the expansion of their control backwards down the supply chain. These factors led to a boom in the 1980s of third-party contractors to handle distribution (Fernie 1997), and the domination of the supply chain by retailers at the expense of

16 The development of these generic IT systems was coordinated in the UK by the Institute of Grocery Distributors (IGD), a trade body founded in 1975 comprised of retailers, manufacturers and distributors (Bamfield 1994; de Angeli 1995). Indeed, the logistics literature has detailed how retailers have turned around the management of the supply chain. The IGD, for example, set-up the Article Numbering Association (ANA) in 1976, which set common standards for bar-coding, leading eventually to the adoption of an e-standard in 1997.

17 Information as to customer buying patterns and trends has been gathered from store data and loyalty card information. Data warehousing was becoming common in the late 1990s, as retailers continued to gather information on the buying patterns of consumers. Data mining technologies allowed them to develop bundles of products and promotions to exploit consumer demand. The retailers have used this knowledge for product development. They have been in the sole position to gather this information, and it must be noted that in a system of transparent information, this critical information is guarded closely within the organization.

manufacturing firms, who saw their distribution services decimated (Whiteoak 1993; Cooper *et al.* 1994). By moving their direct management backwards into the chain of logistics (Fernie and Sparks 1998), retailers were able to gather information regarding the role of wholesaling much more effectively and to introduce their own computer-controlled stock management systems into this aspect of the value chain. As a result, retailers have been able to unbundle many of the costs of services that were supplied by wholesaling subcontractors and gain much more precise information over a variety of costs that had previously been beyond their purview.

This unbundling process is especially significant. Traditional subcontracting relationships are complicated by the provision of a bundle of value-added services, asset specificity, and the problem of contractor-based risk. In such cases, bilateral negotiation is undertaken. In contrast, the removal of these questions simplifies the process of negotiation, lowering the costs of individual transactions. The management of RDCs has in many cases been subcontracted to third parties in a system that effectively involves reverse-franchising. The retailer retains direct ownership of the asset (such as a warehouse or fleet) and the computer-controlled stock management system, but subcontracts out the operation and various other support services that the physical management of the asset requires. Thus the integrated information system underpins and provides control over an organizational structure that actually constitutes a network of independent firms revolving around the hub played by the retailer's head office. This arrangement represents the inverse of the concept of "hollowing-out", since it allows the company to maintain control over the critical system-wide information whilst enabling it to relinquish direct responsibility for its management. And whilst this arrangement requires the management of many times the number of discrete transactions than would be involved in conventional subcontracting, the costs of managing these transactions has been sharply reduced by the development of computerized information management systems.

In relation to distribution, subcontractors and the management of RDCs, the traditional problems of opportunism and bounded rationality are circumvented by three means. First, subcontractors' management fees do not include risks associated with building idiosyncratic assets (such as RDCs), because the retailers have either internalized these costs, or given guarantees to agents by means of extended and relational contracts. Second, manufacturers are not able to conflate distribution costs into the cost of manufacture because they no longer undertake these functions. Third, because of retailers' involvement in controlling the flow of supply-chain information through the system, they are very aware of the real costs involved. This also applies, as was observed in the innovation network, to the costs of development and the manufacture when retailers are directly involved in the process. The outcome of these changes in logistics and RDC management subcontracting is a move towards open book negotiation with retailers, a system based on low management fees in conjunction with reward structures for efficiency improvements.

Retailer A: unbundling costs and managing multiple relationships

A close examination of Retailer A's supply chain illustrates the operation of the linkages within the control network. Retailer A's logistics department is formed by a

TABLE 5: RETAILER A'S RDC AND PCC STRUCTURE

	RDCs		PCCs	
		No. of contractors		No. of contractors
Self-managed	9	Nil	Nil	
Managed by third party	15	8[a]	13	10[b]
Total	24		13	

[a]The two major contractors manage six RDCs.
[b]Most PCC contractors only operate one PCC (being regionally constrained), and none of them manage RDCs.
Source: Interviews with Retailer A.

director operating with a team of four senior managers, of which one is the manager for ambient and frozen goods and one for chilled and perishable goods. The managers are responsible for the day-to-day running of the supply chain and work with a total staff of 250 employees. Retailer A's distribution network comprises of 24 RDCs and 13 PCCs as shown in Table 5. The supply chain is coordinated by Retailer A's hardware and software systems. Retailer A's logistics manager commented that "If you go to (Contractor O's) RDC it's our hardware even if they own the depot" explaining that this integration makes the supply chain transparent to the retailer.

> Unless you knew that RDC 2 was owned by us and RDC 12 was owned by (Contractor N), you can't see the difference ... you have the same information and the computer systems dictate the processes and methods of working. Throughout the supply-chain really you have our systems.

The same condition applies in the case of physical distribution, where the contractors that operate Retailer A's fleet own only 50 per cent of the RDC-to-store vehicles.

Logistics contractors explained that the transparency afforded to retailers both by the integration of their computer systems and the benchmarking provided by their own operations supplied them with a high level of information about costs: Contractor M relating that Retailer A's "knowledge about costs is as great as ours is. There is nothing hidden there for us to extract margins from." Consequently Contractor M's management fee declined from 15 per cent to 10 per cent to 5 per cent to 2 per cent on each contract renewal. Coupled with increased information transparency, Retailer A's decision to build its own (or buy back) RDCs led to a change in emphasis in contractor's reward structures, moving from management fees based on fixed-volume freight rates to a system based on low management fees with an incentive structure for productivity gains. "Quite often it is the retailer's capital and the fee therefore becomes two tier—a fixed fee and then a sum of money that is deliverable in addition if service or costs are improved." This profoundly alters the nature of relationship between retailer and contractor, and this can be observed in longer contract lengths—Retailers A's contracts with Contractor M having increased from 2 to 5 years. Within this longer-term relationship Retailer A and its suppliers pool information on real incurred costs during negotiation in order to arrive at the mutually acceptable distribution of costs and profits, with the retailer sometimes finding that contractors' actual costs were higher than its own predictions and adjusting rewards to account for this. As a result of this framework, the close relations enable Retailer A to use fewer contractors in more trusted mutually advantageous relationships—indicated by the fact that only two contractors are responsible for managing six out of their eight externally managed RDCs.

Casson (1997: 122) has used the term "communal networks" to describe forms of coordination in which existing high levels of trust act to facilitate price negotiation through the removal of opportunistic threats and uncertainties that usually result from one party bearing irreversible costs. Cooperative price negotiation therefore helps to foster longer-term relationships in contrast to competitive tendering, a situation demonstrated by retailers adopting longer-term contracts, facilitating trust. In this case, however, the mutual trust that develops within such a "communal network" is an *outcome* of the information transparency engendered by the retailer's computer systems rather than being a precursor.

In their management of the RDC-to-store supply chain, Retailer A negotiates contracts with third-party logistics firms to manage specific RDC management contracts.[18] The PCC network is significantly different from the RDC network, and less under the direct control of the retailer. The PCC exists to allow larger manufacturers to make smaller, more regular demand-driven deliveries to RDCs, and to bring smaller suppliers within the supermarket's supply chain, allowing infrequent deliveries of products or regular deliveries of small loads. This capability is critical for chilled foods because the production volumes on some lines are already relatively small, in the case of Retailer A 90 per cent of products selling less than six units a week per store. Large and medium food manufacturers with their own distribution systems (such as Northern Foods and Geest) and small regional logistics companies are in the ideal position to collect small crate loads from suppliers and make consolidated deliveries into PCCs. This is only efficient if these small loads are consolidated for multiple retailers, so the job of Retailer A's logistics manager

> is to go round and convince the suppliers that it is in their interest to become part of this network, because [Contractor O] is not just going to a supplier and picking up for us but for Retailer C and Retailer D as well.

The composition of the PCC network means that it is regionally constrained and local in nature. In operational terms this means that Manufacturer X's Midlands PCC is run by Contractor O, which collects goods from local suppliers (within a limited $1-1\frac{1}{2}$ hour road time from the PCC). Manufacturer X then delivers to Retailer A's eight regional RDCs. For Retailer A this means that managing and extending the PCC network entails recreating and managing many relationships with local firms. As in the innovation network, Retailer A manages multiple relationships with suppliers and adds value by central coordination.

Information exchange and innovation

The supply chain described in the previous section can be represented by the flow of physical goods shown in Figure 2. Through POS information, retailers respond to demand by ordering from their suppliers the stock needed to fulfil or, increasingly,

18 The main suppliers are: Excel Logistics, Christian Salversson, NFT, BOC Transshield, Tibbet & Britten, and Wincanton. Tibbet & Brittan was formerly Unilever's internal logistics division, and BOC Transhield was established as a joint-venture between BOC and M&S to develop the chilled supply chain.

FIGURE 2: THE CHILLED READY-MEAL SUPPLY CHAIN: PHYSICAL FLOWS.

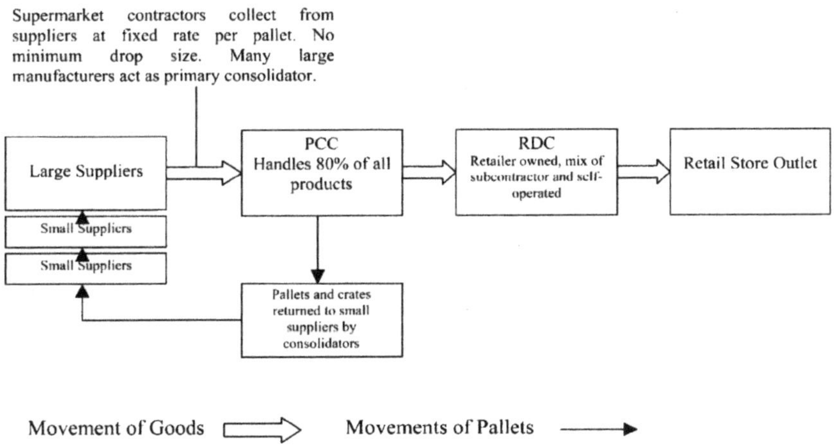

anticipate demand. Orders are passed directly to suppliers' computer systems through the EDI network, where they are tracked by the retailer's control of the IT information system through primary and secondary consolidation points before delivery to individual outlets. This control over the supply chain is fundamental to the existence of the chilled ready-meal market. It allows retailers to correlate supply with demand (vital for extremely short-life products where wastage tends to vary between 20 and 40 per cent of output) through the delivery of small batches and allows small specialist suppliers to be incorporated into the supply chain. The transparent information system coordinating the supply chain has changed the nature of relationships, and the potential structure of linkages, between manufacturers and retailers. Integration of the information network allows retailers to work more closely with suppliers and contractors than typical contractual models suggest. The POS data is the critical information that drives the supply chain, and is tightly controlled by the retailer. This is because the POS information can be exploited not only to match supply and demand, but in the case of chilled ready-meals, to develop and innovate new products for markets revealed by this data. The potential for close relationships in the supply chain allows retailers to form supply-chain-based networks with firms that own complementary assets and the capabilities to exploit these revealed consumer demands.

CONCLUSION

This paper has used insights drawn from Casson's reformulation of the economic theory of the firm based on information requirements to explore the changing structure of inter-firm relations in the UK's food processing and retailing industry. In Casson's view, the structure of institutions at any given time can be interpreted as a rational response to the social need to economize on information costs (Casson 1997: 3). The importance of such an approach is that it provides a starting point for embedding a variety of organizational forms of economic coordination—firms, markets, networks—into an integrated theoretical framework. In this framework, relationships between firms that are not mediated purely by the price mechanism (i.e. inter-organizational networks) can be treated as a response to the changing imperatives of information management within an economic system. The present paper, however, attempts to move beyond the idea of treating networks purely as an efficiency response and considers how the possession of certain critical information may confer enduring forms of competitive advantage on specific actors within a given industry, particularly within the vertical value-adding chain.

In the food processing and retailing industry, the emergence of sophisticated computerized information management systems has placed the leading retailers in a potentially dominant position. In the case of the vertical supply chain, ownership of inventory management software extends the reach of supermarket chains through the distribution process and has enabled them to exert a significant degree of control over the strategies of food producers and manufacturers as well. We have termed this a network of control. In addition, data generated and recorded at the point of sale on customer preferences and purchasing patterns has given British supermarkets access to information that can be utilized, in conjunction with food processors and packaging firms, to directly initiate aspects of NPD. These firm alliances we have termed a network of innovation.

The implications of these information-centred networks of control and innovation for the structure of the food processing and retailing industry are particularly well exemplified by the development of the chilled ready-meals sector. These meals represent a type of product in which accurate management of the supply chain and stock replenishment process is a critical determinant of success, and where the high profit margins that are achievable stand to be undermined by high wastage rates. Only with the ability to effectively manage both the production and distribution of these items are the supermarkets able to exploit this potentially lucrative market segment. Moreover, the financial benefits to be gained from the successful management of these products are further enhanced by the reputation advantages that the supermarkets receive through the continued development of these relatively expensive, high-quality items that carry the brand name of the retailer. Indeed, the perception of British supermarkets as innovative businesses has been built to an important degree on the ever-extending range and quality of these chilled ready-meals, despite the well-known fact that the products are manufactured by independent (but anonymous) suppliers. Thus the reputation of the retailer actually depends upon its quality control system, which represents the fulcrum of the networks of control and innovation. Retailer A's NPD manager made this point clearly by stating that:

> when you look at our competitors ... the only thing that's different is the own-brand offering because Heinz baked beans are Heinz baked beans ... so the big point of difference we offer our customers in own-brand is really through quality. Chicken Tikka Masala is the perfect example—everybody's got it but who has the best one?

Thus, both the NPD and supply-chain management systems represent inter-firm networks that are ultimately driven by consumer demands. Access to data on purchasing patterns stands at the centre of each network and is, in each case, under the control of supermarkets. However, the structure of the two networks differs. In terms of NPD, the alliances formed between supermarkets, packaging companies and manufacturers are based on an open exchange of information as the effective competitive pressures are horizontal in nature, i.e. between competing alliances of such collaborative networks. No formal ownership links need to be developed between these firms who are bound together via gentlemen's agreements of mutual benefit. Information may be freely shared, although the retailer's access to the end customer remains of crucial importance.

The institutional structure of the control networks is more complex. Effective management of the supply chain by supermarkets requires the extension of its computer-based information management system along the length of the vertical chain. Thus, some degree of vertical integration has historically been a pre-requisite for the development of this network of control. In this case it has involved direct management by retailers of the final tier of distribution through the provision of RDCs and vehicle fleets. Over time, however, supermarkets have subcontracted the management of these services to independent contractors, and have ultimately transferred ownership of some of these facilities whilst retaining control over the management of the information system embedded within them. Indeed, the more recent development of PCCs has been an initiative in which retailers have promoted a new layer of distribution that incorporates supermarkets' supply-chain information systems but in which they hold no ownership or management responsibilities whatsoever. The transparency afforded to the supermarkets through the operation of these management information systems has had the effect of removing information asymmetries between actors along the supply chain and allowed for much higher levels of trust in inter-firm negotiations.

There is no doubt that the changes outlined in this paper have served to enhance the competitive position of retailers in the UK relative to other actors in the industry. The decision by the Director General of Fair Trading to refer the operations of the leading supermarket chains for investigation by the Competition Commission in April 1999 was provoked by a general sense of unease about their competitive strength relative to both suppliers and consumers (Dobson *et al.* 1998). In fact, the findings of the Commission suggested that neither the prices charged nor the profits made by the supermarkets were excessive (Competition Commission 2002: 6). Within the supply chain, the buying power and control exerted by the supermarkets created, according to the Commission's summary, "a climate of apprehension among many suppliers in their relationship with the main parties" and also appeared to discourage suppliers from investing in NPD and innovation (Competition Commission 2002: 5). In a more detailed assessment, however, the relationship between the supermarkets and their suppliers was shown to be more complex. In the case of own-brand suppliers, there was evidence of supermarkets encouraging and collaborating in product innovation and of good, long-term supplier relations. On the other hand, producers of undifferentiated goods and branded manufacturers exhibited less harmonious relations with the large multiple retailers (Competition Commission 2002: 240–241).

A critical finding of the Commission's report was the growing importance in the food processing and retailing industry of efficient consumer response (ECR). This involves both supply management, through continuous replenishment and automated store ordering, and demand management in which retailers and suppliers jointly manage product categories. Both of these activities are based on the use of information systems of the kind discussed in this paper (Competition Commission 2002: 241–243). In similar fashion, a recent analysis of the sector has noted that added value will continue to be the major driver in the food market, citing a spokesman from the large retailers as follows: "consumers change enormously and out of that comes opportunity. What we have to do is become the one that realises that opportunity . . ." (Key Note Report 2002: 49).

The observations made in this paper have implications both for theory and the study of network organizations. In particular, they highlight the limitations of transaction cost theory's focus on firm boundaries and emphasize the need to place information flows at the heart of institutional analysis. Clearly, the increasing incidence of inter-firm collaboration points to a general need to analyse networks as systems rather than focusing on specific manifestations such as subcontracting, alliances and joint ventures. Our paper shows that the networks underpinning the chilled ready-meals sector are dynamic structures, which evolve in relation to technical change and involve elements of both control and innovation. It is our contention that the example of the ready-meals sector is an indication of the potential role of IT more generally and a signal of the growing importance of consumer information to the competitive process. Such long-term relationships between those firms whose activities are close to customers and their suppliers using ICT-driven networks are poised to become still more prevalent in industries where competition is fundamentally demand-driven.

ACKNOWLEDGEMENTS

The authors are grateful to the Leverhulme Trust for providing an Institutional Grant F/00 533/C in support of this research and to Marion Frenz for research assistance on the project. The development of this paper would not have been possible without the contribution of interviewees from food retailers' new product development and logistics departments, contract logistics companies, food processing trade bodies and journals. The authors would like to express their gratitude to these contributors, whilst absolving them from responsibility for any misinterpretations or mistakes contained in the paper.

REFERENCES

Abernathy, F.H., Dunlop, J.T., Hammond, J.H. and Weil, D. 1999: *A Stitch in Time: Lean Retailing and the Transformation of Manufacturing: Lessons from the Apparel and Textile Industries*. New York: Oxford University Press.

Bamfield, J. 1994: The adoption of electronic data interchange by retailers, *International Journal of Retail and Distribution Management*, 22(2): 3–11.

Bourlakis, M. 1998: Transaction costs, internationalisation and logistics: the case of European food retailing, *International Journal of Logistics*, 1(3): 251–265.

Bowersox, D. 1998: Logistics: the route to quality, *Focus*, 7.

Buck, D. 1990: Changing to contract distribution, *International Journal of Retail and Distribution Management*, 18(1): 35–41.

Burt, S. and Sparks, L. 1997: Performance in food retailing: a cross-national consideration and comparison of retail margins, *British Journal of Management*, 8(2) (June): 133–150.

Casson, M. 1997: *Information and Organisation*. Oxford: Clarendon Press.

Casson, M. and Cox, H. 1997: An economic model of inter-firm networks, in M. Ebers (ed.), *The Formation of Inter-organisational Networks*, pp. 174–197. Oxford: Oxford University Press.

Casson, M. and Wadeson, N. 1998: Communication costs and the boundaries of the firm, *International Journal of the Economics of Business*, 5(1): 5–27.

Chandler Jr, A.D. 1977: *The Visible Hand: The Managerial Revolution in American Business*. Cambridge, MA: The Belknap Press of Harvard University Press.

Chandler Jr, A.D. 1990: *Scale and Scope: The Dynamics of Industrial Capitalism*. Cambridge, MA: The Belknap Press of Harvard University Press.

Chandler Jr, A.D. 2000: The information age in historical perspective: introduction, in A.D. Chandler Jr and J.W. Cortada (eds.), *A Nation Transformed by Information: How Information has Shaped the United States from Colonial Times to the Present*. New York: Oxford University Press.

Clark, K.B., Chew, W.B. and Fujimoto, T. 1987: Product development in the world auto industry, *Brookings Papers on Economic Activity*, 3: 729–781.

Coase, R.H. 1937: The nature of the firm, *Economica*, 4(4): 386–405.

Competition Commission 2002: *Supermarkets: A Report on the Supply of Groceries from Multiple Stores in the United Kingdom*. London: HMSO (http://www.competition-commission.org.uk/reports/446super.htm).

Cooper, J., Browne, M. and Peters, M. 1994: *European Logistics: Markets, Management and Strategy*, 2nd edn. Oxford: Blackwell.

Cox, H., Mowatt, S. and Prevezer, M. 2002: The firm in the information age: organizational responses to technological change in the processed foods sector, *Industrial and Corporate Change*, 11(1): 135–158.

de Angeli, T. 1995: IGD: forum for change and action, *Grocer*, 217(7220) (16 September): 18–20.

Dicken, P. 1998: *Global Shift*, 3rd edn. London: Paul Chapman.

Dobson, P., Waterson, M. and Chu, A. 1998: The welfare consequences of the exercise of buyer power. Office of Fair Trading Research Paper 16, London.

Ebers, M. (ed.) 1997: *The Formation of Inter-organisational Networks*. Oxford: Oxford University Press.

Fernie, J. 1997: Retail change and retail logistics in the United Kingdom: past trends and future prospects, *The Service Industries Journal*, 17(3): 383–396.

Fernie, J. and Pierrel, F. 1996: Own branding in UK and French grocery markets, *Journal of Product and Brand Management*, 5(3): 48–59.

Fernie, J. and Sparks, L. 1998: *Logistics and Retail Management*. London: Kogan Page.

Gereffi, G. 1994: The organization of buyer-driven global commodity chains: how U.S. retailers shape overseas production networks, in G. Gereffi and M. Korzeniewicz (eds.), *Commodity Chains and Global Capitalism*, pp. 95–122. Westport, CT: Praeger.

Grabher, G. (ed.) 1993: *The Embedded Firm: On the Socioeconomics of Industrial Networks*. London: Routledge.

Grandori, A. and Soda, G. 1995: Inter-firm networks: antecedents, mechanisms and forms, *Organisation Studies*, 16(2): 183–215.

Grocer, The, 1997: *The Grocer Food and Drink Directory: 1997*. London: William Reed.

Harabi, N. 1998: Innovation through vertical relations between firms, suppliers and customers: a study of German firms, *Industry and Innovation*, 5(2): 157–181.

Hughes, D. and Merton, I. 1996: Partnership in produce: the J Sainsbury approach to managing the fresh produce supply chain, *Supply Chain Management*, 1(2): 4–6.

Jarillo, J.C. 1993: *Strategic Networks*. Oxford: Butterworth-Heinemann.

Key Note Report 2001: *Ready Meals*. ICM.

Key Note Report 2002: *Supermarkets and Superstores*. ICM.

Lane, C. and Bachmann, R. (eds.) 1998: *Trust Within and Between Organizations: Conceptual Issues and Empirical Applications*. Oxford: Oxford University Press.

MacDonald, J. 1994: Quality in retail distribution, *The TQM Magazine*, 6(4): 11–14.

Mason-Jones, R. and Towill, D. 1998: Time compression in the supply chain: information management is the vital ingredient, *Logistics Information Management*, 11(2): 93–104.

McKinnon, A. 1989: *Physical Distribution Systems*. London: Routledge.

Mintel 2000: *Chilled Ready Meals*. London: Mintel International Group Limited.

Nohria, N. and Ghoshal, S. 1997: *The Differentiated Network*. San Francisco, CA: Jossey-Bass.

Ody, P. and Newman, S. 1991: Speeding up the supply chain, *International Journal of Retail and Distribution Management*, 19(5): 4–7.

Powell, W. 1990: Neither a market nor hierarchy: network forms of organisation, *Research in Organisational Behaviour*, 12: 295–336.

Quarmby, D. 1998: The importance of quality in retailing, *Focus*, September: 7.

Ross, D.F. 1997: *Competing Through Supply Chain Management*. London: Chapman & Hall.

Sachwald, F. 1998: Co-operative agreements and the theory of the firm: focussing on barriers to change, *The Journal of Economic Behaviour and Organization*, 35: 203–225.

Senker, J.M. 1986: Technological co-operation between manufacturers and retailers to meet market demand, *Food Marketing*, 2(3): 88–101.

Senker, J.M. 1988: *A Taste for Innovation: British Supermarkets Influence on Food Manufacture*. Bradford: Horton.

Smart, R. 1995: Quick response supply-chain management from the bottom-up!, *Logistics Focus*, 3(5): 26–28.

Swann, P., Prevezer, M. and Stout, D. 1998: *The Dynamics of Industrial Clustering: International Comparisons in Computing and Biotechnology*. Oxford: Oxford University Press.

Tether, B. 2000: Who co-operates for innovation within the supply-chain and why?: an analysis of the United Kingdom's innovation survey. CRIC Discussion Paper No. 35, The University of Manchester and UMIST.

Vickers, R. 1999: *The European Chilled Foods Market*. London: Leatherhead Food Research.

Whiteoak, P. 1993: The realities of quick response in the grocery sector: a supplier viewpoint, *International Journal of Retail and Distribution Management*, 21(8): 3–10.

Williamson, O.E. 1975: *Markets and Hierarchies: Analysis and Anti-trust Implications*. New York: Free Press.

Williamson, O.E. 1985: *The Economic Institutions of Capitalism*. New York: Free Press.

Winters, T. 1996: The effective implementation of co-managed inventory, *Logistics Focus*, 4(7): 2–7.

[8]

Regional Blocs or Global Markets? A World Accounting Approach to Analyze Trade and Financial Linkages

By

Niek de Jong and **Rob Vos**

Contents: I. Introduction. – II. The Word Accounting Matrix. – III. Trade and Financial Linkages: β and δ-coefficients. – IV. Regional Trade Linkages. – V. Global Financial Linkages. – VI. Linkages between Trade and Finance. – VII. Some Conclusions. – Appendix.

I. Introduction

International finance has grown rapidly in recent decades. This growth has been associated with a gradual process of deregulation of restrictions on capital movements since the 1950s. This move towards freer and growing international capital flows could be seen as a sign of the emergence of a fully integrated global capital market (e.g. Harberger 1980). Together with the dismantlement of restrictions on trade, sealed by the signing of GATT, one might expect that the world has become one big market place for trade in commodities and financial instruments. Put in historical perspective, it would appear that after more than half a century the world economy is saying goodbye to the strong tendency towards regionalization which occurred in the 1930s. The regionalization of international trade and payments patterns during the post-1929 slump have usually been associated with world-wide intensified protectionism and international exchange rate policies splintering the gold standard into currency blocs.

However, recent research has callenged the central role of policies in the move towards regionalization in the 1930s and has claimed that this shift is more properly attributed to ongoing historical forces establishing commercial and financial links between countries forged

---

Remark: The authors are grateful to Elio Londero and an anonymous referee for helpful comments on a draft of this paper. Views expressed in this article are those of the authors and do not necessarily coincide with those of the institutions they are affiliated with. This article is based on research carried out for the United Nations, Department of Economic and Social Information and Policy Analysis (DESIPA), and Project LINK.

over many years (Eichengreen and Irwin 1995). It is also unclear whether the deregulation of international commodity and financial markets of more recent date has led to an increasing integration of these markets. The notion of an integrated global capital market has been investigated empirically, among others, by looking at cross-country savings-investment correlations, but these have yielded conflicting evidence [1] and have been subject to methodological critique.[2] The degree of financial integration of developing countries with external capital markets has been assessed by an evaluation of alternative tests of capital mobility.[3] The empirical literature, however, can provide, at best, evidence on the degree of capital mobility, but does not tell us whether international capital flows take place in regionalized markets or in an integrated global capital market. Looking at institutional factors, one could also believe that there has been a trend towards increasing regionalization, rather than globalization of trade and investment, as reflected in the revival of regional trade agreements, such as NAFTA, Mercosur and the strengthening of the European Union.[4]

The question thus emerges to what extent commercial policies and regulations of capital flows determine regional patterns of trade and finance. Do liberalization and deregulation lead to a disintegration of regional networks? Or, are other factors such as historical processes and structural characteristics such as size, distance and continguity at least equally important?[5] Do savers and investors move capital merely in response to cross-country rate-of-return differentials, as predicted by models assuming a fully integrated capital market? Or, do market imperfections such as asymmetrical information, and other structural factors, such as distance and historically grown political ties, lead investors to follow certain historically established regional

[1] See, for instance, Feldstein and Horioka (1980) who initiated a large debate and found evidence contradicting the notion of an integrated capital market. This result has been by and large reproduced by others, e.g. Sachs (1981), Feldstein (1983) and Dooley et al. (1987). Frankel (1992) gives evidence in support of a near-integrated global capital market, while Vos (1988) only finds some evidence towards increased integration of capital markets among industrialized countries, not world wide.

[2] See, among others, Bryant (1987) and Vos (1988, 1994).

[3] See Montiel (1994). Apart from Feldstein–Horioka correlations of savings and investment, Montiel evaluates measures of gross capital flows and tests of arbitrage conditions and Euler equation tests to measure capital mobility.

[4] See, for example, De Melo and Panagariya (1993) and UNCTAD (1993).

[5] The latter type determinants characterize gravity models of the pattern of international trade. The seminal reference is Linnemann (1966).

patterns of trade and finance, making interest rates a less reliable guide of how capital will move?

The purpose of the present paper is not to provide an analytical model in search for an answer to these questions. The analysis of global linkages will be of a much more preliminary and descriptive nature. The novel feature is the use of a consistent *global accounting framework* to show the degree of regionalization of international trade and finance. Such a framework is required to overcome the shortcomings of existing data sources for adequate empirical analysis. The accounting framework may serve as a starting point for subsequent more analytical applied research. Global data inconsistencies are visible, for instance, from the fact that the sum of the current account balances of all countries in the world does *not* equal zero, as consistent accounting rules would require. IMF *Balance of Payments Statistics*, for instance, have shown global statistical discrepancies in the order of US $ 100 billion (IMF 1987, 1992; De Jong et al. 1993a, 1993b). Another shortcoming is the absence of systematic data sources that specify both the origin and destination of various current account and capital account components. To detect discrepancies and to account for them to the best knowledge available, as well as to partly overcome the problem of gaps in information, a consistent global accounting framework – labelled *World Accounting Matrix* (WAM) – has been developed and applied to existing data sources. We will use WAMs for 1985 and 1990 and some descriptive indicators to analyze the degree of regionalization of commodity and capital flows. The results show that strong regional patterns in both trade and finance persist, though there was a slight weakening in the latter half of the 1980s.

The remainder of this paper is organized as follows. The basic principles of the WAM framework are outlined in Section II. A set of coefficients describing regional linkages in trade and finance are defined in Section III. These coefficients are subsequently estimated for trade (Section IV) and finance (Section V), using WAMs for 1985 and 1990. Section VI investigates to what extent regional patterns of trade and finance coincide. The final section provides conclusions and some suggestions for further analysis.

II. The World Accounting Matrix

Accounting rules command that commodity and financial flows balance at the global level. Such rules are consistently defined in a framework labelled World Accounting Matrix (WAM), developed originally by Vos (1989) and elaborated further in collaboration with others (Luttik 1992; De Jong et al. 1993a, 1993b; Vos and De Jong 1995).[6] The WAM connects international transactions of each economy with the internal balance (reflected in the savings-investment balance) and identifies the interactions between economies. Since at the world level all incoming and outgoing flows must balance, it should hold that:

$$\sum_i^n (S_i - I_i) \equiv \sum_i^n (E_i - M_i + R_i) \equiv 0 \tag{1}$$

and

$$\sum_i^n [(\Delta FA_i - \Delta FL_i) + (\Delta RES_i + EO_i)] \equiv 0\,, \tag{2}$$

where

S = gross national savings
I = gross domestic investment
E = exports of goods and services
M = imports of goods and services
R = net factor income and current transfers from abroad
ΔFA = change in total external financial assets
ΔFL = change in total external financial liabilities
ΔRES = net change in reserves
EO = net errors and omissions.

In other words, the global savings-investment account should balance. Similarly, the global current account balance and the aggregate change in the *net* external asset position should both be *zero*, ex post. In addition, for each financial instrument the external asset position should equal the external liabilities position at the global level. Existing data sources, such as the *Balance of Payments Statistics* compiled by the IMF or *National Accounts* collected by the UN or the World Bank, do not show such a consistency at the global level and show huge discrepancies.

The WAM is designed to cross-check and reconcile data on trade, finance and accumulation and to specify international transactions on a source-use and origin-destination basis. The WAM is outlined in matrix format in Table 1. The matrix presentation permits the identi-

[6] See also Vos (1995) for an assessment of the consistency between the WAM framework and the 1993 System of National Accounts and the new IMF Balance of Payments Manual. The WAM could be seen as the global consistency framework to be added to the external account of individual economies.

Table 1 – *Schematic Presentation of the World Accounting Matrix (WAM)*

	Current Account country groups (1..n)	Capital Account country groups (1..n)	Change in Reserves	Total
Current Account country groups (1..n)	CA (Matrix of current account transactions)	I (Diagonal matrix of domestic investment)		$CA_i + I_i = (E + R^R + I)_i$ (Total current receipts)
Capital Account country groups (1..n)	S (Diagonal matrix of national savings)	ΔFA – ΔFL (Flow of funds matrix, liabilities in rows, assets in columns)		$S_i + \Delta FL_i$ (Total investment finance)
Change in Reserves and Errors and Omissions (E&O)		ΔRES + EO (Row vector of adjusted net changes in reserves[a] and E&O)		$\Sigma(\Delta RES_i + EO_i) = 0$ (Global net change in reserves[a] and E&O)
Total	$CA_i + S_i = M_i + R_i^P + S_i$ (Total current payments to abroad and national savings)	$I_i + \Delta FA_i + \Delta RES_i + EO_i$ (Total investment, domestic and foreign)		

[a] The accounting of (changes in) reserve assets contains adjustment with respect to the standard balance-of-payments accounting rules to obtain symmetry in the recording of those reserve assets held abroad in the form of portfolio investment and other financial assets. The reserve holdings are a separate item in the flow of funds matrix, the remaining reserve transactions (gold, SDRs and use of IMF credits are in the special account for reserve changes. See De Jong et al. (1993a, Appendix A.1) for further details on this adjustment.

fication of the origin and destination of each transaction included in the accounting identities of equations (1) and (2). The WAM consists of four blocks. The Current Account (CA) block is placed in the upper left quadrant. The rows of this block define exports of goods and services plus all factor income and current transfers received from abroad for country (group) $i = 1 \ldots n$; the columns in CA define commodity imports plus factor and current transfer payments to abroad. The CA block is a consolidated matrix which is decomposed of a set of transactions matrices with the same dimensions. The *S* and *I* blocks in the first and third quadrant are *diagonal* matrices, defining national savings and domestic investment per country group. The FOF (flow of funds) block in the second quadrant defines the total international financial transactions between countries and regions. The change in external liabilities are to be read in the rows and the change in external assets in the columns. The FOF block is also built up from a set of matrices that identify origin and destination of different types of international capital flows (direct investment, long-term capital, short-term capital, etc.). An exception to this form of presentation concerns the net changes in international reserves and errors and omissions, which for each country (group) are the closing item of the balance of payments, but cannot be identified by origin and destination.

WAMs for the years 1985–1990 are now available for a classification of 23 countries and country groups and an entry for international organizations. Matrices of beginning and end-of-year foreign asset positions are included in satellite tables (De Jong et al. 1993a, 1993b; Vos and De Jong 1995). In general, the WAMs reconcile data from all relevant data sources,[7] after a careful assessment of the nature of data discrepancies and of differences in reliability of official estimates. The large global discrepancies emerging from official sources imply the need for substantial adjustments to obtain the required world accounting balances.[8]

---

[7] The main data sources are IMF *Balance of Payments Statistics*, UN *Trade Statistics*, the World Bank *Debt Reporting System*, IMF/BIS *Banking Statistics*, UNTCT *World Investment Directory* and *National Accounts* data on savings and investment. Additional data sources include UNCTAD data on maritime shipment and Central Bank reports of the main industrialized countries on the geographical distribution of external claims and liabilities of banks and of direct foreign investment. See De Jong et al. (1993a, 1993b) for a complete listing of data sources.

[8] As explained at length in De Jong et al. (1993a, 1993b) and Vos and De Jong (1995), the balancing of the accounts in the WAM was achieved in several steps, making use of all available data. First, identified global imbalances were cross-checked, using data on capital, trade and payments flows by origin and destination. Where no direct data were available, the interiors of sub-matrices were derived indirectly from several sources and on the basis of specific construction methodologies, building on other variables in the system. The discrepancies that arose between the row (or column) totals of the derived matrix and their reference totals were adjusted later on as part of an overall (controlled) mathematical balancing procedure. For example, the sub-matrices for direct investment income were constructed on the basis of an assumed link between bilateral investment income receipts and corresponding bilateral direct investment stocks at the beginning of the year.

Unallocated totals and unknowns in, for example, the capital account sub-matrices were apportioned by distributing the unallocated part of total asset changes of country i in correspondence with the distribution of total changes in liabilities of countries j. For flows (and stocks) of DFI, outward recordings were the primary data source, because they are generally considered more accurate than those of inward DFI. In contrast, the data on inward flows (and stocks) were the starting points in the construction of the matrices of portfolio investment and other capital (except for the entries based on direct

Compared with primary data sources, the WAM shows substantially lower current account deficits for some industrial countries (USA and the UK) and some developing countries (Latin America, in particular, due to higher merchandise export earnings) and higher current account surpluses in offshore banking centers and other industrial countries (except Japan for which the WAM shows a surplus lower than the official recordings). An important part of these adjustments are due to a re-estimation of investment income flows.

Net asset positions in the satellite tables of financial stocks changed as a result of the adjustments required to arrive at globally consistent financial claims and liabilities. On balance, these changes tend to follow the pattern of the current account adjustments, as logically follows from the world accounting methodology. In the reconciliation process of the international assets and flow matrices, the reporting of direct foreign investment abroad and of liabilities of both portfolio investment and other capital are considered to be more reliable than the reporting of direct investment at home and of external claims of both portfolio investment and other capital respectively (see footnote 8).

It is difficult to tell to what extent the geographical pattern of the international flow of funds as obtained in the WAM differs from existing data sources. This is so simply because existing sources only provide bits and pieces of the puzzle and never a complete and globally consistent picture. In this sense, the WAM provides a value added to our existing knowledge. Comparisons can be made on a country-by-country basis and deviations from primary sources, but these are obviously biased by the assumptions, indicated above, about the reliability of the various sources and forms of recording. We have no established benchmarks (that is, other than our assumptions about

estimates from the World Bank's Debtor Reporting System), since a significant part of portfolio investment consists of international bonds and bond issues are presumably recorded better on the debtor side, as purchases may be spread over many creditors. Also for other equity investment, it may be held that there is greater accuracy in the recording on the liability side. The geographical distribution of other capital flows for the industrialized countries were derived from official data sources of the major OECD countries. Most of these sources only provide *stock* data with a geographical breakdown. Due to a lack of information it was not possible to single out changes in assets and liabilities due to new transactions (flows) and other than revaluation of stocks due to exchange rate changes and other value adjustments. The difference between end-of-year stocks had to be taken as a proxy for the distribution of the flow during the year. The geographical breakdown of the changes in stocks served as proxy distributions of the flows and have been applied to the relevant reference total of flows.

the quality of the data sources) to assess whether the adjusted flows and stocks in the WAM are more accurate than those according to the primary data sources. We believe that the consistent and comprehensive global data framework provided by the WAM yields additional insight and in that sense a better view of the structure of the world economy.

In this paper we use the WAMs for 1985 and 1990 and focus on trade and financial linkages in both years. We also investigate whether the pattern of exports coincides with the pattern of outward direct investment. For the comparison of linkages in both years, the 1990 WAM has been estimated at 1985 constant prices, using export prices to deflate international transactions of country *i* with country *j*. The choice of the appropriate deflator(s) is not obvious in this integrated framework of trade and finance and depends on the purpose of the analysis. Here export prices were chosen to define real (foreign exchange) earnings of countries and regions. An implicit import price deflator was used to deflate DFI. The Appendix provides more detail on the followed procedure and discusses alternative considerations for the deflator choice.

III. Trade and Financial Linkages: β and δ-coefficients[9]

If global commodity and financial markets were fully integrated and characterized by perfect competition, trade and financial flows between countries should be responses to comparative advantages and rates of return differentials. Smooth price and interest rate adjustment mechanisms would restore equilibria and lead to equalization of prices and rates of return in all parts of the world. In reality, commodity and capital markets do not operate this way, as they are characterized by imperfections. Some markets, particularly international financial markets, tend to be characterized by oligopolistic behaviour and asymmetric information (see e.g. Vos 1994). Transport costs also play a role in international trade. If transaction costs are taken into account, the outcome of market forces is likely to be different from the picture sketched above. Further, there may be regulations, such as

[9] In De Jong and Vos (1994) also α- and γ-coefficients are defined and estimated. The α-coefficient identifies whether the tendency of a country *j* to invest in a particular type of asset (say DFI) in country *i* deviates from the average bilateral investment linkage. The γ-coefficient is the ratio of bilateral capital flows and bilateral current account balances.

tariffs and non-tariff barriers to trade and legal restrictions, which may hinder the flow of commodities and capital.

Transaction costs and regulations could underlie the hypothesis that stronger than average linkages may exist between particular pairs of countries (e.g. those within regional blocs), because of a larger flow of information, proximity of markets (smaller geographical distance leading to lower transaction costs), or other reasons, and weaker than average linkages between other pairs of countries. To study this, a coefficient β_{ijk} is defined as:[10]

$$\beta_{ijk} \equiv \frac{S_{ijk}}{S_{jk}} \equiv \frac{X_{ijk}/X_{ik}}{X_{jk}/X_k} \equiv \frac{X_{ijk}/\sum_i X_{ijk}}{\sum_i X_{ijk}/\sum_i \sum_j X_{ijk}}, \qquad (3)$$

where:

X_{ijk} = exports of k from country i to country j
S_{ijk} = share of importer j in exports k of country i
S_{jk} = share of importer j in exports k of all countries.

The deflation method of the WAM is not neutral for the estimation of the β-coefficient, but in practice the implied bias appeared to be only small.[11] Exports of k can be interpreted as sales of a type of commodity (e.g. classified according to the SITC) or as sales of a type of financial liability (e.g. DFI). If the share of an importing country j in the exports of a commodity or financial liability k of country i is the same as the share of j's imports in world trade in that commodity, then the β-coefficient is equal to 1. A deviation of β_{ijk} from unity is called:

a "positive bias" (or stronger than average linkage), if $\beta > 1$
a "negative bias" (or weaker than average linkage), if $\beta < 1$.

[10] See also FitzGerald and Luttik (1991) and Luttik (1992, pp. 143–146). Note that here, for trade shares in rows (exports) of a matrix are considered, while for financial variables, shares in columns (changes in assets or foreign investments) are considered.
[11] For each row in the trade matrix a single export price deflator (of country i) is used. Therefore, deflating rows in the matrix of merchandise trade does not affect the shares of country j in country i's exports. Aggregating the deflated trade values columnwise results in total imports of each country j from all countries i in the world. Imports of country j as a share of world trade will be affected by deflating. Consequently, the β-coefficients – the ratios of shares in a country's exports to shares in world imports – differ from those on the basis of trade measured in nominal values. In practice, however, the differences in the β-coefficients are very small, if deflated figures instead of nominal values are used.

The implications are, for instance, that if Japan would have positive trade biases (β's > 1) with other Asian countries only, and negative trade biases (β's < 1) with all other countries in the world, a higher rate of economic growth in Japan – implying increased import demand – would, other things being equal, result in a growth of exports of other Asian countries that is larger than the average rate of growth of exports of all countries.

Capital flows in the WAM are defined as net changes in assets and net changes in liabilities. Consequently, cell entries can be negative. As coefficients calculated on the basis of negative shares tend to provide interpretation difficulties, we have calculated β-coefficients for the financial stock matrices.

In order to obtain a more systematic view of the relationships between foreign investment and trade between countries, a coefficient δ is defined as the ratio of the share in outward investment to the share in merchandise exports:[12]

$$\delta_{ijlm} = \frac{S_{ijl}}{S_{ijm}}, \tag{4}$$

where:

S_{ijl} = share of country j in outward investment in instrument l of country i

S_{ijm} = share of country j in exports of commodity m of country i.

To illustrate the meaning of the δ-coefficient, we compare the link between direct foreign investment (DFI) and trade in commodities. If $\delta = 1$, the shares of countries in the outward direct investment position of other countries are equal to their shares in the exports of those countries. Put differently, if all δ's were equal or close to 1, the concentration in foreign investment would reflect the concentration in export markets. This could be interpreted as a situation in which investors from one country prefer to invest in countries with which the home country already has strong trade linkages. It could also be

[12] Unlike the β-coefficients, the δ-coefficients are not affected by deflation. The shares in investment are calculated columnwise and the shares in exports rowwise; since investment is deflated columnwise and export values rowwise, deflation does not alter the shares. This becomes immediately clear after rewriting (4):

$$\delta_{ijlm} = \frac{S_{ijl}}{S_{ijm}} = \frac{X_{ijl}/X_{il}}{X_{ijm}/X_{jm}} \equiv \frac{(X_{ijl}/d_l)/(X_{il}/d_l)}{(X_{ijm}/d_m)/(X_{jm}/d_m)},$$

where d_l is the deflator used to deflate outward investment and d_m the export price deflator.

interpreted the other way round, of course: the foreign investment contributes to establishing or expanding export markets.[13] If $\delta > 1$, it means that the investment linkage is stronger than the trade relationship. This may be the case if, for example, the foreign investments are concentrated in (financial) services or are used to circumvent trade restrictions.[14] Another reason why (direct) foreign investment and trade relationships may not be closely associated could be the existence of discrimination in trade relationships or the threat of future discrimination experienced by non-members of a regional trade arrangement. Non-members would be induced to establish or expand DFI relationships with such a region, either to avoid future discrimination or to defuse the threat of it.[15] If $\delta < 1$, the financial linkage is weaker than the trade relationship. This could reflect a case of countries which have liberalized their trade, so there may be less need to establish subsidiaries in each other's economies. Of course, if $\delta = 0$, there is no bilateral DFI relationship at all.

IV. Regional Trade Linkages

This section addresses the following questions: Do we find regional trading blocs? Have patterns of trade shifted during the 1980s? The results of the analysis suggest a substantial degree of regionalization of trade, which, however, tended to decrease slightly in the latter half of the 1980s.

The USA is the major importing country in the world in the second half of the 1980s and by far the largest export market of Canada and Latin America. The β-coefficients for the major trading partners presented in Tables 2a (1985) and 2b (1990) indicate that within the Western Hemisphere there are clear positive biases in US-Canadian trade and US-Latin American trade (that is, β's > 1).[16] The positive biases in both US exports to Latin America and Latin American exports to the USA have become stronger between 1985 and 1990 (as can be seen from the increase of the β-coefficients from 2.1 to 2.4 and from 2.5 to 2.8, respectively), whereas there has been a weakening of the bias in the US exports to Canada.

---

[13] This hypothesis is maintained by UNCTAD (1993), for instance.

[14] See UNCTAD (1993) for a discussion of this possibility.

[15] This is discussed, for instance, in World Bank (1993).

[16] For presentational purposes, we have excluded in the tables the following regions and accounts that form part of the WAM: Other European OECD countries (including Yugoslavia), Other developed countries (Israel and South Africa), Offshore Banking Centers, and Multilateral agencies.

Table 2 – *Main Trade Linkages 1985 and 1990 (Beta's based on values in 1985 dollars)*

	1	2	3	4	5	6	7	8	9	10	11	12	13	14	15	16	17	18	19
	a. Beta's for 1985																		
Western Hemisphere																			
1 USA	0.0	5.5	2.1	1.6	1.6	0.6	0.8	1.0	1.3	0.4	0.4	0.5	0.8	0.6	0.4	0.3	0.1	0.7	0.6
2 Canada	4.4	0.0	0.8	0.8	0.5	0.1	0.5	0.5	0.3	0.1	0.1	0.1	0.4	0.2	0.1	0.4	0.1	0.4	0.2
3 Latin America	2.5	0.4	3.0	0.8	0.2	0.5	0.4	0.8	0.5	0.5	0.4	0.7	0.3	0.7	0.3	1.5	0.4	0.7	0.8
Asia-Pacific																			
4 Japan	2.0	0.6	0.9	0.0	2.5	1.5	1.2	3.7	2.4	0.5	0.2	0.1	0.5	0.3	0.4	0.4	0.1	0.5	0.7
5 Australia & New Zealand	0.8	0.3	0.3	4.4	4.5	1.4	1.6	2.3	2.5	0.3	0.4	0.5	0.9	0.3	0.1	0.7	0.2	1.1	0.3
6 Middle East	0.2	0.1	1.9	4.3	0.6	2.1	3.8	0.0	2.5	0.3	0.6	1.4	0.2	0.7	0.1	0.1	0.4	0.8	0.9
7 South Asia	1.2	0.3	0.1	1.8	1.0	3.5	2.1	0.4	0.9	0.7	0.4	0.6	1.2	0.7	0.4	2.4	0.6	1.2	1.1
8 China	0.5	0.2	0.5	3.6	0.5	1.5	1.3	0.0	1.2	0.3	0.3	0.3	0.2	0.1	0.2	1.0	0.8	0.8	0.4
9 Southeast Asia	1.7	0.6	0.5	3.6	1.3	0.8	1.2	0.4	1.6	0.4	0.3	0.2	0.5	0.3	0.2	0.3	0.1	0.4	0.8
Western Europe																			
10 Germany	0.6	0.2	0.4	0.2	0.7	0.8	0.7	0.6	0.4	0.0	2.0	1.7	1.5	1.8	2.5	0.5	0.8	0.9	0.7
11 France	0.5	0.3	0.7	0.2	0.4	0.9	0.6	0.4	0.3	1.9	0.0	2.5	1.5	1.8	1.3	0.5	0.2	3.0	2.7
12 Italy	0.7	0.3	0.5	0.2	0.7	1.6	0.4	0.5	0.2	2.0	2.5	0.0	1.3	1.0	1.5	0.5	0.3	2.6	1.2
13 United Kingdom	0.9	0.5	0.4	0.2	1.4	1.4	1.1	0.3	0.3	1.4	1.7	1.0	0.0	2.1	1.4	0.2	0.2	0.7	1.7
14 Other EC	0.4	0.2	0.4	0.2	0.4	0.8	0.6	0.3	0.2	2.9	2.4	1.4	2.1	1.5	1.3	0.3	0.2	1.1	1.0
15 EFTA	0.5	0.3	0.5	0.3	0.6	0.8	0.5	0.4	0.3	2.2	1.0	1.1	2.6	1.2	2.4	1.1	0.6	0.8	0.8
Former CMEA																			
16 USSR	0.0	0.0	1.5	0.2	0.0	0.3	1.5	0.6	1.3	0.7	0.6	0.9	0.4	0.5	1.1	0.0	11.4	0.6	0.7
17 Other Eastern Europe	0.1	0.0	0.5	0.1	0.0	0.8	0.4	1.0	0.2	0.9	0.2	0.5	0.4	0.3	1.2	11.0	4.9	1.5	0.2
Africa																			
18 North Africa	0.5	0.2	0.4	0.2	0.0	0.2	0.4	0.1	0.1	1.2	3.0	5.9	0.5	1.8	0.4	0.2	1.1	0.4	0.3
19 Sub-Saharan Africa	1.0	0.2	0.1	0.3	0.1	0.3	0.2	0.2	0.4	1.3	2.8	2.0	1.3	1.6	0.5	0.3	0.2	0.6	5.1

(Table continued on next page)

(Table 2 – continued)

	1	2	3	4	5	6	7	8	9	10	11	12	13	14	15	16	17	18	19
	b. *Beta' for 1990*																		
Western Hemisphere																			
1 USA	0.0	4.2	2.4	1.5	1.7	0.9	0.8	0.8	1.4	0.5	0.6	0.4	0.9	0.5	0.5	0.4	0.2	0.8	0.5
2 Canada	4.4	0.0	0.8	0.8	0.5	0.3	0.4	0.6	0.4	0.2	0.2	0.2	0.5	0.2	0.2	0.4	0.1	0.4	0.2
3 Latin America	2.8	0.6	3.0	0.7	0.2	0.5	0.3	0.5	0.4	0.6	0.5	0.6	0.4	0.6	0.5	1.9	0.4	0.6	0.4
Asia-Pacific																			
4 Japan	1.6	0.7	0.8	0.0	1.9	1.4	1.1	1.5	2.7	0.7	0.5	0.3	0.6	0.4	0.6	0.3	0.2	0.4	1.1
5 Australia & New Zealand	0.7	0.4	0.4	3.4	4.6	1.7	2.0	1.7	2.7	0.4	0.3	0.5	0.9	0.3	0.2	0.2	0.3	0.9	0.3
6 Middle East	0.9	0.2	–	3.7	1.0	0.9	5.0	0.3	1.3	0.3	0.8	0.9	0.5	0.8	0.3	0.6	0.2	0.7	0.4
7 South Asia	1.1	0.3	0.2	1.3	1.0	4.0	2.0	0.5	1.2	0.8	0.5	0.7	1.2	0.7	0.5	2.9	1.2	1.4	1.9
8 China	1.2	0.4	0.4	1.9	1.1	0.8	0.8	0.0	0.9	0.7	0.5	0.5	0.2	0.3	0.3	1.0	1.0	0.3	0.6
9 Southeast Asia	1.6	0.5	0.5	2.6	1.5	1.0	1.1	1.4	1.6	0.5	0.4	0.3	0.5	0.3	0.4	0.3	0.1	0.4	0.7
Western Europe																			
10 Germany	0.4	0.2	0.5	0.3	0.5	0.9	0.6	0.4	0.4	0.0	1.6	1.8	1.4	1.9	2.4	1.1	1.0	0.9	0.7
11 France	0.4	0.2	0.7	0.4	0.4	1.0	0.3	0.4	0.4	1.9	0.0	2.2	1.5	1.8	1.1	0.3	0.4	2.9	2.3
12 Italy	0.5	0.2	0.5	0.4	0.5	1.2	0.4	0.3	0.3	1.9	2.4	0.0	1.1	1.3	1.5	0.6	0.8	2.8	1.1
13 United Kingdom	0.7	0.6	0.5	0.4	1.2	2.1	1.0	0.4	0.5	1.3	1.4	1.0	0.0	1.9	1.2	0.3	0.5	0.7	2.0
14 Other EC	0.3	0.1	0.4	0.2	0.3	0.7	0.6	0.2	0.2	2.2	2.1	1.5	2.1	1.6	1.3	0.2	0.5	1.1	1.1
15 EFTA	0.4	0.4	0.5	0.4	0.6	0.9	0.4	0.3	0.4	2.1	1.1	1.4	1.9	1.2	2.1	1.0	1.4	0.7	0.7
Former CMEA																			
16 USSR	0.1	0.1	2.2	0.7	0.0	0.4	1.3	1.9	0.8	1.0	0.8	1.3	0.4	0.7	1.3	0.0	19.0	1.2	0.5
17 Other Eastern Europe	0.2	0.1	0.3	0.2	0.1	0.5	0.9	1.3	0.2	1.6	0.7	1.0	0.5	0.6	1.4	15.7	4.5	1.4	0.3
Africa																			
18 North Africa	0.6	0.1	0.3	0.2	0.1	0.5	0.6	0.1	0.2	1.3	2.4	5.0	0.6	1.4	0.6	1.3	0.7	2.2	0.4
19 Sub-Saharan Africa	1.6	0.4	–	0.4	0.1	0.1	0.9	0.4	0.3	0.9	2.0	1.1	0.7	1.7	0.6	0.3	0.2	0.4	6.6

In Asia and the Pacific there is also a strong regional concentration of trade, with Japan and Southeast Asia being the major importers. Strong bilateral trade linkages existed between most of the countries within the Pacific Basin. A comparison of the β's for trade in 1985 and in 1990 suggests a weakening of the positive biases in trade within the Asian-Pacific bloc, particularly between Japan and most of its Asian trading partners.

There are positive biases in trade within the bloc of Western European countries (β's > 1), but these have also weakened somewhat between 1985 and 1990, as a result of the fact that imports from within the region grew less than overall imports of the region.

Exceptions to these typical hemispheric trade concentrations are the positive biases that existed in trade between the USA and countries in the Asian-Pacific region and between Europe and Africa, as well as in trade between South Asia and the former USSR. Within the former communist trading bloc (CMEA), the positive biases in trade between the former USSR and Other Eastern Europe are stronger in 1990 than in 1985, despite a shift in orientation towards Western Europe as a market for Eastern European exports. This reflects the larger decline of the shares of Eastern European countries in world imports than the shares of intra-CMEA trade.

Africa's contribution to world trade is very small and its exports account for only 2 or 3 per cent of global imports. African exports are largely directed towards Western Europe (which is likely to be related to the institutional ties between ACP countries and the European Union) and towards the USA. This trade dependence had not changed much over time. Another salient feature is the positive bias in trade between the Sub-Saharan African countries ($\beta > 5$). This bias is partly a result of data construction, rather than necessarily reflecting great success in African integration. The coefficient reflects relatively high intra-group imports: the share of Sub-Saharan African exports going to countries within the group is much higher than the share of world exports going to Sub-Saharan African, which is very small (about 1 per cent). Nevertheless, despite all the stories about failing African trade integration, intra-regional trade in the region is not unimportant.

These findings show the persistence of regional biases in trade, despite moves towards worldwide trade liberalization. The strong regional concentrations of trade are reflected in the high β-coefficients for the trade blocs in the Western Hemisphere, Asia and the Pacific, Western Europe, Eastern Europe and Sub-Saharan Africa. The degree of regional trade linkages is larger within some blocs (e.g. in North and South America) than in others. Another general finding is that there has been a weakening of these linkages in most regions in the second half of the 1980s, which might be associated with more liberal trade policies. However, this tendency has been stronger in some parts of the world (such as Asia) than in others (e.g., the Americas or Europe). Despite a redirection of former CMEA exports towards Western Europe, the WAM for 1990 still shows a strong bias towards intra-CMEA trade.

V. Global Financial Linkages

The novelty of the WAM is that it allows to analyze bilateral and regional trade *and* financial linkages within the same, coherent framework. We also estimate β-coefficients for financial transactions to assess patterns in the global capital market. Because the WAMs (and the primary data sources used for its construction) include *net* changes in financial assets and liabilities, certain entries may be negative, making β-coefficients difficult to interpret. Instead of using the net flows of the FOF block of the WAM, we estimate the β-coefficients using the matrices of international asset and liability positions.[17] The β-coefficients are estimated for various types of financial assets; in the analysis below, we concentrate on the findings for the 1990 WAM data of direct foreign investment (DFI) (Table 3a) and other finance (portfolio investment and official and bank credits) (Table 3b), though we will also point at some changes between 1985 and 1990.

Like trade, DFI is heavily concentrated regionally. The β-coefficients in Table 3a indicate that DFI linkages within North and South America tend to be (slightly) stronger than with countries outside the bloc. Japanese DFI within the Asian-Pacific bloc is also characterized by positive biases, while within the Western European bloc the DFI relationships are generally strong (β's >1). Within the CMEA bloc there are hardly any DFI linkages, but in contrast relatively strong credit ties do exist (Table 3b). The relatively small amounts of DFI within the African region do show a strong intra-regional concentration.

[17] For the matrices of investment positions of DFI, see De Jong et al. (1993a, 1993b). The international investment positions in current end-of-year prices were deflated on the basis of average implicit import price deflators, which were derived from the matrices of merchandise exports in current and constant price export values.

Table 3 – *Main Financial Linkages (Beta's based on values in 1985 dollars)*

	1	2	3	4	5	6	7	8	9	10	11	12	13	14	15	16	17	18	19
	a. Foreign direct investment position 1990																		
Western Hemisphere																			
1 USA	0.0	2.0	1.9	1.7	0.9	2.1	1.9	1.5	0.7	0.9	0.8	0.1	1.6	1.6	0.8	–	0.9	0.1	0.0
2 Canada	1.8	0.0	0.3	0.3	0.2	0.8	0.9	0.0	1.1	0.4	0.5	0.1	0.7	0.4	0.7	–	0.9	0.1	0.1
3 Latin America	1.1	1.3	0.7	0.8	1.2	0.7	0.7	1.0	1.0	0.7	0.5	0.4	0.5	0.0	2.2	–	1.0	1.4	1.5
Asia-Pacific																			
4 Japan	1.8	0.6	0.3	0.0	0.4	0.3	0.4	0.4	0.4	1.0	0.2	0.7	0.5	0.5	0.4	–	0.4	0.5	0.6
5 Australia & New Zealand	0.8	0.8	1.0	1.3	3.1	0.0	0.0	0.0	1.5	0.2	0.2	0.1	1.8	0.5	0.4	–	0.0	0.0	0.0
6 Middle East	1.0	0.2	2.5	1.4	0.0	2.5	2.6	3.2	3.3	0.4	0.5	0.4	0.2	1.9	0.9	–	3.3	4.2	4.4
7 South Asia	0.9	0.9	0.7	1.0	0.0	0.7	0.7	0.8	0.8	1.2	0.0	0.1	1.7	0.4	0.7	–	0.8	1.0	1.0
8 China	0.2	0.0	2.9	2.5	0.0	2.9	3.0	0.0	3.7	0.2	0.2	0.4	0.5	1.9	2.9	–	3.8	4.8	5.0
9 Southeast Asia	0.8	0.4	0.6	3.1	1.6	0.6	0.6	0.8	0.8	0.3	0.1	0.1	0.3	0.4	0.6	–	0.8	1.0	1.1
Western Europe																			
10 Germany	1.1	0.2	0.8	0.3	0.0	0.8	0.8	0.2	1.1	0.0	1.0	1.7	0.6	1.9	1.1	–	1.1	0.7	0.5
11 France	0.7	0.4	0.8	0.3	0.0	0.8	0.9	1.1	1.2	1.7	0.0	2.7	1.0	1.6	1.5	–	1.2	1.6	1.7
12 Italy	0.9	0.2	1.3	0.1	0.2	1.3	1.3	1.7	1.8	1.6	2.8	0.0	0.5	0.5	2.1	–	1.8	2.4	2.5
13 United Kingdom	1.1	1.2	0.8	0.6	3.0	0.8	0.9	1.7	1.7	0.8	0.7	1.2	0.0	0.8	1.6	–	1.8	2.9	3.1
14 Other EC	0.6	0.3	0.5	0.5	0.3	0.4	0.5	0.7	0.8	1.9	2.5	1.8	0.8	0.9	0.7	–	0.8	1.2	1.2
15 EFTA	0.9	0.3	0.6	0.2	0.0	0.6	0.7	0.9	0.9	1.6	1.2	4.7	0.4	1.0	1.0	–	0.9	1.3	1.4
Former CMEA																			
16 USSR	0.9	0.0	0.0	0.0	0.0	0.0	0.0	0.0	0.0	0.0	0.0	0.0	4.1	0.0	0.0	–	0.0	0.0	0.0
17 Other Eastern Europe	0.0	0.2	0.9	0.1	0.0	0.9	0.0	1.0	1.0	5.2	0.0	0.1	2.6	0.8	0.5	–	0.0	1.3	1.3
Africa																			
18 North Africa	0.9	0.3	2.3	0.7	0.0	2.3	2.4	2.9	2.9	1.2	1.0	0.4	0.6	1.0	1.8	–	2.9	3.7	3.8
19 Sub-Saharan Africa	0.5	0.2	1.5	0.4	0.0	1.5	1.5	1.8	1.8	0.4	2.4	0.3	2.2	0.6	1.1	–	1.9	2.3	2.4

(Table continued on next page)

(Table 3 – continued)

	1	2	3	4	5	6	7	8	9	10	11	12	13	14	15	16	17	18	19
	b. Portfolio and other investment 1990																		
Western Hemisphere																			
1 USA	0.0	2.2	2.9	0.8	1.7	0.7	1.4	1.3	1.8	0.3	0.8	0.8	1.1	0.4	0.9	0.0	1.5	0.6	0.6
2 Canada	1.0	0.0	1.4	1.4	0.8	0.8	0.7	0.7	0.5	0.7	0.4	0.9	0.9	0.9	0.7	0.3	0.5	0.7	0.7
3 Latin America	4.3	0.7	0.8	0.5	0.0	0.0	0.0	0.1	0.0	0.5	0.6	0.4	0.1	0.3	0.4	2.3	1.0	0.0	0.0
Asia-Pacific																			
4 Japan	1.2	0.9	0.7	0.0	1.0	0.8	0.7	0.8	0.6	0.7	1.4	1.1	1.3	1.0	0.9	0.2	0.5	0.8	0.8
5 Australia & New Zealand	0.8	0.8	0.6	1.3	0.8	0.7	0.7	0.7	0.5	1.1	0.5	0.9	1.1	0.9	1.0	0.3	0.5	0.7	0.7
6 Middle East	0.3	0.0	0.0	0.3	2.8	2.3	0.0	1.2	0.0	0.3	1.2	0.5	0.2	0.0	0.0	66.2	26.1	0.2	0.0
7 South Asia	0.6	1.3	0.0	1.4	0.0	0.4	0.2	1.7	0.6	1.1	0.6	0.2	0.3	0.1	0.2	2.2	1.4	0.1	0.0
8 China	0.1	0.9	0.0	3.6	0.0	0.3	0.0	0.0	0.0	1.2	0.0	0.1	0.0	0.2	1.2	0.0	1.3	0.0	0.0
9 Southeast Asia	0.9	0.4	0.0	3.4	0.7	0.1	0.1	0.1	0.2	0.5	0.2	0.0	0.1	0.1	0.4	1.3	0.3	0.0	0.0
Western Europe																			
10 Germany	0.5	0.3	0.4	0.4	0.7	1.2	0.7	0.4	1.1	0.0	0.9	0.8	1.6	3.0	1.8	0.9	1.6	0.9	0.4
11 France	0.7	1.2	0.3	0.7	0.8	0.9	0.8	1.9	1.7	1.1	0.0	1.5	1.2	1.8	1.5	0.4	1.2	2.8	2.3
12 Italy	0.5	0.8	0.6	1.3	0.8	0.7	0.7	0.7	0.5	1.6	1.1	0.0	1.1	0.8	1.0	0.3	0.5	0.7	0.7
13 United Kingdom	1.3	0.6	0.4	0.8	1.5	2.2	1.9	1.7	1.4	1.7	1.1	1.1	0.0	1.2	2.1	0.4	1.0	1.6	2.8
14 Other EC	0.4	0.8	0.6	1.3	0.8	0.7	0.6	0.7	0.5	1.6	1.1	0.9	1.1	0.8	1.0	0.2	0.4	0.7	0.7
15 EFTA	0.8	0.8	2.6	0.2	0.9	2.1	2.8	1.1	2.9	1.1	1.2	2.1	1.1	1.3	0.3	1.7	0.8	2.5	1.7
Former CMEA																			
16 USSR	0.0	0.0	0.0	0.3	0.0	0.2	0.0	0.0	0.0	4.7	2.0	1.0	1.8	1.0	1.7	–	0.0	0.0	0.0
17 Other Eastern Europe	0.5	2.6	0.7	0.6	0.0	0.0	0.0	0.8	0.1	2.7	1.5	0.7	0.7	2.2	1.7	4.0	0.5	0.0	0.0
Africa																			
18 North Africa	1.1	1.8	0.0	1.0	2.3	2.6	0.2	1.9	0.0	1.7	2.1	1.2	0.2	0.4	0.6	2.8	4.9	1.0	0.0
19 Sub-Saharan Africa	0.4	0.5	0.2	0.5	0.7	1.6	1.2	4.0	0.2	0.7	3.4	1.4	0.5	0.5	0.4	11.7	2.7	2.2	1.1

These observed DFI linkages confirm the alleged regional associations of developing countries with members of the so-called Triad – the United States, Japan and the EC – reported elsewhere (see UNCTAD 1993 and World Bank 1993). Indeed, the results suggest that the USA has stronger DFI relationships with Latin America than with other developing countries, whereas outward DFI of Japan was more concentrated in Southeast Asia and Western European DFI more in Africa than in other developing countries.

Table 3b shows that other types of capital flows equally show an important degree of regional concentration. It cannot be established, however, whether DFI tends to be more strongly concentrated regionally than portfolio and other financial flows. This pattern is somewhat diverse, as appears from a comparison of both panels of Table 3. DFI links between the USA and Latin America, for instance, are strong, but the degree of intra-regional concentration is even stronger for credit flows and portfolio investment. In contrast, the positive biases in the financial relationships between the USA and Western Europe are in general stronger for DFI than for the portfolio investment position. In turn, the positive biases in the financial relationships between Western European countries and Africa are in several cases weaker for DFI than for portfolio and other investment.

In De Jong and Vos (1994) we also made a comparison of the financial linkages in 1990 and 1985. The empirical analysis revealed slightly higher positive biases both for direct investment and for portfolio and other investment within the Western Hemisphere, somewhat decreased biases in Japanese investment in other Asian-Pacific countries, but no substantial changes within Western Europe (except for some shifts between countries). From the analysis we concluded that – in general – (i) within the three main regions the positive biases are less pronounced than the trade linkages; (ii) the financial linkages between Japan and Asia-Pacific and within Western Europe weakened between 1985 and 1990; and (iii) these linkages became stronger within the Western Hemisphere. Apparently, there is no generalized trend towards globalization.

These results confirm the existence of fairly strong regional patterns of capital movements. This holds as much for DFI as for other, more liquid forms of capital movements. These patterns prevail despite the fact that capital is free to move in most parts of the world. As it appears, there is no fully integrated global capital market place, and numerous capital market imperfections and location-specific decision factors are likely behind this (see e.g. Vos 1994). However, the descriptive parameters derived from the WAM do not permit the testing of any particular capital market theory hypotheses. The β-coefficients can only provide a first indication of the degree of capital market integration and of the prevailing regional patterns of capital movements based on a consistent data set.

VI. Linkages between Trade and Finance

Do trade and investment follow the same regional patterns? The link between trade relationships and DFI relationships can be measured by a δ-coefficient (see Section III). The results in Table 4 reveal that in the Western Hemisphere the coefficients are near unity, except in the case of the economic ties between Canada and Latin America, where Canadian DFI is much stronger biased towards Latin America than Canadian merchandise exports. Other regions show a less clear picture. The only more or less general finding is that the concentration of trade is stronger than that of DFI within most regional blocs; the δ-coefficients are generally smaller than 1 within these blocs, while they are larger than 1 for many observations for the DFI-trade links with other countries and regions (that is, for the off-block diagonal elements in both panels of Table 4). In the Western Hemisphere, the DFI relationships between the USA and Canada are weaker than their trade relationships. Japan has both strong trade and DFI ties with China, the Middle East and Southeast Asia, but the trade (export) linkages are stronger, hence the small δ. In contrast, Latin America is more important to Japan as an investment haven than as an export market.

The finding that the regional concentration of DFI is lower than trade, could suggest that international production, more so than trade, is the preferred means of globalization. Liberalization of DFI flows, lower information costs, and the like, could be factors explaining such a trend. However, the evidence is not strong enough to make such a conclusion. The findings in the previous section pointed at an important degree of regional concentration of DFI and no systematic trend at a reduction of regional biases. We are more inclined to conclude that trade and investment both show substantial degrees of regional concentration, but, clearly they do not appear to be as congruent as they seem to have been in the 1930s (Eichengreen and Irwin 1995).

Table 4 – *Direct Foreign Investment-Trade Linkages 1985 and 1990 (Delta's based on values in 1985 dollars)*

	1	2	3	4	5	6	7	8	9	10	11	12	13	14	15	16	17	18	19
									a. Linkages for 1985										
Western Hemisphere																			
1 USA	–	0.8	1.1	1.1	2.9	13.2	1.7	0.0	1.6	2.9	2.9	0.6	2.7	6.8	3.2	119.9	27.8	0.0	3.4
2 Canada	0.8	–	0.8	0.8	1.1	41.1	10.9	0.0	3.6	3.6	1.9	0.0	3.5	4.3	6.1	0.0	37.3	0.7	0.4
3 Latin America	1.1	1.7	0.6	2.0	9.0	0.8	13.6	3.6	2.6	3.3	1.4	6.0	3.0	0.0	4.6	1.0	2.9	9.7	19.0
Asia-Pacific																			
4 Japan	0.3	0.1	0.1	–	0.0	0.0	0.1	0.2	0.0	1.0	0.5	0.6	0.7	0.8	0.4	0.5	1.7	1.2	0.3
5 Australia & New Zealand	1.4	3.7	17.1	1.1	1.6	0.0	3.1	0.0	1.9	1.2	1.7	1.3	5.2	2.4	1.5	0.0	0.0	0.0	0.0
6 Middle East	0.6	0.7	1.7	0.6	0.0	0.4	0.3	0.8	1.1	0.1	0.1	0.3	0.0	0.6	0.1	2.5	1.1	8.3	3.3
7 South Asia	0.2	0.2	0.2	0.1	0.0	0.0	0.0	1.0	0.1	0.3	0.1	0.1	0.4	0.1	0.2	0.0	0.2	0.4	0.4
8 China	0.1	0.0	0.4	0.0	0.0	7.3	0.8	–	0.7	0.0	0.1	0.4	0.3	0.5	0.9	0.5	0.3	9.4	1.8
9 Southeast Asia	0.6	0.0	1.2	1.2	0.0	0.2	0.0	0.0	0.3	0.3	0.8	1.2	0.9	1.0	1.0	0.0	2.5	8.3	1.3
Western Europe																			
10 Germany	1.8	1.1	0.9	0.4	0.2	1.5	0.7	0.6	1.0	–	0.4	0.2	0.3	0.4	0.4	0.6	0.4	0.2	0.1
11 France	1.3	0.7	1.7	0.8	0.0	1.1	2.0	0.2	2.3	0.7	–	0.6	0.3	0.4	1.0	1.1	2.6	0.5	0.2
12 Italy	1.1	0.9	1.0	0.3	0.0	0.4	0.1	0.1	2.8	0.5	0.4	–	0.2	0.2	1.1	0.0	1.1	0.2	0.3
13 United Kingdom	2.8	4.5	5.8	1.3	4.1	9.5	1.6	0.1	2.8	0.6	1.0	0.7	–	0.5	1.0	4.0	3.0	8.1	1.2
14 Other EC	1.2	2.7	1.0	1.5	0.5	1.0	1.3	6.4	2.1	1.0	1.3	2.7	0.4	0.6	1.1	1.3	1.9	1.0	0.5
15 EFTA	3.5	2.0	2.0	0.4	0.0	4.1	1.4	7.2	2.0	0.7	1.6	2.4	0.4	0.7	0.2	0.4	0.4	2.4	1.0
Former CMEA																			
16 USSR	0.0	0.0	0.0	0.0	0.0	0.0	0.0	0.0	0.0	0.0	0.0	0.0	0.0	0.0	0.0	–	0.0	0.0	0.0
17 Other Eastern Europe	0.0	0.0	0.0	0.0	0.0	0.0	0.0	0.0	0.0	0.0	0.0	0.0	0.0	0.0	0.0	0.0	0.0	0.0	0.0
Africa																			
18 North Africa	0.9	0.2	0.5	0.3	0.0	0.4	0.3	1.2	0.8	0.8	0.1	0.2	0.3	0.4	0.6	0.5	0.2	1.2	0.6
19 Sub-Saharan Africa	1.0	0.6	1.3	0.9	0.0	1.1	1.0	25.3	1.1	1.0	0.6	0.5	1.3	0.5	0.7	1.4	4.1	6.5	0.2

(Table continued on next page)

(Table 4 – continued)

	1	2	3	4	5	6	7	8	9	10	11	12	13	14	15	16	17	18	19
	b. *Linkages for 1990*																		
Western Hemisphere																			
1 USA	–	0.7	1.1	1.5	2.0	3.4	2.8	1.9	0.7	3.1	3.1	0.4	3.8	8.2	3.0	0.0	9.5	0.1	0.0
2 Canada	0.9	–	0.6	0.6	0.8	8.0	4.9	0.0	3.7	3.6	4.0	0.5	2.2	5.5	3.5	0.0	12.3	1.4	0.3
3 Latin America	1.0	4.8	0.4	1.7	5.5	–	6.8	4.4	4.0	2.6	1.2	1.4	2.4	0.0	8.6	0.0	7.0	9.2	–
Asia-Pacific																			
4 Japan	0.3	0.2	0.1	–	0.0	0.0	0.1	0.0	0.0	0.6	0.1	0.5	0.3	0.6	0.2	0.0	0.6	0.7	0.3
5 Australia & New Zealand	1.4	4.5	11.5	1.8	1.9	0.0	0.0	0.0	2.7	1.3	1.6	0.6	4.4	5.1	1.6	0.0	0.0	0.0	0.0
6 Middle East	0.4	0.2	1.4	0.3	0.0	0.9	0.2	1.3	1.0	0.1	0.2	0.1	0.0	0.8	0.3	0.0	2.1	2.5	10.9
7 South Asia	0.2	0.3	0.3	0.1	0.0	0.0	0.1	0.2	0.1	0.3	0.0	0.0	0.3	0.1	0.3	0.0	0.1	0.3	0.2
8 China	0.0	0.0	1.2	0.4	0.0	2.5	1.3	–	0.6	0.1	0.1	0.3	0.3	2.1	2.1	0.0	0.6	10.7	3.0
9 Southeast Asia	0.3	0.6	0.6	0.5	0.3	0.2	0.2	0.4	0.2	0.3	0.1	0.1	0.3	0.8	0.7	0.0	1.7	2.7	1.4
Western Europe																			
10 Germany	1.2	0.5	0.6	0.2	0.0	1.2	0.5	0.1	0.9	–	0.3	0.4	0.2	0.4	0.2	0.0	0.3	0.3	0.3
11 France	0.9	1.7	1.1	0.4	0.1	0.7	1.1	1.7	2.1	0.7	–	0.8	0.5	0.5	1.0	0.0	1.3	0.5	0.6
12 Italy	1.5	0.4	1.2	0.2	0.2	0.8	1.0	1.9	3.0	0.5	0.7	–	0.3	0.2	0.8	0.0	1.0	0.3	1.3
13 United Kingdom	2.6	4.9	3.8	1.9	6.5	3.2	1.4	13.1	6.0	1.0	0.9	2.0	–	0.7	1.6	0.0	7.4	9.7	9.1
14 Other EC	1.8	2.4	0.9	1.6	1.5	0.7	0.9	3.4	2.8	1.2	1.7	1.7	0.6	0.7	0.8	0.0	1.6	1.0	0.9
15 EFTA	2.0	1.4	1.4	0.3	0.0	2.7	1.5	2.7	2.7	0.7	1.2	3.1	0.4	0.9	0.5	0.0	0.7	2.3	2.2
Former CMEA																			
16 USSR	0.0	0.0	0.0	0.0	0.0	0.0	0.0	0.0	0.0	0.0	0.0	0.0	0.0	0.0	0.0	–	0.0	0.0	0.0
17 Other Eastern Europe	0.0	0.1	0.0	0.0	0.0	0.1	0.0	0.0	0.2	0.1	0.0	0.0	0.1	0.0	0.0	0.0	0.0	0.0	0.1
Africa																			
18 North Africa	0.5	0.3	1.6	0.6	0.0	1.4	0.7	3.3	3.2	0.5	0.1	0.1	0.3	0.4	1.0	0.0	0.9	0.7	3.4
19 Sub-Saharan Africa	0.5	0.5	1.9	0.2	0.0	1.8	0.4	1.5	1.2	0.3	0.5	0.1	0.6	0.3	0.8	0.0	2.6	3.0	0.2

VII. Some Conclusions

The analysis of the patterns of trade and finance based on the reconciled WAMs for 1985 and 1990 suggest that: (a) strong regionalized patterns of trade and investment exist; (b) the regional concentration of commodity trade seems to have weakened somewhat during the 1980s; (c) DFI and other capital flows both show a fair degree of regional concentration, suggesting that the WAM does not provide evidence to support a hypothesis of the existence of a highly integrated global capital market; and (d) there is no particular strong congruence between the relative degree of regional concentration of trade and DFI.

These are the findings from the application of a consistent global accounting framework, the WAM, which reconciles inter-country linkages of trade and finance. The WAM can provide the basic data base for global models. In this paper, however, we have merely tried to show how the WAM can be used as a tool for a descriptive analysis of global linkages. Safeguarding for possible shortcomings regarding possible sensitivity of the results to the choice of deflators and the omission of exchange rate shifts, the exploratory data analysis points at important segmentation and regionalization in the pattern of trade and finance. The subsequent step would be to use these findings in the specification of behavioural models of commodity and financial markets. This was not the aim of this paper. Hopefully, what it has made clear, however, is the relevance of the WAM as a tool for consistent global accounting and identification of global linkages and, thereby, as the basis for the explicit modelling of these linkages.

Appendix

Methodology for Deflating the WAMs

The balanced WAMs give merchandise trade and financial flows (and financial stocks in satellite tables) measured in current prices. To study changes in the patterns of trade and finance over time, it is necessary to isolate the effects of changes in prices. Bilateral deflators, however, are not available. Neither available are deflators for different commodity groups for each of the years covered. One could use export price indices of country i to estimate trade (exports) of country i with any country j at constant prices. By deflating the values in each cell of a row of the trade matrix by a single export price index, it is implicitly assumed that the composition of imports in terms of commodities is the same for each importing trading partner *j* of country *i*.[18]

It is less clear what would be appropriate deflators for international financial variables (see, e.g., FitzGerald and Vos 1991). The choice of a particular deflator depends on the purpose of the analysis. For example, if the import capacity of countries is considered, import price deflators are probably the most appropriate ones, whereas a study of portfolio decisions could make use of deflators of domestic investment. If creditworthiness is the focus of the analysis, a possible deflator could simply be the export price of country (group) *i*. In this case, values in the rows of the matrix in constant prices can be interpreted as the liabilities of a country vis-à-vis its trading partners, measured in terms of real exports required for repayment of the debts. Another possibility would be to deflate external financial claims on the basis of derived import price indices. In this case, we would interpret the constant price values as a future claim on commodities (real imports). Clearly, this is only valid if current price changes form the basis for price expectations. A further complication is caused by the fact that all transactions of the WAM are valued in dollar terms. This would require not only to adjust for price changes, but also for exchange rate changes. However, the existing data sources used for the WAM only specify for very few entries the currency composition of trade and finance. Hence, it is virtually impossible to make corrections for exchange rate changes. This is a shortcoming of the current analysis and is a subject for future research.[19] In the exercises carried out in the text, it is not the purpose to claim that the deflators that are used are definitely the best ones that can be chosen, but rather to illustrate what can be done with the WAM data if a particular deflator is used.

Merchandise trade in 1990 in current prices has been deflated on the basis of export price indices derived from the World Tables 1992 (World Bank 1992). For country groups in the WAM weighted aver-

---

18 This assumption is to be preferred to the assumption that the commodity composition is the same for each exporting country *i* to a country *j*, which would be implicit in the use of import price indices to deflate columns of the trade matrix.

19 Note that since the value of trade is expressed in US dollars, deflating trade values by indices based on export prices in US dollars accounts for both changes in export prices (in local currency) and exchange rate changes. Of course, changes in export prices and changes in exchange rates are interrelated, because prices of commodities may be formed at world markets and quoted in US dollars. Because in the current exercise only one export price deflator is used for each (group of) country's exports, the bilateral exchange rate changes may not be fully accounted for.

age export price indices have been calculated on the basis of World Tables 1992. The export price indices for the former USSR have been taken from the DEC Analytical Database (Riordan 1991).

Implicit import price deflators for year $t (d_{pmjt})$ can be calculated from trade matrices in current and in constant prices as follows:

$$d_{p_{mjt}} \equiv \frac{M_{jt}}{M^*_{jt}} \equiv \frac{\sum_i p_{x_{ijt}} x_{ijt}}{\sum_i p_{x_{ijt-n}} x_{ijt}} = \frac{\sum_i X_{ijt}}{\sum_i \left(\frac{p_{x_{it-n}}}{p_{x_{it}}} \right) X_{ijt}}, \tag{5}$$

where:

M_{jt} = value of imports of country j
M^*_{jt} = value of imports of country j expressed in period $t-n$ prices on the basis of relevant export price deflators of its trade partners
X_{ijt} = value of exports from country i to country j
x_{ijt} = volume of exports from country i to country j
$p_{x_{ijt}}$ = price indices of exports from country i to country j.

Under these assumptions, it can be deduced that the balancing items of the constant price WAMs are terms-of-trade changes (see FitzGerald and Vos 1991).

References

Bryant, R. (1987). *International Financial Intermediation*. Washington, D.C.: The Brookings Institution.

De Melo, J., and A. Panagariya (1993). *New Dimensions in Regional Integration*. Cambridge: Cambridge University Press.

Dooley, M., J. A. Frankel, and D. Mathieson (1987). International Capital Mobility: What Do Investment-Savings Correlations Tell Us? *IMF Staff Papers*, Vol. 34, pp. 503–530.

Eichengreen, B., and D. Irwin (1995). Trade Blocs, Currency Blocs and the Reorientation of World Trade in the 1930s. *Journal of International Economics*, Vol. 38, pp. 1–24.

Feldstein, M. (1983). Domestic Saving and International Capital Movements in the Long Run and the Short Run. *European Economic Review*, Vol. 21, pp. 129–151.

Feldstein, M., and C. Horioka (1980). Domestic Saving and International Capital Flows. *Economic Journal*, Vol. 90, pp. 314–329.

FitzGerald, E. V. K., and R. Vos (1991). Deflating the WAM. Some Preliminary Notes. Institute of Social Studies. The Hague, April 1991 (Mimeo).

FitzGerald, E. V. K., and J. Luttik (1991). A Note on the Measurement of Trade and Financial Linkages in the WAM. Working Paper – Sub-Series on Money, Finance and Development – No. 40. Institute of Social Studies, The Hague.

Frankel, J. A. (1992). International Capital Mobility: A Review. *American Economic Review*, Vol. 82, pp. 197–202.

Harberger, A. (1980). Vignettes on the World Capital Market. *American Economic Review, Papers and Proceedings*, Vol. 70, pp. 331–337.

IMF (1987). *Report on the World Current Account Discrepancy*. Washington, D.C.: International Monetary Fund.

IMF (1992). *Report on the Measurement of International Capital Flows*. Washington, D.C.: International Monetary Fund.

Jong, N. de, and R. Vos (1994). Patterns of International Finance Between Major Trading and Investment Partners: A World Accounting Approach. Working Paper Series on Money, Finance and Development No. 56. Institute of Social Studies, The Hague.

Jong, N. de, R. Vos, T. Jellema, and H. Zebregs (1993a). Trade and Financial Flows in a World Accounting Framework – Balanced WAMs for 1985–88. Paper prepared for UN-DESIPA and Project LINK. Institute of Social Studies and GDUI, The Hague, June 1993.

—, Jong, N. de, R. Vos, T. Jellema, and H. Zebregs (1993b). Trade and Financial Flows in a World Accounting Framework – Balanced WAMs for 1989–90. Paper prepared for UN-DESIPA and Project LINK. Institute of Social Studies and GDUI, The Hague, October 1993.

Linnemann, H. (1966). *An Econometric Study of International Trade Flows*. Amsterdam: North-Holland.

Luttik, J. (1992). *Trade and Finance in a World Accounting Matrix*. PhD Dissertation, University of Amsterdam.

Montiel, P. J. (1994). Capital Mobility in Developing Countries: Some Measurement Issues and Empirical Estimates. *The World Bank Economic Review*, Vol. 8, pp. 311–350.

Penati, A., and M. Dooley (1984). Current Account Imbalances and Capital Formation in Industrial Countries, 1949–1981. *IMF Staff Papers*, Vol. 31, pp. 1–24.

Riordan, E. J. (1991). DEC Analytical Database. Diskette from the World Bank, International Economics Department/Analysis and Prospects Division, Washington, D.C.

Sachs, J. D. (1981). The Current Account and Macroeconomic Adjustment in the 1970s. *Brookings Papers on Economic Activity*, No. 1, pp. 201–268.

UNCTAD (1993). *Explaining and Forecasting Regional Flows of Foreign Direct Investment*. United Nations Conference on Trade and Development, Programme on Transnational Corporations, New York.

Vos, R. (1988). Savings, Investment and Foreign Capital Flows: Have World Capital Markets Become More Integrated? *Journal of Development Studies*, Vol. 24, pp. 310–334.

—, (1989). Accounting for the World Economy. *The Review of Income and Wealth*, Vol. 35, pp. 389–408.

—, (1994). *Debt and Adjustment in the World Economy. Structural Asymmetries in North-South Interactions*. London and New York: Macmillan and St. Martin's Press.

Vos, R. (1995). External Sector Transactions: Toward a World Accounting Matrix. In J. W. Kendrick (ed.), *The New System of National Accounts*. Dordrecht: Kluwer Academic Publishers (forthcoming).

Vos, R., and N. de Jong (1995). Trade and Financial Flows in a World Accounting Framework: A Balanced WAM for 1990. *The Review of Income and Wealth*, Vol. 41, pp. 139–159.

World Bank (1992). World Tables 1992 Update. Diskette. Washington, D.C.

—, World Bank (1993). *Global Economic Prospects and the Developing Countries 1993*. Washington, D.C.

* * *

Abstract: Regional Blocs or Global Markets? A World Accounting Approach to Analyze Trade and Financial Linkages. – Do we live in a world of globalized capital and commodity markets or do regional networks dominate trade and financial linkages between economies? This paper addresses the question, using an integrated and consistent data system of trade and financial flows, called the World Accounting Matrix (WAM). This framework overcomes many of the data discrepancies and shortcomings in official statistics sources. Simple descriptive parameters are derived from the WAM to define the degree of trade and financial linkages between countries and regions. It is found that regional ties continue to be a predominant feature of the structure of the world economy. JEL No. F02, F15, F36

[9]

ENTREPRENEURSHIP & REGIONAL DEVELOPMENT, 14 (2002), 117–134

National differences in entrepreneurial networking

SARAH DRAKOPOULOU DODD and ELENI PATRA
The American College of Greece, Gravias Street, Aghia Paraskevi, Athens, Greece; e-mail: sarahdrakopouloudodd@yahoo.co.uk

The paper reports findings of a study into the personal contact networks of Greek entrepreneurs and compares these to results already published for other countries (Canada, Japan, Italy, Northern Ireland, Sweden, the UK, and the USA). Findings show that generic behaviour across borders cannot be assumed, although similarities exist in the under-representation of women as network members, the average age of network contacts, duration of relationships, and average monthly meetings. A clear example has also been provided of a culture where business networks are very deeply embedded in social structures, and where little or no evidence of an instrumentalist neo-classical model can be found. From a theoretical perspective, adaptation of Hofstede's four-dimensional model provides a generally robust interpretive framework for the results.

Keywords: entrepreneurship; culture; networks; international; Greece.

1. Introduction

The subject of networking has long been the subject of considerable interest to the disciplines of organizational behaviour and management studies, particularly since Granovetter's observation that 'economic action is embedded in ongoing networks of personal relationships rather than carried out by autonomous actors' (Granovetter 1973, Gatley *et al.* 1996: 78). Indeed, some writers have maintained that networks or 'hybrid organisational forms' offer an alternative structure for the allocation of resources to compete with the dominant economic models of markets and formal organization (see, for example, Powell 1987, 1990).

Entrepreneurship, in particular, has embraced networking theory as a mechanism for exploring the creation and development of new ventures.[1] Entrepreneurial networks can be defined as the sum total of relationships in which an entrepreneur participates, and which provide an important resource for his, or her, activities. These relationships may be articulated through the mechanism of membership in formal organizations, through the links an entrepreneur develops with suppliers, distributors and customers, or through the utilization of social contacts, including acquaintances, friends, family and kin. Entrepreneurial networks have been shown to act as providers of psychological and practical support (Johannisson 1996, 1997), of access to opportunities (Burt 1992, Hills *et al.* 1997), and of a host of other resources, including finance and information (Ostgaard and Birley 1994). Indeed, it is difficult to see how venture creation is possible without access to an effective set of network relationships (see, especially, Szarka 1990).

Curran and colleagues have argued that 'networks are best seen as primarily cultural phenomena, that is as sets of meanings, norms and expectations usually linked with behavioural correlates of various kinds' (Mitchell 1973, Curran *et al.* 1993: 77).

Entrepreneurship and Regional Development ISSN 0898–5626 print/ISSN 1464–5114 online © 2002 Taylor & Francis Ltd
http://www.tandf.co.uk/journals
DOI: 10.1080/08985620110111304

Cultural variations contingent upon entrepreneurs can therefore be posited to result in networks of quite differing characters. Cultural differences can be sharply perceived at the national level, with most nation states exhibiting (at least some) unique socio-cultural structures and norms (Hofstede 1980, 1983, 1991: 10). The level of the national society, then, may be an appropriate one at which to examine how culturally determined and diverse entrepreneurial networks are, while not precluding the impact which other levels of mental-programming[2] may have on networking activity. Although the network developed by each entrepreneur is *de facto* unique to that individual, it is reasonable to hypothesize that 'proprietors in different countries may exhibit different networking styles' (Birley *et al.* 1991: 61).

2. International differences in entrepreneurial networks – hypotheses

Recent years have seen a debate in the literature between those who argue that entrepreneurship is essentially universal, or generic, and those who emphasize the importance of international cultural divergence. The universalists argue that entrepreneurs have more in common with their international counterparts than with non-entrepreneurs from their own cultures (McGrath and MacMillan 1992, McGrath *et al.* 1992, Baum *et al.* 1993).

The second group of scholars maintain that national differences, alongside other cultural variables, impact significantly upon the level and nature of entrepreneurship (Shane *et al.* 1991, Shane 1992, Johannisson and Monsted 1997, Dana 1995, Thomas and Mueller 2000). Both sides of the divide have marshalled empirical and theoretical arguments to cogently support their position. Thomas and Mueller (2000) suggest that the universalists hold a position that implicitly imposes an Austrian-American hegemony upon our understanding of entrepreneurship, being based upon notions of achievement (McClelland 1961) work-ethic (Weber 1930), and the economic significance of creative destruction (Schumpeter 1934). A resolution to this dilemma may be emerging through new developments in cognitive processes, which are increasingly suggesting that while some cognitive scripts may be broadly generic across cultures, the values that shape and give rise to those scripts nonetheless vary considerably (Busenitz and Lau 1996, Mitchell *et al.* 2000). This study contributes to the above debate, by examining the extent and nature of international differences in entrepreneurial networking. The greater the differences, the more support is provided for the contextualist position, whereas broadly generic findings would add weight to the universalist position. Empirical work carried out to date comparing networking behaviour in different countries has, in fact, provided evidence of some international similarities, as well as some national-level characteristics.

Aldrich *et al.* (1989) examined the differences and similarities between samples of entrepreneurs from the USA (North Carolina Research Triangle) and Italy (Milan). Matched studies were carried out in Sweden (Johannisson and Nilsson 1989) and Northern Ireland (Birley *et al.* 1991). Aldrich and Sakano (1995) then utilized an adapted version of the earlier questionnaire to compare Japanese and US entrepreneurs, adding data drawn from the Italian, Irish and Swedish studies. Finally, Staber and Aldrich (1995) present data comparing the US sample with entrepreneurs from Atlantic Canada. It should be noted that differences within the samples selected (with some studies focusing on young entrepreneurs, some on women, some on urban and some on rural groups) limit the confidence that we can place on these results. Equally, a range of sample construction and questionnaire administration techniques were utilized, which restricts conclusions based on direct comparisons to indications of overall trends. Nonetheless, as an initial foray into national differences, the material has merit, and considerable interest. Staber and Aldrich (1995: 443) find broad similarities exhibited across these international samples, suggesting that 'At least some aspects of business networking are generic, and that owners approach some tasks in similar ways in different environments.'

Staber and Aldrich (1995) paint a picture of broad homogeneity, in some areas, periodically interrupted by evidence of national divergence. For example, women are not well represented in the entrepreneurial networks of any nation studied. The time expended on maintaining and developing contacts was found to be similar internationally (except for Italy and Japan). The proportion of family, friends and business ties were very similar in all samples (except for Canada). Network density is a measure of the interconnectedness of network members. The studies reviewed here measure the percentage of strangers in the network to assess network density. Specifically, respondents were asked to review which of their network contacts (alters) also knew each other. Density, reported as proportion of alters[3] who did not know each other, was almost identical for all nations studied (40–45%). The network contacts were, on average, in their early forties, for all countries except Japan, where an older group of entrepreneurs was studied. Relationships with these strong-tie contacts had endured, on average, from 10–12 years for all country samples except Northern Ireland (NI; 8 years) and Japan (14 years).

However, given the socially-embedded nature of networking activities, differences between cultures could be anticipated, and, indeed, plenty are to be found within the studies, as Birley *et al.* (1991) emphasized. For example, US entrepreneurs had larger personal contact networks than other countries (9.5 members, on average), although they did not meet with them very often (10 times per month), and were the most likely to include business ties within their networks. Japanese entrepreneurs spent the least time of all developing and maintaining their networks (7.9 hours a week), and were, overall, the least alike to the other nations studied, as might well have been hypothesized. Even Aldrich and Sakano (1995: 43) conclude that 'Japanese networks are a more closely tied, relatively circumscribed systems than networks in other nations'.

In summary, the results from this series of linked (although not methodologically identical) studies indicate some homogeneity, suggesting a degree of generic universal entrepreneurial behaviour, and some heterogeneity, highlighting the importance of cultural differences. Why might this be the case, and how can the issue be clarified?

Many of the countries studied (the USA, NI, Sweden, Canada, especially, and to a lesser degree Northern Italy) have a fairly high degree of cultural commonality. Without minimizing the relevance of their differences, they are all developed Western democracies, with dominant Anglo-Saxon/Nordic Protestant majorities, high levels of education, to name but a few shared variables. It is possible that these cultural similarities have impacted upon entrepreneurial networking so as to make some differences too subtle to be detected by the methodology utilized in the studies. A comparison with a culturally independent country could thus be anticipated to throw into sharper relief differences in entrepreneurial networking, and thereby to clarify whether universalism or contextualism might better explain this entrepreneurial phenomenon. Greece offers just such a contrast to the countries in the study, having, for example, far higher scores for Hofstede's power-distance, uncer-

Table 1. Hofstede's 4 Dimensions.

	Power distance	*Uncertainty avoidance*	*Individualism*	*Masculinity*
Canada	39	48	80	52
Greece	60	112	35	57
Italy	50	75	76	70
Japan	54	92	46	95
Sweden	31	29	71	5
USA	40	46	91	62
UK	35	35	89	66

Adapted from Hofstede (1991)

tainty avoidance and collectivism than the remaining six nations (Hofstede 1980, 1983, 1991). The combination of these factors is likely to create a divergent, highly-contextualized style of entrepreneurial networking.

The main objective of the present work, then, is to test the extent and nature of possible divergences in entrepreneurial networking, given a group of extant studies that are claimed to show broadly generic behaviour. To operationalize this aim, hypotheses were developed from Hofstede's four-dimensional model, with regard to the likely nature of Greek entrepreneurial networking, as compared to that of the other nations for which data is available. Hofstede's model was adopted as our theoretical framework in part because of its widespread recognition, in particular as a framework for international investigations of entrepreneurship (McGrath *et al.* 1992, Shane 1992, Busenitz and Lau 1996, Mitchell *et al.* 2000, Thomas and Mueller 2000). It also recommended itself for the additional, more prosaic, reason that amongst the 53 countries and regions in Hofstede's field study are included the seven of special interest to ourselves (table 1). Since Greece does not diverge from the group for the masculinity dimension, and since this dimension has proved a less strong explanatory variable than the other three (Hostede and Bond 1988), no hypotheses will be drawn relating to masculinity. Each of the remaining three dimensions will now be taken in turn, and hypotheses relating to the likely nature of Greek entrepreneurial networks drawn from each.

2.1 Power distance

Power distance (PDI) is a cultural variable which expresses the acceptance a society exhibits for power inequalities within, among other things, organizations. Greece, Japan and Italy show a fairly high power distance score, in comparison to the low power distance scores of Canada, the USA, Sweden and the UK. Mitchell *et al.* (2000: 6–7) argue that:

> Power distance may influence venturing scripts by shaping an individual's perspective on the availability of opportunities to venture. For example, in high-power-distance countries, people in the lower classes may view venturing as something that only the elite do... who you know and their positions or status tend to count more than their capabilities. Thus, arrangements scripts are likely different than in low-power-distance countries.

Observing Greeks at work and play provided anecdotal evidence supporting this. Personal and professional problems are typically solved not by asking '*what shall we do'*, but rather '*who should we call?*' or '*do we **have** anyone?*'. This personalized problem-solving approach demands a large set of weak-tie acquaintances, typified by an atmosphere of muted caution.

Networks from countries with a high power distance are likely to exhibit the need to show deference to contacts, so that additional time may be required to pay the appropriate respects to network members, including time spent outside working hours in social activities. This in turn will probably restrict the feasible number of personal contacts within the immediate strong-tie network, while, paradoxically, increasing the need for a large set of weak-tie acquaintances ready to assist with personalized problem-solving in a wide range of areas. (Strong-ties, following Granovetter (1973), are defined as those with whom the entrepreneur interacts at least twice a week. Weak-ties are relationships that are enacted less than twice a week, but at least once a year.) It therefore seems reasonable to suppose that entrepreneurs in Greece will be able to manage only relatively small strong-tie networks. They can also be expected to expend a substantial amount of time maintaining and developing these network contacts, in contrast to entrepreneurs from countries with a lower power distance score. Aldrich *et al.* (1987) have demonstrated that a network of strong-ties, for their sample at least, was a better predictor of profitability than a mostly weak-tie network. Predominantly very strong-tie networks may, however, lead to a degree of sterility, and redundancy since friends and family are likely to hold common attitudes, beliefs, objectives, problem-solving techniques, and so forth, whatever their occupation (Burt 1992).

Hypothesis 1. Comparatively large amounts of time are spent on networking by Greek entrepreneurs.

Hypothesis 2. Greek entrepreneurs will report comparatively small, strong-tie personal networks.

2.2 *Uncertainty avoidance*

Uncertainty avoidance (UAI) measures the extent to which a society is comfortable with lack of formal rules, an open, questioning approach to new ideas and the future. Again, a grouping of Canada, the USA, UK, and especially Sweden, is found showing low scores for uncertainty avoidance. Italy, Japan, and especially Greece show high scores for this dimension. Indeed, Greece has the highest score of any of the 53 countries in Hofstede's study for this dimension.

Thomas and Mueller (2000: 5) have demonstrated that risk-taking propensity decreases as uncertainty avoidance increases. A very high level of uncertainty avoidance is likely to lead to networks that closely follow long established norms of social behaviour. This will govern whom a person may contact in given circumstances, how much help it is appropriate to ask for, what he or she should offer in return, and the time-scale needed for the network to provide the sought resources. This provides further support for the argument that Greek entrepreneurs can thus be expected to expend a considerable amount of time maintaining their existing, probably small, set of strong-tie contacts (Hypotheses 1 and 2), and are unlikely to change their immediate action set with ease.

In a society which has an affinity for regulation, state bureaucracy, and in particular legislation, may be highly developed. When entrepreneurs are required to spend a high percentage of their time dealing with state administration and securing licences, permits, and so on, the need for access to a large network of relevant weak-tie contacts to 'oil the machine' may also be prevalent. Time must also be spent on cultivating new, and potentially useful, acquaintances. For a country where high power distance and uncertainty avoidance combine, this is likely to be especially so. Although these weaker ties are unlikely to enter the small in-groups which comprise Greek entrepreneurs' main action sets, they are important in facilitating the entrepreneur's interaction with the external environment, and will require some social servicing. Equally, it is probable that one of the major functions of the entrepreneur's strong-tie alters will be to provide links into large networks of their own. These secondary networks, 'friends of friends' or, at least, 'acquaintances of friends', are likely to play a vital role in accessing information, propitious service, and 'favours', in a society such as Greece, characterized by high levels of uncertainty avoidance and power distance. A heterogenous and large set of weak-ties, and secondary ties, provide access to diverse information and opportunities, by bridging structural holes (Granovetter 1973, 1978, Burt 1992). The networking literature has placed substantial emphasis upon their overall importance, in strategic terms, to the entrepreneur.

It should be noted that UAI has been shown to have a poor explanatory effect for Asian countries, thus the Japanese data is not anticipated to fit well with the hypotheses generated from this dimension (Hofstede and Bond 1988). Overall, Hofstede's model fits less well for Asian cultures, and the Japanese data are thus less likely than that for other countries to fit the model.

Hypothesis 3. Greek entrepreneurs will report comparatively large secondary networks (the contacts of their own strong-tie alters).

2.3 *Individualism*

The individualistic-collectivist dimension measures the dependence of individuals upon the group. A collectivist society (*gemeinschaft*) is one in which people are integrated into in-groups, to which they are fiercely loyal, and which shelter and protect them throughout their lives. In-groups include those based on kin-ties, shared village or region of origin, political ties, caste groups, or a combination of these. Such a society is essentially relationship-based, with 'traditional' concepts such as trust and loyalty being valued, and a high level of interplay between private and business lives. In an individualistic society (*Gesellschaft*) more emphasis is placed upon contracts, meritocracy, and the task-based achievements of individuals in competition with each other.

According to Welford and Prescott (1996: 351)

> Great store is placed upon management values such as *entrepreneurship*, industry champions and individual effort. People are encouraged to operate alone, and often can only get on at work by usurping others and competing for jobs and recognition.

Greece and Japan show a very low score for individualism, which is in marked contrast to the high scores recorded for the USA, UK (in first and second place overall, respectively, for this dimension), Canada, Italy and Sweden (listed in descending order of score).

Mitchell *et al.* (2000: 7) have suggested that in collectivist cultures entrepreneurs may find it harder to identify individual decision-makers, may have reduced motive for, and role-models of, individual success, and may find it harder to gain access to collectively-held resources. Thomas and Mueller (2000: 5) have demonstrated that internal locus of control decreases as collectivism increases, although they note that this reduction in the belief that they can manipulate their environment does not *de facto* reduce 'their entrepreneurial propensity'.

In nations with a highly collectivist perspective, strong-tie networks are likely to be based extensively upon kinship and friendship ties, or, to use Hofstede's terminology, with members of their in-group. Probably, such networks also involve the spending of social time with business contacts, to bring the private and public aspects of their lives closer together. Network contacts may be difficult to terminate, given the close personal nature of relationships that develop in such a context, leading to a longer average lifespan for network relationships. In Greece, typical strong-tie networks are often composed of immediate family and close friends, the latter often becoming 'adopted' family through participation in marriage and baptism rituals. In order for 'contacts' to become friends, a lengthy courtship must take place, involving time spent in social settings. The wooing of business contacts, to solidify relationships, is known as 'public relations', and may even extend to shared holidays.

Collectivist societies also exhibit a heightened awareness of the possibility of losing and maintaining face, which in Greece, as Hofstede notes, is encapsulated in the word *philotimo*. The desire not to 'let the side down', not to bring shame upon the in-group, may make it difficult for entrepreneurs to reveal anxieties, weaknesses, and problems to any but a very close circle of immediate contacts. Further theoretical support is thus forthcoming for the hypothesis relating to small, tightly-knit strong-tie networks, with whom the entrepreneur will spend a great deal of time.

It is also likely that Greek entrepreneurs will develop networks in which the contacts are well-known to each other, drawing on family, friends, and colleagues extensively. This will be heightened by social interaction, in which personal contacts are brought together for entertainment, rather than professional, pursuits. Hansen has demonstrated that the *degree* of an entrepreneur's action set (the web of interactions between the networks' alters), also referred to sometimes as *network density*, has a positive effect upon venture growth. He argues that this is because high levels of density speed the transmission of information through a network (Hansen 1995: 15).

The difficulty in identifying decision-makers, and the need to bring social and business life close together, once again led to the conclusion that the small strong-tie circle will be complemented by a larger than usual weak-tie set of acquaintances, and large secondary networks. Greek entrepreneurs will probably also draw proportionally more of their personal contact network from in-groups, which will be illustrated by a higher number of family and friends in their networks, at the expense of business contacts. Given this, it is even more likely that these networks will be dense, that the entrepreneur's alters will also be well-known to each other. Few of the network members are likely to be strangers to each other, if the bulk of strong ties are based on kin or friendship bonds.

Also, this argument provides additional weight for the hypothesis that the strong-tie alter relationships, in a collectivist society such as Greece, will be of long duration, on average. Our relationships with family and friends are more likely to endure than those with business contacts. The benefits of long-lived relationships include a very high degree of mutual trust and support, and a thorough understanding of the personal and professional needs of other network members. The major disadvantage of such relationships is that they may inhibit the development of new ties, which fit better with the changing needs of the business.

Hypothesis 4. Greek entrepreneurs will report comparatively high proportions of family and friends in their entrepreneurial networks.

Hypothesis 5. Greek entrepreneurial networks will show a higher density, and a lower percentage of strangers.

Hypothesis 6. Greek entrepreneurs will report relatively long-lived relationships.

3. Method

So as to permit comparisons with earlier work, the questionnaire used in the Northern Irish study by Birley *et al.* (1991), which is in important respects that used for all the earlier studies, was utilized.

The questionnaire was translated into Greek, and a handful of additional questions added (concerning growth intentions and membership of formal networks). The questionnaire[4] gleans basic demographic information (entrepreneur's age, education, gender, type and age of business, etc.), before progressing to solicit number of network contacts, their age, occupation, and the length and nature of the relationship. Also requested was information about how many of these contacts were shared with employees, and about the frequency of meetings, network density, and hours per week spent developing new and existing contacts. (The variation used by Birley *et al.* (1991) was followed, separating contacts into customers and non-customers.) A question was added asking where the contacts took place, to attempt to unravel the social-professional issue. Answers to questions were solicited in formats susceptible to quantitative analysis, and most, as the questions outlined above indicate, sought a number as an answer (for example, of meetings per month, or hours expended). The use of this questionnaire permits international comparisons, although the number of other countries for which data is available on any given area varies from one to all seven.

The sample construction was the weakest part of the study, from a technical perspective. Without access to a large database of potential respondents, a convenience sample was generated by utilizing students from our entrepreneurship classes to identify and recruit entrepreneurs known to them. The students also undertook to administer the questionnaire in a structured interview setting. This approach was intended to allow data to be gathered in an atmosphere of pre-existent trust, encouraging honest and open responses from the entrepreneurs.[5] This unorthodox approach nevertheless generated a fairly large sample (149 entrepreneurs), although it resulted in a sample with somewhat older, better-established businesses than is the norm in Greece.[6]

Table 2 presents data on the seven country samples, covering age of the entrepreneurs, their gender, business age and business size by employee. Many of the differences across samples, for example the proportion of women, or age of the businesses, are a result of sample design in earlier studies skewed towards areas of special interests for the researchers involved.

Table 2. The samples.

Country	*Japan*	*Canada*	*Northern Ireland*	*USA*	*Italy*	*Sweden*	*Greece*
Sample size	142	119	244	264	59	206	149
Age of respondents (%)							
17–34 years	10	29	36	20	71	32	22
35–44 years	29	39	35	41	19	36	18
45–54 years	39	24	23	25	2	22	42
55+ years	22	8	6	13	8	9	17
Total	100	100	100	99	100	99	99
N	142	119	244	142	52	206	147
Mean age	47.8	41	39.2	43	34.6	39.8	45
Gender (%)							
Women	38	61	23	15	36	18	21
N	776	119	240	142	52	200	149
Business age (%)							
0–1.9 years	4	37	13	13	31	56	9
2–4.9 years	27	36	19	38	42	44	18
5+ years	68	27	68	49	27	0	73
Business Size (%)							
0–4 emp	21	75	75	44	46	71	46
5–9 emp	18	5–24 emp: 22	10	18	12	6	21
10–19 emp	21		5	13	17	3	13
20–49 emp	18	25–49 emp: 2	7	14	8	9	9
50+ emp	22	2	3	11	17	11	11
Total	100		100	100	100	100	100
N			244	142	52	206	142

4. Results and discussion

Hypothesis 1. Comparatively large amounts of time are spent on networking by Greek entrepreneurs.

Table 3 presents data relating to the approximate mean meetings per month with the named key personal contacts of the respondents. The Japanese figure is so low as to cause Aldrich and Sakano to worry whether the question has been correctly understood. All the other figures fall into a fairly tight group (from 10 to 16 meetings per month), and, although the Greek figure is the highest reported to date (an average of 17 meetings per month reported), it is not significantly higher than for Canada, Italy and Sweden.

Information on frequency of meetings needs supplementing with some measure of total time expended on networking activities. In the Greek and Northern Irish studies,

Table 3. Monthly discussions with key contacts.

	Japan	*Canada*	*Northern Ireland*	*USA*	*Italy*	*Sweden*	*Greece*
Mean contact per month (approx.)	3.5	16	11	10	15	15	17

Table 4. Average hours per week expended on network maintenance and development.

	Japan	*Northern Ireland*			*Greece*			*USA*	*Italy*
		Customers	*Others*	*Total*	*Customers*	*Others*	*Total*		
Existing contacts	4.3	10.4	6.0	16.4	15.7	8.9	24.6	5.8	12.0
New contacts	3.6	8.3	4.7	13	9.2	9.8	19.0	5.6	11.5
Total	7.9	18.7	10.7	29.4	24.9	18.7	43.6	11.4	23.5

Chi-square test, NI against Gr: $\chi^2 = 36.98$, $p < 0.0001$.

respondents were asked to estimate how many hours they spent a week in communication with each of four groups, new and existing customers, and new and existing non-customer contacts. The Japanese, American and Italian studies did not differentiate between customer and non-customer contacts. Statistically testable data is therefore available only for the Northern Irish sample, who expend many fewer hours per week, on average, in developing and maintaining their networks (table 4). The Greek sample report, on average, that some 25 h a week are devoted to network maintenance, and 19 h to network development. Almost 44 h a week are therefore estimated to be allocated to this task, or 6 h a day, 7 days a week! This finding indicates a dramatically different pattern of entrepreneurial networking in Greece, and the overall difference is statistically significant at the 0.0001 level.

So as to investigate the social-business interplay, Greek respondents were asked to name where communication with their alters took place. An average of two 'venues' per contact were reported, with 21.5% of discussions taking place over the telephone, 36.5% in business offices, and 43% in a social setting (the home of one of the parties, or over a drink, a coffee or a meal).

These data establish strong support for our initial hypothesis that Greek business life and social life are strongly intertwined. Spending an abundance of time with network contacts, many of whom are family and friends, away from the business setting, is a hallmark of Greek business communication.

Hypothesis 2. Greek entrepreneurs will report comparatively small, strong-tie personal networks.

Respondents were asked to report the number of people with whom they had discussed their business in the last 6 months, so as to generate an indication of the size of personal contact networks. Greek entrepreneurs report the smallest personal contact networks of all nations for which data is available (table 5). However, the average size of their networks is very close indeed to that reported by the Italian and Irish samples.

Table 5. Mean number of contacts reported in respondents' networks of personal contacts.

Country	*USA*	*Northern Ireland*	*Italy*	*Greece*
Mean	9.5	7.2	7.7	7

Table 6. Percentage of sample with more than 10 reported personal network members.

Country	*Sweden*	*Northern Ireland*	*Greece*
Percentage with >10 personal network members	28%	19%	19%
N	206	244	149
χ^2, Sw and NI against Gr	$\chi^2 = 10.84$ $p < 0.0001$	$\chi^2 = 0$ (no difference inferred)	

It is noteworthy that, in subsequent questions, some of our respondents were unable to name more than two or three people with whom they routinely discuss their business. These small circles, however, were utilized very extensively – with often more than 50 contacts taking place per month.

The nature of the Swedish data requires that, in order to compare network size for Sweden, Greece, and Northern Ireland, the percentage of the samples with more than 10 reported personal network members were analysed. Birley and colleagues note that the Northern Irish have significantly smaller personal networks (at the 0.05 level) than the Swedish entrepreneurs do (Birley *et al.* 1991: 64). The Greek sample reports identically with the Irish sample on this variable, both showing much lower propensity towards large networks than the Swedish (table 6, $p < 0.0001$). Indeed, 48% of the Greek sample claimed to have discussed their business with less than five people in the previous 6 months.

The overall picture is of small networks being reported for Italy, Ireland and Greece, and larger networks for Sweden and the USA. Some weak support is thus forthcoming for Hypothesis 2.

Hypothesis 3. Greek entrepreneurs will report comparatively large secondary networks.

It was hypothesized that small, strong-tie networks in Greece would be complemented by larger than normal secondary networks. The available data allows us to test this only with regard to the Swedish and Northern Irish samples, who, like the Greek sample, were asked to assess the size of the networks for each of (up to) five named strong-tie alters.

Greek entrepreneurs reported that they believed that some 56% of their five closest contacts had access to very big networks, with higher percentages (81% and 62%, respectively) being reported for Contacts 1 and 2, on average. These percentages are very much higher than those reported for Sweden, as table 7 illustrates, and the differences between these sample proportions, for each of the five named contacts, are highly statistically significant, for both Northern Ireland and Sweden. It does indeed appear that Greek entrepreneurs combine small, strong-tie circles, with much larger weak-tie networks, providing support for Hypothesis 3.

Hypothesis 4. Greek entrepreneurs will report comparatively high proportions of family and friends in their entrepreneurial networks.

Only the Northern Irish findings can be directly compared with those for the Greek sample, since for the other nations multiple responses were permitted, except for Canada, where the totals reported do not add up to 100%. Nonetheless, the results shown in table 8 indicate that the Greek sample does show markedly more kin

Table 7. Percentage of secondary networks perceived as very big.

	Personal network contact					
	1	*2*	*3*	*4*	*5*	*N*
Greece, %	81	62	53	40	44	659
Northern Ireland, %	31	21	21	15	15	785
Chi-square, NI against Gr, by contact, for contacts 1–5						
χ^2	255	112.02	64.54	40.88	54.38	
$p <$	0.0001	0.0001	0.0001	0.0001	0.0001	
Sweden, %	50	33	33	27	28	799
Chi-square, NI against Sw, by contact, for contacts 1–5						
χ^2	99.79	56.89	25.61	10.59	16.6	
$p <$	0.0001	0.0001	0.0001	0.001	0.0001	

Table 8. The nature of strong-ties.

	Japan	*Canada*	*Northern Ireland*	*USA*	*Italy*	*Sweden*	*Greece*
Family	13	18	13	14	24	23	**31**
Friends	45	45	32	50	28	32	**35**
Business ties	60	14	55	65	54	54	**34**
Other	4	N/a	0	6	2	22	N/a
Total	122	77	100	135	108	131	100
N	571	N/a	785	615	235	799	608

Directly comparable data only available for Northern Ireland.
χ^2 (Northern Ireland against Greece) = 17.972, $p > 0.0001$.

members than other nation-samples, and a lower percentage of primarily business contacts than other countries. The differences between Greece, and Northern Ireland, for proportions of family and business contacts, are significant at the 0.0001 level. Almost one-third of the members of Greek strong-tie networks were reported to be family. Two-thirds of ties were primarily social in nature. The Greek respondents also noted that 6% of their full-time employees, and 19% of their part-time employees, were relatives.

The very high dependence upon family and friends in the provision of business advice raises serious concerns about the usefulness of Greek entrepreneurial networks in functional terms. Are these strong-tie networks offering much to the entrepreneur besides very high levels of emotional support? In order to examine this issue in a little more detail, we compared the occupation of the Greek strong-tie contacts with those reported by the Northern Irish sample, who exhibit the lowest proportion of social ties in their network.

As table 9 shows, counter-intuitively, Greek entrepreneurs appear to have more appropriately structured networks, from the occupational perspective, than the Irish sample. The occupation of the two sets of alters is statistically significant, at the 0.0001 level. Importantly, a higher percentage of professionals is evident in the Greek sample. This group includes bankers, lawyers, accountants, but also marketing, production and quality control specialists, and technical experts. Many of these professionals are also, of course, members of the entrepreneur's family, or group of friends. Such

Table 9. Occupation of personal contact network members (percentages).

	Northern Ireland	*Greece*
Owner-Manager	4	39
Employed	67	25
Unemployed/Retired	2	3
Academic/Student	2	3
Professional	23	30
Small Firms' Agency	1	0
N	812	634

$\chi^2 = 841.6$, $p > 0.0001$.

professional specialists help to compensate for deficiencies in the entrepreneur's own managerial competence range. There are far fewer employed network members in the Greek study, and many more owner-managers, whose experience of business ownership should make them sound sources of advice, information and other resources.

The importance of socially-derived ties, therefore, does not appear to diminish the functional usefulness of the Greek networks, and almost certainly increases levels of trust. For the Greek sample, small heterogenous strong-tie networks also seem to be offset by the complementary large secondary networks.

Hypothesis 5. Greek entrepreneurial networks will show a higher density and a lower percentage of strangers.

Aldrich *et al.* (1989) have argued that the denser, or more inter-related, a network, the faster information and other resources can move through it. This is measured by asking entrepreneurs how many of his/her personal network contacts are also known to each other, and reporting this finding as a percentage of the total possible cross-relationships. However, this area has stubbornly resisted showing any significant transnational differences. For Sweden, the USA, Northern Ireland and Italy, no significant difference exists between the reported levels of network density (Birley *et al.* 1991: 68).

Table 10 demonstrates that Greek entrepreneurs have disrupted the established pattern by reporting a significantly lower level of strangers in their networks than all other nations studied to date. Given the proportion of kin and friends within the Greek networks, this is to be expected, although note that the Canadian networks are no more dense than other nations, in spite of their relatively low level of business

Table 10. Percentage of strangers.

	Japan	*Canada*	*Northern Ireland*	*USA*	*Italy*	*Sweden*	*Greece*
Percentage of strangers		42	40.6	42.6	45.4	42	24
Chi-square test performed for each country reported, against Greece							
χ^2	Data not available	Data not available	107.17	109.39	75.32	190.283	
$p >$			0.0001	0.0001	0.0001	0.0001	

Table 11. Duration of ties.

	Japan	*Canada*	*Northern Ireland*	*USA*	*Italy*	*Sweden*	*Greece*
Mean years known	13.9	10	8.1	10.6	11.9	11.6	15.8
Mean age of Entrepreneurs	47.8	41	39.2	43	34.6	39.8	45
Mean age of personal contacts	49.8	42	42.3	43.4	40.4	42.5	42.7

contacts. Here we have clear evidence that for some aspects of network composition and activity, national differences can override even previously well established generic task performance. Greek entrepreneurial networks are very tightly held together, with almost every member of the network knowing the others, in contrast to all other nations.

Hypothesis 6. Greek entrepreneurs will report relatively long-lived relationships.

Greek entrepreneurs have known their contacts for somewhat longer than the remainder of the sample, as would be anticipated given the high proportion of kin and friends within their networks (table 11). However, they are also, along with the Japanese, an older group, and it is likely that the established international trend of ties aging with the entrepreneur has been replicated here. Some limited support is thus provided for Hypothesis 6. (The nature of the data prevented the use of statistical tests, so all that can be claimed is the identification of a broad trend.)

With relation to average age of the personal contact network, note that the Greek sample is unique in reporting a younger mean age for personal contacts, than for the main sample of entrepreneurs. It is suggested that this reflects the tendency for discussion of business matters with the family's next generation, perhaps with a view to succession.[7]

5. Conclusions

In summary, a degree of success has been enjoyed in the testing of our six hypotheses, as table 12 illustrates. Greek entrepreneurs include many more family and friends in their strong-tie networks, which are also very tightly tied together by contacts between other network members. Although small in size, their strong-tie networks are perceived to give them substantial access to larger secondary networks than normal.

The business networks of Greek entrepreneurs are firmly embedded in their social existence, as their composition and the time expended on them indicates. Indeed, the excessive amount of time spent on network maintenance and development must surely carry considerable opportunity cost. The occupation of personal contact members, however, appears to be appropriate to the needs of the entrepreneurs. Benefits of such network activity, typical of collectivist societies, are likely to be concentrated upon 'resource leveraging . . . relying on extended associations for the acquisition and supply of the needed resources for the enterprise' (Tiessen 1997). Strong levels of support and trust will also be forthcoming, and their strong density, or degree, may well impact positively upon venture growth (Hansen 1995). The negative aspects of such networks are in their sterility, their failure to offer variety of thought, perspective and oppor-

Table 12. Summary of findings.

	Hypothesis	*Finding*
Hypothesis 1	Comparatively large amounts of time spent developing and maintaining networks in Greece.	Strongly supported
Hypothesis 2	Comparatively small Greek strong-tie personal networks.	Weakly supported
Hypothesis 3	Comparatively large Greek weak-tie personal networks.	Strongly supported
Hypothesis 4	A higher proportion of family and friends, and a smaller proportion of business ties, in Greek networks.	Strongly supported
Hypothesis 5	Greek strong-tie networks will be very dense, with a small proportion of strangers.	Strongly supported
Hypothesis 6	Greek strong-ties will be of relatively long duration.	Weakly supported

tunity. These are likely to be overcome by the large weak-tie sets which the Greek sample reported, providing them with access to a variety of different social and professional contexts. In sum, the results provide a picture of an effective mixture of dense, well-structured, socially-embedded, small strong-tie groups, balanced by larger than normal weak-tie sets for the Greek entrepreneurs studied.

Our study has demonstrated that not all national samples of entrepreneurs network in the same way, and that generic behaviour across borders cannot be assumed. This is true in spite of the persistent proximity of some nations studied to date in terms of the under-representation of women as network members, the mean age of network contacts, duration of relationships, and mean monthly meetings. The Greek study has clearly demonstrated that culture is significant in shaping the nature of entrepreneurial networks. The weight of evidence provided by the Greek data, and especially the tight fit with the hypotheses generated from Hofstede's work, provide considerable support for the contextualist approach to entrepreneurial activities, and suggest that the generic universalist theories are erroneous. National differences exist. Culture matters.

As has been argued elsewhere (Gibb 1999, Thomas and Mueller 2000, Drakopoulou Dodd and Anderson 2001), there are policy and research dangers inherent in the application of the unproven universalist position. Specifically, imported motivation or training programmes, based on assumptions about entrepreneurs derived from 'foreign' models, are unlikely to meet with success in 'contexts where the task and psychic environments may be vastly different' (Curran 2000, Curran and Blackburn 2000, Thomas and Mueller 2000: 2). A strong understanding of national (regional, ethnic, sectoral or gender) cultures will enable the avoidance of such dangers, and lead to the development of context-appropriate policies and practices, such as those described by Dana (1995) with relation to India, and Johannisson and Monsted (1997) for Scandinavia.

In research terms, findings from the USA and North-Western Europe cannot be grafted onto other national cultures without considerable prior empirical verification. It must never be assumed that what holds true for entrepreneurs in one part of the world can therefore, *de facto*, form a legitimate basis for studies elsewhere. Beyond national divergence, other cultural variables such as gender, class, race, industry norms, and religion can be expected – and have often been demonstrated – to impact upon the degree and nature of entrepreneurship in a given group. While the pursuit of a unified theory of entrepreneurship is understandable (see, for example, MacMillan and Katz 1992, Shane and Venkataraman 2000), it should not be permitted to force data, or model-building, into an inappropriately universalistic straitjacket (Steyaert 1997, Thomas and Mueller 2000).

The pronounced embeddedness of Greek entrepreneurs within their social context also mitigates against neo-classical instrumentalism as providing a coherent, holistic explanation of entrepreneurial functions. Hybrid structures, like networks, have been argued elsewhere to better explain modern economic transactions, as well as allowing theories of entrepreneurship to remove themselves from the rhetorical and political stranglehold of neo-classical enterprise culture models (Powell 1987, Gray 1998, Stanworth and Curran 1999: 328, Drakopoulou Dodd and Anderson 2001). Examining co-operation and alliance may offer us greater understanding than the concept of competition, for example. In particular, the implicit (and sometimes explicit) ideological halo around the supposed freedom and independence of the entrepreneur may be reduced.

National averages disguise the fact that large variance may exist within a sample. In order to increase our understanding of Greek entrepreneurial networks, future research will concentrate on examining differences within the sample, as well as adding qualitative data collection, in an attempt to more clearly understand the special conditions under which Greek entrepreneurs operate. Equally, a better understanding of the content of network exchanges is needed, to offset the overly structural approach adopted in this study. It is hoped that such insights will facilitate support agencies as they attempt to develop programmes suitable for Greek entrepreneurs.

Acknowledgements

Special thanks are due to Professor Sue Birley of Imperial College for generously trusting us with the questionnaire. We are also grateful to our students, for their enthusiastic assistance with field data collection, and to the participants of the Eighth Global Entrepreneurship Research Conference, for their comments on an earlier version of this paper. We would also like to thank Professor Bengt Johannisson, and two anonymous referees for their substantial advice and guidance.

Notes

1. Scandinavian scholars, in particular, have found the network metaphor useful in terms of its bridging function between social and economic dimensions of human conduct when analysing entrepreneurship, as Johannisson and Monsted's (1997) review amply illustrates.
2. Other relevant levels of mental programming include gender, race, regionality, and education.
3. In the networking literature, the person whose network is being studied, or discussed, is termed the 'ego'. They form the centre, or core, of the network. His, or her, personal contacts, are termed 'alters'.
4. The questionnaire is reported in detail in the earlier papers in the series, and has not escaped criticism, most notably from Hansen (1995).
5. A degree of cynicism and mistrust is attached to postal and telephone questionnaires, and one is likely to be suspected of being a tax agent!
6. The American College of Greece is a private non-profit institution, which tends to attract the sons and daughters of entrepreneurs from the middle classes.
7. A 1997 study of Belgian entrepreneurs found that those with the longest business experience tended to discuss business matters most with their relatives, and ascribed their finding to 'the succession issue. The

entrepreneurs sound out their relatives in order to know whether they are interested in the business; they may also try to prepare their children for entrepreneurship' (Donckels and Lambrecht 1997: 20).

References

Aldrich, H. and Sakano, T. 1995 Unbroken ties: how the personal networks of Japanese business owners compare to those in other nations, in Fruin, M (ed.), *Networks and Markets: Pacific Rim Investigations* (New York: Oxford University Press) pp. 17–45.

Aldrich, H., Rosen, B. and Woodward, B. 1987 The impact of social networks on business foundings and profit: a longitudinal study, in N. C. Churchill, J. A. Hornaday, B. A. Kirchoff, C. J. Krasner and K. H. Vesper (eds), *Frontiers of Entrepreneurship Research 1998* (Wellesley, MA: Babson College).

Aldrich, H., Reese, P., Dubini, P., Rosen, B. and Woodward, B. 1989 Women on the verge of a break-through: networking between entrepreneurs in the United States and Italy, *Entrepreneurship & Regional Development*, **1**: 339–356.

Baum, J., Olian, J., Erez, M., Schnell, E., Smith, K., Scully, J. and Smith, K. 1993 Nationality and work role interactions: a cultural contrast of Israeli and US entrepreneurs' versus managers' needs, *Journal of Business Venturing*, **8**: 499–512.

Birley, S., Cromie, S. and Myers, A. 1991 Entrepreneurial networks: their emergence in Ireland and overseas, *International Small Business Journal*, **9**(4): 56–73.

Burt, R. 1992 The social structure of competition, in Nitkin, N. and Eccles, R. (eds), *Networks and Organizational Structure, Form and Action* (Boston, MA: Harvard Business School Press).

Busenitz, L. and Lau, C. 1996 A cross-cultural cognitive model of new venture creation, *Entrepreneurship Theory and Practice*, **20**(4): 25–39.

Curran, J. 2000 What is small business policy in the UK for? Evaluation and assessing small business policies, *International Small Business Journal*, **00**: 36–50.

Curran, J. and Blackburn, R. A. 2000 Panacea or white elephant? A critical examination of the proposed new small business service and response to the DTI consultancy paper, *Regional Studies*, **34**(2): 181–206.

Curran, J., Jarvis, R., Blackburn, R. and Black, S. 1993 Small firms and networks: constructs, methodological strategies, and some findings, *International Small Business Journal*, **11**(2): 13–25.

Dana, L. P. 1995 Entrepreneurship in a remote sub-arctic community, *Entrepreneurship Theory and Practice*, **Fall**: 57–72.

Donckels, R. and Lambrecht, J. 1997 The network position of small businesses: an explanatory model, *Journal of Small Business Management*, **35**(2): 13–25.

Drakopoulou Dodd and Anderson 2001 Enterprise culture as economic development: paradox and paradigm, *The International Journal of Entrepreneurship and Innovation*, **2**(1): 13–25.

Ford, D. (ed.) 1990 *Understanding Business Markets. Interaction, Relationships, Networks* (London: Academic Press).

Gatley, S., Lessem, R. and Altman, Y. 1996 *Comparative Management, A Transcultural Odyssey* (London: McGraw-Hill).

Gibb, A. 1999 Creating an entrepreneurial culture in support of SMEs, *Small Enterprise Development*, **10**(4).

Granovetter, M. 1973 The strength of weak ties, *American Journal of Sociology*, **78**: 1360–1380.

Granovetter, M. 1985 Economic action and social structure: the problem of embeddedness, *American Journal of Sociology*, **91**: 481–510.

Gray, C. 1998 *Enterprise and Culture* (London: Routledge).

Hansen, E. 1995 Entrepreneurial networks and new organization growth, *Entrepreneurship Theory and Practice*, **19**(4): 7–17.

Hills, G.,. Lumpkin, G. and Singh, R. 1997 Opportunity recognition: perception and behaviors of entrepreneurs, in P. D. Roynolds, W. O. Bygrave, N. M. Carter, P. Davidsson, W. B. Gartner, C. M. Mason, P. P. McDougall (eds), *Frontiers of Entrepreneurship Research 1997* (Wellesley, MA: Babson College) pp. 168–182.

Hofstede, G. 1980 *Culture's Consequences: International Differences In Work Related Values* (Beverly Hills, CA: Sage).

Hofstede, G. 1983 National cultures in four dimensions: a research theory of cultural differences among nations, *International Studies of Management and Organisation*, **13**: 46–74.

Hofstede, G. 1991 *Cultures and Organisations* (London: McGraw-Hill).

Hofstede, G. and Bond, M. 1988 The Confucian connection: from cultural roots to economic growth, *Organizational Dynamics*, **16**(4): 4–21.

Johannisson, B. 1986 Network strategies: management technology for entrepreneurship and change, *International Small Business Journal*, **5**(1): 19–30

Johannisson, B. 1987 Beyond process and structure: social exchange networks, *International Studies of Management and Organization*, **17**: 3–23.

Johannisson, B. and Monsted, M. 1997 Contextualising entrepreneurial networking: the case of Scandinavia, *International Studies of Management and Organization*, **27**(3): 109–137.

Johannisson, B. and Nilsson, A 1989 Community entrepreneurs: networking for local development, *Entrepreneurship & Regional Development*, **1**: 3–19.
MacMillan, I. and Katz, J. 1992 Idiosyncratic milieus of entrepreneurial research: the need for comprehensive theories, *Journal of Business Venturing*, **7**: 1–8.
McGrath, R. and MacMillan, I. 1992 More like each other than anyone else? A cross-cultural study of entrepreneurial perceptions, *Journal of Business Venturing*, **7**: 419–429.
McGrath, R., MacMillan, I., Yang, E. and Tsai, W. 1992 Does culture endure or is it malleable? Issues for entrepreneurial economic development, *Journal of Business Venturing*, **7**.
McLelland, D. C. 1961 *The Achieving Society* (Princeton NJ: Van Nostrand).
Mitchell, J. 1973 Networks, norms and institutions, in Boissevain, J. and Mitchell, J. (eds), *Network Analysis: Studies in Human Interaction* (The Hague: Mouton) pp. 00–00.
Mitchell, R., Smith, B., Seawright, K. and Morse, E. 2000 Cross-cultural cognitions and the venture creation process, *Academy of Management Journal*, **43**(1): 974.
Ostgaard, T. and Birley, S. 1994 New venture growth and personal networks, *Journal of Business Research*, **36**: 37–50.
Powell, W. 1987 Hybrid organisational arrangements: new form or transitional development? *California Management Review*, **30**(1): 67–87.
Powell, W. 1990 Neither market nor hierarchy: network forms of organization, *Research in Organizational Behavior*, **12**: 295–336.
Schumpeter, J. 1934 *The Theory of Economic Development* (Cambridge, MA: Harvard Press).
Shane, S. 1992 Why do some countries invent more than others? *Journal of Business Venturing*, **7**: 29–46.
Shane, S. and Venkataraman, S. 2000 The promise of entrepreneurship as a field of research, *Academy of Management Review*, **25**(1): 217–235.
Shane, S., Kolvereid, L. and Westhead, P. 1991 An exploratory examination of the reasons leading to new firm formation across country and gender, *Journal of Business Venturing*, **1**: 129–140.
Staber, U. and Aldrich, H. 1995 Cross-national similarities in the personal networks of small business owners: a comparison of two regions in North America, *Canadian Journal of Sociology*, **20**: 441–465.
Stanworth, J. and Curran, C. 1999 Colas, burgers, shakes and shirkers: towards a sociological model of franchising in the market economy, *Journal of Business Venturing*, **14**: 323–344.
Steyaert, C. 1997 A qualitative methodology for process studies of entrepreneurship: creating local knowledge through stories, *International Journal of Management and Organization*, **27**(3): 13–34.
Szarka, J. 1990 Networking and small firms, *International Small Business Journal*, **8**(2): 10–22.
Thomas, A. and Mueller, S. 2000 A case for comparative entrepreneurship: assessing the relevance of culture, *Journal of International Business Studies*, **31**(2): 287–295.
Tiessen, J. H. 1997 Individualism, collectivism and entrepreneurship: a framework for international comparative research, *Journal of Business Venturing*, **12**: 367–384.
Weber, M. 1930 (translation; reprinted 1990) *The Protestant Ethic and The Spirit Of Capitalism* (Trans. Parsons, T.) (London: Allen Unwin).
Welford, R. and Prescott, K. 1996 *European Business* (London: Pitman).

[10]

Information exchange and the robustness of organizational networks

Peter Sheridan Dodds*†, Duncan J. Watts*‡§, and Charles F. Sabel¶

*Institute for Social and Economic Research and Policy, Columbia University, 420 W. 118th Street, New York, NY 10027; ‡Department of Sociology, Columbia University, 2960 Broadway, New York, NY 10027; §Santa Fe Institute; 1399 Hyde Park Road, Santa Fe, NM 87501; and ¶Columbia Law School, Columbia University, 435 W. 116th Street, New York, NY 10027

Communicated by Harrison C. White, Columbia University, New York, NY, July 24, 2003 (received for review March 15, 2003)

The dynamics of information exchange is an important but understudied aspect of collective communication, coordination, and problem solving in a wide range of distributed systems, both physical (e.g., the Internet) and social (e.g., business firms). In this paper, we introduce a model of organizational networks according to which links are added incrementally to a hierarchical backbone and test the resulting networks under variable conditions of information exchange. Our main result is the identification of a class of multiscale networks that reduce, over a wide range of environments, the likelihood that individual nodes will suffer congestion-related failure and that the network as a whole will disintegrate when failures do occur. We call this dual robustness property of multiscale networks "ultrarobustness." Furthermore, we find that multiscale networks attain most of their robustness with surprisingly few link additions, suggesting that ultrarobust organizational networks can be generated in an efficient and scalable manner. Our results are directly relevant to the relief of congestion in communication networks and also more broadly to activities, like distributed problem solving, that require individuals to exchange information in an unpredictable manner.

Information exchange is central to the performance of a wide range of networked systems, including infrastructures such as the Internet (1), airline, postal, and transportation networks, as well as peer-to-peer file sharing systems, communication networks, and organizations such as public bureaucracies (2, 3) and business firms (4, 5). Despite considerable recent exploration of the structure of real-world networks (6–8) and a long established organizational complexity literature in sociology (9–11), the dynamics of information exchange in networks has attracted limited attention (12, 13). In this paper, we introduce a model of what we call "organizational networks," networks whose purpose is to organize and coordinate the decentralized exchange of information. In focusing on information exchange, our general aim is to construct a framework for exploring organizational robustness with respect to a range of environmental stresses.

The topic of optimal organizational architecture has long been of concern to economists (4, 14–17), but their emphasis has been on efficiency rather than robustness. As a result, the economics literature on organizations has focused almost exclusively on multilevel hierarchies: acyclic, undirected branching networks that originate at a single root node and descend through a series of levels or ranks to their terminal leaf nodes. By connecting N nodes together with the minimum required number of $N - 1$ links and creating a chain of command that is only $L \propto \log N$ links in depth, hierarchies are almost as efficient as possible. Unlike hub-and-spoke networks (a special case of a hierarchy with a single subordinate level), multilevel hierarchies require each node to interact directly with, on average, only b other nodes, where $b \ll N$ and is generally called the "span of control." Hierarchies are therefore attractive, scalable architectures whenever individual capacity is bounded (e.g., managers in business firms) or else not easily augmented (e.g., terminals in airline networks). Numerous variations on this basic argument have been invoked to justify the optimality of hierarchical organizational networks for exerting control (2, 14, 18), performing decentralized computations (4), distributing processing load (16), making decisions (15), and accumulating knowledge (17).

However, a critical, and often unstated, assumption of this line of investigation is that the organization's task is decomposable into simpler subtasks, such that each subtask can be completed independently and therefore in parallel with others (19). Radner (4), for example, analyzes the case of summing a set of integers, a linearly associative task that is trivially decomposable. In contrast, most modern business firms and public bureaucracies face problems that are not only large and multifaceted but also ambiguous: objectives are specified approximately and typically change on the same time scale as production itself, often in light of knowledge gained through the very process of implementing a solution (9). As a result, problem solving is almost always a collective activity (20), embodied in strategies such as mutual monitoring (21, 22) and simultaneous design (23) in which initial designs or solutions are regularly adjusted on the basis of information-rich collaboration between individuals, teams, departments, and even different organizations.

Under these circumstances, the chief problem facing an organization is not efficiency, understood roughly as being maximized by minimizing the number of costly links needed to support a defined burden. Rather, the challenge is robustness: on the one hand, protecting individual nodes from being overtaxed by the direct and indirect effects of changing and unpredictable patterns of collaboration; and on the other hand, protecting the organization as a whole from disintegration in cases where individual failures occur regardless. More specifically, when task definitions are ambiguous, individual collaborators will often exchange information with other problem solvers (10), if only to ask after and obtain information about potential partners or to keep abreast of design changes relevant to their immediate task. In cases where the information is exchanged indirectly (e.g., via a superior), the relevant intermediaries incur an information processing burden. The burden imposed by any single coordinating message may be small, but high rates of message passing in combination with concentration of traffic will tend to overload key nodes. An analogous problem arises in other kinds of organizational networks, such as the Internet, airline networks, or the postal system, which must redistribute information, personnel, or materials while simultaneously minimizing the likelihood of overload. Organizational networks that minimize the probabilities of such failures exhibit what we call "congestion robustness."

In addition to resisting failure at the level of individual nodes, contemporary organizational networks must continue to function even when individual elements do fail. The Internet, for example, suffers little performance loss in the event that individual routers fail. Business firms can display remarkable resilience with respect to (seemingly) catastrophic breakdowns in their supply chains (20), involving loss of key component pro-

†To whom correspondence should be addressed. E-mail: peter.dodds@columbia.edu.

 www.pnas.org/cgi/doi/10.1073/pnas.1534702100

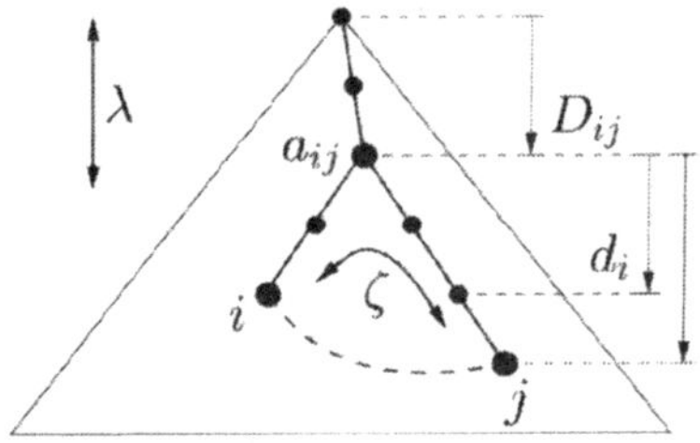

Fig. 1. Schematic of the network construction algorithm. Links to be added are chosen stochastically according to Eq. 1 (without replacement) to a hierarchical backbone with L levels and branching ratio b. Eq. 1 takes as its arguments the organizational distance x_{ij} between two nodes i and j, as well as the depth D_{ij} of their lowest common ancestor a_{ij}. Organizational distance is defined as $x_{ij} = (d_i^2 + d_j^2 - 2)^{1/2}$, where d_i and d_j are measured relative to a_{ij} (see text for details). The two parameters λ and ζ set characteristic lengths in D_{ij} and x_{ij}, respectively, beyond which links are unlikely to form, thus embodying the influence of rank and homophily on link formation within an organizational network. Because links are chosen without replacement, links that are initially unlikely to be chosen will eventually be selected. This means that although λ and ζ control the order in which links are added, they do not have a simple interpretation in the resulting networks formed by the addition of many links. The alternative of choosing links with replacement and taking only the set of unique links so chosen would mean that the number of links added would no longer be conserved.

ducers, equipment, personnel, and office space (24, 25). In contrast, under conditions of environmental uncertainty and catastrophe recovery, hierarchies are extremely prone to cascading breakdowns because the failure of nodes near the top of the hierarchy effectively severs large subnetworks from the main organization, thereby impairing global coordination. Organizations that reduce the adverse consequences of externally driven failures exhibit what we call "connectivity robustness." Finally, we call organizational networks that exhibit both congestion and connectivity robustness "ultrarobust."

Our approach to the design of organizational networks through the lens of information exchange under conditions of ambiguity follows naturally from a long line of work in organizational sociology in which issues such as the interaction between an organization and its environment (9–11), the role of uncertainty in necessitating communication (9, 10), and the importance of adaptability to innovation and crisis management (9, 24, 26) have frequently been emphasized. By operationalizing the performance of organizations in ambiguous environments in terms of robustness, we hope to extend the optimality approach of the economics literature on firms to the richer domain of organizational sociology.

Modeling Organizational Networks

Our model requires four components: (*i*) an algorithm for constructing organizational networks, (*ii*) a specification of the task environment from which the requirement for information exchange is derived, (*iii*) a precise description of information exchange in terms of an algorithm for passing messages, and (*iv*) a well defined way of measuring congestion and connectivity robustness.

Network Construction Algorithm. Our algorithm takes as its point of departure the simplest version of an organizational network: a pure hierarchy with branching ratio b and L levels. The number of nodes is therefore $N = (b^L - 1)/(b - 1)$, where the lth level possesses b^l nodes and $l = 0, \ldots, L - 1$. The algorithm proceeds by sequentially adding links, chosen stochastically, until a prescribed total of m have been added. The probability $P(i, j)$ that two nodes i and j will be connected depends on the depth D_{ij} of their lowest common ancestor a_{ij} in the backbone and also their own depths d_i and d_j, respectively, beneath a_{ij} (in Fig. 1, for example, $D_{ij} = 2$, $d_i = 2$, and $d_j = 3$). We choose links without replacement, and $P(i,j)$ is therefore always normalized over all remaining pairs of unconnected nodes. We treat links that are added in this manner differently from links that are part of the hierarchical backbone: backbone links define a node's coordinates in the network and also transmit information; added links only transmit information. Thus, the hierarchical backbone may be thought of as the formal organization (chain of command), whereas added links correspond to the informal organization, a common distinction in the sociological literature of organizations (9, 10, 26, 27).

We thus map the theoretical problem of how organizational networks should be structured into the question of what is the corresponding functional form of P. Furthermore, whatever form of P that is appropriate for one kind of organization in a given environment (e.g., an early 20th automobile manufacturing firm) may well be inappropriate elsewhere (e.g., an early 21st century software manufacturer). We therefore seek a class of functions that is sufficiently general to explore a wide range of alternative topologies, but not so general that the resulting space of networks cannot be explored systematically.

To restrict the possible form of P, we make the following assumptions that we claim are plausible for the case of organizational networks. (*i*) Because it is a probability, we require that P is nonnegative for all values of D_{ij}, d_i, and d_j. (*ii*) Because immediate subordinates and superiors in the underlying hierarchy ($d_i + d_j = 1$) are connected by default, P is effectively constrained to be non-zero for values of $d_i + d_j \geq 2$ (we disallow self-connections and duplicate links). (*iii*) We assume that individuals are identical aside from their relative position in the hierarchy; hence, P is symmetric with respect to d_i and d_j. (*iv*) All else being equal, we assume that individuals of the same rank are "closer" than individuals of different ranks; thus, for fixed $d_i + d_j$, distance is minimized when $d_i = d_j$. Incorporating assumptions *i–iii*, we define *organizational distance* x_{ij} between two nodes i and j to be $x_{ij} = (d_i^2 + d_j^2 - 2)^{1/2}$ (valid for $d_i + d_j \geq 2$). (*v*) We assume that P decreases monotonically with increasing x_{ij}, a familiar property of social networks known generically as homophily (28), or the tendency of "like to associate with like" (we note that together, assumptions *iv* and *v* effectively incorporate two kinds of homophily that can be roughly attributed to similarity in class and profession, respectively). (*vi*) P is also assumed to decrease monotonically with respect to increasing lowest common ancestor rank D_{ij}; that is, all other things being equal, nodes of higher rank are more likely to interact. (*vii*) Because both homophily (assumption *v*) and lowest common ancestor rank (assumption *vi*) effects will apply to varying extents across different organizations, we introduce two tunable parameters, λ and ζ, that can be interpreted as characteristic lengths in x_{ij} and D_{ij}, respectively, beyond which connections become unlikely.

Incorporating assumptions *i–vii*, we propose the following stochastic rule governing the formation of new interactions:

$$P(i, j) \propto e^{-D_{ij}/\lambda} e^{-x_{ij}/\zeta}. \quad [1]$$

We use Eq. 1 to choose (without replacement) the sequence of m links to be added to an initial hierarchical backbone, where different choices of λ and ζ will result in different network topologies for the same choice of b, L, and m (i.e., the same number of links added to the same backbone).

We immediately observe four stylized classes of organizational networks that arise for limiting values of (λ, ζ), as depicted in Fig. 2.

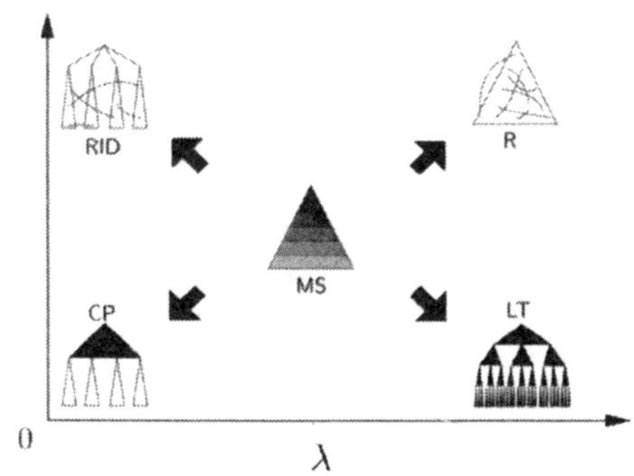

Fig. 2. Classes of networks realized in different regions of (λ, ζ)-space. Multiscale networks occupy a broad interior region of space, whereas random (R), random interdivisional (RID), local team (LT), and core-periphery (CP) networks arise when one or both parameters approach their limiting values. Technically, the upper limit for both λ and ζ is ∞, and these limits would typically be approximated by numbers sufficiently larger than the maximums of x_{ij} and D_{ij}. However, because λ and ζ only set the order in which links are likely to be chosen, and hence are nontrivially related to the resulting networks, these parameters effectively reach ∞ at values less than the maximums of x_{ij} and D_{ij}.

Random: For $(\lambda, \zeta) \to (\infty, \infty)$, links are allocated uniformly at random; that is, neither lowest common ancestor rank nor homophily has any influence on link selection.

Local team: For $(\lambda, \zeta) \to (\infty, 0)$, links are allocated exclusively between pairs of nodes that share the same immediate superior, regardless of their superior's rank. Hence, homophily is important to link selection, but lowest common ancestor rank is not. The result is that "teams" form at all levels of the hierarchy.

Random interdivisional: For $(\lambda, \zeta) \to (0, \infty)$, links are allocated exclusively between nodes whose lowest common ancestor is the single node at the top of the hierarchy. Links therefore only form between nodes in different "divisions" (the largest subunits) of the organization, but otherwise they are allocated randomly, meaning that lowest common ancestor rank is important but homophily is not.

Core-periphery: For $(\lambda, \zeta) \to (0, 0)$, links are added exclusively between subordinates of the top node alone. The resulting networks are characterized by a fully connected central core from which pure branching hierarchies extend. For non-zero, but small, values of λ and ζ (i.e., in the vicinity of the origin in Fig. 2), the core-periphery dichotomy continues to pertain, but the core extends beyond the top layer. Hence, both homophily and lowest common ancestor rank matter.

Multiscale: Finally, we identify a fifth, qualitatively distinct class of networks that arise in the central region of Fig. 2 [i.e., intermediate values of (λ, ζ)]. We call this class *multiscale networks* because, unlike the four classes of networks defined above, whose connectivity is dominated by a single scale [either local (team) or global (random) ties], these networks display connectivity at all scales simultaneously. Multiscale networks, however, do not display uniform density of links at all scales: link density decreases monotonically with depth, such that the top rank (the core) exhibits the highest density, thus distinguishing multiscale networks from earlier "small-world" network models (29) in which random links are distributed homogeneously. This difference is critical for the problem at hand because, in a wide variety of environments, the hierarchical nature of organizational networks tends to place the burden of information exchange disproportionately on higher ranks. Thus multiscale networks and core-periphery networks have much in common. But by exhibiting connectivity across all other ranks as well, multiscale networks also embody the salient features of local team and random networks, a combination that, as we show below yields desirable robustness properties.

Task Environment. We specify the organization's task environment in terms of the rate and distribution of messages to be exchanged between individual problem solvers in the course of completing some global task. Stable environments correspond to a low rate of information exchange μ (defined as the average number of messages initiated by each individual at each time step), whereas volatile environments are equivalent to high μ. In addition to volatility, the environment may also allow for varying task decomposability: tasks that are nearly decomposable correspond to a pattern of message passing that requires only individuals within the same team (i.e., nodes with the same immediate superior) to communicate; tasks that cannot be decomposed even approximately require constant communication between remote, as well as nearby, individuals. In practice, for each message initiated at a node s at rate μ, a corresponding target node t is selected by weighting all nodes at distance x from s with a factor $\exp\{-x/\xi\}$, normalizing appropriately, and then choosing t at random according to the resulting distribution. Thus, for $\xi = 0$ (local dependencies only), all messages are to be delivered to local targets, whereas for $\xi = \infty$ (global dependencies), t is chosen uniformly at random.

Information Exchange. Once initiated, a message is passed from source to target through a chain of intermediaries. Each node in the chain must process each message that it initiates or receives in the same time step by forwarding it to an immediate neighbor, choosing the neighbor who has the lowest common ancestor with the target node (in case of equally distant neighbors, one such neighbor is chosen at random). Thus each node i is assumed to have complete information regarding its own location in the hierarchy, as well as the locations of its neighbors. Each node also understands general information about targets beyond its immediate neighborhood, an assumption we call "pseudoglobal knowledge." If node i is an indirect superior of t in the hierarchy, then pseudoglobal knowledge implies that i knows in which of the subunits t belongs but not specifically where (in which case i could send the message directly); similarly, if t is not beneath i but subordinate to one of i's neighbors along an informal link, i knows to send the message "across" the hierarchy to that neighbor; if neither of these cases hold, then i must pass the message up the hierarchy to its immediate superior. Pseudoglobal knowledge therefore embodies an inherent tradeoff between quantity and quality of information: high ranking nodes tend to possess general information about more subordinates than nodes in lower ranks but have less specific information about any one subordinate.

Pseudoglobal knowledge can also be interpreted in terms of distributed problem solving, where the target's address, rather than being the location of an individual in an organization, can be thought of instead as a complete description of the solution required by a particular problem (by analogy, the call number of a book in a library characterizes the knowledge contained therein). Neither the knowledge itself nor its address, however, is initially available to the problem solver (the sender) who must therefore poll his or her contacts in the organization for a relevant recommendation. The closer a contact is to the eventual target, the more accurately he or she can direct the problem solver, and the fewer subsequent intermediaries are required to conclude the search (we do not consider the case where the relevant knowledge does not exist in the organization). The progress of a message therefore corresponds to a problem solver acquiring increasingly specific knowledge about the problem to be solved; a process that can only succeed with the cooperation of increasingly knowledgeable intermediaries.

Measures of Robustness. The property of ultrarobustness requires an organizational network to exhibit both congestion robustness (the capacity to protect individual nodes from congestion) and connectivity robustness (the capacity to remain connected even when individual failures do occur). To measure congestion robustness, we initiate an average of μ messages per node each time step over a total of T time steps, where messages are removed from the system on reaching their designated target. Assuming that each node i can process a maximum of R_i messages per time step without failure, then an organizational network will, on average, remain free of failures only if $R_i > r_i = \mu N \rho_i$ for all i, where r_i is the rate of messages to be processed by node i and *congestion centrality* ρ_i is the probability that any given message will be processed by i. Although congestion centrality is similar to other centrality measures in graph theory (30) and social network analysis (31), it is more appropriate to the problem of information exchange in that it depends on task decomposability (ξ) and the message passing algorithm as well as a node's position in the network. [For example, when message passing is sufficiently global (ξ is large), high-ranking nodes will be more central than low-ranking nodes, as would be the case for betweenness centrality (31). But when message passing is purely local ($\xi \rightarrow 0$), nodes at all ranks (other than the bottom rank) will be equally central.] Assuming that environmental volatility (μ) and individual capacities (R_i) are beyond the control of the organization, a robust architecture is one that reduces the congestion centrality, hence the likelihood of failure, of its constituent nodes. We therefore associate congestion robustness with the reduction of maximum congestion centrality ρ_{max} over the entire network (we have also considered $\langle \rho \rangle$, obtaining qualitatively similar results).

Even a network that is highly robust with respect to congestion related failures can suffer failures, such as sickness, accidents, sabotage, attack, and natural disasters, that are imposed on it from the outside (20, 24, 25). In accordance with previous work (32–34), we therefore define connectivity robustness in terms of the fractional size $C = S/(N - N_r)$ of the largest connected component (size S) remaining after the removal of N_r nodes. Because different removal strategies have previously been shown to yield dramatically different conclusions regarding the connectivity robustness of other classes of networks (32), we have examined a number of such strategies: preferential elimination of nodes by rank (top-down); elimination of nodes radiating out from a random start point (cascade); preferential elimination of highly connected nodes (hubs); and uniformly random elimination (random).

Results and Discussion

We now investigate the congestion and connectivity robustness of organizational networks as measured by ρ_{max} and C respectively, as a function of both environmental conditions (μ, ξ) and network topology (m, λ, ζ). Before commencing, we note that when $\mu = 0$ (i.e., a static environment) and in the absence of exogenous failures, all networks perform identically. Efficiency arguments similar to those outlined above therefore dictate that pure hierarchies ($m = 0$) will be superior to all other network topologies. Thus, in the trivial limit of an unchanging environment, our model is consistent with the standard economics literature on organizations (e.g., refs. 4 and 14).

Congestion Robustness. We first consider information congestion associated with an intermediate level of task interdependency, $\xi = 1$. Fig. 3*A* shows ρ_{max} for a fixed network density $m = N$ as a function of the network topology parameters λ and ζ. Equating

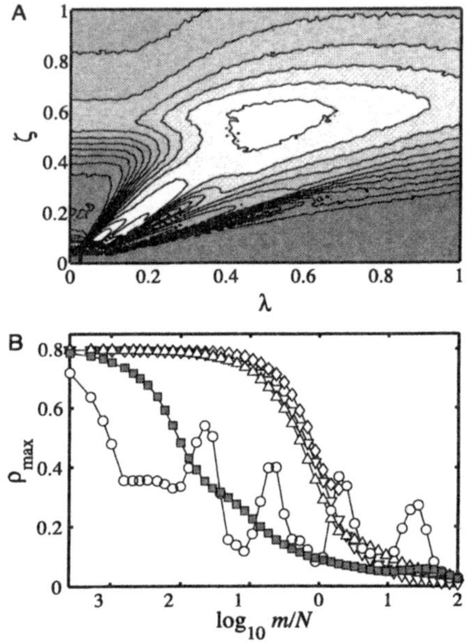

Fig. 3. Congestion centrality ρ_{max} as a function of the network parameters (m, λ, ζ). For both plots, the underlying hierarchy of the networks examined here has $N = 3905$ nodes with branching ratio $b = 5$ and depth $L = 6$. (*A*) Contour plot of $\rho_{max}(\lambda, \zeta)$ for $\xi = 1$ averaged over an ensemble of 100 networks. Lighter regions correspond to lower values of $\rho_{max}(\lambda, \zeta)$. For each parameter pair (λ, ζ), $m = N$ links are added and the resulting network is tested by initiating messages at each node with probability $\mu = 2.561 \times 10^{-3}$ for $T = 10^3$ time steps (i.e., an average of 10 messages are generated per time step). The broad local minimum centered around $(\lambda, \zeta) = (0.5, 0.5)$ corresponds to multiscale networks. (*B*) Change in ρ_{max} with the addition of links. The networks tested here are random ($\lambda = \infty$, $\zeta = \infty$, ▽), local team ($\lambda = \infty$, $\zeta = 0$, ◇), random interdivisional ($\lambda = 0$, $\zeta = \infty$, △), core-periphery ($\lambda = 0.1$, $\zeta = 0.15$, ○), and multiscale ($\lambda = 0.5$, $\zeta = 0.5$, □). Each data point is the average of 100 realizations. In the case of multiscale networks, most of the reduction of ρ_{max} is obtained by the addition of only $m = N$ links (the same holds for $\langle \rho \rangle$).

the axes of Figs. 2 and 3*A*, we can infer that multiscale networks minimize congestion (hence maximize congestion robustness) at least as well, and generally much better than, the other four generic network classes. Furthermore, the congestion robustness property of multiscale networks persists over a broad region of the parameter space, ensuring that it is stable with respect to small changes in parameters. Core-periphery networks (Fig. 2, bottom left) can also exhibit desirable congestion properties. But because their performance depends so heavily on the relatively small population of nodes in the core, they suffer from extreme sensitivity to parameter selection, with the best and worst performing networks arising for almost identical choices of parameters (Fig. 3*A*, lower left).

Fig. 3*B* generalizes the above result by comparing ρ_{max} for the different network classes over the full range of network density m (where particular choices of parameters have been used as proxies for each class). We note that ρ_{max} eventually decreases as a function of increasing network density m, regardless of the procedure used to add links, and that when m is sufficiently large, all networks perform similarly. However, Fig. 3*B* also points to

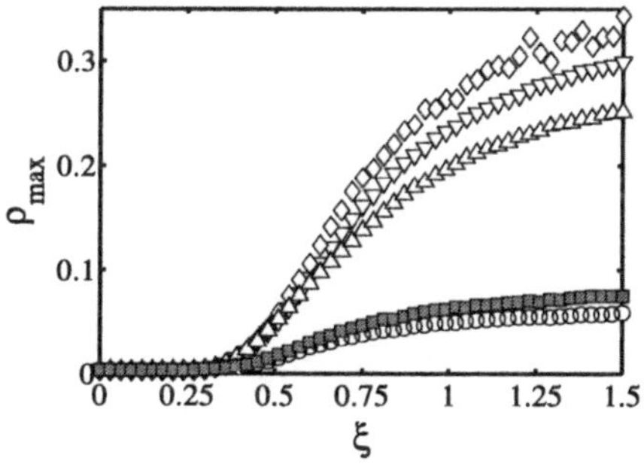

Fig. 4. Variation of congestion centrality ρ_{max} as a function of ξ, where increasing ξ corresponds to decreasing task decomposability. Symbols correspond to the same parameter choices of (λ, ζ) as in Fig. 3*B*, with 100 samples per data point. Multiscale networks perform almost as well as core-periphery networks over the entire range of ξ, and significantly better than all other classes (random, random interdivisional, and local team) for any but completely decomposable ($\xi \rightarrow 0$) tasks.

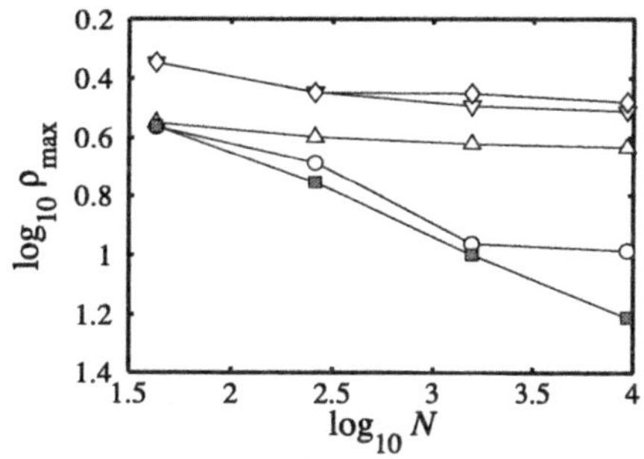

Fig. 5. Scaling of ρ_{max} with increasing network size N. Symbols represent the same choices of (λ, ζ) as in Fig. 3*B*. The task environment is given by $\xi = \infty$ and constant μ (i.e., individual nodes send the same number of messages independent of network size), and N is increased by fixing the branching ratio b = 6 and increasing the number of levels L = 3, 4, 5, and 6 (i.e., N = 43, 259, 1,555, and 9,331). Congestion centrality ρ_{max} rapidly approaches a constant for local team, random, and random interdivisional networks, and also appears to approach a constant at large N for core-periphery networks, whereas for the multiscale example given, ρ_{max} decreases roughly as $N^{-0.28}$.

some less obvious conclusions: (*i*) ρ_{max} does not necessarily decrease monotonically with m. In particular, the congestion experienced by the most congested node in a core-periphery network can increase significantly as more edges are added, before falling again, giving rise to oscillations periodic in $\log(m/N)$ (a consequence of the sensitivity to parameters noted above). (*ii*) The drop in ρ_{max} occurs an order of magnitude earlier for multiscale networks than for random, random interdivisional, and local team networks. In fact, almost all of the drop in ρ_{max} for multiscale networks occurs for $m \approx N$, which for large N is negligible compared with $m_{max} = O(N^2)$.

Fig. 4 continues the comparison between multiscale and other classes of organizational networks, extending it across the entire range of environmental complexity ξ, for fixed $m = N$ and for the same representative choices of (λ, ζ) as in Fig. 3*B*. In the limit of full task decomposability $\xi \rightarrow 0$, at which messages are passed exclusively between closely separated individuals, all types of organizational networks perform equally well. As decomposability decreases, however, large differences in congestion robustness manifest themselves, with multiscale networks always performing almost as well as any other class, and much better than most. Furthermore, although core-periphery networks can also perform well, outperforming multiscale networks for some parameter choices, they continue to exhibit the same sensitivity to parameter choices mentioned above (i.e., a slightly different choice of parameters would generate much worse core-periphery results, circles in Fig. 4). Multiscale networks display no such sensitivity; hence, they represent a more reliable solution to congestion robustness.

Finally, for fixed μ (volatility), congestion increases, regardless of topology, as a function of organizational size; that is, an organization can break simply under the burden of its own coordination requirements (35). However, the manner in which congestion increases with N can vary across different network topologies, leading to large differences in the maximum size that an organization can attain in any particular environment. In particular, for large N the maximum congestion $r_{max} = \mu N \rho_{max}$ at any one node scales linearly with N for random, random-interdivisional, local team, and core-periphery networks but scales sublinearly for multiscale networks. Thus, multiscale networks display the surprising property that maximum congestion centrality ρ_{max} actually decreases with the size of the system (while approaching a constant for the other network classes), a result we confirm in Fig. 5. Another way to interpret the scaling of r_{max} is in terms of the maximum size N_{max} attainable by an organization, given some constraint R_{max} above which failures become inevitable. In Fig. 5, for example, setting R_{max} = 570 yields estimates of $N_{max} \approx$ 1,600 for random networks, $N_{max} \approx$ 1,800 for local team networks, $N_{max} \approx$ 2,400 for random interdivisional networks, $N_{max} \approx$ 5,500 for core-periphery networks,

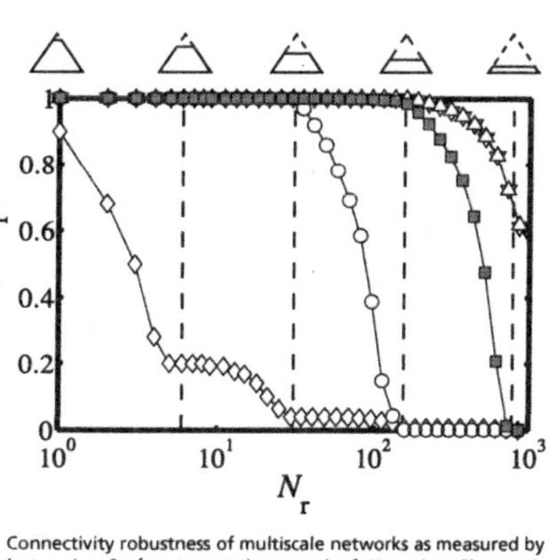

Fig. 6. Connectivity robustness of multiscale networks as measured by the largest cluster size S after targeted removal of N_r nodes. Cluster size is normalized by the size of the remaining network N–N_r. The networks are the same as those described in Fig. 3*B* with 10 samples per data point. Nodes are removed according to a top-down targeting strategy (see text) where N_r is increased until the top five levels of a possible six have been eliminated. The hierarchies depicted and dashed vertical lines correspond to complete removal of nodes down to a depth of 1, 2, . . . , 5. Random and random interdivisional networks are the most resilient to this form of network degradation, whereas local team networks perform poorly. Multiscale networks, however, are almost as robust as random networks. In the case of (λ, ζ) = (0.5,0.5), disintegration of the remnant components begins only after four of the six levels of the hierarchy are removed.

and $N_{max} \approx 9{,}300$ for multiscale networks. In other words, given the same individual-level capacities and the same environmental conditions, multiscale networks can grow to nearly twice the size of the next best class without incurring failures.

Connectivity Robustness. The second aspect of robustness that is of interest to organizational networks is their capacity to remain connected and thereby functional in the event of failures, whether induced endogenously (as with congestion) or exogenously. To quantify connectivity robustness we measure $C = S/(N - N_r)$ after the targeted removal of N_r nodes, where we have studied a number of different targeting strategies, specified above. In Fig. 6, we present the results for the "top-down" elimination strategy, because it results in the most damaging choice of targets, and also is the most likely result of congestion-related failures (even in multiscale networks, congestion is concentrated in the top ranks). Local team networks are by far the least robust of the five classes, followed by core-periphery networks, whereas random and random interdivisional are the most robust. Multiscale networks, however, are almost as robust as random networks, performing measurably worse only after all of the organization but the bottom rank has been eliminated. The other targeting strategies yield similar results, except that all classes of networks perform better than in the top-down case, and that core-periphery networks replace local team networks as the worst performing class when the "hubs" strategy is used.

Taken together, the above results suggest that multiscale networks display a remarkable combination of properties. (*i*) Over a wide range of environmental conditions, multiscale networks minimize the likelihood of congestion related failure. (*ii*) Even in the event that failures occur anyway, multiscale networks remain extremely resilient to disconnection. (*iii*) No other class of organizational networks studied exhibits both congestion and connectivity robustness: core-periphery networks handle congestion well but are easily disconnected; random and random-interdivisional networks are difficult to disconnect, but easy to congest; and local team networks are bad in both senses. Hence, multiscale networks are not only ultrarobust but appear to be uniquely so. (*iv*) Multiscale networks achieve ultrarobustness efficiently in the sense that most of the attendant benefits are generated by a relatively small number $O(N)$ of additional links. (*v*) The superior robustness of multiscale networks also conveys better scaling properties than other classes of networks in that, for a given level of environmental volatility μ, multiscale networks can grow to much larger sizes before suffering failure. (*vi*) The properties of multiscale networks are themselves robust in the sense that they are insensitive to small (or even quite large) changes in the network parameters λ, ζ, and m. Networks resembling multiscale networks may therefore be expected to arise in real-world business firms and bureaucracies, at least some of which do appear to display properties that resemble our notion of ultrarobustness (20, 24, 25).

This work was supported in part by the Office of Naval Research, National Science Foundation Grant 0094162, Legg Mason Funds, and the Intel Corporation.

1. Faloutsos, M., Faloutsos, P. & Faloutsos, C. (1999) *Comput. Commun. Rev.* **29,** 251–262.
2. Gerth, H. H. & Mills, C. W., eds. (1946) *From Max Weber: Essays in Sociology* (Oxford Univ. Press, New York).
3. Taylor, F. W. (1911) *The Principles of Scientific Management* (Harper and Row, New York).
4. Radner, R. (1993) *Econometrica* **61,** 1109–1146.
5. Van Zandt, T. (1998) in *Organizations with Incomplete Information* (Cambridge Univ. Press, New York), pp. 239–305.
6. Strogatz, S. H. (2001) *Nature* **410,** 268–276.
7. Albert, R. & Barabási, A.-L. (2002) *Rev. Mod. Phys.* **74,** 47–97.
8. Newman, M. E. J. (2003) *SIAM Rev.* **45,** 167–256.
9. Burns, T. & Stalker, G. M. (1961) *The Management of Innovation* (Tavistock, London).
10. Lawrence, P. R. & Lorsch, J. W. (1967) *Organization and Environment* (Harvard Business School Press, Boston).
11. Thompson, J. D. (1967) *Organizations in Action* (McGraw Hill, New York).
12. Arenas, M., Bertossi, L. & Chomicki, J. (2001) *Lecture Notes Comput. Sci.* **1973,** 39–53.
13. Goh, K.-I., Kahng, B. & Kim, D. (2001) *Phys. Rev. Lett.* **87,** 278701.
14. Williamson, O. E. (1975) *Markets and Hierarchies: Analysis and Antitrust Implications* (Free Press, New York).
15. Sah, R. K. & Stiglitz, J. E. (1986) *Am. Econ. Rev.* **76,** 716–727.
16. Bolton, P. & Dewatripont, M. (1994) *Q. J. Econ.* **109,** 809–839.
17. Garicano, L. (2000) *J. Polit. Econ.* **108,** 874–904.
18. March, J. G. & Simon, H. A. (1958) *Organizations* (Wiley, New York).
19. Simon, H. A. (1962) *Proc. Am. Philos. Soc.* **106,** 467–482.
20. Nishiguchi, T. & Beaudet, A. (2000) in *Knowledge Creation: A New Source of Value*, eds. Von Krogh, G., Nonaka, I. & Nishiguchi, T. (MacMillan, London), pp. 199–230.
21. Helper, S., MacDuffie, J. P. & Sabel, C. F. (2000) *Ind. Corp. Change* **9,** 443–483.
22. Sabel, C. F. (1994) in *Handbook of Economic Sociology*, eds. Smelser, N. & Swedberg, R. (Princeton Univ. Press, Princeton), pp. 137–165.
23. Ward, A., Liker, J. K., Cristiano, J. J. & Sobek, D. K. (1995) *Sloan Manage. Rev.* **36,** 43–51.
24. Kelly, J. & Stark, D. (2002) *Environ. Plan. A* **34,** 1523–1533.
25. Beunza, D. & Stark, D. (2003) *Socio-Economic Rev.* **1,** 135–164.
26. Krackhardt, D. & Stern, R. N. (1988) *Soc. Psychol. Q.* **51,** 123–140.
27. Granovetter, M. (1985) *Am. J. Sociol.* **91,** 481–510.
28. Lazarsfeld, P. & Merton, R. (1954) in *Freedom and Control in Modern Society*, eds. Berger, M., Abel, T. & Page, C. (Van Nostrand, New York), pp. 18–66.
29. Watts, D. J & Strogatz, S. J. (1998) *Nature* **393,** 440–442.
30. West, D. B. (1996) *Introduction to Graph Theory* (Prentice Hall, Upper Saddle River, NJ).
31. Wasserman, S. & Faust, K. (1994) *Social Network Analysis: Methods and Applications.* (Cambridge Univ. Press, Cambridge, U.K.).
32. Albert, R., Jeong, H. & Barabási, A.-L. (2000) *Nature* **406,** 378–382.
33. Callaway, D. S., Newman, M. E. J., Strogatz, S. H. & Watts, D. J. (2000) *Phys. Rev. Lett.* **85,** 5468–5471.
34. Cohen, R., Erez, K., ben Avraham, D. & Havlin, S. (2000) *Phys. Rev. Lett.* **85,** 4626–4628.
35. Coase, R. H. (1937) *Economica* **4,** 386–405.

[11]

Mika Kallioinen

Information, Communication Technology, and Business in the Nineteenth Century: The Case of a Finnish Merchant House

ABSTRACT

Historically, access to recent and reliable information has been a central problem in business. The present paper is concerned with the role of information and communication technology in international trade in the nineteenth century. The world's first modern instrument of information technology, the telegraph, had a wide-ranging impact on business, though to refer to it as a revolution is an exaggeration. For centuries, prices and other data were obtained by postal correspondence, and this method remained unchanged after the introduction of the telegraph. As the path dependence theorem would suggest, the adoption of the telegraph was not a straightforward process. In the nineteenth century the availability of business information was improved because of the progress in information technology and also because of the extension of the merchants' personal business networks. This reduced the information costs by improving the quality of information, in particular the speed, reliability and the intervals – how frequently it was possible to receive messages from the market.

1. Introduction: Information in Business

Today, rapid changes in information technology continue to reduce the unit costs of acquiring, analysing, and presenting information. At the same time, increasingly global markets and rapid changes in all types of products and technologies are augmenting the demand for information. Changes in the supply of information are particularly salient, with computer and telecommunications technologies evolving at an extremely rapid rate. Modern information technologies have radically improved the speed and reduced the cost of collecting, transmitting, storing and retrieving, and analysing information. These stages of information handling have also, at least in theory, become more integrated, allowing information to flow from one to the next without pause or re-entry of data.

Today's information society derives from a long history. In the first half of the nineteenth century most transactions were still, for the most part, coordinated by small local and regional markets, in a non-integrated organisational mode. By the 1880s, the introduction of such revolutionary transport and information systems as the railway, telegraph, steamship and cable systems enabled the faster and less expensive flow of goods and information at an unprecedented volume, creating what historians have properly termed the Second Industrial Revolution.[1]

Relevant and recent information is necessary for interaction. The fundamental theoretical problem underlying co-operation is the manner in which individuals attain knowledge of each other's preferences and likely behaviour. In the real world, information is neither complete nor free of cost. On the contrary, given the cost of information and the need for it, people typically make predictions about the behaviour of the economy and the behaviour of individuals based upon a limited number of easily observable characteristics. Treating information like other scarce goods has many powerful implications. The deepest and most significant is that economic decision-makers will generally not choose to acquire all the information available, any more than they will want to have all of any other goods or services in the economy. They may not want, or even be able, to process all the information to which they do have access. As a result, entrepreneurs typically have to make decisions on the basis of less than complete information.[2]

This paper examines the role of information and communication technology in international trade in the nineteenth century. In particular, interest is focused on the question whether the new information technology led to changes in traditional business conduct. The introduction of the telegraph in the mid-nineteenth century gave entrepreneurs for the first time the opportunity to obtain and to dispatch information to and from remote places very rapidly. What kind of information was transmitted by the telegraph, and did it displace correspondence as a means of communication between business partners? Did the new information technology have an impact on the old forms of business?

The empirical object of the study is Turku, the second biggest town in Finland and one of its leading businessmen, Carl Magnus Dahlström.[3] The peripheral Finland is an interesting case, because the connections to the most important markets in the Central and Western Europe were distant in temporal and also in geographical terms. The telegraph was adopted in Finland relatively late (1855). Thus, in obtaining information, Finnish businessmen were behind their foreign colleagues. Dahlström's entire foreign correspondence during his career as an independent businessman, including telegraph messages, has been analysed for the years between 1836 and 1869, a period that saw the breakthrough of the new

1 Chandler, A. D. Jr., What is a Firm? A historical perspective, *European Economic Review*, vol. 36, 1992, 483–492.

2 Du Boff, R. B., Business Demand and the Development of the Telegraph in the United States, 1844–1860, *Business History Review*, vol. LIV, 1980, 478; Picot, A., Ripperger, T., Wolff, B., The Fading Boundaries of the Firm: The Role of Information and Communication Technology, *Journal of Institutional and Theoretical Economics*, vol. 152, 1996, 72–73.

3 C. M. Dahlström (1805–1875) was among the five leading ship-owners in Turku, and according to the standards of the town, his business networks were extensive. At the end of his career, he had the second biggest income in Turku. See Kallioinen, Mika, *Verkostoitu tieto. Informaatio ja ulkomaiset markkinat Dahlströmin kauppahuoneen liiketoiminnassa 1800-luvulla*. Helsinki: Suomen Kirjallisuuden Seura 2002, 28–39, 167–171.

information technology. A total number of about 7700 letters and messages have been preserved from this period.

This paper will first discuss the role of traditional correspondence between business partners. It will then describe the adoption of the new information technology, and the telegraph in particular, in the mid-nineteenth century. The third section will explore the use of new information technology in the everyday business of the Dahlström merchant house. Finally, some concluding remarks are made.

2. Traditional Communication: Correspondence Between Networks and Partners

Carl Magnus Dahlström worked as the head of the merchant house founded by himself. This form of enterprise was typical until the late nineteenth century, when the modern limited company replaced it. In Finland, merchant houses usually operated over a wide range of commercial activities, and dominated the country's foreign trade and shipping. The import and export of goods was the fundamental characteristic and sphere of activities of the merchant houses. In his foreign trade, Dahlström specialised in importing goods for the domestic market. He paid for the imported merchandise mainly out of the income he made in the domestic trade, whereas his export trade was rather modest.

Soon after Dahlström became an independent merchant in 1836, he deliberately formed networks of business partners in the most important commercial centres abroad. He had business partners in most parts of Europe and in the Mediterranean, and even as far away as Rio de Janeiro in Brazil. Most of the partners were in Stockholm, Hamburg, St Petersburg, and Lübeck; this illustrates the direction of his business transactions. With some of his business friends Dahlström had close relations, lasting over many decades, whereas with many he dealt only occasionally. The organisation of foreign trade in the nineteenth century was indeed based on the networks between the merchant houses and their managers. Inside these networks the managers were dealing with fellow merchants of the same level, so that hierarchies were almost completely lacking in entrepreneurship. In the market almost complete competition prevailed. Since many competitors of about same size and volume existed in all towns and in all countries, no one of these actors was able to decide prices alone.

These networks moved not only goods but also information for entrepreneurs; the business networks were, at same time, also networks of information. Although the businessmen obtained information from newspapers and other public sources, for instance, from the consuls stationed in foreign towns, they placed special value on the letters received directly from their foreign partners. This is precisely the key to the existence of a network relationship: the parties were dependent on the resources controlled by both parties, both goods and information, so by mutual co-operation both parties gained mutual benefits. Long-term, personal networks were particularly well suited for transmitting information that required high reliability. Only rarely can the most valuable information be obtained through public sources or the price mechanism of the markets. The useful sources of information are precious, often consisting of particular contacts that have turned out to be reliable previously.[4] We can assume that those actors possessing the most extensive personal networks of business partners from which to obtain information had the best chances to succeed.

Up to the 1850s, Carl Magnus Dahlström received information through his foreign business networks in two ways: by meeting his partners or their agents personally, or by corresponding with them. Even though Dahlström made a combined business and holiday trip to Central Europe almost every summer, and although his partners' agents occasionally visited him in Turku, by far the largest proportion of information was transmitted by letter. The importance of correspondence is illustrated by the fact that letters flowed to Dahlström's office in a continuous stream, on average more than 150 per a year. The regularity of correspondence meant that Dahlström was constantly receiving information from abroad, during the busiest periods even on a daily basis.[5]

Correspondence made it possible for entrepreneurs to gain a rather good picture of the markets in the entire region in which they were trading. Most of the information in the letters was about prices. The business partners used to tell each other prices for their commodities that typically were valid only for a certain period or for the present. These letters can in a way be considered as advertisements, whose function was to lead to an order from the recipient. The price information was not a binding offer, but the final prices were determined at the time of the order. Often partners offered their own estimates of the future development of prices based on the expected liveliness of business and on the size of the stocks, for example, which was very valuable from the recipient's point of view. The estimates of future prices were useful in deciding what the best time for the order would be.

In general, partners wrote about all relevant matters in the business, for instance the yield of the crops or changes in the political situation in their country. Usually business partners sent information without the recipient asking for it, in the hope that Dahlström would give an order, but sometimes Dahlström deliberately asked for specific information, for example on prices of certain goods, if he had planned to send them an order in the near future.

Although the correspondence transmitted to Finland continuous market information from over a wide geographical area, the problem was its slowness. The rapid changes in prices were made it very difficult to find the optimal timing for the orders. As a local newspaper in Turku wrote in 1846, "for a commercial and industrial city, rapid correspondence with the neighbouring regions is far from being least important".[6] Letters from the rest of Europe were carried to Finland either by ship or land through St Petersburg or Sweden. From Turku the regular mail was carried to Stockholm twice a week, but to St Petersburg, from 1848 on-

4 Casson, Mark, *Information and Organization. A New Perspective on the Theory of the Firm.* Oxford: Clarendon Press 1997, 69, 118–122; Milne, Graeme J., Knowledge, Communications and the Information Order in Nineteenth-Century Liverpool, *International Journal of Maritime History*, vol. XIV, 2002, 209–224; Ojala, Jari, The Problem of Information in Late Eighteenth- and Early Nineteenth-Century Shipping: A Finnish Case, *International Journal of Maritime History*, vol. XIV, 2002, 189–208; Powell, W. W., Neither Market nor Hierarchy: Network Forms of Organization: *Markets, Hierarchies and Networks. The Coordination of Social life.* London: Sage 1991, 272.

5 Kallioinen, *Verkostoitu tieto*, 46–57.

6 *Åbo Tidningar*, 18 March 1846.

Table Transmission speeds of Dahlström's correspondence from selected places to Turku, Finland. Median figures in days

Geographical area	1837	1838	1842	1843	1844	1845	1846	1847	1848	1849	1850	1851	1852	1853	1854	1855	1856	1857	1858	1859	1860	1861	1862	1863	1864	1865	1866	1867	1868
Stockholm			4		4	3	4	2	3	3	3	4	3	3	5	8	3	4	3	3	4	3	3	3	6	3	2	2	2
St Petersburg			3		4	3		7	3	3	4	4		5	4	5	4	4	4	4		4	5	5	4	4	4	3	4
Riga									7	6	7	7	7	7	9	7	7	7	7	9		7	5		7				
Danish straits			7					6		9		8	7	8	15	14	7	10	10	9		9	10		8	8	11		4
Lübeck	16	10	10		12	10	19	11	11	10	13	11	15	11	12	10	11	12	11	11	10	9	9	9	9	8	8	8	8
Hamburg	15	11	11		11	11	13	11	11	11	11	11	11	11	11	10	12	11	11	10	11	9	8	9	8	8	8	8	7
Other Germany			24			9	17		21	14	12	11	13	10	11	12	13	13	12	12	13	10	7	8	8	7	8	8	8
Amsterdam						13				10		13		11	12				12	13									
London											14	15	12	12	13	15	13	12	11	12	12	10	9	9	9	10	9	8	8
Other Britain					15	16	18		15	14	15	15	17	13	12		14	13	13	14	13	12	11	11	10	9	9	10	10
Paris												18		12			11	13	15			11	9	10	8	8	9	9	9
Other France											17	16	15	14				14	13	14	13				10				
Mediterranean			26		26				18	21	22	22	22	20	22	21	18	19	20	18	20	16	14	14	13	11	11	11	10
Rio de Janeiro								63	67	74	78	62	58	56				47	42	50	45	41	37	38	37	36	37	37	36
Observations	109	87	88	31	140	178	208	217	209	252	242	212	203	290	161	181	285	366	340	347	246	396	412	296	422	453	377	453	303

Source: Turku Provincial Archives, Finland, *C. M. Dahlström's archive, correspondence* 1836–1869.

wards, three times a week, which was more often than on any other mail route in Finland.[7]

Because it was a practice in the office of the Dahlström merchant house to mark the day of arrival on the letters, it is possible to calculate how many days it took for a letter to travel to Turku. This information is shown in the adjoining table. The correspondence became faster in the 1840s and 1850s, though in the 1860s the shortening of the mailing times was most rapid. In the 1860s, on many routes the letters reached Turku in half the time needed two or three decades before. From St Petersburg and Stockholm, letters arrived in the 1860s in two, three or four days, but from Lübeck and Hamburg they took on average of about one week. For letters from the Mediterranean one normally had to wait for more than ten days, and from Rio de Janeiro for up to five to seven weeks.[8]

Turku was favourably situated compared with many other towns in Finland, since letters that travelled by sea, or via St Petersburg or, in particular, Stockholm, often arrived there faster than in other places in Finland. The differences were, however, not substantial. From Oulu in Northern Finland it easily took two weeks in the 1870s for a letter to travel to Liverpool in England. In the 1840s, in Pietarsaari in Ostrobothnia the merchants had to wait about twelve weeks for a letter from Bahia in Brazil, from Rio about eighteen weeks, and from Batavia in Java once even for almost twenty-five weeks.[9]

Besides the slowness of correspondence, another occasional problem was its reliability. Sometimes letters disappeared en route without trace, as happened with at least three of Dahlström's letters.[10] As a ship-owner Dahlström considered it of utmost importance that the captains of his ships wrote to him every time when the ship arrived at a foreign port and again at the time of departure. In 1853 he wrote to one of his captains: "we are here always worried if we do not receive information about the ship, if it has not arrived at its destination in due time". He insisted that in the future the captain should send a letter every time he arrived at or left a port. Another of Dahlström's captains had not confirmed by letter that he had received instructions sent by his employer, "which may never again happen, since otherwise I will not have the knowledge whether my letters have fallen into your hands". It was often difficult to reach captains, since letters did not always arrive at a foreign port while the ship was staying there. Dahlström normally addressed letters to his captains to a business associate in the port where the ship was expected to arrive. If the ship had already left the port, the business associate was asked to forward the letter after the ship to its new destination.[11]

7 Pietiäinen, J.P., *Suomen postin historia I*. Helsinki: Valtion painatuskeskus 1988, 317, 326.

8 Yrjö Kaukiainen has shown that in the speed of communication, quite a substantial improvement took place a few decades before the introduction of the telegraph. Kaukiainen, Yrjö, Shrinking the world: Improvements in the speed of information transmission, c. 1820–1870, *European Review of Economic History, vol.* 5, 2001, 5–6.

9 Nikula, Oscar, *Malmska handelshuset i Jakobstad*. Helsingfors: Svenska litteratursällskapet 1948, 173.

10 See for example Turku Provincial Archives, Finland, C. M. *Dahlström's archive, correspondence* 1836–1869 (TPA), Dahlström to Stockmayer & Co (Rio de Janeiro) 23.10.1853; Meyer & Co (Hamburg) to Dahlström 25.11.1853; Dahlström to K. A. Almgren (Stockholm) 6.11.1855.

11 TPA, Dahlström to his captains F. W. Fagerlund (Falmouth) 12.8.1853; G. A. Weckman (Hull) 23.10.1853.

In business, correspondence was so vital that constant efforts were made to improve its speed and especially its reliability in every way. It was not simple, it is true, to better the speed of correspondence; reliability was more easily improved. Communication was speeded up a little by taking into consideration of the times of arrival of the ships carrying mail. For example, a merchant house in Hamburg asked Dahlström to mail his orders for coffee at once, because the next mail to Rio de Janeiro was due in twenty days.[12] The merchants tried to make sure that letters arrived in their destination by entrusting mail to the care of the ship's captain, so that the delivery of the mail was the captain's responsibility.

In correspondence directed outside Europe, in particular, it was customary to send two letters via different routes, the original and a hand-written copy. Dahlström's coffee orders to Rio de Janeiro were backed up in this way. For example, in 1860 the original letter of order went by boat from Turku to Hamburg, then by normal mail to Bordeaux in France and continued by steamboat to the final destination, whereas the duplicate was sent two weeks later directly from Hamburg to Rio.[13] From Rio to Finland letters were usually mailed via Falmouth in England, and duplicates via Lisbon in Portugal, some French port, or Hamburg. Exceptionally, the same technique was employed during the Crimean War in the postal traffic between Finland and Stockholm: in case the ship was captured by the enemy, a copy of the letter was often sent via the long and slow land-route around the Gulf of Bothnia.

3. New Transport and Information Technology in the Nineteenth Century

In international trade, correspondence had been the dominant means of communication since the Middle Ages. Since the thirteenth century, writing letters and exchanging commercial information had been one of the techniques that contributed to the success of the Italian merchants, for instance. According to Woodruff Smith, most of the market information that flowed to Amsterdam in the seventeenth century was transmitted by letter.[14] The techniques of communication remained almost unchanged until the nineteenth century, when several technological innovations offered new opportunities besides traditional correspondence.

From the Finnish point of view, one of the first changes that affected communication and international connections was the beginning of steamship traffic in the Baltic Sea during the first part of the nineteenth century. The new steam-driven ships were not only faster but also more regular than sailing packets. A steamer company founded by some entrepreneurs from Turku started to operate between Turku, Stockholm, and St Petersburg by the 1830s, and in the 1850s, a direct shipping line was opened from Turku and Helsinki to Lübeck. In good conditions, letters were carried by the steamers quite rapidly: the voyage from Stockholm to Turku took at its best only fourteen hours, and it usually took about the same time from St Petersburg.

12 TPA, Lipman & Geffcken (Hamburg) to Dahlström 12.11.1860.

13 TPA, Lipman & Geffcken (Hamburg) to Dahlström 23.11.1860.

14 Smith, Woodruff, The Function of Commercial Centres in the Modernization of European Capitalism: Amsterdam as an Information Exchange in the Seventeenth Century, *Journal of Economic History*, vol. XLIV, 1984, 990–991.

In 1858, the new steam ship *Svea* ran from Stockholm to Lübeck in forty hours, which gave occasion to some merchants from Lübeck to call the ship "the Sprinter". Other international connections also became faster. Between American and European ports, the westbound trip of a sailing ship took on average thirty-five days; steam reduced the time to ten days or two weeks. Even on eastbound trips, where the prevailing winds meant an average sailing voyage of about twenty-five days, steamships still far outpaced the fastest clippers.[15]

Steamers especially affected the flow of information, since in the Baltic Sea commodities were carried by steam only in modest quantities in the mid-nineteenth century. Merchants appreciated the new means of transport. New steamer lines from Hamburg to New York, Rio de Janeiro, and Barcelona were introduced in the 1850s, and some of Dahlström's business partners optimistically predicted that this would "have a favourable influence on business".[16] One must, however, bear in mind that sailing ships too could, at their best, be quite fast. Dahlström's captains sometimes boasted in their letters about their rapid voyages. One captain sailed from the Turku archipelago to Cadiz in Spain in only fifteen days, which was maybe one week faster than the normal speed of a letter via the land-route to the same destination. The same captain later mentioned another voyage, from Shields in England to Genoa in Italy, which took only twenty-five days.[17] It is not likely that a steamer could have made the same trip much faster.

Undoubtedly steam ships speeded up overseas communications, but equally important was the building of the European railway network from the 1840s onwards. The process was fast, for by around the year 1870 in Continental Europe (including Russia) there were about 90 000 kilometres of railways.[18] The railway had a great influence on the postal services between Finland and the Mediterranean ports, where the mail usually went by land across the continent.

In addition to steam ships and the railways, a third new means of communication in the first part of the nineteenth century was the telegraph, which introduced a crucial distinction between the transport of goods and the communication of information. The importance of the telegraph was not only its rapidity, but also the fact that negotiation now became possible between remote places. This had far-reaching effects on, for instance, the concentration of companies. Established commercial centres like London grew considerably once company head offices, with the assistance of the telegraph, were able to make decisions almost as effectively as the local agents, who now became less independent. At the same time, the global economy was centralising, as the prices of more and more commodities were determined by demand and supply on a global level. The impact of the telegraph in this process of structural change was powerful, if less widely documented than the effects of the railroads on market and factor productivity.

15 TPA, Halterman & Brattström (Lübeck) to Dahlström 27.7.1858 and 29.8.1858; Chandler, Alfred Jr., *The Visible Hand. The Managerial Revolution in American Business.* Cambridge: The Belknap Press of Harvard University Press 1977, 190; Kaukiainen, Yrjö, *A History of Finnish Shipping*, London: Routledge 1993, 66.

16 TPA, Lipman & Geffcken (Hamburg) to Dahlström 13.1.1857.

17 TPA, capt. F. W. Fagerlund to Dahlström 31.5.1859 and 4.5.1860.

18 Pollard, Sydney, *Peaceful Conquest. The Industrialisation of Europe 1760–1970.* Oxford: Oxford University Press 1974, 1981, 129.

As Richard Du Boff has pointed out, telegraph technology, after all, represented a breakthrough without precedent.[19]

The world's first telegraph line was opened in 1844, in the United States between Baltimore and Washington. Telegraph systems, which achieved commercial practicability in 1845–1846, had blanketed the east and west and reached the principal northern and southern cities by early 1851. The transcontinental line to California was completed in 1861. Similarly, in Europe the first telegraph lines were built in the 1840s in France and in Prussia, but a permanent submarine line connecting the two continents was not completed until 1866–1876. Like the other Nordic countries, Finland introduced the telegraph later than in the United States or Continental Europe. The line connecting Helsinki with St Petersburg was opened in July 1855, and one year later it was extended to Turku. All of Finland's telegraph connections with the rest of Europe went via St Petersburg, until a new line through Stockholm was introduced in 1869.[20]

In Europe, government played a much larger role in financing, locating, and even operating the telegraph systems than it did in the United States. In Finland, the telegraph lines were built and operated by the Russian government, which needed the communication technology for its military and administrative purposes. In the United States, on the other hand, conditions favoured a weeding out of smaller telegraph companies and successive rounds of consolidation within the industry. There the railway and the telegraph marched across the continent in unison. The telegraph companies used the railroad for their rights-of-way, and the railroad used the services of the telegraph to coordinate the flow of trains and traffic. A clear difference between the rise of modern business enterprise in the USA and Europe was, therefore, the role central government played in providing the communication infrastructure.[21]

In the United States, the extraordinary speed of introduction of the telegraph was due to the prevailing system of small competitive enterprise and independent merchants, wholesalers, and speculators, who were quick to grasp the opportunities that the new means of communication offered. In other words, the demand for telegraph services came above all from the business sector. In the 1880s, it was estimated that in the United States, eighty per cent of messages were on business matters. In Finland, although the telegraph lines were in the first place built for the needs of government, business started soon to use it extensively. Initially, the Russian bureaucracy was a problem, although the transmission of private messages was also permitted. However, the language of foreign messages was strictly regulated, and because the telegraph officials were mostly Russians, sending and receiving messages written in the Latin alphabet was for a long time difficult. Finn-

19 Du Boff, Business Demand and the Development of the Telegraph, 461. See also Ahvenainen, Jorma, Telegraphs, Trade and Policy. The Role of the International Telegraphs in the Years 1870–1914. *The Emergence of a World Economy 1500–1914. Papers of the IX International Congress of the Economic History*. Wiesbaden: Steiner 1986, 505, 514; Chandler, *The Visible Hand*, 218.

20 Pollard, *Peaceful Conquest*, 53; Risberg, Einar, *Suomen lennätinlaitoksen historia 1855–1955*. Helsinki: Posti- ja lennätinhallitus, 1959, 63–70, 72–95, 122–130.

21 Chandler, *The Visible Hand*, 195, 205; Du Boff, Business Demand and the Development of the Telegraph, 462–465; Field, A. J., The Magnetic Telegraph, Price and Quantity Data, and the New Management of Capital, *The Journal of Economic History*, vol. 52, 1992, 406–408; Risberg, *Suomen lennätinlaitoksen historia*, 64, 72–80; Uselding, P., Business History and the History of Technology, *Business History Review*, vol. LIV, 1980, 447.

ish businessmen were well aware of the competitive advantages given by the telegraph. Local merchants soon realised that they were falling behind competitors who already had access to the telegraph in their own towns, and business communities around Finland therefore pressed for the installation of a telegraph line to their town.[22]

Availability of almost instant communication dramatically improved the functioning of markets, above all else by extending price information. Increasingly, the telegraph allowed businessmen to obtain up-to-date information on market prices and quantities and to reduce inter-market uncertainties of all kinds. Such price data are essential when producers and buyers have several potential markets, or suppliers, at their disposal, and the superiority of the telegraph for executing these transactions seems to have been recognised almost at once. As A. J. Field comments, "the rapid growth of telegraph service speaks to the intense economic demand for sending and receiving information having high time value".[23] The rapid spread of the telegraph indeed implies that considerable demand. There is almost no sign of any of the technological resistance that usually takes place when new technological innovations are introduced.[24] Those who developed and used the telegraph did not display reluctance to transfer from the traditional communication technology, probably simply because there was no such technology except correspondence. Contemporary commentators saw the telegraph as a totally new and revolutionary means of communication, so that there were no grounds for resisting it. Although in the early days of the telegraph some doubts were expressed about its practicality, people generally accepted it with amazement and enthusiasm, even with pride. Finnish businessmen, too, awaited the telegraph with impatience even years before the lines were finally connected to their town.[25]

4. The Use of New Information Technology in Everyday Business

The rapid adoption of the telegraph in business had long-ranging effects in commerce. The logic of business expansion, a search for enlarged total profits, pushed firms to reach out for larger markets before and after the telegraph, but this "constant" of entrepreneurial behaviour was constrained by the costs of establishing wider ranges of commercial contact. The first impact of the telegraph on public consciousness was its distance-shrinking potential. In a large, decentralised country (USA) or continent (Europe) the commercial advantages of the telegraph were obvious. The effect of the telegraph was a simple one: it evened out markets in space. To some extent, the telegraph put everyone who had access to it in the same

22 Du Boff, Business Demand and the Development of the Telegraph, 461, 466–467, 471; Risberg, *Suomen lennätinlaitoksen historia*, 91–92, 98. C.f. also Grossman, S. J. – Stiglitz, J. E., On the Impossibility of Informationally Efficient Markets, *The American Economic Review*, vol. 70, 1980, 404.

23 Field, The Magnetic Telegraph, 403. See also Du Boff, Business Demand and the Development of the Telegraph, 476–477.

24 E.g. Joel, *The Lever of Riches. Technological Creativity and Economic Progress*. Oxford: Oxford University Press 1992, 115, 162–165.

25 Czitrom, D., Lightning Lines. *Communication in History. Technology, Culture, Society*, Ed. David Crowley, Paul Heyer. New York: Longman 1995, 151.

place for purposes of trade.[26] Even in the eighteenth century, merchants of Turku tried to extend their sailing network to areas where they could buy the goods directly from the producers, to the Mediterranean and the transatlantic ports. There the commodities were cheaper than in the traditional towns of middleman sellers, like Hamburg, Lübeck, and Stockholm. Carl Magnus Dahlström had the same goal, though in the beginning of his career he still relied heavily on the services of agents in the Baltic Sea ports. Starting in the 1840s, he extended his direct commercial connections from the Baltic to the Mediterranean and to Rio de Janeiro, for example. The introduction of the telegraph made it easier to operate over a wider geographical area, despite the fact the telegraph did not reach Rio until 1875.[27]

The telegraph was, of course, significantly faster than the traditional correspondence, even though it can hardly be described as real-time communication, as some historians have claimed.[28] It usually took only minutes for a message to be transmitted between nearby towns, but longer distances could take hours. In 1855, when the very first telegraph dispatch was received in Finland, it took nineteen minutes for the message to be transmitted from St Petersburg to Viipuri. The telegraph was introduced in Turku a year later, and in the interim, the town was clearly out in the cold compared to Viipuri and Helsinki in terms of information access. For instance, when the peace that ended the Crimean War was concluded in Paris on 30 March 1856, Turku received the news in five days, whereas in Viipuri people had received the news by telegraph within one day. Differences in the flow of information as huge as these could, of course, have a crucial impact on decisions made in business.[29]

From 1856, Carl Magnus Dahlström received telegraph dispatches from many parts of Europe. For example, from Helsinki it took on average about half an hour for the dispatch to reach Turku, from Hamburg eight or nine hours, and from England often more than twelve hours, although differences between the fastest and the slowest times remained substantial. Still, even this was a decisive improvement in the speed of communication.[30]

Dahlström sent or received in 1856–1869 about 160 telegraph messages, which was only five per cent of the total volume of his correspondence. Most of the messages were orders for captains, and the speed of the telegraph indeed gave the ship-owner greatly improved opportunities to control his ships and their captains compared with traditional correspondence. From the beginning, Dahlström realised the possibilities that the telegraph gave to him as a ship-owner. In 1856, only a few months after the line had reached Turku, he wrote to one captain in Odessa:

26 Carey J., Time, Space, and the Telegraph, *Communication in History. Technology, Culture, Society*, Ed. David Crowley, Paul Heyer. New York: Longman 1995, 195; Du Boff, Business Demand and the Development of the Telegraph, 460–462.

27 See Ahvenainen, Telegraphs, Trade and Policy, 507.

28 See Ahvenainen, Telegraphs, Trade and Policy, 514.

29 Risberg, *Suomen lennätinlaitoksen historia*, 87.

30 Kallioinen, *Verkostoitu tieto*, 79–80.

> "You must inform me several times a month about the freight charges, and if the matter is urgent and important, I must be informed by telegraph, so that the answer can be given in a few days."[31]

Price information was the second biggest group in Dahlström's telegraph traffic. Usually these messages related to the ordering of goods, if Dahlström considered the price appropriate. Knowing the prevailing prices in different geographical areas made it easier not only to order goods but also to choose the best destination for a ship. For example, Dahlström's business partner from Alicante, Spain, lauded Alicante for its excellent telegraph connections. According to this partner, Alicante was one of the most important commercial centres for Nordic products in the Mediterranean, because it was easy for captains arriving there to check the current prices in other ports by telegraph, and to decide their final destination accordingly.[32]

Besides orders for captains and price information, Dahlström also made use of the telegraph to follow the progress of the Crimean War, and, in particular, the development of the naval blockade in the Baltic in 1855–1856, although in these cases his foreign business partners wrote him letters about information they had originally received by telegraph. Later on Dahlström sometimes used the telegraph to inform about payments he had paid and that were already on their way.

The telegraph brought some problems, too, because it proved more difficult to control its manipulative uses. In the United States, two newspapers vented indignation in 1846 over false information on the price of flour transmitted after the arrival of the *Britannia* in Boston Harbor.[33] In Dahlström's case, there are no examples of such false information, but other problems occurred at times. In the beginning one difficulty was the obligatory transliteration of the messages into Russian. In Dahlström's very first messages, sent through St Petersburg to Hamburg and to Newcastle, England, only one month after the telegraph had reached Turku, the dispatches changed on the way into unreadable form. The name "Johan Granfeldt", for example, had changed into "Ragano Granfeldt".[34] Later on there were no confusions on this scale, but the parties involved still had to bear in mind the possibility of errors. It was therefore a common custom to secure the delivery of the message by also sending an exact copy in a letter.[35]

There is no doubt that the telegraph benefited business, but nowhere did it displace correspondence as a means of communication. It has been mentioned above that in Dahlström's foreign communications the telegraph only represents five per cent of the total volume. By contrast, Scovill Manufacturing Company from Connecticut, USA, gradually came to use the telegraph fairly frequently. According to Yates, by 1877 one in ten communications in the press book of outgoing correspondence was a telegraph message, almost exclusively to exchange price and

31 TPA, Dahlström to capt. F. W. Fagerlund 24.11.1856; Kallioinen, *Verkostoitu tieto*, 62–65, 79–82.

32 TPA, Dahlander & Co (Alicante) to Dahlström 26.2.1859.

33 Du Boff, Business Demand and the Development of the Telegraph, 476.

34 TPA, Gustaf Sterky & Son (St. Petersburg) to Dahlström 8.7.1856; Dahlström to Gustaf Sterky & Son 9.7.1856.

35 See for example TPA, Johan Thesen & Co (Bergen) to Dahlström 30.9.1857; Dahlström to capt. C. A. Lindqvist 13.4.1859; Dahlström to capt. F. W. Fagerlund 9.11.1860.

timing information about specific, urgent orders. Because of the high cost it was not used for less time-sensitive communication, which continued to take place by correspondence.[36]

This point applies to Dahlström, too, and, as it seems, to all his business partners around Europe. It was clearly cost that restricted the use of the telegraph. Around 1865, to send a telegraph dispatch from Finland to Denmark cost roughly fifteen times the price of a standard letter. In the United States, the first ten words of a message between New York and Chicago cost $1.55, while most letters cost only $0.03, that is, the telegraph was about fifty times more expensive than a letter. The price, obviously, made the telegraph unattractive for more routine uses.[37]

5. Conclusions: Path Dependence Theorem and the Adoption of Telegraph

The results of this paper suggest that the telegraph had influences on business, though to call this a revolution is an exaggeration. The data concerning one Finnish merchant house indicates that the new information technology was greeted with enthusiasm, and entrepreneurs started to use it as soon it was introduced in their town. Nevertheless, due to the difficult Russian bureaucracy and the high costs involved, the telegraph was employed only to a limited extent. Besides, personal correspondence remained the most reliable way to send delicate massages, for instance those related to reputation or liquidity of another party. One must also remember that the telegrams were extremely brief, which made them impractical in conveying detailed information. It was rational to use the telegraph only if obvious advantage was to be expected from its great speed.

Because of these weaknesses, the telegraph did not displace correspondence as the dominating means of communication in foreign trade in the 1850s and 1860s. Surprisingly, even as late as the middle of the twentieth century, expensive telephone conversations overseas were not a daily practice in international business, and contacts were usually maintained by correspondence. As the path dependence theorem would suggest, the adoption of the telegraph was not a straightforward process.

Path dependency refers to the view that technological change depends primarily on its own past. It was Paul David who first called the attention of economic historians to this issue. In his article, David attempts to explore how the peculiar organisation of letters on the typewriter and computer keyboard became standardised and fixed and to explain what accidental set of happenings appears to have caused this result to persist, even in the face of more efficient alternatives. Technological anomalies of this kind are not hard to find. Incremental changes in technology, once begun on a particular track, may lead one technological solution to win out over another, even when, ultimately, this technological path may be less efficient than the abandoned one would have been. It is misleading to think that nothing leads to technological progress like technological progress. Ex-

36 Yates, Y., Investing in Information: Supply and Demand Forces in the Use of Information in American Firms, 1850–1920. *Inside the Business Enterprise. Historical Perspectives on the Use of Information*, Ed. Peter Temin. Chicago: The University of Chicago Press 1991, 133–134.

37 Risberg, *Suomen lennätinlaitoksen historia*, 183; Pietiäinen, *Suomen postin historia*, 395; Yates, Investing in Information, 124.

amples of successful innovation gradually petering out show the inadequacy of this thought.[38]

It seems that during the first decade after the introduction of the telegraph, the traditional correspondence was considered more suitable for business communication than the telegraph. It was not so much about resistance towards the new technology than the fact that during this period correspondence was de facto, in most business purposes, considered preferable to the new technology. The businessmen had a long tradition of correspondence based on established trust-based networks, so it was not likely that they would all the sudden have abandoned this well-functioning path. The benefits of the telegraph must accordingly be interpreted with caution. It had a limited impact on the traditional forms of business. The development of logistical control by telegraph affected the character and practice of business management in those sectors that could benefit from it. The telegraph was mostly used in communication between ship-owners and their captains. By the new technology the management of the employees became easier. The speed of communication was of particular advantage in the monitoring of ship movements.

The telegraph reduced the agents' autonomy, because it was now easier to do business directly between the seller and the buyer and not any more through an intermediary. The captains, for instance, soon realised that their status had become more limited, since they were no longer able to close deals in a way they had been used to. The new technology does not seem to have changed the entrepreneurs' understanding of information as such. In the beginning at least it did not increase the demand for information or create new expectations for it. Rather the telegraph was an addition to the old forms of communication; despite its speed the telegraph was used to transmit the very same kind of information that was recently sent in postal letters.

Besides, the speed of communication was probably not very crucial as it comes to the different components in the increasing efficiency of communication. Because the movement of freight traffic did not speed up at the same pace as communication, in normal shipments rapid communication was not necessarily so important. Business still had to adjust to the slow annual rhythm, in which the biggest orders had to be scheduled according to the freezing and the reopening of the waterways. It is possible that the telegraph had the biggest impact on business from the late nineteenth century onwards, when the transmitting of dispatches became more routine as the prices were lowered.

One conclusion is certain: during the period of research the availability of information was improved because of the progress in information technology and also because of the extension of Dahlström's personal business network. This reduced the information costs by improving the quality of information, in particular the speed, reliability and the intervals – how frequently it was possible to receive messages from the market. All this increased the efficiency of business, especially when the foreign correspondence and, in the course of time, also the sending of telegraph dispatches became cheaper, which accordingly reduced the information costs. The information that was received more quickly, cheaply, and from

38 David, Paul A., Clio and the Economics of Qwerty, *American Economic Review*, vol. 75, 1985, 332–337. See also Mokyr, *Lever of Riches*, 164–165; North, Douglass C., *Institutions, Institutional Change and Economic Performance*. Cambridge: Cambridge University Press 1990, 93.

a wider geographical area made it easier to compare price- and other data and to seek more profitable deals.

It is as yet uncertain how much growth was fostered by telegraphic transmission as opposed to correspondence on commodity prices and other data. For centuries, price data had been obtained by correspondence, and this method continued unchanged after the introduction of the telegraph. Most valuable for entrepreneurs were personal, confidence-based networks, that transmitted reliable information that was difficult, or, even impossible to acquire by other means. During the middle of the nineteenth century at least, this traditional organisation was not yet changed by the telegraph, but it is likely that there were changes in the long run. An understanding of this process, its consequences, and its selective impact is an important precondition for assessing modern innovation in information technology and its influence on business organisation and economic growth.

[12]

Understanding Mexican Migration to the United States[1]

Douglas S. Massey
University of Pennsylvania

This article draws on prior theory and research in the fields of sociology, economics, and anthropology to specify six basic propositions about international migration. These are examined using data specially collected from migrants in four Mexican communities. The migration process is divided into four phases corresponding to different events in the migrant career—departure, repetition, settlement, and return—and logit probability models are estimated to study the determinants of each event. Empirical estimates show that the likelihood of out-migration to the United States rises during stages of the life cycle when household dependence is greatest and is increased by prior migrant experience and a lack of access to productive resources. The probability of repeat migration increases with each U.S. trip and is primarily affected by characteristics of the prior trip. The likelihood of settlement grows steadily with the accumulation of U.S. migrant experience and is principally determined by variables surrounding the migrant experience itself. The likelihood of return migration declines steadily over time but is increased by owning property in Mexico and advancing age. These results support the conceptualization of migration as a dynamic social process with a strong internal momentum.

I begin this article with the view that Mexican migration to the United States is a developmental social process governed by a well-defined internal logic that unfolds in a predictable way over time. From prior theory and research in the fields of sociology, anthropology, and economics, I distill six basic principles that together capture key aspects of this social process. I then employ these six propositions as a general framework in studying patterns of U.S. migration from four Mexican communities. For

[1] The research presented in this article was sponsored by Grant HD15166 from the National Institute of Child Health and Human Development and is based on chapter 10 of the book *Return to Aztlán,* written by myself with Rafael Alarćon, Jorge Durand, and Humberto González, which will be published in 1987 by the University of California Press. Requests for reprints should be sent to Douglas S. Massey, Population Studies Center, University of Pennsylvania, 3718 Locust Walk, Philadelphia, Pennsylvania 19104-6298.

0002-9602/87/9206-0003$01.50

analytic purposes, I divide the migration process into four distinct phases that correspond to important events in the migrant career—departure, repetition, settlement, and return—and use multivariate logit models to estimate the effects of determinants at each stage. This procedure isolates the dynamic links in the migrant process and helps to explain why Mexican migration has become the mass phenomenon it is today.

MIGRATION AS A SOCIAL PROCESS

Neoclassical economists view migration as a means of allocating workers between low- and high-wage areas (Lewis 1954; Ranis and Fei 1961; Borts and Stein 1964; Todaro 1976; Greenwood 1981). However, secular fluctuations in the Mexican-American wage gap are not strongly correlated with temporal shifts in the volume of international migration (Frisbie 1975; Jenkins 1977; Blejer, Johnson, and Prozecanski 1978); and a wage gap cannot explain why poor communities that are equally distant from the United States send vastly different numbers of migrants or why migration suddenly begins after a wage differential has existed for years (Piore 1979). To explain these things, one must consider structural relations within sending and receiving societies.

In receiving societies, migration stems from economic segmentation, which creates a class of unstable, poorly paid jobs with limited opportunities for advancement (Piore 1979; Portes and Bach 1985). Since natives shun these jobs, employers turn to foreign workers and typically initiate migration streams through recruitment. Mexican workers were actively recruited into the United States at the turn of the century, during the First World War, throughout the 1920s, and especially during the Bracero Program of 1942–64 (Galarza 1964; Samora 1971; Cardoso 1980).

In sending countries, migration represents an adjustment of inequalities in the distribution of land, labor, and capital that arise in the course of economic development (Furtado 1970; Balan, Browning, and Jelin 1973). Processes of enclosure and mechanization displace rural workers from agriculture, while capitalization displaces urban operative workers from factories, generating underemployment and unemployment, leading to international migration. Such a process is occurring now in Mexico (Alba 1978; Hewitt de Alcantara 1976; Arizpe 1981) and has occurred historically, both in Mexico (Cardoso 1980) and in western Europe (Thomas 1954).

International migration may originate in the structure of sending and receiving societies, but, as my second proposition states, once it has begun, it eventually develops a social infrastructure that enables movement on a mass basis. Over time, the number of social ties between sending and receiving areas grows, creating a social network that progressively reduces the costs of international movement. People from the same community are enmeshed in a web of reciprocal obligations, and new migrants draw on these to enter and find work in the receiving society. Each new migrant becomes part of the network, and his entry expands its range of social contacts, which encourages still more migration, leading ultimately to the emergence of international migration as a mass phenomenon (Reichert 1979; Mines 1981, 1984; Mines and Massey 1985; Massey et al. 1985).

The idea that social networks are central to migration is not new. Research in the 1920s demonstrated a tendency for migrants from particular sending areas to be channeled to specific districts in American cities (Zorbaugh 1929; Gamio 1930). Similarly, Tilly and Brown (1967) refer to the "auspices" of migration, by which they mean "social structures which establish relationships between the migrant and the receiving community before he moves." Others have called these relationships "migration chains" (MacDonald and MacDonald 1974; Graves and Graves 1974; Tilly 1978). Anthropological studies have long underscored the importance of assistance provided to migrants by relatives and friends (Lomnitz 1977; Arizpe 1978; Roberts 1974, 1978). Economists, too, have demonstrated the importance of network connections in household migration decisions (Stark and Levhari 1982; Taylor 1984).

A third generalization from the research literature is that as international migration becomes more widely accessible, it is increasingly adopted by families as part of larger strategies for survival, with the timing of migration being determined by life-cycle changes that affect the relative number of dependents and workers in the household. The importance of life-cycle changes in promoting migration has long been documented by sociologists (Rossi 1955; Simmons 1968; Speare 1974; Findley 1977); and recent studies from anthropology (Lomnitz 1977; Roberts 1978; Wood 1981; Pressar 1982) and economics (Stark and Levhari 1982; Stark 1983; Taylor 1984) suggest that households do formulate and implement strategies for survival in a changing economic world. Once networks have developed to the point where a foreign job is within easy reach, international migration becomes a preferred strategy among poor families seeking to alleviate pressing economic needs caused by many dependents and few workers.

My fourth proposition is that international migration is strongly disposed to become a self-sustaining social process. The experience of migration affects individual motivations, household strategies, and community structures in ways that lead to more migration. At the individual level, one trip has a way of breeding another, as high wages and living standards change tastes and expectations among people who initially plan only one trip (Bohning 1972; Piore 1979; Reichert and Massey 1979; Massey 1985). Within households, families adapt to the routine of international migration and make it a permanent part of their survival strategies. At the community level, studies show that migration alters social and economic structures in ways that encourage more migration (Paine 1974; Rhoades 1978, 1979; Reichert 1981, 1982; Mines and de Janvry 1982; Roberts 1984; Wiest 1984).

A fifth generalization from the research literature is that, no matter how temporary a migration flow may seem, settlement of some migrants within the receiving society is inevitable. Although people may begin as seasonal commuters, over time they acquire social and economic ties that draw them into permanent residence abroad (Piore 1979; Mines 1981; Massey 1985). These settlers form cohesive daughter communities in the receiving society, thereby greatly strengthening the networks by providing a firm anchor for social relations abroad and a secure context within which migrants can arrive and adjust.

Finally, my last proposition is that networks are maintained by an ongoing process of return migration, in which recurrent migrants regularly go home for varying periods each year and settled migrants reemigrate to their communities of origin. It is a sociological truism that every migration stream breeds a counterstream (Ravenstein 1885, 1889). The process of settlement is partially countered by a concomitant process of return migration (Cornelius 1978; Mines 1981). Even among those who have lived abroad for a long time, many eventually return to live and work in their home communities (Rhoades 1979). Although Mexican migrants may be drawn north for economic reasons, they retain a strong sentimental attachment to their native culture, which is expressed in a powerful ideology of return migration (Cornelius 1976; Reichert and Massey 1979), a finding that has been observed among migrant groups in a variety of settings (Philpott 1973; Bovenkerk 1974; Bretell 1979; Rubenstein 1979).

These, then, are the basic propositions that shape the ensuing analysis: that migration originates in the socioeconomic structure of sending and receiving societies; that, once begun, migrant networks form to support migration on a mass basis; that, as international migration becomes widely accessible, families make it part of their survival strategies and use it during stages of the life cycle when dependency is greatest; that individual motivations, household strategies, and community structures are altered by migration in ways that make further migration more likely; that, even among temporary migrants, there is an inevitable process of settlement abroad; and that, among settlers, there is a process of return migration.

DATA

My examination of this perspective on Mexico-U.S. migration is based on data gathered, using a combination of ethnographic and survey methods, in four Mexican communities, two rural and two urban. The first community is a traditional agricultural town of about 6,100 located in the state of Jalisco, and the second is a larger, more commercialized farm center of 9,900 situated in the state of Michoacan. The two urban communities are urban in the sense that neither has significant agricultural employment. One is an industrial town of 9,400 just south of Guadalajara, Mexico's second largest city, and the other is a working-class neighborhood of 4,800 in Guadalajara itself. All four communities lie more than 500 miles from the nearest border crossing and more than 1,200 miles from California, where the vast majority of migrants from each place work.

Within each community, a simple random sample of 200 households was drawn—large enough to provide cases for analysis yet small enough so that intricate, ethnographically informed interviews could be conducted. The questionnaire design was semistructured and was applied in two phases. In the first phase, basic social and demographic data were collected on all household members. The second phase compiled a complete life history from household heads with migrant experience in the United States. The life history included a labor history, a marital history, a fertility history, and a property history. The unit of observation in each case was the person-year; for each year of a respondent's life, the occurrence of important events and transitions was noted and personal background characteristics recorded. Interviews were conducted by three Mexican anthropologists and by assistants they specially trained for the project.

Interviewing took place from November 1982 through February 1983 but was concentrated in the months of December and January, when most seasonal migrants are back from the United States. However, because samples of returned migrants inevitably underrepresent those who have settled abroad, the four community samples were supplemented by additional interviews conducted in 60 migrant households—households in California whose members did and did not have documents—during August and September of 1983. Twenty households from each of the two rural towns and the industrial community were located using the chain-referral method (Goodman 1961). A household was eligible for inclusion in the California sample if its head had been in the United States for three continuous years and had been born in the home community. Out-migrants from the Guadalajara neighborhood were not included in the

California sample because most of the household heads had been born somewhere else.

In all, some 6,312 people were enumerated in 885 households,[2] providing data on some 780 U.S. migrants. Since only one life history was taken per household, and since many households contained multiple migrants, the total number of migrants exceeded the number of life histories. Most of the analyses that follow are based on the life histories of 357 migrants. I present a more detailed account of sampling methods and interviewing procedures, together with a justification of the research design, in Massey (1985) and Massey et al. (1987).

STEPS IN THE MIGRATION PROCESS

In order to examine the social process of migration, I divide the migrant career into four segments corresponding to fundamental decisions that migrants and their families confront at key points in their lives: whether to begin migrating, whether to continue migrating, whether to settle in the United States, and whether to return to Mexico. Statistical analyses were conducted separately for each step. A multivariate logit model (Hanushek and Jackson 1977) was estimated to measure the impact of different variables on the probability of each event (departure, repetition, settlement, and return). In all but the departure model, the units of analysis were person-years, making the studies discrete-time event history analyses (Allison 1982, 1984).

In these event history models, time-varying explanatory variables were specified as such. That is, variables that normally change from year to year—whether regularly, for example, age, or irregularly, for example, household dependency—were allowed to vary across years in the event history. Only fixed characteristics such as sex or rural origin remained constant over all person-years of observation. However, statistical identification of the models did require making several restrictive assumptions. Right-hand censoring was assumed to be random, making the time between the beginning and end of observation independent of the timing of events. Moreover, while the underlying risk of events was not

[2] In the industrial town, relatively few migrants turned up in early interviews of sample households. In order to secure enough migrants for detailed analysis, an additional 25 migrant households from outside the sample were located and interviewed. The total sample thus contains 800 households selected by randomly sampling the four communities, 60 California-based households selected using the chain-referral method, plus 25 extra households from the industrial town. Migrants from these 25 extra households are included in analyses throughout this paper. However, their inclusion or exclusion does not markedly change the pattern of results.

assumed to be constant over time, it was assumed to change monotonically. Although the models typically included some measure of exposure time on the right-hand side of the equation, so that steadily falling or rising event probabilities could be detected, they did not contain separate dummy variables for each year of observation, so that repeated secular fluctuations in these probabilities could not be measured. These simplifications are warranted by the exploratory nature of the analyses and by the limited size of the data sets, so the conclusions reported here should be regarded as preliminary.

Departure

In work reported elsewhere, my colleagues and I use data from a variety of sources to argue that migration from the four communities originates in profound structural transformations that have occurred historically in Mexico (Massey et al. 1985, 1987). In particular, the capitalization of agriculture in the 1960s created widespread unemployment and underemployment in the two rural communities. This development coincided with the maturation of migrant networks at the end of the Bracero Program, and the probability of U.S. migration rose steadily, until by the late 1970s a young man had a 90% chance of going to the United States during his lifetime. In the urban communities, a wave of factory mechanization in 1954–55 similarly spawned a period of widespread out-migration to the United States that lasted until 1970, with lifetime migration probabilities of around .50.

Ideally, the effects of these transformations should be quantified at the individual level using methods of event history analysis. Unfortunately, such an analysis cannot be undertaken because complete life histories were gathered only from U.S. migrants. It is therefore impossible, with retrospective data, to contrast those who did and did not go to the United States in a given year. However, the process of out-migration can be studied cross-sectionally by comparing migrants and nonmigrants during 1980–82.

Two logit models were estimated to predict the likelihood of different household members going to the United States during this period. The first model predicts the probability of U.S. migration for male household heads (fathers), and the second predicts migration probabilities for other family members (primarily wives, sons, and daughters). Models were specified separately for rural and urban areas, and members of the California sample were excluded in each case. This exclusion reduced the number of households from 885 to 825 and the number of individuals from 6,312 to 4,520. The dependent variable was whether the household member in question went to the United States between 1980 and 1982. It was coded 1 if a trip was made and 0 otherwise. Predicting this outcome is equivalent to predicting a person's probability of migration over the period.[3]

The models employed three sets of explanatory variables: household characteristics (dependency, land ownership, business ownership, and home ownership), personal characteristics (age, sex, education, labor force status, and occupation), and characteristics of the migrant experience itself (here, months of prior U.S. experience and father's migrant experience; later analyses broaden the list to include legal status, U.S. wages, and the migrant status of other family members). Mexican wages were not included in the analyses because a large share of workers did not work for pay. In rural areas, many were independent farmers or sharecroppers, and in urban areas they were often self-employed service or handicrafts workers.

Measurement of most independent variables was straightforward. Dummy variables were defined to equal 1 if a subject displayed the trait in question and 0 otherwise. Thus, business owners, males, workers, and documented migrants were all coded as 1, and landownership was coded as 1 if households owned at least five hectares of farmland, roughly the smallest plot able to support a family (Stavenhagen 1970). Occupation was coded differently in rural and urban areas. In the former, it was coded as 1 if the subject was a farmworker and 0 otherwise; and in the latter, skilled workers were coded as 1 and others as 0. The variable of father's prior experience was coded as 1 if a respondent's father had migrated before 1980 and as 0 otherwise. Dependency equaled the number of dependents per household member, age was age at last birthday, education was measured as years of formal schooling, and total migrant experience was expressed in months. When wages are employed in subsequent analyses, they are measured in constant dollars.

[3] There is an inevitable risk of sample-selection bias in such a research design (Berk 1983). The population at risk of migrating between 1980 and 1982 consists of all those residing in the communities in January 1980, but the data were gathered in December/January 1982–83. Thus, migrants who were at home in January 1980 but who had not returned as of January 1982 would be selectively excluded from the sample. Although such a bias is inherent in the study's design, it is not likely to be large. We kept records on dwellings that were selected into the sample but empty at the time of the survey. Since migrants rarely sell their property in Mexico, even when spending long periods abroad, vacant homes are a good indicator of a nonreturned U.S. migrant. Only 4% of homes selected into the sample were vacant, and, of these, many undoubtedly belonged to migrants who left before 1980 and were not at risk of migrating during the interval under consideration. Thus, systematic selection out of the sample through nonreturn is probably on the order of 2% or less. The risk of selection bias is low because most migrants' U.S. jobs are seasonal and the workers return home each year for the winter months.

For the purposes of this analysis, variables such as age, education, and occupation are viewed as human capital variables that determine the potential returns to migration and, hence, the propensity to migrate. Household characteristics such as ownership of land or businesses are assumed to represent a family's structural position relative to the means of production, and dependency indicates its stage in the life cycle. Migration indicators probe the social dynamics of the migration process. My general hypothesis is that migration originates in the structure of society but that, over time, variables associated with the migrant experience itself assume larger and more important roles in shaping the course of migration.

Table 1 presents, for different household members in rural and urban areas, coefficients that measure the partial effect of each independent variable on the logit of the probability of U.S. migration between 1980 and 1982. In the equations for fathers, labor force status was not included as a variable in the equations because virtually all were employed, and age squared was omitted because of excessive colinearity with age. The values in the first column indicate that property ownership is negatively related to the probability of rural fathers migrating to the United States, with the owning of farmland being an especially strong determinant. The coefficients also show that the probability of out-migration falls steadily with age. On the other hand, the propensity to migrate increases sharply with rising household dependency and with increasing migrant experience.

This pattern of coefficients is consistent with the view that migration originates in the structural organization of society. For rural fathers, the strongest determinants of migration reflect the influence of social and economic institutions rather than individual characteristics such as education or occupation.[4] Access to such productive resources as land and commerce stems from structural arrangements in society, such as the system of land tenure, the availability of credit, the extent of urban primacy, and the social organization of agriculture. Among individual variables, only age is significantly related to out-migration, with other human capital variables playing small and insignificant roles.

From the first column of table 1, it is obvious that the kind of rural father most likely to migrate to the United States is a landless farm worker with many dependents, no business, and prior migrant experience. While this conclusion follows from the table, it is difficult to visu-

[4] This finding is quite robust with regard to the way that education and occupation were specified. We tried a variety of discrete specifications for education and experimented with different occupational groupings—and always obtained much the same results.

TABLE 1

LOGIT MODELS PREDICTING THE 1980–82 MIGRATION PROBABILITY OF DIFFERENT HOUSEHOLD MEMBERS BY RURAL-URBAN STATUS

	RURAL				URBAN			
	Fathers		Others		Fathers		Others	
VARIABLE	B	P	B	P	B	P	B	P
Household characteristics:								
Dependency	2.296**	.045	−.593	.468	−1.086	.420	2.108	.258
Land owned	−4.464**	.004	−1.432**	.003	...	...	...	...
Business owned	−2.359**	.005	−.238	.512	.486	.404	−.131	.853
Home owned	.068	.863	−.080	.808	.083	.875	−.133	.818
Personal characteristics:								
Sex	...	...	1.040**	.008	...	...	1.407**	.045
Age	−.055**	.000	.104**	.024	−.028	.132	.192*	.105
Age squared	...	...	−.001**	.056	...	...	−.002	.237
Schooling	.044	.542	.108**	.014	.061	.381	.108	.193
Farmworker	.538	.233	.917**	.018	...	...	...	...
Skilled worker	...	...	...	...	−.226	.659	−2.055**	.016
Nonworker	...	...	−1.011**	.023	...	...	−2.186**	.004
Migrant characteristics:								
U.S. experience	.025**	.000	.061**	.000	.014**	.000	.187**	.031
Father migrant	...	...	.473*	.082	...	...	−.617	.442
Intercept	−1.629	.196	−5.071**	.000	−1.661	.220	−8.739**	.000
χ^2 [a]	203.9**		452.2**		141.1**		131.1**	
N of fathers or others	327		1,897		375		1,921	

[a] Difference between χ^2 for model and χ^2 for intercept alone; $df = N$ of cases minus N of variables.
* $P < .10$.
** $P < .05$.

TABLE 2

ESTIMATED MIGRATION PROBABILITIES FOR A 25-YEAR-OLD FARM WORKER WITH THREE YEARS OF SCHOOLING, AN OWNED HOME, AND SELECTED OTHER CHARACTERISTICS

	HOUSEHOLD DEPENDENCY RATIO					
CHARACTERISTIC	.0	.2	.4	.5	.6	.8
No U.S. experience:						
No land or business	.056	.087	.130	.159	.192	.273
Business and no land	.006	.009	.014	.018	.022	.034
Land and no business	.001	.001	.002	.002	.003	.004
Both business and land	.000	.000	.000	.000	.000	.000
Two years experience:						
No land or business	.166	.239	.332	.385	.442	.555
Business and no land	.018	.029	.045	.056	.069	.105
Land and no business	.002	.004	.006	.007	.009	.014
Both business and land	.000	.000	.001	.001	.001	.001
Four years experience:						
No land or business	.397	.511	.623	.675	.723	.805
Business and no land	.059	.090	.135	.164	.198	.281
Land and no business	.008	.012	.019	.023	.029	.046
Both business and land	.001	.001	.002	.002	.003	.004

alize what it really means in terms of concrete migration probabilities. In order to estimate actual migration probabilities, independent variables were given values corresponding to different assumed traits, and these values were inserted into the following equation to generate predicted probabilities: $P = 1/(1 + e^{-\mathbf{BX}})$, where **B** is the vector of coefficients estimated in table 1, **X** is the vector of assumed characteristics, and P is the predicted probability. This procedure is an appropriate means of conveying the social significance of results from a logit model (Petersen 1985). The resulting probability estimates are presented in table 2.

The basic case in this table is a 25-year-old farm worker and homeowner (the modal categories) with three years of education (the average level). The table shows how property ownership, dependency, and U.S. experience affect such a person's likelihood of migration. For example, a privileged property owner with few dependents—that is, a father owning his own business and farmland, with a working wife and no children—had practically no chance of becoming a migrant during 1980–82, regardless of his level of prior migrant experience. In contrast, a young father from the rural proleteriat—with four years of prior U.S. experience, a nonworking wife, three small children, and no land or business—had an 81% chance of migrating.

Migration

In general, those without property have high probabilities of migration, especially during periods of peak dependency. For example, a typical case of a father with three young children generates a dependency ratio of .60 if the wife works and .80 if she does not. Without land or business, the father's probability of migration would be .19 at the former dependency level and .27 at the latter. If we assume that he had previously spent two years in the United States, the respective probabilities grow to .44 and .56. Given that it is quite common for young men to spend a year or two in the United States before marriage, and that two-thirds of the fathers in the rural communities do not own either land or businesses, the potential for out-migration from these towns is considerable.

The estimated probabilities also suggest the powerful momentum inherent in the migration process. Even if there were a radical restructuring of Mexican society giving all 25-year-old fathers access to farmland, those with four years of U.S. experience would still display a .05 probability of migration at the highest dependency levels. Similarly, giving them access to businesses would still leave a migration probability of .20 during periods of peak dependency. In other words, once U.S. migration is incorporated into a family's survival strategy, it shows remarkable persistence. Even with access to resources sufficient for the general support of a family, once migration has been experienced, there is a strong tendency to use this well-known and secure resource again.

The second column of table 1 presents the logit equation for other family members in rural areas. In contrast to the fathers', their migrations are determined more by personal than by household factors. Among household characteristics, only land ownership is statistically related to the likelihood of other members migrating, and the strength of this effect is only about a third of that for fathers, a difference that is highly significant. On the other hand, all personal characteristics are strongly related to the propensity to migrate abroad. The likelihood of migration is strongly increased by being male, by being in the agricultural work force, and by education. Age increases the probability of migration, but at a decelerating rate as it advances. Applying the method of table 2, we see that the probability of migration for a 15-year-old son with a primary school education who has begun to assist his parents in farmwork is about .24, assuming the household has no property and contains no one with migrant experience.

The model also shows a significant connection between the migration of fathers and sons and a strong positive effect of prior migrant experience. Both these findings suggest the self-perpetuating nature of international migration. If to the above case of an educated son from a landless family we add a year of migrant experience, the boy's probability of migration increases from .24 to .40. If we further assume that the boy's father has also migrated, the migration probability increases to .52. This connection between the migration of fathers and sons documents the intergenerational transmission of the migrant tradition.

The third and fourth columns of table 1 display the logit models for fathers and other household members from urban areas. Compared with the rural models, they provide a much less satisfying explanation of out-migration. The only variable significantly related to the likelihood of fathers migrating is prior migrant experience. The lack of significant effects for any of the other individual or household variables probably reflects economic conditions around Guadalajara at the time of the survey. Although the displacement of labor through recession and mechanization had led to migration in the past, during 1980–82 Guadalajara's economy was booming, and unemployment among men in my sample was about 1%. While prior migrant experience was widespread, most male household heads were inactive as migrants during the reference period. The only fathers who did migrate were those with prior U.S. experience, supporting my view of migration as a self-perpetuating process.

The various effects of personal variables on the migration behavior of other family members generally parallel those in the rural model, except that education's effect is not significant. Those most likely to migrate are unskilled males who have entered the work force. The probability of migration predicted for a 15-year-old son with a primary education and working as an unskilled laborer is about .01. As in the rural model, having prior experience substantially elevates the probability of migration, but in this case having a migrant father does not. A year of prior U.S. experience raises chances of migration of the subject above to around .12.

In sum, results from the departure model are broadly consistent with the social process of migration outlined at the beginning of this article, especially in rural areas. First, migration is strongly determined by access to productive resources such as land and commerce, which reflects the structural organization of Mexican society. Second, prior migrant experience or having a migrant parent greatly increases the propensity to migrate, reflecting in part the influence of network connections. Third, the timing of migration is primarily determined by life-cycle factors such as age and the relative number of dependents. Finally, migration tends to be a self-perpetuating phenomenon. Having prior U.S. experience greatly increases the probability of migrating again, and the link between the migration of fathers and sons implies an intergenerational transmission of the migrant tradition.

Repeat Migration

In prior work (Massey 1985), I have used the data employed here to show that the probability of making an additional trip rises with the number of trips that have already been made. Among rural origin migrants, the probability of making another trip increases from .77 after the first trip to .93 after the ninth, and, among urban origin migrants, the respective figures are .59 and 1.0 (Massey 1985, p. 292). Here I examine determinants of repeat migration.

The conception of migration as a social process suggests that, while structural factors may initiate migration, once it has begun, they fade into the background. As the migrant career develops and trips are repeated, aspects of the migrant experience itself come increasingly to dominate the decision to make another trip. Table 3 tests this conceptualization of the migration process by conducting a logit regression analysis of trip-progression probabilities. The model was estimated for all migrants who reported a life history on the survey, including those interviewed in California.

After each trip, a set of independent variables is employed to predict the likelihood of making another trip. For each year, the dependent variable is measured as 1 if a new trip was made and as 0 if not. The units of analysis are therefore person-years of experience subsequent to the most recent trip. As before, three sets of explanatory variables are considered: characteristics of the household, characteristics of the person, and characteristics of the latest trip. The present model also controls for the period when migration began. This and all subsequent models include the California respondents and pool data from rural and urban respondents, indicating the effect of rural background with a dummy variable.[5]

[5] Some reviewers expressed concern that the design for studying repeat migration might be biased by sample selection, because the models are estimated only for people who have taken at least one trip to the United States and exclude those of migrant age who have not yet begun to migrate. In expressing this concern, they draw an analogy with the common econometric problem of measuring wage discrimination (i.e., whether two racial groups are offered different wages by employers). Since only workers have wages whereas the population "at risk" of wage offers includes all those of labor-force age and not just those with jobs, there is a selection problem in using wages paid to infer wages offered. In the present case, the presumed analogy is that nonmigrants who are old enough to migrate could potentially become repeat migrants; but they are not in the sample. However, this analogy is inappropriate because we estimate probabilities of repeat migration independently after each successive trip. Rather than controlling for a confounding selection process while trying to estimate a separate statistical model, we are modeling the selection process itself, estimating how different variables act to *select* which migrants progress from trip n to trip $n + 1$. Thus, people at risk of making a second trip are those who have made their first trip, while those at risk of making three trips are those who have taken two, and so on. Our models estimate the *conditional* probability of making trip $n + 1$, contingent on having taken trip n. An extended discussion of selection bias for sociologists may be found in Berk (1983).

TABLE 3

LOGIT MODELS PREDICTING THE PROBABILITY OF MAKING AN ADDITIONAL U.S. TRIP, BY NUMBER OF TRIPS

	TRIPS ALREADY MADE (N)					
	One Trip		Two Trips		Three or More Trips	
EXPLANATORY VARIABLE	B	P	B	P	B	P
Household characteristics:						
No children	.158	.669	−.465	.333	−.501	.248
Land owned	−1.113	.115	.075	.894	.572	.207
Business owned	.174	.671	−.747	.247	−.131	.776
Home owned	−.695**	.008	−.473	.158	−1.185**	.001
Personal characteristics:						
Never married	.341	.340	−.381	.427	.577	.194
Age	−.096	.236	.108	.558	−.017	.814
Age squared	.001	.308	−.001	.294	.001	.699
Years of schooling	.000	.994	.020	.711	.013	.791
Rural origin	.400	.168	−.231	.489	−.735**	.020

Characteristics of last U.S. trip:						
Years since trip	−.113**	.001	−.107**	.004	−.104**	.001
Months U.S. experience	.018**	.001	.004	.231	.008**	.001
Wife a migrant	4.426**	.001	.995	.184	.802*	.090
Children migrant	−.029	.965	.802	.236	1.337**	.001
Farm worker	.272	.323	.345	.311	.619**	.050
Documented	1.787**	.001	.829**	.044	.183	.621
Bracero	.049	.728	−.953**	.008	−.748**	.023
Period of first trip to U.S.:						
1950–59	.103	.747	−.024	.949	.651**	.030
1960–69	.258	.460	−.065	.873	.796**	.027
1970–82	.572	.131	−.159	.708	1.150**	.004
Intercept	−.526	.719	−1.507	.453	−.240	.878
χ^{2a}	625.8**		458.4**		615.0**	
Person years	1,011		819		1,193	

[a] Difference between χ^2 for model and χ^2 for intercept alone; df = N of cases minus N of variables.
* $P < .10$.
** $P < .05$.

While a household's access to productive resources and its level of dependency strongly influence the probability of out-migration, after the first trip these variables play a minor role in the migration process. The ownership of a business or farmland and the presence of minor children, key variables in explaining the commencement of migration, are unrelated to the likelihood of subsequent trips being made. Only home ownership has a significant impact, that of strongly reducing the likelihood of making more trips. Studies have repeatedly shown that the purchase of a home is a favored way of investing migrant earnings. The present results suggest that, once a home is owned, migrants tend to stop making additional trips. Personal variables are also unimportant in accounting for repeat migration. Marital status, age, and education are all unrelated to the likelihood of making an additional trip, and being of rural origin only influences the process after the third trip, when it begins tc reduce the probability of going again.

For the most part, the progression from one trip to the next is determined by variables connected with the migrant experience itself. Having a migrant wife strongly increases the probability of subsequent trips and, after the third trip, so does having children with U.S. experience. As one would expect, the number of years since the last trip has a negative effect on the probability of going again, the longer one waits after a trip, the smaller the chances of making another. In contrast, the effect of prior migrant experience is strongly positive; the more time accumulated abroad, the more likely another trip. Moreover, migrants who work in U.S. agriculture are more likely to make another trip than those who hold nonagrarian jobs. Since it is inherently seasonal, farm work is more conducive than urban employment to repeat migration.

Not only do variables connected with the migrant experience play a predominant role in determining whether a migrant makes another trip, but their influence increases from trip to trip. Of the seven trip-related variables, four are significant after the first trip and three after the second, but six are significant in predicting trips after the third. Only the impact of legal status declines steadily as the number of trips grows, until it is no longer significant after the third trip. Apparently, after gaining familiarity with the migrant network on the first couple of trips, the migrant finds that a lack of legal documents no longer acts as a barrier to further U.S. migration.

Finally, after the third trip, the period in which a person began migrating has a strong influence on the probability of his or her doing so again. The more recently one began migrating, the higher the probability of one's making additional U.S. trips. This pattern reflects the ongoing development and maturation of the migrant networks. People who began migrating during the 1970s are more likely to make trips after the third because they have better developed and more extensive networks at their disposal, greatly facilitating a strategy of recurrent migration (Massey et al. 1985).

Thus, evidence on the repetition phase indicates that migration is indeed a self-perpetuating process. The probability of migrating again increases with each subsequent trip and with each month of accumulated migrant experience. Moreover, as the social process unfolds, the factors that originally spurred migration become less relevant. Over time, the social process of migration acquires its own momentum, and the structural causes of migration fade into the background. The importance of social networks in this process is suggested by the irrelevance of legal status after the first two trips and by the higher probability of repeat migration among those who began migrating recently, when the networks were most fully developed.

Settlement

A prominent view is that Mexican migrants are temporary rather than permanent immigrants to the United States. Cornelius (1978, pp. 24–28), in particular, argues that Mexican migrants are "sojourners" rather than "settlers" and that their long-term impact on the nation will be much less than their large numbers now suggest. "While it is quite likely that the number of *temporary* Mexican migrants to the U.S. has increased substantially in recent years, . . . there is no evidence indicating the number of new *permanent* additions to the illegal migrant population has risen dramatically" (1978, p. 13). Consonant with this view, surveys show that Mexican migrants typically remain in the United States for very short periods (North and Houstoun 1976; Bustamante 1978; Ranney and Kossoudji 1983); and several field studies have described entire communities of temporary migrants who regularly shuttle back and forth between the two countries (Wiest 1973; Reichert and Massey 1979, 1980; Reichert 1981).

However, as temporary migrants make repeated trips northward and accumulate time in the United States, many can be expected to settle (Piore 1979). Any analysis of the settlement process requires a definition of when "settlement" occurs, and among Mexican migrants the concept of settlement is highly ambiguous. Even after many years in the United States—and ownership of a house and a car here—families still make annual trips back to their home communities, and they may invest substantial sums there. "Settled" migrants may even own land and a house in Mexico and continue to play a significant role in community affairs. Moreover, nearly all settled migrants swear they will return, even though mounting evidence suggests that they will not return.

This study adopts an arbitrary criterion for settlement and then considers return as a possible fourth step in the migration process. Here a settler is defined as a migrant who has been in the United States for three *continuous* years. That is, someone had to report a solid block of 36 contiguous months' residence in the United States in order to be defined as a settler. While some such settlers may have returned to Mexico for brief visits, unless these visits were reported in the life history, the respondents would be considered settled. This definition excludes seasonal migrants who reported working several months in the United States during successive years.

As before, the determinants of settlement are studied using a logit model in which units of analysis are person-years lived in the United States and the outcome is whether settlement occurred in a given year. Migrants receive a score of 1 in the last of three successive years in the United States and 0 otherwise. The U.S. person-years need not occur consecutively; a migrant can accumulate five years of experience by migrating every other year for 10 years or by staying abroad for two years, returning home, and then making three successive one-year trips. However, only person-years spent in the United States, and only those after the second U.S. year, are included in the analysis, since only then are migrants at risk of settling. Again, the model is estimated for all migrants who reported a life history, including those in the California sample.[6]

Settlement does not necessarily mean the same thing as accumulation of U.S. experience. It is quite possible for migrants to accumulate 20 years of experience in the United States without ever settling; and, indeed, 34 migrants from the four communities did exactly that. However, as migrants move back and forth and accumulate time, settlement tends to become increasingly likely. After accumulating 10 years of migrant experience, 42% of rural migrants and 53% of urban migrants have settled in the United States (Massey 1985, p. 290).

Coefficients associated with each predictor variable are shown in table 4. As with repeat migration, factors related to the household's economic

[6] Obviously, using the community samples by themselves would severely underestimate the probability of settlement, so the California sample is included in order to capture the experience of settled migrants. This solution is not ideal, because we have no way of knowing how representative this sample is of all settled out-migrants. It does not include migrants who settled in other states (probably a relatively small number), nor is it representative in a statistical sense. If the sample we selected understates or overstates the relative number of settled migrants, then estimated settlement probabilities may be too low or too high. Moreover, if migrants in the California sample differ in some systematic way from settled migrants in general, the estimated effects of variables may also be biased. The inclusion of a nonrandom sample of settlers from California represents a practical solution to a difficult design problem and underscores the preliminary nature of the results.

Migration

TABLE 4

LOGIT MODEL PREDICTING THE PROBABILITY OF U.S. SETTLEMENT FROM SELECTED VARIABLES

Explanatory Variable	B	SE	P
Household characteristics:			
No children	1.460**	.681	.032
Land/business owned	−.574	1.115	.607
Home owned	.115	.418	.783
Personal characteristics:			
Never married	.708	.602	.240
Age	.516**	.183	.005
Age squared	−.008**	.003	.005
Years of schooling	.042	.056	.447
Rural origin	−1.277**	.412	.002
Characteristics of U.S. trip:			
Months U.S. experience	.050**	.008	.001
Wife a migrant	.311	.695	.655
Children migrant	1.048	.679	.123
Farm worker	.648*	.384	.091
Documented	.791**	.357	.027
Bracero	−2.978**	.054	.002
Initial U.S. wage	.101*	.054	.063
Intercept	−12.268**	3.077	.001
χ^{2a}	287.5**		
Person years	524		

[a] Difference between χ^2 for model and χ^2 for intercept alone; *df* = *N* of cases minus *N* of variables.
* $P < .10$.
** $P < .05$.

position are not very important in the settlement process. Ownership of farmland or a business is not significantly related to the propensity to settle, nor is home ownership. While a lack of access to the means of production may spark migration in the first place, it has little to do with the direction the migration process takes once it has begun, playing no real part in the decision to settle. The household characteristic that is of primary importance is the presence or absence of children. The probability of settlement is considerably enhanced by a lack of children.

Among personal characteristics, marital status itself is not strongly related to the propensity to settle; married and single men have roughly the same settlement propensities. As we have seen, it is the presence or absence of children that is important. Age, however, is strongly related to the likelihood of settlement, with such a likelihood being low in the teen ages, rising through the twenties to a peak in the early thirties, and then falling steadily thereafter. In general, then, settlement is most likely to occur at early stages of the life cycle, just before or just after marriage, before family formation has really gotten under way. Being from a rural area strongly decreases the likelihood of settlement, suggesting that rural networks are better adapted to recurrent than to settled migration. Education plays an insignificant role in the process.

In addition to its association with life-cycle factors, the propensity to settle is strongly associated with trip characteristics, and particularly with greater U.S. experience. The strong impact of the experience variable reflects two complementary effects, one statistical and one social. Statistically, the cumulative probability of settlement grows with greater experience because more total time in the United States implies more exposure to the risk of settling. Someone with 15 years of experience has been exposed to the risk of settling five times longer than someone with three years of experience. At the same time, growing experience brings the accumulation of social and economic ties to the United States, connections that progressively draw migrants into settled residence abroad (Massey 1985, 1986). Whatever the mechanism, the probability of settlement rises steadily as temporary migrants accumulate time abroad, contrary to the arguments advanced by Cornelius (1978).

Another trip characteristic associated with settlement is legal status, although whether it is a consequence or a determinant of settlement is open to debate. While legal status clearly facilitates settlement by removing barriers to employment and opportunity, the three years required for settlement to occur also facilitate the establishment of connections leading to documentation: marriage to a citizen or legal migrant, or sponsorship by an employer. However, while settlement may lead to documentation, that situation is not as plausible as that of documentation leading to settlement. Three years is not enough time for most migrants to meet a wife, get married, and apply for and receive a resident visa, and for an unskilled worker without family connections, the prospects of obtaining documentation through an employer are dim and extremely time consuming. Therefore, the possession of legal documents probably acts more as a determinant than as a consequence of settlement.

The likelihood of settlement is also increased by employment in agriculture and by a high initial wage in the United States (the survey did not ask the wage of each U.S. job, just of the first and the last). The prospects for settlement are similarly enhanced by having children who are migrants. Bracero migrants were very unlikely to settle, which is not surprising, since the Bracero Program ended before the networks had really come into their own and was explicitly designed to discourage settlement by limiting visas to six months.

In order to illustrate the relative importance of variables in the settlement process, table 5 presents probabilities of settlement for a typical Mexican migrant: a married, 25-year-old man with no property in Mexico

TABLE 5

PROBABILITY OF U.S. SETTLEMENT FOR A MARRIED MALE MIGRANT AGED 25 WITH NO PROPERTY AND AN INITIAL U.S. WAGE OF $3.40

CHARACTERISTIC	YEARS OF U.S. MIGRANT EXPERIENCE 3	4	5	6	7	8	9	10	15
Rural origin farm worker:									
Documented:									
No children	.354	.500	.646	.768	.858	.917	.953	.973	.999
Migrant children	.267	.399	.547	.688	.801	.880	.930	.960	.998
Nonmigrant children	.113	.188	.297	.435	.584	.719	.823	.895	.994
Undocumented:									
No children	.199	.312	.453	.601	.733	.833	.901	.943	.997
Migrant children	.141	.230	.352	.498	.643	.766	.857	.916	.995
Nonmigrant children	.055	.095	.161	.259	.389	.537	.679	.794	.987
Urban origin nonfarm worker:									
Documented:									
No children	.507	.642	.774	.862	.919	.954	.974	.986	.999
Migrant children	.404	.552	.692	.804	.882	.932	.961	.978	.999
Nonmigrant children	.193	.304	.443	.591	.725	.828	.898	.941	.997
Undocumented:									
No children	.319	.460	.608	.739	.838	.904	.945	.969	.998
Migrant children	.235	.359	.505	.650	.772	.861	.918	.953	.998
Nonmigrant children	.098	.165	.265	.397	.545	.686	.799	.879	.993

who earned the current minimum wage on his first U.S. trip. Using the same procedure as in table 2, this table estimates the effect of origin, occupation, documentation, and children on such a person's probability of settlement.

The striking aspect of this table is that migrant experience ultimately overcomes the effect of all other variables, to make settlement all but inevitable in the long run. After accumulating 15 years of U.S. experience, our typical migrant would have a 99% chance of settlement, irrespective of his legal status, origin, U.S. occupation, or whether he had children. Differences in the likelihood of settlement with respect to these variables occur primarily within the first 10 years of the migrant experience. After three years, the probability of settlement within any year ranges from a low of about .06 for undocumented rural farm workers with nonmigrant children to a high of .51 for documented urban nonfarm workers without children. After five years, the settlement probability for the former rises to only .16, while that of the latter rises to .77; and after 10 years of experience, the gap between the two figures narrows considerably, to .99 versus .79. By the 15-year mark, all the original differences are erased.

Thus, while having legal documents, no children, and being a nonfarm worker of urban origin all substantially increase the probability of settlement early in the migrant career, as experience accumulates, these variables matter less and less. As the social process of migration runs its course and migrants build up increasing time abroad, the probability of settlement eventually becomes so great that other variables become irrelevant. In short, the logit models provide dramatic evidence of an ongoing settlement process among Mexican migrants to the United States.

Return

In spite of the fact that the probability of U.S. settlement becomes very great when migration is extended indefinitely, the act of settling abroad rarely implies a break with social life in the home community. Social networks are maintained and reinforced by a constant circulation of people, goods, information, and capital between sending and receiving areas. Most of this circulation involves the temporary migration of people who work seasonally in the United States. However, the networks are also reinforced by another kind of return migration involving people who once adopted a settled migrant strategy. Even after many years in the United States, migrants may sell their foreign assets and return to live either in the community where they were born or in a Mexican urban area. Thus, return is the last phase in the social process of migration.

Using the life history data, I selected all migrants who had ever settled in the United States (that is, who had ever lived abroad for three consecutive years) and then looked to see whether they returned to Mexico in the years subsequent to their settlement.[7] Return occurred when a former settler spent three consecutive years back in Mexico. As before, person-years were the units of observation, with the outcome variable being coded as 1 in the last of three consecutive years spent in Mexico and as 0 otherwise. Migrants were only considered to be at risk of returning two years after they had settled in the United States. By this definition, 31% of migrants reemigrated to Mexico 10 years after settlement, and after 20 years the figure is about 60% (Massey et al. 1987).

Table 6 presents the results of a logit analysis of return migration. The key variables in the process seem to be property ownership, age, and marital status. When a family owns a home in Mexico or operates some productive enterprise there, the likelihood of return migration is substantially increased. Return tends to occur as migrants approach old age, a finding that fits with casual field observation of many ex-migrants who live in Mexico and receive their U.S. pensions and social security payments. The probability of return is significantly lower if a man is married, although this effect is partially offset if the wife is herself a migrant.

All factors relating to aspects of the migrant's stay in the United States are negatively related to the probability of return migration. As the length of the stay grows and wages increase, the probability of return steadily diminishes. Having a migrant wife or children also lowers the likelihood of return (although not significantly), as does working in agriculture. The omission of legal status from the list of trip characteristics does not imply that the possession of documents is unrelated to the probability of return. On the contrary, it is so highly related that, in the years following settlement, not one legal migrant in our sample returned to Mexico for three consecutive years. That is, the probability of return migration among settled migrants with documents was zero. Since the logit estimation method requires that at least some documented migrants return, the effect of this variable could not be estimated statistically. Nonetheless, it is

[7] In modeling the process of return migration, there are three important groups whose experience must be represented. First are former settled migrants who have returned to live in their communities of origin, a group we represent with the random community samples. Second are settled migrants currently living abroad, who are represented by the snowball sample of Californians. Finally, there are former U.S. settlers who have returned not to their community of origin but to a location elsewhere in Mexico. Migrants from the states of Michoacan and Jalisco are most likely to return to Guadalajara, if not to their home community. Although we cannot trace former settlers from our three towns back to Guadalajara, the experience of such people is reflected in the neighborhood sample taken in that city, which contains several former U.S. settlers from small towns who have returned to found businesses there. Again, the sample design represents a practical solution to a difficult design problem.

TABLE 6

LOGIT MODEL PREDICTING RETURN MIGRATION FROM SELECTED VARIABLES

Explanatory Variable	B	SE	P
Household characteristics:			
No children	.454	.444	.307
Land/business owned	1.289**	.494	.009
Home owned	.684**	.349	.050
Personal characteristics:			
Never married	−.904**	.462	.050
Age	.041**	.018	.024
Years of schooling	−.071	.058	.220
Rural origin	.505	.344	.142
Characteristics of U.S. stay:			
Months U.S. experience	−.008**	.003	.001
Wife a migrant	−.667	.591	.259
Children migrant	−.442	.464	.341
Farm worker	−.705**	.330	.033
Most recent wage	−.220**	.079	.005
Intercept	−2.658**	.809	.001
χ^{2a}	404.5**		
Person years	1,557		

[a] Difference between χ^2 for model and χ^2 for intercept alone; *df* = *N* of cases minus *N* of variables.
* $P < .10$.
** $P < .05$.

clear that the possession of legal documents strongly discourages, if not precludes, return migration to Mexico.

Thus, the kind of settled migrant most likely to return to Mexico is an older married undocumented migrant who has a wife, children, house, and property in Mexico and who has been in the United States less than five years working at near the minimum wage in an urban job. However, it is not very common for settled migrants to leave their wives and children in Mexico. Settled migrants are usually either single or have their families with them, and they usually work at something more than the minimum wage. Table 7 therefore presents probabilities for two typical rural migrants—one single and one married with a migrant family, both earning $5.00 per hour in an urban job—and then examines the effect of property ownership, age, and time in the United States.

In general, property ownership has the greatest impact on return migration. Among those without any property in Mexico, the ***highest*** yearly probability of return was only .04, compared with .07 among those with a home, .13 among those with land or a business, and .22 among those with both. In essence, once settlement has occurred, return migration is not very likely unless a migrant owns property in Mexico, and, even then, the

TABLE 7

PROBABILITY OF RETURN MIGRATION FOR SETTLED RURAL ORIGIN NONFARM WORKERS EARNING $5 PER HOUR ON THEIR LATEST U.S. JOB

	YEARS OF U.S. MIGRANT EXPERIENCE				
CHARACTERISTIC	5	10	15	20	25
Single, age 25 with no children:					
No property	.017	.011	.077	.004	.003
Home only	.034	.021	.013	.008	.005
Land/business only	.060	.038	.024	.014	.009
Home, land, and business	.112	.072	.046	.029	.018
Married with migrant wife and children:					
Aged 25 years:					
No property	.014	.009	.005	.003	.002
Home only	.028	.009	.011	.003	.002
Land/business only	.050	.031	.020	.012	.008
Home, land, and business	.094	.060	.038	.023	.015
Aged 50 years:					
No property	.038	.024	.015	.009	.006
Home only	.074	.047	.029	.019	.012
Land/business only	.127	.082	.053	.033	.021
Home, land, and business	.224	.152	.100	.064	.041

prospects for return steadily diminish with time in the United States. The highest probability of return, .22, is for an older property owner with a migrant family and five years' residence abroad. But his probability of return falls rapidly the longer he remains in the United States. At 10 years it is only .15, falling to .10 after 15 years, to .06 after 20 years, and finally to .04 at 25 years.

Thus, long periods of U.S. residence considerably reduce the chances of return migration, even among those who are otherwise disposed to leave. Although the existence of a clear process of return migration has been confirmed, the generally slow pace of reemigration, the steady decline, over time, in the likelihood of return, and the fact that most settled migrants own nothing more than a home in Mexico do not suggest substantial reverse migration for settled migrants in the short term.

DISCUSSION

The pattern of results obtained from the estimated models of departure, repetition, settlement, and return generally supports the interpretive framework developed at the outset of this article. Findings suggest that U.S. migration is not just a matter of high wages attracting poor workers, although this clearly happens. Instead, migration seems to originate in structural arrangements within sending societies, which generate unequal access to productive resources. (It is probably also related to structural relations in receiving societies, but we lack the data to confirm this view). The most powerful predictors of whether a household head migrates are not human capital variables, which determine the potential economic returns to migration, but land and business ownership, which reflect institutional arrangements in society. Traditional human capital variables such as education and occupation only affect the migration propensities of people who are not responsible for household support, for example, older sons.

Once begun, migration tends to develop a life of its own because of its inherently social nature. Social networks develop from kin and friendship relations and link migrants with U.S. employers, labor contractors, and other migrants abroad. Knowing or being related to a migrant gives access to these connections, thereby greatly reducing the cost of migration. The models provide a glimpse of how these networks form. Fathers initiate sons into the migrant process, which, by giving them foreign work experience, increases the probability that they, in turn, will migrate when they have families of their own. The migration of sons also increases the probability of migration among their friends and acquaintances and, later, their in-laws, by giving them a social tie to someone with foreign connections. In this way, migration spreads from person to person and from family to family. The gradual development of such networks is suggested by the steadily increasing probabilities of repeat migration from the 1940s through the 1970s.

As the networks develop and mature, U.S. employment is brought within easy reach of most households, and families respond by making international migration a regular part of their survival strategies. It becomes a well-known and trusted resource to be employed when family needs are most acute. As findings show, the precise timing of migration is associated with life-cycle changes that affect the level of dependency within the household, suggesting that migration is employed in a conscious, strategic way by families during times of pressing need.

While international migration begins at critical points in the life cycle and in households with limited access to productive resources, over time it tends to become self-perpetuating. The reasons that originally sparked migration fade into the background as characteristics pertaining to the migrant experience itself come to dominate decisions about whether to go north again. In particular, each month of accumulated U.S. experience strongly increases the likelihood of migrating again, and the probability of making an additional trip rises steadily as the number of prior trips increases.

The growth of migrant networks is greatly facilitated by an inevitable process of settlement that leads directly to the formation of daughter communities abroad. These communities provide a firm anchor for the social connections that comprise the network and create a secure context within which new migrants can arrive, adjust, and find work. Results from the settlement model confirm the existence of an ongoing settlement process whereby migrants are progressively drawn into settled life abroad, a process that is greatly encouraged by childlessness and the possession of legal documents but is unaffected by the structural factors that originally led to the migration.

Finally, the social process of network migration is further enabled by an inevitable process of return migration, whereby formerly settled migrants reemigrate to their home communities. The presence at home of these former U.S. settlers who have friends and relatives abroad gives other community members access to an unusually extensive array of social and economic ties in the receiving country. The likelihood of return migration is strongly decreased by long residence abroad and high foreign wages but is markedly increased by advancing age and the ownership of property in the sending society.

Thus, structural factors and life-cycle variables seem to play key roles during the first and final phases of the migration process. Not having access to productive resources and being young with a growing family strongly encourage departure, while owning Mexican property late in life strongly fosters return. Those least likely to leave—people with access to productive wealth—are also those most likely to return. In the intervening stages, the course of the migration process is most strongly shaped by whether a migrant's origins are rural or urban and by various aspects of his experience in the United States, especially the amount of time he has accumulated abroad.

An appreciation of the momentum inherent in the migration process has profound implications for the future course of Mexico-U.S. migration. After 40 years of steady development, migration is now so institutionalized, so widespread, so much a part of family strategies, individual expectations, and community structures, in short, so embedded in social and economic institutions, that the idea of controlling it is probably unrealistic. Although that facet of it is not specifically studied here, migration also causes long-term adjustments in the United States that encourage migration. Given the accumulated weight of four decades of steady Mexican immigration, the social process is probably now so advanced that it will play itself out no matter what the United States does, with trends being determined by shifting economic conditions and the ongoing elaboration of the networks.

One last issue implicit in the conclusions presented here is their generalizability. Obviously, with data from only four sending communities, we cannot extend specific coefficients and probabilities to Mexico-U.S. migration in general. The estimates in this article do not shed light on the true probabilities of migration, repetition, settlement, and return. What they do provide is a way of understanding and interpreting the social processes that underlie these parameters.

REFERENCES

Alba, Francisco. 1978. "Mexico's International Migration as a Manifestation of its Development Pattern." *International Migration Review* 12:502–13.

Allison, Paul D. 1982. "Discrete-Time Methods for the Analysis of Event Histories." Pp. 61–98 in *Sociological Methodology 1982*, edited by S. Leinhardt. San Francisco: Jossey-Bass.

———. 1984. *Event History Analysis: Regression for Longitudinal Event Data*. Sage University Paper Series on Quantitative Applications in the Social Sciences, no. 56. Beverly Hills and London: Sage.

Arizpe, Lourdes. 1978. *Migración, Etnicismo y Cambio Economico: Un Estudio sobre Migrantes Campesinos a la Ciudad de México*. Mexico City: El Colegio de México.

———. 1981. "The Rural Exodus in Mexico and Mexican Migration to the United States." *International Migration Review* 15:626–49.

Balan, Jorge, Harley L. Browning, and Elizabeth Jelin. 1973. *Men in a Developing Society: Geographic and Social Mobility in Monterrey, Mexico*. Austin: University of Texas Press.

Berk, Richard A. 1983. "An Introduction to Sample Selection Bias in Sociological Data." *American Sociology Review* 48:386–98.

Blejer, Mario I., Harry G. Johnson, and Arturo C. Prozecanski. 1978. "An Analysis of the Economic Determinants of Legal and Illegal Mexican Migration to the United States." *Research in Population Economics* 1:217–31.

Bohning, Wolf R. 1972. *The Migration of Workers in the United Kingdom and the European Community*. London: Oxford University Press.

Borts, G. H., and J. L. Stein. 1964. *Economic Growth in a Free Market*. New York: Columbia University Press.

Bovenkerk, J. 1974. *The Sociology of Return Migration*. The Hague: Mouton.

Brettell, Caroline. 1979. "Emigrar para Voltar: A Portuguese Ideology of Return Migration." *Papers in Anthropology* 20:1–20.

Bustamante, Jorge A. 1978. "Dimensions of the Migration Phenomenon in Mexico and the Caribbean Basin." Pp. 22–40 in *Proceedings of the Brookings–El Colegio de México Symposium on Structural Factors in Mexican and Caribbean Basin Migration*. Washington, D.C.: Brookings Institution.

Cardoso, Lawrence. 1980. *Mexican Emigration to the United States 1897–1931*. Tucson: University of Arizona Press.

Cornelius, Wayne A. 1976. "Outmigration from Rural Mexican Communities." *Interdisciplinary Communications Program Occasional Monograph Series* 5 (2): 1–39. Washington, D.C.: Smithsonian Institution.

———. 1978. *Mexican Migration to the United States: Causes, Consequences, and U.S. Responses*. Migration and Development Monograph C/78-9. Cambridge, Mass.: MIT Center for International Studies.

Findley, Sally. 1977. *Planning for Internal Migration: A Review of Issues and Policies in Developing Countries*. Washington, D.C.: Government Printing Office.

Frisbie, Parker. 1975. "Illegal Migration from Mexico to the United States: A Longitudinal Analysis." *International Migration Review* 9:3–13.

Migration

Furtado, Celso. 1970. *Economic Development of Latin America*. New York: Cambridge University Press.

Galarza, Ernest. 1964. *Merchants of Labor: The Mexican Bracero Story*. Santa Barbara, Calif.: McNally & Loftin.

Gamio, Manuel. 1930. *Mexican Immigration to the United States*. Chicago: University of Chicago Press.

Goodman, Leo A. 1961. "Snowball Sampling." *Annals of Mathematical Statistics* 32:148–70.

Graves, Nancy B., and Theodore D. Graves. 1974. "Adaptive Strategies in Urban Migration." *Annual Review of Anthropology* 3:117–51.

Greenwood, Michael J. 1981. *Migration and Economic Growth in the United States*. New York: Academic.

Hanushek, Eric A., and John E. Jackson. 1977. *Statistical Methods for Social Scientists*. New York: Academic.

Hewitt de Alcantara, Cynthia. 1976. *Modernizing Mexican Agriculture: Socioeconomic Implications of Technical Change, 1940–1970*. Geneva: United Nations Research Institute for Social Development.

Jenkins, J. Craig. 1977. "Push/Pull in Recent Mexican Migration to the U.S." *International Migration Review* 11:178–89.

Lewis, W. Arthur. 1954. "Economic Development with Unlimited Supplies of Labour." *The Manchester School of Economic and Social Studies* 22 (2): 139–91.

Lomnitz, Larissa. 1977. *Networks and Marginality*. New York: Academic.

MacDonald, John S., and Leatrice D. MacDonald. 1974. "Chain Migration, Ethnic Neighborhood Formation, and Social Networks." Pp. 226–36 in *An Urban World*, edited by Charles Tilly. Boston: Little, Brown.

Massey, Douglas S. 1985. "The Settlement Process among Mexican Migrants to the United States: New Methods and Findings." Pp. 255–92 in *Immigration Statistics: A Story of Neglect*, edited by Daniel B. Levine, Kenneth Hill, and Robert Warren. Washington, D.C.: National Academy Press.

———. 1986. "The Settlement Process among Mexican Migrants to the United States." *American Sociological Review* 51:670–84.

Massey, Douglas S., Rafael Alarcon, Jorge Durand, and Humberto Gonzalez. 1987. *Return to Aztlañ: The Social Process of International Migration from Western Mexico*. Berkeley and Los Angeles: University of California Press, in press.

———. 1985. "The Social Organization of Mexican Migration to the United States." Paper presented at the Annual Meetings of the Population Association of America, Boston.

Mines, Richard. 1981. *Developing a Community Tradition of Migration: A Field Study in Rural Zacatecas Mexico and California Settlement Areas*. Monographs in U.S.-Mexican Studies, no. 3. La Jolla: Program in United States–Mexican Studies, University of California, San Diego.

———. 1984. "Network Migration and Mexican Rural Development: A Case Study." Pp. 136–55 in *Patterns of Undocumented Migration: Mexico and the United States*, edited by Richard C. Jones. Totawa: N.J.: Rowman & Allanheld.

Mines, Richard, and Alain deJanvry. 1982. "Migration to the United States and Mexican Rural Development: A Case Study." *American Journal of Agricultural Economics* 64:444–54.

Mines, Richard, and Douglas S. Massey. 1985. "Patterns of U.S. Migration from Two Mexican Communities." *Latin American Research Review* 20:104–23.

North, David S., and Marion F. Houstoun. 1976. *The Characteristics and Role of Illegal Aliens in the U.S. Labor Market: An Exploratory Study*. Washington, D.C.: Linton.

Paine, Suzanne. 1974. *Exporting Workers: The Turkish Case*. London: Cambridge University Press.

Petersen, Trond. 1985. "A Comment on Presenting Results from Logit and Probit Models." *American Sociological Review* 50:130–31.
Philpott, Stuart B. 1973. *West Indian Migration*. London: London School of Economics Monographs in Migration Series.
Piore, Michael J. 1979. *Birds of Passage: Migrant Labor and Industrial Societies*. New York: Cambridge University Press.
Portes, Alejandro, and Robert Bach. 1985. *Latin Journey: A Longitudinal Study of Cuban and Mexican Immigrants in the United States*. Berkeley and Los Angeles: University of California Press.
Pressar, Patricia R. 1982. "The Role of Households in International Migration and the Case of U.S.-Bound Migration from the Dominican Republic." *International Migration Review* 16:342–64.
Ranney, Susan, and Sherrie Kossoudji. 1983. "Profiles of Temporary Mexican Labor Migrants in the United States." *Population and Development Review* 9:475–93.
Ranis, Gustav, and J. C. H. Fei. 1961. "A Theory of Economic Development." *American Economic Review* 51:533–65.
Ravenstein, E. G. 1885. "The Laws of Migration." *Journal of the Royal Statistical Society* 48:167–277.
———. 1889. "The Laws of Migration." *Journal of the Royal Statistical Society* 52:241–302.
Reichert, Joshua S. 1979. *The Migrant Syndrome: An Analysis of U.S. Migration and Its Impact on a Rural Mexican Town*. Ph.D. diss. Department of Anthropology, Princeton University.
———. 1981. "The Migrant Syndrome: Seasonal U.S. Wage Labor and Rural Development in Central Mexico." *Human Organization* 40:56–66.
———. 1982. "Social Stratification in a Mexican Sending Community: The Effect of Migration to the United States." *Social Problems* 29:422–33.
Reichert, Joshua S., and Douglas S. Massey. 1979. "Patterns of Migration from a Mexican Sending Community: A Comparison of Legal and Illegal Migrants." *International Migration Review* 13:599–623.
———. 1980. "History and Trends in U.S.-Bound Migration from a Town." *International Migration Review* 14:475–91.
Rhoades, Robert E. 1978. "Intra-European Return Migration and Rural Development: Lessons from the Spanish Case." *Human Organization* 37:136–47.
———. 1979. "From Caves to Main Street: Return Migration and the Transformation of a Spanish Village." *Papers in Anthropology* 20:57–74.
Roberts, Bryan R. 1974. "The Interrelation of City and Provinces in Peru and Guatemala." *Latin American Urban Research*: 4:207–35.
———. 1978. *Cities of Peasants: The Political Economy of Urbanization in the Third World*. London: Arnold.
Roberts, Kenneth D. 1984. "Agricultural Development and Labor Mobility: A Study of Four Mexican Subregions." Pp. 74–92 in *Patterns of Undocumented Migration: Mexico and the United States*, edited by Richard C. Jones. Totawa, N.J.: Rowman & Allanheld.
Rossi, Peter H. 1955. *Why Families Move*. Glencoe: Free Press.
Rubenstein, Hymie. 1979. "The Return Ideology in West Indian Migration." *Papers in Anthropology* 20:21–38.
Samora, Julian. 1971. *Los Mojados: The Wetback Story*. Notre Dame, Ind.: University of Notre Dame Press.
Simmons, James W. 1968. "Changing Residence in the City: A Review of Intraurban Mobility." *Geographical Review* 58:622–51.
Sjaastad, Larry A. 1962. "The Costs and Returns of Human Migration." *Journal of Political Economy* 70:80–93.

Speare, Alden, Jr. 1974. "Residential Satisfaction as an Intervening Variable in Residential Mobility." *Demography* 11:173–88.
Stark, Oded. 1983. "Migration Decision Making: A Review Essay." *Migration and Development Program.* Discussion paper no. 3. Cambridge, Mass.: Migration and Development Program, Harvard University.
Stark, Oded, and D. Levhari. 1982. "On Migration and Risk in LDC's." *Economic Development and Cultural Change* 31:191–96.
Stavenhagen, Rodolfo. 1970. "Social Aspects of Agrarian Structure in Mexico." Pp. 225–70 in *Agrarian Problems and Peasant Movements in Latin America,* edited by R. Stavenhagen. Garden City, N.Y.: Anchor.
Taylor, J. Edward. 1984. "Differential Migration, Networks, Information, and Risk." *Migration and Development Program.* Discussion paper no. 11. Cambridge, Mass.: Migration and Development Program, Harvard University.
Thomas, Brinley. 1954. *Migration and Economic Growth.* London: Cambridge University Press.
Tilly, Charles. 1978. "Migration in Modern European History." Pp. 48–72 in *Human Migration,* edited by William H. McNeil and Ruth S. Adams. Bloomington: Indiana University Press.
Tilly, Charles, and C. H. Brown. 1967. "On Uprooting, Kinship, and the Auspices of Migration." *International Journal of Comparative Sociology* 8:139–64.
Todaro, Michael P. 1976. *Internal Migration in Developing Countries.* Geneva: International Labour Office.
Wiest, Raymond E. 1973. "Wage-Labor Migration and the Household in a Mexican Town." *Journal of Anthropological Research* 29:180–209.
———. 1984. "External Dependency and the Perpetuation of Temporary Migration to the United States." Pp. 110–35 in *Patterns of Undocumented Migration: Mexico and the United States,* edited by Richard C. Jones. Totowa, N.J.: Rowman & Allanheld.
Wood, Charles C. 1981. "Structural Changes and Household Strategies: A Conceptual Framework." *Human Organization* 40:338–44.
Zorbaugh, Harvey W. 1929. *The Gold Coast and the Slum.* Chicago: University of Chicago Press.

[13]

Financial History Review, vol. 8, part 1, April 2001. Printed in the United Kingdom

Networks of information, markets, and institutions in the rise of London as a financial centre, 1660–1720

LARRY NEAL
Department of Economics, University of Illinois at Urbana-Champaign, Urbana, IL 61801, USA

and

STEPHEN QUINN
Department of Economics, Texas Christian University, Fort Worth, TX 76129, USA

International market integration during the late seventeenth century required an ability to take advantage of favourable exchange rate differentials with regard to geographic location and types of payment. London-based bankers acquired this ability by using a network of merchants and bankers that spanned nations, religions and trade specialisations. This business web was more diverse than the kin groups, religious connections or guilds that had supported the rise of international trade since the Middle Ages. Rather, its constituent members were bound by financial interaction revolving around the hub of banking in London. By using bills of exchange written between a banker and his agent, merchants became stakeholders in the monitoring and enforcement of agency relationships. However, the network's efficacy varied with the nature of various nations' legal systems. The autocratic tendencies of France diminished agents' credibility, while the commitment of the Dutch and English to international commercial law strengthened overseas enforcement.

With information flows criss-crossing northern Europe, London-based bankers could successfully specialise in the supply of international finance. Merchants secured the system for the bankers and, in turn, benefited from bankers' services. Essential to the character of London's emerging financial system was the lack of a singular institution to coordinate information. A substantial network was in place as early as 1670. By the time the Bank of England was founded in 1694, London finance did not require a Dutch-style exchange bank to support the system of international payments. Instead, the Bank of England was designed along the lines of the other fractional reserve banks that already comprised a hub in London. At the turn of the century, no single bank in London dominated the bill market. Rather, deepening channels of finance enmeshed the bankers of Lombard Street with agents in various ports and the many merchants who connected them.

An examination of the late seventeenth-century ledgers of Edward Backwell, a pre-eminent goldsmith-banker, shows that he relied on the existing network of foreign merchants for connecting himself to overseas agents. The goldsmith made merchants his stakeholding partners in the processes of moving funds and monitoring the behaviour of his primary agents with whom he held covering balances in foreign currencies. With his arrangement of primary agents and multiple monitors, Backwell, and other London bankers, were by 1670 supplying bills, offering discounts and arranging bullion shipments. Although London had not yet become the dominant hub of international finance, its constituents were creating a new style of banking and a payment system that would form an integral part of the 'financial revolution'. The English system was oriented to an active market in bills of foreign exchange, which was unregulated but disciplined by English law, itself based upon the existing law merchant for dealings in goods. Even after the establishment of the Bank of England, this payment system continued to flourish, albeit focused increasingly upon Amsterdam and Hamburg rather than Paris or Madrid. In the merchant-controlled cities of Amsterdam, Hamburg and London, the law merchant governed the settlement of disputes arising from protested bills of exchange. By contrast, in the royal cities of Paris and Madrid, the often arbitrary law of the monarch could disrupt the web of credit that supported Western Europe's prospering trade.

The practices of arbitrage in foreign exchange – making foreign payments that took advantage of minor fluctuations in cross-exchange rates from mint par ratios – were already emerging in Restoration London and so well before the post-1688 revolution in public finance. The evidence arises again from the complex payments arranged by Backwell among his agents in Cadiz and Amsterdam. By the mid-eighteenth century, Postlethwayt's *Universal Dictionary of Trade and Commerce* could devote many pages to describing these payment alternatives taken by London merchants. That this system survived the systemic shocks of several major wars and the financial crisis of 1720 testifies to the inherent durability of trade networks when credit and payment networks sustain them. We conclude that it was the credit nexus established during the seventeenth century, more than the preceding webs arising from kinship, or religion or politics, which sustained the long-run development of trade relationships in northern Europe.

Finally, we examine in detail how enforcement procedures in case of credit default could be invoked in the London-Amsterdam nexus in contrast to the arbitrary rules set in Paris. The evidence derives from the systemic crisis that affected all of Europe with the collapse of both the Mississippi bubble in France and the South Sea bubble in England. During the general breakdown of the European payments system, a diamond merchant in Amsterdam tried to force payment on bills drawn by a local merchant banker on a goldsmith-banker in London. At the same time, the Amsterdam diamond merchant had to deal with the default of a merchant banker in London. The different procedures followed in the two cases of default, and the different outcomes that emerged in London and Amsterdam, demonstrate the long-run viability of the merchant-oriented legal system. The 'bubbles' episode was a defining moment for the competing systems of London and Paris. Thereafter during the eighteenth century, financial relationships flourished between London and Amsterdam, with spillovers to Hamburg and the Baltic, while French and Mediterranean connections languished.

I

With the development of networks of European trade centred upon Amsterdam, the supply of bills of exchange became a viable commercial specialisation, not only in Amsterdam but also at each of the outlying nodes. Bills were orders to pay in a foreign port in a foreign currency at some time in the future. They were similar to modern travellers cheques and were the dominant means of international payment during the early modern era. Instead of merchants arranging all the elements required for a bill, third-party intermediaries supplied credit or other services. This innovation in financial intermediation liberated individual traders from the costs arising from maintaining foreign contacts, settling their offsetting accounts, acquiring credit information on foreign traders and other burdensome activities. As the number of European merchants dealing with foreign markets increased, the greater became the value added by the suppliers of financial intermediation. In London, at least, these services became concentrated in the hands of bankers. From the mid-seventeenth century, such economic actors were transforming themselves from being goldsmiths to undertaking purely financial business.

The supply of international services required agents in foreign ports. The principal-agent problem faced by London-based bankers was of particular importance because the City was developing into a new kind of hub for international finance – one without an exchange bank. An exchange bank, like that at Amsterdam, held specie deposits upon which bills of exchange could be written.[1] Such banks brought many advantages to suppliers of bills. Transaction costs for settling bills were reduced by the clearing of accounts within the bank (in *banco*). Risk was also reduced because default meant expulsion from the exchange bank. Both of these features – the reduction of transaction costs and the reduction of default-risk – enjoyed increasing returns as increasing numbers of merchants participated in an exchange bank. Since the exchange bank acted as a clearing house for international payments, it both centralised information on default and orchestrated the ostracism of the defaulter. The Amsterdam municipal authorities required all bills of exchange for more than 300 guilders to be processed through the city's exchange bank, so network economies of scope were enjoyed.[2] Indeed, funds on deposit at the Wisselbank enjoyed a persistent premium (agio) over circulating coins.[3]

[1] J. G. van Dillen, 'The Bank of Amsterdam', in idem (ed.), *History of the Principal Public Banks* (The Hague, 1934).

[2] W. D. H. Assar, 'Bills of exchange and agency in the 18th century law of Holland and Zeeland', in idem, *The Courts and the Development of Commercial Law* (Berlin, 1987).

[3] J. McCusker, *Money and Exchange in Europe and America, 1600–1775: A Handbook* (Chapel Hill, 1978), pp. 46–51.

The differences between London and Amsterdam were translated into divergent paths of development. Founded in 1609, the Amsterdam Exchange Bank (Wisselbank) replaced the paper notes then being issued by cashiers and money changers.[4] As a result, the development of Amsterdam's private banking system appears to have been constrained for a century.[5] In the absence of an exchange bank, London witnessed the development of a strong banking industry. Individual bankers supplied deposits, means of payment, lending and money changing.[6] As a group, they offered mutual acceptance and systemic monitoring.[7] In order to offer overseas services, London bankers had to arrange a network of international monitoring without the benefit of a centralised institution. A measure of success in this regard is that the Bank of England was founded in 1694 as a fractional reserve, note-issuing institution, modelled on existing banks. The City's financial system had developed to the point that, when the new corporate bank was established, it was not created to dominate the bill market or act as a clearing house.

Individual London bankers could handle their respective foreign contacts in a variety of ways. The most secure was to send an employee abroad. However, such staff were expensive to maintain and, consequently, were limited to primary markets.[8] An alternative was to retain correspondents on a for-fee basis. This reduced costs relative to maintaining employees. For an individual banker in London, the cost of placing staff in numerous continental cities was prohibitive. As goldsmiths ran shops with only a few apprentices or clerks, the agent-based system was adopted.

The archetypal principal-agent relationship was based upon merchants who agreed to accept each other's bills for a fee and then settle the balance by creating an offsetting bill.[9] 'In such cases, Amsterdam merchants accepted bills drawn on them for the account of others and covered themselves by redrawing.'[10] Transaction costs were kept low because offsetting bills meant that there was no need for specie to be transported. However, vesting overseas agents with fiduciary power created the risk of misbehaviour. Kinship or religious ties were often insufficient to cover the wide network of commerce that had then developed. The creation of reputation effects by repeated business was another important tool. Agents with much to gain from future business were less likely to cheat. When the goldsmith-banker Edward Backwell developed a web of foreign agents, he usually concentrated his foreign business on only one correspondent per city. In this way, the banker generated

4 P. W. N. M. Dehing and M. C. 't Hart, 'Linking the fortunes: currency and banking, 1550–1800', in 't Hart, J. Jonker and L. van Zanden (eds), *A Financial History of the Netherlands* (New York, 1997), p. 43.

5 ibid., pp. 43–4.

6 R. D. Richards, *The Early History of Banking in England* (New York, 1927), pp. 23–4.

7 S. Quinn, 'Goldsmith-banking: mutual acceptance and interbanker clearing in Restoration London', *Explorations in Economic History*, 34 (1997), p. 412.

8 J. Price, 'Transaction costs: a note on merchant credit and the organization of private trade', in J. D. Tracy (ed.), *The Political Economy of Merchant Empires* (Cambridge, 1991), p. 279.

9 L. Neal, *The Rise of Financial Capitalism* (New York, 1990), pp. 5–9.

10 Price, 'Transaction costs', p. 28.

considerable business with a trusted agent. Building this reputation was a service that Backwell supplied to customers who could not manage such levels of activity on their own.

Concentrated business, however, still left risk for the banker. The London banker had to be aware of business troubles before the punishment of the perpetrator could be pursued. The arrangement would be more effective if news of malfeasance could be spread to damage the agent's reputation with other principals. London-based bankers needed to generate a flow of information sufficient to extend reputation effects to a network of bankers and merchants. In this way, a default to one member became known and punished by the whole. By the mid-eighteenth century, such reputation effects were well established.

The conduits for this information were merchants. Seventeenth-century merchants constantly passed information between ports and one family firm was subsequently found to have saved 10,500 letters between 1668 and 1680.[11] Merchants' correspondence brimmed with all manner of information. News of market conditions, war, exchange rates, bankruptcies and anything else of interest was routinely shared. The letters were kept because they formed a record of advice given, orders received and actions taken. If a merchant had to explain why a shipment was lost, or why a venture was unprofitable or why he could not pay his bills, the letters could clear his good name. Published price currents complemented this effort by providing a third-party record.[12] Even though Amsterdam was clearly then the hub for distributing commercial information,[13] London-based merchants were able to exploit effectively the information channels that existed in northern Europe.

The financial side of this correspondence was the bill of exchange. Merchants saved copies of bills for the same reasons they kept letters. Unlike letters, bills represented payments and merchants named in the bills became stakeholders in the payment process. A default, like a bounced cheque, affected all named parties. Individuals, added by their respective endorsements after the bill had been drawn, were also dragged into any failed performance because, if the bill was not redeemed, everyone else who had endorsed it became liable for its payment. The Dutch developed transfer by endorsement during the sixteenth century specifically as a means to involve merchants in the quality of the bills that they passed. The English adopted this system.[14]

By using merchants to pass funds to agents abroad, bankers like Edward Backwell took advantage of the incentives bills created. When the banker accepted or wrote

[11] H. Roseveare, *Markets and Merchants of the Late Seventeenth Century* (Oxford, 1987), p. 14.

[12] C. Gravesteijn and J. J. McCusker, *The Beginnings of Commercial and Financial Journalism* (Amsterdam, 1991), pp. 43–53.

[13] W. D. Smith, 'The functions of commercial centers in the modernization of European capitalism: Amsterdam as an information exchange in the seventeenth century', *Journal of Economic History*, 44 (1984); and M. Morineau, *Incroyables Gazettes et Fabuleux Metaux* (Cambridge, 1985).

[14] J. Rogers, *The Early History of the Law of Bills and Notes* (Cambridge, 1995) and J. M. Holden, *The History of Negotiable Instruments in English Law* (London, 1955).

bills involving his foreign agents, his ledger clearly named the merchants concerned. For example, on 28 March 1670, Backwell drew a bill of exchange ordering Henry and Charles Gerard to pay William Jarret 2,080 guilders.[15] The Gerards were Backwell's agents in Amsterdam. Should the Gerards have failed to pay as ordered, Jarret would become a party to the dispute. Similarly, any merchant to whom Jarret had transferred the bill would also become involved. Jarret had a clear incentive to know that the bill was honoured and settled. Endorsing merchants had a stake in monitoring Backwell's agent and would spread word of default on the bill to their colleagues.

London bankers and their agents employed a large number of different merchants at each port to send and receive bills. Although a banker might want to transfer large sums overseas, individual merchants preferred small bills in line with their less significant transactions. Thus a number of merchants were used which thickened the credit nexus and created multiple monitors for each agent. The arising effect was strengthened through integrating different religious and geographic communities. Each added its particular internal system of monitoring and reputation to the whole. For example, on 15 October 1669, Backwell paid Abraham Doportos for a bill drawn and sold by the Gerards in Amsterdam to Simon Nunes Enriques & Simon Soares of Hamburg.[16] Comparably, on 23 August of the same year, Backwell had paid Jo. Patters for a bill drawn by the Gerards on Jo. Vandercloet of Rotterdam.[17] Furthermore, George and Robert Shaw of Antwerp drew bills on Backwell by way of Engeld Muyhuk, Albertus Lunden and Barnardo Bree, all of Brussels, and Bartholomew van Berchen of Bruges.[18] Backwell had a wide range of merchants also moving between London and Middelburg, Hamburg, Cadiz, Seville and Paris.

The problem with a diverse body of merchants was passing news of default on to others and organising collective action. Here London banks helped solve the problem. In Amsterdam, the Exchange Bank monitored and enforced all bills clearing through the city. In London, the system of individual banks mimicked that role. Word of an agent's behaviour would pass back to the banker through the injured merchant and protested bill. The banker then spread the word to the numerous other merchants who held accounts in London. The banker also had a regular channel to other bankers in the City via regular, bilateral clearing arrangements.[19] The web tightened further because merchants banked with more than one shop. For example, on 13 July 1669, Backwell paid Sir John Frederick & Co. for a bill drawn by the Gerards in Amsterdam after it had passed through the shop of another

[15] Royal Bank of Scotland, Archive, London [hereafter RBS]: Backwell Ledger, S 1670–71, folio 41.
[16] RBS: Backwell Ledger, R 1669–70, folio 481.
[17] RBS: Backwell Ledger, R 1669–70, folio 63.
[18] RBS: Backwell Ledger, S 1670–1, folios 76, 328.
[19] Quinn, 'Goldsmith-banking', pp. 418–24.

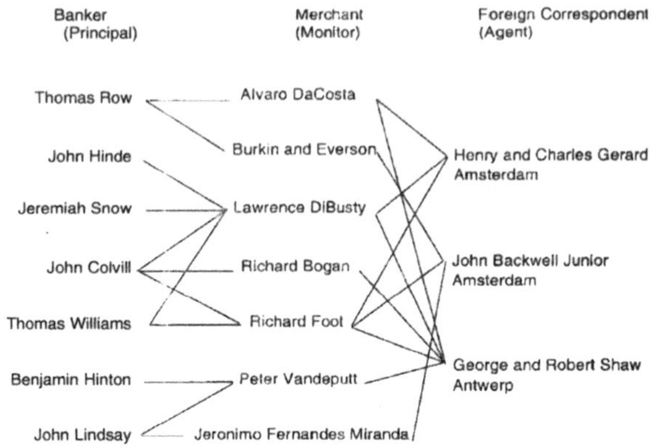

Figure 1. *Examples of connections between bankers, merchants and foreign agents in Edward Backwell's 1670 ledger*

goldsmith-banker, John Lindsay.[20] A number of other London bankers also appear in the process of moving bills to Backwell.

Use of multiple merchants per banker and of multiple bankers per merchant expanded the network's ability to spread information. For example, the Gerards of Amsterdam received bills from Backwell from over 20 different merchants during the 12 months from March 1670 to March 1671. Any default by the Gerards would have spread to a large number of merchants, which would extend the scope of damage to the Gerards' reputation. In addition, these merchants often banked with more than one goldsmith in London. Again, these contacts would disseminate knowledge of improper behaviour. Figure 1 connects seven merchants that presented bills from the Low Countries to Backwell in London and then transferred their resulting credit on the banker's ledger to other goldsmith-bankers. These examples are very exclusive because they do not consider the many merchants who presented bills to Backwell but did not bank with him. Such bills would have been settled in cash, by note or by some other form of payment rather than by ledger credit. Furthermore, the examples in Figure 1 do not include merchant transactions with goldsmiths other than Backwell (listed in Backwell's ledger), who were not directly associated with a bill of exchange. Merchants banking with Backwell regularly transferred funds to other bankers. Even under these restrictive terms, a substantial number of goldsmith-merchant-agent connections existed in 1670.

The British East India Company also used the same arrangements. When engaged in continental bullion purchases in 1675, the Company used the same agents as Backwell, namely: Gerards in Amsterdam; Banks in Hamburg; Rowland Dee in

[20] RBS: Backwell Ledger, R 1669–70, folio 62.

Cadiz; and Benjamin Bathurst in Seville.[21] Moreover, the Company used numerous prominent merchants and London goldsmith-bankers to pass the funds.[22] The strong similarities between the banker and the East India Company in their respective payments procedures suggest that this was common practice in late seventeenth-century London.

Another common element between the East India Company and the goldsmith-banker was the covering balances with agents. In contrast to a correspondent relationship premised on credit, both the Company and the banker regularly built up balances with their respective agents in advance of drawing bills payable by those agents. This was an expensive arrangement because neither operation earned interest on funds placed abroad. However, when the Company or Edward Backwell sent a bill, the agent already owed that amount. Covering balances made an agent's failure to honour a bill a failure to retire debt rather than a failure to extend credit. One benefit was that the agent would not have to create an offsetting bill, so the likelihood of acceptance would increase. A second benefit was that not honouring an order to pay backed by a debt was a more serious matter than failing to extend credit. By analogy, today a credit card has more latitude in denying funds than a demand deposit. The law regarding debt was well advanced by the seventeenth century, while that binding agents to credit-granting commitments was less clear.[23]

The potential problem of establishing that an agent in Amsterdam actually owed a principal in London was mitigated by the use of merchants to transfer funds. Merchants witnessed the transfer of funds and had incentives to see that those transfers were honoured and remembered. Merchants formed the spokes and bankers the hub of the London network. The flow of information was necessary for London-based bankers to conduct overseas finance.

II

The incentive for bankers and merchants to cooperate in operating the web of credit and information lay in the profits to be earned, and shared, in the arbitrage of foreign exchange. For example, bankers could offer bills between pairs of ports to capture favourable exchange rate differences. By increasing demand for bills denominated in weaker currencies and increasing the supply of bills denominated in stronger currencies, banker networks created a flow of funds that narrowed exchange rate differentials. While the integration of eighteenth-century exchange markets has been quantitatively established, data to perform similar tests for the seventeenth century are not available.[24] In place of market data on exchange rates, we have used the accounts of leading banking firms to show that bankers and

21 India Record Office, London [hereafter IRO]: East India Company Ledger, 1673–5, L/AG/1/1/6.

22 ibid.

23 Assar, 'Bills of exchange and agency'; and Rogers, *Early History of Law*.

24 E. Schubert, 'Arbitrage in the foreign exchange markets of London and Amsterdam during the 18th century', *Explorations in Economic History*, 26 (1989); and Neal, *Rise of Financial Capitalism*.

merchants took advantage of differences between direct rates and cross-rates throughout the network of leading European ports well before 1700. This, incidentally, shows that the origins of international market integration arose well before 1700 and before the revolution in English public finance during the 1690s.

A network of agents was necessary for taking advantage of exchange rate and cross-exchange rate opportunities. Moreover, such networks could provide spatial economies of scale. The marginal effect of adding one more information node to a network increased geometrically with the increased size of the network. Adding Hamburg to a London-Amsterdam network added two cross-connections: Hamburg-London and Hamburg-Amsterdam. Adding Paris to the Hamburg-London-Amsterdam network would add three links and so on. Each new link expanded the returns from the fixed investment embodied in existing nodes and opened new cross-market opportunities. The profits to be shared among participants engaged in effective arbitrage maintained the credit network's cohesion as it expanded.

With regular correspondence, dealers in bills of exchange would know when differences in rates developed between ports. 'When such local disequilibria occurred it was natural for the more adventurous dealers to practice arbitrage – dealing with a third centre whenever rates on a second centre might prove more advantageous.'[25] Henry Roseveare found that the London merchant Jacob David moved his funds from Amsterdam to Antwerp to take advantage of cross-rate imbalances in 1676.[26] Moreover, David did this on the advice received by letter from his underwriter Claude Hays. At other times, David routed funds to Hamburg via Amsterdam and Venice.[27]

Edward Backwell engaged in similar arbitrage behaviour and at an even earlier date. Much of Backwell's foreign transactions involved supplying funding for the English fleet provisioned out of Cadiz. Backwell provided banking services to the famous diarist Samuel Pepys and other purchasing agents for the Royal Navy.[28] For example, on 9 February 1671, Backwell drew bills due on Rowland Dee, Jr, of Cadiz for 15,000 pieces of eight (£3,375). Dee's account with Backwell recorded payment of the bill to Sir Hugh Cholmely at 20 days sight, value of Samuel Pepys. Because of his various agents, the banker could also supply bills directly between Spain and the Low Countries. After supplying the Royal Navy with silver and honouring bills drawn in London by Backwell, Rowland Dee balanced his accounts with the banker by drawing bills both on London and on Backwell's agents in Amsterdam. Over the 12 months from March 1670, Dee drew bills totalling £6,000 directly on London. The Cadiz agent drew an additional £3,769 worth of bills on

25 Roseveare, *Markets and Merchants*, p. 53.

26 ibid., p. 593.

27 ibid.

28 Richards, *Early History of Banking*, pp. 74–5.

Figure 2. *Arbitrage between Cadiz and London via Amsterdam in 1670*
Source: See note 34

the banker's agents in Amsterdam and £4,474 on the goldsmith's agents in Antwerp.[29]

The timing of Dee's bills, however, was most important. He switched from drawing bills on London to only drawing bills on the Low Countries in autumn 1670. This would have benefited Backwell in London. During summer 1670, Dee had drawn bills on London at a rate of 48.5 pence/peso (two-month bills). When Dee switched to Amsterdam and Antwerp in September and October, the Dutch schellingen had already depreciated against the pound by 2.5 per cent since May (34.6 Sch/£ in May to 35.5 in September). When the Dutch schellingen reached 36 to the English pound in October 1670, Dee's pesos-via-Holland were only costing Backwell 47 English pence a piece as opposed to 48.5 during the summer.[30] That was a three per cent gain. Over winter 1670–71, the Dutch rate strengthened relative to Spain as well, so the cross-rate differential favouring the Low Countries was eliminated. In February 1671, Rowland Dee resumed drawing bills directly on London. Figure 2 has presented a schematic of Backwell's arbitrage behaviour.

The ability to switch financial channels was evident. Merchants and bankers had the means to capture favourable cross-rates. Moreover, the information the network provided would have been essential for the successful manipulation of exchange rate differentials. Eric Schubert has described arbitrage between markets for bills as uncertain.[31] From the perspective of pricing bills, uncertainty entered into the demand for bills. Consider a market for bills in London. Information regarding the supply of pounds would be apparent to all parties in London. The demand side, however, was composed of agents for merchants in Amsterdam, and other cities,

[29] RBS: Backwell Ledger, S 1670–71 with Dee in Cadiz, folios 300, 320, 593, 595; Gerard in Amsterdam, folios 41, 443, 444; and Shaws in Antwerp, folios 76, 328, 573.

[30] The calculation was (117 grooten/ducata)(0.72533 ducata/peso)(0.08333 schellingen/grooten)[1/(36 schellingen/£)](240 pence/£) = 47.15 pence/peso. Denominational relationships from McCusker, *Money and Exchange*, pp. 44, 61, 99–100, 107.

[31] Schubert, 'Arbitrage'.

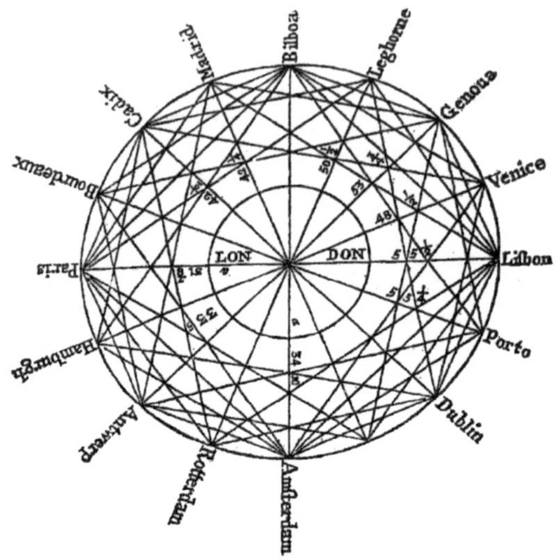

Figure 3. *The opportunities for arbitrage profits in the exchange network of Europe*
Source: M. Postlethwayt, *The Universal Dictionary of Trade and Commerce*, 4th ed. (London, 1774; reprinted New York, 1971), vol. I, *Arbitrage*

wanting to buy pounds with their schellingen, pesos, etc. For those trying to price a bill in London, information on actual demand would be as old as the most recent vessels crossing the channel. Expectations of demand arriving from foreign ports would play a discriminating role. A supplier of bills in London with better information about conditions in Amsterdam would have an advantage. 'Good manners, if not explicit instructions, required merchants in most European centres to keep their customers informed of the current rates of exchange.'[32] The better the information, the faster markets would tighten the weave of cross-rates. The same information was also essential for financial speculation as well. The implicit rate of return on bills was speculative because it relied on re-exchange.[33] Returns to 'dry exchange' – rolling over the value of a bill into a bill due back at the initial port – depended upon the exchange rate at the foreign port when the first bill fell due. Information from abroad reduced the risk of speculation by improving estimates of where foreign exchange markets were moving.

The network also aided the flow of bullion (Figure 3). In late 1669, Backwell drew down some of his account with the Gerards of Amsterdam by having them buy bullion and coin. On the banker's behalf, the Gerards acquired Spanish pistols

[32] Roseveare, *Markets and Merchants*, p. 592.

[33] R. DeRoover, 'What is dry exchange? A contribution to the study of English mercantilism', in idem, *Business, Banking, and Economic Thought* (Chicago, 1974).

and pieces of eight, French crowns, Venetian ducats and Dutch rixdollars, along with ingots and bars of silver and gold.[34] Market-integrating arbitrage between bills and bullion required both access to, and knowledge of, foreign markets, with Amsterdam being the key market.[35] Thus the network of bankers and merchants provided the means to connect the many European markets for bills of exchange, gold and silver. One question remains. How could this credit network survive repeated shocks inflicted upon it by the succession of wars, revolutions, and financial crises that characterised both the closing decades of the seventeenth century and the eighteenth century?

III

A detailed example of enforcement in action is provided by the surviving correspondence of an Amsterdam diamond merchant, Bernard van der Grift, with his principal client in London, Lord Londonderry (Thomas Pitt, Jr), 1720–25.[36]

Van der Grift was trying to collect sums owed to Londonderry by John Law, arising from Law's spectacular loss through speculating against stocks traded on the London stock market.[37] From Paris, Law had instructed his agent in London, the goldsmith-banker George Middleton, to pay Londonderry in Amsterdam. To make this payment, Law told Middleton to draw five bills on his Amsterdam agent, Abraham Mouchard, the representative of the French Compagnie des Indes. Middleton drew the bills and tendered them to Londonderry as partial payment of Law's debts to Londonderry. Londonderry then endorsed the bills to his agent in Amsterdam, the diamond dealer Bernard van der Grift.

Middleton had asked Mouchard on each bill to pay a stated sum in Dutch bank money to Londonderry, based upon value received from John Law. Londonderry, in turn, endorsed every bill to his agent in Amsterdam, van der Grift, so that van der Grift could receive the sum and credit it to Londonderry's account with him. Middleton would write a letter of advice to Mouchard, explaining the source of funds from Law that Mouchard should use in making the payment, while Londonderry wrote to van der Grift explaining how, and when, he wanted the funds used for his account. Mouchard was expected to accept each bill when

[34] RBS: Backwell Ledger, R 1669–70, folios 64, 481–2.

[35] S. Quinn, 'Gold, silver, and the Glorious Revolution: arbitrage between bills of exchange and bullion', *Economic History Review*, 49 (1996), pp. 474–82.

[36] This correspondence is contained in a bundle of letters in Chancery Masters Exhibits at the Public Record Office, Kew, London [hereafter PRO]: C108/420. All dates on van der Grift's letters are Gregorian calendar, New Style, and correspond to 11 days earlier in Britain, still on the Julian calendar, Old Style.

[37] Details of this episode are in L. Neal, 'George Middleton: John Law's goldsmith-banker, 1727–1729', in Paul Klep and Eddy van Cauwenberghe (eds), *Entrepreneurship and the Transformation of the Economy (10th–20th Centuries)* (Leuven, 1994); and L. Neal, ' "For God's sake, remitt me": the adventures of John Law's goldsmith-banker in London, 1712–1729', *Business and Economic History*, 23 (1994), pp. 27–60.

presented to him by van der Grift. After signing his acceptance, the bill would become a negotiable instrument in Amsterdam so that van der Grift could either discount it for immediate cash or hold it for the two months usance allowed to Mouchard to raise the sums and pay off the bill. Londonderry had made the acquaintance of van der Grift while acting as the overseas agent for his father, Thomas Pitt, Sr – Governor Pitt – perhaps the wealthiest diamond merchant in London. One of the largest capital transfers of the time ultimately had to be made through the credit network previously established by traders – in this case diamond merchants in London and Amsterdam.

Earlier in 1720, Londonderry had sent van der Grift five bills drawn on Mouchard by John Lambert, another goldsmith-banker. In a letter of 14 June to Londonderry, van der Grift explained that Mouchard had not accepted the bills for payment. Instead of protesting the bills with a notary public in Amsterdam as the first step in pursuing legal remedies against Mouchard, van der Grift returned the bills as unpaid and unaccepted to Londonderry. Here he was simply following Londonderry's instructions, who had suspected the bills might not be covered by funds Lambert had on account with Mouchard.

When van der Grift received the new set of bills drawn on Mouchard, this time by Middleton, he was naturally concerned for his client Londonderry. Despite his reservations about the ability of both Middleton and Mouchard to carry on payments in this manner, van der Grift promised to pay the bills Londonderry drew on him 'on account of the value, and credit I have for your Lordship (and I assure your Lordship on no other accounts)'.[38] Wanting to retain the business of Londonderry, his principal in London, van der Grift was volunteering to pay out his own cash to Londonderry's creditors whether or not he received cash from Mouchard. All he asked was that the bills drawn by Middleton on Mouchard be dated payable before those that Londonderry drew on van der Grift, a reasonable precaution in the uncertain circumstances of the time. Van der Grift intended to cover his payments on Londonderry's behalf by drawing on money owed him in London by a Lewis Johnson and to have this remitted to him via bills of exchange. It would be in Londonderry's interest to assist van der Grift in collecting the sums Johnson owed him, if any difficulty arose in completing that contract.

As matters developed, van der Grift found in October 1720 that his speculations on South Sea stock with his agent in London, Lewis Johnson, had come to nothing. Johnson stopped payments on bills drawn on him. Nevertheless, van der Grift insisted that he could continue to meet Londonderry's drafts on him through other balances he had owing to him in London. But now Londonderry became van der Grift's agent in London to help resolve his claims on Lewis Johnson. Meanwhile, van der Grift continued to pay off Londonderry's partners in Amsterdam by accepting bills drawn on him by Londonderry, as Mouchard had accepted the bills drawn on him by Middleton. Both sets of accepted bills were negotiable instruments

[38] PRO: Chancery Masters Exhibits, Pitt v. Cholmondeley, C108/420, letter of 24 Sep. 1720.

but van der Grift was retaining the bills accepted by Mouchard. Due to the general knowledge within Amsterdam of the payments difficulties that Mouchard was facing as his source of funds in Paris dried up, any discount of one of Mouchard's acceptances would have incurred a heavy risk premium. There would also be a hefty interest charge, given the then general shortage of credit in Amsterdam.

So far, all that required appeal to enforcement mechanisms, whether formal or informal, was van der Grift's claim on Lewis Johnson, which he wished to use for making payments to Londonderry in London. To initiate proceedings against Johnson while still maintaining a flow of payments to Londonderry, van der Grift suggested that Londonderry return the protested bills of van der Grift on Johnson and sell £1,000 of South Sea stock that van der Grift had bought earlier through Londonderry. In order to maintain Londonderry's business, van der Grift had previously sent him funds to buy stock of the South Sea Company, which had then been rapidly rising on the London market, and these were still being held by Londonderry on van der Grift's account. The Dutchman subsequently assured Londonderry that, even if he was not inclined to sell the South Sea stock due to its now low and continually falling price, he would remit him immediately against it, in effect pledging the stock as collateral for whatever payments Londonderry made on his behalf, 'for his honour'.[39]

In a letter of 29 October, van der Grift gave Londonderry his first hint of future troubles with Mouchard. He noted, first, that Mouchard was only obtaining means to make payment on the bills drawn on him through gold continually sent from France in monthly shipments, which he had pawned immediately at the Wisselbank. Neither silver nor any other form of exchange with France was being transferred, either to, or from, Amsterdam. While Mouchard had considerable amounts of coffee and indigo in his warehouse, it was being held on account of the French Compagnie and consequently was not available for sale or to be pawned on his account. The bills, that he had accepted earlier and was supposed to pay the day before, had not yet been paid.[40] All this information on Mouchard's affairs was readily available to all concerned bankers and merchants in Amsterdam and could be easily confirmed by Londonderry from London.

In the next letter of 1 November 1720, van der Grift enclosed his protests on three of the bills on Mouchard that he had accepted but not paid when due. While van der Grift considered Mouchard to be an honest man, if the Compagnie in France did not continue to support him, he would be unable to pay the large amount of bills he had already accepted. A week later, van der Grift was informed by Mouchard that the gold he had received from the Compagnie was much less in amount than he needed and expected. There were hundreds of bills running on him so, if he failed, there

[39] PRO: Chancery Masters Exhibits, C108/420, letter of 22 Oct. 1720.
[40] PRO: Chancery Masters Exhibits, C108/420, letter of 29 Oct. 1720.

would be serious trouble in Amsterdam since two of the very best houses in the Dutch city had already stopped payments on their accepted bills.[41]

To give some assurance about Mouchard to Londonderry, van der Grift persuaded Mouchard to give him some bills due to Mouchard over the coming month. Even though van der Grift was apprehensive over whether these bills would, in turn, be paid, he felt it was 'better security than none at all'. His 12 November letter was largely taken up with his reasoning over how to deal with his defaulter in London, Lewis Johnson, and giving instructions to Londonderry about how to act as his attorney in resolving that matter. Van der Grift proposed to pay cash out to Londonderry's creditors in Amsterdam but then have them return to London the accepted, but unpaid, bills drawn on Lewis Johnson with a counter-protest. As van der Grift would have by then paid off the obligation of Lewis Johnson, he would become Johnson's creditor in London and have legal standing to sue him in London courts and possibly force him to be declared a bankrupt. It was more the threat of bankruptcy and imprisonment, rather than the practice, that van der Grift desired. In this way, he could force Johnson to make a full account of what he could pay.[42]

As conditions worsened in France, especially for the personal circumstances of John Law, van der Grift found himself in the middle of yet another transaction between Londonderry and his father. This time, Law had directed Middleton to draw bills on his agent in Hamburg, Alexander Bruquier, and give them to Governor Pitt as payment for his share in the wager. The Governor, in turn, sent them to his trusted agent in Amsterdam, van der Grift, to collect on his behalf. Bruquier had informed Middleton by letter that he had accepted the bills for payment but van der Grift knew that actually Law's Hamburg agent had only accepted them when they were presented to him a second time. There was then no negotiation of bills between Hamburg and Amsterdam due to the systemic financial crisis enveloping all of Europe. Consequently, there was a problem of how to get the payment back to Governor Pitt's account with van der Grift in Amsterdam even if Bruquier paid in Hamburg. Van der Grift proposed in a letter of 26 November to send the bills accepted by Bruquier to a friend of his in Hamburg, Lucas Backman, whose character he vouched for, for re-exchange back to van der Grift in Amsterdam. In this way, Backman would end up being paid by Bruquier in Hamburg, Governor Pitt would be paid by van der Grift in Amsterdam, after the completion of intermediate steps involving van der Grift creating a claim on Backman and Backman then, in turn, discharging it with a bill drawn on van der Grift. The contract between the principals, Pitt and Bruquier, was to be fulfilled by Bruquier paying out in Hamburg and Pitt receiving payment in Amsterdam. The intermediaries involved – van der Grift and Backman – would receive commissions for their services and some interest derived from the exchange rate spreads in

[41] PRO: Chancery Masters Exhibits, C108/420, letter of 8 Nov. 1720.

[42] PRO: Chancery Masters Exhibits, C108/420, letter of 12 Nov. 1720.

Amsterdam and Hamburg. In short, van der Grift was recommending that Governor Pitt should rely on the proven network of merchant credit built up over the years instead of trusting the new network of agents established by John Law on behalf of the French Compagnie des Indes.

Regardless of this side play, Londonderry still needed to pay off his father and his powerful partners in Amsterdam for their part in the wager with Law. He evidently proposed that van der Grift pawn some of his merchandise that lay unsold in Amsterdam to pay the bills Londonderry had drawn, in turn, on van der Grift. Van der Grift dismissed this, noting that prices of such goods had fallen dramatically and, therefore, their sale or pawn would not begin to cover the sums required to honour the bills drawn by Middleton on Mouchard. Rather, he recommended that Londonderry return the protested bills on Mouchard to Middleton, who would then be obliged to reimburse Londonderry, just as van der Grift had reimbursed the Amsterdam partners of Londonderry when Lewis Johnson had defaulted in London.[43] Van der Grift had not evidently perceived that Middleton was, in turn, about to fail at nearly the same time Londonderry would have received his letter.

Middleton's desperate situation in London, reflecting that of John Law in Paris, became clear when the next post brought a batch of bills drawn by Middleton on Law's agent in Genoa, M. Chavigny. Van der Grift agreed to send the first bills to Genoa to have them accepted but asked Londonderry to send the seconds endorsed to van der Grift. These the Dutchman would hold until their usance was nearly up before then sending them to Genoa. This way, van der Grift would get the shortest dated bills possible, which would be the most secure for payment back in Amsterdam.

Meanwhile, it became ever clearer that Mouchard would be unable to pay the bills that he had accepted. As van der Grift was growing tired of his procrastination and repetitive excuses, he finally recommended initiating legal action. As earlier with Lewis Johnson in London, this was intended to frighten Mouchard to exert himself more seriously to make payment if at all possible. Otherwise, Mouchard could be made bankrupt and imprisoned.[44]

Before accepting van der Grift's advice, Londonderry had to cope with the shock of Middleton's stoppage of payments on 13 December in London (but 24 December, Christmas Eve, in Paris and Amsterdam). Middleton himself wrote to van der Grift, to explain that the dismissal of John Law in Paris had made it impossible for him to cover any of Law's bills in expectation that Law could eventually reimburse him.[45] From Paris, Londonderry sent van der Grift a power of attorney that enabled the Dutchman to put Londonderry's name to the unendorsed bills that Londonderry had already sent to Amsterdam. Van der Grift noted that this unusual method, apparently recommended to Londonderry in Paris, was not lawful

43 PRO: Chancery Masters Exhibits, C108/420, letter of 3 Dec. 1720.

44 PRO: Chancery Masters Exhibits, C108/420, letter of 20 Dec. 1720.

45 Coutts & Co., Archives, London: Letter Book 'O-14', Foreign Letters 1720, f. 509.

in Amsterdam. Therefore, he suggested that Londonderry endorse the second copies of the bills and send them to him in Amsterdam. Even so, these bills would be no good if Mouchard still lacked funds on account for John Law.[46]

The next ploy by Mouchard was to suggest to van der Grift and Londonderry that he draw bills on Compagnie des Indes in Paris payable to Londonderry's agent in Paris, Sir John Drummond. However, French law required such bills always to state clearly that 'value was received' by the drawer of the bill. A bill of exchange drawn on Paris could be declared null and void if the drawer could not provide proof that he had received value corresponding to the amount being drawn. This was the assurance provided in French law that the ultimate drawer would always be responsible for the amount paid out on his credit. English law was more flexible, requiring only that the original drawer be responsible ultimately for payment, without needing to demonstrate that value had been received for each bill. If van der Grift gave Mouchard either the bills drawn by van der Grift directly on Mouchard or bills drawn to Londonderry and endorsed to van der Grift, he would lose legal leverage on Mouchard under Dutch law in Amsterdam. In any case, he did not trust Compagnie des Indes to pay since the concern had not been providing Mouchard with the necessary means to meet his obligations to date in Amsterdam.[47]

Meanwhile, van der Grift had received payment for the bills drawn by Middleton on Bruquier in Hamburg, and he was remitting the proceeds directly to Governor Pitt. The well-established merchant lines of credit were being sustained to at least this extent in the midst of the financial meltdown of international capital markets during 1720. Ironically, one of the bills sent by van der Grift was drawn on Robert Knight, treasurer of the South Sea Company. Knight was under close investigation by a Secret Committee of Parliament enquiring into the collapse of the South Sea Company and about to abscond to Brussels!

During the next month, van der Grift continued to enquire at least each post day at Mouchard's office to sustain the pressure on him while his protested bills were in process of being sent to Londonderry. Londonderry then obtained a contra-protest on the bills from Middleton, who could rightly claim that he had been informed by his principal, John Law, that provision had been placed with Mouchard for payment of the bills. By mid-February, the contra-protested bills had been received back in Amsterdam by van der Grift, who was now ready to proceed with legal action against Mouchard. Using the contra-protested bills – endorsed originally by Londonderry to van der Grift and then accepted by Mouchard, protested by van der Grift and sent to Londonderry, who had them contra-protested by Middleton and sent them back to van der Grift – Van der Grift's lawyer obtained a *prise de corps* authorisation from the Amsterdam magistrates. Once in effect, the *prise de corps* meant that van der Grift could, at his pleasure, have Mouchard arrested and put in prison. For the *prise de corps* to take effect, Mouchard had to be summoned three

[46] PRO: Chancery Masters Exhibits, C108/420, letter of 14 Jan. 1721.

[47] PRO: Chancery Masters Exhibits, C108/420, letter of 17 Jan. 1721.

times before the magistrate. Within a week this was carried out and van der Grift now had the full force of Dutch law at his disposal to be used against Mouchard on behalf of Londonderry.

Nevertheless, it seemed to van der Grift that the wisest course of action was to keep the threat of imprisonment as an option, rather than to exercise the *prise de corps*.[48] This recommendation by van der Grift was taken and appears to have had the desired effect of terrifying Mouchard. Van der Grift reported that Mouchard was no longer to be found in his office but was hiding in his home. Moreover, he had shown bad faith by first depositing some French bank bills with the notary who was holding the *prise de corps* and then taking the bills back. Despite this show of desperation by Mouchard, van der Grift still counselled patience. Mouchard repaid this kindness by hiding out in a friend's house, which caused van der Grift to recommend declaring him bankrupt and having him arrested. This way he and Londonderry could seize what little effects remained in Mouchard's possession before he had a chance to dispose of them.[49] In the event, another creditor also obtained a *prise de corps* against Mouchard and took out a statute of bankruptcy against him.[50] That creditor turned out to be Londonderry himself, no doubt somewhat to van der Grift's surprise. Londonderry then allowed Mouchard three months' liberty to try to put his affairs in order and Mouchard gratefully accepted. Van der Grift noted that after Londonderry's liberty period expired, his original *prise de corps* would again be in force, so the ultimate threat of imprisonment would remain.

Over the following several years, Mouchard's name only appeared every three months in the weekly letters from van der Grift to Londonderry – upon the renewed extensions of the liberty he allowed to Mouchard from the *prise de corps* still outstanding against him. The *prise de corps*, never being exercised, legally lapsed one year and six weeks after its issue but *sauf conduits* were then issued repeatedly to protect Mouchard from the statute of bankruptcy. The affair ended in March 1724 as Law and Londonderry had come to a separate conclusion of Law's huge debt, after intensive negotiations between the two principals in London.

At the close of 1723, it had appeared that Law would be recalled to France by the Duc d'Orléans, chief adviser to Louis XV then in his teens, and allowed to regain possession of his estates and financial assets. In turn, Law pledged his 3,000 shares in Compagnie des Indes towards payment of his final debt of £92,000 to Londonderry and associates. Law then released all of his agents – in Amsterdam, Genoa, Hamburg and London – of their obligations to pay bills of exchange drawn on them. However, with the death of the Duc d'Orléans in late 1723, the new French ministers turned against Law; they induced his brother also to turn against him and apparently seduced his wife to stay in Paris while Law languished in Venice. But that is another, unhappy

[48] PRO: Chancery Masters Exhibits, C108/420, letter of 14 Feb. 1721.

[49] PRO: Chancery Masters Exhibits, C108/420, letter of 4 Mar. 1721.

[50] PRO: Chancery Masters Exhibits, C108/420, letter of 7 Mar. 1721.

tale of the lack of honour among statesmen and aristocrats. It has no more bearing on our story of the network of credit established among the mercantile community of early modern Europe and the legal apparatus supporting it.

The legal procedures of protest and contra-protest on bills that were either not accepted or, if accepted, were not paid, provided documentary evidence of breach of payment. All parties to a bill also had to supply and preserve the supporting letters of advice with instructions from principals to agents and confirmation of actions taken sent back by agents to their principals. In the case study just presented, Londonderry was both principal and agent to van der Grift. It is unfortunate that Londonderry's letter book for the period is missing but van der Grift was clearly the instructor in the relationship, patiently tutoring his new client in the ways of the mercantile world. Thanks to his expositions, we have been able to reconstruct the legal machinery available and used by merchants during the early eighteenth century. It was also clearly in operation by the mid-seventeenth century.

IV

To become an international financial centre, seventeenth-century London had to overcome at least one comparative disadvantage – the lack of a public bank, a central institution that processed bills of exchange. Such banks were essentially clearing houses for payments by foreigners using bills of exchange drawn on correspondents. Amsterdam's Wisselbank, established in 1609, was the most envied foreign example.[51] Despite considering many schemes to emulate the Wisselbank, London bankers and merchants never created such an institution. Before 1688, the reason no doubt lay in merchants' reluctance to put their specie assets at the potential disposal of a capricious monarch capable of seizing them for reasons of state. Only city-states governed by republican forms of government dominated by merchant interests, such as Venice, Genoa or Hamburg, established such exchange banks in Europe. After the Glorious Revolution of 1688 in England, the Protestant monarch was more tightly constrained by the legislative power of Parliament.[52] Even then, it took the duress of war finance to persuade Parliament to establish a peculiarly British version of a public bank in 1694 – the Bank of England. Unlike the Bank of Amsterdam, the Bank of London (as the Bank of England was popularly, and correctly, known during the eighteenth century) did not dominate the local bill market, it did not act as large-scale clearing house, and no bills were required to pass through it.[53] Instead, the Bank was a fractional reserve, note-issuing bank, committed to serving the British Treasury. In place of a centralised institution such as the Wisselbank, London bankers had to arrange an informal network of

[51] J. K. Horsefield, *British Monetary Experiments 1650–1710* (New York, 1983), p. 94.

[52] D. North and B. Weingast, 'Constitutions and commitment: the evolution of institutions governing public choice in seventeenth-century England', *Journal of Economic History*, 49 (1989).

[53] H. V. Bowen, 'Bank of England 1694–1820', in R. Roberts and D. Kynaston (eds), *The Bank of England, Money, Power and Influence 1694–1994* (Oxford, 1995), pp. 14–16.

mutual monitors operating through the foreign-exchange markets to maintain a viable payments system. This was necessary to support England's growing overseas commerce and public expenditure.

Rather than clear all bills through an exchange bank, London bankers' bills were settled, along with notes and cheques, via bilateral clearing between bankers.[54] The benefit for London's financial development was that the specie deposited in fractional reserve banks was recycled into market lending. In contrast, an exchange bank was required to maintain 100 per cent backing for its deposits. Recycling deposits buttressed a resilient, market-oriented, domestic banking system in London. The cost, however, was that bills drawn on London lacked the firmer backing offered by bills drawn on Amsterdam. Further, because all bill traffic in Amsterdam was directed through the Wisselbank, any default there was immediately observed by all participants and met by universal withdrawal of business from the defaulter. Defaulted bills in London, by contrast, required legal action to be initiated by the aggrieved individual, while the defaulter could continue to do business with other clients.

London bankers reduced their risks in dealing with international bills of exchange by creating a network of responsible agents overseas, each of whom owed a substantial part of his business to the respective London banking house and, therefore, had every incentive to maintain his reputation for fair and prompt dealing with London. Overseas agents, in turn, were constantly monitored by a large number of diverse merchants, both British and foreign, who remitted bills of exchange between London and abroad in part to finance their trading activities. Confronted by a classic principal-agent problem, bankers in Lombard Street focused on establishing accounts with proven and reputable associates in Amsterdam, Paris or Cadiz. As they widened their networks of trade and credit, they rapidly outgrew the possibility of their foreign agents' sanctioning opportunistic behaviour by religious or family ostracism, or by organising collective action with other merchants in a foreign port against an expropriating prince or a mercenary merchant.[55] Both London bankers and their foreign agents were only subject to the domestic law at each port. To enforce contracts across the resulting legal boundaries required the creation of enforcement mechanisms that were both informal and novel.

54 Quinn, 'Goldsmith-banking'.

55 A. Greif, 'Reputation and coalitions in medieval trade: evidence on the Maghribi traders', *Journal of Economic History*, 49 (1989); idem, 'Contract enforceability and economic institutions in early trade: the Maghribi traders coalition', *American Economic Review*, 83 (1993); and P. Milgrom, D. North and B. Weingast, 'The role of institutions in the revival of trade: the medieval law merchant, private judges, and the champaigne fairs', *Economics and Politics*, 2 (1990).

[14]

PHYSICAL REVIEW E **68**, 036122 (2003)

Why social networks are different from other types of networks

M. E. J. Newman and Juyong Park
Department of Physics and Center for the Study of Complex Systems, University of Michigan, Ann Arbor, Michigan 48109, USA and Santa Fe Institute, 1399 Hyde Park Road, Santa Fe, New Mexico 87501, USA
(Received 2 June 2003; published 22 September 2003)

We argue that social networks differ from most other types of networks, including technological and biological networks, in two important ways. First, they have nontrivial clustering or network transitivity and second, they show positive correlations, also called assortative mixing, between the degrees of adjacent vertices. Social networks are often divided into groups or communities, and it has recently been suggested that this division could account for the observed clustering. We demonstrate that group structure in networks can also account for degree correlations. We show using a simple model that we should expect assortative mixing in such networks whenever there is variation in the sizes of the groups and that the predicted level of assortative mixing compares well with that observed in real-world networks.

DOI: 10.1103/PhysRevE.68.036122 PACS number(s): 89.75.Hc, 87.23.Ge, 64.60.Ak, 05.90.+m

I. INTRODUCTION

The last few years have seen a burst of interest within the statistical physics community in the properties of networked systems such as the Internet, the World Wide Web, and social and biological networks [1–4]. Researchers' attention has, to a large extent, been focused on properties that seem to be common to many different kinds of networks, such as the so-called "small-world effect" and skewed degree distributions [5–7]. In this paper, by contrast, we highlight some apparent differences between networks, specifically between social and nonsocial networks. Our observations appear to indicate that social networks are fundamentally different from other types of networked systems.

We focus on two properties of networks that have received attention recently. First, we consider degree correlations in networks. It has been observed that the degrees of adjacent vertices in networks are positively correlated in social networks but negatively correlated in most other networks [8]. Second, we consider network transitivity or clustering, the propensity for vertex pairs to be connected if they share a mutual neighbor [5]. We argue that the level of clustering seen in many nonsocial networks is not greater than one would expect by chance, given the observed degree distribution. For social networks, however, clustering appears to be far greater than we expect by chance.

We conjecture that the explanation for both of these phenomena is in fact the same. Using a simple network model, we argue that if social networks are divided into groups or communities, this division alone can produce both degree correlations and clustering.

The outline of the paper is as follows. In Sec. II we discuss the phenomenon of degree correlation and summarize some empirical results for various networks. In Sec. III we do the same for clustering. We also present theoretical arguments that suggest that the clustering seen in nonsocial networks is of about the magnitude one would expect for a random graph model with parameters similar to real networks. Then in Sec. IV we present analytic results for a simple model of a social network divided into groups. This model, which was introduced previously [9], is known to generate high levels of clustering. Here we show that it can also explain the presence of correlations between the degrees of adjacent vertices. In Sec. V we compare the model's predictions concerning degree correlations against two real-world social networks, of collaborations between scientists and between business people. In the former case we find that the model is in good agreement with empirical observation. In the latter we find that it can predict some but not all of the observed degree correlation, and we conjecture that the remainder is due to true sociological or psychological effects, as distinct from the purely topological effects contained in the model. In Sec. VI we give our conclusions.

II. DEGREE CORRELATIONS

In studies of the network structure of the Internet at the level of autonomous systems, Pastor-Satorras *et al.* [10] have recently demonstrated that the degrees of adjacent vertices in this network appear to be anticorrelated. They measured the mean degree $\langle k_{\mathrm{nn}} \rangle$ of the nearest neighbors of a vertex as a function of the degree k of that vertex and found that the resulting curve falls off with k approximately as $\langle k_{\mathrm{nn}} \rangle \sim k^{-1/2}$. Thus, vertices of high degree tend to be connected, on average, to others of low degree and vice versa. A simple way of quantifying this effect is to measure a correlation coefficient of the degrees of adjacent vertices in a network, defined as follows.

Suppose that p_k is the degree distribution of our network, i.e., the fraction of vertices in the network with degree k, or equivalently the probability that a vertex chosen uniformly at random from the network will have degree k. The vertex at the end of a randomly chosen edge in the network will have degree distributed in proportion to kp_k, the extra factor of k arising because k times as many edges end at a vertex of degree k than at a vertex of degree one [11–13]. Commonly we are interested not in the total degree of the vertex at the end of an edge, but in the "excess degree," which is the number of edges attached to the vertex other than the one we arrived along, which is obviously one less than the total degree. The properly normalized distribution of the excess degree is

$$q_k = \frac{(k+1)p_{k+1}}{\sum_k k p_k}. \tag{1}$$

We then define the quantity e_{jk}, which is the joint probability that a randomly chosen edge joins vertices with excess degrees j and k.

Now consider a network in which the vertices have given degrees (the values of the degrees being called the "degree sequence"), but which is in all other respects random. That is, the network is drawn uniformly at random from the ensemble of all possible networks with the given degree sequence. This is the so-called configuration model [12–15], which we can use as a handy null model for testing our results. In the configuration model the expected value of the quantity e_{jk} is simply $e_{jk}=q_j q_k$, and by its deviation from this value we can quantify the level of degree correlation present relative to the null model. We define [8]

$$r = \frac{1}{\sigma_q^2} \sum_{jk} jk(e_{jk} - q_j q_k), \tag{2}$$

where $\sigma_q^2 = \Sigma_k k^2 q_k - [\Sigma_k k q_k]^2$ is the variance of the distribution q_k. The quantity r will be positive or negative for networks with positive or negative degree correlations, respectively. In the ecology and epidemiology literatures these two cases are called "assortative" and "disassortative" mixing by degree, and this nomenclature has been adopted by many physicists also.

The findings of Pastor-Satorras *et al.* [10] discussed above suggest that the Internet should have a negative value for r, and this indeed is the case. The most recent structural measurements of the autonomous-system graph of the Internet [16] yield a value of $r=-0.193\pm0.002$. It now appears that similar results apply to essentially all other networks *except* social networks. In Refs. [8,17] we found that almost all networks seem to be disassortatively mixed, i.e., have negative values of the coefficient r, except for social networks, which are normally assortative. A small number of networks yield inconclusive results because the error on r is bigger than its value, but other than these few, the pattern appears essentially perfect.

Here we propose that this striking pattern arises because disassortativity is the natural state for all networks, in a sense that we will make clear shortly. Left to their own devices, we conjecture, networks normally have negative values of r. In order to show a positive value of r, a network must have some specific additional structure that favors assortative mixing. In Sec. IV we suggest a possible candidate for such a structure in social networks.

Our conjecture that most networks will be disassortative is motivated by work of Maslov *et al.* [18]. Using computer simulations, they showed that on small networks disassortative mixing is produced if one restricts the network topology to having at most one edge between any pair of vertices. The same result can be demonstrated analytically as well [19]. How small a network needs to be to show this effect depends on the degree distribution; to see significant disassortativity, the highest-degree vertices in the network need to have degree of the order of $\sqrt{n}$, where n is the total number of vertices, so that there is a substantial probability of some vertex pairs sharing two or more edges. (Obviously if there is negligible probability of a double edge occurring anywhere in the network, then the restriction of having no double edges will have no effect.) The Internet is a particularly good example of the effect, since it has a degree distribution that appears approximately to follow a power law, $p_k \sim k^{-\alpha}$ with α constant [16,20], and the fat tail of the power law produces many vertices of sufficiently high degree. However, a number of other networks also fit the bill: the World Wide Web, peer-to-peer networks, food webs, neural networks, and metabolic networks all have vertices of sufficiently high degree, at least in some cases. In their most common representations these networks also have only single edges between vertices, and hence we would expect them to have $r<0$, and calculations of r from structural data confirm that this is the case [17].

In fact, most networks have only single edges between their vertices. Although it is possible to have double edges in some networks, in practice these are usually ignored even where they exist and all edges are represented as single. For instance, in the World Wide Web it is possible, and even common, for a Web page to link twice or more to the same other page, creating a multiple link. Such links are however normally recorded as single by Web crawler programs, and hence any information about multiple links is lost. Thus many networks may have single edges only because that is the way researchers have chosen to represent them, and observed properties such as disassortativity may be purely a product of this choice of representation rather than a fundamental law of nature. Other networks may truly have single edges—metabolic networks and food webs are possible examples of this.

Social networks also usually have only single edges between vertex pairs. Two people are either acquainted with one another or not—we do not normally have a concept of being "doubly acquainted" with a person. Nonetheless, the assortativity coefficient r is positive, and sometimes very positive, for almost all social networks measured [8,17]. This appears to indicate some special structure in social networks that distinguishes them from other types of networks. A revealing clue about what this special structure might be comes from network transitivity, as we now describe.

III. CLUSTERING

Watts and Strogatz [5] have pointed out that most networks appear to have high transitivity, also called clustering. That is, the presence of a connection between vertices A and B and another between B and C, makes it likely that there will also be a connection between A and C. To put it another way, if B has two network neighbors, A and C, they are likely to be connected to one another, by virtue of their common connection with B. In topological terms, there is a high density of triangles, ABC, in the network, and clustering can be quantified by measuring this density:

$$C=\frac{3\times(\text{number of triangles on the graph})}{\text{number of connected triples of vertices}}, \quad (3)$$

where a "connected triple" means a vertex connected directly to an unordered pair of others. In physical terms, C is the probability, averaged over the network, that two of your friends will be friends also of one another. (This is in fact only one definition of the clustering coefficient. An alternative definition, given in Ref. [5], has also been widely used. The latter however is difficult to evaluate analytically, and so we avoid it here.)

The value of the clustering coefficient in the null configuration model can be calculated in a straightforward fashion [21,22]. Suppose that two neighbors of the same vertex have excess degrees j and k. The probability that one particular edge in the network falls between these two vertices is $2(j/2m)(k/2m)$, where m is the total number of edges in the network. The total number of edges between the two vertices in question is m times this quantity, or $jk/(2m)$. Both j and k are distributed according to Eq. (1), since both vertices are neighbors of A and, averaging over this distribution, we then get an expression for the clustering coefficient:

$$C=\frac{1}{2m}\sum_{jk} jkq_jq_k=\frac{1}{n}\frac{[\langle k^2\rangle-\langle k\rangle]^2}{\langle k\rangle^3}, \quad (4)$$

where averages are over all vertices and we have made use of $2m=n\langle k\rangle$.

Normally this quantity goes as n^{-1} and so is very small for large graphs. However, some graphs are not large, and hence C is not negligible. Consider, for example, the food web of organisms in Little Rock Lake, WI, which was originally analyzed by Martinez [23] and has been widely studied in the networks literature. This network has $n=92$, $\langle k\rangle=21.0$, and $\langle k^2\rangle=655.2$. Plugging these figures into Eq. (4) gives $C=0.47$. The measured value of C is 0.40. Thus it appears that we need invoke no special clustering process to explain the clustering in this network. Similar results can be found for other small networks.

This argument can also be applied to some larger networks as well, particularly those with power-law degree distributions. The fat tail of the degree distribution in power-law networks can affect the value of the clustering coefficient strongly. To see this consider first how the degree of the highest-degree vertex in the configuration model varies with system size [4].

The probability of there being exactly m vertices of degree k in the network and no vertices of degree greater than k is $\binom{n}{m}p_k^m(1-P_k)^{n-m}$, where

$$P_k=\sum_{k'=k}^{\infty} p_{k'} \quad (5)$$

is the probability that a vertex has degree greater than or equal to k. Then the probability h_k that the highest degree in the network is k is

$$h_k=\sum_{m=1}^{n}\binom{n}{m}p_k^m(1-P_k)^{n-m}$$
$$=(p_k+1-P_k)^n-(1-P_k)^n, \quad (6)$$

and the expected value of the highest degree is $k_{\max}=\Sigma_k kh_k$.

The value of h_k tends to zero for both small and large values of k, and the sum over k is dominated by the terms close to the maximum. Thus, in most cases, a good approximation to the expected value of the maximum degree is given by the modal value. Differentiating and observing that $dP_k/dk=p_k$, we find that the maximum of h_k occurs when

$$\left(\frac{dp_k}{dk}-p_k\right)(p_k+1-P_k)^{n-1}+p_k(1-P_k)^{n-1}=0, \quad (7)$$

or $k_{\max}$ is a solution of

$$\frac{dp_k}{dk}\simeq -np_k^2, \quad (8)$$

where we have made the assumption that p_k is sufficiently small for $k\gtrsim k_{\max}$ that $np_k\ll 1$ and $P_k\ll 1$. For a degree distribution with a power-law tail $p_k\sim k^{-\alpha}$, we then find that

$$k_{\max}\sim n^{1/(\alpha-1)}. \quad (9)$$

(As shown by Cohen *et al.* [24], a simple rule of thumb that leads to the same result is that the maximum degree is roughly the value of k that solves $nP_k=1$.)

Most networks of interest have $\alpha<3$, which means $\langle k^2\rangle\sim k_{\max}^{3-\alpha}\sim n^{(3-\alpha)/(\alpha-1)}$ and $\langle k\rangle$ is independent of n. Then Eq. (4) gives

$$C\sim n^{(7-3\alpha)/(\alpha-1)}. \quad (10)$$

If $\alpha>\frac{7}{3}$, this means that C tends to zero as the graph becomes large, although it does so slower than the explicit $C\sim n^{-1}$ of Eq. (4). At $\alpha=\frac{7}{3}$, C becomes constant (or logarithmic) in the graph size. And remarkably, for $\alpha<\frac{7}{3}$ it actually increases with increasing system size, becoming arbitrarily large as $n\to\infty$. Thus for $\alpha\lesssim\frac{7}{3}$, we might expect to see quite large values of C even in large networks.

Taking the case of the World Wide Web, for example, we find the predicted value of the clustering coefficient for the configuration model is $C=0.048$ [21], while the measured value is 0.11—certainly not perfect agreement, but of the right order of magnitude. Other examples err in the opposite direction. Maslov *et al.* [18], for instance, cite the example of the Internet, for which they show using numerical simulations that the observed clustering is actually lower than that expected for an equivalent random graph model.

It is worth noting that Eq. (10) implies the clustering coefficient can be greater than 1 if $\alpha<\frac{7}{3}$. Physically this means that there will be more than one edge on average between two vertices that share a common neighbor. This is perhaps at odds with the conventional interpretation of the clustering coefficient as the probability that there exists *any* edge between the given two vertices—normally one would not distinguish between the case where there are two edges and the case where there is one. (Indeed, as mentioned in Sec. II, in many networks, one ignores double edges altogether.) If one takes this approach, then the value of the clustering coefficient is modified for networks that would otherwise have $C > 1$ as follows.

Consider again two vertices that are neighbors of vertex A, with excess degrees j and k. The probability that a particular edge falls between them is $2(j/2m)(k/2m)$, as before, and the probability that it does not is 1 minus this quantity. Then the probability that no edge falls between this pair is

$$\left[1-\frac{jk}{2m^2}\right]^m \simeq e^{-jk/2m}, \qquad (11)$$

where the equality becomes exact in the limit of large m. Thus the probability of any edge falling between the two vertices is $1-e^{-jk/2m}$, and the correct expression for the clustering coefficient is the average of this

$$C=\sum_{jk} q_j q_k (1-e^{-jk/2m}). \qquad (12)$$

In fact, however, using this expression makes only the smallest of differences to the expected value of C on, for example, the World Wide Web.

All of this demonstrates that for many nonsocial networks, including food webs, the Internet, and the World Wide Web, clustering can be explained by a simple random model. The same however is not true for social networks. It turns out that social networks in general have a far higher degree of clustering than the corresponding random model. We give four examples: the widely studied network of film-actor collaborations [5,7], collaboration networks of mathematicians [25,26] and company directors [27], and an email network [28]. For these four networks the theory presented above predicts values of the clustering coefficient of 0.0098, 0.000 15, 0.0035, and 0.017. The actual measured values are 0.20, 0.15, 0.59, and 0.17, in each case at least an order of magnitude greater than the prediction. The implication appears to be that there is some mechanism producing clustering in social networks that is not present at a significant level in nonsocial networks (or not at least in the examples studied here). Recent work [9,29–32] suggests a possible candidate theory that social networks contain groups or "community structure" [41].

IV. COMMUNITY STRUCTURE IN NETWORKS

In Ref. [9] one of us proposed a simple model of a network with community structure and showed that this structure produces substantial clustering, with values of C that do not go to zero as the network size becomes large. Thus the results of the preceding section could be explained if social networks possess community structure and other types of networks do not (or they possess it to a lesser degree). We now show that the same distinction can also explain the observed difference in degree correlations between social and nonsocial networks.

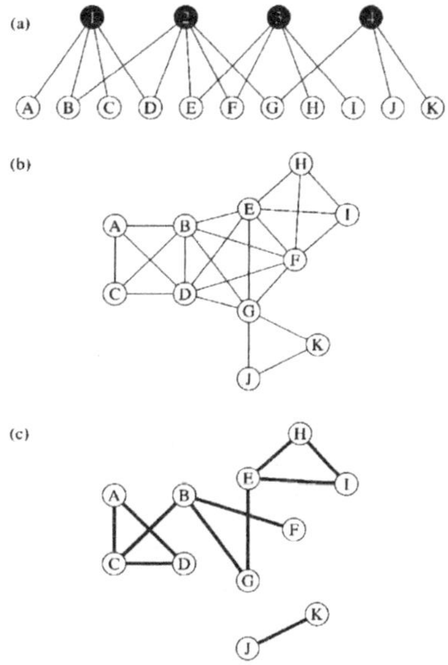

FIG. 1. The structure of the network model studied in Sec. IV. (a) We represent individuals (A–K) and the groups (1–4) to which they belong by a bipartite graph structure. (b) The bipartite graph is projected onto the individuals only, giving a network with edges between any pair of individuals who share a group. (c) The actual social connections between individuals are chosen by bond percolation on this projection with bond occupation probability p. The net result is that individuals have probability p of knowing others with whom they share a group.

In our model the network is divided into groups and each individual can belong to any number of groups. Individuals do not necessarily know all those with whom they share a group, but instead have probability p of acquaintance. They have probability zero of knowing those with whom they do not share a group. Mathematically the model can be represented as a bond percolation process with occupation probability p on the network formed by the projection of a suitable bipartite graph of individuals and groups onto just the individuals, as shown in Fig. 1. The percolation properties of the model can be solved exactly using generating function methods.

In Ref. [9] the model was studied in a simple version in which the size of all groups was assumed the same. This case can account for the presence of clustering in the network, and is straightforward to treat mathematically. However, it is inadequate for our purposes here, since it does not produce any degree correlation. Degree correlation arises because individuals who belong to small groups tend to have low degree and are connected to others in the same group, who also have low degree. Similarly those in large groups tend to have higher degree and are also connected to one another. Thus, the model should give rise to assortative mixing provided there is enough variation in the sizes of groups. As we will see, this is indeed the case.

In addition to the parameter p, we characterize the model by two probability distributions: r_m is the probability that an individual belongs to m groups and s_n is the probability that a group contains n individuals. Subject to the constraints imposed by these distributions, the assignment of individuals to groups is entirely random.

To proceed we calculate the joint distribution e_{jk} of the excess degrees of vertices at the ends of an edge. Noting that the total number of edges in groups of size n goes as $s_n n(n-1)$, we write

$$e_{jk}=e_0\sum_n s_n n(n-1)P(j,k|n), \tag{13}$$

where $P(j,k|n)$ is the probability that an edge that belongs to a group of size n connects vertices of excess degrees j and k, and e_0 is a constant whose value can be calculated from the requirement that e_{jk} be normalized, so that $\Sigma_{jk}e_{jk}=1$.

We now decompose j and k in the form $j=j_{\text{in}}+j_{\text{out}}$, $k=k_{\text{in}}+k_{\text{out}}$, where j_{in}, k_{in} are the numbers of connections to vertices within the group to which the edge in question belongs, and j_{out}, k_{out} are the numbers of connections outside that group. The distributions of j_{in} and k_{in} are simply binomial, and hence $P(j,k|n)$ factors into terms depending separately on j_{in}, j_{out} and k_{in}, k_{out} thus

$$P(j,k|n)=\sum_{j_{\text{in}}}\binom{n-2}{j_{\text{in}}}p^{j_{\text{in}}}q^{n-2-j_{\text{in}}}P(j_{\text{out}}) \times\sum_{k_{\text{in}}}\binom{n-2}{k_{\text{in}}}p^{k_{\text{in}}}q^{n-2-k_{\text{in}}}P(k_{\text{out}}), \tag{14}$$

where $P(j_{\text{out}})$ is the probability distribution of j_{out}, which is independent of j_{in}, and similarly for k_{out}.

To evaluate this expression we introduce the following generating functions for the distributions r_m and s_n:

$$f_0(z)=\sum_{m=0}^{\infty} r_m z^m, \quad f_1(z)=\frac{1}{f_0'(1)}\sum_{m=0}^{\infty} m r_m z^{m-1}, \tag{15}$$

$$g_0(z)=\sum_{n=0}^{\infty} s_n z^n, \quad g_1(z)=\frac{1}{g_0'(1)}\sum_{n=0}^{\infty} n s_n z^{n-1}. \tag{16}$$

Physically, $f_0(z)$ is the generating function for the number of groups an individual belongs to and $f_1(z)$ is the generating function for the number groups that an individual in a randomly selected group belongs to, other than the randomly selected group itself. Similarly $g_0(z)$ generates the group sizes and $g_1(z)$ generates the number of other individuals in a group to which a randomly selected individual belongs. Of these, our randomly selected individual is connected to a number binomially distributed according to the probability p and thus generated by the simple generating function $pz+q$, where $q=1-p$. Averaging over the group sizes, the number of neighbors of a randomly chosen individual within one of the groups to which they belong is generated by $g_1(pz+q)$, and an individual belonging to a randomly chosen group will have a number of neighbors in other groups generated by $f_1(g_1(pz+q))$. This then gives us the quantity $P(j_{\text{out}})$ of Eq. (14), which is equal to the coefficient of $z^{j_{\text{out}}}$ in $f_1(g_1(pz+q))$, and similarly for $P(k_{\text{out}})$.

Combining Eqs. (13) and (14) we find that e_{jk} is generated by the double probability generating function

$$\begin{aligned}E(x,y)&=\sum_{jk} e_{jk}x^j y^k\\ &=g_2((px+q)(py+q))f_1(g_1(px+q))\\ &\quad\times f_1(g_1(py+q)),\end{aligned} \tag{17}$$

where

$$g_2(z)=\frac{1}{g_0''(1)}\sum_{n=0}^{\infty} s_n n(n-1)z^{n-2}. \tag{18}$$

Then, making use of Eqs. (1) and (2) and the fact that $q_k=\Sigma_j e_{jk}$, we can write the assortativity coefficient r as

$$r=\left.\frac{\partial_x\partial_y E-(\partial_x E)(\partial_y E)}{\partial_x(x\,\partial_x E)-(\partial_x E)(\partial_y E)}\right|_{x=y=1}=\frac{\mathcal{P}}{\mathcal{Q}}, \tag{19}$$

where the numerator and denominator $\mathcal{P}$ and $\mathcal{Q}$ are

$$\mathcal{P}=p\mu_1^2\nu_1^2[(\nu_4-\nu_3)(\nu_2-\nu_1)-(\nu_3-\nu_2)^2], \tag{20a}$$

$$\begin{aligned}\mathcal{Q}={}&\mu_1\nu_1(\nu_2-\nu_1)[(\mu_2-\mu_1)(\nu_2-\nu_1)^2\\ &+\mu_1\nu_1(2\nu_1-3\nu_2+\nu_3)]+p[(\mu_1^2-\mu_2^2-\mu_1\mu_2+\mu_1\mu_3)\\ &\times(\nu_2-\nu_1)^4+\mu_1\mu_2\nu_1(\nu_2-\nu_1)^2(2\nu_1-3\nu_2+\nu_3)\\ &+\mu_1^2\nu_1\{\nu_1^2(2\nu_2+\nu_3-\nu_4)-\nu_1(\nu_3-\nu_2)^2\\ &-\nu_1\nu_2(\nu_4-5\nu_2)+\nu_2^2(3\nu_2-\nu_3)\}].\end{aligned} \tag{20b}$$

In this expression the quantities μ_i and ν_i are the ith moments of the distributions r_m and s_n, respectively. Thus, given the distributions and the probability p it is elementary, if tedious, to calculate r. Below we apply this expression to two real-world example networks. First, however, a few points are worth noting.

It is straightforward to show, though certainly not obvious to the eye, that the expression for r, Eq. (19), is non-negative for all distributions r_m and s_n, so that our model always produces an assortatively mixed network, as our intuition suggests.

Now consider the simple case in which each individual belongs to exactly one group, and the group sizes have a Poisson distribution. In this case, Eq. (19) gives $r=p$, and we can achieve any value of r by tuning the parameter p. In particular, if each individual knows all others in their group then $p=1$ and we have perfect assortativity. This is reasonable, since in this case each individual in a group has the exact same number of neighbors. This case is a rather pathological one, however, since if everyone belongs to only one group, then the network consists of many isolated groups and most people are not connected to one another. To make things more realistic, let us allow the number of groups to which individuals belong also to vary according to a Poisson distribution. Then we find that

$$r=\frac{p}{1+\mu+\nu\mu p}, \tag{21}$$

where $\mu\equiv\mu_1$ and $\nu\equiv\nu_1$ are the means of the two distributions. Thus as the two means increase, the correlation decreases. The decrease with μ is easily understood—the more groups an individual belongs to, the less the relative within-group degree correlation upon which the assortativity depends: the within-group correlation is diluted by all the other groups the individual belongs to. The behavior with ν is a little more subtle. The width of the Poisson distribution of group sizes goes as $1/\sqrt{\nu}$ as a fraction of the mean, and hence the effective variation in size between groups decreases with increasing ν. It is this decrease that drives r towards zero.

V. EXAMPLES

We now apply our model to two real-world example networks. In the first case, as we will see, it gives a value of r in excellent agreement with the real network. In the second it underestimates r by about a factor of 2, indicating that group structure can account for only a portion of the observed assortativity, the rest, we conjecture, being due to true social effects.

A. Collaboration network

Networks of coauthorship of scientists or other academics provide some of the best-documented examples of social networks [25,33]. Using bibliographic databases it is possible to construct large coauthorship networks with high reliability, and these networks are true social networks, in the sense that it seems highly likely that two authors who write a paper together are acquainted.

Figure 2 shows a coauthorship network of physicists who conduct research on networks. The network was constructed using names drawn from the bibliography of the recent review by Newman [4] and coauthorship data from preprints submitted to the condensed matter section of the Physics E-print Archive at arxiv.org between Jan 1, 1995 and June 30, 2003. To find the groups in the network, we fed it through the community structure algorithm of Girvan and Newman [29], producing the division shown by the colors in the figure [42]. The figure shows only the largest component of the network. There are also 41 smaller components, which are not shown but which were included in our calculations.

The moments of the distributions r_m and s_n are easily extracted from the network by direct summation. To find the value of p, we counted the number of edges in the network and divided by the total number of possible within-group edges, giving $p=0.168$. Feeding this value and our figures for the moments into Eqs. (19) and (20), we then find a predicted value of $r=0.183$. The measured value for the real network is 0.154 ± 0.044. (The error is calculated according to the prescription given in Ref. [17].) These two figures are in agreement within the statistical error on the latter [43].

This result by no means proves that the group structure is responsible for assortativity in this network. Certainly it is reasonable to suppose that the actual process of forming collaborative contacts is more complicated than that depicted in our model. The value of p, for example, could vary with group size, or there could be a nonzero probability of contact with individuals outside the groups to which one belongs. However, our results tell us that no more complicated model is necessary to explain the observed value of r. With group structure as shown in the figure and otherwise random mixing, we would get a network with exactly the assortativity that is observed in reality, within expected error.

B. Boards of directors

Davis and co-workers [27,34] have studied networks of the directors of companies in which two directors are considered connected if they sit on the board of the same company. They studied the Fortune 1000, the one thousand U.S. companies with the highest revenues, for 1999, and assembled a near-complete director network from publicly available data. The network consists of 7673 directors sitting on 914 boards. It provides a particularly simple example of our method, for two reasons. First, the groups in the network through which individuals are acquainted are provided for us—they are the boards of directors. Second, it is assumed that directors are acquainted with all those with whom they share a board, so that the parameter p in our model is 1.

The distributions of boards per director and directors per board have been studied before [13]. We note that most directors (79%) sit on only one board and that there is considerable variation in the size of boards (from 2 to 35 members). Thus we would expect strong assortative mixing in the network, and indeed we find that $r=0.276\pm0.004$. Taking the moments of the measured distributions r_m and s_n for the network and setting $p=1$, Eq. (19) gives a value of $r=0.116$ for our model. So it appears that the presence of groups in the network can explain about 40% of the assortativity we observe in this case, but not all of it. There is some further assortativity in addition to the purely topological effect of the groups, and we conjecture that this is due to true sociological or psychological effects in the way in which acquaintanceships are formed. One possibility is suggested by the analysis of the directorships data by Newman *et al.* [13], who found that directors who sit on many boards tend to sit on them with others who sit on many boards. Since those who sit on many boards will also tend to have high degree, we would expect this effect to add assortativity to the network, but the effect is missing from our model in which board membership is assigned at random.

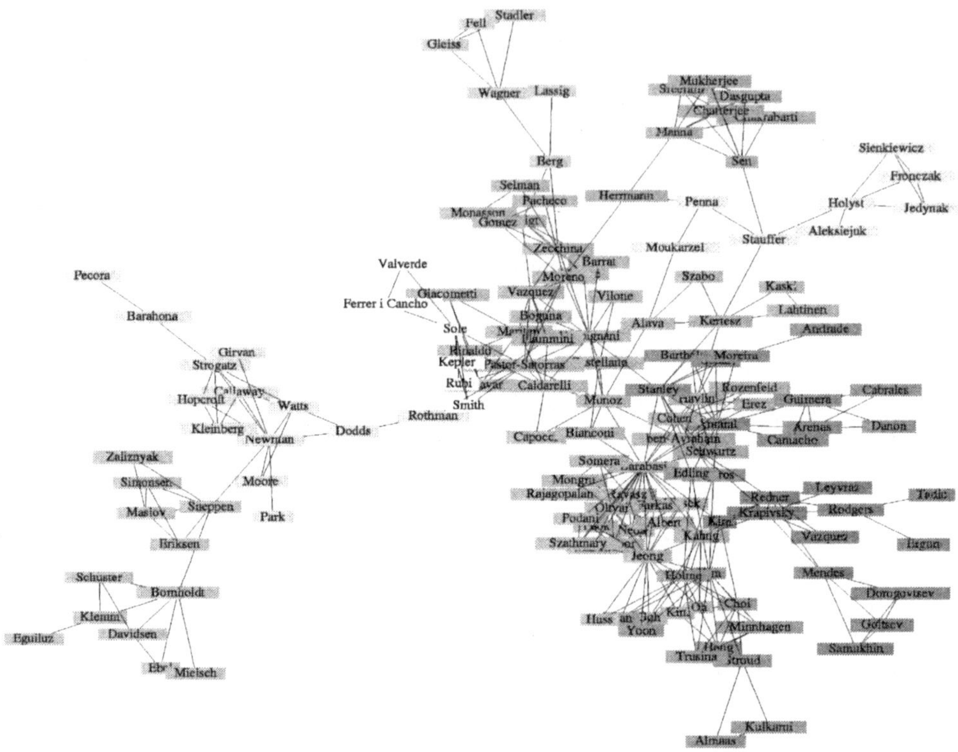

FIG. 2. (Color online) The largest component of the network of coauthorships described in the text. This component contains 145 scientists, and there are 41 other components, of sizes ranging from 1 to 5, containing 90 more. The vertices are grouped according to the communities found using the algorithm of Ref. [29]. The communities correspond reasonably closely to geographical and institutional divisions between the scientists shown.

In a sense, our model is giving a baseline against which to measure the value of r; it tells us when the value we see is simply what would be expected by random chance, as in the collaboration network above, and when there must be additional effects at work, as in the boards of directors.

VI. CONCLUSIONS

In this paper we have argued that social and nonsocial networks differ in two important ways. First, they show distinctly different patterns of correlation between the degrees of adjacent vertices, with degrees being positively correlated (assortative mixing) in most social networks and negatively correlated (disassortative mixing) in most nonsocial networks. Second, social networks show high levels of clustering or network transitivity, whereas clustering in many nonsocial networks is not higher than one would expect on the basis of pure chance, given the observed degree distribution.

We have shown that both of these differences can be explained by the same hypothesis, that social networks are divided into communities and nonsocial networks are not. We have studied a simple model of community structure in social networks in which individuals belong to groups and are acquainted with others with whom they share those groups. The model is exactly solvable using generating function techniques, and we have shown that it gives predictions that are in reasonable and sometimes excellent agreement with empirical observations of real-world social networks.

ACKNOWLEDGMENTS

The authors thank Duncan Watts for useful conversations. This work was funded in part by the National Science Foundation under Grant No. DMS-0234188 and by the James S. McDonnell Foundation and the Santa Fe Institute.

[1] S.H. Strogatz, Nature (London) **410**, 268 (2001).
[2] R. Albert and A.-L. Barabási, Rev. Mod. Phys. **74**, 47 (2002).
[3] S. N. Dorogovtsev and J. F. F. Mendes, *Evolution of Networks: From Biological Nets to the Internet and WWW* (Oxford University Press, Oxford, 2003).
[4] M.E.J. Newman, SIAM Rev. **45**, 167 (2003).
[5] D.J. Watts and S.H. Strogatz, Nature (London) **393**, 440 (1998).
[6] A.-L. Barabási and R. Albert, Science **286**, 509 (1999).
[7] L.A.N. Amaral, A. Scala, M. Barthélémy, and H.E. Stanley, Proc. Natl. Acad. Sci. U.S.A. **97**, 11149 (2000).
[8] M.E.J. Newman, Phys. Rev. Lett. **89**, 208701 (2002).
[9] M.E.J. Newman, Phys. Rev. E **68**, 026121 (2003).
[10] R. Pastor-Satorras, A. Vázquez, and A. Vespignani, Phys. Rev. Lett. **87**, 258701 (2001).
[11] S. Feld, Am. J. Sociol. **96**, 1464 (1991).
[12] M. Molloy and B. Reed, Random Struct. Algorithms **6**, 161 (1995).
[13] M.E.J. Newman, S.H. Strogatz, and D.J. Watts, Phys. Rev. E **64**, 026118 (2001).
[14] B. Bollobás, Eur. J. Comb. **1**, 311 (1980).
[15] T. Łuczak, in *Proceedings of the Symposium on Random Graphs, Poznań, 1989*, edited by A. M. Frieze and T. Łuczak (Wiley, New York, 1992), pp. 165–182.
[16] Q. Chen, H. Chang, R. Govindan, S. Jamin, S. J. Shenker, and W. Willinger, in *Proceedings of the 21st Annual Joint Conference of the IEEE Computer and Communications Societies* (IEEE Computer Soc. Press, London, 2002).
[17] M.E.J. Newman, Phys. Rev. E **67**, 026126 (2003).
[18] S. Maslov, K. Sneppen, and A. Zaliznyak, e-print cond-mat/0205379.
[19] J. Park and M.E.J. Newman, Phys. Rev. E **68**, 026112 (2003).
[20] M. Faloutsos, P. Faloutsos, and C. Faloutsos, Comput. Commun. Rev. **29**, 251 (1999).
[21] M. E. J. Newman, in *Handbook of Graphs and Networks*, edited by S. Bornholdt and H. G. Schuster (Wiley-VCH, Berlin, 2003), pp. 35–68.
[22] H. Ebel, L.-I. Mielsch, and S. Bornholdt, Phys. Rev. E **66**, 035103 (2002).
[23] N.D. Martinez, Ecol. Monogr. **61**, 367 (1991).
[24] R. Cohen, K. Erez, D. ben-Avraham, and S. Havlin, Phys. Rev. Lett. **85**, 4626 (2000).
[25] J.W. Grossman and P.D.F. Ion, Congr. Numer. **108**, 129 (1995).
[26] V. Batagelj and A. Mrvar, Soc. Networks **22**, 173 (2000).
[27] G. F. Davis, M. Yoo, and W. E. Baker, Preprint, University of Michigan Business School, 2001.
[28] M.E.J. Newman, S. Forrest, and J. Balthrop, Phys. Rev. E **66**, 035101 (2002).
[29] M. Girvan and M.E.J. Newman, Proc. Natl. Acad. Sci. U.S.A. **99**, 8271 (2002).
[30] R. Guimerà, L. Danon, A. Díaz-Guilera, F. Giralt, and A. Arenas, e-print cond-mat/0211498.
[31] E. Ravasz and A.-L. Barabási, Phys. Rev. E **67**, 026112 (2003).
[32] J.R. Tyler, D.M. Wilkinson, and B.A. Huberman, e-print cond-mat/0303264.
[33] M.E.J. Newman, Proc. Natl. Acad. Sci. U.S.A. **98**, 404 (2001).
[34] G.F. Davis and H.R. Greve, Am. J. Sociol. **103**, 1 (1997).
[35] D.L. Banks and K.M. Carley, J. Math. Sociol. **21**, 173 (1996).
[36] D.J. Watts, Am. J. Sociol. **105**, 493 (1999).
[37] E.M. Jin, M. Girvan, and M.E.J. Newman, Phys. Rev. E **64**, 046132 (2001).
[38] J. Davidsen, H. Ebel, and S. Bornholdt, Phys. Rev. Lett. **88**, 128701 (2002).
[39] K. Klemm and V.M. Eguíluz, Phys. Rev. E **65**, 036123 (2002).
[40] J. Jost and M.P. Joy, Phys. Rev. E **66**, 036126 (2002).
[41] An alternative theory is that individuals introduce pairs of their acquaintances to one another, thus completing network triangles and increasing the clustering coefficient. Several models of this "triadic closure" process have been studied in the literature [35–40].
[42] Since our model requires all connected pairs of individuals to belong to at least one common group, we define the groups to include both the core members shown by the colors in Fig. 2 and all individuals connected directly to those core members. This makes the group memberships overlap, as they do in the model.
[43] We deliberately chose to define the groups in our calculation using an algorithmic method—the method of Ref. [29]—to avoid possible subjective biases in the calculation. Some might argue however that, for a network such as this, group membership could be better assigned by a knowledgable human experimenter. We have performed calculations in this way also, assigning groups according to the authors' personal knowledge of the field. This results in somewhat different group assignments, though not grossly so, and a slightly higher value for p of 0.178. The final value of r extracted from the model is however unchanged within errors, at $r = 0.183$. Thus, the agreement between empirical observation and model is again good.

[15]

Capital networks in the Sheffield region, 1850–1885[1]

Lucy Newton

Introduction

Recent literature in business history has focused upon the viability of an alternative model of capitalist development to that put forward by Chandler. Rather than championing the 'big business', US-orientated approach, others have argued in favour of capitalist development in the form of industrial districts or 'clusters', involving small and medium-sized business units and flexible specialisation.[2] A key element of such districts is that they possess an internal homogeneity in comparison with other regions, and have well-developed networks of internal connections. They also manufacture a variety of products for domestic and international consumption utilising flexible technology. Furthermore, within these districts the formations of institutions occur that promote both cooperation and competition among enterprises, therefore stimulating innovation in the business environment.

This paper aims to examine such an industrial district, but with the focus upon internal connections, most particularly business and capital networks. While business networks are notoriously difficult to define and research, they are characterised here as 'high-trust linkages connecting to a series of entities',

---

[1] I would like to thank the following people for the support given and helpful comments made in the writing of this chapter: Phil Cottrell, John Wilson, Josephine Maltby and all those present at the Preston 'Networks and Clusters' conference in September 2001. All errors and omissions are my own.

[2] M.J. Piore and C.F. Sabel, *The Second Industrial Divide: Possibilities for Prosperity* (Basic Books, 1984); M.E. Porter, *The Competitive Advantage of Nations* (Macmillan, 1990); C. Sabel and J. Zeitlin, 'Historical Alternatives to Mass Production: Markets, Politics and Production in the Nineteenth Century', *Past and Present*, No. 108 (1985); P. Scranton, *Figured Tapestry: Production, Markets and Power in Philadelphia Textiles, 1855–1941* (Cambridge University Press, 1989); P. Scranton, 'Diversity in Diversity: Flexible Production and American Industrialisation, 1880–1930', *Business History Review*, 65, (Spring 1991); P. Scranton, '"Build a Firm, Start Another": The Bromley's and Family Entrepreneurship in the Philadelphia Region', *Business History*, 35 (Oct. 1993); M. Storper and S. Christopherson, 'Flexible Specialisation and Regional Industrial Agglomerations: The Case of the U.S. Motion Picture Industry', *Annals of the Association of American Geographers*, Vol. 77, No. 1 (1987).

with linkages based on information flow.[3] As the intricate networks amongst business elites and supplies of capital have important repercussions upon both individual enterprises and the economic performance of a region as a whole, they are therefore worthy of closer inspection.

The region under examination here is that of Sheffield and its surrounding towns and villages in South Yorkshire and North Derbyshire. The city, towns and villages were all involved in the same manufacturing and mining industries of iron, steel, engineering, secondary metals and coal mining. It was a region defined by common economic activity, rather than by geographical or political boundaries. Sheffield and its neighbours formed a specialist centre for domestic production and international exports during the nineteenth century, and into the twentieth. Its manufacture of special steels, tools and cutlery involved a highly differentiated system of production that required flexibility of labour and technology. Such flexibility, along with an emphasis on quality, ensured that the region remained an international leader in these products into the twentieth century.

During the period under examination, business within the region experienced boom and slump, large variations in demand for their products, growing competition from abroad, important innovations in technology and changes in the scale and organisation of production. This paper aims to analyse the role of business networks in managing changing economic and institutional conditions, especially the ability to obtain finance in order to expand, to purchase new technology, or merely to survive. In particular, companies that adopted limited liability during the period are considered.

Following the Joint Stock Companies Act of 1855, enterprises were allowed to adopt limited liability and call upon shareholders as a source of finance. Sheffield, along with Oldham, was a centre of limited liability company formations, following the liberalisation of company law, whereas much of the rest of England was slow to adopt joint-stock form. This paper considers groups of individuals who consistently purchased shares in the region's joint stock companies to form a 'capital network'. Networks of investors are especially pertinent when examining issues of financial provision in an era when funds from family and friends formed a crucial source of supply. In this way, social networks can be seen to impact upon business networks. The aim of the paper is to provide a rigorous analysis, based upon empirical evidence, of the operation of networks as channels of information and resources (in this case, finance) and their impact upon the economic performance of a particular industrial district.

Initially, the paper will examine the institutional framework of share ownership in England and Wales during the period under consideration, namely, the changes in company law and the uptake of limited liability. The following sections will then analyse limited company promotion and

---

[3] Chapter 2, in this volume.

shareholding patterns in the Sheffield region. A final section will attempt to draw some conclusions from the analysis.

Institutional framework

Following the liberalisation of company law in 1855 and 1856, limited liability became increasingly adopted in Great Britain as a form of company organisation.[4] With limited liability, a company's shareholders were only liable for its debts to the extent of the nominal value of their shareholdings and, furthermore, each shareholder could freely transfer his/her holding in such a company without reference to any other shareholder. This method of company organisation also, potentially, allowed a firm to raise capital publicly and therefore, in theory, to draw upon a broader capital market than had hitherto been available. However, despite the ruling permissive code of company law from 1855, the use made of limited liability by English manufacturing concerns was not very widespread before 1885. Within industry there was some concentration of conversions in the cotton, iron, steel, and coal sectors, while, more rapidly and generally, the number of joint-stock companies only increased from the 1880s. In addition, conversion to the limited form was not always accompanied by public appeals for capital; in an effort to prevent the divorce of ownership from management, those previously in control of the firm and/or their friends and relatives often retained shares.[5] The majority of firms in England and Wales relied upon internal sources of finance, usually the plough-back of company profits.

By 1886, Sheffield and Oldham had become two of the most important centres of joint stock company formation in England.[6] By the mid-1880s, contemporaries estimated that Sheffield had a total of 44 limited companies with a paid up capital of just over £12 million.[7] In this study, a sample of 90

[4] For a full discussion of nineteenth century company law reform see P.L. Cottrell, *Industrial Finance 1830–1914: The Finance and Organisation of English Manufacturing Industry* (Methuen, 1980), pp. 39–79; J.B. Jefferys, *Trends in Business Organisation in Great Britain since 1856* (1938. Reprinted by Arnos Press, 1977), pp. 19–53; H.A. Shannon, 'The Coming of General Limited Liability' (1931) in E.M. Carus Wilson (ed), *Essays in Economic and Social History* (Edward Arnold, 1946), pp. 358–79.

[5] P.L. Payne, 'Family Business in Britain: An Historical and Analytical Survey' in A. Okochi and S. Yasuoka (eds), *Family Business in the Era of Industrial Growth* (Tokyo University Press, 1984), pp. 171–3.

[6] L.A. Newton, *Credit and Capital in Sheffield: The Finance of Industry in Nineteenth Century England* (Ashgate, forthcoming); W.A. Thomas, *The Provincial Stock Exchanges* (Frank Cass, 1973); D.A. Farnie, *The English Cotton Industry and the World Market, 1815–1896* (Oxford University Press, 1979).

[7] *The Accountant*, 1887, p. 17.

companies based in and around Sheffield that adopted limited liability between 1855 and 1885 have been identified and their shareholders analysed.[8]

Company promoters played an important role in the adoption of the new limited liability company form. Firms wishing to adopt joint-stock status could call upon the services of such individuals, who would then market the company and its shares through a prospectus, and by utilising their personal and business contacts in order to ensure that adequate subscriptions were raised. In examining the 90 companies that adopted limited liability in Sheffield during the third quarter of the nineteenth century, three such promoters have been identified and will be discussed in detail below.

Despite the comparatively rapid uptake of limited liability in Sheffield, as compared to the rest of England and Wales, the mixed industrial structure of Sheffield, with a predominance of small-scale operations alongside large-scale industrial concerns, must be emphasised. Flexible production; family control; low barriers to entry; and a cheap supply of highly skilled labour all impacted upon the structure of Sheffield's manufacturing industry, in that it encouraged small-scale, niche manufacturers, rather than large-scale mass producers. Moreover, large-scale operations were not necessarily fully integrated factories of the 'modern' type. The system of production in Sheffield remained dependent upon the mixed system of large-scale production, middlemen and outworkers. A highly differentiated and flexible manufacturing system, particularly in the secondary metal trades, thus dominated production in the Sheffield area in during the nineteenth century and beyond.[9] This is a classic portrait of an industrial district, first identified by Marshall, and one which has been studied in detail by Lloyd-Jones and Lewis.[10] Therefore, by 1885 a very complex industrial structure had developed in the Sheffield region, whereby small-scale firms which required only low levels of capital investment existed in considerable numbers alongside a relatively few large joint stock concerns, mainly in heavy industries, which required large capital investments. Methods of business also remained parochial for large and small-scale firms alike.

8 The companies from this particular study were initially selected by viewing the summary Parliamentary Papers concerned with London registrations of limited liability companies. *British Parliamentary Papers*, 'Returns of the names, objects, places of business, date of registration, nominal capital, number of shares etc. of all joint-stock companies formed or registered...': 1864, LVIII; 1866, LXVI; 1867, LXIV; 1867-68, LIV; 1868-9, LVI; 1874, LXII; 1875, LXXI; 1876, LXVIII; 1877, LXXVI; 1878, LXVIII; 1878-80, LXVII; 1881, LXXXIII; 1881-82, LXIV; 1882-83, LXIV; 1884, LXXII; 1884-85, LXXI. Further companies were consequently identified during searches in the Public Record Office indexes and file series. The sources consulted for the subsequent analysis are located at the Public Record Office, Kew, London: Board of Trade Papers, file series 31. These files include the following documents: Articles of Association, Memorandum of Association, a Summary of Capital and Shares and any Articles of Agreement associated with the conversion of an existing company, all of which were returned to the Registrar of Joint Stock Companies.

9 Newton, *Credit and Capital*.

10 R. Lloyd-Jones and M.J. Lewis, 'Personal Capitalism and British Industrial Decline: The Personally Managed Firm and Business Strategy in Sheffield, 1880–1920', *Business History Review*, Vol. 68 (1994), pp. 364–411.

Conducting business in the fluctuating economic climate of nineteenth century Britain was a risky affair.[11] The introduction of limited liability was one method by which those companies wishing to expand their capital bases could reduce their personal risk. However, the persistence of the 'private' limited company in Britain demonstrated the reluctance of owners to fully relinquish control of their enterprises. 'Private' limited companies tended to sell their shares to family members, friends or business associates from the local area. Even many of the 'true' public companies in Britain maintained a high degree of family control.[12] Managers of nineteenth century limited companies were thus ensuring a degree of continuity between the new joint-stock firm and the private partnership.

In addition to maintaining control of their companies, it is likely that the managements of limited companies were attempting to reduce the potential risks that resulted from calling upon external sources of funding. Shareholders known by the promoter or vendor, and who were knowledgeable of, and participated in, the region's industry would have been likely to engender a greater sense of commitment to an enterprise than would be demonstrated by a shareholder from outside the region. Retaining control amongst family and friends meant the maintenance of trust in a business environment which remained uncertain. The entry into a business of persons who stood outside such a circle of kinship or friendship ties would probably be viewed as an increase in risk.[13]

Casson has highlighted the benefits that such 'committed' shareholders could bring to a company, especially with regard to financial support. He has argued that 'if shareholders themselves experience a sense of moral obligation then they may consent to sacrifices over and above this level'. This may be contrasted with 'shareholders who are concerned purely with profit-maximisation [who] will, of course, require that any financial sacrifices made' must generate savings and benefits for the investor.[14]

> Shareholders are ... unlikely to participate emotionally in the goals of the enterprise if they only hold a small shareholding for speculative purposes, which they can liquidate at any time ... In small firms, where each shareholder usually holds a significant stake on a long-term basis, emotional rewards to owners are likely to be much greater. Greatest of all are likely to be the rewards in the owner-managed firm, and in the family firm.[15]

---

[11] M. Lester, *Victorian Insolvency* (Oxford University Press, 1995); J. Maltby, 'UK Joint Stock Companies Legislation 1844–1900: Accounting Publicity and "Mercantile Caution"', *Accounting History*, Vol. 3, No. 3 (1998), p. 15.

[12] M.B. Rose, 'The Family Firm in British Business, 1780–1914' in M.W. Kirby and M.B. Rose (eds), *Business Enterprise in Modern Britain* (Routledge, 1994), p. 68.

[13] Ibid., p. 67.

[14] M. Casson, 'Culture as an Economic Asset' in A.C. Godley and O.M. Westall (eds), *Business History and Business Culture* (Manchester University Press, 1996), p. 68.

[15] Ibid.

This is not to say that those investing in limited concerns in the Sheffield region were not concerned with making a profit upon their shareholdings. However, Casson's analysis highlights the potential benefits of attracting investors who had a greater commitment to the company – through personal or business contacts – and to the region's industry through their participation in local business networks. This can be applied to large nineteenth century joint-stock firms as equally as to small-scale, modern enterprises.

The concept of business networks has been examined in the introduction to this volume. Such theories appear to be applicable to a nineteenth century business environment in which transactions frequently occurred at a local level and consequently often took place amongst those who were known to each other. Wilson has stressed that the 'highly localised and personal nature of relationships was the bedrock of eighteenth and nineteenth century organisation and finance'.[16] Despite the international nature of Sheffield's export trade, production took place at a local level and would have frequently involved face-to-face contact between economic actors. Indeed, Tweedale's comprehensive studies of Sheffield have emphasised the localised/parochial nature of nineteenth century business in and around the city.

The stamping ground of these men was not the national scene, but their own locality, where they could pursue their personal values and maintain their old-established networks.[17] Tweedale thus confirms the highly embedded nature of the networks that existed in Sheffield.

> Sheffield's cluster of steel firms ... nurtured a close-knit community of shared values. The fact that few of these men ran totally integrated mills intensified an industrial network of complex linkages. These linkages were of course reflected socially, by intermarriage and a complex networking of families ... that often extended into the banking and financial scene in the city.[18]

Institutions such as the *Company of Cutlers*, the *Sheffield Assay Office*, *Sheffield Chamber of Commerce*, the *Freemasons* and the *Sheffield Club*, along with religious and political affiliations, were part of the fabric that constituted a complex network structure of the business community in the region.[19] How did these networks apply to the limited companies under examination here?

---

[16] J.F. Wilson, *British Business History, 1720–1994* (Manchester University Press, 1995), p. 47.

[17] G. Tweedale, *Steel City: Entrepreneurship, Strategy and Technology in Sheffield, 1743–1993* (Oxford University Press, 1995), p. 144.

[18] Ibid., p. 145.

[19] C. Binfield and D. Hey (eds), *Mesters to Masters: A History of the Company of Cutlers in Hallamshire* (Oxford University Press, 1997); C. Binfield, R. Childs, G. Harper, D. Hey, D. Martin and G. Tweedale (eds) *The History of the City of Sheffield, 1883–1993*, 3 Vols. (Sheffield Academic Press, 1993).

Company promoters

Company promoters were responsible for bringing joint-stock firms 'to life' and were crucial to the spread of limited liability during the second half of the nineteenth century. Potentially, such individuals could draw upon considerable networks of contacts in order to facilitate the uptake of company shares in particular and limited liability in general. They could therefore improve the efficiency of the new form of company organisation and capital flows.

However, promoters had a notoriously bad reputation. Fear of the corrupt company promoter had been voiced in the debates concerning the reform of company law in the first half of the nineteenth century. An article in *The Times* in 1844 gave a dramatic warning to the innocent investor of the unscrupulous promoter's ability to:

> stimulate avarice by representations of unimpeachable security, and hope by the promise of boundless wealth – to lull the suspicions of the aged, and rouse the cupidity of the young – to guaranty secrecy and large dividends to all. As director, he must simply lie ... always lie.[20]

The freedom granted promoters to establish limited companies by the reform of company law between 1855 and 1862 increased the activity of promoters. Cottrell has argued that:

> It is highly likely that the extreme freedom that the law gave to company promoters led ironically to limited companies getting a 'bad name', with their formation being regarded with disfavour by manufacturers and industrialists.[21]

Indeed, Armstrong has emphasised that, in terms of regulation: '[t]here were few rules. Neither company law nor the regulations of the Stock Exchange placed many restrictions on the methods the predatory promoter might employ'.[22] The system was thus open to abuse and unscrupulous company promoters furnished the occupation with a rather dubious reputation. Burn assesses the record of the company promoter, arguing that public prejudices against them after the 1870s 'were clearly well grounded, though some of the promoter's errors were doubtless the result not of knavery but of a pardonable failure to forecast the change of price trend in the 'seventies'.[23] Kynaston has

[20] Quoted in B.C. Hunt, *The Development of the Business Corporation in England 1800–1867* (Harvard University Press, 1936), p. 90–2.

[21] Cottrell, *Industrial Finance*, p. 54.

[22] J. Armstrong, 'The Rise and Fall of the Company Promoter and the Financing of British Industry', in J.J. van Helten and Y. Cassis (eds), *Capitalism in a Mature Economy. Financial Institutions, Capital Exports and British Industry, 1870*–1939 (Ashgate, 1990), p. 115.

[23] D.L. Burn, *The Economic History of Steelmaking* (Cambridge University Press, 1940, reprinted 1961), p. 256.

been more critical, surmising of company promoters that: 'Some ... were more or less honourable; most were not'.[24]

Despite their tarnished reputation, promoters played an increasing and important role in promoting joint-stock companies. 'The period 1870 to 1914 was the heyday of the individual company promoter working on domestic industrial floatations.'[25] The growing numbers of investors and growth in demand for capital from business called for professional intermediation in the establishment of joint-stock concerns.[26] Unfamiliarity with the new company legislation was also a reason to turn to the promoter.[27]

The employment of company promoters grew from the 1860s onwards, especially by enterprises where capital requirements were large and more public calls for capital were required, or where a business was new and the connections necessary to sell shares were inadequate. Promoters did not usually persuade companies to convert to joint-stock status, but rather assisted the process of conversion. Indeed, the company that was to adopt limited liability would usually be a conversion, rather than a brand new venture.[28] Company promoters were engaged in order to utilise their networks of contacts and raise the necessary capital. As the volume of capital required for these conversions rose, the importance of promoters in securing adequate subscriptions from public sources and/or their contacts grew correspondingly. Armstrong has emphasised the importance of such a role when asserting that: '[f]loating a company was primarily a marketing exercise'.[29] As the marketer of company shares, it was important for the promoter to have 'an appreciation of the mood of the market', but Armstrong has also stressed that 'a market could be stimulated, in shares as in any other commodity, and the company promoter needed to be adept at this if he was to be successful'.[30] The prospectus was an important document to be utilised in the attempt to enhance the sales of shares and it was here that 'the company promoter had a fairly free rein to indulge his creative-writing talents'.[31] Promoters would also frequently attempt to ensure the success of a joint-stock venture by the 'underwriting' of floatations, either formally or informally. This was usually achieved through a group of affluent associates who would invest money in a promoter's conversions. A successful history of conversions enhanced the reputation of the promoter and his associated investors.[32]

---

24 D. Kynaston, *The City of London, Vol. 1. A World of its Own, 1815–1890* (Chatto and Windus, 1994), p. 344.

25 Armstrong, 'The Rise and Fall of the Company Promoter', p. 115.

26 Jefferys, *Trends in Business Organisation*, pp. 294–5.

27 Armstrong, 'The Rise and Fall of the Company Promoter', p. 115.

28 Ibid., p. 116; Newton, *Credit and Capital*, Chapter 5.

29 Armstrong, 'The Rise and Fall of the Company Promoter', p. 117.

30 Ibid., p. 117.

31 Ibid., p. 117 and 124; Cottrell, *Industrial Finance*, pp. 62–3 and 68–9.

32 Armstrong, 'The Rise and Fall of the Company Promoter', pp. 117–18 and 126–7.

In terms of the type of industry in which these promoters operated, in the 1860s and 1870s 'the most conspicuous industry of the first type in which the embryo promoter or agent appeared, was iron and steel'.[33] Indeed, such company promoters operated in the iron and steel trades in the Sheffield region. The involvement of promoters in the floatation of a limited company may be discerned by examining the legal documentation contained in the Board of Trade files. These documents also included the names of vendors and initial subscribers to the company, revealing an interesting portrait of a group of capitalists/entrepreneurs operating in the region. This is the initial step in identifying those involved in a network of capital provision for the region's industry.

Promoters of Sheffield companies

When reviewing the names of vendors and promoters of companies adopting limited liability in the Sheffield region, three dominant promoters were identified: Alfred Allott, John Unwin Wing and David Chadwick, all accountants. Alfred Allott, from Sheffield, was the sole promoter of eight companies[34] and a joint promoter of one other[35] – all were conversions of existing undertakings. Four of Allott's promotions took place in 1872, four in 1873 and one in 1874 – a concentrated burst of activity, occurring during the boom years in the iron and steel industries. All the companies with which Allott was involved were iron or steel firms, eight located in Sheffield and one in Rotherham. John Unwin Wing, also from Sheffield, was the promoter of seven companies – one in 1872, three in 1873, two in 1874 and one in 1876.[36] Again, all were conversions. Wing's period of promotions activity was also intense, although not as concentrated as that of Allott, and his promotions again mainly coincided with the iron and steel boom of the early 1870s. Six of the companies were manufacturers and processors of iron, steel or other metals and metal goods, and one was located just over the county border on the Derbyshire coalfield. Of the other Wing companies, four were located in Sheffield and two in Rotherham. The Manchester accountant David Chadwick promoted four companies: Charles Cammell, Parkgate Iron, Yorkshire Engine Company and Vickers. These flotations took place in 1864, 1865 and 1867, involving iron, steel and engineering firms in Sheffield and Rotherham. Thus, the activities of the promoter who was based outside the region took place in the 1860s, in

---

[33] Jefferys, *Trends in Business Organization*, p. 297.

[34] Albion Steel & Wire & Co. Ltd., Charlton Iron Works Ltd., Davy Bros. Ltd., Hallamshire Steel & File Co. Ltd., Hydes & Wigfull Ltd., Phoenix Bessemer Steel Co. Ltd., Saville St Foundry & Engineering Co. Ltd. and William Cooke & Co. Ltd..

[35] Jarvis William Barber was the joint promoter of Henry Wilkinson & Co. Ltd. with Alfred Allott.

[36] Cardigan Iron & Steel, G & J Brown, James Fairbrother, Kelham Rolling Mills, Sheffield Nickel & Silver Plate, Tinsley Rolling Mills, and Whittington Silkstone Colliery Ltd.

contrast to the local promotions of the 1870s, and one of Chadwick's undertakings was not a conversion but a completely new venture (Yorkshire Engine Company Ltd.).

Who were these men that played such a prominent role in the movement towards limited liability by manufacturing industry in the Sheffield region before 1885? Much has already been written about David Chadwick.[37] He was not only an accountant, with offices in both Manchester and London, but had been the Treasurer to the Corporation of Salford, a writer on urban living conditions and a statistician. He was involved in the creation of 47 limited companies, most importantly iron, steel and coal concerns, and was a forceful advocate of limited liability as a method of industrial organisation and finance. Jefferys estimated that the total share capital involved in these floatations was over £40 million. His firm of Chadwick, Adamson and Collier 'was the most important financial agent for industrial companies in the first twenty-five years of the Limited Liability Act'.[38] Morgan and Thomas also argue that 'Chadwick's business was a very conservative one', in that he would check the accounts of a company before taking on its conversion and 'he admitted that other promoters were less strict in their selection'.[39] Chadwick's firm was 'in touch with some of the most important investors in the country'.[40] In 1867, Chadwick claimed that his contacts numbered in the hundreds; in 1874, he claimed that they had reached 4000, and by 1878 the figure was 5000.[41] Even allowing for some exaggeration for the sake of publicity, the volume of such contacts remains impressive. Jefferys estimates that the investors in all of Chadwick's promotions, not only those in Sheffield, provided approximately £10,000,000 to £15,000,000 for domestic manufacturing companies up to 1877.[42] He utilised prospectuses and letters in order to generate subscriptions. In evidence to a parliamentary committee investigating the progress of the 1862 and 1867 Companies Acts, he asserted that: 'We have no connection with the Stock Exchange, no jobbing, and very seldom any advertising'.[43] Rather, he sent out prospectuses and letters marked 'private and confidential' which invited his 'friends to subscribe'.[44] The reputation of Chadwick preceded him and companies using his services were virtually guaranteed to raise sufficient external capital.

---

37 Cottrell, *Industrial Finance*, pp. 113–4, 153, 186–7 and 252; D.J. Jeremy (ed), *Dictionary of Business Biography* (Butterworths, 1984), pp. 652–3.

38 Jefferys, *Trends in Business Organization*, p. 298.

39 E.V. Morgan and W.A. Thomas, *The Stock Exchange. Its History and Functions* (Elek Books, 1962), p. 136.

40 Jefferys, *Trends in Business Organization*, p. 317.

41 *British Parliamentary Papers*, 'Report of the Select Committee on the Companies Acts', X (1867), q. 869 and *British Parliamentary Papers*, 'Report of the Select Committee on the Companies' Acts' of 1862 and 1867, VIII (1877), q. 2079.

42 Jefferys, *Trends in Business Organization*, p. 318.

43 *PP* Report, 1877: q. 2045.

44 Jefferys, *Trends in Business Organization*, p. 318.

The backgrounds of John Unwin Wing and Alfred Allott are harder to discern. Alfred Allott was an accountant and partner in Allott, Hadfield, Kidner & Hawson, 'auditors, financial agents, and public accountants' and insurance agents, a firm with an office in both Sheffield and London. He also had a private residence in London.[45] John Unwin Wing was a partner in Wing, Wing & Co., 'accountants, auditors, etc.' of Sheffield and London. John Wing was also secretary to the Sheffield Wagon Co. Ltd., author of *Mercantile Book-keeping* (published in 1865) and resided in Abbeydale, an affluent Sheffield suburb.[46] Both Allott and Wing were active members of the Society of Accountants in England and served on its council during the Council's formative years.[47] They were also founding Fellows of the Sheffield Institute of Accountants, established in 1877, and Allott was the first President of this organisation.[48] John Unwin Wing's career failed to develop smoothly, as in July 1882 he was convicted at Leeds Assizes for felony.[49] This must have been a major setback to the career of an accountant and company promoter. Indeed, Wing did not promote any companies in the 1880s and no information has been found about him after this date.

Sheffield accountants were unusual in their 'very close affiliation and virtual dominance of the Stock Exchange in Sheffield'.[50] Early nineteenth century sharebrokers in Sheffield operated as accountants and this practice continued into the twentieth century. In 1880, almost half of the membership of the Sheffield Stock Exchange offered accountancy services.[51] The importance of such individuals in the region's industrial and financial networks was therefore long-standing. In the case of Allott, Wing and Chadwick, their significance is also apparent by the number of industrial companies in which they participated – 20 of the 90 companies examined – and by the volume of capital involved in their Sheffield promotions (see Table 7.1). These three men taken together were responsible for the promotion of twenty companies with a combined nominal capital of £2,885,000. Chadwick promoted the fewest companies numerically, but they involved the greatest volume of nominal capital. They were therefore financially powerful individuals within the region during the 1860s and 1870s and the volume of capital involved in their promotions implies an importance within this industrial sector on a national level. In addition, their influence was crucial in the success, or failure, of the new limited companies, most particularly in the initial sale of their shares.

---

45 *White's Directory of Sheffield* (White, 1962 and 1879).

46 A.M. Hoe, *The Sheffield & District Society of Chartered Accountants. The First Hundred Years Centenary, 1877–1977* (The Sheffield & District Society of Chartered Accountants, 1977), p. 6; *White's Directory of Sheffield* (1962 and 1879).

47 Hoe, *Sheffield and District Society of Chartered Accountants*, pp. 3–4.

48 Ibid., pp. 7–9.

49 HSBC Group Archives: AD5, Sheffield Union Banking Company, Board of Directors Minutes, f. 227.

50 Hoe, *Sheffield and District Society of Chartered Accountants*, p. 4.

51 Ibid., p. 4; Thomas, *Provincial Stock Exchanges*, p. 50.

Table 7.1
Capital involved in promotions by Allott, Wing and Chadwick

Name	No. of Companies	Total Nominal Capital (£)	Average Nominal Capital (£)
Allott	9	795,000	88,333
Wing	7	435,000	62,143
Chadwick	4	1,655,000	413,750

The three promoters also often owned shares in their prodigies, once a full allotment had been made, such shares being then potentially available on the open market. Table 7.2 shows the shareholdings of Allott, Wing and Chadwick in their companies following initial subscription. This gives some indication as to the extent of their interest once a company was established. These have been extracted from the first available annual return made to the Registrar of Joint Stock Companies from the summary of capital and shares of the company following registration. It should be emphasised that these figures show actual subscribed capital, rather than nominal capital, thus demonstrating their 'real' involvement in the listed companies. In addition, the Table shows the investments of these promoters in companies other than those in which they were involved in floating.

Chadwick subscribed a total of £12,500 to three of the companies he promoted, a sizeable amount of personal capital. However, £9000 of this was invested in vendors' shares of Yorkshire Engine Co. Ltd., an indication of Chadwick's commitment to the success of this new company. A relatively large amount of capital was also subscribed by Alfred Allott - £4838 to seven out of the nine companies he promoted – but, in addition, £4504 to four where he was not the promoter and to which he made large subscriptions.[52] Therefore, Allott appears to have been committed to investing in Sheffield's manufacturing industry *per se*, rather than merely confining his funds to his own promotions. In contrast, John Unwin Wing was not as supportive to the companies that he had promoted in terms of funds he subscribed once they had been registered. He took up shares in five out of seven companies he promoted, but the total amount of money involved was only £2985.[53] Thus, Wing's involvement appears to have been with regard to the legal and financial aspects

[52] £1000 to Brown Bayley & Dixon, £1280 to London & Sheffield Nickel Silver Plate, and £2200 to The Whittington Freehold Colliery.

[53] He also subscribed £150 to The Sheffield Steel & Manufacturing Co. Ltd., a company he did not promote.

of promotion, and less to actual personal investment in the companies themselves.

Table 7.2
Shareholdings of Allott, Wing and Chadwick

Company	Year	Type of Share	No. of Shares	Capital Subscribed by Promoter (£)	Capital Subscribed by Promoter as % of Total Subscribed Capital per Co.
Allott					
Whittington Freehold Colliery	1864	Ordinary	500	2200	14.6
Midland Iron Co.	1865	Ordinary	160	1280	6.4
Joseph Peace & Co.	1869	Ordinary	12	24	0.2
Albion Steel & Wire	1873	Ordinary	100	500	0.8
Brown, Bayley & Dixon	1873	Ordinary	50	1000	0.6
Charlton Iron Works	1873	Ordinary	20	550	0.8
Davy Bros.	1873	Ordinary	50	750	2.5
Henry Wilkinson	1873	Ordinary	20	100	0.5
Hydes & Wigfull	1873	Ordinary	50	188	1.5
Phoenix Bessmer	1873	Ordinary	50	2000	2.5
William Cooke	1873	Ordinary	50	750	1.1
Wing					
James Fairbrother	1869	Ordinary	100	100	6.7
G. & J. Brown	1873	Ordinary	2	90	0.2
Sheffield Nickel & Silver Plate	1873	Ordinary	20	80	0.8
Sheffield Steel & Manufacturing Co.	1874	Ordinary	25	150	1.2
Chadwick					
Charles Cammell	1865	Vendors	180	9000	2.3
Parkgate Iron	1865	Ordinary	100	2000	3.3
Yorkshire Engine	1865	Ordinary	100	1500	8.1

The involvement of Allott, Wing and Chadwick in their promotions clearly went beyond merely registration. Jefferys has described a commitment whereby promoters 'did not collect their commission and pass on to another company, but stayed with the company as auditors and felt to a certain degree responsible to their clients whom they had persuaded to invest'.[54] Indeed, of the 20 companies that Allott, Wing and Chadwick were involved in promoting, all bar one utilised the services of the men's accountancy firms as their company auditors.[55] Such responsibility was also demonstrated in the Monthly Circular that Chadwick's accounting firm sent to all its clients.[56] However, it is difficult to assess the extent to which they influenced the subsequent success of the companies they had promoted.

Chadwick claimed that nine out of every ten companies he promoted were a success, when the overall failure rate of joint-stock firms during the 1860s and 1870s was being calculated at between 30 and 50 per cent.[57] However, it was unlikely that Chadwick himself would provide an accurate measurement of success, given the need to publicise his activities in a positive light. An attempt has been made to measure the success of the promoters' companies from the data available in the Board of Trade files.

None of the companies promoted by Allott, Wing or Chadwick were 'abortive' or rather did not commence operations. This would indicate success for the companies in terms of initial promotion. The viability of a company might also be gauged by the proportion of capital subscribed from its first share issue, possibly indicating how attractive the venture was to investors. The promoter was likely to have had a major influence upon the sale of the first issue of shares, although the precise extent cannot be measured. All three promoters under discussion were accountants and therefore were likely to have had well-developed networks of financial contacts and potential investors.

The actual amount of capital subscribed to Allott's, Wing's and Chadwick's promotions in the Sheffield region, as a percentage of nominal capital, is shown in Table 7.3. This indicates that for each of the three groups of companies, the subscribed capital amounted to less than half of the aggregate nominal capital. Cottrell found that the limited companies he sampled between 1866 and 1882 had, on average, only 25 per cent of their nominal capital called up, whilst during the 1860s boom the average was even lower at 18.9 per cent.[58] Chadwick himself claimed that 25 per cent paid on shares was common for industrial concerns.[59] Therefore, comparatively, the amount of capital called by the companies of Chadwick, Wing and Allott was high. The willingness of investors to subscribe to these companies and fulfil the relatively high calls made on the shares would indicate that these promotions were successful.

---

54 Jefferys, *Trends in Business Organization*, pp. 298–9.

55 The only firm not to use the services of its company promoter as auditor was Davy Bros. Ltd, promoted by Allott, who instead used the services of John Watson & Son, a Sheffield practice.

56 Jefferys, *Trends in Business Organization*, pp. 298–9.

57 Ibid., p. 320.

58 Cottrell, *Industrial Finance*, pp. 84–5.

59 Maltby, 'UK Joint Stock Companies Legislation', p. 20.

Table 7.3
Capital subscribed to industrial promotions of Allott, Wing and Chadwick

Name	Total Nominal Capital (£)	Capital subscribed as % of Nominal Capital (£)	Average Share denomination
Allott	435,000	40.7	24
Wing	795,000	48.4	17.5
Chadwick	1,655,000	34.2	100

Share denominations had an impact upon their attractiveness to investors. Jefferys has argued that share denominations were high in the early days of the general availability of limited liability, but thereafter gradually decreased. The introduction of lower denominations made shares potentially more widely available, especially with the increase in denominations of £5 or less. The earlier company registrations of Chadwick had a high average share denomination of £100, whereas the later registrations of Wing and Allott had lower average share denomination of £24 and £34 respectively. Yet, despite their relatively high nominal values – not one average share denomination for any set of the promoters companies is below £20 – there does not appear to have been a reluctance to subscribe to shares offered by these companies. The attraction of investing in these companies must, in some part, have been due to Wing, Allott and Chadwick acting as financial agents, using both business and personal connections to ensure that subscriptions were plentiful. There may also have been an element of trust involved in purchasing shares of this nature; either trust in the promoter of the firm and its management. The role of Allott, Wing and Chadwick in the consequent success, or otherwise, of the companies that they promoted is impossible to gauge, but providing a successful floatation and attracting 'solid' investors was likely to have provided a positive contribution to the future progress of the newly converted businesses.

Shareholders in nineteenth century limited companies

What of those that purchased shares in the limited companies – the men and women who 'owned' the concerns? Before considering the shareowners of the 'Sheffield' companies, it is important to consider some general trends in share ownership during the nineteenth century.

Due to the existence of limited companies before 1855, most notably railways that had been incorporated through Acts of Parliament, by the mid-century: 'Investment had become a fairly respectable occupation for landed gentry and merchant alike'.[60] Who were the investing classes? High share denominations meant that only the wealthy, those with money to invest over the long-term, could purchase such shares.[61] Wealthy shareholders were the type most desired by limited companies. They were a high 'quality', safe type of investor, with plenty of money to spend and credentials that were known in the locality or by brokers and financial agents. For industrial companies, who rarely applied for a quotation on the London Stock Exchange, large shares and stable investors were the aim in the early days of limited liability.[62]

Yet the wealthy investor was not the only type who purchased shares in industrial concerns. The middle classes, professionals and traders were also investors in limited companies and, according to Jefferys, tended to be interested in regular dividends and marketable shares.[63] Spinsters, widows and the gentry were another group of investors who gradually came to purchase shares in domestic industrial companies. Jefferys described this group as the 'rentier', 'safe' or 'steady and legitimate' investor, believing that they formed 'the base of the Victorian investment market'.[64] Such investors would usually shy away from riskier enterprises such as new industrial concerns: 'Limited liability only affected them indirectly'. In contrast, it was 'the more enterprising "commercial classes" and members of the "native trading" community which had to lead the way in the new limited companies before the "safe" investor would follow'.[65] While these 'commercial classes' were to be found in large commercial centres and had accumulated volumes of capital, they were not familiar enough with industrial enterprise to set up such ventures by themselves. They tended to be far more adventurous than the 'safe' investor.[66]

The industrial capitalist was another type of shareholder. They were usually entrepreneurs who had conducted businesses on a partnership basis before the coming of general limited liability and who, following the 1855, 1856 and 1862 Companies Acts, were able to convert to limited liability and to potentially raise some level of external finance.

> The typical shareholders of the early joint stock companies was wealthy, tended to confine his investments to two or three companies and was

---

[60] S.A. Broadbridge, 'The Sources of Railway Share Capital', in M.C. Reed (ed), *Railways in the Victorian Economy: Studies in Finance and Economic Growth* (David and Charles, 1968); Jefferys, *Trends in Business Organization*, p. 47–8; J.R. Killick and W.A. Thomas, 'The Provincial Stock Exchanges', *Economic History Review*, XXIII (1970); M.C. Reed, *Investment in Railways in Britain, 1820–1844: A Study in the Development of the Capital Market* (Oxford University Press, 1975).

[61] Jefferys, *Trends in Business Organization*, p. 384.

[62] Ibid., pp. 173–4.

[63] Ibid., p. 175.

[64] Ibid., p. 385.

[65] Ibid., p. 387.

[66] Ibid., pp. 389–90.

> interested to a certain degree in the running of these companies. This applied particularly to the shareholders in industrial concerns.[67]

Thus, the investment of these individuals was largely personal; they invested in the firms in which they had been proprietors or sometimes extended their shareholdings to other industrial concerns in the sector or location with which they were familiar. By delegating the floatation of a limited company to promoters such as Chadwick, Allott and Wing, a less 'personal' element to investment in industrial firms was sometimes introduced. The type of company in which this type of investor took shares, according to Jefferys, tended to be iron, steel, coal and shipping firms; they had few shareholders per company; they had large individual shareholdings; and larger enterprises in which they were involved were likely to have been quoted on the London or provincial stock exchange lists, although the buying and selling of shares in these enterprises tended to be restricted.[68] Jefferys went on to argue that: 'As a whole ... the home industrial companies retained their "personal" investment character and that despite the role of the company promoter, investors in these domestic manufacturing concerns tended to be the vendors and their friends and families'.[69]

The work of Maltby confirms these findings. She has argued that, from the perspective of accounting history, any financial publicity concerning a limited company was not only undesirable for those large investors who wished to keep details of their personal wealth private, but also unnecessary due to the close relationships between many shareholders and the directors of these concerns. Accounting publicity was not important for large investors who possessed:

> financial expertise and ready access to management ... Personal knowledge, fostered by a shared background and membership of the same social network, did the same job, and did not have the drawback of exposing shareholders' financial affairs to the world at large.[70]

Moreover, the accounting profession was encouraged to underplay the profits of limited companies, again in the interests of limited company directors and their large investors and to the detriment of the small, 'outside' investor. Maltby argues that 'corporate governance was designed to accommodate the interests of large "insider" shareholders'.[71] Directors would also vet share

---

67 Ibid., p. 173.

68 Ibid., pp. 391-2.

69 Ibid., p. 393; *Chadwick's Investment Circular*, 1871: p.115.

70 Maltby, 'UK joint Stock Companies Legislation', p. 26.

71 J. Maltby, 'The Origins of Prudence in Accounting', *Critical Perspectives on Accounting*, Vol. 11 (2000), p. 63.

applications in order to ensure that shares were allocated to desirable or known individuals.[72]

Was this the case in the Sheffield region? In order to answer this question, the shareholders in those companies promoted by Allott, Wing and Chadwick have been analysed. The data used were taken from the Memorandum of Association and the first annual return of the 'Summary of Capital and Shares' made by each company to the Registrar of Joint Stock Companies.

Firstly, the seven signatories to the Memoranda of Association, or initial shareholders, will be considered. Chadwick regarded initial shareholders in a company as the 'promoters' of the company.[73] They were often important to the management of the company, as they usually included the vendors, if it was a conversion; sometimes the promoter; the Directors of the company; and, if additional names were required, family members or business colleagues of the vendors. Certain 'names' recurred amongst the signatories to the Memoranda of Association of the companies being examined. How active they would be in terms of management is hard to discern, but many were owners of the companies prior to conversion and maintained such involvement after floatation.

Alfred Allott was an initial subscriber to only two of his promotions, but he appears to have used a group of people to sign the Memorandum of Association for his companies. Five names appear as initial subscribers for more than one company – William Cooke (ironmaster), David Davy (engineer), Alfred Davy (engineer), George Haywood (ironfounder), and Joseph Pickering (polish manufacturer). Considering these individuals will provide a better picture of the financial networks operating in the region.

Both Alfred and David Davy were the vendors of Davy Bros. & Co. Ltd., but only David was an initial subscriber to that company. David also signed the Memorandum of Association of another of Allott's companies – the Charlton Iron Works – and Alfred gave his signature to two others – Phoenix Bessemer and Albion Steel & Wire. William Cooke, an ironmaster, was a vendor of William Cooke and Co. Ltd., a company converted in 1873 and for which he was a signatory. He was also an initial subscriber to the Charlton Iron Works, first promoted in 1872. George Haywood was owner of Yates Haywood & Co., which merged with the Rotherham Foundry Co. in 1879 to form a limited concern, a conversion in which Allott was not involved.[74] His connection with Allott's promotions appears, rather, to have been a result of involvement in the iron industry or possibly through a personal connection. Joseph Pickering was a Sheffield polish manufacturer. Unlike the other individuals involved with Allott's companies, he does not appear to have been directly connected with the iron and steel industry. His link with Allott may have arisen through either

---

72 Maltby, 'UK Joint Stock Companies Legislation', p. 17.

73 Cottrell, *Industrial Finance*, p. 115.

74 *White's Directory of Sheffield* (1879), p. 154. The company formed was Yates Haywood & Co. & the Rotherham Foundry Co. Ltd., PRO: BT31/2533/13127.

Allott's accountancy practice, or a personal relationship. However, all those used by Allott in the formation of limited companies as signatures to the Memorandum of Association originated from either Sheffield or Rotherham. Thus, the business and personal contacts of Allott were local.

The companies promoted by John Unwin Wing do not contain the same cluster of common initial subscribers. Wing himself made initial subscriptions to five of the seven companies he promoted, but only two other names appear more than once on the Memoranda of Association of his companies. They are John Easterbrook, signatory to three companies, and John James Brown, signatory to two. Easterbrook was an engineer from Sheffield, a member of the firm of Easterbrook & Allcard, machinists and engineers' tool manufacturers. Brown, an ironmaster from Rotherham, was manager of one of Wing's promotions – G. & J. Brown Co. Ltd. – to which he was an initial subscriber. Brown was also a signatory to Tinsley Rolling Mills, a company that Wing promoted in 1874, two years after G. & J. Brown.

Only two names appear more than once amongst the Memoranda of Association of the 'Sheffield' companies promoted by David Chadwick. William Landsdowne Beale, an ironmaster with a London address and a director/owner of Parkgate Iron and Steel, and George Wood, a Manchester merchant. Both were signatories to two of Chadwick's companies. In terms of initial subscribers, the companies promoted by Chadwick do not show a clear group of men used by the promoter to 'found' or manage these firms, but only four companies are being considered here. However, both Beale and Wood were from outside the Sheffield region and demonstrate the use made by Chadwick of extra-regional capital and management skills, especially that from Manchester and London. This contrasts with Allott's and Wing's multiple signatories, who were all from the Sheffield locality.

To expand upon the exploration of interlocking ownership within the 20 companies promoted by Wing, Allott, and Chadwick, the shareholders, as found in the first summaries of capital and shares returned to the Registrar, have also been analysed. Interlocking shareholdings between the companies promoted by the same financial agent can thereby be established.

Chadwick's four promotions involved 413 shareholdings held by 384 investors. Two men that had been initial subscribers to Chadwick's companies – William Landsdowne Beale and George Wood – retained multiple shareholdings in these companies on the first issue of shares proper. Beale held shares in Yorkshire Engine and Parkgate Iron & Steel, the two companies for which he was an initial subscriber. George Wood, and other individuals with the same surname, figure prominently amongst the shareholdings of Chadwick's companies. George Wood, George Wood Junior and Edward Wood, all cotton dealers from Manchester, each held shares in three of Chadwick's companies. William Newmarch, the economist and manager of the London private bank Glyn Mills, also had shareholdings in three of Chadwick's companies. Eighteen other men held shares in two of Chadwick's companies. Of these, one came from Sheffield, one from Oldham, one from

London, one from Edinburgh, two from Doncaster, with the remaining 12 all from Manchester. Therefore, these multiple shareholders again demonstrate the use of extra-regional capital by Chadwick. There appears to have been a movement of funds generated in the cotton manufacturing North West to the iron, steel and coal producing area of South Yorkshire/North Derbyshire, facilitated by Chadwick and his Manchester associates.

The companies promoted by John Unwin Wing also had a number of investors with cross shareholdings. There were 621 shareholdings in total and 537 investors: thirteen men had shareholdings in three or four of Wing's companies. Of these, seven originated from Sheffield and six from Rotherham, eight were involved in the production of iron and steel and two were colliery proprietors. There were also 50 others that had shareholdings in just two of Wing's companies, of which 38 had Sheffield addresses and nine were from Rotherham. This confirms the local base of Wing's business affiliations.

Alfred Allott's promotions involved the largest amount of subscriptions in numerical terms – 951 shareholdings and 730 investors. The shareholders included individuals with the highest number of multiple shareholdings – 50 people held shares in three to seven companies. Of these multiple shareholders, forty-one originated from Sheffield, three from Rotherham, two from Saltaire, one from Barnsley and only four from outside Yorkshire.[75] All the individuals who were initial subscribers to more than one of Allott's companies retained their shareholdings. William Cooke and George Haywood held shares in three companies and Joseph Pickering held shares in two. The Davy family expanded their investment in Allott's companies after incorporation. Abraham junior, Albert, Charles, Walter Scott and David all had shareholdings in four companies; Dennis in three firms; and Abraham senior, Alfred, and Mary Ann had shareholdings in two companies.[76] All these family members held shares in Davy Bros. Ltd, but their involvement in financial investment in the region's iron and steel production extended to other of Allott's conversions.

Two other men were important investors in the companies promoted by Allott. They were Thomas Hampton and John Kidner, both holders of shares in five of Allott's companies and both co-partners in the same accountancy practice as Allott. The participation of these partners in Allott's accountancy firm demonstrates the personal and professional involvement of accountants in the local share market, as highlighted earlier.

The findings for the 20 companies incorporated by the three promoters came from an initial study of 90 companies floated in and around Sheffield between 1855 and 1885. Multiple shareholdings and cross-holding patterns for all of these 90 companies have also been analysed. Results reveal that there appears to have been a highly localised capital network consisting primarily of iron, steel and engineering industrialists who invested in companies involved in the same manufacturing activities as themselves. Multiple shareholdings and cross-

[75] Bridgenorth (Shropshire), London and Worksop (Nottinghamshire).

[76] In addition, four others with the surname Davy held shares in Davy Bros.

shareholdings occurred primarily in 12 firms that were incorporated in 1872, 1873 and 1874 and were undertaken by 63 core investors. Of these 12 firms, seven were promoted by Alfred Allott and two by John Unwin Wing. This indicates that the 'core' membership of the local capital market comprised individuals connected with the two Sheffield promoters. The concentration of this investment activity by the group of individuals occurred in the boom years of the early 1870s, the period in which Allott and Wing were active. Allott himself was owner of multiple shareholdings, making the highest number of separate investments in companies (twelve) to be found in this regional capital network.

Shareholders in Sheffield: Geographical distribution and occupational analysis

The local nature of share subscriptions in manufacturing firms converting to limited liability has already been emphasised. In the case of the companies promoted by Allott, Wing and Chadwick, this can be clarified through the analysis of the addresses of shareholders as detailed in the share returns to the Registrar. The majority of capital invested in the companies of Wing and Allott originated from Yorkshire, 89 per cent and 84 per cent respectively, and over 50 per cent from Sheffield itself. These men were financial agents, originally based in Sheffield, and capital from their local sphere of influence dominated the companies with which they were involved. However, as mentioned previously, the 1879 *White's Sheffield District Trade Directory* shows that both Wing and Allott were by then members of financial practices which had London offices. The predominance of Yorkshire subscriptions could have been due to the promotions taking place before Wing and Allott opened offices in London, or, rather, have been due to their stronger connections in the Sheffield region.

In contrast, the geographical origins of the funds invested in Chadwick's four companies are predominantly Lancashire and London. Chadwick had both Manchester and London offices and the results reflect the difference compared with Wing's and Allott's companies; 29 per cent of the capital invested in Chadwick's firms originated from Yorkshire, whereas a higher amount of capital (33 per cent) came from Lancashire. Much of this finance came from Manchester (26 per cent). In contrast, only five per cent of the capital subscribed to Wing's companies was from Lancashire and one per cent with respect to Allott's companies. In addition, a substantial amount of capital in Chadwick's companies came from London (21 per cent), as opposed to only one per cent for Wing's firms and seven per cent for Allott's. Before the late 1870s, the London connections of Chadwick, therefore, appear to have been far more highly developed than those of the locally-based Sheffield promoters. Chadwick's influence was therefore far more national than either Allott or Wing.

Were shareholders predominantly those involved in local industrial concerns, as identified in the work of Jefferys? In order to answer this question, Table 7.4 shows the occupational origins of shareholders in the companies promoted by Allott, Wing and Chadwick. The majority of shareholders gave their occupation as 'manufacturing'. This is not surprising, given the nature of the companies being considered. The other dominant groups of investors consist of those from commerce, the professions and those with independent means. After manufacturing, 'commerce' constituted the most important occupational group for those investing both in Chadwick's and Wing's industrial concerns, 25 per cent and 20 per cent respectively. More important for the companies promoted by Allott were investors from the 'Professions', which provided 18 per cent of the capital invested, as opposed to 12 per cent of capital from those in commerce. Investors from the professions were less important to Chadwick's companies (nine per cent). Men and women of independent means were an important source of finance for each three promotional groups – 16 per cent in the case of Allott's companies, 11 per cent of Wing's and 17 per cent of Chadwick's. The only other significant occupation, other than the 'top four', occurs in the enterprises promoted by John Unwin Wing, with ten per cent of capital coming from the mining sector. This is probably due to one of his promotions being a coal mining concern, the only such undertaking converted by any of the three. The remaining balance of capital originated from a wide social group of subscribers with varying occupations.

Table 7.4
Allott, Wing and Chadwick promotions: Occupational distributions of shareholdings

	Per cent of subscribed capital		
	Allott	Wing	Chadwick
Occupational category			
Manufacuring	38.9	37.4	40.0
Professional	18.3	13.1	8.8
Independent	15.9	11.0	17.5
Commerce	12.2	20.0	24.7
Unknown management	3.4	5.0	1.8
Unknown workers	2.9	1.3	0.8
Construction	2.8	0.5	0.1
Mining	2.7	9.8	0.1

These results confirm the trend identified by Jefferys: that investors in Sheffield's manufacturing industry tended to be vendors, other local industrialists, and the family, friends and business associates of these individuals. Thus, the promoters could draw upon a 'pool' of knowledgeable investors through their business and social connections and those of the vendors. It is unlikely that Allott or Wing would have had to advertise widely and seek 'outside' investors, as evidenced by the geographical and occupational profile of shareholders in the sample companies. This conforms to the findings of Wilson, who investigated the patterns of investment of the North West gas industry and discovered that before 1880 'the whole process remained a local affair, with the promoters, management and shareholders coming from the business community to be supplied by an undertaking'.[77]

Conclusions

This study has demonstrated that the promoters Allott, Wing and Chadwick had a very important influence upon the movement towards limited liability made by manufacturing industry in the Sheffield region between 1855 and 1885. The number of companies they promoted, and the capital involved in these formations, clearly shows the significance of their roles. Chadwick's promotions in the 1860s introduced extra-regional capital to the local iron and steel industry, mainly from Lancashire, specifically Manchester, and also London. In contrast, local funds constituted the mainstay of Allott's and Wing's promotions in the iron and steel boom of the early 1870s. All of the promoters were involved with the companies they promoted, as auditors, as signatories to the Memoranda of Association or shareholders thereafter, with both Chadwick and Allott retaining considerable shareholdings in their promotions. The development of a management group by the promoters appears to have been most significant in the case of Alfred Allott, who used a group of men involved in the Sheffield and Rotherham iron and steel industries. In each case, Allott, Wing and Chadwick seem to have used their local connections, be they Mancunian or from South Yorkshire, to provide finance for the expansion of iron and steel manufacturing in the Sheffield region. Furthermore, such company promoters were not only important in terms of the funds they generated for the companies that they promoted, but also in their role in the domestic industrial capital market which developed following the 1855 and 1862 Companies Acts. Jefferys stresses that these promoters 'educated a solid core of wealthy investors into the art of investment'.[78]

---

77 J.F. Wilson, ***Lighting the Town. A Study of Management in the North West Gas Industry, 1805–1880*** (Paul Chapman Publishing, 1991), p. 103. His results (in Chapters 3 and 4) reveal that shareholders originated from the local area and participated in local trades and professions.

78 Jefferys, *Trends in Business Organization*, p. 319.

The analysis of shareholders in these companies has revealed a highly localised capital market which was dependent mainly upon subscriptions from four social groups: those engaged in manufacturing, trade, commerce or the 'professions' (members of the former three groups being chiefly occupied in the major Sheffield trades). Within the local financial capital market, there also existed a specific capital network in the Sheffield companies, identified by the existence of multiple shareholders and their cross-holdings in the sample of 90 limited companies promoted in the region between 1855 and 1885. The company promoters were again influential in this phenomenon, as nine of the early 1870s registrations of Allott and Wing contained a common group of local investors. This capital network consisted mainly of local industrialists who were linked with each other, the promoters and the vendors of the limited companies in which they held shares by their occupations and also by kinship and probably social ties.[79]

In terms of the investment patterns identified, network theory may be usefully applied. It is reasonable to argue that the managements of firms adopting a new form of company organisation were attempting to reduce risk and uncertainty by relying upon resources with which the vendors were familiar, in this case shareholders who resided in the local area; who were known to the owners via business or personal networks; or were known to a company promoter via their local networks. The impersonal investor with no links to the firm or the area may be viewed as having less commitment to their investment, and therefore a greater likelihood to withdraw their funds. By deliberately selling shares only to those investors with links to the company and/or the region, managements were acting to reduce potential exit opportunities by ensuring shareholder 'ties' to the company, therefore reducing the risk and uncertainty inherent in broadening their capital bases. This created a 'high trust' environment, one that was likely to have experienced peer monitoring and the consequent restraint of opportunistic behaviour. Indeed, further results have shown that lists of shareholders remained relatively static during the first five to ten years of a limited company's existence, indicating the continuing commitment of investors.[80] It can be further argued that such networks reduced transaction costs and advanced economic efficiency by improving information flows and reducing the risks of opportunistic behaviour.

In addition to providing the company with committed investors, the 'high trust' environment may be considered from the perspective of the shareholder. These investors were usually highly informed, as they were active in and/or connected to local industry and it was unlikely that they would have been 'duped' by a dishonest promoter. They were also purchasing shares of high denominations and with a large amount left unpaid, therefore demonstrating a

[79] An examination of institutions such as the *Company of Cutlers*, the *Sheffield Club* and political parties will prove useful in exploring networks in Sheffield in more detail. A comparative examination of financial networks in Oldham would also be fruitful. Such work was beyond the scope of the paper but will be pursued in future.

[80] Newton, *Credit and Capital*, Chapters 5 and 6.

high level of trust in the promoters, vendors and management of the enterprises in which they invested. In turn, it was necessary for those involved in the promotion of such local firms to be known, trustworthy and credible in the eyes of such knowledgeable shareholders and vendors.

This research has therefore demonstrated that capital networks existed in the investing community that developed in the Sheffield region between 1855 and 1885. Such networks were undoubtedly of vital importance to the proliferation of limited liability as a form of company organisation, but also, correspondingly, to the development of the region's industry in terms of its ability to raise finance, to adopt new technology, to increase in scale and to survive cyclical downturns in the economy. Financial networks allowed an initial broadening of the region's capital base, albeit within restricted parameters which maintained local control of industry and a low risk use of external forms of finance. The movement towards a broader capital market was thus tentative but significant, nonetheless.

In this light, these networks may be described as successful: they attracted solid investors and raised finance for local industry. Unfortunately, it has not been possible to measure the 'success' in terms of company performance, such as dividend values, as it has not been possible to consult such data. However, many of the companies considered had a very long lifespan and some survived, in one form or another, into the twenty first century. In considering the success or otherwise of these networks, it is also interesting to note that it was the extra-regional financial network of Chadwick, rather than the local networks of Allott and Wing, which ultimately generated more capital both in the region and on a national level. Even at this early stage of the development of financial markets, the potential limitations of local funding were visible.

[16]

INTERNATIONAL MIGRATION, DOMESTIC WORK, AND CARE WORK
Undocumented Latina Migrants in Israel

REBECA RAIJMAN
University of Haifa, Israel
SILVINA SCHAMMAH-GESSER
ADRIANA KEMP
Tel Aviv University

This article discusses three major dilemmas embedded in women's labor migration by focusing on undocumented Latina migrants in Israel. The first is that to break the cycle of blocked mobility in their homelands, migrant women must take jobs that they would have never taken in their countries of origin, despite uncertainty about possible economic outcomes. The second dilemma is that the search for economic betterment leads Latina migrants to risk living and working illegally in the host country, forcing them to remain on the margins of society. The third dilemma relates to the role of mothers who, to secure a better future for their children, are forced to leave them behind, thus subverting the traditional definition of motherhood. The absence of an egalitarian notion and the practice of citizenship for non-Jews leave undocumented labor migrants in Israel without prospects for incorporation into the society.

Keywords: *transnational motherhood; domestic work; Latinas; labor migration; globalization*

Alba is a 45-year-old widow from Colombia who arrived in Israel in 1996 as an undocumented migrant. She came alone, leaving her two sons back home under the care of her sister. In her hometown, where she earned $100 per month as a factory worker, Alba dreamed of having her own home and opening a small business. To achieve these goals, she needed a considerable sum of money, which was hard to save and even harder to get in loans or credit. A window of opportunity was opened when Alba was recommended to a family in Israel as a live-in domestic worker. Alba considered migration as a strategy for saving the money that she required in a relatively

---

AUTHORS' NOTE: *This research was supported by the Israeli Science Foundation founded by the Israel Academy of Sciences and Humanities. The authors wish to thank five anonymous reviewers for their helpful comments and Christine Bose for her editorial suggestions. We are also grateful to Tamara Barsky, Alejandro Paz, and Valentin Nabel for their efficient research assistance and to Deborah Bernstein for her careful reading and helpful suggestions. A preliminary version of this article was presented at the annual conference of the FIELAC in April 1999. Direct all correspondence to Rebeca Raijman, Department of Sociology and Anthropology, University of Haifa, Haifa 31905, Israel; e-mail: raijman@soc.haifa.ac.il.*

GENDER & SOCIETY, Vol. 17 No. 5, October 2003 727-749
DOI: 10.1177/0891243203255762

short period of time. Since her arrival, she has been working without a work permit as a domestic worker in the Tel Aviv suburbs. Although she constantly fears being deported, she hopes that the sacrifices she is making will provide better prospects for her and her children in the future.

Alba's case illustrates the increasingly visible economic presence of immigrant women in the current flows of international migration. This presence undermines the implicit assumption in migration studies that men are the central protagonists in migrant flows, with women only following men's initiative. The rampant feminization of transnational migration in recent decades is challenging this assumption and has motivated a novel line of research in which women become independent social actors making decisions, taking actions, and redefining family and labor roles as they cross international borders in search of a better life in a new globalized world (Hondagneu-Sotelo 1992, 1994, 2001; Morokvasic 1984; Pedraza 1991; Pessar 1999; Phizacklea 1983; Salazar Parreñas 2000, 2001; Wong 1996).

As a foreign domestic worker in Israel, Alba is part of a larger flow of "global reproductive workers" who are imported as cheap labor to occupy gender-specific jobs in Western capitalist societies, in the newly industrialized countries of Asia, and in the oil-rich nations of the Middle East. In this setting, Alba's case exemplifies a relatively neglected aspect of globalization that relates to the consequences of migration for women, children, and their families. These features have been brought to the fore recently by several scholars in the field of international migration, who, moving beyond the "mobility of the capital and labor approach," have stressed the gendered implications of globalization and more particularly the dilemmas resulting from the "globalization of domestic work" and the "globalization of child-care" (Hochschild 2000; Hondagneu-Sotelo 2001; Hondagneu-Sotelo and Avila 1997; Salazar Parreñas 2000, 2001).

Indeed, Alba's story illuminates the dilemmas inherent in the process of female labor migration, namely migration as a strategy for economic mobility on one hand and the inherent cost and strain associated with it on the other. More specifically, we refer to the prices that migrant women have to pay in terms of occupational downward mobility, the "cost" of being illegal in the host society, the disruption of family life, and the contradictory expectations stemming from the need to redefine their roles as mothers and as breadwinners. Drawing on the experiences of undocumented non-Jewish Latina women in Israel as a case study, this article has a twofold purpose: First, we offer an analysis of the fundamental dilemmas faced by migrant women, who, besides being segregated in the labor market by gender, race, class, and nationality, live in perpetual fear of being arrested by state authorities and deported, and second, we delve into the strategies that migrant women develop to cope with their situations.

Although the dilemmas and strategies analyzed in the article are resonant with the female labor migration experience in general, our focus on non-Jewish undocumented migrant women in Israel is novel. Previous research in Israel has mainly concentrated on Jewish migrant women and the "occupational cost" they pay when migrating to Israel (Raijman and Semyonov 1997; Remennick 1999). However, because of their Jewish origin, these migrants' status is substantially different from that of non-Jewish labor migrants. The latter are not entitled to citizenship, not even to "permanent resident" status, and are therefore bound to remain excluded from the dominant regime of incorporation in the host country (Kemp et al. 2000; Raijman and Kemp 2002).

Our argument unfolds as follows: After presenting our theoretical background, we describe the phenomenon of labor migration to Israel and the patterns of informal recruitment in the domestic service sector in which most Latina women concentrate. Next, we describe the research methodology and proceed to data analysis. In the analysis, we first present a profile of the sociodemographic and economic characteristics of Latina labor migrant women, the motives for migration, and the forms of recruitment to Israel. This is followed by a discussion of the dilemmas stemming from the transformation of migration—initially regarded as a short-term strategy for economic betterment—into a more complex and long-term process that entails emotional, social, and economic costs, which are not always foreseen. We conclude by discussing the modes in which migrant women actively cope with uprootedness and structural disadvantages. We suggest that some of the dilemmas that migrant women have to face are not necessarily gendered, but the strategies they develop to cope with them mostly are.

THEORETICAL BACKGROUND: GENDER, DOMESTIC SERVICE, AND INTERNATIONAL MIGRATION

Demand for domestic and care workers has expanded in recent decades, especially in developed countries, as a consequence of the increasing numbers of women entering the workforce and the decline of the welfare state. These factors have caused an escalation in women's burdens, often leading to the reallocation of these responsibilities onto female relatives and/or hired labor. Within this configuration, migrant women—as reproductive workers—constitute the new flow of migration recruited to meet the demands of child care and domestic work as well as care for the elderly and the handicapped in postindustrial nations (Chant 1992; Chant and Radcliffe 1992; Hondagneu-Sotelo 2001; Lim 1993; Tienda and Booth 1991; Truong 1996; Wong 1996). Indeed, First World countries are now importing domestic and care work as they once imported raw material from the Third World (Hochschild 2000).

Inequalities arising from economic globalization, international migration, North-South disparities, and the restructuring of reproductive labor in the household are key factors in explaining the globalization of contemporary paid domestic work and the increasing flow of migrant women to receiving countries. This flow is composed not only of women from lower socioeconomic statuses but also of women of relatively high status (in their countries of origin) for whom migration entails the cost of occupational downward mobility (Salazar Parreñas 2000).

The incorporation of migrant women into domestic service and care work is not only the result of migratory circumstances (a lack of language proficiency, inadequate cultural orientation, and incompatible occupational skills), but rather it reflects the fact that domesticity is one of the few occupations open to migrant women due to gender segregation in the labor market of developed countries (Glenn 1986; Salazar Parreñas 2001). That is, in addition to their migrant status, immigrant women experience further difficulties in the labor force as a result of the "double negative" effect of gender and birthplace (Boyd 1984; Raijman and Semyonov 1997; Robinson 1991).

This situation is more acute in the case of undocumented migrant women, thus adding a significant dimension to their disadvantages in the receiving society. Because of their illegal status, they are excluded from most jobs regardless of their human capital, and they cannot enter occupations for which they have qualifications. The structural constraints within the labor market of the host country compel women to enter the domestic and care work sector. Likewise, their status as undocumented migrants makes female workers particularly vulnerable to discrimination, exploitation, and abuse. These are especially acute in the sphere of domestic and care work in which duties are conducted in isolated households that are closed to public scrutiny (Cheng 1996, 2003; Salazar Parreñas 2001; Wong 1996). Under these conditions, the experience of downward occupational mobility becomes gendered.

As opposed to migrant men, who have a wider spectrum of job opportunities both formal and informal (that do not necessarily imply downward mobility in terms of occupational prestige), migrant women suffer from a double disadvantage. Since domestic work is the only occupational niche available for them, women have to endure a work setting that is small, is unregulated, and involves patriarchal and vertical ties with the employer (Hagan 1998, 65). Likewise, taking domestic jobs represents a more severe decline in social status for women who never envisaged working in such low-prestige jobs in their countries of origin. This is the case even though wages in Israel may be much higher in domestic service than in the construction, light industry, and other service sectors, in which most Latino men work.

In addition to the occupational cost exacted from downward mobility (as women who work at domestic jobs) and their illegal status, women also face the emotional distress associated with the separation from their families, especially those who leave children behind in their countries of origin. During their stays in the host countries, migrants continue to nurture bonds with family and community in their home countries. While most economic migrants tend to maintain close links with their families and households in their native countries, these relations are stronger and more complex in the case of migrant mothers. This phenomenon demands a transnational approach that emphasizes the way in which migrant lives cut across national boundaries and construct a social space of networks, activities, and lifestyles encompassing both the host and the home society (Alicea 1997; Pessar 1999;

Salazar Parreñas 2000, 2001). Building on this perspective, the concept of transnational motherhood refers to the new ways by which migrant mothers redefine their identities as a result of their simultaneous roles in the host and the sending societies.

Hondagneu-Sotelo and Avila (1997, 548) defined transnational motherhood as the variations in organizational arrangements, meanings, and priorities of motherhood that migrant women need to internalize to cope with the spatial and temporal separation from their children left behind in their countries of origin. According to this perspective, the concept of mothering as a universal women's calling disguises the fact that for women of different class, race, and ethnic affiliations, as well as nationalities, their incorporation into the labor market may challenge traditional ways of child raising and motherhood.

As Nakano Glenn (1994, 3) stated, "Mothering—more than any aspect of gender—has been subject to essentialist interpretation: seen as natural, universal, and unchanging." However, for migrant mothers, who leave their children in their homelands, the need arises to switch from an ideology of "family in one place" (glorifying the idea of privatized mothering) to a new rhetoric of transnational motherhood (emphasizing the breadwinner role) (Hondagneu-Sotelo and Avila 1997, 548). Thus, transnational motherhood openly subverts traditional conceptions of mother-child bonds nurtured daily within the home and conventional views that employment and mothering are mutually exclusive. Adjusting to their new role as "overseas mothers" capable of caring for their children by "remote control" forces women to face the paradox that to provide their children with a better future, they are forced to leave home.

The occupational and emotional costs of international migration discussed so far are the price migrant women must pay as they cross international borders looking for economic betterment. Contrary to the widely accepted assumption that migration is a rational strategy to maximize family income and minimize risks associated with a variety of market failures (e.g., labor, credit, and insurance markets) (Stark 1991), we argue that international migration, especially for women, is a strategy abounding with dilemmas that defy instrumental rationales and assumptions (Hondagneu-Sotelo and Avila 1997; Salazar Parreñas 2000, 2001).

Building on previous work by Hondagneu-Sotelo and Avila (1997), Hondagneu-Sotelo (2001), and Salazar Parreñas (2000, 2001), we focus on three main dilemmas faced by undocumented non-Jewish Latina women in Israel. The first is that to break the cycle of economic stagnation and blocked mobility in their homelands, migrant women are forced to take low-status jobs (e.g., domestic work), often positions that they would never have taken in their countries of origin, despite uncertainty about possible economic outcomes (Salazar Parreñas 2000, 2001). The second relates to the search for economic betterment, which leads Latina migrants to risk living and working illegally in the host country and forces them to remain "aliens" and relegated to the margins of society. The third dilemma concerns their role as mothers, who, to secure a better future for their children, are obliged to leave them behind, thus subverting the traditional definition of "motherhood" that emphasizes the presence of the mother at home (Hondagneu-Sotelo and Avila 1997).

Although the second dilemma (the cost of being illegal) is related to the costs of international migration and may apply equally to migrant men and women, the first and third dilemmas (downward occupational mobility and the transnationalization of motherhood) derive from gender segregation in the labor market, the new globalized gendered economy of care, and the gendered domestic division of labor in migrants' countries of origin. As such, they acquire a specific meaning for women. While these dilemmas relate to distinct social issues confronted by Latina migrants, we will show the ways in which they are closely intertwined.

Moreover, whereas men and women both may develop strategies that would help them "rationalize" the "costs" entailed in their migration, the particular strategies chosen by migrants tend to be patterned along distinct gender lines. To demonstrate this, we expand and elaborate on two main strategies used by Latina migrants in Israel. First, we show how women's increased participation in religious activities serves as a compensatory mechanism to counter marginalization, thus opening an alternative path for social mobility in an unfriendly environment. Second, we analyze the conditions that legitimize transnational motherhood among Latina migrants in Israel as they actively engage in redefining their traditional roles as mothers and caregivers.

THE ISRAELI SETTING

Overseas labor migration is a recent phenomenon in Israel. As a self-defined Jewish nation-state, Israel actively encourages immigration of Jews from practically every corner of the globe and is both institutionally and ideologically committed to their successful absorption. The legal platform for the Jewish character of the state is based on the Law of Return of 1950 (reformed in 1970 so as to enlarge the definition of "who is a Jew") and the Israeli Law of Nationality, which came into force in 1952. The former, based on the jus sanguinis principle, confers on all Jews, and only Jews, the right of immigration, while the latter grants them Israeli nationality virtually automatically. At the same time, Israel is an ethnically divided society, with a population of approximately 83 percent Jews and 17 percent Arabs. The Arab citizens, although legally considered equal, actually constitute a subordinate social, political, and national minority. Israel can be viewed as an immigrant-settler society based on an ethno-nationalist structure, defined both ideologically and institutionally.

Labor Migration: The Israeli View

Following the Six Day War in 1967, the government gradually began the recruitment of noncitizen Palestinian workers from the West Bank and Gaza Strip to perform mostly menial, low-status, manual jobs in the Israeli labor market. By 1987, they composed 7 percent of the entire Israeli labor force. The outbreak of the first Intifada (Palestinian uprising) in 1987 created a shortage of labor in low-status positions, when the entry of noncitizen Palestinian workers into Israel was prevented (because of imposed closure or self-imposed strikes). These events set the initial stage for the organized recruitment of overseas labor migrants in 1993, primarily from Rumania (construction sector), Thailand (agriculture sector), and the Philippines (geriatric care, nursing, and domestic services) (Bartram 1998). Currently, foreign workers constitute 10 percent of the Israeli labor force (about 60 percent without work permits),[1] placing Israel at a similar level to that of top labor-importing countries. This massive flow of migrants arriving in a relatively short period of time makes Israel an illuminating setting in which to study labor migration.

Although labor migrants have become an integral part of the economy, they are placed at the bottom of the labor market and the social order. They suffer from the worst working conditions and are generally excluded from the welfare and benefit system accorded to Israeli citizens. Furthermore, since the end of 1995, Israel's declared policy toward migrant workers has been to reduce their number drastically, by arresting and deporting migrant workers without work permits. The overall goal set by the minister of labor was to reduce the proportion of migrant workers to just 1 percent of the labor force. The deportation policy emerged as a patchwork affair and entailed the violation of basic human rights. Many migrants were deported when they tried to demand their rights from their employers or from the National Insurance Institute (social security); hundreds were held in detention for lengthy periods in harsh conditions and without being brought to trial, and although in principle the state has to pay for the deportees' tickets, those who want to avoid lengthy periods of arrest pay for their own (for a thorough discussion of the deportation policy, see Raijman and Kemp 2002).

Although Israel has a democratic regime, its labor migration policy resembles the patterns of labor migration regulation and control in the Gulf system and in the newly industrialized countries in South East Asia, where laws and regulations governing labor migration are much stricter than those prevailing in Western labor-importing countries. Similar to the Gulf states and to Taiwan, in Israel work permits are granted to employers, to whom the migrant worker is indentured, thereby maximizing employers' and the state's control over the foreign population. The state does not allow residence without a work permit; does not recognize any right of asylum or any right of family reunification; does not guarantee access to housing, social benefits, or medical care; and carries out a blatant deportation policy that allows the arrest and expulsion of undocumented migrants at any time by simple administrative decree. In that sense, Israel's labor migration policy reflects the state's continuous anxiety over a changing ethnoscape that may pose a threat to its Jewish character. (For a discussion on labor migration in the Gulf system, see Massey et al., 1998, and Castles, 2000; for a discussion on labor migration in Taiwan, see Cheng, 2003). It is within this scenario that we should understand the unique situation of undocumented Latino labor migrants in Israel.

Domestic Service in Israel

The history of domestic service in Israel is one of ethnic succession. Since the establishment of the state in 1948, several ethnic groups entered this occupational niche. Initially, Jewish migrant women coming from North African and Asian countries during the 1950s joined the domestic sector, but the rapid growth of the Israeli economy created new opportunities for migrant women in clerical work and public services during the 1960s. The resulting shortage of cleaning workers from the Jewish immigrant sector opened the door for the recruitment of rural Arab women from villages within the state of Israel and, to a lesser extent, for men from the territories occupied by Israel since 1967 (Bernstein 1986, 404). By the late 1970s, students and young women from peripheral areas (mainly kibbutzim and development towns) were attracted to this niche because of the time flexibility this type of job permits and the easy accessibility to cash. Still, their joining the domestic sector did not significantly change its ethnic composition.

Since the early 1990s, as the massive wave of Jewish migrants from the former Soviet Union arrived in Israel, many Russian women joined the domestic sector, since they were not able to find a suitable job immediately after arrival and were forced to change their original occupations. By the mid-1990s, the arrival of foreign workers radically changed the ethnic composition of the domestic sector. Filipino migrants were legally recruited by professional (recruitment) agencies to care for the elderly and handicapped, while other migrant women such as Latinas and Black Africans were increasingly incorporated as cleaning and care workers through informal channels.

The existence of a Latina labor force in the domestic service sector (in which the majority of undocumented Latinas work) is a recent phenomenon in Israel. No large, established (non-Jewish) Latin American community existed prior to the arrival of these women in the early 1990s. The entry of Latin American migrant women into the domestic sector is characterized by two informal patterns of recruitment. One way is through Latin American Jewish families living in Israel. Family members or friends residing in the sending country act as recruiters, and the Israeli family sends funds for a plane ticket and other expenses. The Latino migrants come as "counterfeit tourists" and remain in Israel after their tourist visas expire. As tourists, they can stay legally in the country but do not have the right to work. When their visas expire (after three months), they become illegal residents and run the risk of being caught and deported by the Israeli authorities.

The second recruitment pattern involves migrants' own social networks. Pioneering Latino labor migrants in Israel laid the foundations for a social network serving present-day economic migrants from Latin America, mostly from the "southern cone." Individuals in the countries of origin respond to "invitations" from friends and family already living and working in Israel. Others decide to engage in similar experiences, swayed by the rumors of earning "easy" money in Israel, which encourage people to come and "make it in the Holy Land."[2] Relatives and friends already residing in Israel help others to join the migration process by providing them with help and information during their initial period after arrival. As a result of informal recruitment, migration spreads like a "virus" from person to person and from family to family, thus increasing the probability of others migrating to Israel (Massey et al. 1998). Informal labor recruitment helps to explain the peculiar direction of certain migrations, as initial social networks tend to become a central factor in the decision to migrate and the choice of destination for prospective migrants (Repak 1994).

METHOD

Data collection was based on 44 in-depth interviews with migrant women, as well as informal conversations during visits to households and in other social gatherings. Interviews were guided by a semistructured questionnaire, including items relating to premigration background, reasons for migration, occupational history in Israel, patterns of residence, income, leisure time, social networks, and community participation. Supplementary questions were posed to immigrant mothers, including topics relating to child-rearing arrangements in their home countries, monitoring strategies used by transnational mothers, their role as the sole wage earner (especially in the case of single-parent families), and the social stigma attached to migrant mothers who leave their families behind. Besides the interviews, we also conducted focus groups with transnational mothers in which women discussed the topics listed above. All names used in this article are pseudonyms.

We used a multiple-entry snowball sampling technique to detect and construct a sample of undocumented Latina labor migrants in Israel, thus avoiding the danger of interviewing limited personal social networks. We conducted fieldwork in various social and institutional settings (such as soccer games, salsa clubs, chess clubs, religious services, social clubs, organized tours, fairs, kindergartens, schools, etc.), thereby broadening the range of interviewee profiles.

Approximately 40 percent of the women in our sample had come from Colombia, the largest group among Latino migrants in Israel. Almost a quarter had migrated from Ecuador, and the rest were from Bolivia, Peru, Chile, Uruguay, Argentina, Brazil, and Venezuela. The majority of the women had arrived in Israel after 1993, and for most of them, their current stay in Israel was their first trip to this country.

LATIN AMERICAN LABOR MIGRATION TO ISRAEL

Labor Migration: The Latino/Latina View

Whereas undocumented Latin American labor migration to Israel can be explained in terms of pull factors (higher wages, easy entry compared with North America and Western Europe) and informal forms of recruitment, the structural constraints inherent in most Latin American countries provide the general context for understanding Latinos' motivation to migrate. Increasing foreign debt, austerity plans dictated by the International Monetary Fund, high inflation, and the consequent internal recession and economic stagnation have widened social gaps and increased poverty rates (Lijphart and Waisman 1996). The combination of falling incomes, frustrated ambitions, and the restructuring of many Latin American economies has generated powerful pressure for emigration among both skilled blue-collar workers and the educated urban middle classes. Consequently, political and socioeconomic conditions should be considered important factors for emigration from different countries in South America (Massey et al. 1998). In the next section, we provide a socioeconomic profile of Latina migrants in the sample and consider the motivations underlying their decisions to migrate far from home.

Sociodemographic Characteristics

The majority of Latina labor migrants in Israel are undocumented (96 percent). They average 35 years of age, confirming what other studies have shown, that migrants are concentrated in the middle labor force ages. These migrant women are evenly distributed along marital status categories: one-third are single, one-third are married, and one-third are divorced or widows. Almost half of all migrant Latinas left their children behind in their countries of origin under the care of husbands, parents, or other family members. These Latinas in our sample report an average of 11.5 years of formal education, and 15 percent hold a postsecondary degree. The majority (75 percent) were in the labor force in their countries of origin, and two-thirds worked in pink-collar occupations (clerks and sales), mostly in retail and public sectors. Only a minority (10 percent) worked in domestic service prior to migration. This fact suggests that for most of the sampled Latina migrants, migration involves some kind of downward occupational mobility.

The major motivating factors for migration were wage gaps (between their home countries and Israel) and a lack of opportunities for upward social and economic mobility in the sending societies. The average income of the women in their countries of origin amounted to no more than U.S.$250 per month. These levels contrast sharply with the expected income to be earned in Israel, which amounts to around $1,000 or $1,200 per month. This means that the economic incentives for migration to Israel are very strong because most women expect to earn three times what they would get at home.

Several recurrent themes illustrate the driving force behind the decision to migrate to Israel: the opportunity to save large amounts of money in a considerably short period of time; a strong desire for economic independence and a preference for self-employment or business ownership on returning to their home countries; an urge to secure a better future and education for their children, especially higher education; the determination to help their households and relatives pay family debts; and the aspiration to buy a house or a plot of land.

While Latina labor migrants come to Israel searching for a better life and/or to acquire the means of pursuing socioeconomic mobility in their countries of origin, they have to face the costs inherent in the migration process, especially if they are undocumented. These costs are associated with occupational downward mobility, illegality, and the disruption of family life.

THE COSTS AND DILEMMAS OF WOMEN'S LABOR MIGRATION

The Burden of Occupation Downward Mobility: *Aquí nos toca duro: Allá era la señora aquí soy la sirvienta* (We Are Really Having a Hard Time: Over There We Were Ladies and Here We Are Servants)

In his pioneer book on labor migration, Piore (1979) argued that the way migrant men minimize their status inconsistency is through rationalizing their taking hard, oppressive jobs with the prospects of returning home with money in hand that will secure the economic future of their families. Although Piore's study refers only to men, it is already well known that similar patterns exist among migrant women as well (Salazar Parreñas 2000).

Undocumented Latina migrants in Israel told us that the income they earn is also intended to bolster their family status at home. However, the mismatch between their skills and the jobs they perform still remains a major source of distress. That is because for the majority domestic work is the only option available in the host labor market.

Among these Latinas, the negative connotations attached to this type of work stem not only from the nature of the work itself, and the context of the work (especially in the case of live-in arrangements), but also because in Latin America domestic workers are located at the bottom of the social ladder. Even the term of reference, *las sirvientas* (the servants), with its class connotation of social distance and inequality, reflects their marginal status.

Consequently, for the majority of these women, taking a cleaning job was traumatic, even though they saw their stay in Israel as a transitional experience. This feeling was more pronounced among newly arrived migrants who, for the first time, took a live-in job (*internas*) in private households. The trauma of having to work as internas is exemplified in the words of Veronica, a 24-year-old Latina, who prior to her arrival had completed the second year of her studies in the faculty of dentistry in Ecuador. She came to Israel following her mother and aunt, who had also taken cleaning jobs. In Quito, Veronica worked as a clerk earning $100 per month to finance her studies. While higher education was considered a strategy for socioeconomic betterment in her family, she admitted that

> education is no longer a guarantee for a better future in Ecuador. . . . There are no possibilities for young professionals to make a decent living out of their skills . . . no matter how hard they work. [Prior to migration, her aunt warned her,] "Work in Israel

would no longer be office work. . . . I am telling you this in advance so you will not be taken by surprise. Then, it will be up to you whether to come or not."

For Veronica, the cool and calculated assessment of the prospects of earning around $1,000, compared with the meager $100 per month she got at home, won out. Still, no matter how prepared she was to endure the new working conditions, she felt a real shock on her arrival:

> I started right away working as a live-in caretaker of an old man. The first week was a nightmare. For someone like me who had never done this type of job and, on top of it, in a completely unknown country and without knowing a single word in Hebrew!! . . . I was supposed to be at his side round the clock and stay at home. I could not help but cry the whole week. The disappointment of initially seeing Tel Aviv with tourists' eyes and then turning to the real thing, to what you have come to. . . . Even though I knew that cleaning was the only type of job available for me and Mom, I could not stand seeing my mother or myself working as servants. It was degrading.

This feeling of shame was also expressed by Carmen, who worked as a dressmaker in Ecuador. Prior to migration, she had never considered the possibility of working in domestic service. When she informed her family about her migration plans, her relatives, distressed, tried to discourage her from taking this path to economic mobility. Still, she did not give up her plans. The economic incentives proved to be strong enough for her, as a divorced mother and sole provider for her children. Even under these conditions, she felt humiliated working as a domestic servant and complained, "This type of job is not meant for me."

The experience of downward mobility is further deepened among migrant women taking live-in positions. Many, like Veronica, reported the feeling of "being locked up" (*encerradas*), feelings that were exacerbated if their employers did not speak Spanish. Furthermore, the private nature of the work and the asymmetrical relations of power inherent in the employer-employee relationship mean that migrant women have few if any options to negotiate their working conditions. Due to their isolation, they are initially unaware of the salary range for this type of work, and many of them have settled for much lower wages than they should. In several cases, women report being paid only one-fifth of the highest salary available in the sector. In more extreme situations, employers (using the excuse that it is for the sake of the worker's own economic interests) retain the worker's salary, promising to deposit it in a savings account until considerable sums mounted up. Some employers even confiscate passports to prevent workers from changing jobs. As reported in the interviews, there are cases in which workers never got their salaries or passports returned to them.[3] Yet very few Latinas have considered the possibility of taking legal action against their employers due to the fear associated with their nonlegal status.

Be that as it may, with tenure in the country and the establishment of social networks, many female domestic workers have managed to move from live-in to live-out domestic service and to rent an apartment with friends or family members. These new residential arrangements allow them to have multiple employers, usually attending to two houses per day, an average of 12 hours of work per day (many of them work seven days a week). Although having multiple employers enables them to earn more money, they also incur extra expenses (e.g., rent, food, utilities). Nevertheless, live-out arrangements are viewed by migrant women as a substantial improvement in their quality of life, allowing them to control their time and private life, to mix with the Israeli society, to learn the Hebrew language, and to get first-hand information regarding both the Latino community and the wider Israeli context (see Hagan, 1998, and Hondagneu-Sotelo, 1994, for similar findings regarding the U.S. case).

Yet their employment remains unstable, and domestic workers are still vulnerable to their employers' demands, as their contracts are limited to mere verbal agreements. Under these conditions, Latina migrants are permanently seeking and maintaining a large number of jobs with the result that job searching is not merely a limited strategy for employment but part of the job itself. Despite the fragility of domestic work conditions, social interaction with other migrant women in different settings (church, salsa nightclubs, soccer games, and other informal social or community gatherings) helps these women develop a particular set of values, practices, and collective advice that act as a basic work culture, thereby establishing a more structured framework to their position as domestic workers (Salzinger 1991).

With the passage of time, many Latinas realize that what they considered a temporary job has turned into a dead-end position with no prospect for change. The frustration is even greater for those who understand that returning home is no longer a viable alternative, given the endemic socioeconomic and political problems in their countries of origin. They feel lost: "*No somos de aquí, ni somos de allá: somos parias.*" ("We belong neither here nor there. We are pariahs.")

Being at the crossroads, many are planning to migrate to a European country (primarily Spain). This step is seen as an alternative strategy—as the opportunity to become a legal resident in Israel is almost nonexistent, and the hope of finding a more suitable job, if not for them at least for their children, is doomed to failure. As a Latina migrant residing in Israel with her husband and two children told us, "*Si nos quedamos aquí, que les puedo ofrecer a mis hijos cuando cumplan 18 años: una escoba?*" ("If we stay here, what could I offer to my children when they are 18: a broom?")

As the stories of Veronica and Carmen testify, what compensates for occupational downward mobility is the idea that their current domestic jobs are an instrumental, short-term strategy. Their purpose is not to develop a career but to save for their futures and contribute to the household income. For many women, the autonomy and economic independence their new income allows provide sufficient incentive for enduring the costs of occupational downward mobility. Some of them become the major source of financial support not only for their children but also for their extended family. Yet seeing themselves as economic providers and considering the prospects of enjoying the fruits of their efforts in their countries of origin are not the only way to cope with downward mobility. Despite their extreme marginality and absolute exclusion, migrants develop other modes of dealing with the painful reality resulting from their marginal positions in the host society. As we will discuss later, one central strategy among Latina migrant women becomes participation in ethnic associations, especially religious organizations.

The Cost of Being Illegal:
Diosito, haznos invisibles a los ojos de la policía
(God, Make Us Invisible to the Eyes of the Police)

This saying was the climax of a "petition" prayer offered by a group of Evangelical Latino migrants who regularly meet to celebrate their weekly mass in a shabby old house turned into a church, near the old Central Bus Station in Tel Aviv, where most undocumented labor migrants live. Singing frantically, tightly holding their hands up, and immersed in deep concentration, these women were sharing their anxieties and pouring out their fears of being caught by the police. Able to experience some kind of relief and empowerment through religious rites, these women desperately craved a miracle.

Because Latino migrants in Israel must join the local labor force without work permits, they are forced to remain at the margins of the host society. As undocumented residents and workers in the informal sector of the economy, they do not have access to employment benefits, although they are supposed to be protected by local labor laws (Raijman and Kemp 2002). Employers can exploit this asymmetrical situation to their own benefit in a number of ways. As already mentioned, prearranged rates of payment may be lowered, earnings may be paid much later than previously agreed, or earnings may not be paid at all. Although undocumented workers have the right to claim their share, they rarely take this option even when nongovernmental organizations are ready to act on their behalf. As a rule, they prefer to lose their money and change jobs rather than take legal action that may entail the risk of being caught by the police and deported.

Being "illegal" has become a permanent burden affecting migrants' everyday lives, and it constitutes a recurrent theme in community gatherings. Viviana, a labor migrant from Bolivia, shared her consternation regarding her illegal status.

> I live with tension. We never have a moment of peace. We are not free to act and interact as normal people. People take advantage of this situation. Take for instance the question of renting an apartment. You know that they charge you more just because you are illegal and you cannot say a word. I already left two apartments and my money guarantee was not returned. Again, I couldn't complain. If you need a medicine, you cannot get it because illegal workers don't have medical insurance. Most employers do not want to pay for that.

Since the beginning of the deportation policy in 1995, as police arrest and deportation campaigns became a daily routine, illegality has become the daily nightmare for every migrant. Suddenly, home and street turned into dangerous places. Fearing arrest and deportation, migrants tried to avoid even the most casual encounter with the police. "I never take the same path on my way back home. Even the Tel Aviv marketplace that was a meeting place for Latinos on Friday afternoon has become a taboo place. You never know who is haunting you" (Gloria).

Police raids targeting the old and new Central Bus Station area in Tel Aviv led many migrants to move out to the surrounding areas with a lower concentration of foreign workers, hoping to reduce the chances of being caught. A case in point is Irene, a migrant from Venezuela, who moved to a northern suburb of Tel Aviv:

> Although living in the suburbs makes me feel a little more secure I know that the police can catch me on any bus at any time. To be on the safe side, I always have a sum of money reserved for the ticket in case of deportation. You know, when I leave my house I never know if I'll be back. (Irene)

In other cases, many women working as live-out domestics considered the possibility of taking a live-in position as a strategy to avoid being arrested on their way to work. It is particularly striking that for undocumented migrants in Israel, the fear of arrest and deportation exceeds their anxiety about terrorist attacks and the deteriorating security situation in the country. A clear and painful example that spotlights the fears and anxieties of undocumented labor migrants in Israel is the bomb attack perpetrated in southern Tel Aviv in January 2003. Several of the dead and injured were labor migrants who lived in the area. The local media seized on the fact that some of the survivors refused to go to the hospital out of fear of being deported, despite having sustained serious injuries. Government officials tried to assure the workers—through televised messages in English—that they would not be in danger and that they would be granted assistance. But this was not of much help. For days after the attack, foreign workers were reported to be more afraid of deportation and of the Israeli police than they were concerned about their medical conditions (Mualam and Sinay 2003).

Still, for most the fear of deportation and the need to find a shelter from the vicissitudes of everyday life bring labor migrants, especially migrant women, to the Catholic churches and the Evangelical churches newly established by the migrants themselves. The specific significance of religious participation as a gendered strategy to cope with illegality is further elaborated below.

Redefining Motherhood in the Context of International Migration: *Para procurar por el bien de los hijos uno se debe separar de ellos* (To Secure the Future of Our Children We Have to Leave Them Behind at Home)

Migrant mothers redefine their roles and conceptions of family life as they are forced to deal with great temporal and spatial separation from home and to endure novel arrangements for child raising. The concept of transnational motherhood helps understand the manner in which the meaning of motherhood shifts, to adapt to the new circumstances created by international migration in the era of globalization (Hondagneu-Sotelo and Avila 1997, 549).

The heuristic value of this concept is especially relevant in the case of Latina migrants. As overseas mothers, they are breaking away from the "cult of domesticity" and the rigid role models rooted in Latin American traditions as well as in Spanish Catholicism (Hondagneu-Sotelo and Avila 1997). Traditional conceptions of family and gender roles in Latin America have been strongly shaped by the Catholic Church's ideology, which confines women to the private sphere as the core of family life, in the home, caring for the children. Conversely, the husband as the head of the family and the sole provider is portrayed as ruling the public sphere of economy and polity (Wainerman, Jelin, and Feijoo 1983).

An ideology that places mothers solely in the "private" realm creates serious conflicts for migrant mothers who are forced to work far away from home (Glenn 1994). Consider the case of Marta, a divorced mother who came to Israel from Latin America three years ago, leaving behind two adolescent children in the care of her mother and sisters, as the father had cut all ties with her and evaded his economic responsibilities. Reflecting on her decision to come to Israel, she admitted that migrant mothers have a difficult choice to make.

> We are at a crossroads. On the one hand, we are supposed to be at home looking after the well-being of our family and children. On the other hand, the economic needs push us to look for a better future abroad . . . because, you know, that in Latin America it is impossible to make it. You cannot have everything at once. Sometimes you have to choose. In our case we have to make the best of a bad job and go to work. What else is left for us? I do miss my children. I always think about them. . . . What are they doing right now? Who is taking care of them? My mother was right in saying that they need me. But what can I do? You cannot have your cake and eat it.

Estela, a Black Latina single mother who left her eight-year-old boy with her family in Colombia, expressed a similar dilemma. She pointed out that coming to Israel was a difficult decision to make:

> [You have to decide] either to go out, fight for life, and make a living, or stay at home with the children but without the possibility of having a better future. It is especially difficult if you are a single or a divorced mother, as in my case. If I had a husband to share the burden with me, it would have been a completely different story. I would never have left.

While aware that their redefinitions of the female role, family life, and child-rearing arrangements transgress traditional family conventions in their home countries, these women propose a new conception of motherhood, in which taking economic responsibility is as important as—or even more important than—their daily presence in the home. As Marta told us,

> We have been taught that mothers are to stay with their kids. That is why we may feel bad about leaving our children. But I am a different type of mother. I have left them but they are having a little bit more than other children there [in her country of origin]. My mother thinks that I am irresponsible, but why? I am here working and I am not avoiding my duties. I am the same mother I was before, even a better one because I can help them. My commitment as a mother has not changed.

Sometimes, reference to the "sacrifice" of downward occupational mobility helps diminish the fears and anxieties caused by the transition to transnational mothering and the criticism that may rise from home, as made explicit by Yolanda, a separated migrant woman from Bolivia:

> In Bolivia I used to sell jewelry but I only made $60 a month. . . . When I decided to separate from my husband I realized that migration was the only available alternative for me in order to earn a living for me and my children. Since my arrival I have been working in domestic service. It is hard for me. In Bolivia I had a maid myself!! It is even harder to be away from my children! But for me it is the only possible way to economic independence.

The emphasis on their economic role helps migrant mothers reevaluate their own definitions of mothering, as expressed in the words of Rocío, a divorcee who left her four-year-old daughter with her sister in her home country:

> Very few mothers are ready to make the sacrifice of those women who go abroad and leave their children behind. It takes a mother to dare to do so. Many women don't do anything in order to overcome the difficult situations. Instead, those who leave [their children] really give their best [for them]. *Uno se siente mas madre.* [One feels more of a mother.]

In making the assessment of the costs and benefits of mother-child separation, Estela is convinced that the sacrifice is worthwhile:

> We are not with our children but this is a sacrifice for their own benefit. We miss many things [by being far away] but we are doing more, helping more. I am a responsible mother because I am taking charge of the economic well-being of my son as well as my family. I am doing my bit. I feel at ease with my conscience because I am doing my best to support my child.

The articulation of a new rhetoric of transnational motherhood proves to be critical as women attempt to make sense of their new situations. Notwithstanding their discursive significance, transnational practices of motherhood and child care have to meet two conditions to become a fully legitimate and viable strategy for migrant mothers. The first condition, as we have already shown, is economic need. The second is to have a suitable family arrangement for the children. All the women we interviewed emphasize the fundamental role their families have in raising their children. They concurred that without the willingness of their families (mothers, sisters, brothers) to care for them, they could not have come to Israel and stayed for lengthy periods of time. Thus, when the arrangements are satisfactory and the well-being of the child is guaranteed, the separation is considered as a viable option.

Still, separation is not accepted in all cases as a legitimate solution. When the home arrangements fail and their children are not taken care of properly, migrant mothers are confronted with a new dilemma. Should they return home to take charge of their own children and give up their economic aims? What are the alternatives these migrant women construct for themselves?

Most women agree that the first option is to search for an adequate alternative arrangement for the children in the home country since the priority for transnational mothers is to remain in Israel and earn money. The second option is to bring the child to live with them in Israel. However, this alternative is considered problematic because, according to their own testimonies, Latino migrant children living in Israel are left without supervision most of the day, and the older ones, being free to roam the streets, run the risk of exposure to criminal activities (e.g., drugs).

If these two options are not viable, the appropriate way to cope with the situation would be to return home. Transnational mothers openly criticized those migrant mothers who know that their children are not receiving proper care at home but decide to remain in Israel. There is a line that cannot be crossed when it comes to motherhood: the well-being of the children.

Reflecting on the overwhelming responsibility of raising her child as a single mother, Estela made the following statement.

> Women who stay despite being aware of their children's problems at home are wrong to do so. The children come first. If one makes lots of money but returns home and the child is either sick or dies one will regret the decision of staying. The responsibility of a mother is the care of her children. Our priest in Colombia says that many parents risk losing their children to get money and when they have the money they may no longer have their children to enjoy the dollars they have earned. Money is not everything.

Despite the self-redeeming discourse that transnational mothers may adopt, the complexities of new child-rearing arrangements are a major source of distress and ambivalence. Rocío expressed these feelings, as she maintained that no mother can be at ease having left her children behind since "the love of a mother cannot be replaced and yet, I am afraid she will forget me. There is always the fear that time and distance will make her forget me." Missing her small daughter has turned into an emotional burden she cannot overcome. Monitoring her daughter's daily activity by making constant long-distance calls, sending gifts, and writing letters has become her way to cope with the spatial distance. Be that as it may, migrant women like Rocío face the paradoxical situation that to secure a better future for their children, they have to leave them behind.

One Solution: Religion

The question remaining is how Latina migrants in Israel deal with these pressing difficulties and dilemmas. For the majority, the trauma of downward occupational mobility and illegal status has been somewhat diminished since they consider these a transitory cost they are ready to pay to achieve economic independence and financial resources for themselves and their families. Deprived of social status, prestige, and power in the occupational and social spheres, many migrants search for alternative spaces within their ethnic communities. Latino migrant organizations in general provide mobility pyramids for those who are active members. Organizing group activities, becoming a community leader, or just being an active part of these organizations is a way to regain self-esteem and prestige within the migrant community.

Although the strategy of participation in ethnic organizations is common to both men and women, the range of public spaces available to migrant men is much wider than to migrant women. Men are active in soccer clubs, chess clubs, and other informal networks organized around sport and business activities. Conversely, women tend to engage and be more active in social activities that cater to cultural and spiritual needs of the community.[4]

Religious organizations constitute the main social space open for women's initiatives and active participation. There are two main kinds of churches: long-established Catholic churches that serve a wide local and foreign audience and newly established Evangelical churches created by and for the labor migrants themselves. A most striking characteristic of religious congregations is that they overwhelmingly consist of women, even though according to the 1995 Israeli population census women compose 46 percent of the Latino labor migration. Women's participation is strongly felt also in the organization of religious and communitarian activities as they form the core group of "leaders" in both the Catholic and Evangelical churches, which first and foremost serve labor migrant congregants.

According to Latina migrants, the church constitutes a "surrogate family" and provides an alternative space for the production of a "sense of belonging," which stands in stark contrast to the experiential context of uprootedness and displacement in which they live and work. According to Maria, for example, the Evangelical church, where she is an active congregant, constitutes "a form of self-help. It gives me the strength to go on."

Latina migrants' participation and self-initiatives are particularly salient in Evangelical churches. The theological principles nurtured in these churches, though pragmatic and adaptive to changing conditions, are at the same time extremely strict in regard to discipline and personality control (a ban on alcohol, drugs, and sexual promiscuity). As such, religious spaces provide migrant women with a sense of "safety" and "well-being" that is not always found in other types of community activities. They constitute "protected spaces" for undocumented migrants where the police still do not dare enter in search of illegal workers and where migrant women acquire their own space of public visibility (for a detailed discussion on Evangelical migrant churches in Israel, see Raijman and Kemp forthcoming).

CONCLUSIONS

Our aim has been to delineate the major dilemmas and costs undocumented Latina migrants face as they cross international borders looking for better economic opportunities that eluded them in their homelands, as well as the strategies they develop to cope with these dilemmas. Drawing on the literature that stresses the gendered implications of globalization, and more particularly the dilemmas resulting from the "globalization of domestic work" and the "globalization of child-care" (Hochschild 2000; Hondagneu-Sotelo 2001; Hondagneu-Sotelo and Avila 1997; Salazar Parreñas 2000, 2001), we have focused on the costs that emerge as women, in their search for new paths of socioeconomic mobility, are forced to take undesirable jobs (despite unknown economic outcomes), to work and live as aliens on the margins of the host society, and to endure indeterminate spatial and temporal separation from their families and communities.

We suggest that while the cost of being illegal may apply equally to migrant men and women, downward occupational mobility and the transnationalization of motherhood are distinctly gendered as they derive from gender segregation in the labor market, the new globalized gendered economy of care, and the gendered domestic division of labor in migrants' countries of origin. Not only are the dilemmas gendered, but also the particular strategies chosen by migrants tend to be patterned along distinct gender lines. How do migrant women cope with their loss of social status, with the experience of illegality, and with the disruption of family life for those mothers who leave their children behind?

In answering this question, we singled out two main gendered strategies: religious participation and transnational motherhood discourse. We argue that Latina migrants' participation in religious activities opens an alternative path for social mobility and a public space, perhaps the only one available to undocumented migrant women, where they can acquire visibility within their community. Churches offer Latina migrants a space for the production of a "sense of belonging" within the experiential context of uprootedness and marginality. The significance of religious activities and participation for Latina migrants should be understood against the backdrop of the constant threat of arrest and deportation and the ability of migrant churches to provide, albeit only for fragmented moments, a protected space for doubly disadvantaged migrant women.

Transnational mothering rhetoric is another important strategy that Latina migrants use in their attempts to cope with family life disruption. In this article, we have expanded on the concept of transnational motherhood, on the circumstances that allow for the reconstitution of mothering across borders, and on the limits and boundaries of transnational mothering. As we have shown, a redefinition of mothering that stresses the economic responsibility for their children as equally important to—or even more important than—their daily presence at home becomes a central strategy that legitimizes separation from their children. Their rhetoric of transnational motherhood creates a new discourse that subverts traditional conceptions of mothering. In that way, Latina migrants in Israel remind us that "privatized" mothering and child rearing are cultural constructs deeply embedded in class, race, ethnicity, marital status, and citizenship divides.

In some cases, the lengthy disruptions in family life lead to the routinization of the separation, meaning that transnational mothers are forced to come to terms with the fact that they do not raise their own children. Separations may last longer than the women had originally planned as they keep on delaying their return home. Delays are mainly explained in economic terms, as many find it hard to save the amount of money they initially set for themselves. Many migrant women are also tempted to stay longer to save larger amounts of money as the economic situations in their countries of origin continue to deteriorate. In some cases, the migrants' families urge them to stay as their remittances become the families' major source of income. Because of their undocumented status, Latina migrant women cannot afford to visit their families in Latin America as they know that reentering Israel is difficult (given the strict visa controls). Some migrant women have not seen their children since they came to the country.

Whatever the costs and dilemmas migrant women face in Israel, in the final analysis many of them critically evaluate the chances they have of becoming permanent residents in Israel. They realize that migrant workers in Israel are considered temporary workers and not prospective citizens. The Israeli case seems to be more problematic than that of other Western countries regarding the integration prospects of non-Jewish migrants. Foreign workers in Israel are considered outsiders in the cultural, social, and political spheres. Even the term by which they are known, *ovdim zarim* (foreign workers), with a biblical connotation of profanity, exemplifies their marginal position.

Unwillingness to accept labor migrants is expressed through exclusionary immigration policies (especially severe limitation of family reunion and refusal to grant residence status), restrictive naturalization rules, and a double standard: an exclusionary model for non-Jews (foreign workers) as opposed to an "acceptance-encouragement" model for Jews. The ethno-national nature of the state and the absence of an egalitarian idea and practice of citizenship for non-Jews make Israel a society without prospects for the incorporation of non-Jewish immigrants.

NOTES

1. Undocumented non-Jewish labor migrants come from a variety of countries: East Europe (15 percent), the former Soviet Union (25 percent), South Asia (20 percent), Arab countries (11 percent), Africa (14 percent), and Latin America (15 percent). Most of them reside on the south side of Tel Aviv, where they compose around 20 percent of the local population.

2. Being the "Holy Land," Israel uniquely attracts Christians from all over the world aspiring to visit as pilgrims. As the millennium approached, many migrants expressed their wish to settle in Israel, yearning for the coming of the Messiah (Raijman et al. 2001; Raijman and Kemp forthcoming; Schammah-Gesser et al. 2000).

3. Similar findings were reported by Cheng (2003, 173-75) in her analysis of state control and foreign Filipina domestic workers in Taiwan.

4. An example is the creation of La Escuelita, a Sunday-like framework for Latino migrant children, organized mostly by Latina migrant women.

REFERENCES

Alicea, M. 1997. A chambered nautilus: The contradictory nature of Puerto Rican women's role in the social construction of a transnational community. *Gender & Society* 5:597-626.

Bartram, D. 1998. Foreign workers in Israel: History and theory. *International Migration Review* 32:303-25.

Bernstein, D. 1986. The subcontracting of cleaning work: A case in the casualisation of labour. *Sociological Review* 34:396-422.

Boyd, M. 1984. At a disadvantage: The occupational attainment of foreign-born women in Canada. *International Migration Review* 18:1091-120.

Castles, S. 2000. *Ethnicity and globalization*. London: Sage.

Chant, S. 1992. *Gender and migration in developing countries*. New York: Belhaven.

Chant, S., and S. A. Radcliffe. 1992. Migration and development: The importance of gender. In *Gender and migration in developing countries*, edited by Sylvia Chant. New York: Belhaven.

Cheng, S. A. 1996. Migrant women domestic workers in Hong Kong, Singapore and Taiwan: A comparative analysis. *Asian and Pacific Migration Journal* 5:139-52.

———. 2003. Rethinking the globalization of domestic service: Foreign domestics, state control and the politics of identity in Taiwan. *Gender & Society* 17 (2): 166-86.

Glenn, E. Nakano. 1986. *Issei, Nisei, warbride*. Philadelphia: Temple University.

———. 1994. Social constructions of mothering: A thematic overview. In *Mothering: Ideology, experience, and agency*, edited by Evelyn Nakano Glenn, Grace Chang, and Linda Rennie Forcey. New York: Routledge.

Hagan, J. M. 1998. Social networks, gender, and immigrant incorporation: Resources and constraints. *American Sociological Review* 63:55-67.

Hochschild, A. R. 2000. The nanny chain. *American Prospect* 4:32-36.

Hondagneu-Sotelo, P. 1992. Overcoming patriarchal constraints: The reconstruction of gender among Mexican immigrant women and men. *Gender & Society* 6:393-415.

———. 1994. *Gendered transitions: Mexican experiences of immigration*. Berkeley: University of California Press.

———. 2001. *Domestica. Immigrant workers cleaning and caring in the shadows of affluence*. Berkeley: University of California Press.

Hondagneu-Sotelo, P., and E. Avila. 1997. I'm here, but I'm there. The meanings of Latina transnational motherhood. *Gender & Society* 11:548-71.

Kemp, A., R. Raijman, J. Resnik, and S. Schammah-Gesser. 2000. Contesting the limits of political participation: Latinos and Black African migrant workers in Israel. *Ethnic and Racial Studies* 23 (1): 94-119.

Lijphart, A., and C. Waisman. 1996. *Institutional design in new democracies in Eastern Europe and Latin America*. Boulder, CO: Westview.

Lim, L. L. 1993. Effects of women's position on their migration. In *Women's position and demographic change*, edited by N. Federici, K. Oppenheim Mason, and Solvi Sogner. New York: Clarendon.

Massey, D., J. Arango, G. Hugo, A. Kouaouci, A. Pellegrino, and J. Taylor. 1998. *Worlds in motion. Understanding international migration at the end of the millennium*. New York: Oxford University Press.

Morokvasic, M. 1984. Birds of passage are also women. *International Migration Review* 18:886-907.

Mualam, M., and R. Sinay. 2003. Wounded foreign workers were afraid of being arrested and hid from the policemen. *Ha'aretz*, 6 January.

Pedraza, S. 1991. Women and migration: The social consequences of gender. *Annual Review of Sociology* 17:303-25.

Pessar, P. 1999. Engendering migration studies. *American Behavioral Scientist* 42:577-600.

Phizacklea, A. 1983. *One way ticket: Migration and female labor*. Boston: Routledge Kegan Paul.

Piore, M. 1979. *Birds of passage: Migrant labor in industrial societies*. Cambridge, UK: Cambridge University Press.

Raijman, R., and A. Kemp. 2002. State and non-state actors: A multi-layered analysis of labor migration policy in Israel. In *Public policy in Israel*, edited by D. Korn. London: Lexington Books.

———. Forthcoming. Consuming the Holy Spirit in the Holy Land: Evangelical churches, labor migrants and the Jewish state. In *Consumption and market society in Israel*, edited by Y. Carmeli and K. Applebaum. Oxford, UK: Berg.

Raijman, R., A. Kemp, S. Gesser, and J. Resnik. 2001. *Searching for a better future: Latino labor migration.* Discussion paper 105. Tel Aviv, Israel: Tel Aviv University, Golda Meir Institute for Social & Labor Research.

Raijman, R., and M. Semyonov. 1997. Gender, ethnicity and immigration: Double-disadvantage and triple-disadvantage among recent immigrant women in the Israeli labor market. *Gender & Society* 11 (1): 108-25.

Remennick, L. 1999. Women with a Russian accent in Israel: On the gender aspects of migration. *European Journal of Women's Studies* 6 (4): 441-61.

Repak, T. A. 1994. Labor and the lure of the capital: Central American migrants in Washington, DC. *Gender & Society* 8:507-24.

Robinson, K. 1991. Housemaids: The effects of gender and culture on the internal and international labor migration of Indonesian women. In *Intersexions: Gender/class/culture/ethnicity*, edited by Gill Bottomley, Marie de Lepervanche, and Jeannie Martin. Sydney, Australia: Allen & Unwin.

Salazar Parreñas, R. 2000. Migrant Filipina domestic workers and the international division of reproductive labor. *Gender & Society* 14 (4): 560-81.

———. 2001. *Servants of globalization: Women, migration, and domestic work.* Stanford, CA: Stanford University Press.

Salzinger, L. 1991. Maid by any other name: The transformation of "dirty work" by Central American immigrants. In *Ethnography unbound: Power and resistance in the modern metropolis*, edited by Michael Burawoy et al. Berkeley: University of California Press.

Schammah-Gesser, S., R. Raijman, A. Kemp, and J. Reznik. 2000. "Making it" in Israel? Non-Jewish Latino undocumented migrant workers in the Holy Land. *Estudios interdisciplinarios de America Latina y el Caribe* 11 (2): 113-36.

Stark, O. 1991. *The migration of labor.* Cambridge, UK: Basil Blackwell.

Tienda, M., and K. Booth. 1991. Gender, migration and social change. *International Sociology* 6:51-72.

Truong, T. 1996. Gender, international migration and social reproduction: Implications for theory, policy, research and networking. *Asian and Pacific Migration Journal* 5:27-52.

Wainerman, C., E. Jelin, and M. del C. Feijoo. 1983. *Del deber ser y el hacer de las mujeres*. Mexico City: El Colegio de Mexico, Pispal.

Wong, D. 1996. Foreign domestic workers in Singapore. *Asian and Pacific Migration Journal* 5:117-38.

Rebeca Raijman is a senior lecturer in the Department of Sociology and Anthropology at the University of Haifa, Israel. She received her Ph.D. in sociology from the University of Chicago. She is currently conducting comprehensive research regarding the emergence on new (migrant) ethnic minorities in Israel, the sociopolitical organization of undocumented migrant communities, and the politics and policy of labor migration in Israel.

Silvina Schammah-Gesser received her M.A. degree from the Department of Sociology and Anthropology at Tel Aviv University. She is a Ph.D. candidate at the School of History at the University of Tel Aviv. Her research interests focus on cultural studies and international migration. She is currently conducting research on the Spanish cultural context prior to the Civil War.

Adriana Kemp is a lecturer in the Department of Sociology and Anthropology, Tel Aviv University. Her fields of research are labor migration, citizenship and identity, boundaries, and nationalism. She has published several articles on non-Jewish and non-Palestinian labor migration in Israel.

[17]

Fortune, Risk, and Remittances: An Application of Option Theory to Participation in Village-Based Migration Networks[1]

Kenneth D. Roberts
Southwestern University

Michael D. S. Morris
University of New Orleans

Fortune and Risk are contending conceptions of the role of chance in the universe. From Chance ... there issues both "hazard" and "opportunity" ... The conception of Fortune is founded on the possibility of exercising some measure of choice over the outcomes one will accept from Chance.

Paul A. David, 1974

Altruism, insurance, and investment are three potential motives for migrant remittances that have been explored in the literature. The model developed in this paper posits an additional motive – that remittances are necessary for the migrant to participate in the employment networks that are based in the village, and thus are partially a payment for the option to change jobs within this network. The model is tested with data on Mexican migrants to the United States and finds support in that network strength and diversity increase remittances, whereas the insurance motive predicts stronger networks will decrease remittances.

Two concepts – risk and networks – have become essential components of the tool kit used in analyzing migration processes in developing countries. These concepts converge when membership in a network reduces the costs and risks of migration. But implicit in much of the discussion of migrant networks is the idea that networks provide not only security but also opportunity – that the jobs held by other members in the network become more accessible to the migrant, so that network relationships represent "social capital" that migrants

[1]This article has benefited greatly from the comments of anonymous reviewers at several stages since its presentation at the annual meetings of the Population Association of America in New Orleans in May, 1996. The authors give special thanks to Doug Massey for his encouragement throughout the process.

0198-9183/04/3704.0144

can draw upon to enhance their economic mobility (*see* Astone *et al.*, 1999, 1987; Massey and Espinosa, 1997). One of the earliest studies to recognize the importance of networks for undocumented Mexican migrants in the United States says, "the network receives its signals from the larger society and in turn creates options for its members" (Mines and de Janvry, 1982:446). This article develops the concept of options more fully, both as broadly-construed alternatives as in the quote above and as an economic asset with value to the migrant, by integrating options theory into the literature on migration, risk and networks.

An option is a contract which entitles, but does not oblige, its owner to a particular course of action. Options expand opportunities, and so are valuable. Like diversification, their value is embodied in common wisdom: "don't burn your bridges" is as meaningful as "don't put all your eggs in one basket." This wisdom is perhaps even more important for small-scale producers in developing countries, where the margin for failure is small. A review of research in the 1960s concluded: "In the game against an uncertain world, peasant strategy is to keep the range of options open and to widen the range whenever possible" (Brookfield, 1970, quoted in Chapman and Prothero, 1983:615).

Because options can be used to manage risk, they are often confused with insurance. In fact, a put option that gives its owner the right to dispose of an asset at a specific price, in conjunction with ownership of that asset, "is functionally equivalent to an insurance policy that protects its owner against economic loss from a decline in the asset's value below the exercise price" (Merton, 1998:337) Insurance is thus a type of option – one that is concerned only with the downside of an asset's distribution of potential returns, or "hazard" – while options more generally can take advantage of the upside, or "opportunity." In both, the potential for loss is fixed, but with insurance the potential for gain is limited to the value of the insured asset, while with an option the potential for gain can be unlimited.

Another difference between options and insurance is that insurance is triggered by a specific set of circumstances, while when to exercise an option is, within limits, at the discretion of the decision maker. For example, home insurance pays only upon a specified loss; a home mortgage with the privilege of prepayment, in contrast, gives one the option to pay off the mortgage at any time. The flexibility given by this temporal dimension has been recognized in discussion of the strategies of small-scale agricultural producers in developing countries, where "decision makers may respond to uncertainty not only with diversification, reduction of cash inputs, or risk diffusion, but by adoption of strategies that have enough flexibility to adjust to unforeseen or stochastic events" (Roumasset, 1979:16).

Because they are valuable, options usually have a cost. Just as one pays for the option to buy a stock if its price rises, one might pay more for a health insurance program that allows choice of doctors, take a lower paying job in a company with greater potential for growth, or sow an early-maturing but lower-yielding grain variety to maintain the flexibility to sow a second crop if the rains come early enough. Likewise, we will argue that access to the employment options provided by a migrant's network is conditional upon engaging in activities that affirm the migrant's membership in the community where the network is based, including visits home, gifts, remittances, and contributions to community projects. Option theory thus posits a reason beyond altruism and insurance for the links which endure between migrants and their communities of origin.

Option theory applied to migrant networks is rooted in the theoretical and empirical analysis of households, risk and migrant networks, and the first section of this article reviews aspects of this literature relevant to the issues at hand. It will provide support for the propositions that networks are valuable to migrants because they expand opportunities, that these networks are anchored in the home community, and that support of kin in the community is essential for membership in the network. The second section reviews the growing literature on remittance motivations. The third section translates and applies the variables of financial option theory to the remittance decision of migrants, and the last section tests the model with data on Mexican migrants to the United States. The paper concludes with a brief discussion of the implications of the model for the retention of rural ties under different circumstances.

NETWORKS, RISK AND OPPORTUNITY

Circular Migration, Risk and Households

The advancement of theory to explain population mobility in developing countries has often been in response to what were considered anomalies to conventional cost-benefit calculations by individuals. Todaro's pioneering contribution explained the first obvious paradox – that of continuing migration to the urban areas of developing countries despite high rates of urban unemployment – by showing that if the migrant considers expected wages, the high wages of the formal sector might more than offset the low probability of securing a job there (Todaro, 1969).

The second anomaly to be explained was that of circular migration, which had emerged in the 1970s as a major form of mobility in developing countries. It was apparent that the individual might not be the most appropriate unit of analysis in a model designed to illuminate this process, because the individual migrant would have no reason to return to the rural area unless the difference between expected rural and urban incomes were to narrow. There followed a shift in the unit of analysis from the individual to the household, which was said to develop "strategies" that include sending out members to earn money that would be pooled for the joint consumption of all (Wood, 1981).

Two reasons were given for households to engage in circular as opposed to permanent migration: it was cheaper to maintain the family in the country than in the city, and the household could reduce risk by pooling the earnings from several activities. Risk reduction was accomplished by diversification, which involved consideration not only of the distribution of the returns of different occupations, but also of the correlation between these returns (Stark, 1982). Inclusion of this second dimension of risk led to powerful and often surprising conclusions: an occupation that might by itself be extremely risky, such as undocumented migration to the United States, could actually reduce the risk of the household income portfolio if the returns from that occupation were relatively uncorrelated with other sources of household income (Roberts, 1982). Other decisions made within households in developing countries, including the accumulation of livestock (Binswanger and McIntire, 1987), marriage (Rosenzweig and Stark, 1989), and fertility (Cain, 1983), were also shown to be partly motivated by diversification. These household-based strategies were employed to compensate for the lack of market-based alternatives, especially credit and insurance.

Employing the concept of the household as a decisionmaking unit without considering gender, age, and the process by which decisions are negotiated among the individuals that comprise it has been sharply criticized (Hart, 1992; Pessar, 1999). Rather than assume its members engage in a common strategy, it was necessary to examine the household's internal dynamics. Is a cohesive family structure maintained over space in developing countries? If so, why does the individual maintain economic links to other household members when breaking them could increase his or her individual income?

An answer to this paradox was provided by the theory of household economics: the family was preferred over other forms of economic organization because altruism limited opportunistic behavior by individuals (Becker,

1981), while ease of monitoring the actions of family members reduced the costs of transactions among them (Ben-Porath, 1980). Identity is particularly important for transactions that extend over long periods of time and about which information on the quality of what is being exchanged is imperfect, such as insurance. Migrants might want to retain ties to their rural households after having gone to work elsewhere because they are insuring themselves against unemployment, sickness, and old age in situations where good markets for these services are not available. The household was perceived to be a risk-reducing machine, binding members together by providing mutual insurance at low cost, and then leveraging the power of the larger unit through diversification. Economic theory combined with an understanding of the social context of these households led again to an enrichment of migration theory.

Networks and Risk

The most significant "stylized fact" to emerge in the recent literature on migration in developing countries is that it takes place within well-defined village and community networks. The importance of social networks had been percolating in the anthropological and immigration literature for some time, especially concerning European migration streams. But it was not until the late 1970s, when Mexican migration to the United States came under intense scrutiny, that networks were recognized to be so central to contemporary labor migration. It became obvious that most Mexican migrants traveled, lived and worked with fellow villagers, and that these social networks were very specific from village to destination (Mines and de Janvry, 1982). Research in Thailand (Fuller, Kamnuansilpa and Lightfoot, 1990), East Africa (Elkan, 1967), India (Banerjee, 1982), and China (Zhao, 2000) confirmed the importance of networks for circular migrants in other developing countries.

More recently, the network itself has been elevated to the status of an independent unit of analysis with the introduction of the concept of a transnational community. These are migrants' networks connecting origins and destinations "woven together so tightly that, in an important sense, they have come to form a single community spanning the various locales ... a 'transnational migrant circuit.'"(Rouse, 1992:45). Chavez (1988) calls families with close ties to communities in both Mexico and California "binational families" and found that the majority of families living in the United States continue to send money to families in Mexico (Chavez, 1994). Over 65 percent of the households in the small Dominican village of Miraflores have relatives in Boston and establish such close social and economic ties that "it is as if village life takes place in two settings" (Levitt, 1998:22). Based upon overwhelming evidence that this phenomenon is not abating, Goldring (1998:166) asks, "Why do transmigrants maintain ties to their place of origin? Why do so many continue to send and spend money (in Mexico), even after appearing to have 'settled' in the United States?"

The formation of transnational networks has been explained by their ability to reduce both the costs and the risks of migration (Massey *et al.*, 1987; Espinosa and Massey, 1994). The main means by which they are said to reduce risks is by enlarging the solidarity unit beyond the household, providing an incentive for individuals and families to share risks with others facing uncertainties that are less covariant (Bromley and Chavas, 1989:731). The advantages of networks are thus the same as those of households – through interpersonal relationships, individuals acquire "relation-specific" information within social networks that reduces monitoring and transaction costs, allowing these larger units to more effectively insure against risks (Fafchamps, 1992:148).

But empirical research has found no evidence to support either function. Longitudinal data collected in Mexico and the United States do not provide evidence that the accumulation of social capital lowers the costs of migration (Espinosa and Massey, 1999:11). If networks were to reduce risks, then stronger networks should reduce the need for village-based insurance, which should have the effect of lowering remittances as payments for this insurance (motivations to remit will be discussed in detail in the next section). But analysis of the same data found that, "contrary to the predictions, social capital tends to increase the probability of remitting, which rises as the number of relatives living in the United States increases" (Massey and Basem, 1992:197). Why continue to maintain these ties to the home community when networks are so strong in the destination? This is the latest paradox in migration theory.

The answers provided so far – altruism and risk reduction – seem incomplete, mere extensions of the benefits of household membership. Even together, they lack the power of expected income to explain migration in the face of urban unemployment; of diversification to explain circular migration; or of altruism and insurance to explain household strategies. The emergence of transnational networks is neither the historical norm nor inevitable: a theory that explains their growth must explore as well the question "under what conditions do networks weaken and/or disappear?" (Boyd, 1989:655). The answer that this study proposes – that networks offer mobility as well as security and that network membership is contingent upon the maintenance of rural ties – extends the concept of risk once more to include fortune, the upside of the distribution of potential returns.

Networks and Opportunity

Many studies have noted that membership in a network enhances a migrant's opportunities. An important reason for the prevalence of circular migration in Southeast Asia was that permanent migrants would lose their village contacts, restricting future job opportunities (Fan and Stretton, 1985). More than half the rural migrants to Delhi got information on jobs from friends and relatives already working in the city, thus undertaking a rural-based search for urban jobs (Banerjee, 1984b). Migrants to Mexico City made frequent trips home, not only to maintain old social alliances, but also to continue or to establish critical economic linkages (Kemper, 1981:222). And while networks might not reduce the costs of migration from Mexico to the United States, they did raise the benefits by increasing both wages and the number of hours worked (Espinosa and Massey, 1999).

Employee referral of friends and relatives is the major way that networks enhance the economic mobility of participants, both in internal (Banerjee, 1984a:243) and international (Philpott, 1968:47) migration. Even high-paying jobs held by later generations of Mexican migrants to the United States were usually obtained through the network; "in each case a similar process was repeated, with one person finding a job and then inviting other *paisanos* (people from the village) to come and work in the same firm" (Massey *et al.*, 1987:167). It appears from this evidence that membership in a network not only reduces risk but also increases economic mobility, "joining security and mobility in a single goal continuum" (Greenhalgh, 1988:638). Security and mobility, risk and fortune, insurance and options: all express the two sides of chance.

There is, however, a significant conceptual difference between these two sides of chance, which has implications for how the migrant views the distribution of earnings of the jobs held by members of the network. A migrant who can "sample" different jobs within a labor market before making a final choice of destination will choose the destination with the highest variance in earnings, for it is there that repeated sampling will result in the highest payoff (David, 1974; McCall and McCall, 1987). Risk involves acquiescence to the distribution of potential outcomes, accepting its mean; fortune involves exercising a measure of choice from among potential outcomes.[2] In the former case, for the same level of average earnings, a risk-averse migrant would prefer a smaller variance of earnings, while in the latter a larger variance would be preferable.

Following a similar line of reasoning, membership in a network will not only lower risk by easing a migrant's entry into the jobs held by other members, but also increase the range of jobs from which the migrant may choose. The former could be construed as insurance against unemployment, with the average earnings of other network members for the period of extra employment representing the expected insurance payoff. The latter increases opportunity: the migrant, through membership in the network, may have more occupational alternatives through the varying fortunes of its members. Therefore, a migrant who is able to choose from among the jobs held by other network members will prefer the higher variance in earnings that would result from network members working in a variety of occupations and locations. The larger and more diverse the network in the destination area, the greater its value to the migrant as a vehicle for economic mobility.[3]

Networks and the Community

The locus of migrant networks is the community of origin: migrants from the same community are called *paisanos* in Mexico, where "the community of origin is the organizing element in transnational social space" (Goldring, 1996:78), and *tongxiang* in China, where "the concept of native place was a critical component of personal identity" (Goodman, 1995). Migrants maintain close contact with their communities of origin through visits, remittances and gifts to family, and donations to community projects. Granting that the network provides important benefits to the migrant, would it not be possible to enjoy these benefits without having to maintain these contacts? The

[2]The temporal dimension of options mentioned earlier is essential to this choice. In Mexico, "typically, a letter arrived one day, or a return migrant uncle or brother appeared, and an opportunity – an invitation or a proposition to migrate – suddenly materialized.... Instead of careful household calculation, it appears that often migration is the result of a social opportunity which must be grasped and acted upon immediately" (Hondagneu-Sotelo, 1995).

[3]The reader will recognize the similarity of the argument about the advantages of diversity in destinations within the network with that of "the strength of weak ties" (Granovetter, 1983). Because community networks bridge geographic clusters within a network, "weak ties tend to be stronger bridges to new information about employment opportunities than strong ties" (Wilson, 1998:397).

advantages of such a strategy are obvious: not only the savings in travel costs, remittances and gifts, but the accrual of more job-specific human capital if it were not necessary to disrupt employment by returning for regular visits to the community (Lindstrom, 1996:359).

The answer to the question is negative, because network membership is contingent upon community membership, and community membership requires regular reaffirmation. For migrants to Shanghai, "native-place identity was invoked less as a birthright than as a delicate plant which demanded constant cultivation" (Goodman, 1995:8). In Taiwan during the 1960s, migrants took "care in maintaining their relationships with each other (because) these relationships are considered voluntary, not obligatory, and laborers believe they must be nurtured" (Gallin and Gallin, 1974:355). Trips home affirm the migrant's place in the Mexican community: "when (migrants) return with gifts for their family, extended and fictive kin, and friends, they are asserting and maintaining their community membership" (Goldring, 1998:181). In contrast, "women who marry out, men who abandon their families, or people who do not maintain contact with fellow villagers" are no longer considered part of the community and the network based there (Goldring, 1996:81).

The community of origin is not only the conceptual locus of the network but also the place where much of the interchange of information concerning opportunities actually occurs. Because of this, circular migrants often return to their villages at a particular time of year. Mexican migrants to the United States usually return for the celebration of their village's patron saint (Massey *et al.*, 1987). In China, despite overcrowded railways and strenuous attempts by the government to spread out the flow, most rural migrants return from the cities during the Spring Festival (Roberts, 1997), and one of the three most significant variables explaining urban job mobility among Chinese labor migrants was if the migrant returned home each year (Liu and Chan, 1998). The exchange of information among migrants from diverse locations and occupations that occurs during these gatherings is instrumental in maintaining and expanding the network, and it increases the value of the option to move within it. Were altruism or insurance from one's own family the only motives for returning to the village, there would be no need for migrants to synchronize their journeys.

Another reason that the community is central to the migrant network is because the network encompasses former migrants who reside there. Mexican migrants were found to have closer ties to previous migrants than to those currently living in the United States, prompting speculation that ties to former migrants might provide access to a broader array of employment options than do ties to U.S. residents (Espinosa and Massey, 1999:18).

The community is also the social and geographical locus of the valorization of the migrant's status. Returning with expensive gifts for family or with money to share in celebration, contributing to community projects, and investing earnings in cattle and land "are material expressions of shared, but negotiated, ideas about community status" (Goldring, 1996:88) that offer individuals and families an opportunity for social mobility (Goldring, 1998:182). The status conferred by the flow of goods and services to family and community enhances the value of a migrant's employment options within the network, because it makes it more likely that he or she will be the first to hear of a new opportunity.

So far we have explored how the migrant gains from membership in the community and the network anchored there. What the community gains from the migrant network is more obvious – in the case of most of the communities we have cited, their continued existence is dependent upon the remittances and expenditures generated by migration. In a community in Michoacán, Mexico, "*compadrazgo* (godparent) relationships ensure villagers of material advantages from migrants.... Rather than their smallholdings being their security, their networks, into which they invest much effort and time, are their principal form of security and flexibility" (Fletcher, 1999:48). It would indeed be strange if membership in such a community-based network, providing tangible benefits to the migrants that comprise it, should not be used by that community to enforce the major benefit conferred by migrants to the community, their support. This leads to the question posed by Philpott (1968:472) regarding Caribbean migrants to Britain: "What mechanisms of social control operate to induce migrants to meet their obligations to the home community, mainly by sending back money?"

Although there are important exceptions, such as direct contributions to community projects,[4] the majority of migrant spending flows to and through family at the place of origin. In developing countries, family loyalty is "an important cultural norm ... maintained by assessing strong sanctions against those who deviate from them and by offering rewards for those who

[4]In Mexico, "migrants' financial contributions to fiestas, their support of church and school projects, and their annual return to the Fiesta of the Virgin of Guadalupe maintain social and cultural ties. There are requisite amounts of money and time migrants must contribute to remain in good standing with the local community" (Fletcher, 1999:49).

adhere to them" (Nugent, 1985:78). Individuals who fulfill family obligations are rewarded with respect and esteem, while those who do not are punished by a loss of reputation (Pollack, 1985:586).

Remittances, the results of which are easily visible in the form of improved housing, clothes and appliances (Banerjee, 1984b:241), are the strongest evidence to the community that the migrant is providing support for close relatives at home. On the Caribbean island of Montserrat, migrants anticipate the general community approval of a man who "never sent an empty letter all the time he was out." Even children there are taught the appropriate behavior expected of migrants, through the praise of those who send remittances and condemnation of those who do not (Philpott, 1968:472, 468).

A disloyal migrant suffers a loss of reputation not only in the village but also in the destination, for the constant circulation of migrants means that people in one locale are aware of actions taken by individuals in the other (Fletcher, 1999:49). In China, "custom requires male migrants to mantain their social ties and status in the village community by sending regular remittances to support their families. Otherwise, they risk losing face not only among relatives and neighbors in the home village, but also within the emigrant network of fellows villagers in the city" (Matthews and Nee, 2000:613). Thus, punishment of disloyal migrants can be decentralized, with sanctions imposed by well-informed family members used as a signal that other villagers should punish as well (Fafchamps, 1992:159). Portes and Sensenbrenner (1993:1332) call the social capital emerging from the monitoring capacity of immigrant communities "enforceable trust," where "predictability in the behavior of members of a group is in direct proportion to its sanctioning capacity."

The links between the community and the migrant's support of his own family are reinforced though kinship relations within the network. Many members are related by marriage, so that if a migrant were to fail to support his immediate family he would likely hurt members of the families of his fellow migrants. The community is more than one end of a bundle of linear relationships between each migrant and his immediate family: it rather comprises the intertwined relationships among migrants, kin and others at both origin and destination.

This section has provided support for the ideas that networks are valuable to migrants because they expand opportunities, that these networks are anchored in the home community, and that support of kin in the community is essential for membership in the network. Together, these provide the foundation of the option motive for remittances. If (in addition to altruism) insurance provided by the family were the only motive for remittances, the loss of insurance benefits should be a sufficient sanction if the migrant were to cease remitting, and it would not be necessary for the community to impose additional sanctions. But if there exists additional benefits of network membership that the migrant could enjoy without paying their costs, the community has an incentive to impose additional sanctions in order to prevent "free-riders" on the network, for the community as a whole suffers when migrants cease support.

MOTIVATIONS TO REMIT

Remittances provide the most direct and measurable form of support from the migrant to home, and this section examines more closely the contrast between the option motive to remit and other remittance motivations. The primary motives for remittances identified in the literature are altruism and exchange, with exchange encompassing both insurance and investment. Altruism and insurance strongly complement one another, for altruistic families help to insure their members against disaster.

An altruistic migrant derives utility from increasing the utility of those at home; with conventional assumptions concerning the utility of income, remittances will rise with an increase in the migrant's income and fall with an increase in family income (*see* Table 1). The first prediction is supported by data from Botswana (Lucas and Stark, 1985), Kenya (Hoddinott, 1994), India (Banerjee, 1982), and Mexico (Massey and Basem, 1992). However, as incomes increased beyond a certain point, remittances stayed constant in Kenya and actually declined in India. If other motives would cause remittances to fall with increased income, a declining marginal utility of extra income remitted could cause even altruistic migrants to reduce remittances at high levels of income.

The second prediction, that migrants will remit more to families in need, also generally receives support. Kaufman and Lindauer (1986) found that, for a given loss in income, needier families received higher transfers, and Malaysians in poor health received more remittances than those in good

TABLE 1
EFFECTS OF VARIABLES ON REMITTANCES UNDER DIFFERENT REMITTANCE MOTIVATIONS

Variable	Altruism	Insurance	Investment	Option
Migrant's income	+	?		-
Family's income	-	?	+	+
Migrant's income variability	-	+		
Family's income variability	+	?		+
Migrant's age		+		-
Migrant's education			+	
Network size and diversity	+	-		+

health (Bommier, 1996). Need and thus remittances should increase with more dependents at home, a prediction supported by Massey and Basem (1992) in Mexico, but not by Hoddinott (1994) in Kenya. In both Rwanda (Clay and Vander Haar, 1993) and Malaysia (Bommier, 1996), the contribution of each migrant child to their parents did not decrease as the number of migrant donors increased, as would be expected if these remittances were primarily intended to meet parental need.

Because income variability of migrants and their families makes both worse off by increasing their insecurity, the altruism motive predicts the opposite sign for this variable than that for increases in income. Cox and Jimenez (1998) found support for this hypothesis among migrants in urban Colombia, where a stable income significantly reduced the probability of receiving transfers and raised the probability of giving transfers. Likewise, migrant networks, by decreasing risk, should make migrants better off and increase remittances.

According to the insurance motive, migrants negotiate an implicit contract with their families to send remittances in exchange for support in times of unemployment, illness, and old age. The predictions about remittances resulting from the insurance motive are less straightforward than those resulting from altruism. Higher migrant income would increase remittances if insurance is a normal good (more is consumed at higher levels of income), or if the level of subsistence benefits considered acceptable during unemployment or old age increases with higher levels of current income. However, if higher levels of income make the migrant less risk-averse, remittances could decrease. Thus, the net effect of higher migrant income on remittances is indeterminate, as indicated by the "?" in Table 1.

The migrant must also be concerned with the effect of remittances upon the family's ability and willingness to provide insurance. In a one-way insurance contract, where the migrant remits in exchange for insurance, higher family income should increase remittances because the family is more capable of providing that insurance. If, however, the insurance contract is reciprocal (the migrant insures the family as well as the family insuring the migrant) (Stark and Lucas, 1988), or if hard times were to undermine the long-term viability of family enterprises were remittances not received and thereby endanger the family's ability to fulfill its insurance obligations to the migrant, the migrant may well remit more when family income declines, making the net effect indeterminate, another "?" in Table 1.

Income variability is the primary variable affecting remittances under the insurance motive. The reasoning in the previous paragraph applies equally to the variability of family income: more variability may increase remittances as an insurance payment to the family, or decrease remittances because the family is less capable of providing insurance. Riskier migrant income, on the other hand, increases the migrant's need for insurance and should unequivocally raise remittances if insurance, rather than altruism, is the primary motive. Cox and Jimenez's (1998) finding that income stability raises the probability of giving money and gifts thus supports the altruism over the insurance motive.

Because it is difficult to measure income variability, proxy variables have often been used in empirical analysis. If the variability of migrant income decreases over time as the migrant gains more experience and location-specific human capital, remittances should be negatively related to length of time in the destination. In India the probability of remitting was positively related to length of time in the city, and there was no evidence of ties weakening over time (Banerjee, 1982:351), and for Pacific Islanders in Australia "the remittance-decay hypothesis has no empirical validity" after controlling for age and other variables (Brown, 1997). The legal right to live and work in a country or city should make it easier to get a job and reduce income variability, but Massey and Basem (1992) found the possession of documents by Mexican migrants in the United States increased remittances even after controlling for income.

A relatively simple prediction of the insurance model focuses on old-age security: remittances will increase as the migrant ages and approaches retirement. Remittances in Kenya did increase with the age of the migrant, but after a certain age they leveled off (Hoddinott, 1994). Older Thai migrants remitted a lower percentage of their income (Fuller, Kamnuansilpa and Lightfoot, 1990), while the percentage of Philippine migrants who remitted declined with age, from 60 percent of those between 26 and 35 to only 37 percent of those over age 45 (Trager, 1984). Separation of the decision to remit from the amount remitted for Salvadorian migrants showed that while the amount remitted was an inverted U that traced an earnings profile as migrants aged, those in their middle ages were the least likely to remit at all (Menjívar *et al.*, 1998).

If the principal function of networks is to provide insurance, then stronger networks should decrease the need for insurance provided by the family and reduce remittances. Massey and Basem, measuring the strength of Mexican migrant networks by the number of the migrant's relatives living in the United States, found the probability of remitting was significantly increased by having more family members in the United States: "rather than indicating a growing orientation to the United States and a lower propensity to remit, ties to relatives in the United States appear to indicate a stronger commitment to Mexico and a higher probability ... of remitting." They address this paradox by pointing out that "migrant networks improve access to employment," which "might indicate the existence of a broader family strategy for socioeconomic improvement through migration" (Massey and Basem, 1992:204). Migrants' ties to networks afford them mobility, but require that they maintain strong links to home.

A third category of remittance motivations is investment. One view of investment is that it represents the fulfillment of one side of an implicit mutual contract with the family. In this context, remittances from children to parents may be a repayment of the investment made in their education.[5] Remittances from children to parents may also be an investment by the migrant in potential parental bequests; if this is true, then greater household income and wealth should increase remittances. Land held by the family, the principal and most measurable component of household wealth in rural areas, was found to positively affect remittances in Kenya (Hoddinott, 1994), but not in India (Banerjee, 1982).

A second connotation of investment is that the migrant is investing in real assets that will provide an income flow upon return. Where capital markets are underdeveloped, migrants might remit more for investment purposes to dynamic rural communities with greater possibilities for the productive employment of capital than to poor communities. In Mexico, 19 percent of remittances to dynamic communities were spent on productive investments, such as farm land, businesses and livestock, while only 5 percent of remittances to poor communities went for productive investment (Lindstrom, 1996).[6]

[5]Banerjee (1982), Hoddinott (1994) and Bommier (1996) all found that higher levels of education increased remittances, while Massey and Basem (1992) found that completion of primary school lowered remittances from Mexican migrants to the United States. Since education should increase job stability and reduce risk, it might be argued that the reduced need for insurance overwhelmed the repayment of education motive or, as Taylor (1986) suggests, education might hold less relevance for Mexican migrants in the United States, where the jobs they hold do not usually require high levels of education. An alternative approach is to question the repayment of education motive altogether: "it is difficult to accept that when a child goes to school and invests in human capital, he or she is consciously entering into an informal agreement voluntarily, *i.e.*, that the child could refuse the agreement or modify the terms" (Lianos, 1997:74).

[6]However, it should be noted that classification of the uses of remittances as consumption or investment may not capture their underlying purpose: remittances destined for housing and weddings could actually be productive investments: a good marriage can expand the family's influence and its chances of economic prosperity, while housing can provide security in old age (Mooney, 2001).

FINANCIAL OPTION THEORY APPLIED TO REMITTANCES

The analysis of options was first developed to determine the value of financial options like puts and calls, and later applied as "real options" to decision processes where the costs and benefits of maintaining flexibility are explicitly considered (Trigeorgis, 1996). A major type of application has been to capital investment decisions, where the decision should rarely be construed as "invest all" or "invest nothing," but instead may involve an incremental investment that maintains the possibility of future action, exploiting the temporal dimension of options. Making this incremental investment is the equivalent of buying an option to expand in the future, and the value of the option (what the decisionmaker should be willing to pay for the incremental investment) can be rigorously derived by application of the Black-Scholes model (Black and Scholes, 1973), developed to price options sold in financial markets. In this model, the value of a call option, which permits its owner to buy a stock at a specified price, depends upon five variables: the current price of the stock, the time until expiration of the option, the interest rate, the volatility of the stock's price, and the specified price at which the call's owner can buy the stock, called the exercise price (*see* Merton, 1998).

The effect of most of these variables upon the value of a call option is intuitively obvious. An increase in the stock's price allows for greater profit from owning the call and raises its value, while an increase in the exercise price lowers potential profit and decreases its value. The owner of a call does not own the stock itself but only right to buy it, and thus will profit from upward movements in the stock's price while being protected from downward movements. Therefore, greater volatility, by increasing the dispersion of future stock prices, increases the value of the call option. Similarly, a longer time until expiration, because it allows for greater movement in the stock's price, increases the value of the call. Because variability generally equates to risk and risk usually reduces value, these last two conclusions are not so intuitive as the first two.

Translating these variables to migration networks is rather straightforward (*see* Table 2). The asset which the migrant can claim is one job within the portfolio of potential jobs available through the network at a future time. The price that the migrant pays for the option on this asset is the support given to family and community that is paid to maintain membership in the network, which can be measured by a portion of remittances. The higher the present earnings in these jobs (the current stock price in the Black-Scholes model), the higher the value of the option. The higher the migrant's earnings

TABLE 2
PRINCIPAL VARIABLES AND THEIR EFFECTS ON REMITTANCES IN MODELS OF FINANCIAL OPTIONS AND NETWORK MOBILITY OPTIONS

Financial Model		Network Mobility Model	
Dependent Variable		Dependent Variable	
Option Price		Remittances	
Independent variables	Effect	Independent variables	Effect
Current stock price	+	Current earnings in network	+
Exercise Price	-	Current earnings of migrant	-
Stock Volatility	+	Dispersion of network earnings	+
Time until expiration	+	Time until retirement	+

in his or her current job (the exercise price that will be given up by exercising the option and taking another job), the lower the value of the option. Because the migrant will only exercise the option when higher paying jobs are available through the network, greater potential dispersion of network earnings (the stock's volatility) will increase the value of the option.

According to the model, a migrant will continue to send remittances in order to maintain the option to change jobs within the network. In exercising the option, the migrant utilizes the network to obtain employment in a better job. If that job is stable, the migrant could cease remitting without effective sanctions (those resulting in restricted mobility). This would be the case for permanent migration, when the potential benefits provided by the network in obtaining future employment would no longer be enough to offset the cost of network membership. However, since jobs held by migrants are often unstable and cannot be relied upon to provide permanent employment, or because an even better job may become available later through the network, or finally because the migrant's mobility within the new occupation might be dependent upon maintaining a good relationship with the person who provided the referral, the migrant will often obtain another option at the same time as exercising the old by continuing to remit, thus retaining membership in the network. Only when the migrant approaches retirement (the time of expiration of the last potential option) will the value of the option decline significantly.

The option motive thus provides unambiguous predictions about the effect of major variables upon migrant remittances (*see* Table 1). Higher migrant income will decrease remittances, unlike under the altruism motive. The interaction of the altruism and option motives provides one possible explanation for the empirical findings discussed earlier, where remittances increase with more income (the altruism motive dominates) until income is high enough to reduce the potential benefits from changing jobs (the option motive dominates). Higher and more variable family income, by increasing the range of earnings from which the migrant can choose, will increase remittances. Older migrants will remit less because the value of the option declines as the migrant approaches retirement, while the insurance motive predicts increased remittances. And most relevant for our analysis linking options and networks, larger and more diverse networks – that is, networks that provide contact with more persons working in a wider variety of occupations and destinations – will, by enhancing the value of the network as a vehicle for economic mobility, increase remittances.

This is an important conclusion, for it provides a testable hypothesis that is the opposite of that found in the insurance motive. There, stronger networks provide an alternative to insurance provided by the family: while access to the network might still be dependent upon remitting under the insurance motive, the size and density of the network works in the opposite direction, leading to a negative or at best ambiguous prediction of the net effect of network strength on remittances.

The link between the option motive and networks is that the migrant will be sanctioned by removal from the network if remittances are not sent to the household. This link is dependent upon monitoring of the migrant's actions, which should be more effective within "small, stable communities (where) disloyalty can be easily detected and communicated" (Nugent, 1985:91). Thus, remittances should be greater to households in small communities than to those in large communities.

THE MODEL APPLIED TO MEXICAN MIGRATION TO THE UNITED STATES

In this section, data from the Mexican Migration Project (1995), which by 1995 was collected on a random sample of 5,680 households in 30 communities in Western Mexico, are used to examine the different motivations to remit.[7] A definition of the variables we will be considering and the basic statistics describing them appears in Table 3. The altruism motive can be exam-

[7]The Mexican Migration Project survey is an ongoing survey that gathers information about family characteristics and migration experience, including detailed data on the wages and remittances sent by the household heads who had migrated to the United States. Of the households in the 30 communities surveyed at the time of this analysis, 2,776 of them reported a household head who had been or was currently a migrant. Data on remittances was obtained from 84 percent of these migrant households, and 69 percent of those with valid remittance data did actually remit on a monthly basis. The final sample was limited to those 1,009 migrants who had remitted since 1929 and who had provided valid information on the other variables in the model. All data are reported for the period of the migrant's most recent trip to the United States.

ined by the number of dependents and/or a spouse left behind to measure need and the migrant's earnings to measure ability to provide. The investment motive can be investigated with number of years of education, for which remittances could be a repayment, and the amount of land owned by the family, which could represent either a potential bequest or an asset that remittances are intended to maintain. The insurance motive can be analyzed with the migrant's earnings, age, amount of experience in the United States, whether the migration was legal or illegal, and the network variables: the size of the network, the dispersal of the network, and whether the migrant used the network to get a job. The option motive can be examined with these same variables, as well as the size of the origin community.

TABLE 3
DESCRIPTIVE STATISTICS FOR VARIABLES DETERMINING MIGRANT REMITTANCES

Variable	Definition	Mean	Standard Deviation
Remittance	Natural log of migrant's monthly remittances in 1982-1984 dollars	4.69	1.38
Age	Age of the migrant in years	35.1	12.1
Education	Years of school completed	4.1	3.8
Dependents	Number of children left behind	3.2	3.1
Illegal	Dummy variable = 1 if illegal, 0 if legal	0.56	0.50
Land	Hectares of land owned by the household	2.3	16.4
SpouseLeft	Dummy variable = 1 if married and spouse left behind, 0 otherwise	0.66	0.47
NwkDisp	Index of the number of locations in which the migrant's community had migrants in the year the migrant was abroad	8.7	4.2
NwkJob	Dummy variable = 1 if migrant used network to obtain job, 0 otherwise	0.58	0.49
NwkExp	Number of relatives and friends with U.S. migration experience	16.2	19.5
Pop	Population of the migrant's home community	43,752	148,713
USExper	Total number of months of migrant's U.S. experience	54.4	73.8
Wage	Migrant's monthly wage in dollars	805	1,124
WageSqd	Square of the migrant's monthly wage in dollars	1.91e+06	2.77e+07

Using this data, we regress these variables on the log of remittances. Because the equation only uses information on those who did remit money, we include a variable to correct for this selection bias.[8] The results are summarized in Table 4, with the coefficients multiplied by 100 indicating the per-

[8]We correct for the selection bias of looking only at those who remitted by including a lambda coefficient (Heckman's sample correction estimator) in the multiple regression model, derived from a probit regression estimated to predict a dichotomous variable equaling one if the migrant remitted and zero otherwise.

TABLE 4
DETERMINANTS OF LEVELS OF MIGRANT REMITTANCES

Variable	Coefficient	T-statistic (Absolute Value)
Age	0.009	1.21
Education	0.088	6.71[b]
Dependents	0.001	0.03
Illegal	0.159	1.72[a]
Land	-0.001	0.26
SpouseLeft	-0.987	1.66[a]
NwkDisp	0.052	6.12[b]
NwkJob	0.285	3.75[b]
NwkExp	0.004	1.76[a]
Pop	3.43e-07	0.67
USExper	0.004	3.96[b]
Wage	0.0009	10.85[b]
WageSqd	-2.39e-08	10.74[b]
Lambda	-2.71	1.95[a]
Constant	4.25	4.74[b]
R-square	0.46	
Number of observations	1009	

Notes: [a]Significant at the 10% level
[b]Significant at the 1% level

centage change in the amount remitted due to an increase of one unit of the variable, holding all else constant.

The major goal of the analysis is to investigate the impact of networks on remittances; the insurance motive suggests a negative relationship because a strong network increases the migrant's security, while the option motive suggests a positive relationship due to the opportunities provided by network connections.

The network coefficients strongly support the option motive. Migrants who found their jobs through a network remit 28.5 percent more than those who did not, with a high level of statistical significance. The number of locations in which the migrant's home community has placed migrants, which is relevant for testing the hypothesis that the range and diversity of the network are of value to the migrant in providing options for economic mobility, significantly impacts the level of remittances, with each additional location increasing remittances by 5.2 percent. Furthermore, each additional friend or relative with U.S. experience significantly increases remittances by 0.4 percent, indicating the value of a larger, stronger network. Given that the average size of a village in the sample was 189 households, and in 49 percent of these the household head was a migrant or ex-migrant, this network effect would increase remittances by at least 37 percent (many households had more than one migrant) for migrant households who knew one another in these villages.

In addition to the network variables, the data permit examination of several other predictions of the option and/or insurance motives for migrant remittances. The total number of months that the migrant has worked in the United States positively and significantly affects the level of remittances. The option motive would suggest that time spent in the United States, by giving the migrant experience and confidence, would enhance geographic mobility and effective utilization of the network, while the insurance motive predicts that U.S. experience should increase the migrant's security and therefore lower remittances. Illegality raises remittances, which is consistent not only with the insurance motive but with the option motive as well. The option motive is contingent upon the network being the primary avenue of economic mobility; this would be the case for illegal migrants, while legal migrants can use more formal channels. The positive signs for age and community size fail to point in the direction predicted by the option motive, but neither is significant.

The altruism and investment motives receive mixed support. The increase in remittances from an increase in earnings supports altruism, but the negative sign of the square of wages suggests that after a certain point this relationship levels off. This is consistent with the argument that altruism dominates remittance decisions when income is low, but that above a certain level of income either the migrant becomes less risk-averse or the high level of current income decreases the value of the option. The insignificance of the number of children left behind and the negative impact of leaving a wife behind do not support altruism. The model gives mixed support for different versions of the investment motive: an additional year of education significantly increases remittances by 8.8 percent, suggesting the possibility of repayment for prior investments in education, while the amount of land owned by the household has no significant impact on the level of remittances.

DISCUSSION

Altruism, insurance, and investment are three potential motives for migrant remittances that have been explored in the literature. The model developed in this paper posits an additional motive – that remittances allow migrants to participate in employment networks based in the village and thus are in part a payment for the option to change jobs within this network. The social capital of network membership is an asset that has value, for it makes jobs held by other network members accessible to the migrant through the exchange of information and referrals. However, this asset has a cost: to maintain mem-

bership in the network the migrant has to be a part of the larger village community where it is based, which requires meeting socially-prescribed obligations of family support through remittances, gifts to family and community, and regular visits home. A part of these costs can be considered as the price the migrant pays for the option to change jobs within the network.
Option theory, developed in financial economics, provides concrete hypotheses about the effect of key variables upon the value of this option, which are tested using data on Mexican migrants to the United States. The data support the key hypothesis that network connections increase remittances: specifically, a more disperse network, more friends and relatives with migration experience, and the migrant's use of network connections to get a job all increase the amount the migrant remits to Mexico. If insurance were the primary motive, remittances should fall because network connections reduce risk.

The option model of migrant remittances is firmly grounded in the literature on migration, networks and remittances in three ways. First, the option motive complements other motivations for remittances – all can operate together, or one can dominate in particular circumstances. Altruism and insurance reinforce one another because altruistic family members help one another and thus provide mutual insurance; insurance and investment because by investing in assets at home, insurance benefits are protected. Likewise, the option motive complements these other motives because an option provides insurance in case of loss of current income, because investment in assets at home expands employment options, and because remittances are partly dependent upon the community enforcing altruism upon the migrant.

Second, the option motive builds upon the insights from financial economics concerning risk and flexibility, some of which have already been applied to migration in analyzing the diversification of household income sources. As in that case, where the addition of a risky income source could reduce the risk of the household income portfolio, the results of this application are somewhat counterintuitive. According to option theory, stronger networks should increase remittances rather than decrease them, and ties to the origin community may remain important even though the migrant's economic position in the destination is made more secure by these networks. These counterintuitive predictions result from having deepened our understanding of uncertainty: in the case of diversification by incorporating the correlation among returns, and in the case of options by considering fortune as well as hazard. This may help us to understand the enduring ties between mature migrant streams and their places of origin, especially in circumstances where economic mobility is restricted in either origin or destination.

Third, the option motive completes the integration of networks into the analysis of migration, networks and remittances. The migration-remittance and migration-network links have been well established both theoretically and empirically. The option motive links remittances and networks, and by so doing not only highlights the importance of networks in providing mobility, but also provides an explanation for previous empirical findings that stronger networks increase remittances.

The option motive predicts that networks and support for the community in which they are based will be particularly strong where personal contacts are the main avenue for economic mobility. When alternative information or mobility channels become available through education or job markets that are less network-dependent, ties to home could be broken unless maintained by the other motives. Perhaps this might help explain why remittances to communities in Mexico with a preparatory school were found to be lower than to those without (Durand *et al.*, 1996), or why education increases the probability of frequent trips home for undocumented migrants, who encounter strong barriers to economic mobility in the United States, while decreasing that probability for migrants within Mexico (Massey and Espinosa, 1997).

The model of network participation based on employment options is consistent with a particular dynamic that has been observed in longitudinal studies of migration networks – that the diversity of destinations within the network increases and then decreases over time. During the early stages of network formation, the network provides incomplete information about job opportunities in the destination, prompting migrants to try their luck in new destinations without network connections: "as more people are drawn into the process, some migrants inevitably seek out better opportunities in new places and occupations. In this way the diversity of foreign destinations, jobs, and strategies increases." As this process continues, "someone from the sending community achieves a position of responsibility that enables him or her to channel employment, housing, and other resources to fellow townspeople," and "the migration stream begins to focus more narrowly and the diversity of jobs, destinations and strategies to constrict (Massey, Goldring and Durand, 1994:1501). This constriction of network diversity is consistent with migrants using the network as a ladder for economic mobility, honing in on the best jobs available within the network. Yet the very success of the network in enhancing mobility eventually undermines this function, as destinations converge and the development of migrants' human capital replaces networks as the primary determinant of their economic success. The locus of the network moves to the destination or evaporates altogether, and "settlement" as it is conventionally defined occurs.

One implication of the model is that anything that weakens the information flow within the network will reduce the value of the option, both because sanctions for nonremitting migrants will be less effective and because knowledge of alternative employment opportunities is limited. Thus, the option value of village-based networks should be particularly strong if migrants are working in imperfect labor markets where personal relationships are important in obtaining jobs and if frequent contact between the migrant and disperse members of the network is possible through visits and other means of communications. These are precisely the conditions that have characterized migration between Mexico and the United States, and so it is not surprising that migrants have maintained particularly strong ties there. Where migrants are effectively cut off from their villages, as in the Chinese Diaspora during the first half of the twentieth century, the link between remittances and employment options provided by village-based networks is severed, and transnational communities are less likely to emerge.

It follows from the above that remittances to home may not diminish over time, as hypothesized by the altruism and insurance motives, as the migrant establishes emotional and financial ties to the destination. This lends theoretical support to evidence that remittance streams worldwide have not declined as migration networks have matured (Taylor, 1999).

Insurance and diversification have proved to be useful concepts because they point empirical research toward the examination of particular types of behavior. While it is sometimes difficult to test these propositions empirically (in the case of the diversification hypothesis, there is scant empirical evidence to support the deliberate pooling of occupations with noncovariant earnings within households), this does not diminish the conceptual utility of the theory as a tool to understand labor allocation decisions. Likewise, the evidence that we have used to support option theory is by no means conclusive. The data on remittances are imperfect and can support a number of interpretations, and the key propositions of the model – that networks are valuable to migrants because they expand opportunities, that these networks are anchored in the home community, and that support of kin in the community is essential for membership in the network – have been supported mainly by anecdotal evidence from several settings.

These limitations do not diminish the conceptual utility of option theory to aid in understanding the value of networks to migrants; instead, they underscore the importance of closely examining how networks actually function. How is membership in the network gained and lost? How do migrants communicate information about opportunities to one another? Under what conditions do networks based in the village shift their locus to the destination? These are important questions that are emerging in current research, which could form the foundation for future theoretical development.

REFERENCES

Astone, N. M., C. A. Nathanson, R. Schoen and Y. J. Kim
1999 "Family Demography, Social Theory, and Investment in Social Capital," *Population and Development Review*, 25(1):1–31.

Banerjee, B.
1984a "Information Flow, Expectations and Job Search," *Journal of Development Economics*, 15:239–257.

____
1984b "Rural to Urban Migration and Conjugal Separation: An Indian Case Study," *Economic Development and Cultural Change*, 32(4):767–780.

____
1982 "Rural-Urban Migration and Family Ties: An Analysis of Family Considerations in Migration Behaviour in India," *Oxford Bulletin of Economics and Statistics*, 323–355.

Becker, G. S.
1981 *A Treatise on the Family*. Cambridge, MA: Harvard University Press.

Ben-Porath, Y.
1980 "The F-Connection: Families, Friends, and Firms and the Organization of Exchange," *Population and Development Review*, 6(1):1–30.

Binswanger, H. P. and J. McIntire
1987 "Behavioral and Material Determinants of Production Relations in Land-abundant Tropical Agriculture," *Economic Development and Cultural Change*, 36(1):73–99.

Black, F. and M. Scholes
1973 "The Pricing of Options and Corporate Liabilities," *Journal of Political Economy*, 81(3):637–654.

Bommier, A.
1996 "Intergenerational Transfers and Intra-Household Allocation of Resources: Evidence from Malaysia." Paper presented at the annual meetings of the Population Association of American, New Orleans, May 9–11.

Boyd, M.
1989 "Family and Personal Networks in International Migration: Recent Developments and New Agendas," *International Migration Review*, 23(3):638–670.

Bromley, D. W. and J. P. Chavas
1989 "On Risk, Transactions and Economic Development in the Semiarid Tropics," *Economic Development and Cultural Change*, 37(4):719–736.

Brookfield, H. C.
1970 "Dualism and the Geography of Developing Countries." Paper presented at the meetings of the Australian and New Zealand Association for the Advancement of Science, Port Moresby, Papua New Guinea.

Brown, R. P. C.
1997 "Estimating Remittance Functions for Pacific Island Migrants," *World Development,* 25(4):613–626.

Cain, M.
1983 "Fertility as an Adjustment to Risk," *Population and Development Review,* 9(4):688–702.

Chapman, M. and R. M. Prothero
1983 "Themes on Circulation in the Third World," *International Migration Review,* 17(4):597–632.

Chavez, L. R.
1994 "The Power of the Imagined Community: The Settlement of Undocumented Mexicans and Central Americans in the United States," *American Anthropologist,* 96(1):52–73.

———
1988 "Settlers and Sojourners: The Case of Mexicans in the United States," *Human Organization,* 47(2):95–108.

Clay, D. C. and J. E. Vander Haar
1993 "Patterns of Intergenerational Support and Childbearing in the Third World," *Population Studies,* 47(1):67–83.

Cox, D. and E. Jimenez
1998 "Risk Sharing and Private Transfers: What About Urban Households?" *Economic Development and Cultural Change,* 46(3):621–637.

David, P. A.
1974 "Fortune, Risk, and the Microeconomics of Migration." In *Nations and Households in Economic Growth: Essays in Honor of Moses Abramovitz.* Ed. P. A. David and M. W. Reder. New York: Academic Press. Pp. 21–88.

Durand, J., W. Kandel, E. A. Parrado and D. S. Massey
1996 "International Migration and Development in Mexican Communities," *Demography,* 33(2)249–264.

Elkan, W.
1967 "Circular Migration and the Growth of Towns in East Africa," *International Labor Review,* 96:81–89.

Espinosa, K. E and D. S. Massey
1999 "Undocumented Migration and the Quantity and Quality of Social Capital." In *Migration and Transnational Spaces.* Ed. L. Pries. Aldershot: Ashgate. Pp. 106–137.

Fafchamps, M.
1992 "Solidarity Networks in Preindustrial Societies: Rational Peasants with a Moral Economy," *Economic Development and Cultural Change,* 41(1):147–174.

Fan, Y. K. and A. Stretton
1985 "Circular Migration in South East Asia: Some Theoretical Explanations." In *Labour Circulation and the Labour Process.* Ed. G. Standing. London: Croom Helm. Pp. 338–357.

Fletcher, P. L.
1999 *La Casa de Mis Sueños: Dreams of Home in a Transnational Migration Community.* Boulder, CO: Westview Press.

Fuller, T. D., P. Kamnuansilpa and P. Lightfoot
1990 "Urban Ties of Rural Thais," *International Migration Review,* 24(3):534–562.

Gallin, B. and R. S. Gallin
1974 "The Integration of Village Migrants in Taipei." In *The Chinese City between Two Worlds.* Ed. M. Elvin and G. W. Skinner. Stanford, CA: Stanford University Press. Pp. 331–358.

Gardner, K.
1995 *Global Migrants, Local Lives: Travel and Transformation in Rural Bangladesh.* Oxford: Clarendon Press.

Goldring, L.
1998 "The Power of Status in Transnational Social Fields." In *Transnationalism from Below.* Vol. 6. *Comparative Urban and Community Research.* Ed. M. P. Smith and L. E. Guarnizo. New Brunswick, NJ: Transaction Publishers. Pp. 165–195.

____
1996 "Blurring Borders: Constructing Transnational Community in the Process of Mexico-U.S. Migration," *Research in Community Sociology,* 6:69–104.

Goodman, B.
1995 *Native Place, City, and Nation: Regional Networks and Identities in Shanghai, 1853–1937.* Berkeley, CA: University of California Press.

Granovetter, M.
1983 "The Strength of Weak Ties: A Network Theory Revisited," *Sociological Theory,* 1:201–233.

Greenhalgh, S.
1988 "Fertility as Mobility: Sinic Transitions," *Population and Development Review,* 14(4):629–674.

Hart, G.
1992 "Imagined Unities: Constructions of 'The Household' in Economic Theory." In *Understanding Economic Processes.* Ed. S. Ortiz and S. Lees. Lanham, MD: University Press of America. Pp. 111–130.

Hoddinott, J.
1994 "A Model of Migration and Remittances Applied to Western Kenya," *Oxford Economic Papers,* 46(3):459–476.

Hondagneu-Sotelo, P.
1995 *Gendered Transitions: Mexican Experiences of Immigration.* Berkeley: University of California Press.

Kaufman, D. and D. L. Lindauer
1986 "A Model of Income Transfers for the Urban Poor," *Journal of Development Economics,* 22:337–350.

Kemper, R. V.
1981 "Obstacles and Opportunities: Household Economics of Tzintzuntzán Migrants in Mexico City," *Urban Anthropology,* 10(3):211–229.

Levitt, P.
1998 "Transnational Politics: A Dominican Case," *LASA Forum,* 29(2):22–23.

Lianos, T. P.
1997 "Factors Determining Migrant Remittances: The Case of Greece," *International Migration Review*, 31(1):72–87.

Lindstrom, D. P.
1996 "Economic Opportunity in Mexico and Return Migration from the United States," *Demography*, 33(3):357–374.

Liu, Q. and K. W. Chan
1998 *Rural-Urban Migration Processes in the Transitional Era in China: Job Search Process, Wage Determination and Occupational Attainment.* Chinese Academy of Social Sciences, Beijing. Unpublished manuscript.

Lucas, R. E. B., and O. Stark
1985 "Motivations to Remit: Evidence from Botswana," *Journal of Political Economy*, 93(5):901–918.

Massey, D. S., R. Alarcón, J. Durand and H. González
1987 *Return to Aztlán: The Social Process of International Migration from Western Mexico.* Berkeley: University of California Press.

Massey, D. S. and L. C. Basem
1992 "Determinants of Savings, Remittances, and Spending Patterns among U.S. Migrants in Four Mexican Communities," *Sociological Inquiry*, 62(2):185–207.

Massey, D. S. and K. E. Espinosa
1997 "What's Driving Mexico-U.S. Migration? A Theoretical, Empirical, and Policy Analysis," *American Journal of Sociology*, 102(4):939–999.

Massey, D. S., L. Goldring and J. Durand
1994 "Continuities in Transnational Migration: An Analysis of Nineteen Mexican Communities," *American Journal of Sociology*, 99(6):1492–1533.

Matthew, R. and V. Nee
2000 "Gender Inequality and Economic Growth in Rural China," *Social Science Research*, 29:606–632.

McCall, B. P. and J. J. McCall
1987 "A Sequential Study of Migration and Job Search," *Journal of Labor Economics*, 5(4):452–476.

Menjívar, C., J. DaVanzo, L. Greenwell and R. Burciaga Valdez
1998 "Remittance Behavior among Salvadorean and Filipino Immigrants in Los Angeles," *International Migration Review*, 32(1):97–126.

Merton, R. C.
1998 "Applications of Option-Pricing Theory: Twenty-Five Years Later," *American Economic Review*, 88(3):323–349.

Mexican Migration Project
1995 "MIGFILE," Population Studies Center, University of Pennyslvania, <http://lexis.pop.upenn.edu/mexmig>.

Mines, R. and A. de Janvry
1982 "Migration to the United States and Mexican Rural Development: A Case Study," *American Journal of Agricultural Economics*, 64(3):444–454.

Mooney, M.
2001 "Migrants' Social Ties in the U.S. and Investment in Mexico." Paper presented at annual meetings of the Population Association of America, Washington, DC, March 29–31.

Nugent, J. B.
1985 "The Old-Age Security Motive for Fertility, *Population and Development Review*, 11(1):75–97.

Pessar, P.
1999 "The Role of Gender, Households, and Social Networks in the Migration Process: A Review and Appraisal." In *The Handbook of International Migration: The American Experience*. Ed. C. Hirschman, P. Kasinitz and J. DeWind. New York: Russell Sage Foundation. Pp. 53–70.

Philpott, S. B.
1968 "Remittance Obligations, Social Networks and Choice among Montserratian Migrants in Britain," *Man*, 3(3):465–476.

Pollack, R. A.
1985 "A Transaction Cost Approach to Families and Households," *Journal of Economic Literature*, 23(2):581–608.

Portes, A. and J. Sensenbrenner
1993 "Embeddedness and Immigration: Notes on the Social Determinants of Economic Action," *American Journal of Sociology*, 98(6):1320–1350.

Roberts, K. D.
1997 "China's 'Tidal Wave' of Migrant Labor: What Can We Learn from Mexican Undocumented Migration to the United States?" *International Migration Review*, 31(2):249–293.

———
1982 "Agrarian Structure and Labor Mobility in Rural Mexico," *Population and Development Review*, 8(2):299–322.

Rosenzweig, M. R. and O. Stark
1989 "Consumption Smoothing, Migration and Marriage: Evidence from Rural India," *Journal of Political Economy*, 97(4):905–926.

Roumasset, J. A.
1979 "Introduction and State of the Arts." In *Risk, Uncertainty and Agricultural Development*. Ed. J. Roumasset, J. M. Boussard and I. Singh. Laguna, Philippines: Southeast Asia Regional Center for Graduate Study and Research in Agriculture and the Agricultural Development Council. Pp. 3–21.

Rouse, R.
1992 "Making Sense of Settlement: Class Transformation, Cultural Struggle, and Transnationalism among Mexican Migrants in the United States," *Annals of the New York Academy of Sciences*, 645:25–52.

Stark, O.
1982 "Research on Rural-to-Urban Migration in LDC's: The Confusion Frontier and Why We Should Pause to Think Afresh," *World Development*, 10(1):63–70.

Stark, O. and R. E. B. Lucas
1988 "Migration, Remittances and the Family," *Economic Development and Cultural Change*, 36(3):465–481.

Taylor, J. E.
1999 "The New Economics of Labour Migration and the Role of Remittances in the Migration Process," *International Migration*, 37(1):63–86.

Taylor, J. E.
1986 "Differential Migration, Networks, Information and Risk. In *Research in Human Capital and Development: Migration.* Vol. 4. *Human Capital and Migration.* Ed. O. Stark. Greenwich, CT: JAI Press Inc. Pp. 147–171.

Todaro, M. P.
1969 "A Model of Labor Migration and Urban Unemployment in Less Developed Countries," *American Economic Review,* 59(1):138–148.

Trager, L.
1984 "Migration and Remittances: Urban Income and Rural Households in the Philippines," *Journal of Developing Areas,* 18(3):317–340.

Trigeorgis, L.
1996 *Real Options: Managerial Flexibility and Strategy in Resource Allocation.* Cambridge, MA: The MIT Press.

Wilson, T. D.
1998 "Weak Ties, Strong Ties: Network Principles in Mexican Migration," *Human Organization,* 57(4):394–403.

Wood, C. H.
1981 "Structural Changes and Household Strategies: A Conceptual Framework for the Study of Rural Migration," *Human Organization,* 40(4):338–344.

Zhao, S.
2000 "Organizational Characteristics of Rural Labor Mobility in China." In Rural Labor Flows in China. Ed. L. A. West and Y. Zhao. University of California, Berkeley: Institute of East Asian Studies. Pp. 231–250.

[18]

ELSEVIER

Women's Studies International Forum 27 (2004) 149–162

WOMEN'S STUDIES INTERNATIONAL FORUM

www.elsevier.com/locate/wsif

Can women's social networks migrate?☆

Janet W. Salaff[a,*], Arent Greve[a,b]

[a] Department of Sociology, University of Toronto, 725 Spadina Ave, Toronto, Canada M5S2J4

[b] Department of Strategy and Management, The Norwegian School of Economics and Business Administration, Breiviksveien 40, 5045 Bergen, Norway

Synopsis

This paper analyzes how dual-career couples from the People's Republic of China (PRC) organize care for their children prior to and following immigration to Canada. Using the concepts of social capital and life course, we examine the problems that Chinese immigrant women face in rebuilding their professional careers due to loss of social capital. In the PRC, childcare is provided by a dense web of formal institutional and informal arrangements, with the family playing an important role. After immigrating, most need to rebuild their careers and develop social capital to help them combine childcare and career rebuilding. Women's careers suffer more than that of their husbands. Our data come from interviews with 50 PRC couples, aged in their 30s and 40s, with young children, who immigrated to Canada after 1996 in the skilled worker class.

Introduction: work and family networks

With the globalization of production and services, professionals from Asia increasingly migrate to enrich their work experiences and their family economies in new countries (Castells, 1989; Sassen, 1991). These moves often disrupt their professional employment and family support networks, which they must mobilize anew (Levitt & Schiller, 2003; Portes & Borocz, 1989). Our "Immigration from China" project explores how social networks bridge settlement of professionals who immigrated to Canada in the skilled worker category. We look for those features in their social networks which they share with others and those which are distinctly rooted in dual-career families. This paper analyzes how migration alters the family support system, how couples adapt to reduced social capital for childcare, and how this impedes career opportunities of skilled women in particular.

A number of writers have studied how social networks meet the needs of working class women migrants (Hondagneu-Sotelo & Avila, 1997). We need to learn more about the social networks of skilled workers, a significant category of international migrants (Kofman, 2000). Canada's immigration policies grant permanent status to "independent" immigrants. Typical People's Republic of China (PRC) immigrants to Canada are married professionals who apply to immigrate based on their skills, without having been offered jobs or preceded by other family members. In China, they had built collegial social networks during their education and careers (Lin, Ensel, & Vaughn, 1981). After immigration to Canada, to get appropriate positions, they search for local

☆ Submitted to: Women's Studies International Forum.

* Corresponding author.

0277-5395/$ - see front matter © 2004 Elsevier Ltd. All rights reserved.
doi:10.1016/j.wsif.2004.06.005

work-related network partners which are rooted in the occupation, not in kinship or the ethnic enclave (Gold, 2001; Poros, 2001).

Family needs also require social network support but of a different sort. Professionals are likely to marry other professionals, and both want to develop their careers. To do so, parents with young children draw on complex support systems which, unlike job networks, are based on kinship. Like other migrants, they also have to mobilize family-related social networks over immense physical distances (Hondagneu-Sotelo & Avila, 1997).

Rebuilding work-related and childcare social networks after they migrate is difficult, partly because this reconstruction occurs at the same time. Furthermore, these multiple social networks are based on different types of relationships, intended for different purposes, entailing even more work to revamp them (Man, 1997; Preston & Man, 1999). These problems affect women and men differently and hit the careers of professional immigrant women the hardest (Willis & Yeoh, 2000).

Drawing on work and family biographies collected from 50 PRC couples who immigrated to Canada from 1996 to 2001 in the skilled worker class, we first outline concepts of migration, social networks, and the life course. We then introduce some background materials on family support systems in China and Canada. Part II discusses our sample and qualitative research procedures. Case studies in Part III describe parents' strategies in mixing formal structures and informal relations in China and Canada to get help with young children.

Social networks: migration and social support

Social networks play diverse functions in international migration (Delechat, 2001; Portes & Borocz, 1989). International migrants depend on social networks to find a job, start a business, or other career needs (Burt, 1992; Min, 1988). In addition to career exigencies, new arrivals need to find a place to live, get information and advice, emotional support, and help with childcare from others, the topic of this paper (Man, 2002; Parrenas, 2001; Preston & Man, 1999; Willis & Yeoh, 2000).

There are social class distinctions; while kinship ties are important extra-market resources for working class immigrants, highly educated people are more likely to seek collegial and organizational ties for equivalent positions in a host country (Gold, 2001; Meyer, 2001; Poros, 2001; Wong & Salaff, 1998). Furthermore, between spheres differ by gender. For instance, women's social networks join work and family spheres but may fall short of getting them good jobs. But at the same time, women rely on those networks to enable them to work. Men's social networks more effectively join work and community spheres (Stoloff, Glanville, & Bienenstock, 1999; Wellman, 1992).

Social networks can supply or fail to deliver help, and we reserve the term social capital for the successful provision of scarce resources through membership in networks or broader social structures (Portes, 1995: 257). Social capital is embedded in specific social contexts, and the structure of their social networks and types of relations within the networks shape the kind of help people get (Aldrich, Elam, & Reese, 1997; Granovetter, 1985; Wellman, 1999). Depending on the resources that the network contacts can offer, they can provide different types of support, but one contact can rarely cover a broad specter of services. Support may be located in diverse parts of a person's network. Furthermore, different forms of social networks give diverse kinds of assistance over time (Poros, 2001). Therefore, people need a variety of contacts to get the kind of support they need. Childcare is one of many services that people can get through their social networks. However, this delicate type of service involves considerable trust, and only a few members of a social network can offer the different types of assistance that childcare encompasses. This can be seen when we discuss types of relations and social networks that offer these resources.

First among the relations that build trust are multiplex relations. Multiplex relations involve more than one type of tie between people. People interact in several contexts, each surrounded by others who reinforce the relationship. By bridging more than one type of a relation in a dyad, multiplex ties connect several different networks, which open access to a wider number of trusted people. Strong multiplex ties generate trust and are fundamental in mobilizing informal social support. We more readily trust the friend of a friend than we do an unconnected stranger. Indeed, if they have analogous shape, a friend's network relations may be seen as equivalent to our own and thus broaden the specter of help that a social network can offer (Ibarra, 1992; Krackhardt, 1992).

Most social networks that offer tangible services such as childcare depend on location and proximity. These are difficult to mobilize across continents, and when people migrate, they leave this kind of social capital behind. However, some network ties, for example kinship relations, are institutionalized roles. Strong kinship ties are fixed at birth and hence not easily entered or left behind. Such ties contain a set of expectations and obligations and they are the basis of help in childcare. Precisely because they are committed, people may make extraordinary efforts to maintain their kinship ties. Hence, many have found that kin-related social networks may be portable across the seas. Most of these studies have covered working class migrants. Therefore, we need to know more about how skilled immigrants deal with their childcare needs and how they can adapt their networks to new requirements. Skilled or professional migrants participate in very different network structures than working class migrants. The networks of skilled migrants are mainly centered on their professions and careers, and we question if they can mobilize kin to the same extent as working class migrants.

Life course structure

In each society, family and career trajectories unfold in an expected timing, figuring in the immigrant family dilemma. A career is one's work-life history, with long-term progression structured by the institutional and normative arrangement of roles (Scott & Burchell, 1994). The profession sets the expected timing of employment and career development (Pfeffer, 1997). There are also expected family sequences based on parents' and children's biological maturation, articulated with marriage, school, and other institutions (Clausen, 1986).

Because the biggest demands from work and family come at the same time, a crucial problem for dual-career couples is balancing their work and family careers. State-legislated family policies to support social reproduction often fail to provide effective support to dual-career families. Few countries effectively organize public childcare and employment to support dual-career families. Those that do may favor some sections of the work force with childcare more than others (Buchmann & Charles, 1995; Moen & Firebaugh, 1994).

It is typically women who try to mesh these dual work–family demands. Women may adopt sequential work and family courses, focusing more on each role at different times. They might first study, then raise children, then return to the labor force. This staggered approach often runs against the demands of expected professional career sequences. Simultaneous roles allow attention to both family and career courses. Here, role conflict takes a toll on women's ability to do both without substantial help (Heinz, Kruger, & Verma, 2001; Moen & Yu, 1999). Men commonly adjust their family life to their careers, while wives employ long-term, reciprocal support strategies to bridge formal and informal structures and attain work and family goals.

The difficulties that PRC immigrants to Canada encounter when they transfer between two different social contexts is central to their reconstructing work and family lives as new immigrants. Social structures, typical ways of building careers, and state family policies designed to support social reproduction differ from one setting to another and entail considerable readjustments. Without flexible informal social networks, parents have trouble bridging formal structures, and women assume most of this integrating work.

Work–family roles in China

Educated Chinese women have public and private roles that are both sequential and simultaneous (Giele, 1998). The education of young Chinese professionals and skilled workers is sequential, determined by examinations that lead from one stage to the next. State educational and job placement systems and their own performance and interests channel the educated elite into their adult roles. In force when most of our respondents got their first jobs, this system began to change in the 1980s following the introduction of a private labor market with great consequences for their careers (Bian, 1994; Nee & Matthews, 1996). After graduation from college, they find jobs and begin to build careers. They marry and bear a child within the first year (Robinson, 1985; Whyte & Parish, 1984). Having few children is a political requirement, allowing them to devote themselves to work. The family is now seen as a smaller, leaner, even residual unit, whose tasks have lessened (Croll, Kane, & Davin, 1985).

Women and men remain in the labor force throughout their working lives. Educated women have made inroads into demanding professional, administrative, and skilled manual occupations, although assignments are gendered and males and females work in different sectors (Ngo, 2000). With the market reforms, successful professional and skilled workers increasingly earn high incomes, rewarding women for remaining on the job (Meng & Kidd, 1997).

Women take on the primary responsibility for child rearing and other caring roles. While they downplay their careers when it conflicts with their families, institutional and personal support systems help ease balancing simultaneous careers and work family roles (Moen & Yu, 1999; Zhan & Montgomery, 2003). Chinese family policy helps parents combine public and private roles. The city and the largest state work units operate day care and nursery school places. Although there are institutional shortages, there are adequate places for professional dual-career families. Moreover, with flexible hours, parents can use around-the-clock services.

Mutual obligations between family members also provide social capital to ease the meshing of work–family systems. These norms are traced back to the patrilineal Chinese family. Respect for broad family obligations continues but is more mutual and negotiated today, giving family members a range of social supporters (Whyte & Parish, 1984). Each generation expects to benefit in the long run from mutual assistance (Yang, 1996). The elder generation wants to help professional sons and daughters, substantial earners in the family, meet their work responsibilities. The professional wife's job earning potential is worth more than the time she might spend at household and other reproductive chores. At the same time, children are the whole family's responsibility (Chen, Short, & Entwisle, 2000).

Many parents of our elite couples were themselves professionals who worked in the urban state sector and retired early while still in good health. With small families themselves, grandparents are not overwhelmed with care requests. Coresidence also contributes to shared reproductive tasks. There was no private housing market until the mid-1980s, and housing, provided by their work unit, was in short supply (Walder, 1986). Couples delayed marriage until they had an apartment or accepted living with the older generation, who often had better housing than the younger generation. The seniors first give young mothers childcare help; later, they receive personal care (Zhan & Montgomery, 2003). As a result, in the 1980s, an estimated 25% of younger parents lived together with their own parents (Chen et al., 2000; Davis, 1993).

In these ways, features of the wider context ease reciprocal care between generations. If proximity, social norms, and structures underlay the social exchanges between female generations, how do transnational migrants get the help they need to work from kin?

Work–family roles in Canada

North Americans integrate their work and family life courses in diverse patterns. Women go in and out of school and paid work at different times (Gerson, 1985; Giele, 1998:234–5; Partridge, in press). Jones, Marsden, and Tepperman (1990) point out that Canadian women adapt to paid work by individualizing their life patterns, including an increasingly fluid movement between adult statuses in domestic work, full-time and part-time work, and education.

North American working class women finish school, start their careers, marry and bear children, then leave the labor force to cope with household burdens (Sanchez & Thomson, 1997). In 1995, one third of Canadian women did not work when their children were infants. Other working mothers look to kin or neighbors for help or take alternate shifts to care for their children (Deutsch, 1999). Immigrants may have split households, in which the mother works in North America while the children live with their kin in the home country, sometimes until they are teenagers (Hondagneu-Sotelo & Avila, 1997; Parrenas, 2001).

Earlier cohorts of educated women returned to work after their children were older, often in new careers (Ginzberg, 1967). Professionally trained women today postpone having children until finishing their training. They may then stay in the labor force, finding other caregivers, paying for nannies, often new immigrants of color, work part time, or telework (Parrenas, 2001).

Lack of state commitment to childcare facilities contributes to this fluidity. Due to the incoherent and costly early childhood education system, Canadian childcare has become largely the private responsibility of parents (Doherty, Rose, Friendly, Lero, & Hope, 1995; Vanier Institute of the Family, 2000). Parents engage in considerable private strategizing in order to combine professional work and family roles (Hochschild, 1990). Much of this is the work of women.

Methods

To understand how they reconnect social networks to do their employment and family roles, we studied 50 dual-career couples from China over time. We contacted approximately half of our sample through a large NGO immigration agency in Toronto. The other half was composed of "snowball" contacts, introduced by the original sample. While our small sample cannot represent the many Chinese immigrants in Toronto, our respondents are typical of emigrants from China's urban centers (Liang, 2001; Statistics Canada, 2001). With dependents to support, all needed to earn money immediately. We excluded those that originally came on student visas and investment immigrants who do not immediately enter the labor force.

They averaged 35 years of age at immigration, most with BA degrees or higher. Two thirds have careers in engineering, medicine, accountancy, and computer science. Men, somewhat better educated, were concentrated in engineering and computer fields. Women were also well trained and working in careers in accounting, computer, engineer, humanities, and medicine.

In China, these parents had only a single child, as dictated to the urban elite; had a second child while living outside China. Over half the parents, children 10 and under, have to find childcare in order to work.

We interviewed couples in their native language. In the first 3-hours session, we gathered material on the husband's and wife's work, family histories, other personal experiences, and their social networks. Follow-up interviews and phone calls brought us up-to-date on these topics. We translated the taped interviews and analyzed them for themes, using N-Vivo, a qualitative software package. The text draws on our latest information for the respondents, unless otherwise noted. We maintained contact with nearly all of them through December 2002 and continued to correspond with many through December 2003. In this paper, we quote directly from their comments, giving them pseudonyms and adding their gender in brackets after the comments.

Work–family roles in China and Canada

Social support for work–family roles in China

These parents met their range of childcare needs through complex patterns of family obligations and institutional care in China. If their elders are available, the young couples initially turn to them. Seventy-one percent of the couples received substantial childcare help from their seniors. Grandparents might take over the entire childcare burden to help their children build their professional careers. A recognized career advancement. Their child stayed behind with its grandparents.

Housing and childcare

Complex arrangements to get this help begin before marriage and included moving in with their parents. Parents might prefer more authority over their children, but few had the time or the skills.

Ying Ying (F), a computer scientist, married to Chen Hung, an architect, relied considerably on her kin because of their international moves.

> My husband's working unit was going to assign apartments, so we got married. But even after we had the baby, we hadn't got the apartment yet. My father-in-law held a senior position, so he had a large apartment, and we lived with them. It was close to my work place. Later my working unit assigned me an apartment, but we didn't move there [so as not to lose their parents' help]. We lent it to my colleague.

Getting help for further study

The help received went well beyond occasional babysitting. Although they finished their basic training before marriage, several returned to school for postgraduate studies. Wives' increased dual burden brought several family members into play.

Cheng Li (M) was a metallurgical engineer whose parents were retired teachers. First an engineer in a large public metal works, he transferred to a trading firm in charge of technical products. When the firm went downhill, Cheng Li returned to school for an MSc in another city. Throughout, his wife, Xing Ying, who worked as an administrative assistant, remained in her in-law's home to get help with family. Her own mother, a retired factory worker, was ill and could not care for grandchildren. Xing Ying explained: "We could have gotten our own flat if we wanted (from the enterprise). But how could I take care of my baby on my own? I needed the help of my mother-in-law." Xing Ying's mother-in-law continued to care for the little girl in China for 2 years after the couple moved to Canada. With her burden reduced, Xing Ying became a student and reoriented her career.

Studying abroad created even more demands on their kin. When his son was 4 years old, Chen Hung (M) won a coveted job in the Office of the Japanese architecture branch where he worked. His wife Ying Ying visited for a year, leaving their son in Beijing. Unable to find work in Tokyo, she returned to Beijing. A year later, she went to Holland to take an MSc in Computer Sciences. The whole family reunited in Toronto several years later. Throughout the couple's overseas sojourns, Chen Hung's mother cared for her grandson.

Some coordinated their housing, further studies, and child bearing plans in an all-round support system. Liuma (F), a doctor married to Zhu Ji, an electrical engineer, lived with Liuma's parents after marriage, until Liuma's father, a plant director, arranged a nearby apartment for them. When Liuma had a son, she moved back to her parents' home, hired a babysitter, and her mother also helped after work. Liuma's family continued their help for a year after the couple immigrated to Canada and could get on their feet. She recalled, "I never felt the burden of raising a child!"

Multiplexity

Our couples could rarely designate one grandparent to take responsibility throughout the child's early years. Grandmothers have their own life course and it was not always possible to meet patrilineal goals. As a result, most combined helpers from either side, or both, at different times. The main caregiver was usually a grandparent, the second a grandparent on the other side, or a servant. Arrangements were flexible. If they sent their child to nursery school, they might use fewer helpers. If they delayed school until kindergarten, they drew on more helpers. Of the 32 parents that gave help to their grandchildren, two thirds were the wife's parents.

For example, QuPing (F), with a BA in social science, and her husband, Hu, a computer scientist, grew up in Beijing, and got good private firm jobs in Shenzhen. After their son was born, Hu's mother came to care for the baby. At the same time, she brought her youngest son, a recent graduate, to look for a job in Shenzhen with Hu's help. When QuPing's son was 2 1/2 years old, he was sent to Beijing, where QuPing thought schools were better, and lived with QuPing's parents. But the boy could not adjust to the nursery school routine and returned to Shenzhen. QuPing took care of him, sent him to school in the morning, and fetched him after work. Servants were hard to find, and QuPing was afraid of bringing a stranger into her home. The many services available made it easy for QuPing to handle her household responsibilities after her child returned from school. "There wasn't so much household work to do, so I could handle it. When we returned home late, we could easily find a place to grab a bite."

Wei Li (F) and her husband Jigan (M) likewise used a number of helpers, mainly arranged through the wife's kin. Jigan grew up in Hangzhou and went to a university in Jilin province where he met Wei Li, who was born in Jilin. Wei Li took a government job in Beijing and worked up to the position of vice-director of the division of a ministry. From that position, she helped Jigan get his first job in a research institute. Now, they were some distance from both their parents. The couple married and when they had a daughter, complex childcare arrangements began.

1988–Wei Li gave birth to her daughter in Hangzhou. Jigan's mother helped care for her.

mid-1988–Wei Li and her child returned to Beijing. She took a further half-year leave to care for the child.

1989–Wei Li returned to her government job. Her daughter went to Hangzhou to stay with her paternal grandparents.
1990–Daughter returned to Beijing for nursery school. Wei Li and Jigan took turns sending and fetching her. Jigan recalled: "I stayed at the state-owned research enterprise for five and a half years and took very good care of my daughter. Sometimes I skipped work and was often late. At state-owned enterprises, you make less money but you have a lot more free time."
1992–Daughter was sent to Hangzhou for primary school.
1993–Jigan went to work at a foreign company. The couple moved into a larger apartment. Jigan's mother moved to Beijing and lived with them and took care of her granddaughter for half a year.
1993 to 1998–Live-in servants cared for the child.

Jigan recalled,

> We changed several babysitters. Wei Li's relatives introduced three helpers, including my wife's niece. We paid her, but she didn't work much; she was lazy at our place. My wife ended up doing a lot of housework. Luckily, the other two babysitters from Jilin did a lot of work. So for five years, I never bought groceries or cooked. My wife seldom did any work, either.

In these ways, their wider kin and a range of helpers backed the career moves of these young parents.

Caring for their own children

Nine percent of our couples, primarily those with no elders available, took primary responsibility for their child. The amount of time they spent on the job was central to how they combined work and family roles. When both spouses held state sector posts, they often had a more relaxed schedule. In contrast, professional mothers who worked long hours could not squeeze in much childcare. Conditions in the private sector were especially demanding.

For instance, Hung's (F) son was born during her light teaching stint in a Communist Party College, and flexible job freed her to care for her child for a year. When her son turned 2, Hung's mother had retired from her factory job and helped look after her grandson. When, by the third year, he was old enough for nursery school, Hung and her husband shared responsibility for dropping him off and picking him up.

Many private sector and some state jobs required long hours or travel. Xu Fang (F) and her husband helped manage a branch of Xu Fang's family's private paint products firm. She "... didn't have Saturday or Sunday free, every day was busy." She hired two people to take care of him.

Scaling back

With overall responsibility for their children, despite the help of others, many women altered their professional goals. Some wives deliberately slowed their careers, taking jobs that did not demand long hours and travel or transferred to more flexible jobs to care for their children. Reluctant to leave the stable state sector, fewer moved over to private sector jobs. For instance, a couple, both engineers, grew up in large peasant households and met when both were assigned to the same factory in Beijing, far from their families. The wife recalled,

> Both of us needed to work and no one helped us to take care of our child, so I shifted to teach in a secondary technical school. Because there were winter and summer holidays, it was more convenient for me to look after a child. I didn't totally give up my major, but used it just in a supplementary way.

Education was another example. Had further training after they had married, including all the PhDs (four men, one woman). While their husbands returned to school, wives maintained the family, enabling their husbands to have both a family and career. Nevertheless, wives still continued their careers.

Wives quit their formal employment entirely and cared for their children, in only three cases. However, working from home, they continued to use their professional skills in the private market. For instance, one woman quit her engineering job when one of her twin sons fell and broke his arm. She traded stocks from home, while caring for her toddlers.

Institutional care

A minority of our respondents that used state day care facilities for very young infants and toddlers did so when there were no kin available.

Lei Min (F), a pediatrician who came from Szechuan, lived in Beijing. She recalled her long hours and the difficulties of balancing demands. "In China, I was so tired. When I had seriously ill patients, I couldn't go home for days until their babies were out of danger. My husband took care of home and the child, when he was available. His parents were busy and couldn't help us. Once, when I picked my daughter up from the kindergarten, she was the last one left. She was crying. Sometimes I asked my neighbor to pick her up."

Part of women's mothering roles of bridging work and family was ensuring their child had a supportive home environment. School was often strict, instilling moral training, and requiring much independence. Parents wanted their children to have intimacy and personal care. Moreover, they did not want to deny the older generation the chance to care for a grandchild. Hence, most placed their children in formal childcare institutions only after they were 3 or older.

Institutional care lacked the flexibility of grandparental care and the contrast was hard to bridge. However, it was possible to use formal day care for short-term needs to fill the breach. When their kin were ill or when both parents' jobs suddenly required them to travel, some turned to crèches as their last minute support system.

After maternity leave of 4 months, Ye He stopped breastfeeding and went to work. She left her daughter to her mother-in-law's care. After work, she fetched her daughter home. It was tiring for her because the little girl awoke at night. At age 3, Ye He's daughter went to a kindergarten near mother's home. It was difficult for the first several days because her daughter had been used to her grandmother's ways. The child would cry and He had to bring her back home early. Eventually, Ye He's mother decided to take her granddaughter to the kindergarten herself.

Few women were on their own caring for their children. The majority drew on their social capital. They expected to work, and their kin expected to help them work as a boost to the family earnings and future. Most got help from their personal relations or others connected through them. Past that, they could draw on the state-run crèches for childcare. By supplementing kin support with their own work and scaling back on their demanding jobs, they carried work and family responsibilities first sequentially, then simultaneously.

Social support for work–family roles in Canada

From positions of relative gender equality, where they were embedded in structures that backed their careers and family roles, wives have trouble gaining professional acknowledgment abroad. They have to get Canadian professional certification, which in several cases entails doing most of the education they have over again. They also bear much of the family responsibilities. No longer in a sequential stage as in China, if they have young children to care for, they have heavy simultaneous roles. Although their kin relations are far away, building supportive social networks for their reproductive roles is central to their career edifice, and it is their double burden.

Their experiences as new immigrants in Canada

Foreign-earned credentials are rarely recognized by Canadian organizations. Few immigrants locate well-paying jobs, and most revise their career goals (Basran & Zong, 1998; Salaff, Greve, & Xu, 2002; Spitze, 1984). Eighty-four of our 100 respondents have experienced downward mobility compared to their position in China.

With their professional credentials and experiences unrecognized, they need to retrain. Their choice is dyadic, both parents' skills need upgrading, both are responsible for their child and need to combine their household resources. Couples decide whether both should try to break into the labor force at the same time, each carrying simultaneous roles, caring for their children, working, and retraining. Or should they negotiate a sequential life course—going to school full time, finding alternative care for their child, then getting a suitable job?

By engaging in sequential roles in turn, one spouse works full time even at a minimal wage job to support the family, while the other returns to school to upgrade the credentials needed to adapt to the local labor market. They then switch. When the wife's English proficiency is better than her husband's and the job she seeks does not need long-term reaccreditation, she may be the first to try. If her English is worse and she has trouble fitting her technical and professional job experiences into the acceptable Canadian jobs for women, she waits. Most working parents compromise. Scale back, reducing their goals, changing jobs slowly, finding help where they can, and building new relationships in Canada—turning acquaintances into multiplex relations (Hochschild, 1990).

For instance, Jun (F), a dedicated manager and computer programmer in a private company, lived with her husband's parents and even with their help, she lessened her work in a fast-paced field. She admitted,

> After the baby was born, I changed a lot. Before, I worked like crazy, but now it seems I don't care about it much. Work is not the focus of my life, taking care of the baby and the family is the focus, instead. And it's very demanding.

After moving to Canada, she quickly found a computer programmer's job. No longer under her in-law's thumb, Jun was happy to take on more parenting. However, she has even less time to spend with her son than in China. Because her job earns more than her husband's, he scaled back his career goals. They work their shifts to care for their child. Her husband Tang works 3 days on, and 3 days off duty to help with childcare. In emergencies, they use the help of their neighbor QuPing, a former classmate in China, and one of our respondents. Tang: "I think the public day care environment is best for my son. What we're concerned with most is illness spreads fast. He has been sick three or four times so far."

Q: Then how do you deal with it when he's sick?

Tang: If I'm off, I'll take care of him. If I'm not, my wife will ask for leave from work to take care of him. Once both of us couldn't make it, we asked QuPing to take care of him.

Jun explained that her husband has delayed changing his job,

> [Now] his salary and his working time fit [our family needs]. For example, our baby was sick for a long time. In China, his grandma took care of him. Now, I have to do it on my own. It's so hard. I asked for leave for enough days so my husband could change his shift with somebody else so that he could stay at home and take care of the baby. That's very convenient. So for now, if our parents can't come to help us, it's good that he stays in that company.

A year later, their child had adjusted to day care, and Tang could seek a more demanding job.

Most commonly, the wife's career is placed second. Without a way to care for a child, longer to go to upgrade her degree, wives are more likely to work at low-paying jobs. They shape their job search around their responsibilities to the home and hence their child's age figures in couples' plans. To suit their family roles, those with young children take short-term, English as a Second Language (ESL) courses (a non-degree program) while their children are at school. Short-term accounting courses improve their skills and get them entry-level jobs. By going to school part time, women combine homemaking, reproductive labor, and job preparation.

Lian (F), a former accountant, weaves her ESL study with her son's primary school hours:

> How many hours do I study at school? Everyday I send my son to school at 8:30, then I go to my school from 9:15 am till 2:45 pm. When I get home, I study 10–20 minutes, then I go to pick up my son.

Developing new supports

Those with young children share their childcare responsibilities with kin, friends, and neighbors. Migration has not severed their family relations (Boyd, 1989), and kin are the most important support for those that are upgrading their skills. Just under half had children who were born since 1993 (and are under age 10 at time of writing). Of these, 63% receive care for their children from kin, a proportion close to that in China. The child's grandparents immigrate or apply for shorter-term visitors' visas to help. Parents send infants and toddlers back to China to be reared by their grandparents. Parents plan for the children to remain in China for the 2 years they need to take courses to recertify in professional fields, fetching the youngster back in time to enroll in primary school in Toronto.

In the following two cases, parents depended on their kin to retool. In the first case, both spouses recredentialed at the same professional level they had enjoyed in China. In the next case, however, the wife gave up the quest to continue her profession.

After working for Xu Fang's (F) parents' chemical firm, Xu Fang and Bofu (M) immigrated to Toronto. They took turns recertifying. Bofu first took a low-waged job, while Xu Fang took short-term accounting courses in a local college. Then, Xu Fang got a junior accounting job in a Chinese firm while her husband took a short computer course. During the time that each spelled the other, one earning money while the other taking community college courses and caring for their toddler, neither got well-paid jobs. Finally, the couple enrolled in graduate school to get fully requalified. Bofu brought their 2-year-old son to China to be cared for by Xu Fang's parents until they reestablished their careers. Xu Fang complained:

> We don't have a strong economic base. If you ask someone to help you care for your child, you halve your income. If you ask me what's the most difficult part being here, it's that we've brought our child. Because of this child, we wasted half a year. I feel if I had gone to that school earlier, I could have found a job very soon. I think in your research, [you should point out that] this is the main difficulty. We wasted the time because of the child.

During their first summer in graduate school, Xu Fang's parents and elder brother visited them, bringing their son along. When they saw how both were busy studying, they brought the lad back to China with them. Upon graduation, Xu Fang attained a good accountant's job in a bank. Bofu returned to China to start his own business; the son remains there with him. They will be reunited when the family economy is stronger.

Jun (F) graduated from a leading Shanghai University, majoring in Obs/Gyn, and after graduation, worked as an ophthalmologist in a hospital attached to her university, qualifying by studying on her own. She passed several written English tests for her professional title but seldom practiced English. Although Tang, her husband, was a proprietor of a computer company, Jun did not like to depend on him. She travelled 4 h by public transportation every day to work, and her salary was not even enough for her daughter's expenses. Tang's mother cared for their small child. After landing in Canada, Jun could not find a job. She took care of her daughter herself for 6 months. Then, Tang's parents arrived to stay with them and took over the Jun studied ESL for one year, moving on to electrocardiogram at a career college which gave her work–study experience in Chinese medical clinics. After graduation, she remained in a Chinese clinic which needed a person with an optical background. She accepts the low $12 CAD an hour wage because she can remain in the medical field. The clinic wants her to start working full time, but Tang told us, "I want her to have time to take care of our daughter, and working full time won't bring in a lot more income, just more tax."

On the days that Jun works, Tang sends their daughter to kindergarten, their neighbor whose daughter is in the same class picks her up and she stays there until Tang is off work and fetches her. In exchange, Jun helps the neighbor with their daughter when she is not working.

They also mobilize friends for backup care. Former colleagues have an established base for trust. They meet others, in their course of every day life, who are embedded in similar networks and share a common background, which conveys cultural similarity. These form the new multiplex networks.

Wei Yang (F) has her new roommate as backup support for her 10-year-old daughter. Although in China she was a major in Chinese literature and former Vice-Principal of a high school, Wei Yang cannot get a similar job in Canada. Her husband is an "astronaut" who manages his computer sales business in Beijing. He visits several times a year, leaving childcare entirely to the wife. A virtual sole parent, Wei Yang is reluctant to return to school or take a demanding full-time job. She first tutored her daughter and other youngsters part time in Chinese, as a service to the Chinese community. She next sold products part time in a multilevel marketing position. Wei Yang finally found full-time work at a Chinese job agency, as a receptionist. Her daughter, now used to Toronto, walks to the nearby primary school on her own. Wei Yang's family sublets a room of a 2-bedroom high-rise flat from another Chinese immigrant woman, with a daughter of the same age. Her roommate watches out for Wei Yang's child after school. Unlikely to regain a supervisory position at the level she had left in China, Wei Yang works with what is available in a Chinese environment, turning to sales and service work in the Chinese community. She finds social capital from her Chinese roommate: at age 10, her child does not need a lot of care, and her roommate helps out when needed.

Ying Ying (F) took up an invitation to live temporarily at a friend's that turned into a longer-term responsibility.

> Our first summer in Toronto, my husband's friend—whose wife was still in China—invited us to stay at their place (we had just arrived and had no place to live). After a few days, their son got chicken pox. My son got it, too. So the whole summer I was busy taking care of the two boys.

Although it is part of their social capital, they cannot turn to friends for the even longer-term support needed to return to school to requalify for professional positions. In this manner, neighbors stand in for each other and become social capital. Many negotiate exchanges with neighbors for routine help, such as when women with a neighbor with the same age toddler share childcare. Neighbors are also likely to give emergency help. But there are limits to what friends and neighbors can and are willing to do on a long-term basis.

Children's roles

Children play a role in the family restructuring as well. Some parents send their child to be cared for by its grandparents. Others give up the hope for a professional job for reinvented motherhood. In the end, their children grow up quickly and help the parents.

No longer part of an on-site three-generational household, without additional family help, mothers bear considerable household burdens (Clarkberg & Moen, 2001). Parents demand a lot from their children, justifying coming abroad as a benefit for the youngsters. Their children take on an immigration burden, becoming independent, working hard, and assuming the reason for having left China. Children care for themselves and the family more than they had done in China. Teenagers get their first part-time jobs and they help out in the family business. They study hard, and several parents proudly informed us that their child had gotten into the gifted primary school program. Older children were accepted into universities with scholarships.

A few examples show how children manage on their own. Wei Yang's (F) younger daughter goes to the neighborhood school on her own. Ying Ying's (F) teenage son makes his own lunch in the microwave. On his summer holiday from his computer engineering studies, Jiang Jing's (M) son works in a factory and fills in the family store in the evenings.

> Q: You work at the same shift as your husband, so what about your daughter?
>
> Lei Min (F; with demonstrable pride): We prepare dinner for her and bring our dinner to work. She can take care of herself. She's very independent. My husband said he didn't shed a sad tear over the hard life here, but when I told him that she got second in her class during the first semester although her English was still not so good, his happy tears mixed with the sweat of his laboring job.

When Lei Min opened a hostel for new immigrants in her home, her 14-year-old daughter spent the summer greeting guests.

Intensifying family roles

Some women find new family roles. In contrast to China, where bearing a second child was politically damaging for those with high standing, in Canada, two children are "natural." Six of the couples had a second child in Canada. Nearly all with a second child had first borne a daughter.

Hen Rong (F), a former accountant in China, became a textile laborer in Toronto. Becoming pregnant, her kin and friends pressured the couple to give birth to the second child. "This is your last chance," her mother admonished her pregnant daughter. Her mother had cared for the couple's eldest daughter, and the couple sponsored her to immigrate. The older woman beamed as she toted the baby boy around.

A former pharmacist, now a sales clerk, justified her second pregnancy by what she saw around her,

> "We see Canadians around us having a child, and so decided it was natural."

Unable to resume her profession, she finds a new role in intensified motherhood. Her church members celebrated the pregnancy with showers and gifts.

The second child not only meets a long cherished value of bearing a son for the family. The newborn turns an aborted career, with a confusing prognosis, into the respected career of motherhood. None of the new mothers reestablished their careers. Without childcare support in the new location, gender roles may become entrenched (Lee, Chan, Bradby, & Green, 2002; Willis & Yeoh, 2000).

Discussion

Transnational migration affects women and men in gender-specific ways and places a heavier load of responsibility on women's shoulders. This occurs both in the home and in the host countries, but migration makes this integration work difficult. Women assume more work because they undertake the meshing of work and family systems. Taken-for-granted work institutions, retirement schemes, and formal and informal childcare are rarely well integrated. When they do not easily come together, women's personal actions make these arrangements run in an expected manner. Women must organize support that requires creative reorganization of their social capital, under the new conditions.

Because work and family institutions are organized differently in every country, when catapulted into the new social system, new immigrants' experiences conflict in timing of work and family life courses. In China, professionals completed training before bearing and rearing children, following the sequential life course model. Most drew on multiplex ties to make work–family obligations function while they built their careers. They also obtained public institutional support for childcare, thus lessening the many activities they had to do simultaneously.

Arriving as professionals in Canada, where their qualifications are not recognized, with small children to care for and a household to run, they have heavy burdens. They must both requalify and mobilize support for their family roles at the same time. The formal and informal institutions, personally constructed arrangements that provide childcare support, differ from those in China. When the social arrangements in Canada do not match their needs, women either leave the labor force or call on previous agreements, turning to their multiplex arrangements. They may bring their parents to Canada or send their children to China. For many, social capital is transnational.

Transnational motherhood is not limited to the working-class poor but also is known by middle-class, highly educated Chinese. Professional, career-oriented Chinese immigrants command a future promise of good resources and earnings for their wider families if they get support. They bring their mothers and mothers-in-law or send their children back to China. For some women, this support lets them reconstitute their careers. Others suffer considerable downward professional mobility. Transnational social capital facilitates but does not guarantee a rejuvenated career.

Work–family role conflicts are public issues needing institutional solutions, but few countries define them this way (Folbre, 2001; Mills, 1957). Societies rarely acknowledge the informal work that people do to mesh institutional structures. People draw on personal relations to resolve inconsistent demands. The plight of international migrants outlines the problems encountered in using personal solutions to meet public issues.

Acknowledgements

We acknowledge gratefully the support of the "migration from China" project by The Social Sciences and Humanities Council of Canada. Several centres provided generous homes for our research team. The Centre for Urban and Community Studies, University of Toronto, The Centre for Asian Studies, The University of Hong Kong provided us with helpful support. We wish to thank Stephanie Tang and staff of the CICS for their unstinting help, the many people who generously shared their views and experiences with us. Lynn Xu, Su Zhang, Yan Liu, Ada Choi, Tracy Kennedy, He Huang, and Heather Jiang supplied talented research assistance for this paper. Eleonore Kofman, Evie Tastsoglou, and an anonymous reader for Women's Studies International Forum gave helpful suggestions.

References

Aldrich, Howard E., Elam, Amanda B., & Reese, Pat R. (1997). Strong ties, weak ties, and strangers: Do women owners differ from men in their use of networking to obtain assistance? In Sue MacMillan, & Ian C. MacMillan (Eds.), *Entrepreneurship in a global context* (pp. 1–25). London: Routledge.

Basran, Gurcharn S., & Zong, Li (1998). Devaluation of foreign credentials as perceived by visible minority professional immigrants. *Canadian Ethnic Studies*, *30*(3), 7–23.

Bian, Yanjie (1994). *Work and inequality in urban China*. New York: State University of New York Press.

Boyd, Monica (1989). Family and personal networks in international migration: Recent developments and new agendas. *International Migration Review*, *23*, 638–670.

Buchmann, Marlis, & Charles, Maria (1995). Organizational and institutional in the process of gender stratification: Comparing social arrangements in six European countries. *International Journal of Sociology*, *25*, 66–95.

Burt, Ronald S. (1992). *Structural holes*. Cambridge, MA: Harvard University Press.

Castells, Manuel (1989). *The informational city*. Oxford, UK: Blackwell.

Chen, Feinian, Short, Susan E., & Entwisle, Barbara (2000). The impact of grandparental proximity on maternal childcare in China. *Population Research and Policy Review*, *19*, 571–590.

Clarkberg, Marin, & Moen, Phyllis (2001). Understanding the time-squeeze: Married couples' preferred and actual work-hour strategies. *American Behavioral Scientist*, *44*, 1115–1136.

Clausen, John A. (1986). *The life course, a sociological perspective*. Englewood Cliffs, NJ: Prentice Hall.

Elisabeth Croll, Penny Kane, & Delia Davin (Eds.) (1985). *China's one child family policy*. London: Macmillan.

Davis, Deborah (1993). Financial security of urban retirees. *Journal of Cross-cultural Gerontology*, *8*, 179–195.

Delechat, Corinne (2001). International migration dynamics: The role of experience and social networks. *Labour*, *15*, 457–486.

Deutsch, Francine M. (1999). *Halving it all: How equally shared parenting works*. Cambridge, MA: Harvard University Press.

Doherty, Gillian, Rose, Ruth, Friendly, Martha, Lero, Donna, & Hope, Sharon (1995). *Childcare: Canada can't work without it*. Toronto, Canada: Irwin.

Folbre, Nancy (2001). *The invisible heart: Economics and family values*. New York: The New Press.

Gerson, Kathleen (1985). *Hard choices: How women decide about work, career, and motherhood*. Berkeley, CA: University of California Press.

Giele, Janet Z. (1998). Innovation in the typical life course. In Glen H. Elder, & Janet Giele (Eds.), *Methods of life course research: Qualitative and quantitative approaches* (pp. 231–263). Thousand Oaks, CA: Sage Publications.

Ginzberg, Eli (1967). *Life styles of educated women*. New York: Columbia University Press.

Gold, Steven J. (2001). Gender, class, and network: Social structure and migration patterns among transnational Israelis. *Global Networks*, *1*, 57–78.

Granovetter, Mark (1985). Economic action and social structure: The problem of embeddedness. *American Journal of Sociology*, *91*, 481–510.

Walter R., Heinz, Helga Kruger, & Anil Verma (Eds.) (2001). *Restructuring work and the life course*. Toronto, Canada: University of Toronto Press.

Hochschild, Arlie R. (1990). *The second shift*. New York: Avon.

Hondagneu-Sotelo, Pierrette, & Avila, Ernestine (1997). "I'm here, but I'm there": The meanings of Latina transnational motherhood. *Gender and Society*, *11*, 548–571.

Ibarra, Herminia (1992). Structural alignments, individual strategies, and managerial action: Elements toward a network theory of getting things done. In Nitin Noria, & Robert G. Eccles (Eds.), *Networks and organizations* (pp. 165–188). Boston, MA: Harvard Business School Press.

Jones, Charles L., Marsden, Lorna, & Tepperman, Lorne (1990). *Lives of their own: The individualization of women's lives*. Toronto, Canada: Oxford University Press.

Kofman, Eleonore (2000). The invisibility of skilled female migrants and gender relations in the studies of skilled migration in Europe. *International Journal of Population Geography*, *6*, 45–59.

Krackhardt, David (1992). The strength of strong ties: The importance of philos in organizations. In Nithin Noria, & Robert G. Eccles (Eds.), *Networks and organizations* (pp. 216–239). Boston, MA: Harvard Business School Press.

Lee, Maggy, Chan, Anita, Bradby, Hannah, & Green, Gill (2002). Chinese migrant women and families in Britain. *Women's Studies International Forum*, *25*, 607–618.

Levitt, Peggy, & Schiller, Nina G. (2003). *Transnational perspectives on migration: Conceptualizing simultaneity*. CMD Working Paper #03-09j The Center for Migration and Migration and Development Working Paper Series. Princeton, NJ: Princeton University.

Liang, Zai (2001). Demography of illicit migration from China: A sending country's perspective. *Sociological Forum*, *16*, 677–701.

Lin, Nan, Ensel, Walter M., & Vaughn, John C. (1981). Social resources and the strength of weak ties: Structural factors in occupational status attainment. *American Sociological Review*, *46*, 393–405.

Man, Guida (1997). Women's work is never done: Social organization of work and the experience of women in middle-class

Hong Kong Chinese immigrant families in Canada. *Advances in Gender Research, vol. 2* (pp. 183–226). Greenwich, CT: JAI Press.

Man, Guida (2002). Globalization and the erosion of the welfare state: Effects on Chinese immigrant women. *Canadian Woman Studies, 21/22*(4/1), 26–32.

Meng, Xin, & Kidd, Michael P. (1997). Labor market reform and the changing structure of wage determination in China's state sector during the 1980s. *Journal of Comparative Economics, 25*, 403–421.

Meyer, Jean-Baptiste (2001). Network approach versus brain drain: Lessons from the diaspora. *International Migration, 39*(5), 91–110.

Mills, C. Wright (1957). *The sociological imagination*. New York: Oxford.

Min, Pyong Gap (1988). *Ethnic business enterprise: Korean small business in Atlanta*. New York: Center for Migration Studies.

Moen, Phyllis, & Firebaugh, Francille M. (1994). Family policies and effective families: A life course perspective. *The International Journal of Sociology and Social Policy, 14*, 29–52.

Moen, Phyllis, & Yu, Yan (1999). Having it all: Overall work/life success in two-earner families. *Research in the Sociology of Work, 7*, 109–139.

Nee, Victor, & Matthews, Rebecca (1996). Market transition and societal transformation in reforming state socialism. *Annual Review of Sociology, 22*, 401–435.

Ngo, Hang-yue (2000). Trends in occupational sex segregation in urban China. Paper delivered at the annual meeting of the NACSA (Washington, DC).

Parrenas, Rhacel Salazar (2001). Mothering from a distance: Emotions, gender, and inter-generational relations in Filipino transnational families. *Feminist Studies, 27*, 361–390.

Partridge, May (in press). Managing the struggle: Career strategies of university-educated women. Toronto: University of Toronto Press.

Pfeffer, Jeffrey (1997). *New directions for organization theory: Problems and perspectives*. New York: Oxford University Press.

Poros, Maritsa V. (2001). The role of migrant networks in linking local labour markets: The case of Asian Indian migration to New York and London. *Global Networks, 1*, 243–259.

Portes, Alejandro (1995). Economic sociology and the sociology of immigration: A conceptual overview. In Alejandro Portes (Ed.), *The economic sociology of immigration: Essays on networks, ethnicity, and entrepreneurship* (pp. 1–41). New York: Russell Sage Foundation.

Portes, Alejandro, & Borocz, Jozsef (1989). Contemporary immigration: Theoretical perspectives on its determinants and modes of incorporation. *International Migration Review, 23*, 606–630.

Preston, Valerie, & Man, Guida (1999). Employment experiences of Chinese immigrant women: An exploration of diversity. *Canadian Woman Studies, 19*(3), 115–122.

Robinson, Joan C. (1985). Of women and washing machines: Employment, housework, and the reproduction of motherhood in socialist China. *The China Quarterly, 101*, 32–57.

Salaff, Janet W., Greve, Arent, & Xu, Lynn (2002). Paths into the economy: Structural barriers and the job hunt for professional PRC migrants in Canada. *International Journal of Human Resource Management, 13*, 450–464.

Sanchez, Laura, & Thomson, Elizabeth (1997). Becoming mothers and fathers: Parenthood, gender, and the division of labor. *Gender and Society, 11*, 747–772.

Sassen, Saskia (1991). *The global city: New York, London, and Tokyo*. Princeton, NJ: Princeton University Press.

Scott, Alison, & Burchell, Brendon (1994). "And never the twain shall meet?" Gender segregation and work histories. In Alison Scott (Ed.), *Gender segregation and social change* (pp. 121–156). Oxford, UK: Oxford University Press.

Spitze, Glenna (1984). The effect of family migration on wives employment: How long does it last? *Social Science Quarterly, 46*, 21–36.

Statistics Canada. (2001). Facts and figures: Immigration overview 2001. Available at http://www.cic.gc.ca./english/pdf/pub/facts2001. pdf (Accessed September 22, 2002).

Stoloff, Jennifer A., Glanville, Jennifer L., & Bienenstock, Elisa J. (1999). Women's participation in the labor force: The role of social networks. *Social Networks, 21*, 91–108.

Vanier Institute of the Family (2000). Profiling Canada's families: II. Ottawa, Ontario, Canada, Available at http://www.vifamily.ca/pubs/p2.htm. (Accessed September 22, 2002).

Walder, Andrew G. (1986). *Communist neo-traditionalism: Work and authority in Chinese industry*. Berkeley, CA: University of California Press.

Wellman, Barry (1992). Men in networks: Private communities, domestic friendships. In Peter Nardi (Ed.), *Men's friendships* (pp. 74–114). Newbury Park, MA: Sage Publications.

Wellman, Barry (1999). The network community: An introduction. In Barry Wellman (Ed.), *Networks in the global village* (pp. 1–47). Boulder, CO: Westview Press.

Whyte, Martin K., & Parish, William L. (1984). *Urban life in contemporary China*. Chicago: The University of Chicago Press.

Willis, Katie, & Yeoh, Brenda (2000). Gender and transnational household strategies: Singaporean migration to China. *Regional Studies, 34*, 253–264.

Wong, Siu-Lun, & Salaff, Janet W. (1998). Network capital: Emigration from Hong Kong. *British Journal of Sociology, 49*, 258–274.

Yang, Hongqiu (1996). The distributive norm of monetary support to older parents: A look at a township in China. *Journal of Marriage and the Family, 58*, 404–414.

Zhan, Heying J., & Montgomery, Rhonda J.V. (2003). Gender and elder care in China: The influence of filial piety and structural constraints. *Gender and Society, 17*, 209–229.

[19]

PHYSICAL REVIEW E **68**, 015101(R) (2003)

Topology of the world trade web

Ma Ángeles Serrano and Marián Boguñá
Departament de Física Fonamental, Universitat de Barcelona, Av. Diagonal 647, 08028 Barcelona, Spain
(Received 2 January 2003; published 11 July 2003)

Economy, and consequently trade, is a fundamental part of human social organization which, until now, has not been studied within the network modeling framework. Here we present the first, to the best of our knowledge, empirical characterization of the world trade web, that is, the network built upon the trade relationships between different countries in the world. This network displays the typical properties of complex networks, namely, scale-free degree distribution, the *small-world* property, a high clustering coefficient, and, in addition, degree-degree correlation between different vertices. All these properties make the world trade web a complex network, which is far from being well described through a classical random network description.

DOI: 10.1103/PhysRevE.68.015101 PACS number(s): 89.75.Hc, 87.23.Ge, 05.70.Ln, 89.65.Gh

The world is facing a challenging era. Social, political, and economic arrangements initiated after the end of the Second World War are now culminating in the recognition of globalization, a process which has been accelerated by the new technological advances. When applied to the international economic order, globalization involves control of capital flow and liberalization of trade. As a consequence, economies around the world are becoming more and more interrelated, in other words, the world is becoming a *global village* [1,2]. In this scenario, trade plays a central role as one of the most important interaction channels between countries [3]. The relevance of the international trade system goes beyond the fundamental exchange of goods and services. For instance, it can also be the channel for crises spreading [4]. A good example is found in the recent Asiatic crisis, which shows how economic perturbations originating in a country can somehow propagate elsewhere in the world [5,6]. Thus, it seems natural to analyze the world trade system at a global level, every country being important, regardless of its size or wealth. Despite the extremely complex nature of the problem, relevant structural information can be extracted from modeling the system as a network, where countries are represented as vertices and trade channels as links between these vertices. In this way, the global trade system can be examined under a topological point of view. This analysis will reveal complex properties that cannot be explained by the classical random graph theory, first studied by Erdös and Rényi [7].

Complex networks have been the subject of an intense research activity over the last years [8,9]. Examples range from metabolic networks, where cell functionality is sustained by the network structure, to technological webs, where topology determines the system's ability to transmit information [10–13]. The term complex network typically refers to networks showing the following properties: (i) scale-free (SF) degree distribution, $P(k) \sim k^{-\gamma}$ with $2 < \gamma \leqslant 3$, where the degree k is defined as the number of edges emanating from a vertex, (ii) the *small-world* property [14], which states that the average path length between any pair of vertices grows logarithmically with the system size; and (iii) a high clustering coefficient, that is, the neighbors of a given vertex are interconnected with high probability. In addition, degree-degree correlation has been recently added to this list since it appears as a common feature in many real-world networked systems [12,15–17]. This correlation accounts for the probability that a vertex of degree k is connected to a vertex of degree k' and is a key issue for the correct description of the hierarchical organization within the network. This correlation is found to be assortative, that is, highly connected vertices tend to attach to other highly connected vertices, in social networks, such as scientific collaboration networks [15]; conversely, the correlation is disassortative in technological networks such as the Internet [12].

Among all the studied networks, the social and technological networks have become the paradigmatic examples of complex networks. Perhaps, the reason lies in the fact that each type exemplifies human activity working at one of two different levels: the cooperative level, where concepts, such as friendship, are dominant, and the competitive level, where the activity is governed by optimization criteria. These two different levels will probably lead to different attachment mechanisms which could be the origin of the assortative or disassortative degree-degree correlation observed in these networks. As an example of social network working at the competitive level, we study the network of trade relationships between different countries in the world, hereafter referred to as the world trade web (WTW). The topological characterization of the WTW is of primary interest for the modeling of crisis propagation at the global level as well as for the understanding of the effects that the new liberalist policies have on the world trade system. Moreover, we shall show that the WTW is a complex network sharing many properties with technological networks.

In order to perform our analysis, we extracted data from aggregated trade statistics tables in the International Trade Center site [19], which are based on the COMTRADE database of the United Nations Statistics Division. These tables contain, for each country, an import and an export list detailing the forty most important exchanged merchandises in the year 2000. Two major trading partners are also reported for each product. If we consider imports as in degrees and exports as out degrees, it is possible to construct a directed network where vertices represent countries and directed links represent the import and export relations between them. The fact that the number of merchandises is bounded is, *a priori*, a limitation for the analysis. However, it is possible to overcome this problem taking advantage of the symmetry between in and out degrees. Let $\tilde{A}_{ij}^{imp}$ and $\tilde{A}_{ij}^{exp}$ be the import by export adjacency matrices calculated from the import and export databases. Each adjacency matrix is defined so that $\tilde{A}_{ij}=1$ if country i imports from or exports to country j and zero otherwise. These matrices account only for a subset out of the total number of actual connections between countries. The import and export connections that are of little relevance for a given country are not considered in matrices $\tilde{A}$, although they may be relevant to the partners as the symmetric export and import links. In fact, import and export definitions can apply to the same trade flow depending on whether origin or destination is considered. This implies that the complete adjacency matrices satisfy the symmetry relation $A_{ij}^{imp}=A_{ji}^{exp}$, which can be used in order to recover missing information from the original matrices. Thus, we can write

$$A_{ij}^{imp}=\frac{1}{1+\delta_{(\tilde{A}_{ij}^{imp}+\tilde{A}_{ji}^{exp}),2}}[\tilde{A}_{ij}^{imp}+\tilde{A}_{ji}^{exp}], \qquad (1)$$

where $\delta_{.,.}$ is the Kronecker delta function. In this way we obtain an adjacency matrix where each connection is relevant, at least, to one of the two involved countries. At this point, it is worth noticing that we consider the unweighted version of the WTW. Since the weight of a link can be different, depending on the import or export point of view, it is unclear how these weights should be assigned. After this symmetrization procedure, we obtain a directed network with 179 vertices representing countries and 7510 directed links representing commercial channels among them. The average degree of this network is $\langle k_{in}\rangle=\langle k_{out}\rangle=30.9$.

The question that first arises refers to the directed nature of the WTW. In fact, the in and the out degrees of a given vertex are random quantities that may be correlated. A complete description should involve the knowledge of the joint probability $p(k_{in},k_{out})$. This function is often difficult to obtain although relevant information can be extracted from the correlation coefficient $r=(\langle k_{in}k_{out}\rangle-\langle k\rangle^2)/\sigma_{in}\sigma_{out}$, where $\sigma_{in}(\sigma_{out})$ are the in (out) standard deviations (notice that $\langle k_{in}\rangle=\langle k_{out}\rangle=\langle k\rangle$). For the WTW this coefficient is $r=0.91$, pointing to a strong similarity in the number of in and out connections. However, not all these connections run in both directions, that is, the fact that country A imports from country B does not necessary imply that country B imports from country A. In order to quantify this effect we compute the reciprocity of the network, defined as the fraction of links pointing simultaneously to both ends of the link. In our case the reciprocity is 0.61. These results suggest that actually the WTW may be thought of as an undirected network without losing relevant topological information (that is, considering all directed edges as undirected). The average degree for this definition of the undirected WTW is $\langle k\rangle\approx 43$. This value is, indeed, very high if we take into account the size of the network, and, apparently, that could distort the analysis. An alternative way to define the undirected WTW is to consider only bidirectional edges. In this case, the average

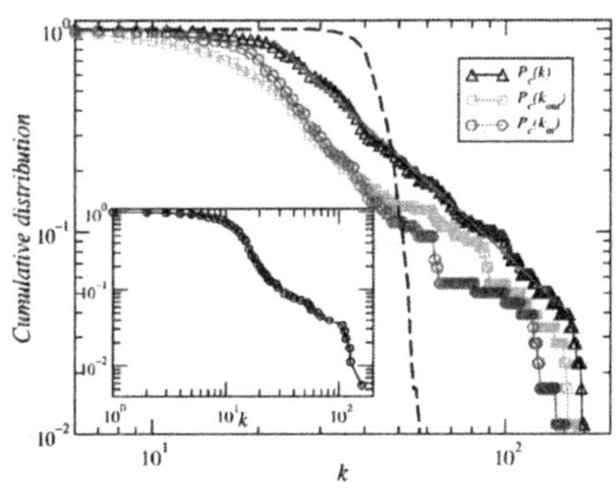

FIG. 1. Cumulative in- and out-degree distributions, $P_c(k_{in})$ and $P_c(k_{out})$, and undirected $P_c(k)$ corresponding to the import and export world trade web. The solid line is a power law fit of the form $P_c(k)\sim k^{\gamma-1}$ with $\gamma=2.6\pm 0.1$. The cumulative distribution of the equivalent random network with the same average degree is also shown. Inset: cumulative distribution for the WTW with reciprocal edges.

degree reduces significantly, $\langle k\rangle\approx 18$, although, as shown in the insets of the figures, the results remain basically unchanged.

One of the most important topological properties of a network is the degree distribution, $P(k)$. This quantity measures the probability of a randomly chosen vertex to have k connections to other vertices. In our case, due to the directed nature of the network, we have to distinguish between in- and out-degree distributions. Figure 1 shows the in, out, and undirected cumulative distributions for the WTW, defined as $P_c(k)\equiv\Sigma_{k'=k}P(k')$. In all cases, the cumulative distribution shows a flat approach to the origin, indicating the presence of a maximum in $P(k)$, at $k\sim 20$, and, in this respect, similar to the Erdös-Rényi network. However, for $k>20$ the cumulative distribution is followed by a power law decay $P_c(k)\sim k^{1-\gamma}$, with $\gamma\approx 2.6$, showing a strong deviation from the exponential tail predicted by the classical random graph theory. The exponent γ is found to be within the range defined by many other complex networks and, thus, we can state that the WTW belongs to the recently identified class of SF networks [8,9]. The SF property implies an extremely high level of degree heterogeneity. Indeed, the second moment of the degree distribution, $\langle k^2\rangle$, diverges in the thermodynamic limit for any SF network.

It may be surprising that the SF region does not extend to the whole degree domain and that, for small values of the degree, the distribution is similar to the Erdös-Rényi network. In fact, the underlying preferential attachment mechanisms [18] could differ depending on the particular political and economic situation of a country. Low-degree countries, most of which turn out to be the poorest, are basically constrained to subsistence trade flows and, therefore, preferential attachment mechanisms could not hold. As expected, there exists a positive correlation between the number of trade channels of a country and its wealth, measured by the per capita Gross Domestic Product (GDP) [19]. This correlation

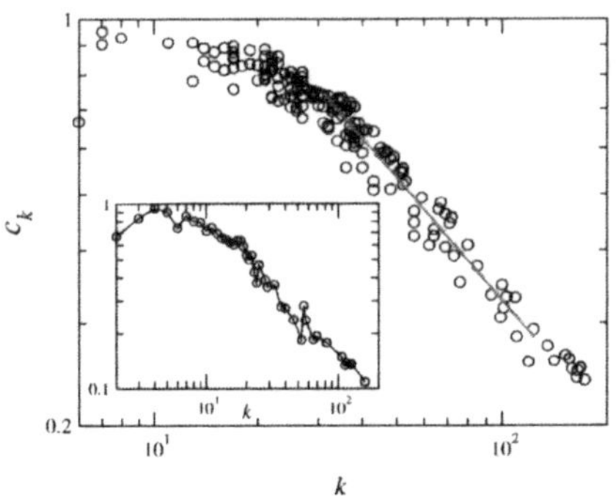

FIG. 2. Clustering coefficient of single countries as a function of their degree for the undirected version of the WTW. The solid line is a power law fit of form $c_k \sim k^{-\omega}$ with $\omega = 0.7 \pm 0.05$. Inset: average clustering coefficient, as a function of the degree, for the WTW with reciprocal edges.

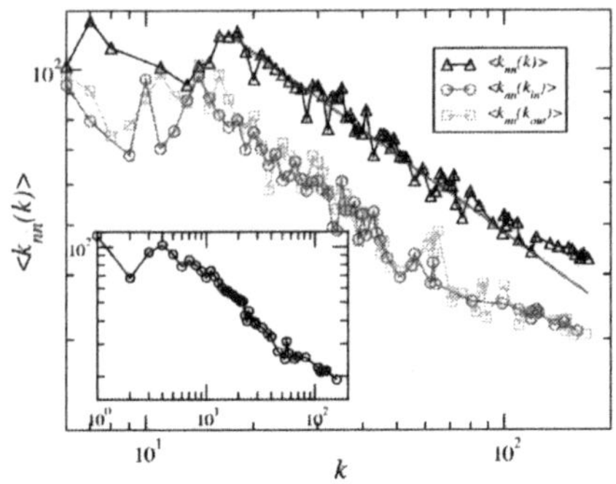

FIG. 3. Average in (out, undirected) nearest neighbors degree as a function of the in (out, undirected) degree of the vertex. The solid line is a fit of the form $\langle k_{nn}(k)\rangle \sim k^{-\nu_k}$ with $\nu_k = 0.5 \pm 0.05$. Inset: the same for the WTW with reciprocal edges.

is found to be high, 0.65, which means that, indeed, most low-connected countries are poor countries—Angola, Somalia, Rwanda, Cambodia . . . —and most high-connected countries are rich countries—the USA, Japan, Germany, and the UK, for example. However, there also exists a significant number of cases in the reversal situation, that is, high per capita GDP countries with a small number of connections and low per capita GDP countries with a large number of trade channels. A germane example for the first circumstance is that of Norway or Iceland, which are among the top ten wealthier countries but only have 56 and 24 trade channels, respectively. For the second case, Brazil, China, or Russia are typical examples.

Thanks to a number of recent studies, it is becoming more and more evident that real networks are not completely random but they are organized according to a hierarchical structure [11,12,17,20]. This hierarchy is usually analyzed by means of the clustering coefficient and the degree-degree correlation. The clustering coefficient of vertex i, of degree k_i, is defined as $c_i \equiv 2n_i/k_i(k_i-1)$, where n_i is the number of neighbors of i that are interconnected. If hierarchy was not present in the system, c_i should be a random quantity independent of any other property. Figure 2 shows the clustering coefficient of the undirected WTW as a function of the vertex's degree. As is clearly seen, this function has a strong dependence on the vertex's degree, with a power law behavior $c_k \sim k^{-\omega}$, with $\omega = 0.7 \pm 0.05$. The clustering coefficient averaged over the whole network is $C = 0.65$, greater by a factor 2.7 than the value corresponding to a random network of the same size.

Hierarchy is also reflected on the degree-degree correlation through the conditional probability $P(k|k')$, which measures the probability of a vertex of degree k' to be linked to a vertex of degree k. Again, this function is difficult to measure due to statistical fluctuations. In order to characterize this correlation, it is more useful to work with the average nearest neighbors degree (ANND), defined as $\langle k_{nn}(k)\rangle \equiv \Sigma_{k'} k' P(k'|k)$ [16]. For uncorrelated networks, this function reads $\langle k_{nn}\rangle = \langle k^2\rangle/\langle k\rangle$, independent of k. However, recent studies have revealed that almost all real networks show degree-degree correlation [12,15] which translates into a k dependence in the ANND. This correlation can be assortative or disassortative depending on whether the ANND is an increasing or decreasing function of the degree. Figure 3 reports the ANND for the directed and undirected versions of the WTW. It can be observed a clear dependency on the vertex's degree, with a power law decay $\langle k_{nn}(k)\rangle \sim k^{-\nu_k}$ with $\nu_k = 0.5 \pm 0.05$. This result means that the WTW is a disassortative network where highly connected vertices tends to connect to poorly connected vertices. This result, together with the scaling law $c_k \sim k^{-\omega}$ reveals a hierarchical architecture of highly interconnected countries that belong to influential areas which, in turn, connect to other influential areas through hubs.

Surprisingly, these results point to a high similarity between the WTW and the Internet. Indeed, the Internet is a SF network, with a critical exponent $\gamma = 2.2$, which is also organized in a hierarchical fashion. The functional behavior found for the clustering coefficient and the ANND is a power law decay as a function of the degree with exponents $\omega_{int} = 0.75$ and $\nu_k = 0.5$ [12], exponents that turn out to be very similar to the ones reported here for the WTW. In some sense, these results are not surprising since both are competitive systems evolving in a quasi free market and, in both cases, there exists, for instance, a geographic limitation that increases the connection costs and thus acts as a constraint in the optimization process of each vertex. Table I presents a summary of the main characteristics of the WTW, the Internet [12], and a random graph of the same size and average degree as the WTW. The average path length, defined as the average of the shortest distances between all pairs of vertices, is $\langle d\rangle = 1.8$, which, in this case, is very similar to the corresponding random network of the same size and average degree.

In conclusion, this first approach to the topology of the

TABLE I. Average degree $\langle k \rangle$, shortest path length $\langle d \rangle$, clustering coefficient C, exponent of degree distribution γ, exponent of clustering, ω, and exponent of the average nearest neighbors degree ν_k, for the world trade web (WTW), the Internet at the autonomous system level, and a random graph (RG) of the same size as the WTW.

	Size	$\langle k \rangle$	$\langle d \rangle$	C	γ	ω	ν_k
WTW	179	43	1.8	0.65	2.6	0.7	0.5
Internet	5287	3.8	3.7	0.24	2.2	0.75	0.5
RG	179	43	1.73	0.24	–	0	0

WTW points out some previously unnoticed features that are of primary importance in the understanding of the new international order. Over the last decades, international trade has grown faster than the world economy as a whole, increasing nation's economic integration. Our research suggests that this evolution is guided by collective phenomena, and that self-organization plays a crucial role in structuring the WTW scale-free inhomogeneities and its hierarchical architecture. These results provide even more evidence that, due to the globalization process supported by the technological advances (which have removed many geographic, economic and technical constraints), the trade system has become a self-organized complex system that must be considered as a whole. It remains an open question if these properties could also be made apparent at other different scales, for instance, in the trade relations between regions, cities, or even individuals. At the country level, the activity is driven by competition. In the same way as it occurs with the Internet, optimization criteria are applied to local decisions made by the individual vertices. The findings in this paper may lead one to consider that there exist underlying mechanisms common to all competitive systems, characterized by disassortative associations, and such mechanisms may differ from the evolutionary processes in social cooperative networks, characterized by assortative associations.

Acknowledgements are due to Romualdo Pastor-Satorras for helpful discussions and advice. This work was partially supported by the European commission FET Open Project No. COSIN IST-2001-33555.

[1] P. Krugman, *The Accidental Theorist, and other Dispatches from the Dismal Science* (Norton, New York, 1998).
[2] S. Amin, *Capitalism in the Age of Globalization: The Management of Contemporary Society* (Zed Books, London, 1997).
[3] B.R. Koka, J.E. Prescott, and R. Madhavan, J. Int. Business Stud. **30**, 127 (1999).
[4] R. Glick and A. Rose, J. Int. Money Fin. **18**, 603 (1999).
[5] M. Noland, L-G Liu, S. Robinson, and Z. Wang, *Global Economics Effects of the Asian Currency Devaluations* (International Institute for Economics, Washington, D.C., 1998).
[6] M. Goldstein, *The Asian Financial Crisis: Causes, Cures and Systemic Implications* (International Institute for Economics, Washington, D.C., 1998).
[7] P. Erdös and P. Rényi, Publ. Math. (Debrecen) **6**, 290-297 (1960); P. Erdös and P. Rényi, Publ. Math. Inst. Hung. Acad. Sci. **5**, 17 (1960).
[8] R. Albert and A.-L. Barabási, Rev. Mod. Phys. **74**, 47 (2002).
[9] S.N. Dorogovtsev and J.F.F. Mendes, Adv. Phys. **51**, 1079 (2002).
[10] H. Jeong, B. Tombor, R. Albert, Z.N. Oltvai, and A.-L. Barabási, Nature (London) **407**, 651 (2000).
[11] E. Ravasz, A.L. Somera, D.A. Mongru, Z.N. Oltvai, and A.-L. Barabási, Science **297**, 1551 (2002).
[12] A. Vázquez, R. Pastor-Satorras, and A. Vespignani, Phys. Rev. E **65**, 066130 (2002).
[13] R. Albert, H. Jeong, and A.-L. Barabási, Nature (London) **401**, 130 (1999).
[14] D.J. Watts and S.H. Strogatz, Nature (London) **393**, 440 (1998).
[15] M.E.J. Newman, Phys. Rev. Lett. **89**, 208701 (2002).
[16] R. Pastor-Satorras, A. Vázquez, and A. Vespignani, Phys. Rev. Lett. **87**, 258701 (2001).
[17] K.-I. Goh, B. Kahng, and D. Kim, Phys. Rev. Lett. **88**, 108701 (2002).
[18] A.-L. Barabási and R. Albert, Science **286**, 509 (1999).
[19] Import and Export databases are publicly avalable at the address http://www.intracen.org/menus/countries.htm and the gross domestic product at http://www.tswoam.co.uk/world
[20] E. Ravasz and A.-L. Barabási, Phys. Rev. E **67**, 026112 (2003).

[20]

World City Networks and Hierarchies, 1977-1997

An Empirical Analysis of Global Air Travel Links

DAVID A. SMITH
University of California, Irvine
MICHAEL F. TIMBERLAKE
Kansas State University

The world's great cities are important nodes in the world economy. Major theorists (Friedman, Sassen, Castells) conceptualize global cities as the command and control centers for contemporary global capitalism. The authors' research offers a view of the global system based on a careful examination of the relations and connections between world cities and how those patterns change over time. Formal network analysis allows the authors to interpret data on flows of airline passengers between the world's great cities for six time points between 1977 and 1997, focusing on the changes in network characteristics (especially centrality hierarchies and clique membership) for the entire global city system. Although New York, Paris, London, Tokyo, and a few other major European and North American metropolises dominate this urban hierarchy throughout the two decades, the network roles and positions of other places shift considerably. The article concludes that research on world city networks once again demonstrates that global urbanization patterns are characterized by the uneven development dynamic anticipated by world-system analysis.

The basic idea of systems of interconnected cities is an old one. Early in the 20th century, some of the theorists associated with the Chicago school of urban sociology offered suggestive sketches of worldwide hierarchies of cities (Gras, 1922; McKenzie, 1927; see Smith, 1995, for a discussion). But it was only in the increasingly interconnected world of the later half of this century, and with explicit grounding in world-system analysis, that fully developed conceptualizations of a global city system emerged (Friedmann & Wolff, 1982; Knox & Taylor, 1995; Sassen, 1991).

Now, as we enter a new millennium, a wide range of commentators claim that the world is experiencing fundamental shifts and restructuring often referred to as *globalization*. As Hargittai and Centeno (2001) explain in the introductory article of this special issue, globalization is a term that is more frequently invoked than explained, and it carries a great deal of definitional uncertainty.

AMERICAN BEHAVIORAL SCIENTIST, Vol. 44 No. 10, June 2001 1656-1678

Rather than delve into the voluminous abstract debates, we will attempt empirically to map the hierarchy of major world cities. Our fundamental premise, quoting Sassen (1998), is that "globalization can be deconstructed in terms of the strategic sites where global processes materialize and the linkages that bind them" (p. 392). A basic assumption of this approach is that global processes are grounded in what geographically situated people do. We also assume that what people are doing often involves relations across space that are constituted by the transport of material goods, the transmission of information, and the movement of the people themselves. Finally, these relations are structured by the historical development of various geographic locales as sites for social interaction, production, reproduction, consumption, and exchange. Furthermore, not only are the world's great cities important nodes in the contemporary global economy, the emergence of centrally positioned global cities in a worldwide dominance hierarchy may be the quintessential weave in the fabric of contemporary globalization.

WORLD CITY NETWORKS AND HIERARCHIES

The pioneering statement on world cities was made by urban planners John Friedmann and Goetz Wolff in 1982. They claimed that world cities are "control centers of the global economy" and share a set of distinct structural characteristics. In a subsequent article, Friedmann (1986) presented a qualitative ranking of key world cities and a figure that schematically maps the linkages between them. His premise is that world cities can be located in a global hierarchy based on their positions in the global geographic nexus of economic power: "World cities can be arranged hierarchically, roughly in accord with the economic power they command. They are cities through which regional, national, and international economies are articulated with the global capitalist system of accumulation" (Friedmann, 1995, pp. 25-26).

Because cities can rise and fall in this hierarchy, it becomes important to recognize "the existence of differences in rank and investigate the articulations of particular world cities with each other" (Friedmann, 1993, p. 5). Friedmann's table listing world cities as either primary or secondary and according to location within the world-system core or semiperiphery is an interesting "first cut" effort to map the world-city system based on the functional importance of the nodes. It has an intuitive appeal (for instance, New York, London, Tokyo, and Los Angeles are among the highest ranking "core primary cities"), but the ranking is ultimately based on the informed opinion of one comparative urban expert rather than on empirical data.

Saskia Sassen's (1991) *The Global City: New York, London and Tokyo* is doubtlessly the most comprehensive explication of the world-city hypothesis. This ambitious treatise combines a global overview, detailed case studies of the three great metropolitan centers, and a synthetic conceptual argument that includes an overview of contemporary globalization processes and the dynamic roles that world cities play in them. She claims that these central nodes both attract and repel: Various functions relating to the command and control of today's world economy concentrate in global cities, even as manufacturing is increasingly dispersed to ever more far-flung regions of the world.

> These cities now function in four new ways: first, as highly concentrated command posts in the organization of the world economy; second, as key locations for finance and specialized service firms, which have replaced manufacturing as the leading economic sectors; third, as sites of production, including the production of innovations, in these leading industries; and fourth, as markets for the products and innovations produced. (pp. 3-4)

There are a number of other case studies that have largely substantiated John Friedmann's notion that there is a distinct category of global or world cities, housing activities and organizations that exert international coordination and control (e.g., King, 1990; Ross & Trachte, 1990; Sassen, 1991). There are also fine examples of more historical comparative case studies of cities, which indicate that we should not assume that situating cities in the global political economy is only useful in the contemporary era (e.g., Feagin, 1988; Feagin & Smith, 1987; Hill & Feagin, 1987; Rodriguez & Feagin, 1986). Recently, in a discussion of European cities, the prominent urban theorist Manuel Castells pulled various strands of the global restructuring/world cities literatures together. Emphasizing the key role of information technology as an underpinning for contemporary globalization, he says, "the national-international business center is the economic engine of the city in the informational global economy" (Castells, 1994, p. 29). Castells's work predicts that dominant global cities will rise to commanding heights by developing the infrastructure that is required to capture the information flows, leading to spatially defined urban hierarchies. The most important implications of this work are that we can better understand urban social structure if we are attentive to how cities are involved in the world economy. Understanding urbanization requires a network-based relational view of how structural similarities among cities and social change within cities are influenced by world-system processes.

Our research follows the lead of Friedmann, Sassen, and other urban political economists who attempted to situate cities in their global contexts. We are convinced that there are great advantages to conceptualizing cities as key nodes in a multilayered network that simultaneously composes the world city system and the core of the command and control system of the entire global economy. But in this particular study, we are not interested in the attributes of particular cases (not even those of such critical ones as New York, Tokyo, or London). Instead, we want to chart the morphology of the entire weblike structure and plot out how it changes over time. To date, only a few quantitative studies have even attempted to identify global hierarchies of cities. Although such studies are suggestive, they are usually based on data measuring the attributes of cities (e.g., population size) rather than using measures of actual relations among cities or between cities and the world economy (e.g., Chase-Dunn, 1985). However, David Meyer's (1986, 1991a, 1991b) work begins to overcome this attributional limitation by examining information having to do with relations among key organizations that are place-bound (in cities). For example, he has studied the distribution of international bank branches linking cities in Latin America to the world's financial centers and each other. Meyer's work suggests that we should study the entire world system of cities, examining many types of important flows among them. This is our strategy.

CONCEPTUALIZING LINKAGES AMONG THE WORLD'S CITIES

Although the most obvious kinds of flows among cities are those of an explicit economic nature, such as commodity flows, it is easy to think of other ways in which cities are connected. Other economic linkages among cities in the human form include flows of labor, sales and producer-services personnel, and managers. When people migrate or immigrate from one city to another to find employment, they represent labor flows. An immigrant from Tijuana to Los Angeles, drawn into the garment industry there, is an example. When a manager travels from corporate headquarters to the site of a branch plant in another city, that represents an economic flow in the human form. The primary material objects linking cities can be traced in the flow of commodities, both in the production process and in the distribution process. Some cities house important value-added processes for commodities that are shipped into the city from other urban locales. Cotton fabric is shipped daily to factories in New York and other cities with garment industries. Other cities house break-of-bulk transportation facilities for moving commodities to smaller cities, where they will be purchased by consumers. Examples of economic flows taking the form of symbolic communication include business-related telecommunications (e.g., telephone calls, faxes, telexes, etc.), mail orders, other business-related mail, and so on. In principle, detailed information measuring different kinds of flows could be used to produce one or more maps of the world system of cities. We now turn to the issue of how we might best use such data to produce such descriptions of the world's city system.

NETWORK ANALYSIS

Both world-system analysis and the literature on global cities rely on network imagery and are filled with allusions to flows, exchanges, nodes, and so on. For example, prominent urbanologists Lo and Yeung (1998) recently described "the functional world city system" in terms of various linkages, claiming that "world cities are at the points of convergence of these networks and thus acquire growing centrality and importance. Network functions are engendered through financial flows, headquarter-branch relations, high-tech service intensity, and telecommunications networks" (p. 10). Although they employ relational imagery, few scholars of global cities attempt to systematically study these types of networks. Most choose instead to focus on case study techniques that describe the ways that particular world cities take on command and control functions within global networks.

Although the leading theorists may be unlikely to turn to high-powered statistical analysis to test their models of global structure and hierarchy, quantitative network analysis is particularly well-suited for this purpose. With appropriate data, this methodology allows us simultaneously to analyze multiple patterns of flows, exchanges, or linkages between cities (or other nodes) in a way that reveals the complex patterning of connections between them as well as the structure of the entire network. It gives researchers a powerful tool to examine global flows of people, commodities, capital, information, and so on. So formal network analysis provides an elegant and rigorous way to operationalize theoretical conceptions about the world economy and the global city system; studies that do so represent a particularly compatible marriage between theory and methodology. Indeed, a number of researchers use network analysis to examine the structure of the world system (Nemeth & Smith, 1985; Sacks, Ventresca, & Uzzi, 2001 [this issue]; Smith & White, 1992; Snyder & Kick, 1979; Steiber, 1979). But, somewhat surprisingly, we alone have used this methodology to map the world-city system.[1]

Network analysis generates measurements of a variety of formal properties of structures and relationships. Two characteristics of networks are of particular interest for studying global city systems. First, the idea of structural or relational equivalence in networks, usually operationalized using various forms of *blockmodeling*, is the most familiar technique in previous network research on the global system. In such research, the goal is to determine which actors (usually nations) fit together into broad groups or blocks according to the way they are similar to each other in terms of their patterns of ties or flows (exchange of diplomats, provision of aid, international trade, migrants, investment, etc.). Snyder and Kick (1979) and Nemeth and Smith (1985) used the popular CONCOR (Convergence of Iterated Correlations) algorithm (see White, Boorman, & Brieger, 1976), which gauged structurally equivalent blocks; more recently, Smith and White (1992) used a relational distance algorithm called REGE, which more accurately captures the idea of role similarity. These measures of equivalence provide a technique for grouping nations or cities (or, in principle, other geographic units for which data are available) together according to similarities in their pattern of exchanges. Theoretical notions about the link between a city's functions and its role in the global urban system suggest that cities should group into rough levels corresponding to their positions in the world-city hierarchy.

In addition to probing overall structures of networks, the methodology also provides insight into the attributes of particular points. One particularly important concept is that of centrality. Sociologists link centrality in communities or interorganizational networks with power, prestige, and economic success (Burt, 1982; Galaskiewicz, 1979; Laumann, Galaskiewicz, & Marsden, 1978; Laumann & Pappi, 1976), whereas anthropologists and geographers have focused on centrality in trade networks between places (for instance, Hage & Harary, 1981; Pitts, 1965, 1979). Formal network methodologists argue that there are several distinct types of centrality, each suggesting different formal measurement algorithms (see Freeman, 1979). Because of technical problems that are only now being solved, quantitative measurement of point centrality is a complex proposition, especially if the data on the flows or relationships between points incorporate information about the amount or value of the exchange (i.e., as opposed to reporting simply the presence or absence of a tie) (see White, 1989). Even without a precise scaled measure of centrality, network analysts often discuss this as an attribute of particular nodes, because it is often discernible when we "eyeball" the matrix data on exchanges. Centrality is obviously relevant to understanding world-city systems (e.g., see quote above from Lo & Yeung, 1998): The key role of world cities as "junctions of flows" (Harris, 1994) should be strongly related to a node's ability to control and broker various types of international exchanges, to serve as a source of information and capital flow, and to act as a magnet for certain types of migrants or high technology. Network analysis, which has developed a precise and concise language for describing such relationships, can help to sharpen our thinking about the webs of relationships among global cities, regardless of whether we actually use the statistical measures or not.

OPERATIONALIZING INTERCITY LINKAGES FOR NETWORK ANALYSIS OF THE GLOBAL CITY SYSTEM

The various types of intercity flows discussed above are not highly abstract. There are fairly clear implications in terms of how we would ideally measure most of these flows. However, obtaining data on actual flows of people, materials, and information among global cities may present a particularly daunting task. Furthermore, the nature of network analysis makes missing data particularly problematic.

Because of the way quantitative data are gathered and compiled, there is an absolute dearth of relational data on all social phenomena. There is growing theoretical interest in the various social sciences on how social structures are generated through the relationships and linkages between people, localities, institutions, nations, and so on (see, e.g., Tilly, 1984). But statistical information still tends to be collected in the attributional form. That is, data report values on the characteristics of particular units (i.e., an individual's income, a city's population, a nation's gross national product) rather than information about their relationship to others (in terms of either connections or flows). Therefore, it is very difficult to obtain data on international flows or links between social units (whether these entities are cities, regions, organizations, corporations, or nations). So although it is easy to get attributional data on various nation-states, and there is some good network data at the international level (commodity trade flows, for instance; see Smith & White, 1992), compilations of networks of interactions or flows between world cities are not readily available. This does not mean that these data do not exist or that pulling them together into a usable format is impossible; it does mean that it is difficult.

The difficulty of this task is compounded by a methodological issue. Although network analysis is a powerful tool to understand social structure, it has some stringent data requirements. Other types of statistical analysis use relatively simple, standardized ways of adjusting for missing cases. But incomplete data in network matrices are much more difficult to accommodate. Although there are some techniques that attempt to deal with this problem, lack of data on the flows between any units of a network means that relational analysis can never adequately capture its multiplex structure in totality. The addition or deletion of information on a single unit can fundamentally alter the configuration of a network. The importance of complete matrices of data, coupled with a serious problem of data availability, makes it imperative to identify possible sources of relevant information.

What sorts of data might this search turn up? Economic flows can be embodied in the movement of people. Labor migration, when people move over long distances for employment, is one form. Periodic surveys of national populations for certain periods of time may allow us to piece together a world-system map of labor flows. Of course, good counts of migrants will not be available for many countries in the world, and when they are, cities of origin may not be coded. But the study of migration is central to demographic inquiry, so this could be a potentially fertile fund of data in the future, which might allow us to begin to chart a migration-based world-city system map.

Economic flows in their material form may be operationalized by describing commodity chains linking geographic locales (see Gereffi & Korzeniewicz, 1994). The required data would consist of some measure of the nature and volume of commodities by cities of origin and destination. Once again, the complete data for all the world's large cities probably do not exist at the present time, but we can begin to piece together a partial map of the world's city system by using the data that are available and making efforts to develop new sources. For example, in the United States, a Commodity Flow Survey is available from the U.S. Department of Transportation (contact the Bureau of Transportation Statistics, www.bts.gov). The survey provides a complete network database (from systematic sampling of commodity flows) on the value and number of commodity flows by zip code. These new data provide exciting possibilities. Once again, the obvious shortcoming is that they will allow researchers to produce only partial maps of the world-city system. But we have just begun to explore the possibilities. It is quite likely that other commodity-flow data for locales are being collected by governments and international agencies. Moreover, we think that it is important to begin the task of mapping the world-city system, if only partially.

Communication among actors in geographic locales remote from one another takes place in the absence of face-to-face contact. Firms, businesses, and business people with far-flung operations and interests use telephone calls, telex messages, faxes, telegraph, and mail for such purposes. In principle, it is possible to sample the volume by locale of origin and destination of some of these communications from existing records. The telephone bills most of us receive indicate that data are kept, at least temporarily, in a form suitable for network analysis. Indeed, according to a Federal Communications Commission official whom we interviewed a few years ago, the best and only source of data for what we really want will be what he called the industries. He pointed out that for the United States, although AT&T is the largest, it carries only 60% of the long distance calls on average, and this varies widely from place to place. He also said that the telephone companies would probably be reluctant to share such information because of the possible implications for their competitive positions in the industry. Scholars of the communications industry and the major telecommunications corporations themselves may be willing to cooperate in generating the necessary data to begin to map the global intercity information network. In principle, with funding and industry cooperation, some kind of sampling procedures could be devised to generate good estimates of the volume and frequency of telephone transmissions between places on the globe. In his recent analysis, Rimmer (1998) provided a survey of the top 25 international telecommunications routes. But the data are only available for a very limited number of cases and are compiled at the national level: The connections between "world cities cannot be traced adequately because the data on global traffic are restricted to the largest country-pairs" (p. 451).

Travelers form other strands in the web linking the world's cities. Corporate emissaries, government trade and commerce representatives, and independent entrepreneurs, for example, move among cities, greasing the wheels of production, finance, or commerce through face-to-face contact. Of these data possibilities, we have begun analyzing those on air travel patterns, using network analysis.

AIR PASSENGER TRAVEL

Like Manuel Castells (1994), Saskia Sassen is convinced that new information technologies binding together major international financial and business centers are critical to understand the phenomena of world cities (and, indeed, to comprehend the crucial underlying logic of current globalization)—"with the potential for global control capability, certain cities are becoming nodal points in a vast communications and market system" (Sassen, 1998, p. 397). At first blush, capturing the essence of that sort of centrality might seem to require examining the architecture of worldwide telematics networks directly (and, if that were possible to do, we would). But she goes on to say,

> One of the ironies of the new information technologies is that, to maximize their use, we need access to conventional infrastructure. In the case of international networks it takes airports and planes. . . . The dominant notion seems to be that telematics obliterates the need for conventional infrastructures. But it is precisely the nature of the production process in advanced industries, whether they operate globally or nationally, that has contributed to the immense rise in business travel in all advanced economies over the past decade, the new electronic era. (Sassen, 1998, p. 403)

Fortuitously, information on air travel (and other forms of transportation data such as the movement of large transoceanic shipping containers, discussed by Rimmer, 1998) is collected for particular ports or nodes, which usually are in or near major cities. Keeling (1995) presented a strong argument both for generic claims about "transport's key role in the world city system" (p. 116) and for specific claims that the air passenger links we will examine are an excellent source of data:

> Airline linkages offer the best illustration of transport's role in the world city system for five reasons: (i) global airline flows are one of the few indices available of transactional flows of inter-urban connectivity; (ii) air networks and their associated infrastructure are the most visible manifestations of world city interactions; (iii) great demand still exists for face-to-face relationships, despite the global telecommunications revolution (Heldman, 1992; Noam, 1992); (iv) air transport is the preferred mode of inter-city movement for the transnational capitalist class, migrants, tourists, and high-value, low-bulk goods; and (v) airline links are important components of a city's aspirations to world city status. (p. 118)

Keeling also points out that airports and air connections often become important political issues in various cities. For symbolic reasons as well as for economic self-interest, members of growth coalitions and of the capitalist class seek to gain public support to develop "their" city's airline capacity.

PREVIOUS RESEARCH ON CITY SYSTEMS AND AIR TRAVEL

A few scholars have used air travel in empirical studies comparing cities. In her study of the degree to which European cities are internationalized, Cattan (1995) argued, "because of its relatively rapid capacity to reply in terms of supply and demand, air traffic provides a pertinent indicator in the quest to evaluate the international character of western European cities" (p. 303). Although she apparently has network-type data, she condenses it to attributional data and shows that variation among European cities' international "attractivity" (in terms of air traffic) is explained by a variety of factors, including each city's relative standing in its national territorial system.

Simon (1995) also used air traffic as one measure of a city's standing in the world system. "The progressive expansion of civil aviation reflects continued growth in business and international tourism" (p. 139). His analysis reveals "the relative insignificance of sub-Saharan African airports relative to those in the NICs"; Cairo is Africa's busiest airport, Johannesburg is sub-Saharan Africa's "gateway," and Lagos is "surprisingly unimportant given (Nigeria's) vast population and considerable potential in view of its economic situation" (p. 139).

Most recently, Rimmer (1998) examined both air passenger and freight movement, with particular interest in the former: "Air passenger travel contributes to economic globalization by bringing people together to acquire *complex knowledge* relatively unburdened by geographical constraints and national borders" (p. 454). Rimmer provides a list of the top 25 metropolitan airports by volume, as well as the top 25 city pairs, based on city-to-city volume; he also traces the changing volumes at these airports and routes for each year between 1984 and 1992. By examining the two-way flows between cities, he is, in effect, doing relational analysis, albeit in a nonrigorous and grossly simplified way. Most of the lead cities he identifies are among those at the top of the world-city hierarchy that we derive from the more sophisticated analysis that follows. But, by ignoring the multiplex linkages between the key nodes and many of the lower order cities (which he presumably does to make his simple comparisons manageable), Rimmer misses out on a key component of global cities' prominence, namely their command and control links to less central parts of the global economy.

ANALYSES OF AIR PASSENGER LINKAGES AMONG GLOBAL CITIES

THE DATA

Network analysis requires data on interactions between all pairs of actors located in the network that have been identified (or hypothesized to exist). Once we became aware of the availability of international airline passenger flows among pairs of cities, our goal was to code these data for as many of the world's important cities as possible. Our primary data source is On-Flight Origin and Destination for 1977 (the earliest available data), 1980, 1985, 1991, 1994, and 1997 (actually, the last two quarters of 1996 and the first two of 1997), published, or otherwise made available, by the International Civil Aviation Organisation (ICAO) in Montreal. Based on reports from states on airline activity to and from each city within their boundaries to or from any city outside of their boundaries, ICAO publishes quarterly and annual figures on numbers of airline passengers traveling between cities in different countries. There are two important limitations to these data. First, to preserve the confidentiality of states and

TABLE 1: Network Prominence Ranking for the Top 30 Cities From the Equivalence Analysis, 1977-1997

	1977		*1980*		*1985*	
Rank	*City*	*Network Eigenvalue*	*City*	*Network Eigenvalue*	*City*	*Network Eigenvalue*
1	London	1	London	1	London	1
2	Paris	0.878	Paris	0.844	Paris	0.914
3	Frankfurt	0.847	Frankfurt	0.804	Frankfurt	0.848
4	New York	0.687	New York	0.652	New York	0.809
5	Amsterdam	0.643	Amsterdam	0.633	Amsterdam	0.612
6	Zurich	0.611	Zurich	0.598	Tokyo	0.608
7	Athens	0.573	Tokyo	0.55	Zurich	0.586
8	Copenhagen	0.526	Copenhagen	0.546	Miami	0.53
9	Tokyo	0.496	Athens	0.516	Singapore	0.482
10	Bangkok	0.439	Bangkok	0.487	Bangkok	0.46
11	Madrid	0.439	Madrid	0.462	Hong Kong	0.446
12	Singapore	0.421	Singapore	0.447	Madrid	0.427
13	Hong Kong	0.393	Hong Kong	0.434	Chicago	0.423
14	Buenos Aires	0.368	Bombay	0.346	Copenhagen	0.417
15	Rio de Janeiro	0.344	Rio de Janeiro	0.345	Athens	0.413
16	Sydney	0.331	Manila	0.342	San Francisco	0.39
17	Brussels	0.32	Brussels	0.334	Brussels	0.368
18	Caracas	0.32	Vienna	0.325	Boston	0.349
19	Toronto	0.309	Karachi	0.309	Manila	0.347
20	Bombay	0.302	Buenos Aires	0.308	Mexico City	0.337
21	Warsaw	0.3	Cairo	0.3	Rio de Janeiro	0.329
22	Lima	0.296	Kuwait City	0.288	Karachi	0.324
23	Karachi	0.293	Sydney	0.275	Bombay	0.321
24	Vienna	0.291	Milan	0.273	Vienna	0.318
25	Tehran	0.288	Caracas	0.264	Cairo	0.316
26	Panama	0.282	Seoul	0.263	Seoul	0.311
27	Kuwait City	0.265	Lima	0.262	Dallas	0.308
28	Stockholm	0.263	Osaka	0.251	Houston	0.296
29	Santiago	0.258	Stockholm	0.251	Sydney	0.29
30	Manila	0.251	Johannesburg	0.248	Buenos Aires	0.288

airlines, the ICAO provides data on travel between international city pairs only when "at least two airlines representing at least two different States have reported" (ICAO, 1993, p. II). Thus, data are missing for city pairs served by only one airline and for city pairs within the same country.

We have managed to find estimates of travel between major cities within the same country for some nations. We have the passenger flows between pairs among the three Canadian cities, Montreal, Toronto, and Vancouver, for 1985, 1991, 1994, and 1996 from Statistics Canada (various years). Beginning in 1985, data on additional U.S. cities (New York, Chicago, Boston, Washington, Miami, Houston, Dallas, Los Angeles, San Francisco, Seattle) are also available from the Air Transport Association of America. The Japanese Ministry of

1991		*1994*		*1997*	
City	*Network Eigenvalue*	*City*	*Network Eigenvalue*	*City*	*Network Eigenvalue*
London	1	London	1	London	1
Frankfurt	0.944	Frankfurt	0.94	Frankfurt	0.859
Paris	0.914	Paris	0.932	Paris	0.767
New York	0.68	New York	0.747	New York	0.672
Tokyo	0.579	Amsterdam	0.677	Amsterdam	0.614
Amsterdam	0.575	Miami	0.575	Miami	0.533
Zurich	0.537	Zurich	0.572	Zurich	0.533
Miami	0.53	Tokyo	0.571	Los Angeles	0.516
Los Angeles	0.524	Los Angeles	0.551	Hong Kong	0.515
Bangkok	0.492	Hong Kong	0.537	Singapore	0.502
Singapore	0.492	Singapore	0.528	Tokyo	0.494
Hong Kong	0.457	Bangkok	0.504	Seoul	0.463
Madrid	0.429	Madrid	0.416	Bangkok	0.444
Vienna	0.352	Seoul	0.416	Madrid	0.405
Brussels	0.349	Brussels	0.415	Vienna	0.374
Chicago	0.325	Vienna	0.409	San Francisco	0.372
Toronto	0.325	Chicago	0.397	Chicago	0.369
San Francisco	0.316	San Francisco	0.378	Dubai	0.367
Mexico City	0.311	Copenhagen	0.347	Osaka	0.364
Milan	0.305	Milan	0.324	Brussels	0.363
Dubai	0.301	Athens	0.294	Milan	0.361
Copenhagen	0.3	Mexico City	0.294	Copenhagen	0.356
Taipei	0.287	Manila	0.285	Mexico City	0.344
Buenos Aires	0.284	Buenos Aires	0.28	Kuala Lumpur	0.311
Rio de Janeiro	0.281	Dubai	0.28	Athens	0.303
Manila	0.261	Sydney	0.28	Istanbul	0.302
Karachi	0.257	Istanbul	0.276	Cairo	0.295
Sydney	0.254	Toronto	0.275	Manila	0.292
Cairo	0.252	Karachi	0.265	Buenos Aires	0.282
Athens	0.25	Cairo	0.263	Sydney	0.277

Transportation provided the data for Nagoya, Osaka, and Tokyo in answer to an e-mail inquiry, and a contact in Sao Paulo was able to find the volume of traffic between Sao Paulo and Rio de Janeiro for some years. Finally, we estimated the volume of air passenger traffic between one pair of cities, London and Hong Kong, which the ICAO apparently does not consider an international pair—at least not until 1997. We did this by assigning passenger totals between this pair at levels comparable to other similar pairs and based on patterns of air traffic between each of London's and Hong Kong's other partners. Still, we are left without several important cities, including Shanghai and Guangzhou in China (we use Beijing), Rome in Italy (following Friedmann, we use Milan), Munich and Berlin in Germany, Calcutta and Delhi in India (we use Bombay), and others. Our resulting matrix of network data, thus, includes about 100 cities, depending on the year, with each city listed as both a destination and an origin. Admittedly, some of these cities are far from being world cities in Friedmann's sense. Our goal was to maximize the geographic coverage of the data by including cities from as many different countries as we could. This strategy resulted in including several small cities with very low levels of air passenger traffic.

Not surprisingly, many of the cells in the resulting matrix contain zeros, indicating no air passengers traveled directly between many of the pairs. On the other hand, among cities that are linked, some have very large number of passengers (e.g., 845,781 flew from Dublin to London, and 840,530 flew from London to Dublin). Because the distribution of numbers in these cells is rather skewed, we logarithmically transformed them before running the network analysis. (Of course, we left the zeros alone; only nonzero numbers were transformed.) We should note, too, that although we have an in-flow/out-flow matrix, not much new information is added by including both. The numbers of passengers who traveled one way between each pair are usually very close, in proportional terms, to the number who traveled in the other direction, as indicated by the London-Dublin numbers given above. In fact, many of them are undoubtedly the same individuals, having obtained round-trip tickets. Other types of flows among cities in which we are interested are likely to be less symmetrical. For example, commodity flows (measured in monetary value) would almost certainly be asymmetrical, because most products or components that are shipped by air would presumably be consumed (or perhaps incorporated into another transportable product) at their destinations. Analyzing these kinds of flows in addition to air passengers would allow a more nuanced description of the world's city system, and we look forward to moving in this direction in future work.

THE METHOD AND HYPOTHESES

We have used Burt and Schott's (1991) STRUCTURE network analysis software program to analyze the passenger flow matrices for the five time points. Primarily, two types of analysis will be used, equivalence and cohesion. *Cohesion analysis* helps the research discern groups of actors in a network on the basis of having interactions with each other at levels that set them apart from other actors (with whom they may also be interacting). In our earlier research, we presented cliques of cities for a single year based on airline passenger flows between pairs in the matrix of world cities. Here, we will be able to chart changes (or stability) in clique membership over time, from 1977 to the present. We will also use STRUCTURE's *equivalence analysis*. This identifies actors that are structurally equivalent in the whole network, regardless of their degree of interaction with one another. Actors are equivalent to the extent they are functionally important (or central) to the whole system. Actors that have high levels of interactions with many other actors are equivalent, and those with few interactions with only a few partners are also equivalent. Thus, at the same time equivalence is gauged, so too is centrality. For our purposes, cities that are high on the measures of centrality are relatively equivalent to one another and relatively central to the world system of cities. In Friedmann's terms, these are the world cities, and those two to four most central cities should include Sassen's global cities. The research reported here will chart changes in the composition of cities that can be classified as world cities on the basis of their positions in the network of air passenger travel.

Restricted as we are by our one measure of cities' relative position in, and importance to, the world system, we are nevertheless able to address several hypotheses that are relevant both in terms of the literature on world cities and world-system research. First, over the 20-year time period under consideration, we would expect cities in rising regions of the world economy to occupy increasingly important positions in the world-city hierarchy, and we would expect this to be reflected in our airline data. At the same time, cities in declining regions should fall in this hierarchy. Specifically, over this period of time, we would expect key Asian cities to become more central to the world economy, with the recent Asian crisis not yet being reflected in the overall trends from 1977 to 1997. We would also expect leading Latin American cities to become less central to the world economy. Within Asia, if we focus on Asian cities only, we would expect the increased competition among the leading national economies to be reflected in a flatter hierarchy among the most central Asian cities, as they become more distinct from lesser cities of Asia. Hong Kong, Singapore, and, more recently, Seoul are expected to become more equivalent to Tokyo and more central to the world system of cities, pulling ahead, in relative equivalence terms, of cities like Jakarta and Kuala Lumpur (although these may be rising relative to other cities of the periphery). Although the distribution may be less hierarchical among the most central Asian cities, the distribution should be more hierarchical among a larger number of Asia's world cities. We also expect to see the Chinese capital, Beijing, begin to rise from the lower periphery after 1985 to somewhere in the middle by 1997, reflecting China's reintegration into the world economy. On the other hand, it is unlikely that significant changes will be observed in the relative positions of the leading core cities over this period of time. Consistent with previous research, we posit that New York, London, and Tokyo will remain at or near the very top of the hierarchy, joined by European metropolises such as Paris and Frankfurt and, perhaps, some U.S. cities.

Comprehensive clique analysis is also expected to reveal changes consistent with shifting regional economic and geopolitical patterns. For instance, key cities of the former Soviet bloc may show interesting changes indicative of recent geopolitical realignments; or Asian cities may coalesce during this period into more distinct regional patterns. But in this article, our discussion of the results of the cohesion analyses we have done will be very limited. Just listing all these groupings for each year would take considerable space; presenting a real analysis of the stability and change in these patterns between 1977 and 1997 would require a separate article. So, here, we will simply provide some illustrative examples.

FINDINGS

The results of the network analysis of airline passenger flows among the world's leading cities for six 1-year time periods between 1977 and 1997 indicate both stability and change in the global city hierarchy. Table 1 is based on matrices of quantitative data on the volume of air travelers between each of the major cities for which we have data in each year, ranging from 83 in 1997 to a high of 97 in the most recent years. To simplify our presentation of the data, we only list the top 30 cities, ranked according to their estimated degree of prominence or centrality in the system of passenger flows. In any case, it is this upper echelon that is of the most interest, because these are the true global cities. For each year's data, London is the most prominent node. The combination of the volume of air passenger arrivals and departures, plus the diversity of links to other cities throughout the world, places the British capital at the top of the world city hierarchy. Of course, although London's airports lie at the confluence of many flights, they are not the final destination for many air travelers. Arguably, data on initial departure/final destination might be "better" and give us a somewhat different image of the network. Unfortunately, the data that are available simply do not allow us to differentiate between passengers who are passing through a hub and transferring to different flights and those who are on the final leg of their air travel. Although we need to keep in mind that the "hub phenomena" might bias our results in certain ways, the very presence of this sort of airport in a major metropolitan area is probably indicative of that city's central place in the national and international system of cities.

Joining London in the group of four most prominent cities for each of the six time periods are Paris, Frankfurt, and New York, with Frankfurt moving up to replace Paris in the Number 2 position beginning in 1991. Among these leading cities, Frankfurt's estimated centrality is the most likely inflated by its role as the long-distance hub for travelers to a wide array of other cities in Europe and beyond. On the other hand, it is hardly surprising that a German city should be among the most important in our late 20th-century world-city hierarchy. Germany is among the largest economies in the world, its banks and bureaucrats have become leading voices in the European Community (now European Union), and German investments and business interests are globally extensive. In addition to being a major transportation crossroads, Frankfurt became the nation's financial center during the postwar period. Friedmann (1995) labeled Frankfurt a *multinational articulation* just a step below London, New York, and Tokyo. Kunzmann (1998) argued that Frankfurt fits into the pantheon of European world cities just under London and Paris (and a notch ahead of Amsterdam, the city that holds fifth spot for all but one of our years). This author suggests that Frankfurt and "the Rhine-Main conurbation," despite being a fairly low-profile central city with a relatively modest population (less than a million), epitomizes an emergent form in the global urban hierarchy that is more accurately called "a world city region." In any case, with the reunification of Germany at the end of the 1980s, more attention has turned to restoring Berlin to its historical position as the leading German city (and now reconstructed seat of national government). In the coming decade, Berlin may join (or perhaps replace) Frankfurt as Germany's preeminent node in international networks, including the flow of travelers. In the meantime, Frankfurt's centrality in the air passenger network suggests that it is, indeed, a leading global city.

Paris's high ranking in our world-city hierarchies deserves some comment, as well, because it is not one of Sassen's prototypical global cities (New York, London, and Tokyo), and other scholars (cf. Friedmann, 1995) rank it a step below even Frankfurt. In our results, however, the French capital is always in the top three, above New York. Most of the serious conceptualizations of elite world cities focus on their command and control functions vis-à-vis the global economy, arguing that financial headquarters and high-level producers' services are critical (Sassen, 1991). "The City of Lights" is almost surely nearer to the top than it might otherwise be because of its status as *the* prime urban tourist destination in the Western world. Conceivably, we could try to parse out this sort of disturbance by developing estimates of the ratio of tourist travel to passengers who come and go for business or who are migrating in or out; we have not done that yet. However, it is unlikely that tourism alone accounts for Paris's position in our results. That status may also have to do with Paris's enormous demographic and functional primacy in France (Paris is center for both French capital and government). Like Germany, France is one of the world's giant economies, and French investment worldwide is significant, extending throughout its far-flung former empire and beyond. Our findings suggest that Paris, like Frankfurt, probably deserves more attention than it has received in the literature on world cities.

Consistent with this literature, New York City holds steady near the top of the hierarchy at the Number 4 position for the duration of the 20-year period. New York is home to the most important financial institutions in the United States (and some of the leading ones in the world), a number of international agencies (including but not limited to the United Nations), and all the associated high-level business services that these corporations and bureaucracies require. Like the other leading cities in the hierarchy, New York is also an important tourist destination for domestic and international travelers and a port of entry to many immigrants. Given its dominance in other estimations of "world-cityness" (e.g., Sassen, 1991, 1994), one might expect it to rank even higher. One difference between New York and cities like London or Paris is that it is not the national capital, which may make it less central in air traffic flows.

Two other European cities are among the top 10 throughout the time period: Amsterdam ranks 5th every year except 1991 (when it slips to 6th), and Zurich is consistently either 6th or 7th. Amsterdam is the lead city of the Randstad conurbation (which also includes Rotterdam and The Hague), a world center for transnational flows of oil and grain, global headquarters to leading transnational corporations (Polygram, Elsevier), and a major research and development center (Kunzmann, 1998); Zurich owns a well-deserved reputation as a center for international banking and insurance (Kunzmann, 1998). Athens (7th) and Copenhagen (8th) also ranked in the top 10 in 1977, but they both decline in prominence in subsequent years, ending up barely maintaining top 25 status in 1997 (at 25th and 22nd, respectively). Because both are known as tourist destinations, their higher rank at the beginning of the period and subsequent decline probably reflect dramatic increases in the volume of airline passengers traveling for business purposes worldwide over the past two decades. Other European cities that are established regional centers also consistently ranked in the top 25 over the period. Madrid is 11th in 1977 and 14th in 1997, Vienna rises from 24th to 14th during that period (perhaps reflecting its growing importance as a center for culture and consumption, see Kunzmann, 1998, p. 43), whereas Brussels holds fairly steady (17th from 1977 until 1985, 15th in 1991 and 1994, falling a bit to 20th in 1997).

In 1977, two East Asian cities, Tokyo and Bangkok, round out the top 10 in the world-city hierarchy, with Singapore (12th) and Hong Kong (13th) also in the top 15. Tokyo, of course, is one of Sassen's 3 top global cities; in our results, the Japanese capital climbs as high as 5th in 1991 before sliding to 8th in 1994 and 11th in 1997. Although Tokyo seems to rank a bit lower than we might expect,[2] the East Asian region is strongly represented. By 1997, Hong Kong is up to 9th in our prominence rankings, with Singapore right behind in 10th place; this is not surprising, because these cities are major finance and trade centers for China and southeast Asia, respectively. Bangkok holds onto 13th place (but we should point out that all these cities' positions are affected by the addition of two U.S. cities other than New York to the data after 1985). Probably the most dramatic mobility among East Asia urban centers is the meteoric rise of Seoul, which rises from 46th in 1977 to 12th in 1997. Following the lead cluster of East Asian cities in 1997 are Osaka (19th), Kuala Lumpur (24th), Manila (28th), and Beijing (lurking just off our table at 32nd). The Chinese capital's case is particularly interesting: It holds 73rd position in 1977. In fact, Seoul and Beijing are the two cities that have moved up the most in the entire network over the 20-year period. This mobility is emblematic of the tremendous economic dynamism of East Asia in the past two decades. Indeed, if we shift our focus just a little—to the rise of the Pacific Rim—we can add the two major cities of California: By 1997, Los Angeles is 8th and San Francisco is 16th in rank.

The remarkable rise of East Asian cities is matched by a precipitous decline in the prominence of several Latin American cities. Buenos Aires, Rio de Janeiro, and Caracas had all disappeared from the top 20 by 1985. Mexico City had risen to the 20th position by 1985 and remained the highest ranked Latin American city in 1997 at 23rd. In spite of the economic downturn in Latin

America in the late 1980s, Mexico's close relationship with the U.S. economy (solidified further by the NAFTA of the mid-1990s) probably helped maintain Mexico City's position in the world-city hierarchy, even as the traditionally dominant cities of South America became increasingly peripheral to the global system of cities. Arguably, the locus of dominance in the regional system has shifted to the north, as the arguably Latin American cities of Miami (see Portes & Stepick, 1993, for a rich case study) and Los Angeles become increasingly central nodes. Migration plays a central part in both cases, as Miami developed increasingly strong ties with the Caribbean basin during this period, whereas Los Angeles became increasingly linked to Mexico and Central America (see our discussion of cliques below for more evidence of this).

Many other trajectories can be traced from Table 1, as well. At the level of world regions, one obvious lesson is that some parts of the world have very few high-ranking cities, and even those may be declining in prominence. Africa's representation in the top 30 cities for most of the period is Cairo (arguably more aptly seen as the leading Islamic center of the Middle East, see Yousry, Abu-Zekry, & Yousry 1998), with Johannesburg breaking into that group once, in 1980. By 1997, Johannesburg had dropped all the way to 67th, the third biggest drop in rank among all our cities. This result is consistent with a recent case study of the South African capital, which Beavon (1998) called a "troubled" city in a "dying" region (exemplified by serious discussion of closing down its national stock exchange). The two cities that declined even more than Johannesburg are also indicative of dramatic regional decline, in this case, of the Indian subcontinent. Both Bombay and Karachi begin the period in the top 25, with the Indian city rising to 14th in 1980 and the Pakistani capital 19th that year. By 1994, Bombay is 50th and still falling, whereas Karachi ranks 73rd in 1997.

We can also relate the prominence of particular cities to recent research on their world-city status. Chicago has recently been touted as one of "America's global cities" (Abu-Lughod, 1999). Indeed, our results provide some evidence that this classification has merit: After we add additional U.S. cities to our network in 1985, Chicago appears, initially in the 13th spot, declining a little to 17th in 1994 and 1997. Agricultural exports are a key component of U.S. foreign trade, and the midwestern metropolis plays a central role in world and national agricultural commodity markets. On the other hand, our findings suggest that Chicago is not a global city on the same order as New York, or even Miami or Los Angeles. Instead, its global prominence is closer to that of San Francisco.

Cohesion analysis. In addition to the structural equivalence analysis that yields the world-city rankings, we also looked at the clique structure of the data over the six time periods. In this article, we will only touch on these results in a very preliminary way. For each year, between 20 and 23 cliques were identified, with between 14 and 23 cities not falling within any clique at all. Once again, clique membership is based on common interactions at similar levels (in terms of the volume of air traffic). The composition of most of the cliques is tied to geographic proximity. This is not surprising. It reflects the commonsense fact that travel is usually to relatively nearby destinations rather than to distant ones, and it means that some of the patterns that emerge are rather uninteresting. However, although the composition of most cliques is fairly stable over time, we can observe some changes in the locations of a few key cities that illustrate the descriptive power of our methodology. For example, in 1977, Mexico City is located in a clique with two other cities, both in Central America, San Salvador and Guatemala City. With shifting affiliations across most time periods, by 1997, we find it located with Los Angeles, Houston, and Dallas, which is where it was identified in 1991. This is consistent with the hypothesis that Mexico City (as suggested above) is becoming more integrated with the cities of the western United States in recent years. In 1994, we find Mexico City and Los Angeles grouped with San Salvador and Guatemala City.[3]

Central European cities of the Soviet bloc countries are split into two cliques in 1977, with Budapest and Prague forming one clique and Moscow and Warsaw the other. The same pattern holds 3 years later, in the 1980 data. However, by 1985, Warsaw joins Prague and Budapest, leaving Moscow 1 of about 20 cities that are isolated from cliques.[4] This is quite possibly the result of the success of the Solidarity-led democratization movement in Poland, separating Warsaw from Moscow's influence. This had all changed by 1991, however. The passenger-exchange data for this year place both Moscow and Warsaw in a larger, more cosmopolitan clique with Vienna and Zurich. Glasnost seems to have reunited the Polish and Russian capitals and brought them both into the European fold in the early 1990s, but by the middle of the decade economic realities had rearranged the relations among these cities once again. Both in 1994 and in the most recent data (1997), Moscow is once again isolated, and Warsaw and Prague form a two-city clique. Budapest is also unaligned.

CONCLUSION

Population flows connect distant geographic places around the world. To the extent that such flows are stable, they can be said to link places in a web-like pattern that constitutes part of the fabric of the world system. The world's great cities are important destinations and departure points for both short-term population flows (e.g., tourism and business travel) and long-term migration. The way in which population flows are structured to link the world's cities reflects patterns of interaction, dominance, and subordination in a world system of cities that both overlays and undergirds the world system of nations with which we are more familiar. Moreover, changes in these patterns reflect the changing fortunes of cities. In a sense, cities vie with one another to become truly global cities, centers of control in the world economy. Of course, cities do not really "do" anything. They are places in which human activity is carried out; they are spaces with attributes, both man-made and natural, that social actors seek to use (or exchange) in their own short-run interests. That local elites often act to enhance the value of "their" cities (and that this is often at the expense of the public good) is a long-standing subject of urban sociology, the "new urban sociology" that is not any longer all that new (Smith, 1995). To the extent that local elites of a given city are the national elites of a particular country, these cities will often be promoted as important hubs in the world system, and national resources will likely be used in this effort.

Certainly, the worldwide patterns of air passenger travel in the latter part of the 20th century provide one important measure of a city's relative success in becoming a world city. What we have shown is perhaps not all that surprising, but nevertheless, it provides a new way to map an important aspect of the world system. Key cities of Western Europe and North America have continuously maintained their positions as central nodes in the international flow of population by air travel. Indeed, the relative stability of the world-city hierarchy, and the long-standing integration of the top cities, provides more evidence for skepticism about the thesis that current globalization is really new or novel (Arrighi 1999; Wade, 1996; see Hargittai & Centeno, 2001, this volume, for an overview of this debate).

If continuity is a major theme in our results, there are also interesting temporal changes over the 20-year period we study. A few cities that, a little more than a decade ago, were marked as lower echelon work cities by John Friedmann show dramatic declines in importance in the global city network.[5] But corresponding to the diminished prominence of cities such as Bombay or Buenos Aires is the remarkable rise in importance of several East Asian cities; in spite of the recent Asian economic crisis, we doubt that this is a transitory phenomenon. There are at least six or seven East Asian cities that would now have to be classified as world cities. Other regions, such as Africa, Latin America, and South Asia, seem to have few cities high in the world-city system, and those seem to be losing ground in terms of prominence. Global urbanization patterns still are characterized by the uneven development dynamics familiar to world-system analysts (see Smith, 1996). However we wish to characterize recent world changes, our results provide evidence of polarization rather than convergence (contrary to more sanguine images in some versions of globalization or the older modernization theory perspective on world urbanization).

Clearly, our research remains at a rather primitive, descriptive stage. Nevertheless, we believe it holds promise. In future work, we hope to combine this global analysis with a few targeted case studies of specific cities, particularly one or two cities that have changed significantly in terms of either their importance to the network or in terms of the cliques in which they have been located. What have local elites done to promote their city? What would analysis of the Hong Kong "growth machine" reveal, for example? What are the relative roles of local, national, and international capital in a city's ascendency to world-city status? And with what consequences for ascending or descending cities' populations? Another direction we would like to proceed is to deepen our understanding of the global city network by analyzing other types of flows among cities, especially those related to oceanic shipping and telematics. These are also important sinews of the new global geography.

NOTES

1. Meyer (1986) and Rimmer (1998) both use the network analogy and quantitative data in attempts to provide approximations of world-city hierarchy and rankings. But both of these studies, ultimately, fall back on attributional data: the particular city's functions on such indicators as concentration of international bank offices (Meyer) or the sheer volume of total trade or traffic (Rimmer); neither uses network analytical techniques.

2. Even factoring in Japanese economic problems in the late 1990s, it seems that Tokyo should register as the dominant city in East Asia, in terms of financial clout, corporate power, and technological leadership (Sassen, 1991). Other East Asian cities may fare better based on air passenger data than they might on other indicators (flows of investment, technology, etc.), because of tourist preferences for mainland Asia and the in- and out-flows of Chinese and Korean natives who reside overseas.

3. Although these results may seem rather strange initially, observers of waves of Central American migrants to the barrios of Los Angeles in the 1990s (who all came by way of Mexico) probably would not find them too surprising. We hope to probe a bit deeper into these results and their implications in a future full-fledged analysis of the changing clique structure over time. In fact, trying to explain how and why clique boundaries change, sometimes in ways that may not seem intuitively obvious, is one of the most interesting aspects of cohesion analysis: It can suggest new directions for substantive case research on global city networks.

4. Being isolated by not having membership in cliques does not mean that these cities are not important points of origin and destination for air passengers. Rather, it indicates that the nature of air passenger interaction with other cities is restricted to unlike cities, in terms of the volume of air traffic and the number of cities with which it has air traffic connections.

5. This is not to say that Friedmann would not have—or did not—predict some of these changes.

REFERENCES

Abu-Lughod, J. (1999). *New York, Chicago, Los Angeles: America's global cities*. Minneapolis: University of Minnesota Press.

Arrighi, G. (1999). Globalization, state sovereignty, and the "endless" accumulation of capital. In D. A. Smith, D. J. Solinger, & S. C. Topik (Eds.), *States and sovereignty in the global economy* (pp. 53-73). London: Routledge.

Beavon, K. (1998). "Johannesburg": Coming to grips with globalization from an abnormal base. In F.-C. Lo & Y.-M. Yeung (Eds.), *Globalization and the world of large cities* (pp. 352-388). Tokyo: United Nations University Press.

Burt, R. (1982). *Toward a structural theory of action: Network models of social structure, perception, and action*. New York: Academic Press.

Burt, R., & Schott, T. (1991). *STRUCTURE: A general purpose network analysis program providing sociometric indicies, cliques, structural and role equivalence, density tables, contagion, autonomy, power, and equilibria in multiple network systems* (Version 4.2, reference manual). New York: Columbia University, Center for the Social Sciences.

Castells, M. (1994). European cities, the informational society, and the global economy. *New Left Review, 204*, 18-32.

Cattan, N. (1995). Attractivity and internationalisation of major European cities: The example of air traffic. *Urban Studies, 32*, 303-312.

Chase-Dunn, C. (1985). The system of world cities, A.D. 800-1975. In M. Timberlake (Ed.), *Urbanization in the world-economy* (pp. 269-292). Orlando, FL: Academic Press.

Feagin, J., & Smith, M. P. (Eds). (1987). *The capitalist city*. London: Basil Blackwell.

Feagin, J. R. (1988). *The free enterprise city*. New Brunswick, NJ: Rutgers University Press.

Freeman, L. (1979). Centrality in social networks: Conceptual clarification. *Social Networks, 1*, 215-239.

Friedmann, J. (1986). The world city hypothesis. *Development and Change, 4*, 12-50.

Friedmann, J. (1995). Where we stand: A decade of world city research. In P. Knox & P. Taylor (Eds.), *World cities in a world-system* (pp. 21-47). New York: Cambridge University Press.

Friedmann, J., & Wolff, G. (1982). World city formation: An agenda for research and action. *International Journal of Urban and Regional Research, 6*, 309-344.

Galaskiewicz, J. (1979). *Global shift: The internationalization of economic activity* (2nd ed.). New York: Guilford.

Gereffi, G., & Korzeniewicz, M. (Eds.). (1994). *Commodity chains and global capitalism*. Westport, CT: Greenwood.

Gras, N.S.B. (1922). *Introduction to economic history*. New York: Harper.

Hage, P., & Harary, F. (1981). Mediation and power in Melanesia. *Oceania, 52*, 124-135.

Hargittai, E., & Centeno, M. A. (2001). Defining a global geography. *American Behavioral Scientist, 44*(10), 1545-1560.

Harris, N. (1994). Viewpoint: The emerging global city—Transport. *Cities, 11*(5), 332-336.

Heldman, R. K. (1992). *Global telecommunications: Layered networks' layered services*. New York: McGraw-Hill.

Hill, R. C., & Feagin, J. (1987). Detroit and Houston: Two cities in global perspective. In M. P. Smith & J. R. Feagin (Eds.), *The capitalist city* (pp. 155-177). New York: Basil Blackwell.

International Civil Aviation Organisation. (1977-1997). *On-flight origin and destination*. Montreal: Author.

Keeling, D. J. (1995). Transport and the world city paradigm. In P. Knox & P. Taylor (Eds.), *World cities in a world-system* (pp. 115-131). New York: Cambridge University Press.

King, A. (1990). *Global cities: Post-imperialism and the internationalization of London*. London: Routledge.

Knox, P., & Taylor, P. (Eds.). (1995). *World cities in a world-system*. New York: Cambridge University Press.

Kunzmann, K. (1998). World city regions in Europe: Structural change and future challenges. In F.-C. Lo & Y.-M. Yeung (Eds.), *Globalization and the world of large cities*. Tokyo: United Nations University Press.

Laumann, E., Galaskiewicz, J., & Marsden, P. (1978). Community structures as interorganizational linkages. *Annual Review of Sociology, 4*, 455-484.

Laumann, E., & Pappi, F. (1976). *Networks of collective action: A perspective on community influence systems*. New York: Academic Press.

Lo, F.-C., & Yeung, Y.-M. (1998). Introduction. In F.-C. Lo & Y.-M. Yeung (Eds.), *Globalization of the world of large cities* (pp. 1-13). Tokyo: United Nations University Press.

McKenzie, R. (1927). The concept of dominance and world-organization. *American Journal of Sociology, 33*, 28-42.

Meyer, D. R. (1986). World system of cities: Relations between international financial metropolises and South American cities. *Social Forces, 64*(3), 553-581.

Meyer, D. R. (1991a). Change in the world system of metropolises: The role of business intermediaries. *Urban Geography, 12*(5), 393-416.

Meyer, D. R. (1991b). The formation of a global financial center: London and its intermediaries. In K. Resat (Ed.), *Cities in the world-system, studies in the political economy of the world-system* (pp. 97-106). New York: Greenwood.

Nemeth, R., & Smith, D. (1985). International trade and world-system structure: A multiple network analysis. *Review (Fernand Braudel Center), 8*, 517-560.

Noam, E. (1992). *Telecommunications in Europe*. Oxford, UK: Oxford University Press.

Pitts, F. (1965). A graph theoretic approach to historical geography. *Professional Geographer, 17*(5), 15-20.

Pitts, F. (1979). The medieval river trade network of Russia revisited. *Social Networks, 1*, 285-293.

Portes, A., & Stepick, A. (1993). *City on the edge: The transformation of Miami*. Berkeley: University of California Press.

Rimmer, P. (1998). Transport and telecommunications among world cities. In F.-C. Lo & Y.-M. Yeung (Eds.), *Globalization of the world of large cities* (pp. 433-470). Tokyo: United Nations University Press.

Rodriguez, N., & Feagin, J. (1986). Urban specialization in the world system: An investigation of historical cases. *Urban Affairs Quarterly, 22*, 187-220.

Ross, R., & Trachte, K. (1990). *Global capitalism: The new leviathan*. Albany: State University of New York Press.

Sacks, M. A., Ventresca, M., & Uzzi, B. (2001). Global institutions and networks: Contingent change in the structure of world trade advantage, 1965-1980. *American Behavioral Scientist, 44*(10), 1579-1601.

Sassen, S. (1991). *The global city: New York, London, Tokyo*. Princeton, NJ: Princeton University Press.

Sassen, S. (1994). *Cities in a world economy*. Thousand Oaks, CA: Pine Forge Press.

Sassen, S. (1998). The impact of new technologies and globalization on cities. In F.-C. Lo & Y.-M. Yeung (Eds.), *Globalization of the world of large cities* (pp. 391-409). Tokyo: United Nations University Press.

Simon, D. (1995). The world city hypothesis: Reflections from the periphery. In P. Knox & P. Taylor (Eds.), *World cities in a world-system* (pp. 132-155). New York: Cambridge University Press.

Smith, D. A. (1995). The new urban sociology meets the old: Rereading some classical human ecology. *Urban Affairs Review, 30*(3), 431-456.

Smith, D. A. (1996). *Third world cities in global perspective: The political economy of urbanization*. Boulder, CO: Westview.

Smith, D. A., & White, D. (1992). Structure and dynamics of the global economy: Network analysis of international trade 1965-1980. *Social Forces, 70*(4), 857-893.

Snyder, D., & Kick, E. (1979). Structural position in the world system and economic growth, 1955-1970: A multiple network analysis of transnational interaction. *American Journal of Sociology, 84*, 1097-1126.

Steiber, S. (1979). The world system and world trade: An empirical exploration of conceptual conflicts. *Sociological Quarterly, 20*(1), 23-36.

Tilly, C. (1984). *Big structures, large processes, huge comparisons*. New York: Russell Sage Foundation.

Wade, R. (1996). Globalization and its limits: Reports of the death of the national economy are greatly exaggerated. In S. Berger and R. Dore (Eds.), *National diversity and global capitalism* (pp. 60-88). Ithaca, NY: Cornell University Press.

White, D. (1989). *Measuring role distance: Structural and relational equivalence*. Unpublished manuscript, Social Network Colloquium, University of California, Irvine.

White, H., Boorman, S., & Brieger, R. (1976). Social structure from multiple networks: Block models of roles and position. *American Journal of Sociology, 81*, 730-780.

Yousry, M., Abu-Zekry, T., & Yousry, A. (1998). Cairo as a world city: The impact of Cairo's orientation to globalization. In F.-C. Lo & Y.-M. Yeung (Eds.), *Globalization of the world of large cities* (pp. 270-313). Tokyo: United Nations University Press.

[21]

Urban Studies, Vol. 32, No. 2, 1995 361–378

Telecommunications and the Changing Geographies of Knowledge Transmission in the Late 20th Century

Barney Warf

[Paper first received, March 1994; in final form, July 1994]

Summary. Recent innovations in telecommunications and computing, enhanced by a global wave of deregulation and the emergence of post-Fordist production regimes, have unleashed profound transformations of various service sectors in the global economy. This paper first reviews the geographical repercussions of the explosion of information services, including the birth of electronic funds transfer systems, the growth of global cities and the dispersal of back offices to low-wage sites across the globe. Secondly, it explores the political economy and spatiality of the largest of these systems, the Internet. Thirdly, it summarises how the global division of labour has recently engendered the birth of 'new information spaces', places whose recent growth is contingent upon the introduction of telecommunications, citing as examples Singapore, Hungary and the Dominican Republic.

The late 20th century has witnessed an explosion of producer services on an historic scale, which forms a fundamental part of the much-heralded transition from Fordism to post-Fordism (Coffey and Bailly, 1991; Wood, 1991). Central to this transformation has been a wave of growth in financial and business services linked at the global level by telecommunications. The emergence of a global service economy has profoundly altered markets for, and flows of, information and capital, simultaneously initiating new experiences of space and time, generating a new round of what Harvey (1989, 1990) calls time–space convergence. More epistemologically, Poster (1990) notes that electronic systems change not only what we know, but how we know it.

The rapid escalation in the supply and demand of information services has been propelled by a convergence of several factors, including dramatic cost declines in information-processing technologies induced by the microelectronics revolution, national and worldwide deregulation of many service industries, including the Uruguay Round of GATT negotiations (which put services on the agenda for the first time), and the persistent vertical disintegration that constitutes a fundamental part of the emergence of post-Fordist production regimes around the world (Goddard and Gillespie, 1986; Garnham, 1990; Hepworth, 1990). The growth of traditional financial and business services, and the emergence of new ones, has ushered in a profound—indeed, an historic—transformation of the ways in which information is collected, processed and circulates, forming

Barney Warf is in the Department of Geography, Florida State University, Tallahassee, FL 32306-2050, USA.

0042-0980/95/020361-18

what Castells (1989) labels the 'informational mode of production'.

This paper constitutes an ambitious overview of the development, spatial dynamics and economic consequences of international telecommunications in the late 20th century as they arise from and contribute to the expansion of a global service economy. It opens with a broad perspective of recent changes in trade in producer services, particularly international finance, as the propelling force behind a large and rapidly expanding telecommunications infrastructure. Secondly, it explores the political economy of one of the largest and most renowned electronic systems, the Internet. Thirdly, it dwells upon the spatial dimensions of the mode of information, including the flowering of a select group of global cities, offshore banking centres, and the globalisation of clerical functions. Fourthly, it traces the emergence of what is called here 'new informational spaces', nations and regions reliant upon information services at the core of their economic development strategies. The conclusion summarises several themes that arise persistently in this discussion.

The Global Service Economy and Telecommunications Infrastructure

There can be little doubt that trade in services has expanded rapidly on an international basis (Kakabadse, 1987), comprising roughly one-quarter of total international trade. Internationally, the US is a net exporter of services (but runs major trade deficits in manufactured goods), which is one reason why services employment has expanded domestically. Indeed, it could be said that as the US has lost its comparative advantage in manufacturing, it has gained a new one in financial and business services (Noyelle and Dutka, 1988; Walter, 1988). The data on global services trade are poor, but some estimates are that services comprise roughly one-third of total US exports, including tourism, fees and royalties, sales of business services and profits from bank loans.

From the perspective of contemporary social theory, services may be viewed within the context of the enormous series of changes undergone by late 20th-century capitalism. In retrospect, the signs of this transformation are not difficult to see: the collapse of the Bretton-Woods agreement in 1971 and the subsequent shift to floating exchange rates; the oil crises of 1974 and 1979, which unleashed $375b of petrodollars between 1974 and 1981 (Wachtel, 1987), and the resulting recession and stagflation in the West; the explosive growth of Third World debt, including a secondary debt market and debt–equity swaps (Corbridge, 1984), the growth of Japan as the world's premier centre of financial capital (Vogel, 1986); the explosion of the Euromarket (Pecchioli, 1983; Walter, 1988); the steady deterioration in the competitive position of industrial nations, particularly the US and the UK, and the concomitant rise of Japan, Germany and the newly industrialising nations, particularly in east Asia; the transformation of the US under the Reagan administration into the world's largest debtor, the emergence of flexible production technologies (e.g. just-in-time inventory systems) and computerisation of the workplace; the steady growth of multinational corporations and their ability to shift vast resources across national boundaries; the global wave of deregulation and privatisation that lay at the heart of Thatcherite and Reaganite post-Keynesian policy; and finally, the integration of national financial markets through telecommunications systems. In the 1990s, one might add the collapse of the Soviet bloc and the steady integration of those nations into the world economy. This series of changes has been variably labelled an 'accumulation crisis' in the transition from state monopoly to global capitalism (Graham *et al.*, 1988), or the end of one Kondratieff long wave and the beginning of another (Marshall, 1987). What is abundantly clear from these observations is the emergence of a new global division of labour, in which services play a fundamental role.

The increasing reliance of financial and business services as well as numerous multinational manufacturing firms upon telecommunications to relay massive volumes of information through international networks has made electronic data collection and transmission capabilities a fundamental part of regional and national attempts to generate a comparative advantage (Gillespie and Williams, 1988). The rapid deployment of such technologies reflects a conjunction of factors, including: the increasingly information-intensive nature of commodity production in general (necessitating ever larger volumes of technical data and related inputs on financing, design and engineering, marketing and so forth); the spatial separation of production activities in different nations through globalised sub-contracting networks; decreases in price and the elastic demand for communications; the birth of new electronic information services (e.g. on-line databases, teletext and electronic mail); and the high levels of uncertainty that accompany the international markets of the late 20th century, to which the analysis of large volumes of data is a strategic response (Moss, 1987b; Akwule, 1992). The computer networks that have made such systems technologically and commercially feasible offer users scale and scope economies, allowing spatially isolated establishments to share centralised information resources such as research, marketing and advertising, and management (Hepworth, 1986, 1990). Inevitably, such systems have profound spatial repercussions, reducing uncertainty for firms and lowering the marginal cost of existing plants, especially when they are separated from one another and their headquarters over long distances, as is increasingly the case.

Central to the explosion of information services has been the deployment of new telecommunications systems and their merger with computerised database management (Nicol, 1985). This phenomenon can be seen in no small part as an aftershock of the microelectronics revolution and the concomitant switch from analogue to digital information formats: the digital format suffers less degradation over time and space, is much more compatible with the binary constraints of computers, and allows greater privacy (Akwule, 1992). As data have been converted from analogue to digital forms, computer services have merged with telecommunications. When the cost of computing capacity dropped rapidly, communications became the largest bottleneck for information-intensive firms such as banks, securities brokers and insurance companies. Numerous corporations, especially in financial services, invested in new communications technologies such as microwave and fibre optics. To meet the growing demand for high-volume telecommunications, telephone companies upgraded their copper-cable systems to include fibre-optics lines, which allow large quantities of data to be transmitted rapidly, securely and virtually error-free. By the early 1990s, the US fibre-optic network was already well in place (Fig. 1). In response to the growing demand for international digital data flows beginning in the 1970s, the United Nation's International Telecommunications Union introduced Integrated Service Digital Network (ISDN) to harmonise technological constraints to data flow among its members (Akwule, 1992). ISDN has since become the standard model of telecommunications in Europe, North America and elsewhere.

The international expansion of telecommunications networks has raised several predicaments for state policy at the global and local levels. This topic is particularly important because, as we shall see, state policy both affects and is affected by the telecommunications industry. At the international level, issues of transborder data flow, intellectual property rights, copyright laws, etc., which have remained beyond the purview of traditional trade agreements, have become central to GATT and its successor, the International Trade Organization. At the national level, the lifting of state controls in telecommunications had significant impacts on the profitability, industrial organisation and spatial structure of information services. In the US, for example, telecommunications underwent a profound reorganisation following the dissolution of ATT's monopoly in 1984, leading to secular declines in the price

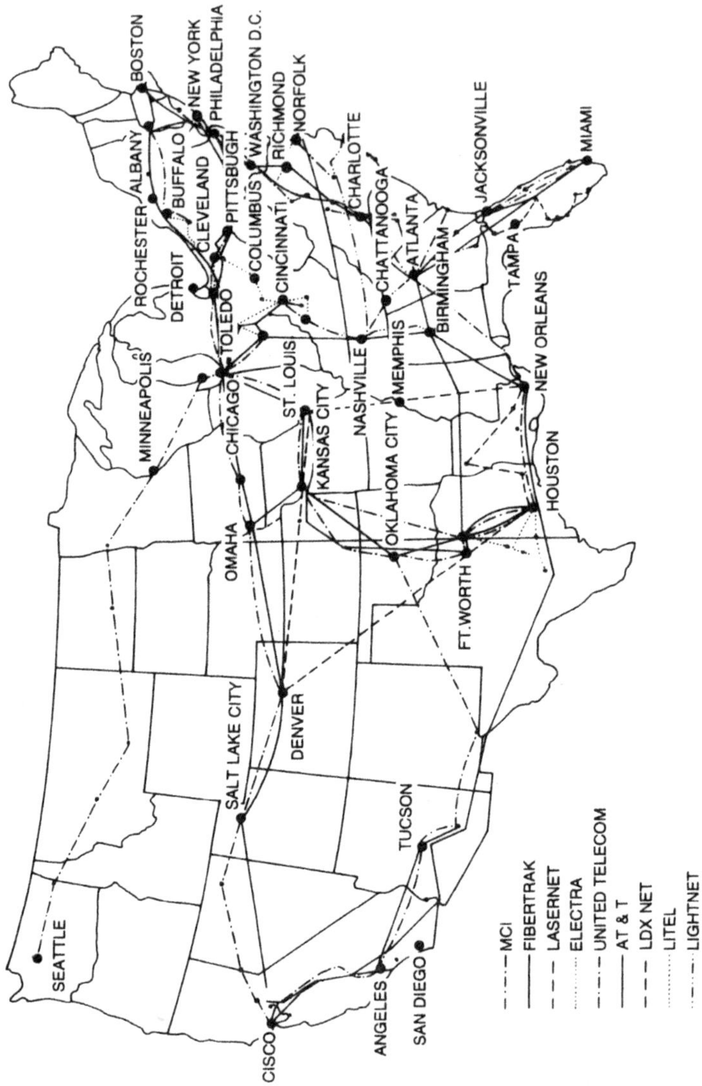

Figure 1. The US fibre-optics network, 1992. *Source:* Office of Technology Assessment (1993).

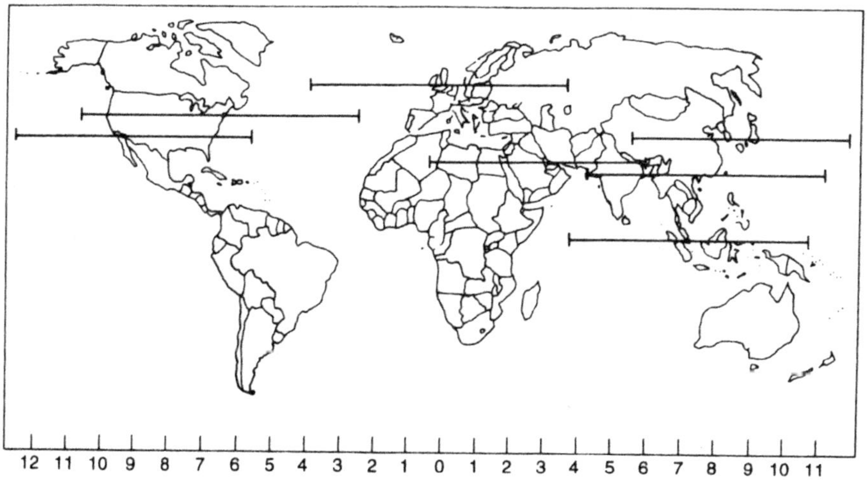

Figure 2. Trading hours of major world financial centres.

of long-distance telephone calls. Likewise, the Thatcher government privatised British Telecom, and even the Japanese began the deregulation of Nippon Telegraph and Telephone.

Telecommunications allowed not only new volumes of inter-regional trade in data services, but also in capital services. Banks and securities firms have been at the forefront of the construction of extensive leased telephone networks, giving rise to electronic funds transfer systems that have come to form the nerve centre of the international financial economy, allowing banks to move capital around a moment's notice, arbitraging interest rate differentials, taking advantage of favourable exchange rates, and avoiding political unrest (Langdale, 1985, 1989; Warf, 1989). Citicorp, for example, erected its Global Telecommunications Network to allow it to trade \$200bn daily in foreign exchange markets around the world. Such networks give banks an ability to move money—by some estimates, more than \$1.5 trillion daily (*Insight*, 1988)—around the globe at stupendous rates. Subject to the process of digitisation, information and capital become two sides of the same coin. In the securities markets, global telecommunications systems have also facilitated the emergence of the 24-hour trading day, linking stock markets through the computerised trading of stocks. Reuters and the Chicago Mercantile Exchange announced the formation of Globex, an automated commodities trading system, while in 1993 the New York stock exchange began the move to a 24-hour day automated trading system. As Figure 2 indicates, the world's major financial centres are easily connected even with an 8-hour trading day. The volatility of stock markets has increased markedly as hair-trigger computer trading programmes allow fortunes to be made (and lost) by staying microseconds ahead of (or behind) other markets, as exemplified by the famous crashes of 19 October 1987. It is vital to note that heightened volatility, or the ability to switch vast quantities of funds over enormous distances, is fundamental to these capital markets: speculation is no fun when there are no wild swings in prices (Strange, 1986).

Within the context of an expanding and ever more integrated global communications network, a central role in the formation of local competitive advantage has been attained by teleports, which are essentially office parks equipped with satellite earth stations and usually linked to local fibre-optics lines (Lipman *et al.*, 1986; Hanneman, 1987a, 1987b and 1987c). The World Teleport Association defines a teleport as:

> An access facility to a satellite or other long-haul telecommunications medium, incorporating a distribution network serving the greater regional community and associated with, including, or within a comprehensive real estate or other economic development. (Hanneman, 1987a, p. 15)

Just as ports facilitate the transshipment of cargo and airports are necessary for the movement of people, so too do teleports serve as vital information transmission facilities in the age of global capital. Because telecommunications exhibit high fixed costs and low marginal costs, teleports offer significant economies of scale to small users unable to afford private systems (Stephens, 1987; Burstyn, 1986). Teleports apparently offer a continually declining average cost curve for the provision of telecommunications services. Such a cost curve raises important issues of pricing and regulation, including the tendency of industries with such cost structures to form natural monopolies. Government regulation is thus necessary to minimise inefficiencies, and the pricing of telecommunications services becomes complex (i.e. marginal revenues do not equal marginal costs, as in non-monopolistic, non-regulated sectors) (Rohlfs, 1974; Saunders *et al.*, 1983; Guldmann, 1990).

In the late 1980s there were 54 teleports in the world, including 36 in the US (Hanneman, 1987a). Most of these are concentrated in the industrialised world, particularly in cities in which data-intensive financial and business services play a major economic role. In Europe, London's new teleport in the Docklands will ensure that city's status as the centre of the Euromarket for the near future; Hamburg, Cologne, Amsterdam and Rotterdam are extending telematic control across Europe.

Tokyo is currently building the world's largest teleport. In the 1980s, the Japanese government initiated a series of high-technology 'technopolises' that form part of a long-term 'teletopia' plan to encourage decentralisation of firms out of the Tokyo region to other parts of the nation (Rimmer, 1991). In 1993 the city initiated the Tokyo Teleport on 98 ha of reclaimed land in Tokyo harbour (Tokyo Metropolitan Government Planning Department, 1993). The teleport's 'intelligent buildings' (those designed to accommodate fibre optics and advanced computational capacity), particularly its Telecom Centre, are designed to accommodate ISDN requirements. Wide Area Networks (WANs) provide local telecommunications services via microwave channels, as do Value Added Networks on fibre-optic routes. The site was originally projected to expand to 340 ha, including office, waterfront and recreational functions, and employ 100 000 people, but may be scaled back in the light of the recent recessionary climate there.

The world's first teleport is named, simply, The Teleport, located on Staten Island, New York, a project jointly operated by Merrill Lynch and the Port Authority of New York and New Jersey. Built in 1981, The Teleport consists of an 11-acre office site and 16 satellite earth stations, and is connected to 170 miles of fibre-optic cables throughout the New York region, which are, in turn, connected to the expanding national fibre-optic network. Japanese firms have taken a particularly strong interest in The Teleport, comprising 18 of its 21 tenants. For example, Recruit USA, a financial services firm, uses it to sell excess computer capacity between New York and Tokyo, taking advantage of differential day and night rates for supercomputers in each city by transmitting data via satellite and retrieving the results almost instantaneously (Warf, 1989).

In addition to the US, European and

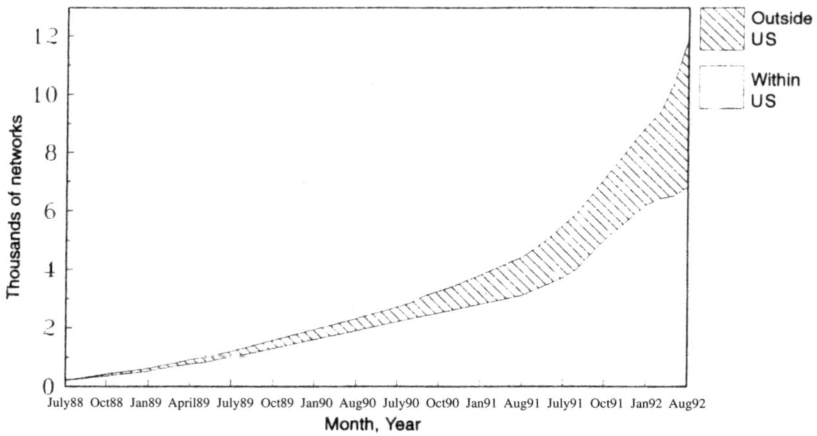

Figure 3. Growth of Internet. *Source:* Broad (1993).

Japanese teleports, some Third World nations have invested in them in order to secure a niche in the global information services economy. Jamaica, for example, built one at Montego Bay to attract American 'back office' functions there (Wilson, 1991). Other examples include Hong Kong, Singapore, Bahrain and Lagos, Nigeria (Warf, 1989).

The Internet: Political Economy and Spatiality of the Information Highway

Of all the telecommunications systems that have emerged since the 1970s, none has received more public adulation than the Internet. The unfortunate tendency in the popular media to engage in technocratic utopianism, including hyperbole about the birth of cyberspace and virtual reality, has obscured the very real effects of the Internet. The Internet is the largest electronic network on planet, connecting an estimated 20m people in 40 countries (Broad, 1993). Further, the Internet has grown at rapid rates, doubling in networks and users every year (Figure 3); by mid 1992, it connected more than 12 000 individual networks worldwide. Originating as a series of public networks, it now includes a variety of private systems of access, in the US including services such as Prodigy, CompuServe or America On-Line (Lewis, 1994), which allow any individual with a microcomputer and modem to 'plug in', generating a variety of 'virtual communities'. By 1994, such services connected almost 5m people in the US alone (Lewis, 1994).

The origins of the Internet can be traced back to 1969, when the US Department of Defense founded ARPANET, a series of electronically connected computers whose transmission lines were designed to withstand a nuclear onslaught (Schiller, 1993). Indeed, the very durability and high quality of much of today's network owes its existence to its military origins. In 1984, ARPANET was expanded and opened to the scientific community when it was taken over by the National Science Foundation, becoming NSFNET, which linked five supercomputers around the US (Figure 4). The Internet, which emerged upon a global scale via its integration with existing telephone, fibre-optic and satellite systems, was made possible by the technological innovation of packet switching, in which individual messages may be decomposed, the constituent parts transmitted by various channels (i.e. fibre optics, telephone lines, satellite), and

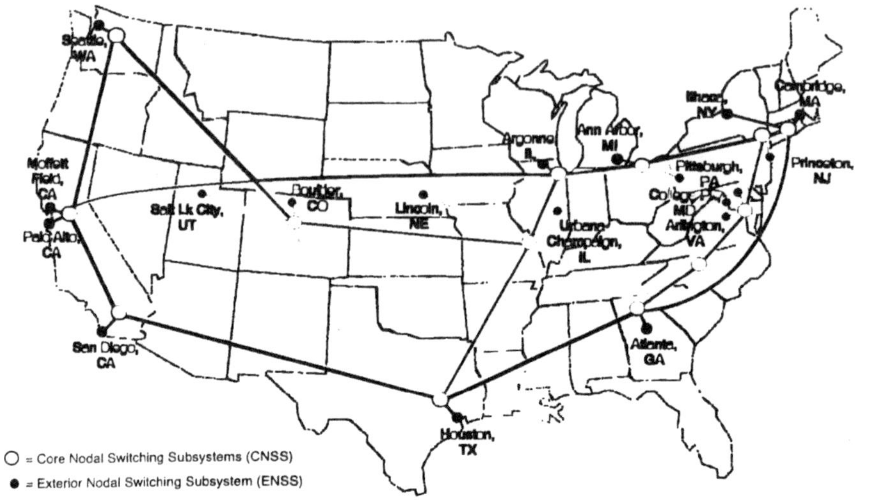

Figure 4. Distribution of NSFNET Backbone Service. *Source:* Office of Technology Assessment (1993).

then reassembled, seamlessly and instantaneously, at the destination. In the 1990s such systems have received new scrutiny as central elements in the Clinton administration's emphasis on 'information superhighways'.

The Internet has become the world's single most important mechanism for the transmission of scientific and academic knowledge. Roughly one-half of all of its traffic is electronic mail, while the remainder consists of scientific documents, data, bibliographies, electronic journals and bulletin boards (Broad, 1993). Newer additions include electronic versions of newspapers, such as the *Chicago Tribune* and *San Jose Mercury News*, as well as an electronic library, the World Wide Web. In contrast to the relatively slow and bureaucratically monitored systems of knowledge production and transmission found in most of the world, the Internet and related systems permit a thoroughly unfiltered, non-hierarchical flow of information best noted for its lack of overlords. Indeed, the Internet has spawned its own unregulated counterculture of 'hackers' (Mungo and Clough, 1993). However, the system finds itself facing the continuous threat of commercialisation as cyberspace is progressively encroached upon by corporations, giving rise, for example, to new forms of electronic shopping and 'junk mail' (Weis, 1992). The combination of popular, scientific and commercial uses has led to an enormous surge in demand for Internet capacities, so much so that they frequently generate 'traffic jams on the information highway' as the transmission circuits become overloaded (Markoff, 1993).

Despite the mythology of equal access for everyone, there are also vast discrepancies in access to the Internet at the global level (Schiller, 1993; Cooke and Lehrer, 1993). As measured by the number of access nodes in each country, it is evident that the greatest Internet access remains in the most economically developed parts of the world, notably North America, Europe and Japan (Figure 5). The hegemony of the US is particularly notable given that 90 per cent of Internet traffic is destined for or originates in that nation. Most of Africa, the Middle East and Asia (with the exceptions of India, Thailand and Malaysia), in contrast, have little or no access. There is, clearly, a reflection here of the long-standing bifurcation between the First and Third Worlds. To this extent, it is apparent than the geography of the Internet reflects previous rounds of capital accumulation—i.e. it exhibits a spatiality largely preconditioned by the legacy of colonialism.

There remains a further dimension to be explored here, however, the bifurcation between the superpowers following World War II. As Buchner (1988) noted, Marxist regimes favoured investments in television rather than telephone systems: televisions, allowing only a one-way flow of information (i.e. government propaganda), are far more conducive to centralised control that are telephones, which allow multiple parties to circumvent government lines of communication. Because access to the Internet relies heavily upon existing telephone networks, this policy has hampered the emerging post-Soviet 'Glasnet'. Superimposed on top of the landscapes of colonialism, therefore, is the landscape of the Cold War.

A rather curious yet revealing byproduct of the Internet's expansion concerns the international transmission of computer viruses, programmes written deliberately to interfere with the operations of other software systems. Although viruses are not new to users of computers, the rapid growth of electronic systems in the 1980s has markedly accelerated their capacity to travel internationally, indicating both the extent and speed with which knowledge circulates through such networks as well as the vulnerability of these systems to unwanted intrusions. In 1992, for example, the Michelangelo virus disrupted software systems of users ranging from South African pharmacists to the San Francisco police department. More ominous is the 'Bulgarian virus machine' (Mungo and Clough, 1993). In the 1980s, Bulgaria was the designated computer producer for the Soviet bloc, and Sofia University produced large numbers of skilled engineers and programmers to serve it. As communism collapsed in the late 1980s, many of such individuals, including bored young men who comprise the vast bulk of hackers, took to writing viruses and releasing them on international networks, including those of the UN. Simultaneously, Sofia University began to export its anti-virus software on the world market. Although some of the worst excesses of Bulgarian hackers have been curtailed, some indications are that they are being joined by Russian, Thai and other counterparts.

Geographical Consequences of the Mode of Information

As might be expected, the emergence of a global economy hinging upon producer services and telecommunications systems has led to new rounds of uneven development and spatial inequality. Three aspects of this phenomenon are worth noting here, including the growth of world cities, the expansion of offshore banking centres and the globalisation of back offices.

World Cities

The most readily evident geographical repercussions of this process have been the growth of 'world cities', notably London, New York and Tokyo (Moss, 1987a; Sassen, 1991), each of which seems to be more closely attuned to the rhythms of the international economy than the nation-state in which it is located. In each metropolitan area, a large agglomeration of banks and ancillary firms generates pools of well-paying administrative and white-collar professional jobs; in each, the incomes of a wealthy stratum of traders and professionals have sent real estate prices soaring, unleashing rounds of gentrification and a corresponding impoverishment for disadvantaged populations. While such predicaments are not new historically—Amsterdam was the Wall Street of the 17th century (Rodriguez and Feagin, 1986)—the magnitude and rapidity of change that global telecommunications have unleashed in such cities is without precedent.

London, for example, boomed under the

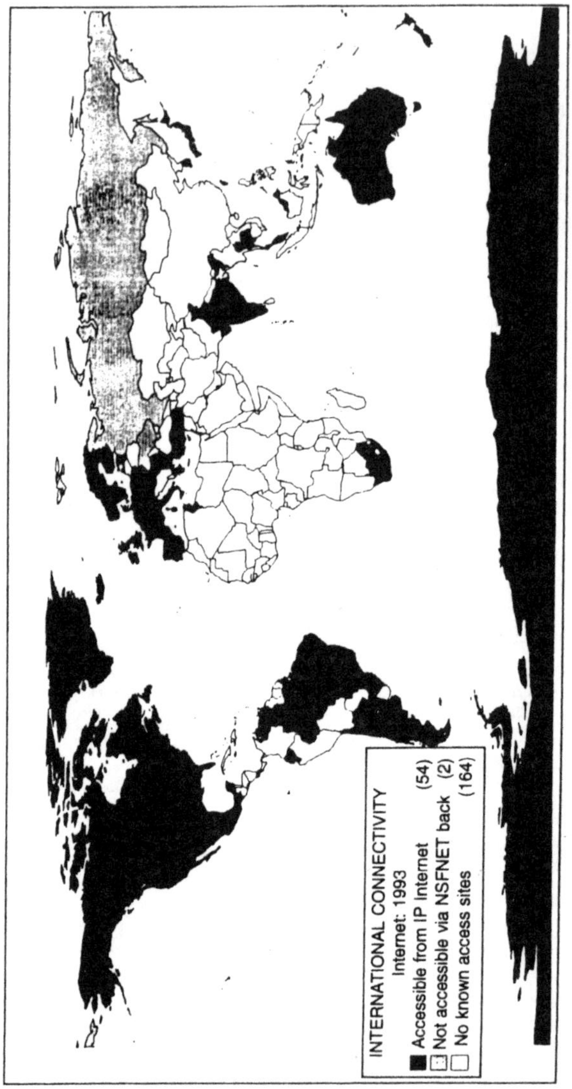

Figure 5. The geography of access to the Internet, 1993. *Source:* unpublished data from the Internet Supervisory Oversight Committee.

impetus of the Euromarket in the 1980s, and has become detached from the rest of Britain (Thrift, 1987; Budd and Whimster, 1992). Long the centre of banking for the British Empire, and more recently the capital of the unregulated Euromarket, London seems to have severed its moorings to the rest of the UK and drifted off into the hyperspaces of global finance. State regulation in the City—always loose when compared to New York or Tokyo—was further diminished by the 'Big Bang' of 1986. Accordingly, the City's landscape has been reshaped by the growth of offices, most notably Canary Wharf and the Docklands. Still the premier financial centre of Europe, and one of the world's major centres of foreign banking, publishing and advertising, London finds its status challenged by the growth of Continental financial centres such as Amsterdam, Paris and Frankfurt.

Similarly, New York rebounded from the crisis of the mid 1970s with a massive influx of petrodollars and new investment funds (i.e. pension and mutual funds) that sustained a prolonged bull market on Wall Street in the 1980s (Scanlon, 1989; Mollenkopf and Castells, 1992; Shefter, 1993). Today, 20 per cent of New York's banking employment is in foreign-owned firms, notably Japanese giants such as Dai Ichi Kangyo. Driven by the entrance of foreign firms and increasing international linkages, trade on the New York stock exchange exploded from 12m shares per day in the 1970s to 150m in the early 1990s (Warf, 1991). New York also boasts of being the communications centre of the world, including one-half million jobs that involve the collection, production, processing, transmission or consumption of information in one capacity or another (Warf, 1991). This complex, including 60 of the largest advertising and legal services firms in the US, is fuelled by more word-processing systems than in all of Europe combined. The demand for space in such a context has driven an enormous surge of office construction, housing 60 headquarters of US Fortune 500 firms. Currently, 20 per cent of New York's office space is foreign-owned, testimony to the need of large foreign financial firms to establish a presence there.

Tokyo, the epicentre of the gargantuan Japanese financial market, is likely the world's largest centre of capital accumulation, with one-third of the world's stocks by volume and 12 of its largest banks by assets (Masai, 1989). The Tokyo region accounts for 25 per cent of Japan's population, but a disproportionate share of its economic activity, including 60 per cent of the nation's headquarters, 65 per cent of its stock transactions, 89 per cent of its foreign corporations, and 65 per cent of its foreign banks (Cybriwsky, 1991). Tokyo's growth is clearly tied to its international linkages to the world economy, particularly in finance, a reflection of Japan's growth as a major world economic power (Masai, 1989; Cybriwsky, 1991). In the 1980s, Japan's status in the global financial markets was unparalleled as the world's largest creditor nation (Vogel, 1986; *Far Eastern Economic Review*, 1987). Tokyo's role as a centre of information-intensive activities includes a state-of-the-art telecommunications infrastructure, including the CAPTAIN (Character and Pattern Telephone Access Information Network) system (Nakamura and White, 1988).

Offshore Banking

A second geographical manifestation of the new, hypermobile capital markets has been the growth of offshore banking, financial services outside the regulation of their national authorities. Traditionally, 'offshore' was synonymous with the Euromarket, which arose in the 1960s as trade in US dollars outside the US. Given the collapse of Bretton Woods and the instability of world financial markets, the Euromarket has since expanded to include other currencies as well as other parts of the world. The recent growth of offshore banking centres reflects the broader shift from traditional banking services (loans and deposits) to lucrative, fee-based non-traditional functions, including debt repackaging foreign exchange transactions and cash management (Walter, 1989).

Today, the growth of offshore banking has occurred in response to favourable tax laws in hitherto marginal places that have attempted to take advantage of the world's uneven topography of regulation. As the technological barriers to capital have declined, the importance of political ones has thus risen concomitantly. Several distinct clusters of offshore banking may be noted, including, in the Caribbean, the Bahamas and Cayman Islands; in Europe, Switzerland, Luxembourg and Liechtenstein; in the Middle East, Cyprus and Bahrain; in southeast Asia, Singapore and Hong Kong; and in the Pacific Ocean, Vanuatu, Nauru and Western Samoa. Roberts (1994, p. 92) notes that such places "are all part of a worldwide network of essentially marginal places which have come to assume a crucial position in the global circuits of fungible, fast-moving, furtive money and fictitious capital." Given the extreme mobility of finance capital and its increasing separation from the geography of employment, offshore banking can be expected to yield relatively little for the nations in which it occurs; Roberts (1994), for example, illustrates the case of the Cayman Islands, now the world's fifth-largest banking centre in terms of gross assets, where 538 foreign banks employ only 1000 people (less than two apiece). She also notes that such centres are often places in which 'hot money' from illegal drug sales or undeclared businesses may be laundered.

Offshore markets have also penetrated the global stock market, where telecommunications may threaten the agglomerative advantages of world cities even as they reinforce them. For example, the National Associated Automated Dealers Quotation System (NASDAQ) has emerged as the world's fourth-largest stock market; unlike the New York, London, or Tokyo exchanges, NASDAQ lacks a trading floor, connecting half a million traders worldwide through telephone and fibre-optic lines. Similarly, Paris, Belgium, Spain, Vancouver and Toronto all recently abolished their trading floors in favour of screen-based trading.

Global Back Offices

A third manifestation of telecommunications in the world service economy concerns the globalisation of clerical services, in particular back offices. Back offices perform many routinised clerical functions such as data entry of office records, telephone books or library catalogues, stock transfers, processing of payroll or billing information, bank cheques, insurance claims, magazine subscriptions and airline frequent-flyer coupons. These tasks involve unskilled or semi-skilled labour, primarily women, and frequently operate on a 24-hour-per-day basis (Moss and Dunau, 1986). By the mid 1980s, with the conversion of office systems from analogue to digital form largely complete, many firms began to integrate their computer systems with telecommunications.

Historically, back offices have located adjacent to headquarters activities in downtown areas to ensure close management supervision and rapid turnaround of information. However, under the impetus of rising central-city rents and shortages of sufficiently qualified (i.e. computer-literate) labour, many service firms began to uncouple their headquarters and back office functions, moving the latter out of the downtown to cheaper locations on the urban periphery. Most back office relocations, therefore, have been to suburbs (Moss and Dunau, 1986; Nelson, 1986). Recently, given the increasing locational flexibility afforded by satellites and a growing web of inter-urban fibre-optics systems, back offices have begun to relocate on a much broader, continental scale. Under the impetus of new telecommunications systems, many clerical tasks have become increasingly footloose and susceptible to spatial variations in production costs. For example, several firms fled New York City in the 1980s: American Express moved its back offices to Salt Lake City, UT, and Phoenix, AZ; Citicorp shifted its Mastercard and Visa divisions to Tampa, FL, and Sioux Falls, SD, and moved its data processing functions to Las Vegas, NV, Buffalo, NY, Hagerstown, MD, and Santa Monica, CA; Citibank moved its cash management services to New Castle, DE; Chase Manhattan housed its credit card operations in Wilmington; Hertz relocated its data entry division to Oklahoma City; Avis went to Tulsa. Dean Witter moved its data processing facilities to Dallas, TX; Metropolitan Life repositioned its back offices to Greenville, SC, Scranton, PA, and Wichita, KS; Deloitte Haskins Sells relocated its back offices to Nashville, TN; and Eastern Airlines chose Miami, FL.

Internationally, this trend has taken the form of the offshore office (Wilson, 1991). The primary motivation for offshore relocation is low labour costs, although other considerations include worker productivity, skills, turnover and benefits. Offshore offices are established not to serve foreign markets, but to generate cost savings for US firms by tapping cheap Third World labour pools. Notably, many firms with offshore back offices are in industries facing strong competitive pressures to enhance productivity, including insurance, publishing and airlines. Offshore back office operations remained insignificant until the 1980s, when advances in telecommunications such as trans-oceanic fibre-optics lines made possible greater locational flexibility just when the demand for clerical and information processing services grew rapidly (Warf, 1993). Several New York-based life insurance companies, for example, have erected back office facilities in Ireland, with the active encouragement of the Irish government (Lohr, 1988). Often situated near Shannon Airport, they move documents in by Federal Express and the final product back via satellite or the TAT-8 fibre-optics line that connected New York and London in 1989 (Figure 6). Despite the fact that back offices have been there only a few years, Irish development officials already fret, with good reason, about potential competition from Greece and Portugal. Likewise, the Caribbean has become a particularly important locus for American back offices, partly due to the Caribbean Basin Initiative instituted by the Reagan administration and the guaranteed access to the US market that it provides. Most back offices in the Caribbean have chosen Anglophonic nations, particularly Jamaica and Barbados. American Airlines has paved the way in the Caribbean through its subsidiary Caribbean Data Services (CDS), which began when a data processing centre moved from Tulsa to Barbados in 1981. In 1987, CDS opened a second office near Santo Domingo, Dominican Republic, where wages are one-half as high as Barbados (Warf, forthcoming). Thus, the same flexibility that allowed back offices to move out of the US can be used against the nations to which they relocate.

New Information Spaces

The emergence of global digital networks has generated growth in a number of unanticipated places. These are definitely not the new industrial spaces celebrated in the literature on post-Fordist production complexes (Scott, 1988), but constitute new 'information spaces' reflective of the related, yet distinct, mode of information. Three examples—Singapore, Hungary and the Dominican Republic—illustrate the ways in which contemporary telecommunications generate repercussions in the least expected of places.

Singapore

Known best perhaps as a member of the East Asian newly industrialised countries (NICs), Singapore today illustrates what may be the most advanced telecommunications infrastructure in the world, creating an 'intelligent island' with high-speed leased circuits, a dense telephone and fibre-optic network, household teleboxes for electronic mail and ubiquitous remote computer access (Dicken, 1987; Corey, 1991). Singapore's government has led the way in this programme through its National Computer Board and Telecommunications Authority. This transformation has occurred as part of a sustained shift in the island's role from unskilled, low-wage assembly functions to exporter of high value-added business services and as the financial hub of south-east Asia, a process hastened by the flight of capital from Hong Kong

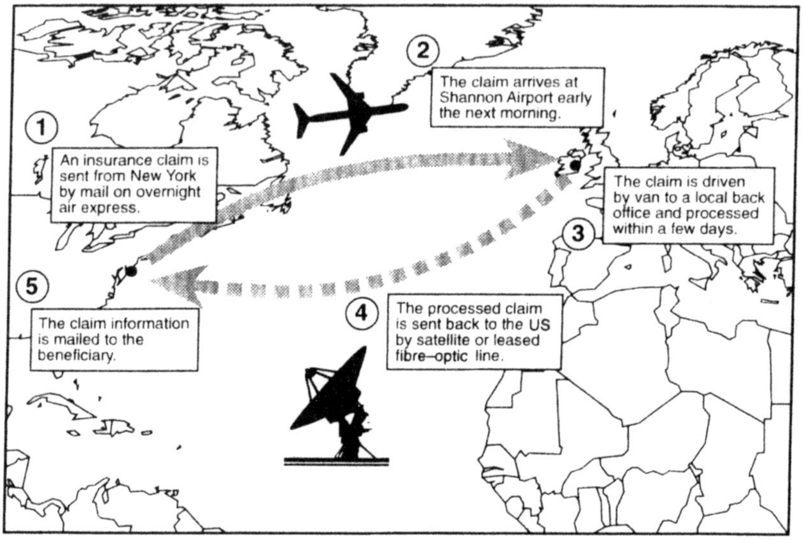

Figure 6. Mechanics of back office relocation to Ireland.

(Jussawalla and Cheach, 1983). Exports of services have now become Singapore's largest industry in terms of employment and foreign revenues. Reuters, for example, uses Singapore as its news hub in south-east Asia. In part, this transformation reflects the island's relatively high wages and fears of competition from its larger neighbours. Today, more than one-third of Singapore's labour force is engaged in skilled, white-collar employment. In addition, Singapore uses its telecommunications network for advanced Electronic Data Interchange (EDI) services to facilitate maritime shipping, in congruence with its status as the world's largest port.

Hungary

Before the collapse of the Soviet Union, Hungary suffered many of the same telecommunications problems as other underdeveloped nations: outdated technology, unsatisfied demand and few advanced services. Today, largely due to deregulation and foreign investment, the Hungarian telecommunications system is the most advanced in the former Soviet bloc, subsuming 10 per cent of the nation's total investment capital. The leader in this process has been the postal service, Magyar Posta, and its successor, the Hungarian Telecommunications Company (Matav), which introduced innovative pricing based on market, not political criteria, fees for telephone connections, time-differentiated and distance-sensitive pricing and bond financing. Concomitantly, an administrative reorganisation decentralised control of the firm, breaking the inefficient stranglehold of the bureaucratic, Communist *apparatchik* (Whitlock and Nyevrikel, 1992). The birth of the new Hungarian telecommunications network was invaluable to the nation's emerging financial system, centred in Budapest, which has expanded beyond simple loans and stocks to include database management and stock transfers (Tardos, 1991). Thus, in this respect, Hungary serves as a model for other nations making the transition from state socialism to market economies.

The Dominican Republic

In the 1980s, the Dominican government introduced a policy designed to develop non-traditional exports, particularly tourism and information services, as part of a strategy to reduce the country's reliance upon agricultural exports. For a small, relatively impoverished nation, the nation possesses a well-endowed information services infrastructure (Warf, forthcoming). The national telephone company Codetel (Compania Dominicana de Telecommunicaciones), for example, has provided the Dominican Republic with near-universal telephone access, high-speed data transmission services on fibre-optics lines, digital switching equipment, cellular telephones and microwave service to all neighbouring nations except Cuba. Codetel also sells a variety of high value-added services such as electronic mail and databases, telex, remote terminals, facsimile services, Spanish–English translations and leased lines. This infrastructure has made the Dominican Republic the most advanced nation in telecommunications in Latin America and has attracted numerous foreign firms. IBM-Santo Domingo, for example, engages in a complex, worldwide system of sub-contracting with its subsidiaries, purchasing, for example, printers from Argentina, disk drives from Brazil, CPUs from the US or Brazil and software, written in Canada, the US and Denmark, through its distributor in Mexico. A similar firm is Infotel, which performs a variety of computer-related functions for both domestic and international clients, including compilation of telephone directories, photocomposition, data conversion, computerised, on-line sale of advertising images, desktop publishing and map digitising. Infotel serves a variety of domestic and foreign clients, including Dominican utilities and municipal governments, the GTE telephone-operating companies, the US Geological Survey and the Spanish telephone network. Another service attracted to the Dominican Republic is back offices. American Airlines, and its subsidiary Caribbean Data Services, processes medical and dental insurance claims, credit card applications, retail sales inventories, market surveys and name and address listings at a Free Trade Zone near the capital.

Concluding Comments

What lessons can be drawn from these observations about the emergence of a globalised service economy and the telecommunications networks that underpin it? As part of the broad sea-change from Fordist production regimes to the globalised world of flexible accumulation, about which so much has already been said, it is clear that capital—as data or cash, electrons or investments—in the context of global services has acquired a qualitatively increased level of fluidity, a mobility enhanced by the worldwide wave of deregulation unleashed in the 1980s and the introduction of telecommunication networks. Such systems give banks, securities, insurance firms and back offices markedly greater freedom over their locational choices. In dramatically reducing the circulation time of capital, telecommunications have linked far-flung places together through networks in which billions of dollars move instantaneously across the globe, creating a geography without transport costs. There can be no doubt that this process has real consequences for places, as attested by the current status of cities such as London, New York, Tokyo and Singapore and the Cayman Islands. Generally, such processes tend to concentrate skilled, high value-added services, e.g. in global cities, while dispersing unskilled, low value-added services such as back offices to Third World locations.

In short, it is vital to note that, contrary to early, simplistic expectations that telecommunications would 'eliminate space', rendering geography meaningless through the effortless conquest of distance, such systems in fact produce new rounds of unevenness, forming new geographies that are imposed upon the relics of the past. Telecommunications simultaneously reflect and transform the topologies of capitalism, creating and rapidly recreating nested hierarchies of spaces technically articulated in the architecture of computer networks. Indeed, far from eliminating variations among places, such systems permit the exploitation of differences between areas with renewed ferocity. As Swyngedouw (1989) noted, the emergence of hyperspaces does not entail the obliteration of local uniqueness, only its reconfiguration. That the geography engendered by this process was unforeseen a decade ago hardly needs restating; that the future will hold an equally unexpected, even bizarre, set of outcomes is equally likely.

References

AKWULE, R. (1992) *Global Telecommunications: The Technology, Administration, and Policies*. Boston: Focal Press.

BLAZAR, W. (1985) Telecommunications: harnessing it for development, *Economic Development Commentary*, 9, pp. 8–11.

BROAD, W. (1993) Doing science on the network: a long way from Gutenberg, *New York Times*, 18 May, B5.

BUCHNER, B. (1988) Social control and the diffusion of modern telecommunications technologies: a cross-national study, *American Sociological Review*, 53, pp. 446–453.

BUDD, L. and WHIMSTER, S. (Eds) (1992) *Global Finance and Urban Living: A Study of Metropolitan Change*. London: Pergamon.

BURSTYN, H. (1986) Teleports: at the crossroads. *High Technology*, 6(5), pp. 28–31.

CASTELLS, M. (1989) *The Informational City*. Oxford: Basil Blackwell.

COFFEY, W. and BAILLY, A. (1991) Producer services and flexible production: an exploratory analysis, *Growth and Change*, 22, pp. 95–117.

COOKE, K. and LEHRER, D. (1993) The Internet: the whole world is talking, *The Nation*, 257, pp. 60–63.

CORBRIDGE S. (1984) Crisis, what crisis? Monetarism, Brandt II and the geopolitics of debt, *Political Geography Quarterly*, 3, pp. 331–345.

COREY, K. (1991) The role of information technology in the planning and development of Singapore, in: B. BRUNN and T. LEINBACH (Eds) *Collapsing Space and Time*, pp. 217–231. London: HarperCollins.

CYBRIWSKY, R. (1991) *Tokyo: The Changing Profile of an Urban Giant*. Boston: G.K. Hall and Co.

DICKEN, P. (1987) A tale of two NICs: Hong Kong and Singapore at the crossroads, *Geoforum*, 18, pp. 151–164.

DICKEN, P. (1992) *Global Shift: The Internationalization of Economic Activity*, 2nd edn. New York: Guilford Press.

FAR EASTERN ECONOMIC REVIEW (1987) Japan banking and finance, 9 April, pp. 47–110.

GARNHAM, N. (1990) *Capitalism and Communication: Global Culture and the Economics of Information*. Beverly Hills: Sage.

GILLESPIE, A. and WILLIAMS, H. (1988) Telecommunications and the reconstruction of comparative advantage, *Environment and Planning A*, 20, pp. 1311–1321.

GODDARD, J. and GILLESPIE, A. (1986) *Advanced Telecommunications and Regional Development*. Newcastle-upon-Tyne: Centre for Urban and Regional Development Studies.

GRAHAM, J. *ET AL.*(1988) Restructuring in U.S. manufacturing: the decline of monopoly capitalism, *Annals of the Association of American Geographers*, 78, pp. 473–490.

GULDMANN, J. (1990) Economies of scale and density in local telephone networks, *Regional Science and Urban Economics*, 20, pp. 521–533.

HALL, P. and PRESTON, P. (1988) *The Carrier Wave: New Information Technology and the Geography of Innovation, 1846–2003*. London: Unwin Hyman.

HANNEMAN, G. (1987a) The development of teleports, *Satellite Communications*, March, pp. 14–22.

HANNEMAN, G. (1987b) Teleport business, *Satellite Communications*, April, pp. 23–26.

HANNEMAN, G. (1987c) Teleports: the global outlook, *Satellite Communications*, May, pp. 29–33.

HARVEY, D. (1989) *The Condition of Postmodernity*. Oxford: Basil Blackwell.

HARVEY, D. (1990) Between space and time: reflections on the geographical imagination, *Annals of the Association of American Geographers*, 80, pp. 418–434.

HEPWORTH, M. (1986) The geography of technological change in the information economy, *Regional Studies*, 20, pp. 407–424.

HEPWORTH, M. (1990) *Geography of the Information Economy*. London: Guildford Press.

Insight. (1988) Juggling trillions on a wire: is electronic money safe? 15 February, pp. 38–40.

JUSSAWALLA, M. and CHEAH, C. (1983) Towards an information economy: the case of Singapore, *Information Economics and Policy*, 1. pp. 161–176.

KAKABADSE, M. (1987) *International Trade in Services: Prospects for Liberalisation in the 1990s*. London: Croom Helm.

LANGDALE, J. (1985) Electronic funds transfer and the internationalisation of the banking and finance industry, *Geoforum*, 16, pp. 1–13.

LANGDALE, J. (1989) The geography of international business telecommunications: the role of leased networks, *Annals of the Association of American Geographers*, 79, pp. 501–522.

LEWIS, P. (1994) A boom for on-line services, *New York Times*, 12 July, C1.

LIPMAN, A., SUGARMAN, A. and CUSHMAN, R. (1986) *Teleports and the Intelligent City*. Homewood, IL: Dow Jones.

LOHR, S. (1988) The growth of the global office, *New York Times*, 18 October, D1.

MARKOFF, J. (1993) Traffic jams already on the information highway, *New York Times*, 3 November, p. 1, C7.

MARSHALL, M. (1987) *Long Waves of Regional Development*. London: Macmillan.

MASAI, Y. (1989) Greater Tokyo as a global city, in: R. KNIGHT and G. GAPPERT (Eds) *Cities in a Global Society*. Newbury Park, CA: Sage.

MOLLENKOPF, J. and CASTELLS, M. (Eds) (1992) *Dual City: Restructuring New York*. New York: Russell Sage Foundation.

MOSS, M. (1987a) Telecommunications, world cities and urban policy. *Urban Studies*, 24, pp. 534–546.

MOSS, M. (1987b) Telecommunications and international financial centres, in: J. BROTCHIE, P. HALL and P. NEWTON (Eds) *The Spatial Impact of Technological Change*. London: Croom Helm.

MOSS, M. and DUNAU, A. (1986) Offices, information technology, and locational trends, in: J. BLACK, K. ROARK and L. SCHWARTZ (Eds) *The Changing Office Workplace*, pp. 171–182. Washington, DC: Urban Land Institute.

MUNGO, P. and CLOUGH, B. (1993) *Approaching Zero: The Extraordinary Underworld of Hackers, Phreakers, Virus Writers, and Keyboard Criminals*. New York: Random House.

NAKAMURA, H. and WHITE, J. (1988) Tokyo, in: M. DOGAN and J. KASARDA (Eds) *The Metropolitan Era, Volume 2: Mega-Cities*. Newbury Park, CA: Sage.

NELSON, K. (1986) Labor demand, labor supply and the suburbanization of low-wage office work. in: A. SCOTT and M. STORPER (Eds) *Production, Work, Territory*. Boston: Allen Unwin.

NICOL, L. (1985) Communications technology: economic and spatial impacts, in: M. CASTELLS (Ed.) *High Technology, Space, and Society*, pp. 191–209. Beverly Hills, CA: Sage.

NOYELLE, T. and DUTKA, A. (1988) *International Trade in Business Services*. Cambridge, MA: Ballinger.

OFFICE OF TECHNOLOGY ASSESSMENT (1993) *Automation of America's Offices*. Washington, DC: US Government Printing Office.

PECCHIOLI, R. (1983) *The Internationalization of Banking: The Policy Issues*, Paris: OECD.

POSTER, M. (1990) *The Mode of Information: Poststructuralism and Social Context*. Chicago: University of Chicago Press.

QUINN, J., BARUCH, J. and PAQUETTE, P. (1987) Technology in services. *Scientific American*, 257(6), pp. 50–58.

RIMMER, P. (1991) Exporting cities to the western Pacific Rim: the art of the Japanese package, in: J. BROTCHIE, M. BATTY, P. HALL and P. NEWTON (Eds) *Cities of the 21st Century*. Melbourne: Longman Cheshire.

ROBERTS, S. (1994) Fictitious capital, fictitious spaces: the geography of offshore financial flows, in: S. CORBRIDGE, R. MARTIN and N. THRIFT (Eds) *Money Power Space*. Oxford: Basil Blackwell.

RODRIGUEZ, N. and FEAGIN, J. (1986) Urban specialization in the world-system, *Urban Affairs Quarterly*, 22, pp. 187–219.

ROHLFS, J. (1974) A theory of interdependent demand for a communications service, *Bell Journal of Economics and Management Science*, 5, pp. 13–37.

SASSEN, S. (1991) *The Global City: New York, London, Tokyo*. Princeton, NJ: Princeton University Press.

SAUNDERS, R., WARFORD, J. and WELLENIUS, B. (1983) *Telecommunications and Economic Development*. Baltimore: Johns Hopkins University Press.

SCANLON, R. (1989) New York City as global capital in the 1980s, in: R. KNIGHT and G. GAPPERT (Eds) *Cities in a Global Society*. Newbury Park, CA: Sage.

SCHILLER, H. (1993) 'The information highway': public way or private road? *The Nation*, 257, pp. 64–65.

SCOTT, A.J. (1988) *New Industrial Spaces*. London: Pion.

SHEFTER, M. (1993) *Capital of the American Century: The National and International Influence of New York City*. New York: Russell Sage Foundation.

STEPHENS, G. (1987) What can business get from teleports? *Satellite Communications*, March, pp. 18–19.

STRANGE, S. (1986) *Casino Capitalism*. Oxford: Basil Blackwell.

SWYNGEDOUW, E. (1989) The heart of the place: the resurrection of locality in an age of hyperspace, *Geografiska Annaler*, 71, pp. 31–42.

TARDOS, A. (1991) Problems of the financial information system in Hungary, *Acta Oeconomica*, 43, pp. 149–166.

THRIFT, N. (1987) The fixers: the urban geography of international commercial capital, in: J. HENDERSON and M. CASTELLS (Eds) *Global Restructuring and Territorial Development*. Beverly Hills: Sage Publications.

TOKYO METROPOLITAN GOVERNMENT PLANNING DEPARTMENT (1993) *Tokyo Teleport*. Tokyo: Tokyo Metropolitan Government Information Centre.

VOGEL, E. (1986) Pax Nipponica? *Foreign Affairs*, 64, pp. 752–767.
WACHTEL, H. (1987) Currency without a country: the global funny money game, *The Nation*, 26 December, 245, pp. 784–790.
WALKER, R. (1985) Is there a service economy? The changing capitalist division of labor, *Science and Society*, Spring, pp. 42–83.
WALTER, I. (1988) *Global Competition in Financial Services: Market Structure, Protection, and Trade Liberalization*. Cambridge, MA: Ballinger.
WALTER, I. (1989) *Secret Money*. London: Unwin Hyman.
WARF, B. (1989) Telecommunications and the globalization of financial services, *Professional Geographer*, 41, pp. 257–271.
WARF, B. (1991) The internationalization of New York services, in: P. DANIELS (Ed.) *Services and Metropolitan Development: International Perspectives*, pp. 245–264. London: Routledge.
WARF, B. (1993) Back office dispersal: implications for urban development, *Economic Development Commentary*, 16, pp. 11–16.
WARF, B. (forthcoming) Information services in the Dominican Republic, *Yearbook of the Association of Latin American Geographers*.
WEIS, A. (1992) Commercialization of the Internet, *Electronic Networking*, 2(3), pp. 7–16.
WHITLOCK, E. and NYEVRIKEL, E. (1992) The evolution of Hungarian telecommunications. *Telecommunications Policy*, pp. 249–258.
WILSON, M. (1991) *Offshore relocation of producer services: the Irish back office*. Paper presented at the *Annual Meeting of the Association of American Geographers*, Miami.
WOOD, P. (1991) Flexible accumulation and the rise of business services, *Transactions of the Institute of British Geographers*, 16, pp. 160–172.

[22]

Human Organization, Vol. 57, No. 4, 1998

0018-7259/98/040394-10$1.50/1

Weak Ties, Strong Ties: Network Principles in Mexican Migration

TAMAR DIANA WILSON

Five network principles are elaborated from literature on Mexican immigrants and from research that I conducted on immigration from a *rancho* in Jalisco state to a variety of destinations within the United States. These principles are, first, that networks are multilocal, encompassing a number of geographical destinations. The importance of destinations, however, may change over time. Second, the anchoring points at any given geographical location are the work sites where immigrants find employment. Thus, labor market conditions structure where immigrants go and where they stay. Third, new geographical locations are often accessed through the "strength of weak ties," leading to geographic dispersion. Over time, some weak ties may be converted to strong ties though marriage or *compadrazgo*. Fourth, both dense networks and diffuse, weak-tie, or acquaintance networks constitute "social capital" for their members. Fifth, given the geographical dispersion at the work site and/or work type clustering found among immigrants from any particular source community, the latter can best be explained by job recruitment primarily through dense network members, especially close relatives.

Key words: migration, networks; Mexico, US

Numerous studies of transnational immigration[1] and internal migration have documented that migration is mediated by kinship and social networks. In order of strength of ties, relatives, friends and *paisanos* (community members) may offer the potential immigrant housing, loans of money, aid in finding employment, and orientation in the destination community (Massey *et al.* 1987). Once at destination, acquaintances made at work or at sites of leisure expand the information members of any given network have about potential employment opportunities (Massey *et al.* 1987; Massey and Espinosa 1997) and possible future destinations. A brief review of the extensive literature on Mexican migration to the United States, "the strength of weak ties," and "social capital," as well as results obtained from a study of transnational immigration from a *rancho* in Jalisco state that I conducted in 1989 and 1990[2] reveal at least five interrelated principles concerning migration networks and their dynamics.[3] These are:

Principle 1: Multilocality of Networks. Networks are multilocal, encompassing a variety of geographical destinations. The importance of destinations in terms of numbers of immigrants received from any one source community may change over time. Once a migration stream has linkages to a destination point, labor market conditions/opportunities become a central variable in explaining the persistence or disappearance of that stream.

Principle 2: Work Sites and Work Types as Anchoring Points of Networks. The magnetic pull of any given destination are the work sites where immigrants manage to find viable employment. Word of mouth information exchange among network members of the first immigrant(s) to land these jobs becomes of primary importance in job placement of later immigrants from the same source community or region.

Principle 3: The "Strength of Weak Ties" in Network Expansion. Networks expand over time to encompass new geographic and work site locations, often through "the strength of weak ties" (Granovetter 1973, 1982), whereby information about employment opportunities is passed from one acquaintance to another. These acquaintances provide an information bridge between more dense network clusters. Alternatively, networks expand to include new members with information about other parts of the transnational social system through the establishment of new strong ties, via, e.g., marriage or *compadrazgo* (fictive kinship established at the time of marked life cycle changes, such as baptism, marriage, etc.). This type of expansion can occur either at the region of origin or at destination(s).

Principle 4: Diffuse Networks as Social Capital. Due to aid extended, information exchanged, and recruitment to jobs that occur among network members, networks can be seen to constitute "social capital" for their members (Coleman 1988; Gold 1994; Massey *et al.* 1987; Massey and Espinosa 1997; Portes 1995; Waldinger 1994, 1995). This is as true of diffuse networks without multiple interactions among members, as it is of "dense" networks.

Tamar Diana Wilson is a research affiliate with the University of Missouri-St. Louis, who currently lives in Mexico. *She would like to thank the Wenner-Gren Foundation for Anthropological Research for the small grant which made the initial research inJalisco state possible. This article was previously presented at the International Congress of Anthropological and Ethnological Sciences, College of William and Mary, Williamsburg, Virginia, July 26-August 1, 1998.*

Principle 5: Dense Networks as Social Capital. Nonetheless, clustering of people from the same origin in specific localities and work sites is due more to the strength of strong ties than due to the weak tie social capital provided by more diffuse migration or ethnic group networks. The former can be called "dense social capital" as opposed to "diffuse social capital." One can envision a continuum between these two types of social capital.

These principles should aid in the analysis of the clustering, dispersion and reclustering of a variety of immigrant groups internationally. In the first part of the paper I will review some of the literature which elaborates upon each of these densely interrelated principles. Due to the overlapping and interlinkage of these principles, much of the information provided in one section will complement information provided in another section. In the second part I will illustrate each of these principles through case studies of transnational wage labor immigrants from the *rancho* in Jalisco which I call "Los Arboles."

Elaboration of Network Principles

PRINCIPLE 1: MULTILOCALITY OF NETWORKS

As concerns multilocality of migration networks, Cornelius has observed:

> "Social network-based migration does not necessarily tie a Mexican sending community to a single receiving area within the United States. While cases of 'specialization'— the migration to a single destination — can be found, the more common pattern entails multiple migration networks leading to a variety of U.S. communities, both urban and rural" (1991:167).

A study he conducted in the early 1970s showed that immigrants from one *pueblo* in Jalisco were working in 110 different locations in the United States, 57 of them in California (Cornelius 1976, 1991).

Migration networks may have nodal points in communities neighboring the source community, in other states within Mexico, and in a variety of destinations within the United States (Kearney 1986; Kearney and Nagengast 1989; Massey *et al.* 1987). Kearney (1986) envisions an "articulatory migrant network" interlinking emigrants from the town of San Jeronimo, Oaxaca to various rural and urban locales in both northwestern Mexico and in California. Such articulatory networks inscribe the geographical space within which individuals can be assured of aid and orientation by relatives, friends, and co-villagers (Wilson 1992).

Multilocality of networks is not a phenomenon peculiar to Mexican immigrants as Ho (1993) shows for the multinational destinations of Afro-Trinidadians, Basch *et al.* (1994) for West Indians, Haitians and Filipinos, Earle (1994) for Guatemalan Mayans, and Margolis (1994) for Brazilians — just to give a few recent examples. Brazilians, most of whom arrived in Canada and the United States in the 1980s, can be found in a variety of destinations in the he states of New York, New Jersey, Connecticut, Massachusetts, Pennsylvania, Florida, California, Virginia and Texas, as well as in Washington, D.C. (Margolis 1994:12-13).

The importance of the various destination points where network members reside and work fluctuates over time and is related to local labor market demands. Massey *et al.* (1987) summarize the history of migration from two rural towns in Jalisco, showing the multilocality of networks, the types of jobs immigrants found, and the changes in destination over time. According to these researchers, at the turn of the century the first migrants from the town of Altamira went to Arizona to work on the expanding railroad lines. In the 1920s Altamirans were recruited by labor contractors to work in the steel mills near Chicago; many also were employed in the California fields (Massey *et al.* 1987:46). Migration to the United States accelerated during the Bracero Program from 1942 to 1965, and many men crossed without bracero contracts, as undocumented workers, at that time as well. Of those without documents who were deported, some settled in the border cities of Tijuana and Mexicali. Meanwhile internal migration took residents of Altamira to Mexico City and Guadalajara. Within the United States popular destinations came to include Arizona, Texas, Illinois and California. In California, Altamirans worked initially in Imperial Valley fieldwork; more recently, they cluster in the San Francisco, Los Angeles, and middle San Joaquín Valley regions (Massey *et al.* 1987: Fig. 6.1, 6.4). Networks may thus encompass multiple home country and transnational interstate and intrastate geographical nodes.

Pioneering immigrants from the town of Chamitlán in the 1912 to 1920 period found work in at least eight states: Illinois, Indiana, Missouri, Montana, New Mexico, Oklahoma, Texas and California. They were employed on the railroads and in foundries, fields, and mines (Massey *et al.* 1987:65). Over the decades between the 1940s and the 1980s, there were changes in destinations, as well as in the numbers of transnational immigrants from Chamitlán choosing these destinations. Clusterings of immigrants, or "daughter communities" were eventually established in several California communities, including in the San Francisco Bay area, Los Angeles, the Salinas Valley and the San Joaquín Valley. These communities acted as "magnets" for ever newer immigrants from Chamitlán (Massey *et al.* 1987:157-161).

The labor market factors involved in the fluctuation of destination points over time have been noted by a number of researchers. As Massey *et al.* (1987) point out, field work in the Imperial Valley ceased to draw Altamirans after the close of the Bracero Program in 1965. A study by Alvarez (1991) documents how the closure of mines in Baja California Sur propelled the immigration of interlinked families first to Mexicali and Tijuana, then eventually to Lemon Grove, California — a network-mediated migration process which took 75 year to complete.

In *Ambivalent Journey*, Jones (1995) describes the shift in U.S. destinations for transnational immigrants from several communities in central Zacatecas and Coahuila. Prior to the end of the Bracero Program, most Coahuilans went to work in the Texas agricultural fields; most Zacatecans entered field work primarily in California and secondarily in Texas. After 1965, and even more so after 1980, immigrants from Zacatecas and Coahuila increasingly shifted into unskilled and skilled urban jobs. A sample of 710 immigrants from three towns in Zacatecas showed that in the 1980s the urban jobs they most often filled, in order of importance, were "restaurant work (busboy, dishwasher), menial factory work, work in bakeries and tortillerías, child care and housekeeping, construction, hotel and casino work, sewing, jobs as mechanics' assistants, gardening, and janitorial work" (Jones 1995:55). Jones also notes that preference's Zacatecans for more distant California, over Texas, is due to higher wages and better working conditions in the former state, thus illustrating the importance of labor market conditions in structuring destination preferences. Nonetheless, Zacatecans can still be found in Texas, as well as in Illinois and other states.

Transnational immigrants from Coahuila, on the other hand, while shifting from rural to urban work sites after 1965, continued to migrate overwhelmingly (86.6% of a sample of 288) to Texas (Jones 1995: Table 6.4). This was due to the presence of "long-standing family ties" in that state, kin who could help them regularize their immigration status. More educated and urbanized than the immigrants from Zacatecas, many found skilled jobs as carpenters, masons, metalworkers and solderers, though the majority remained in unskilled work such as construction, gardening, and cleaning of offices (Jones 1995:95).

That labor market conditions at destinations determine the ebb and flow of immigrants is apparent in historical studies. Summarizing the history of Latinos (Mexicans and Puerto Ricans) in Northwest Indiana, Escobar (1987:3-4; see also Rosales and Simon 1987) recounts how the changes in the steel industry affected migration flows from Mexico. During the Great Steel Strike of 1919, Mexican workers, lacking knowledge of the strike, were actively recruited by the steel mills as strikebreakers. During the Great Depression, steel production sunk to 15% of its former capacity. At the same time, Mexicans were increasingly left unemployed by the steel mills and were both semi-voluntarily and involuntarily repatriated, eroding the Mexican presence in Northwest Indiana. During World War II and for twenty-five years thereafter, the steel industry was reinvigorated and Mexican communities sprung up in strength once more.

Briody (1987) has also shown how fluctuating labor market conditions in South Texas States affected where Mexican immigrants went and what types of jobs they entered in the pre- and post 1974 periods. That labor market demands change over time and affect the type of work new immigrants can find, was also shown by Rodríguez (1987) in his study of Central American immigrants in Houston. While the pre-1980s boom period in construction and petrochemical industries opened up numerous jobs for undocumented Mexicans and Indochinese refugees, by the time undocumented Central Americans arrived there had been a downturn in heavy industry: None found employment in this sector of the economy (Rodríguez 1987:6).

In sum, networks are multilocal, including a variety of destination options where kin and friends can be expected to provide aid. Although some destinations decline in importance over time, newer ones may be accessed. Where employment can be found is one important variable; labor market fluctuations and the positive and/or negative conditions at any particular work site are others. Yet job openings in themselves cannot draw immigrants unless immigrants know about them. Such information flows though kinship and social networks, as well as "acquaintance networks," as will be discussed in greater detail in points 3, 4, and 5 below.

Principle 2: Work Sites and Work Types as Anchoring Points of Networks

Network-mediated recruitment of Mexican laborers, whether documented or undocumented, has existed since Mexican immigrants were incorporated into the U.S. labor force. For example, since the turn of the century, up through the Bracero Program and afterwards, Michigan sugar beet growers have depended on network recruitment by Mexican migrant workers to fulfill their farmworker quotas (Haney 1979). In a study of farmworkers in the Southwestern United States, Thomas (1982) found that existing harvest crews recruit and train new members. Crew members may call upon kin, both near and distant, or community members from the Mexican village of origin, to fill new openings. In addition, if an immigrant achieves the position of foreman or becomes a small business entrepreneur, s/he can recruit employees from among members of his/her personal network (Boyd 1989; Massey *et al.* 1987).

The type of work found by pioneering immigrants influences the employment possibilities of later immigrants, and may select for those who will become immigrants in the future. As Durand and Massey underscore:

> Although the occupational niche of the first migrants from a community is often a matter of chance, one migrants become established in a particular occupational-industrial position, they tend to channel other townspeople into the same structural location, thereby determining the character and composition of the subsequent stream (1992:34).

Jobs may be closed to women or gender-neutral, thus selecting for the sex composition of a particular immigrant stream.

It is well established that immigrants generally locate jobs, whether in agriculture or in urban areas, though the aid of network members. A study of Central American and Mexican immigrants to Austin and San Antonio, Texas showed that they were employed within days of arrival, due to network members' provision of information about available jobs (Browning and Rodríguez 1985:286). Hagan's (1994) research on a Guatemalan Maya community in Houston revealed that 93.3% of her sample of 43 men worked as maintenance or stock men in a retail supermarket chain where a pioneering immigrant from the community had found employment. She notes: "The Maya job network controls the information about the availability of new jobs" in this supermarket chain (Hagan 1994:63).

In a study of wage-labor migrants from a village in Zacatecas, Mines (1981:141-146) found that networks mediated entry into both formal and informal sector jobs in both rural and urban destinations. In Santa Ana, California villagers were concentrated in construction cleanup; in Los Angeles in small dress shops subcontracted to large manufacturers; in San Francisco in restaurants; and in Watsonville as strawberry sharecroppers. Entrepreneurs from this Zacatecas community have also set up small factories processing and packaging cactus leaves. One, in Bell Gardens, Los Angeles County, employed eighteen workers from the source community.

A community in the Los Altos region of Jalisco (Cornelius 1991:177) showed both multilocality in destinations and work specialization at each location: in Oregon villagers worked in orchards and flower fields; in Oklahoma City they were concentrated in bridge and highway construction; in Las Vegas and Palm Springs they found employment in restaurant and hotel work; and in the San Francisco Bay area they were clustered in light industry and services.

Network-mediated recruitment into specific work sites or work types is also found among Brazilian immigrants to greater New York City. Due to word of mouth recruitment, Brazilians have a "near monopoly" in shoe-shining (Margolis 1994:113). A "yuppie" New York Tex-Mex restaurant employs approximately thirty Brazilians, as hostesses, dishwashers, waiters, busboys, cooks, etc: "The first Brazilian was hired around 1985; through word of mouth recruitment, upwards of 200 Brazilians found jobs there over the next six years" (Margolis 1994:133).[4]

Migration networks then, are anchored, however temporarily, in certain geographical locations through access to specific work sites and job types. As access to new work sites and job types expands, so may the geographical nodal points of any given migration network multiply as well. At the same time, channelization to these geographical locations occurs through recruitment into specific work sites and/or through the availability of network members at any given locale to offer aid in the initial "settling in" (Jones 1982; Massey *et al.* 1987). A pattern of initial locational and employment concentration, followed by geographical and occupational dispersion, and then a renewed concentration in several particular geographical and occupational niches has been found for Mexican immigrants from nineteen different communities of origin (Massey *et al.* 1994). With the increase of weak ties (see below) among network members concentrated in several permanent settlement communities in the host society, it can be predicted that the possibilities of further dispersion and reconcentration will be opened.

PRINCIPLE 3: THE "STRENGTH OF WEAK TIES" IN NETWORK EXPANSION

A number of articles by Granovetter (1973, 1982) have explored the importance of the "strength of weak ties" in procuring employment. Strong ties describe the social relations between ego and close friends and/or kin. Together they form a dense network in which members know one another, interact on a routine basis, and are privy to the same shared information regarding the social environment, including job opportunities. Weak ties describe the relationship between ego and his/her "acquaintance network." Such acquaintances are most usually unknown to one another or to members of ego's dense network. Information, for example information about new job possibilities, is held to flow most effectively from more experience distant parts of the social system through weak ties. Acquaintances, then, form information bridges between dense clusters of kin and friends.

In sum, according to Granovetter (1973, 1982) weak ties tend to be stronger bridges to new information about employment opportunities than strong ties. Granovetter (1982) holds, however, that the strength of weak ties is more important among higher socioeconomic groups, because lower socioeconomic groups have little access to high status individuals who can offer them jobs or facilitate their entry into a work site. among the poor, heavily involved in dense reciprocity networks, as documented for a Mexico City squatter settlement (Lomnitz 1977) and among poor Afro-American families (Stack 1974), networks become encapsulating and isolating, and members tend to have few weak ties to other networks (Granovetter 1982).

Concerning specifically Mexican (internal and transnational) migration, modifications to Granovetter's innovative observations are needed among lower socioeconomic groups in Mexico, work is often provided by a *patrón* ("benefactor," employer) who because of his central position in an economic activity can provide jobs to "subordinates." The *patrón* will usually recruit members of his dense network of friends and relatives, and often co-villagers, who may recruit members of *their* dense networks. Thus, Lomnitz (1978) recounts how one in-migrant to a Mexico City squatter settlement became a construction subcontractor, employing between 300 and 400 men over the course of the year. When he needed more workers during periods of peak activity, he recruited them, directly or indirectly through employees, from his village of origin.

Massey *et al.* (1987) provide several cases of transnational immigrant men who were able to establish themselves at a work site, then recruit relatives, friends and *paisanos* (source community members with weaker ties than friends to the pioneering immigrant) into jobs. The greatest clusterings of immigrants from the small town of Chamitlán, Jalisco in California are found primarily in the San Joaquín Valley and secondarily in the San Francisco Bay area. A man who worked as a *bracero* in the San Joaquín Valley was chosen as a foreman on the condition that he recruit farmworkers for the company's fields. Eventually a number of families from Chamitlán, some of whom, from the account given by Massey *et al.* (1987:165) seem to have had relatively "weak ties" to him, went to settle in the Valley," attracted by the employment this paisano could offer." In the San Francisco Bay area, a man who had originally worked as a *bracero* in the California fields became employed as a waiter. Eventually, upon requests by *paisanos* from Chamitlán, he found jobs for approximately 100 other workers in the same restaurant (Massey *et al.* 1987:166).

Once workers are recruited into employment by a *patrón* or a "facilitator," relatively weak ties among those employed in the same work place, become converted through face-to-face interaction to stronger ties. If trusted by the employer, or the bridging employee, workers will often be called upon to recruit more employees from their dense networks. among construction workers whom I observed in Guadalajara in 1992, a subcontractor hired a man from Mexicali who recruited five others from the squatter settlement where he lived; a man from Guanajuato who had migrated to Rosarito, Baja California—the town in which the subcontractor was based, recruited three others from his dense network grounded in León Guanajuato; and a Mexicali-born man in the first network recruited two wife's cousins who were living in Guadalajara. All worked for the same subcontractor at the same work site, and all but the two men from Guadalajara shared an apartment while working in that city.

Mixtec farmworkers in Baja California, who migrate there from Oaxaca accompanied by family members and assisted by relatives, often continue on to work without documents in the fields and orchards of California and Oregon. Most are assisted in their crossing and job placement by labor contractors, coyotes, or acquaintances they have made on their work sites in Baja California (Zabin and Hughes 1995).

Thus, Granovetter's theory must be modified in at least two ways: 1) "weak ties" with individuals who can facilitate finding employment are not absent among internal or transnational wage labor immigrants from Mexico, despite the fact that they generally belong to lower socioeconomic groups; and 2) over time "weak ties" may, (or may not), become "strong ties," or at least stronger ties. What is of primary importance in Granovetter's theory for the study of the geographical spread of transnational immigrants is that ego's "weak ties" can provide information about new job sites, often in different geographical locations, which then may be incorporated into the opportunity space of ego and his/her dense network members.

Principle 4: Diffuse Networks as Social Capital

Networks, as has been widely documented for both immigrant and ethnic groups, and as revealed in Principle 3 above, provide their members with "social capital." Social capital has been described in a variety of ways. Coleman (1988:116) conceptualizes social capital as "the process by which established human relations—such as those rooted in ethnic communities—act as resources for economic cooperation." Social relations form the basis social networks, whether in diffuse or dense networks. Portes (1995:12) defines social capital as "the capacity of individuals to command scarce resources [e.g. employment opportunities] by virtue of their membership in networks or broader social structures."[5] More particularly, Massey *et al.* (1987:170) describe social capital as the access to jobs, housing, and financial assistance [and job information] provided by network members to new immigrants. They make the point that as the volume of social capital increases within any given migration network, risks in migrating decrease, and more source community members are drawn into the migration stream. A study of migration from nineteen Mexican source communities (Massey *et al.* 1994) showed that social capital accumulates with the addition of each new migrant who enters the migration stream; the new migrant provides an additional nodal point for drawing in previously unencompassed potential migrants, from among his/her circle of kin and friends. Notably, social capital also increases in direct proportion to human capital development in the form of learning experiences in the host society by each immigrant within the network. These experiences include, for example, the knowledge of how to find jobs and housing.

Significantly, social capital rests not only on dense network exchanges but also on bridging links between networks ("acquaintance networks") which provide previously unknown information about the social environment, including the economic/employment opportunities in diverse geographical locations. This type of social capital might be called "diffuse social capital."

Principle 5: Dense Networks as Social Capital

Social capital is embedded, then, in networks. Following Granovetter (1973, 1982), weak ties, with their bridging capability to previously unknown or unfamiliar sectors of the social system, could contribute more informational social capital than the more encapsulating strong ties found within dense networks. Nonetheless, a number of studies, including Massey *et al.* (1987) cited above in Principle 3, have shown that direct recruitment into employment is most often provided by family members (Sanders and Nee 1996) or are created through father-son ties (Waldinger 1995). Although these latter studies have focused on self-employment and the family firm, such observations are generalizable to network-mediated entry or recruitment into a specific work site, as seen from various studies cited above. One can represent the increasing diffuseness of networks by drawing at least six concentric circles, with the innermost consisting of the most dense network ties and being composed of close relatives, and the outermost consisting of the most diffuse acquaintance contacts which members of the innermost "circles" have established. The differences between "dense social networks" and "diffuse social networks" must, however, be seen as describing a continuum on an axis of subjective feelings of mutual responsibility. In distributing job information, (subjectively) close relatives would be advised and situated prior to more (subjectively) distant family members, friends prior to *paisanos*, and long term acquaintances prior to short term acquaintances Those with "strong ties" would thus, as a "solidaristic small group" (Sanders and Nee 1996:246) be among the first to share potential employment information and, most importantly, to recruit one another into openings in established employment (Granovetter 1973).

A series of open concentric circles can be envisioned, describing a continuum from the most dense to the most diffuse network members: they are open because a member of the most diffuse network (a mere acquaintance) can eventually become, for example, a brother-in-law, and close family members may, over time, become emotionally and geographically separated, feeling little obligation to those left behind. The first circle consists of the dense network of subjectively (rather than "blood" related) close kin with whom ego enjoys a high level of trust and mutual assistance. The second circle include a less dense network of more distant kin who are tied to ego through feelings of mutual obligation resting on kinship recognition. The third circle includes close friends. The fourth circle is the least dense of the dense networks and includes co-villagers and distant friends in nearby villages. The fifth circle encompasses a diffuse network of long term acquaintances with emergent possibilities of becoming members of the dense network of friends or affinal kin. The sixth, and outer, concentric circle, consists of a diffuse network of still short-term acquaintances. In the latter three cases, ego can potentially tap new information about employment possibilities which is not part of the information bank of the first three dense network groups.

I will now turn to illustrating each of these principle with case studies based on interviews with 115 transnational immigrants from a *rancho* in Jalisco which I call Los Arboles.

Case Study Illustrations of Network Principles

Principle 1: Multilocality of Networks

Networks are multilocal, encompassing a variety of geographical destinations. The importance of destinations in terms of numbers of immigrants received from any one source community may change over time. Once a migration stream has linkages to a destination point, labor market conditions/opportunities become a central variable in explaining the persistence or disappearance of that stream.

Between 1920 and 1990, transnational wage labor migrants from Los Arboles had worked in Illinois, Indiana, Arizona, Texas, Florida, Massachusetts, Wisconsin, and California. In a total of 181 destinations tallied once each for 115 immigrants (108 of which are men), 37% were to California agricultural towns; 34% to work sites in Los Angeles or Orange counties; and 15% of crossings were to Milwaukee. In Los Angeles County, immigrants from Los Arboles have lived and worked in at least 14 named neighborhoods (Wilson 1994). among men who crossed more than twice (involving 44.3% of the total sample), the majority worked in more than one geographical destination. Almost 29% of the 115 immigrants had worked in the United States on four or more occasions, and 13% had crossed the border six or more times. Zenobio, a man in his 60s, had crossed the border to work in Arizona and in southern, central and northern California agricultural fields twenty-five times in twenty-six years. He would have continued this recurrent migration pattern even longer, had he not been hit by a trailer truck and disabled when fleeing from the Border Patrol near San Clemente, California.

The variety of geographical locations and types of work accessed by Los Arboles based immigrants can be illustrated by individual migration histories. A Los Arboles-born recurrent immigrant, whom I call Juan Carlos, first crossed to the United States under *bracero* contract in the late 1950s. On his three crossings under *bracero* contract, accompanied by friends from Los Arboles and nearby *ranchos*, he did fieldwork in Texas, Arizona, and California. In 1969 and again in 1971, he went to Los Angeles, where he joined half-brothers. These half-siblings found him a job in the same fashionable west side restaurant where they were employed. In 1973 he went for the first time to Chicago, accompanying an acquaintance from the state of Guerrero and two other friends; although he had first cousins in Chicago, offspring of father's siblings who had fled Los Arboles at the time of the Cristero rebellion, they stayed with close relatives of the man from Guerrero for several months, before moving on to Milwaukee. In Milwaukee they joined siblings of Juan Carlos' Chicago-based cousins. In Milwaukee they found work in a foundry, an "immigrant niche" (Waldinger 1994) that soon became available to recurrent and "semi-settled"[6] immigrants from Los Arboles. Juan Carlos continued working in the foundry until the mid-1980s; he bought a house in Milwaukee and brought his wife and children to that city. In 1985 he went to California to take a temporary job as a tractor driver. Due to a bad experience there, he decided to return to Mexico. Selling his house in Milwaukee, he bought land and cattle in Los Arboles and opened a slaughter house in Guadalajara. Several of his offspring remain living in Milwaukee.

Notably, the strongest points of attraction for wage-labor migrants from Los Arboles changed over time; these changes were closely related to labor market conditions at destination(s). Pioneering immigrants, pushed out of the *rancho* by the Cristero rebellion and land disputes after the Mexican Revolution of 1910-1917, went to Chicago and to Gary, Indiana. The Great Depression of the 1930s brought a halt to migration streams to these destinations; many Mexicans were repatriated; and only a handful of families from Los Arboles remained in Chicago. These families were "lost" as network members; no one on the *rancho* any longer knows their whereabouts. During and immediately after the Bracero Program, Merced, California became a favored destination. A number of families from Los Arboles have settled there; yet almost no new immigrants from Los Arboles go there now. Over time, some immigrants also established themselves in Los Angeles County. As the labor market for agricultural field work became saturated in Merced, more and more immigrants in the 1970s began to head for the expanding, economically dynamic cities of Los Angeles and Milwaukee. In the 1980s, two more possible destinations opened up: Miami, Florida, where several Los Arboles based immigrants were employed in plant nurseries (having learned their skills in Los Angeles), and Westboro, Massachusetts, where a few immigrants work in a pizza restaurant.

In sum, Los Arboles residents have had a number of geographical sites where network members could provide them aid, orientation, and help in finding jobs. These destinations have changed in importance over time; labor market conditions at destination influenced this change.

Principle 2: Work Sites and Work Types as Anchoring Points of Networks

The magnetic pull of any given destination are the work sites where immigrants manage to find viable employment. Word of mouth information exchange among network members of the first immigrant(s) to land these jobs becomes of primary importance in job placement of later immigrants from the same source community or region.

At each geographical destination specific job sites and/or work types absorbed the immigrants from Los Arboles. In Merced, the overwhelming majority specialized in agricultural field work; in Los Angeles they were employed mainly in restaurants, factories, plant nurseries and on race tracks; in Milwaukee most immigrants tapping aid from the Los Arboles based immigration networks found jobs in foundries and a few in tanneries.

In Merced, Los Angeles County, and Milwaukee, a number of immigrants became settlers. Nonetheless, due to the strength of recruitment networking into foundries, there were more settlers in Milwaukee than in Merced, and due to the a wider array of employment possibilities accessed in greater Los Angeles, more settlers and semi-settlers from Los Arboles there than in Milwaukee.

In Milwaukee, five brothers of a man who became foreman in an iron works foundry found employment in the same foundry for temporary (in two cases) or lengthy (in three cases) period of time. He communicated the job openings to them and to several co-villagers from Los Arboles. Eventually, other co-villagers found jobs in Milwaukee foundries as well.

Notably, of the total sample of 108 migrant *male* heads of household resident on the *rancho* in the 1989 or 1990 study period, 11 (10%) have worked in plant nurseries in Los Angeles County. The reason for the clustering of nursery workers in Los Angeles begins with the migration, in the early 1960s, of the eldest brother of a sibling cluster, whom I will call Everardo. Everardo began working in a nursery in Los Angeles County in the early 1960s; by 1979 he had established a small nursery business of his own, the first and only "ethnic enterprise" found among Los Arboles immigrants. By 1989 he owned three nurseries. One of his brothers crossed to work in the nursery where Everardo was foreman in 1965, later going to work in a nursery owned by a friend of his brothers.[7] In 1968, two father's brother's daughter' sons, second cousins of Everardo, joined him in Los Angeles. Another second cousin, sibling of the first two, arrived in 1978 and found employment in a nearby nursery; and in 1980 a father's father's brother's son joined Everardo to work in a nursery he owned. While Everardo directly employed a number of relatives he also acted as a facilitator to find friends and relatives jobs in nurseries located near his own. Nursery work thus has become an occupational niche of immigrants from Los Arboles to Los Angeles. Nursery work has also been accessed by Los Arboles immigrants to Miami, Florida.

PRINCIPLE 3: THE "STRENGTH OF WEAK TIES" IN NETWORK EXPANSION

Networks expand over time to encompass new geographic and work site locations, often through "the strength of weak ties," whereby information about employment opportunities is passed from one acquaintance to another. These acquaintances provide an information bridge between more dense network clusters. Alternatively, networks expand to include new members with information about other parts of the transnational social system through the establishment of new strong ties, via, e.g., marriage or *compadrazgo* (fictive kinship established at the time of marked life cycle changes, such as baptism, marriage, etc.). This type of expansion can occur either at the region of origin or at destination(s).

Notably, the man from Guerrero who aided three men from Los Arboles to find work in Chicago, and whom they later aided to find work in Milwaukee, had no strong ties to Los Arboles. During one immigration roundup of undocumented workers, he was deported to Mexico with them. Although no one from Los Arboles immigrated to Chicago afterwards, "weak ties" to this man enabled Los Arboles residents to explore new location and job possibilities.

Often weak ties are converted into strong ties through marriage or *compadrazgo*. Thus, one young immigrant from Los Arboles met and married a Mexican-American woman born in Milwaukee. "Weak ties" to her close and distant relatives thus became converted to "strong ties" though this rite of passage. The information his affinal relatives have about job opportunities and other geographical locations, are now available to him, as well as to his "dense network." The same is true for a man from Guanajuato, who married into a family with network ties centered in Los Arboles.

PRINCIPLE 4: DIFFUSE NETWORKS AS SOCIAL CAPITAL

Due to aid extended, information exchanged, and recruitment to jobs that occur among network members, networks can be seen to constitute "social capital" for their members. This is as true of diffuse networks without multiple interactions among members, as it is of "dense" networks.

The examples given in Principle 1, 2, and 3 above, illustrate *how* networks constitute social capital for their members. Network members provided a number of destinations to chose from and access to an array of work sites or job types. Acquaintances made in Mexico or in the United States often provided aid at new destination points, as the man from Guerrero did for Juan Carlos and his two friends in Chicago, and as they in turn did for him in Milwaukee. Francisco and Juan Carlos were neither relatives nor close friends: but they were *paisanos* (co-villagers) with some sense of mutual obligation due to residence in a relatively small community of 207 occupied houses. They can thus be seen as belonging to a fourth level of network density. Residents of Los Arboles have been enabled to access new geographical locations through 'weak ties," however, and have also provided job information to acquaintances whom they met in the migration process. Alternatively, some persons who originally were acquaintances, having only "weak ties" to immigrants from Los Arboles, became spouses or *compadres*, which involved a change from weak to strong ties not only for the parties involved but also for close family members of both.

Wife's relatives may become important sources of information and aid in the migration process of males.[7] In Westboro, Massachusetts a man from Los Arboles tapped aid from his wife's brothers to secure work in the same pizza restaurant where they worked. Wife's brothers also helped the first man who worked in Miami, Florida to find work in a plant nursery there. He later recruited a brother of his into the same work site. Wife's relatives based in Los Arboles also aided a man from Guanajuato who had married a woman from a nearby *rancho* to cross the border and find work.

In the migration process both strong ties and weak ties may be utilized. The migration history of Mateo, one of a cluster of six brothers who migrated into Los Arboles with their parents from Zacatecas in the late 1960s, illustrates the variable ties which can be called upon over an immigrant's migratory career. In the United States, he originally worked in the California fields, crossing the border with friends from Los Arboles who had contacts in several agricultural towns. Later he joined two brothers and a brother-in-law to work in a Pecos, Texas factory. Still later he worked on a Los Angeles County racetrack, calling upon the brother of a friend to place him there. On another crossing he joined his younger brother Francisco (see below) in Milwaukee: both worked there, with two other brothers, in a foundry. On a later crossing he tapped aid from mother's cousins based in Zacatecas, to work picking apples in Michigan. On his last crossing he went with his eldest son, then 17, and a brother in law to Portersville, California, where they joined Mateo's deceased father's sister's sons and worked in agriculture. Notably Mateo had had no face to face interaction for more than two decades with some of the cousins resident in the *rancho* of his childhood in Zacatecas. These ties, appearing "weak" since they had no longitudinal continuity and since these cousins of his were unknown to others in Mateo's contemporary friendship network (or even among his affinal relatives), were reactivated as "strong ties" in the migration process. Although brothers provided aid to Mateo most of the time, friends, relatives of friends, and near and distant cousins also helped Mateo to find work in various locations. Diffuse, or at least less dense, network members often can offer job information and recruitment into work sites and thus aid in the expansion for opportunities of dense network members.

PRINCIPLE 5: DENSE NETWORKS AS SOCIAL CAPITAL

Nonetheless, clustering of people from the same origin in specific localities and work sites is due more to the strength of strong ties than due to the weak tie social capital provided by more diffuse migration or ethnic group networks. The former can be called "dense social capital" as opposed to "diffuse social capital." One can, as outlined above, envision a continuum between these two types of social capital.

In Los Angeles, a cluster of brothers (some of them half-brothers) worked in the 1970s in one Marina del Rey restaurant; another cluster of brothers and first cousins were employed by a Los Arboles immigrant who between 1979 and 1989 had established three plant nurseries in the Los Angeles; a third cluster of brothers worked on a variety of California racetracks throughout the 1970s and early 1980s; a fourth cluster of brothers and sisters have worked in Santa Monica restaurants since the late 1980s. There has thus been both dispersion and clustering among Los Angeles immigrants throughout the Los Angeles area. The clusterings tend to be composed of siblings and are sometimes, if work availability at a specific job site permits, extended to include first and second cousins and friends. While several sibling clusters share the same living quarters, others, especially those accompanied by spouses and children, simply live in the same neighborhood.

In Milwaukee, Juan Carlos was one of the first immigrants from Los Arboles to secure foundry employment. Francisco, a friend who accompanied him in 1973, was born on a *rancho* in the state of Zacatecas but had moved to Los Arboles with his parents and siblings in the late 1960s while he was still an adolescent. Once established in the water pump foundry, he recruited all six of his Los Arboles based brothers to work there. He and four of his brothers have continued to work in the foundry for more than a decade. Three have brought their wives and children to live in Milwaukee. The brothers who left their wives on the *rancho* share the same living quarters with one of their married siblings. Of the other two brothers, Mateo preferred farm work and on subsequent crossings returned to employment in California fields and later in Michigan orchards; the other, with money he earned in the foundry, bought a small piece of land and started to raise pigs in Los Arboles.

Thus, close relatives, especially siblings, are given preference in network recruitment into specific job sites. If more jobs become available, more distant relatives, friends, and lastly acquaintances, may be placed through word of mouth recruitment. Members of dense reciprocity networks will be given preference over members of diffuse contact, or "acquaintance" networks in job placement, however.

Conclusions

This article shows how five network principles can explain the dispersion and clustering of immigrants originally co-resident in a particular source community.[8] Multilocality of networks is the norm among immigrants from a variety of Mexican villages and for residents of Los Arboles. Immigrants are anchored in each geographical location through the work sites and job types they can access. The importance of geographical destinations changes over time and is related to labor market conditions. The conquest of new "activity spaces" (Sassen 1995), leading to multiple choices in destination, is due to the constant expansion of networks though incorporating (and acting upon) information provided by acquaintances. Acquaintances can be held to belong to any given ego's "diffuse network" as opposed to his "dense network(s)" of kin, friends and co-villagers. Diffuse network dynamics lead to geographical and employment dispersion, expanding the field of work opportunities which transnational immigrants can access.

Dense network dynamics, on the other hand, lead to concentration/clustering, as close relatives recruit first close then distant kin, then friends, then *paisanos*, then long-term acquaintances, and last in order of priority, short-term acquaintances into particular job sites. Both diffuse contact and dense reciprocity networks provide social capital to their members in the form of aid, job information and job placement. If work opportunities are limited at a given job site, however, siblings and other close relatives who are members of any ego's dense network will ordinarily be given preference for job recruitment. Thus dense networks provide more social capital to their members; at the same time, however, new information about previously unknown parts of the social system flows mainly from "weak tie" contacts forming the diffuse network of any given individual in the dense network. "Weak ties," converted through marriage, *compadrazgo*, and enduring face-to-face interaction, to strong ties, can come to contribute part of the social capital of ego's dense network. Weak ties and strong ties can be seen to describe a continuum, with some weak ties becoming stronger over time, and, theoretically, some strong ties becoming weaker, (but always retaining the potential to be reactivated as strong ties).

NOTES

[1]I use the term "transnational" immigration instead of "international" immigration for a number of reasons. "International" is a concept which assumes a division of the world into neatly bounded nation-states with exchanges of labor, capital, and commodities between them being regulated according to national and international laws. The concept "transnational immigrants," used in a sense similar to that of "transnational corporations" (Kearney 1995:155), implies processes outside of nation-state control/encapsulation/ identity management. Immigration networks especially have a transnational character since, through their existence, they articulate social spaces legally and politically conceptualized as divided and belonging under the suzerainity of distinct governmental entities (see Basch *et al.* 1994:5-8). Undocumented immigrants, with whom this article is primarily concerned, especially challenge legally bounded spaces through their unregulated border crossings.

[2]The study of the *rancho* was partially funded by a small grant from the Wenner-Gren Foundation, to which I wish to give thanks for allowing me to take two advanced sociology students from the Universidad de Baja California, Mexicali to help me in the preliminary interviewing of 202 male heads of household, or their wives if husbands were absent in the United States. The study revealed that by 1990 more than 76% of male heads of household had migrated to the United States in search of work over the previous six decades. This did not include those immigrants who had settled "permanently" in the United States with their wives and children (see Wilson 1992).

[3]Although I will not discuss the question of the possible negative effects of network recruitment into work sites here, it is notable that many researchers have concluded that network recruitment leads to greater vulnerability and exploitation of workers so recruited, since they accept oppressive labor conditions without protest due to preexisting loyalties to relatives or friends who recommended them for the job (e.g., Browning and Rodríguez 1985; Rodríguez 1987; Thomas 1982). For the divisiveness of networks within the workplace and their manipulation by employers to "divide and rule" the workforce, see Zavella 1987. For the role of networks in fostering competition between various ethnic segments of the secondary labor market, see Waldinger 1994, 1995; Sassen 1995. Network recruitment

of immigrant workers has also been used to undermine unionizing efforts (Thomas 1982) and to erode the power of existing unions (Mines and Avina 1992). In addition, whereas networks constitute "social capital" in enabling network members to find jobs when other workers, including U.S. born workers, may not, networks may merely channel members into devalued and unstable jobs (Waldinger 1994, 1995).

[4]The strength of immigrant networks anchored in certain work sites and employment types explains why immigrants find jobs while many U.S. born minorities remain unemployed (Granovetter 1982; Sassen 1995; Waldinger 1994, 1995). Alternatively, it has been suggested by a number of researchers that immigrants will work for less money than U.S. minorities would find acceptable (e.g., Jones 1995). This is explained by: 1) the propensity of immigrants to compare income earned in the U.S. with the lower income available for the same jobs at origin; 2) the willingness of immigrants to accept difficult labor conditions in the belief by many that their sojourn is only temporary, until they return home, where their consumption possibilities will be greater than prior to migrating; and 3) the fact that maintenance and family reproduction costs, at least among temporary immigrants, are borne by the sending society in times of sickness or unemployment, and for family dependents too young to work. In any case, once pioneering immigrant(s) accept unskilled, underpaid or unstable jobs, they often serve as bridgeheads in recruiting others from their dense network of kin, friends, and co-villagers into the same work site. This is partially explained due to the opportunity to do so and the lack of knowledge of other job openings.

[5]Notably, while networks facilitate the job search for members, they also normally function to exclude outsiders of other ethnicities (Waldinger 1995) and perhaps from other source communities within Mexico. They can be considered the micro-structures which contribute to the ethnic segmentation of labor markets (Bach 1986) or to the appearance of "immigrant niches" (Waldinger 1994).

[6]Although "settlement" may indeed be permanent settlement, it may look permanent even to immigrants involved, yet fail to be so. Thus, as noted above, many Mexican's in Northwest Indiana and Illinois in the 1920s had "settled-in;" but the Great Depression fed into the forcible repatriation of vast numbers, including the U.S. born, and led to the disappearance of Mexican businesses and community organizations (Escobar 1987; Rosales and Simon 1987). Other, more voluntaristic factors, also lead to movement to other locations, or to return to the country of origin. The location of an immigrant at any particular time may be his/her final destination but may also be merely a stopping point in his/her migratory career. Here I mean by "semi-settled" both those immigrants from Los Arboles who spend more time in the United States than in Mexico and plan to continue doing so despite the fact that their wives and children continue living on the *rancho*, as well as those who, while remaining years in Milwaukee, will eventually move to another geographical location in either the source or host country.

[7]Insufficient research has been done on women as nodal links in men's migration networks. A recent study has shown that many Mexican women migrate to the United States, some to join their husbands — even against husbands' wishes — utilizing aid from other women (Hondagneu-Sotelo 1994). Research I conducted of in-migration to a Mexicali squatter settlement showed that more than 46% of the nuclear families migrating to Mexicali tapped aid from wife's kin, and a good number of husband's kin who extended aid were sisters or mothers (Wilson n.d.). Whether a similar pattern can be found among transnational immigrants from Mexico is a question for future research. Whether there would be cultural differences in the utilization of aid from females, and which females, depending on Mexican source region or country of origin, is also open to question.

[8]Notably, dense network ties tend to be used prior to the establishment of a critical mass of people with ever expanding weak ties and concomitant growth of social capital in the country of destination. Alternatively, weak ties in Mexico may aid in initial migration from communities which have no established tradition of immigration to the United States, or, in exploring destinations in the United States not previously accessed by members of the community. Either weak ties or strong ties may be used by any one immigrant on different trips across the border. Which are activated often is determined by preference for a certain type of work (e.g. racetracks as opposed to foundries) or geographic location. There is active agency involved in the decision of whom to ask for or extend aid: the immigrant chooses to activate weak ties or rely on strong ties; chooses to convert weak ties into strong ties through marriage or *compadrazgo*; and, once established in the United States, chooses to whom to extend aid, as structured by cultural definitions of obligations to kin and friends, or at least how much aid to extend.

REFERENCES CITED

Alvarez, Jr., Robert R.

1991 Familia: Migration and Adaptation in Baja and Alta California, 1900-1975. Berkeley: University of California Press.

Basch, Linda, Nina Glick Schiller, and Cristina Szanton Blanc

1994 Nations Unbound: Transnational Projects Postcolonial Predicaments and Deterritorialized Nation States. Basel, Switzerland: Gordon and Breach.

Boyd, Monica

1989 Family and Personal Networks in International Migration: Recent Developments and New Agendas. International Migration Review 23:638-670.

Briody, Elizabeth K.

1987 Patterns of Household Migration into South Texas. International Migration Review 21:27-47.

Browning, Harley L. and Néstor Rodríguez

1985 The Migration of Mexican Indocumentados as a Settlement Process: Implications for Work. *In* Hispanics in the U.S. Economy. George J. Borjas and Marta Tienda, eds. Pp. 277-297. New York: Academic Press.

Coleman, James S.

1988 Social Capital in the Creation of Human Capital. American Journal of Sociology 94 (Supplement): S95-S120.

Cornelius, Wayne A.

1976 Mexican Migration to the United States: The View from Rural Sending Communities. Monograph Series in Migration and Development. Cambridge: Massachusetts Institute of Technology, Center for International Studies.

1991 Los Migrantes de la Crisis: The Changing Profile of Mexican Migration to the United States. *In* Social Responses to Mexico's Economic Crisis of the 1980s. Mercedes González de la Rocha and Agustín Escobar Latapí, eds. Pp. 155-194. La Jolla: University of California, San Diego, Center for US-Mexican Studies.

Durand, Jorge and Douglas S. Massey

1992 Mexican Migration to the United States: A Critical Review. Latin American Research Review 2:3-42.

Earle, Duncan

1994 Constructions of Refugee Ethnic Identity: Guatemalan Mayas in Mexico and South Florida. *In* Reconstrcuting Lives, Recapturing Meaning: Refugee Identity, Gender and Culture Change. Linda A. Camino and Ruth Krulfeld, eds. Pp. 207-234. Basel, Switzerland: Gordon and Breach.

Escobar, Edward J.

1987 The Forging of a Community. *In* Forging a Community: The Latino Experience in Northwest Indiana, 1919-1975. James B. Lane and Edward J. Escobar, eds. Pp. 3-24. Chicago: Cattails Press; Gary, Indiana: Calumet Regional Archives.

Gold, Steven

1994 Patterns of Economic Cooperation among Israeli Immigrants in Los Angeles. International Migration Review 28:114-135.

Ho, Christine G. T.
1993 The Internationalization of Kinship and the Feminization of Caribbean Migration: The Case of Afro-Trinidadian Immigrants in Los Angeles. Human Organization 52:358-375.
Granovetter, Mark
1973 The Strength of Weak Ties. American Journal of Sociology 78:1360-388.
1982 The Strength of Weak Ties: A Network Theory Revisited. *In* Social Structure and Network Analysis. Peter V. Marsden and Nan Lin, eds. Pp.105-130. Beverly Hills: Sage Publications.
Hagan, Jaquilfne Marfa
1994 Deciding to be Legal: A Maya Community in Houston. Philadelphia: Temple University Press.
Haney, Jane B.
1979 Formal and Informal Labor Recruitment Mechanisms: Stages in Mexican Migration into Mid-Michigan Agriculture. *In* Migration Across Frontiers: Mexico and the United States. Fernando Camara and Robert Van Kemper, eds. Pp. 141-149. Albany: State University of New York Press.
Hondagneu-Sotelo, Pierrette
1994 Gendered Transitions: Mexican Experiences of Immigration. Berkeley: University of California Press.
Jones, Richard C.
1982 Channelization of Undocumented Mexican Migrants to the U.S. Economic Geography 58:156-176.
1995 Ambivalent Journey: U.S. Migration and Economic Mobility in North-Central Mexico. Tucson:University of Arizona Press.
Kearney, Michael
1986 From Invisible Hands to Visible Feet: Anthropological Studies of Migration and Development. Annual Review of Anthropology15:331-361.
1995 Borders and Boundaries of State and Self at the End of Empire. *In* Migrants, Regional Identities and Latin American Cities. Teófilo Altamirano and Lane Ryo Hirabayashi, eds. Pp. 151-168. Arlington, Virginia: American Anthropological Association.
Kearney, Michael and Carole Nagengast
1989 Anthropological Perspectives on Transnational Communities in Rural California. Davis: California Institute for Rural Studies.
Lomnitz, Larissa
1977 Networks and Marginality: Life in a Mexican Shantytown. New York: Academic Press.
1978 Mechanisms of Articulation between Shantytown Settlers and the Urban System. Urban Anthropology 7:185-206.
Margolis, Maxine L.
1994 Little Brazil: An Ethnography of Brazilian Immigrants in New York City. Princeton: Princeton University Press.
Massey, Douglas S. and Kristin E. Espinosa
1997 What's Driving Mexico-U.S. Migration: A Theoretical, Empirical, and Policy Analysis. American Journal of Sociology 102:939-999.
Massey, Douglas S., Luin Goldring, and Jorge Durand
1994 Continuities in Transnational Migration: An Analysis of Nineteen Mexican Communities. American Journal of Sociology 99:1492-1533.
Massey, Douglas, Rafael Alarcón, Jorge Durand, and Humberto González
1987 Return to Aztlán: The Social Process of International Migration from Western Mexico. Berkeley: University of California Press.
Mines, Richard
1981 Developing a Community Tradition of Migration: A Field Study in Rural Zacatecas, Mexico and California Settlement Areas. La Jolla: University of California, San Diego, Center for U.S.-Mexican Studies.
Mines, Richard and Jeffrey Avina
1992 Immigrants and Labor Standards: The Case of California Janitors. *In* U.S.-Mexico Relations: Labor Market Interdependence. Jorge A. Bustamante, Clark W. Reynolds, and Raúl A. Hinojosa Ojeda, eds. Pp. 429-448. Stanford: Stanford University Press.
Rodrfguez, Néstor P.
1987 Undocumented Central Americans in Houston: Diverse Populations. International Migration Review 21:4-26.
Rosales, Francisco Arturo and Daniel T. Simon
1987 Mexican Immigrant Experience in the Urban Midwest: East Chicago, Indiana, 1991-1945. *In* Forging a Community: The Latino Experience in Northwest Indiana, 1919-1975. James B. Lane and Edward J. Escobar, eds. Pp. 137-160. Chicago: Cattails Press; Gary, Indiana: Calumet Regional Archives.
Portes, Alejandro
1995 Economic Sociology and the Sociology of Immigration: A Conceptual Overview. *In* The Economic Sociology of Immigration: Essays on Networks, Ethnicity, and Entrepreneurship. Alejandro Portes, ed. Pp. 1-41. New York: Russell Sage Foundation.
Sanders, Jimy M. and Victor Nee
1996 Social Capital, Human Capital, and Immigrant Self-Employment. American Sociological Review 61:231-249.
Sassen, Saskia
1995 Immigration and Local Labor Markets. *In* The Economic Sociology of Immigration: Essays on Networks, Ethnicity, and Entrepreneurship. Alejandro Portes, ed. Pp. 87-127. New York: Russell Sage Foundation.
Stack, Carol B.
1974 All Our Kin: Strategies for Survival in a Black Community. New York: Harper and Row.
Thomas, Robert J.
1982 Citizenship and Gender in Work Organization: Some Considerations for Theories of the Labor Process. American Journal of Sociology (Supplement): 88:S86-S112.
Waldinger, Roger
1994 The Making of an Immigrant Niche. International Migration Review 28:3-30.
1995 The 'Other Side" of Embeddedness: A Case-Study of the Interplay of Economy and Ethnicity. Ethnic and Racial Studies 18:555-580.
Wilson, Tamar Diana
1992 Vamos para Buscar la Vida: A Comparison of Patterns of Outmigration from a Rancho in Jalisco and Internal Migration into a Mexicali Squatter Settlement. Ph.D. Dissertation, UCLA. Ann Arbor: UMI.
1994 What Determines Where Migrants Go? Modifications in Migration Theories. Human Organization 53:269-278.
n.d. Micro-, Meso-, and Macro-Patterns of Women's Migration to Colonia Popular, Mexicali, Baja California. Journal of Borderlands Studies. (Forthcoming).
Zavella, Patricia
1987 Women's Work and Chicano Families: Cannery Workers of the Santa Clara Valley. Ithaca: Cornell University Press.

Name Index

Abernathy, F.H. 101
Abu-Lughod, J. 359
Abu-Zekry, T. 359
Ahvenainen, J. 179, 181
Akwale, R. 367
Alarcon, R. 186
Alba, F. 187
Aldrich, H.E. 148, 149, 151, 155, 159, 325
Aliber, R.Z. 26
Alicea, M. 275
Allison, P.D. 191
Allott, A. 254, 256, 257–60, 262–70
Almgren, K.A. 176
Alvarez, R.R. Jr 384
Anderson 161, 162
Aoki, M. 80
Argyris, C. 2
Arizpe, L. 187, 188
Armstrong, J. 252, 253
Arndt, S.W. 22
Arrighi, G. 361
Assar, W.D.H. 220
Astone, N.M. 295
Avila, E. 272, 275–6, 285–6, 290, 324, 325, 327
Avina, J. 391
Axelrod, R. 48, 50–1, 53–5, 57, 66–7, 70, 71

Bach, R. 187, 391
Bachman, L. 232
Bachmann, R. 100, 107
Backwell, E. 219, 222, 224, 225
Bailly, A. 365
Balan, J. 187
Baldersheim, H. 1, 2, 3
Bamfield, J. 111
Banerjee, B. 298, 300, 304, 305, 307, 308
Barber, B. 47
Barber, J.W. 254
Barsky, T. 271
Bartel, A.P. 15
Bartram, D. 277
Barty-King, H. 33
Basch, L. 384, 390
Basem, L.C. 299, 305–6, 307, 308
Basran, G.S. 331
Bathurst, B. 225
Baum, J. 148
Beale, W.L. 264
Beaverstock, J.V. 35
Beavon, K. 359
Becker, G.S. 297–8
Belanger, A. 15
Belderbos, R.A. 26
Bendor, J. 72
Ben-Porath, Y. 298
Berk, R.A. 193, 199
Bernstein, D. 271, 278
Bian, Y. 326
Bienestock, E.J. 325
Binfield, C. 251
Binswanger, H.P. 297
Birley, S. 147, 148, 149, 154, 157
Blaas 3
Black, F. 309
Blackburn, R. 161
Blau, P.M. 46, 47
Blejer, M.I. 187
Bohning, W.R. 189
Bommier, A. 306, 308
Bond, M. 150, 152
Boone, R.T. 72
Boorman, S. 346
Booth, K. 273
Borjas, G.J. 15, 17, 21
Borocz, J. 324, 325
Borts, G.H. 187
Bose, C. 271
Bourlakis, M. 110
Bovenkerk, J. 189
Bowen, H.V. 236
Bowersox, D. 110
Boyd, M. 275, 300, 385
Bradby, H. 335
Brettell, C. 189
Brieger, R. 346
Briody, E.K. 385
Broad, W. 371, 372
Broadbridge, S.A. 261
Bromley, D.W. 299
Brookfield, H.C. 295
Brown, C.H. 188
Brown, J.J. 264

Brown, R.P.C. 307
Browning, H.L. 187, 385, 390
Bruguier, A. 232
Bryant, R. 122
Buchmann, M. 326
Buchner, B. 373
Buck, D. 110
Budd, L. 375
Burchell, B. 326
Burn, D.L. 252
Burstyn, H. 370
Burt, R.S. 48, 67, 69, 71, 73, 104, 110, 147, 151, 152, 325, 347, 354
Busenitz, L. 148, 150
Bustamente, J.A. 203

Cain, M. 297
Cain, P.J. 93–4
Camerer, C. 51
Cardoso, L. 187
Carey, J. 181
Carus Wilson, E.M. 248
Cassis, Y. 35, 252
Casson, M.C. 78, 81, 86, 94, 100, 102, 114, 116, 174, 250
Castells, M. 32, 324, 344, 349, 366, 375
Castles, S. 15, 277
Cattan, N. 350
Caves, R.E. 25, 36
Centeno, M.A. 342, 361
Chadwick, D. 254–5, 257–60, 262–8, 270
Chan, A. 335
Chan, K.W. 302
Chandler, A. Jr 178, 179
Chandler, A.D. 97, 102, 173
Chang, S.J. 25, 31
Chant, S. 273
Chapman, M. 295
Chapman, S.D. 35, 95
Charles, M. 326
Chase-Dunn, C. 345
Chavas, J.P. 299
Chavez, L.R. 298
Cheah, C. 378
Chen, F. 327
Cheng, S.A. 275, 277, 291
Chevigny, M. 233
Childs, R. 251
Choi, A. 336
Cholmely, H. 226
Christopherson, S. 246
Clark, K.B. 101
Clark, T.N. 2, 8
Clarkberg, M. 334
Clausen, J.A. 326
Clay, D.C. 306
Clough, B. 372, 373
Coase, R.H. 100
Coffee, W. 365
Cohen, R. 240
Coleman, J.S. 47, 48, 69, 383, 387
Cook, Captain 22
Cooke, K. 372
Cooke, W. 263, 265
Cooper, J. 112
Corbridge, S. 366
Corby, T.A.B. 33
Corey, K. 377
Cornelius, W.A. 189, 203, 206, 384, 385
Cottrell, P. 246, 248, 252, 255, 259, 263
Cowell, F.R. 40
Cox, D. 306
Cox, H. 100, 101, 102
Croll, E. 327
Curran, J. 147, 161, 162
Cybriwsky, R. 375
Cyert, R.M. 2
Czitrom, D. 180

d'Orleáns, Duc 235
Dahlström, C.M. 173–8, 181–4
Datta, R. 13
David, J. 226
David, P.A. 183, 184, 294, 300
Davies, P.N. 38
Davin, D. 327
Davis, J.A. 48
Davis, L.E. 93
Davy, A. 263, 265
de Angeli, T. 111
de Janvry, A. 189, 295, 298, 300
De Jong, N. 123, 124, 125–6, 128, 135, 138
De Melo, J. 122
Deardoff, A. 16
Dee, R. 224, 226–9
Dehing, P.W.N.M. 221
Delechat, C. 325
DeRoover, R. 228
Deutsch, F.M. 327
Dicken, P. 101, 377
Dobson, P. 117
Dodd 161, 162
Doherty, G. 328
Donckels, R. 163
Dooley, M. 122
Doportos, A. 223
Drakopoulou 161, 162
Dresher, M. 49

Drummond, J. 234
Du Boff, R.B. 173, 179, 180, 181, 182
Dunau, A. 376
Dunlevy, J.A. 15
Durand, J. 186, 316
Dutka, A. 366

Earle, D. 384
Easterbrook, J. 264
Ebers, M. 100
Eichengreen, B. 122, 139
Ekeh, P.P. 47
Elam, A.B. 325
Elkan, W. 298
Ensel, W.M. 324
Entwisle, B. 327
Erdös, P. 338
Erev, I. 70
Escobar, E.J. 391
España, F.G. 15
Espinosa, K.E. 295, 299, 300, 303, 316, 383

Fafchamps, M. 299, 403
Fagerlund, F.W. 176, 178
Fan, Y.K. 300
Fang, X. 330, 333
Farnie, D.A. 248
Feagin, J. 344, 373
Feenstra, R.C. 23
Fei, J.C.H. 187
Feijoo, M. del C. 286
Feldstein, M. 122
Fennema, M. 35
Fernie, J. 104, 107, 110, 111, 112
Field, A.J. 180
Findley, S. 188
Firebaugh, F.M. 326
Fitzgerald, E.V.K. 129, 143, 144
Flath, D. 26
Fletcher, P.L. 303
Flood, M. 49, 69, 70
Framingham, P. 42
Frankel, J. 13, 14, 17–18, 21, 122
Freeman, L. 347
Frenz, M. 118
Friedman, J. 342, 343, 344, 353–4, 355, 356, 357
Friendly, M. 328
Frisbie, P. 187
Fuller, T.D. 298, 307
Furtado, C. 187

Galarza, E. 187
Galaskiewicz, J. 347
Gallin, B. 302
Gallin, R.S. 302
Gargiulo, M. 47, 48
Garnham, N. 365
Gatley, S. 147
Gerard, C. 223, 224, 228
Gerard, H. 223, 224, 228
Gereffi, G. 101, 347
Gerson, K. 327
Gertler, M.S. 33
Ghoshal, S. 101
Gibb, A. 161
Gibbons, R. 47, 53
Giddens, A. 32
Giele, J.Z. 327
Gillespie, A. 365, 367
Ginzberg, E. 327
Girvan, M. 243
Gladstein, D. 54
Glanville, J.L. 325
Glasberg, D.S. 34
Glenn, N. 274, 275
Goddard, J. 365
Gold, D. 25
Gold, S.J. 325, 383
Goldring, L. 299, 301, 302, 303, 316
Goldsmith, M.J.F. 1
González, H. 186
Goodman, B. 301, 302
Goodman, L.A. 190
Goto, A. 26
Gould, D. 15
Grabher, G. 100
Graham, J. 366
Granovetter, M.S. 47, 48, 147, 151, 152, 301, 325, 383, 386–7, 391
Gras, N.S.B. 342
Graves, N.B. 188
Graves, T.D. 188
Gravesteijn, C. 222
Gray, C. 162
Green, G. 335
Green, M.B. 33, 34
Greenhalgh, S. 300
Greenwood, M.J. 187
Greif, A. 48, 237
Greve, A. 331
Griff, A. 33, 35
Grossman, S.J. 180
Guillén, M.F. 32, 33
Gulati, R. 47, 48
Guldmann, J. 370

Hagan, J.M. 275, 283, 385
Hage, P. 347

Hampton, T. 265
Haney, J.B. 385
Hanneman, G. 370
Hansen, E. 160, 162
Hanushek, E.A. 191
Harabi, N. 101
Harary, F. 347
Harberger, A. 121
Hardin, R. 49
Hargittai, E. 342, 361
Harper, G. 251
Harrigan, J. 16
Harris, N. 347
Hart, G. 297
Harvey, D. 365
Hays, C. 226
Head, K. 15, 25
Hechter, M. 51
Heider, F. 48
Heinz, W.R. 326
Heldman, R.K. 350
Hennart, J.-F. 25, 26, 30–1
Hepworth, M. 365, 367
Hess, M. 34
Hewitt de Alcantara, C. 187
Hey, D. 251
Hill, R.C. 344
Hills, G. 147
Hirschman, A.O. 57
Hirst, P. 33
Ho, C.G.T. 15, 384
Hochschild, A.R. 272, 273, 290, 328
Hodder, J.E. 26
Hoddinot, J. 305–6, 307, 308
Hoe, A.M. 256
Hoffman-Martinot, V. 2, 8
Hofstede, G. 148, 149–50, 152, 153
Holden, J.M. 222
Homans, G.C. 46
Hondagneu-Sotelo, P. 272, 273, 275–6, 283, 285–6, 290, 301, 324, 325, 327, 391
Hope, S. 328
Hopkins, A.G. 93–4
Horioka, C. 122
Horsefield, J.K. 236
Horvath 3
Hoshi, T. 26
Houstoun, M.F. 203
Howe, D. 13
Huang, H. 336
Hughes, D. 107, 111, 386
Hung, C. 328, 329
Hunt, B.C. 252
Hutchinson, W.K. 15
Huttenback, R.A. 93

Ibarra, H. 326
Illner, M. 1, 3
Inchcape, Lord 42
Irwin, D. 122, 139

Jackson, J.E. 191
Jaffee, D. 13
Jarillo, J.C. 101
Jarrett, W. 223
Jefferys, J.B. 248, 253, 254, 255, 258–9, 261, 262
Jelin, E. 187, 286
Jenkins, J.C. 187
Jeremy, D.J. 40
Jiang, H. 336
Jimenez, E. 306, 307
Johannisson, B. 147, 148, 161, 162
Johnson, H.G. 187
Johnson, L. 230–2, 233
Jones, C.L. 327
Jones, G. 42, 94
Jones, R.C. 384–5, 386, 391
Jonker, J. 221
Jussawalla, M. 378

Kakabadze, M. 366
Kallioinen, M. 173, 181
Kamnuansilpa, P. 298, 307
Kane, P. 327
Kashyap, A. 25, 26
Katz, J. 162
Kaukiainen, Y. 176, 178
Kay, J. 33, 40
Kearney, M. 384, 390
Keeling, D.J. 350
Kemp, A. 273, 276, 284, 291
Kemper, R.V. 300
Kennedy, T. 336
Kester, W.C. 26
Kick, E. 346
Kidal, M.P. 327
Kidner, J. 265
Kierzkowski, H. 22
Kieve, J. 33
Killick, J.R. 261
King, A. 344
Kirby, M.W. 250
Kissinger 33
Klausen, K.K. 1
Klep, P. 229
Knez, M. 48, 51, 69, 73
Knox, P. 342
Kofman, A. 324

Kofman, H. 336
Kogut, B. 25, 31
Kojima, K. 25, 26
Kollack, P. 72
Konan, P.E. 16
Korzeniewicz, M. 348
Kossoudji, S. 203
Krackhardt, D. 326
Kreps, D.M. 47, 48
Kroll, C. 13
Krueger, A. 21
Kruger, H. 326
Krugman, P. 15
Kunzmann, K. 356, 358
Kylsant, Lord 42
Kynaston, D. 236, 252–3

Labianca, G. 48
Lambrecht, J. 163
Lane, C. 100, 107
Larson, A. 47
Lau, C. 148, 150
Laumann, E. 347
Law, J. 229, 232–5
Lawler, E.J. 47
Lee, M. 335
Lehrer, D. 372
Lejeune, A. 40
Lero, D. 328
Lester, M. 250
Levhari, D. 188
Levitt, B. 2
Levitt, P. 299, 324
Lewis, A. 33
Lewis, M.J. 40, 249
Lewis, P. 371
Lewis, W. 187
Li, C. 329
Liang, Z. 328
Lianos, T.P. 308
Lightfoot, P. 298, 307
Lijphart, A. 280
Lim, L.L. 273
Lin, N. 324
Lindsay, J. 224
Lindstrom, D.P. 302, 308
Linnemann, H. 122
Lipman, A. 370
Lisle-Williams, M. 35
Liu, Q. 302
Liu, Y. 336
Liuma 329
Lloyd-Jones, R. 249
Lo, F.-C. 346, 347
Lohr, S. 377
Lomborg, B. 70, 72
Lomnitz, L. 188, 386
Londero, E. 121
Louis XV 235
Lucas, R.E.B. 305, 306
Luttik, J. 124, 129

Macauley, S. 47
MacDonald, J.S. 111, 188
MacDonald, L.D. 188
MacMillan, I. 148, 162
Macy, M.W. 70, 72, 73
Magellan 33
Maltby, J. 246, 250, 251, 259, 262, 263
Man, G. 325
March, J.G. 2
Margolis, M.L. 384, 386
Markoff, J. 372
Marks, G. 3
Marsden, L. 71, 327
Marsden, P. 347
Marshall 249
Marshall, M. 366
Martin, D. 251
Martinez, N.D. 240
Marwell, G. 79
Masai, Y. 375
Maslov, S. 239, 240
Mason-Jones, R. 111
Massey, D.S. 15, 188, 189, 191, 192, 199, 203, 204, 206, 209, 277, 279, 280, 294, 295, 299, 300, 302, 303, 305–6, 307–8, 316, 383, 384, 385, 386, 387
Matthei, L.M. 15
Matthews, R. 304, 326
McCall, B.P. 300
McCall, J.J. 300
McClelland, D.C. 148
McCusker, J.J. 220, 222
McDonough, C.C. 15
McGrath, R. 148, 150
McGregor 80
McIntire, J. 297
McKenzie, R. 342
McKinnon, A. 111
Meisel, J.H. 40
Meng, X. 327
Menjívar, C. 307
Mercator 33
Merton, I. 107, 111
Merton, R.C. 295, 309
Meyer, D. 345, 362
Meyer, J.-B. 325

Middleton, G. 229, 230, 232–4
Milgrom, P. 237
Miller, M.J. 15
Mills, G. 264
Milne, G.J. 174
Min, L. 330, 334
Min, P.G. 325
Mines, R. 188, 189, 295, 298, 385, 391
Mitchell, R. 147, 148, 150, 152
Moen, P. 326, 327, 334
Mollenkopf, J. 375
Monsted, M. 148, 161, 162
Montgomery, R.I.V. 327
Montiel, P.J. 122
Mooney, M. 308
Morgan, E.V. 255
Morokvasic, M. 272
Moss, M. 367, 373, 376
Mouchard, A. 229–35
Mualam, M. 285
Mungo, P. 372, 373

Nabel, V. 271
Nagengast, C. 384
Nakakita, T. 25, 30
Nakamura, H. 375
Nakatani, I. 26
Neal, L. 221
Nee, V. 304, 326, 387
Nelson, K. 376
Nemeth, R. 346
Nevill, R.H. 40
Newman, M.E.J. 243
Newman, P.C. 34
Newman, S. 111
Newmarch, W. 264
Newton, L.A. 248, 249, 269
Ngo, H.-Y. 327
Nicol, L. 367
Nikula, O. 176
Nilsson, A. 148
Nixon 33
Noam, E. 350
Nohria, N. 101
Noponen, H. 15
North, D.C. 184, 236, 237
North, D.S. 203
Noyelle, T. 366
Nugent, J.B. 304
Nyevrikel, E. 378

O'Hagan, S.B. 33, 34
Ody, P. 111
Offerdal, A. 1
Ogborn, M. 32
Ojala, J. 174
Okochi, A. 248
Oliver, P. 70
Oskamp, S. 70
Ostgaard, T. 147
Ouchi, W. 80
Ozawa, T. 26

Paine, S. 189
Pallack, R.A. 304
Panagariya, A. 122
Pappi, F. 347
Parish, W.L. 326, 327
Park, Y.R. 25, 30–1
Parrenas, R.S. 325, 327
Partridge, M. 327
Pastor-Satorras, R. 238, 239
Payne, P.L. 248
Paz, A. 271
Pecchioli, R. 366
Pedraza, Z. 272
Pepys, S. 226
Perkins, R. 42
Pessar, P.R. 188, 272, 274, 297
Pfeffer, J. 326
Phelps, B. 40
Philpott, S.B. 189, 300, 303
Phizaklea, A. 272
Pickering, J. 263, 265
Picot, A. 173
Pierrel, F. 104, 110, 111, 112
Pietäinen, T.P. 176
Piore, M.J. 187, 189, 203, 246, 281
Pitt, T. Jr 229
Pitt, T. Sr 230, 232
Pitts, F. 347
Pollard, S. 178, 179
Poros, M.V. 325
Porter, M.E. 246
Portes, A. 187, 304, 324, 325, 359, 383, 387
Poster, M. 365
Postlethwayt 219, 228
Powell, W.W. 100, 147, 162, 174
Prescott, K. 152
Preston, V. 325
Price, J. 221
Prothero, R.M. 295
Prozecanski, A.C. 187
Putnam, R.D. 3, 48

Quarmby, D. 110
Quinn, J. 42
Quinn, S. 221, 223, 229, 237

Radcliffe, S.A. 273
Raijman, R. 273, 274, 277, 284, 291
Ranis, G. 187
Ranney, S. 203
Rapoport, A. 70, 72
Rauch, J.E. 15, 16
Ravenstein, E.G. 189
Ray, R. 13
Reagan 33
Redding, S.G. 90
Reed, M.C. 261
Reese, P.R. 325
Reichert, J.S. 188, 189, 203
Remennick, L. 273
Rényi, P. 338
Repak, T.A. 279
Rhoades, R.E. 189
Richards, R.D. 221
Ries, J. 15, 25
Rimmer, P. 349, 350, 351, 362
Ring 81
Ripperger, T. 173
Risberg, E. 179, 180, 181, 183
Roberts, K.D. 188, 189, 297, 302
Roberts, R. 236
Roberts, S. 376
Robertson, R. 33, 42
Robinson, J.C. 326
Robinson, K. 275
Rodriguez, N. 373, 385, 390
Rogers, A. 15
Rogers, J. 222
Rohlfs, J. 370
Rong, H. 335
Rosales, F.A. 391
Rose, A. 18
Rose, M.B. 250
Rose, R. 328
Rosenberg 40
Rosenzweig, M.R. 297
Roseveare, H. 22, 226, 228
Ross, D.F. 110
Ross, R. 344
Rossi, P.H. 188
Roth, A.E. 70
Roumasset, J.A. 296
Rouse, R. 298
Roy, S. 16
Rubenstein, H. 189
Rubinstein, W.D. 93

Sabel, C.F. 246
Sachs, J.D. 122
Sachs, M.A. 346
Sachwald, F. 100
Sakano, T. 150, 155
Salaff, J.W. 325, 331
Salazar Parreñas, R. 272, 274, 275, 281, 290
Salzinger, L. 283
Samora, J. 187
Sanchez, L. 327
Sanders, J.M. 387
Sassen, S. 15, 324, 342, 343, 344, 349–50, 355, 357, 362, 373, 390, 391
Saunders, R. 370
Saxenian, A. 15
Scanlon, R. 375
Schammah-Gesser, S. 291
Scharfstein, D. 25, 26
Schijf, H. 35
Schiller, H. 371, 372
Schiller, N.G. 324
Scholes, M. 309
Schön, D. 2
Schott, T. 354
Schubert, E. 225, 227
Schumpeter, J. 148
Schwartz, M. 34
Scott, A.J. 326, 377
Scott, J. 33, 34, 35, 38, 40
Scranton, P. 246
Selwood, J. 34
Semyonov, M. 273, 274
Senker, J.M. 101, 102, 103, 107
Sensenbrenner, J. 304
Shane, S. 148, 150, 162
Shannon, H.A. 248
Shaw, G. 223
Shaw, R. 223
Shefter, M. 375
Sherwood, M. 38
Short, S.E. 327
Sihag, B.S. 15
Simmons, J.W. 188
Simon, D.T. 351, 391
Sinay, R. 285
Skinner, T. 34, 35
Sklair, L. 32, 40
Skvoretz, J. 72, 73
Smith, D.A. 342, 346, 348, 361
Smith, M.P. 344
Smith, W.D. 177, 222
Snyder, D. 346
Sobel, J. 48
Soda, G. 100
Sparks, L. 104, 110
Speare, A. Jr 188
Staber, U. 148, 149

Stack, C.B. 386
Stählberg, K. 1, 3
Standage, T. 33
Stanley, B. 93
Stanley, E. 72
Stanworth, J. 162
Stark, O. 188, 275, 297, 305, 306
Stavenhagen, R. 193
Steiber, S. 346
Stein, J.L. 187
Stephens, G. 370
Stepick, A. 359
Steyaert, C. 162
Stinchcombe, A.L. 47
Stokman, F.N. 35, 71
Stoloff, J.A. 325
Storper, M. 246
Strange, S. 369
Stretton, A. 300
Strogatz, S.H. 239
Surazska, W. 2
Suzuki, K. 30
Swann, P. 101
Swenson, D. 25
Swianiewicz, P. 1, 3
Szarka, J. 147

t' Hart, M.C. 221
Tang, S. 336
Tardos, A. 378
Tastsoglou, E. 336
Taylor, J.E. 188, 308, 317
Taylor, P.J. 35, 342
Tepperman, L. 327
Tether, B. 101
Thatcher 33
Thomas, B. 187
Thomas, R.J. 385, 390, 391
Thomas, W.A. 248, 255, 256, 261
Thompson, G. 33
Thomson, E. 327
Thrift, N. 375
Tienda, M. 273
Tiessen, J.H. 160
Tilly, C. 188, 347
Tinkler, S. 16
Todaro, M.P. 187, 296
Tomka, B. 34
Towill, D. 111
Trachte, K. 344
Tracy, J.D. 221
Trager, L. 307
Trigeorgis, L. 308
Truong, T. 273
Tucker, A.W. 49, 70
Tullock, G. 57
Turrell, R.V. 95
Tweedale, G. 251

Urata, S. 25, 30
Useem, M. 38, 40
Uselding, P. 179
Uzzi, B. 47, 346

van Cauwenberghe, E. 229
van der Grift, B. 229–36
Van Dillen, J.G. 220
van Helten, J.-J. 95, 252
van Zanden, L. 221
Vander Haar, J.E. 306
Vaughn, J.C. 324
Venkataraman, S. 162
Ventresca, M. 346
Verma, A. 326
Viaene, J.-M. 16
Vickers, R. 104
Vogel, E. 366, 375
Vos, R. 122, 124, 126, 128, 138, 143, 144

Wachtel, H. 366
Wade, R. 361
Wadeson, N. 100
Wainerman, C. 236
Waisman, C. 280
Walder, A.G. 327
Waldinger, R. 383, 387, 390, 391
Walter, I. 366, 375
Walvin, J. 32
Warf, B. 371, 375, 377, 379
Wassman, V. 27
Watt, J. 33
Watts, D. 239, 244
Weber, M. 148
Weckman, G.A. 176
Weingast, B. 236, 237
Welford, R. 152
Wellman, B. 325
Westall, O.M. 250
Westphal, J.D. 48
Whimster, S. 375
White, D. 346, 347, 348
White, H. 346
White, J. 375
Whiteoak, P. 112
Whitlock, E. 378
Whyte, M.K. 326, 327
Wiest, R.E. 189, 203
Wilamoski, P. 16

Wilkins, M. 33, 94, 95, 97
Willer, D. 73
Williams, H. 367
Williamson, O.E. 16, 100, 102
Willis, K. 325, 335
Wilson, J.F. 246, 268
Wilson, M. 371, 376
Wilson, T.D. 301, 384, 390, 391
Wing, J.U. 254, 256, 257–60, 262–70
Winters, T. 111
Wolf, E.R. 32
Wolff, B. 173
Wolff, G. 342, 343
Wong, D. 272, 273, 274
Wong, S.-L. 325
Wood, C.C. 188, 297
Wood, G. 264
Wood, P. 365

Xu, Z. 331

Yamaguchi, K. 69
Yamamura, K. 27
Yang, H. 327
Yang, W. 333–4
Yasuoka, S. 248
Yates, Y. 183
Yeoh, B. 325, 335
Yeung, Y.-M. 346, 347
Ying, X. 329
Ying, Y. 328, 329, 334
Yoon, J. 47
Yousry, A. 359
Yousry, M. 359
Yu, C.-M. 25, 31
Yu, Y. 326, 327

Zabin 386
Zavella, P. 390
Zeggelink, E.P. 71
Zeitlin, J. 246
Zhan, H.J. 327
Zhang, S. 336
Zhao, S. 298
Zong, L. 331
Zucker, L.G. 47

The International Library of Critical Writings in Economics

1. Multinational Corporations
Mark Casson
2. The Economics of Innovation
Christopher Freeman
3. Entrepreneurship
Mark Casson
4. International Investment
Peter J. Buckley
5. Game Theory in Economics
Ariel Rubinstein
6. The History of Economic Thought
Mark Blaug
7. Monetary Theory
Thomas Mayer
8. Joint Production of Commodities
Neri Salvadori and Ian Steedman
9. Industrial Organization
Oliver E. Williamson
10. Growth Theory
(Volumes I, II and III)
R. Becker and E. Burmeister
11. Microeconomics: Theoretical and Applied (Volumes I, II and III)
Robert E. Kuenne
12. The Economics of Health
(Volumes I and II)
A.J. Culyer
13. Recent Developments in Macroeconomics
(Volumes I, II and III)
Edmund S. Phelps
14. Urban and Regional Economics
Paul C. Cheshire and Alan W. Evans
15. Modern Public Finance
(Volumes I and II)
A.B. Atkinson
16. Exchange Rate Economics
(Volumes I and II)
Ronald MacDonald and Mark P. Taylor
17. The Economic Value of Education: Studies in the Economics of Education
Mark Blaug
18. Development Economics
(Volumes I, II, III and IV)
Deepak Lal
19. The New Classical Macroeconomics
(Volumes I, II and III)
Kevin D. Hoover
20. The Economics of the Environment
Wallace E. Oates
21. Post Keynesian Theory of Growth and Distribution
Carlo Panico and Neri Salvadori
22. Dynamic Labor Demand and Adjustment Costs
Giorgio Galeazzi and Daniel S. Hamermesh
23. The Philosophy and Methodology of Economics (Volumes I, II and III)
Bruce J. Caldwell
24. Public Choice Theory
(Volumes I, II and III)
Charles K. Rowley
25. Evolutionary Economics
Ulrich Witt
26. Economics and Psychology
Shlomo Maital and Sharone L. Maital
27. Social Choice Theory
(Volumes I, II and III)
Charles K. Rowley
28. Non-Linear Dynamics in Economic Theory
Marc Jarsulic
29. Recent Developments in Experimental Economics
(Volumes I and II)
John D. Hey and Graham Loomes
30. Monopoly and Competition Policy
(Volumes I and II)
F.M. Scherer
31. The Economics of Technical Change
Edwin Mansfield and Elizabeth Mansfield
32. The Economics of Exhaustible Resources
Geoffrey Heal
33. The Economics of Institutions
Geoffrey M. Hodgson
34. The Economics of Transport
(Volumes I and II)
Herbert Mohring

35. Implicit Contract Theory
Sherwin Rosen
36. Foundations of Analytical Marxism (Volumes I and II)
John E. Roemer
37. The Economics of Product Differentiation (Volumes I and II)
Jacques-François Thisse and George Norman
38. Economic Growth in Theory and Practice: A Kaldorian Perspective
John E. King
39. Markets and Socialism
Alec Nove and Ian D. Thatcher
40. Recent Developments in the Economics of Education
Elchanan Cohn and Geraint Johnes
41. The Theory of Inflation
Michael Parkin
42. The Economics of Location (Volumes I, II and III)
Melvin L. Greenhut and George Norman
43. Financial Intermediaries
Mervyn K. Lewis
44. The Political Economy of Privatization and Deregulation
Elizabeth E. Bailey and Janet Rothenberg Pack
45. Gender and Economics
Jane Humphries
46. Macroeconomics and Imperfect Competition
Jean-Pascal Bénassy
47. Labor Economics (Volumes I, II, III and IV)
Orley C. Ashenfelter and Kevin F. Hallock
48. The Economics of Altruism
Stefano Zamagni
49. The Economic Analysis of Rent Seeking
Robert D. Tollison and Roger D. Congleton
50. Economics and Biology
Geoffrey M. Hodgson
51. The Economics of Ageing
John Creedy
52. Fiscal and Monetary Policy (Volumes I and II)
Thomas Mayer and Steven M. Sheffrin
53. The Economics of Information (Volumes I and II)
David K. Levine and Steven A. Lippman
54. Transaction Cost Economics (Volumes I and II)
Oliver E. Williamson and Scott E. Masten
55. Agricultural Economics
George H. Peters
56. International Debt (Volumes I and II)
Graham Bird and P. Nicholas Snowden
57. Economics and Discrimination (Volumes I and II)
William A. Darity, Jr
58. Business Cycle Theory
Finn E. Kydland
59. International Trade (Volumes I and II)
J. Peter Neary
60. The Money Supply in the Economic Process
Marco Musella and Carlo Panico
61. Small Firms and Economic Growth (Volumes I and II)
Zoltan J. Acs
62. Producer Cooperatives and Labor-Managed Systems (Volumes I and II)
David L. Prychitko and Jaroslav Vanek
63. Ethics and Economics (Volumes I and II)
Alan P. Hamlin
64. The Economics of the Family
Nancy Folbre
65. The Economics of Training (Volumes I and II)
Orley C. Ashenfelter and Robert J. LaLonde
66. Chaos Theory in Economics: Methods, Models and Evidence
W. Davis Dechert
67. General Equilibrium Theory (Volumes I, II and III)
Gérard Debreu
68. Economic Growth: Theory and Evidence (Volumes I and II)
Gene M. Grossman
69. Long Wave Theory
Christopher Freeman

70. The Economics of Communication and Information
Donald M. Lamberton
71. The Foundations of Public Finance (Volumes I and II)
Peter Jackson
72. The Theory of the Firm
Mark Casson
73. The Economics of Uncertainty (Volumes I and II)
John D. Hey
74. The Economics of Global Warming
Tom Tietenberg
75. The Development of Ecological Economics
Robert Costanza, Charles Perrings and Cutler Cleveland
76. Economic Growth in the Long Run: A History of Empirical Evidence (Volumes I, II and III)
Bart van Ark
77. The Economics of Productivity (Volumes I and II)
Edward N. Wolff
78. The Economics of Population: Key Modern Writings (Volumes I and II)
Julian L. Simon
79. Political Business Cycles
Bruno S. Frey
80. Cultural Economics: The Arts, the Heritage and the Media Industries (Volumes I and II)
Ruth Towse
81. Law and Economics (Volumes I, II and III)
Richard A. Posner and Francesco Parisi
82. Independent Central Banks and Economic Performance
Sylvester Eijffinger
83. Culture, Social Norms and Economics (Volumes I and II)
Mark Casson
84. Industrial Policy and Competitive Advantage (Volumes I, II and III)
David B. Audretsch
85. The Economics of Housing (Volumes I and II)
John M. Quigley
86. Economic Demography (Volumes I and II)
T. Paul Schultz
87. Trade and the Environment: Economic, Legal and Policy Perspectives
Alan M. Rugman and John J. Kirton with Julie A. Soloway
88. The Economics of Fiscal Federalism and Local Finance
Wallace E. Oates
89. Price Theory and its Applications
Bernard Saffran and F.M. Scherer
90. Women in the Labor Market (Volumes I and II)
Marianne A. Ferber
91. Market Process Theories (Volumes I and II)
Peter Boettke and David Prychitko
92. Input–Output Analysis (Volumes I, II and III)
Heinz Kurz, Erik Dietzenbacher and Christian Lager
93. Mathematical Economics (Volumes I, II and III)
Graciela Chichilnisky
94. The Foundations of Regulatory Economics (Volumes I, II and III)
Robert B. Ekelund, Jr.
95. The Economics of Marketing
Martin Carter, Mark Casson and Vivek Suneja
96. Service Industries in the Global Economy (Volumes I and II)
J.R. Bryson and P.W. Daniels
97. Economic Justice (Volumes I and II)
Giorgio Brosio and Harold M. Hochman
98. Foreign Exchange Intervention: Objectives and Effectiveness
Sylvester C.W. Eijffinger
99. Economic Anthropology
Stephen Gudeman
100. Consumer Theory
Kelvin Lancaster
101. The Economics of Famine
Jean Drèze
102. Microeconomic Theories of Imperfect Competition
Jean J. Gabszewicz and Jacques-François Thisse

103. The Economics of Executive Compensation
(Volumes I and II)
Kevin F. Hallock and Kevin J. Murphy
104. The Foundations of Long Wave Theory
(Volumes I and II)
Francisco Louçã and Jan Reijnders
105. The Economics of Commodity Markets
David Greenaway and C.W. Morgan
106. Corporate Governance
(Volumes I, II, III and IV)
Kevin Keasey, Steve Thompson and Mike Wright
107. Economic Welfare: Concepts and Measurement
(Volumes I and II)
John Creedy
108. Economic Forecasting
Terence C. Mills
109. Recent Developments in Game Theory
Eric S. Maskin
110. The Economics of Increasing Returns
Geoffrey Heal
111. The Economics of Corruption and Illegal Markets
(Volumes I, II and III)
Gianluca Fiorentini and Stefano Zamagni
112. The Economics of Price Discrimination
George Norman
113. The Economic Theory of Auctions
(Volumes I and II)
Paul Klemperer
114. The Economics of Regional Policy
Harvey W. Armstrong and Jim Taylor
115. Economic Integration and International Trade
Carsten Kowalczyk
116. The Political Economy of Science, Technology and Innovation
Ben Martin and Paul Nightingale
117. The Economics of Science and Innovation
(Volumes I and II)
Paula E. Stephan and David B. Audretsch
118. Innovation, Evolution of Industry and Economic Growth
(Volumes I, II and III)
David B. Audretsch and Steven Klepper
119. The Economics of Energy
(Volumes I and II)
Paul Stevens
120. Privatisation in Developing Countries
(Volumes I and II)
Paul Cook and Colin Kirkpatrick
121. The Economics of Tourism
(Volumes I and II)
Clem Tisdell
122. The Economics of Unemployment
(Volumes I, II, III and IV)
P.N. Junankar
123. Privatisation and Corporate Performance
David Parker
124. Income Distribution
(Volumes I, II and III)
Michael Sattinger
125. International Finance
(Volumes I and II)
Robert Z. Aliber
126. Welfare Economics
(Volumes I, II and III)
William J. Baumol and Charles A. Wilson
127. The Theory of Trade Policy Reform
Carsten Kowalczyk
128. The Economics of Defence
(Volumes I, II and III)
Keith Hartley and Todd Sandler
129. The Economics of Property Rights
(Volumes I and II)
Svetozar Pejovich
130. Gender and Development: Theoretical, Empirical and Practical Approaches
(Volumes I and II)
Lourdes Benería with Savitri Bisnath
131. The Economics of Politics
(Volumes I and II)
Dennis C. Mueller
132. Economic Theory and the Welfare State
(Volumes I, II and III)
Nicholas Barr
133. The Regulation and Supervision of Banks
(Volumes I, II, III and IV)
Maximilian J.B. Hall
134. The Political Economy of Monetary Union
Paul De Grauwe

135. The Economics of Sport
(Volumes I and II)
Andrew Zimbalist
136. The Economics of Advertising
Kyle Bagwell
137. Regulation, Economics and the Law
Anthony I. Ogus
138. The Economics of Barter and Countertrade
Rolf Mirus and Bernard Yeung
139. The Economics of Technology Transfer
Sanjaya Lall
140. The Political Economy of Development
(Volumes I, II and III)
Amitava Krishna Dutt
141. Macroeconomics and the Environment
Mohan Munasinghe
142. Happiness in Economics
Richard A. Easterlin
143. Speculation and Financial Markets
(Volumes I and II)
Liam Gallagher and Mark P. Taylor
144. Public Procurement
(Volumes I and II)
Sue Arrowsmith and Keith Hartley
145. The Economics of Intellectual Property
(Volumes I, II, III and IV)
Ruth Towse and R.W. Holzhauer
146. Forecasting Financial Markets
(Volumes I and II)
Terence C. Mills
147. The Economics of Labor Unions
(Volumes I and II)
Alison Booth
148. New Developments in Exchange Rate Economics
(Volumes I and II)
Lucio Sarno and Mark P. Taylor
149. Long Term Trends and Business Cycles
(Volumes I and II)
Terence C. Mills
150. The Economics of Language
Donald M. Lamberton
151. The Economics of Migration
(Volumes I, II, III and IV)
Klaus F. Zimmermann and Thomas Bauer
152. Cost–Benefit Analysis
Arnold C. Harberger and Glenn P. Jenkins
153. The Economics of Budget Deficits
(Volumes I and II)
Charles K. Rowley, William F. Shughart II and Robert D. Tollison
154. Alternative Theories of the Firm
(Volumes I, II and III)
Richard Langlois, Tony F. Yu and Paul Robertson
155. The Distribution of Tax Burdens
Don Fullerton and Gilbert E. Metcalf
156. International Financial Integration
(Volumes I and II)
Sylvester C.W. Eijffinger and Jan J.G. Lemmen
157. The Economics of Structural Change
(Volumes I, II and III)
Harald Hagemann, Michael Landesmann and Roberto Scazzieri
158. The Economics of Poverty and Inequality
(Volumes I and II)
Frank A. Cowell
159. The Economics of Schooling
(Volumes I and II)
Eric A. Hanushek
160. Intra-Industry Trade
Peter J. Lloyd and Herbert G. Grubel
161. Economic Analysis of Regional Trading Arrangements
Richard Pomfret
162. The Principal Agent Model: The Economic Theory of Incentives
Jean-Jacques Laffont
163. The Economics of Business Strategy
John Kay
164. Recent Developments in Transport Economics
Kenneth Button
165. The Economics of Higher Education
Clive R. Belfield and Henry M. Levin
166. Constitutional Political Economy
(Volumes I and II)
Stephan Voigt
167. Economics and Religion
(Volumes I and II)
Paul Oslington
168. The Economics of Conflict
(Volumes I, II and III)
Todd Sandler and Keith Hartley
169. Cognitive Economics
(Volumes I and II)
Massimo Egidi and Salvatore Rizzello

170. Comparative Law and Economics (Volumes I, II and III)
Gerrit de Geest and Roger Van Den Bergh
171. Personnel Economics (Volumes I and II)
Edward P. Lazear and Robert McNabb
172. Empirical Industrial Organization (Volumes I and II)
Paul L. Joskow and Michael Waterson
173. Multinationals and Public Policy (Volumes I and II)
Stephen Young
174. Complexity in Economics (Volumes I, II and III)
J. Barkley Rosser, Jr.
175. Time in Economic Theory (Volumes I, II and III)
Stefano Zamagni and Elettra Agliardi
176. The Economics of Affirmative Action
Harry J. Holzer and David Neumark
177. Recent Developments in Environmental Economics (Volumes I and II)
Michael Hoel
178. The Economics of Natural Hazards (Volumes I and II)
Howard Kunreuther and Adam Rose
179. Recent Developments in Growth Theory (Volumes I and II)
K. Daron Acemoglu
180. The Political Economy of Environmental Regulation
Robert N. Stavins
181. The Economics of Nonprofit Enterprises
Richard S. Steinberg
182. Recent Developments in Urban and Regional Economics
Paul C. Cheshire and Gilles Duranton
183. The Economics of Public Private Partnerships
Darrin Grimsey and Mervyn K. Lewis
184. New Economic Geography
J. Vernon Henderson
185. Recent Developments in International Trade Theory
Rod Falvey and Udo Kreickemeier
186. New Developments in Economic Sociology (Volumes I and II)
Richard Swedberg
187. The Psychology of World Equity Markets (Volumes I and II)
Werner De Bondt
188. Spatial Economics (Volumes I and II)
Masahisa Fujita
189. The Economics of Deflation (Volumes I and II)
Pierre L. Siklos
190. Real Options and International Investment
Alan M. Rugman and Jing Li
191. Open Economy Macroeconomics
Norman C. Miller
192. Imperfect Competition, Nonclearing Markets and Business Cycles
Jean-Pascal Bénassy
193. Recent Developments in Economic Methodology (Volumes I, II and II)
John B. Davis
194. Modern Classics in the Economics of Education (Volumes I and II)
Clive Belfield
195. The Economics of Crime (Volumes I, II and III)
Isaac Ehrlich and Zhiqiang Liu
196. The Economics of Public Utilities (Volumes I and II)
Ray Rees
197. The Economics of Patents (Volumes I and II)
John Cantwell
198. The Economics of Biotechnology (Volumes I and II)
Maureen McKelvey and Luigi Orsenigo
199. The Economics of the Mass Media
Gillian Doyle
200. The Economics of Leisure (Volumes I and II)
Clem Tisdell
201. Cartels (Volumes I and II)
Margaret C. Levenstein and Stephen W. Salant
202. New Developments in the Economics of Population Ageing
John Creedy and Ross Guest
203. Recent Developments in the Economics of Training (Volumes I and II)
Francis Green

204. Recent Developments in Behavioral Economics
Shlomo Maital
205. Recent Developments in Cultural Economics
Ruth Towse
206. Islamic Finance
M. Kabir Hassan and Mervyn K. Lewis
207. Recent Developments in Labor Economics (Volumes I, II and III)
John T. Addison
208. The International Monetary Fund and the World Economy (Volumes I and II)
Graham Bird and Dane Rowlands
209. New Developments in Experimental Economics (Volumes I and II)
Enrica Carbone and Chris Starmer
210. International Taxation
James R. Hines Jr.
211. The Foundations of Credit Risk Analysis
Willi Semmler and Lucas Bernard
212. Economic Integration and Spatial Location of Firms and Industries (Volumes I, II and III)
Miroslav N. Jovanovic
213. Innovation and Economic Development
Lynn K. Mytelka
214. The Economics of Modern Business Enterprise (Volumes I, II and III)
Martin Ricketts
215. The Economic Theory of Invention and Innovation
Albert N. Link
216. The Economics of Hazardous Waste and Contaminated Land
Hilary Sigman
217. Recent Developments in Monopoly and Competition Policy
George Norman
218. Financial Crises
Franklin Allen and Douglas Gale
219. Developments in the Economics of Privatization and Regulation
Michael A. Crew and David Parker
220. Applied Welfare Economics
Richard E. Just, Darrell L. Hueth and Andrew Schmitz
221. The Economics of Networks
Mark Casson and Marina Della Giusta

Future titles will include:

The Economics of Health Behaviours (Volumes I, II and III)
John H. Cawley and Donald S. Kenkel

Segmented Labor Markets and Labor Mobility (Volumes I and II)
Michael Reich

The Economics of Innovation Policy (Volumes I and II)
Albert N. Link

Recent Trends in the Economics of Copyright
Ruth Towse and Richard Watt

The Economics of the Hidden Economy (Volumes I and II)
Friedrich Schneider

Incomplete Markets
Michael J.P. Magill and Martine Quinzii

The Economics of Contracts
Patrick Bolton

Neuroeconomics
Paul J. Zak

Feminist Economics
Lourdes Benería, Ann Mari May and Diana L. Strassman

Recent Developments in Monetary Policy
Alec Chrystal and Paul Mizen

The Economics of Knowledge
Robin A. Cowan

Path Dependence
Paul A. David

The Economics of Gambling and National Lotteries
William R. Eadington

The Economics of Transfer Pricing
Lorraine Eden

Equality and Economic Growth
Oded Galor

Economics of Water Resources
R. Quentin Grafton

The Economics of Vouchers
Caroline M. Hoxby

The Economics of Free Trade
Douglas A. Irwin and Arvind Panagariya

The Economics of Organisation and Bureaucracy
Peter M. Jackson

Computational Economics
Kenneth L. Judd

New Developments in Behavioral Economics
Elias L. Khalil

The Phillips Curve
Richard G. Lipsey, Robert Leeson and Edward Nelson

The Economic Role of the State
Steven G. Medema

Recent Developments in Law and Economics
Francesco Parisi and Robert Cooter

The New Evolutionary Economics
Jason Potts and Kurt Dopfer

The Knowledge Economy
Danny T. Quah

New Developments in Public Choice
Charles K. Rowley, Robert D. Tollison and William F. Shughart

The Economics of Traffic Congestion
Eric Verhoef

Controlling Public Expenditure
John Wanna

Tax Competition and Tax Harmonisation
David Wildasin

Recent Developments in Evolutionary Economics
Ulrich Witt

The Economics of Climate Change
Graciela Chichilnisky